36: *British Novelists, 1890-1929: Modernists,* edited by Thomas F. Staley (1985)

37: *American Writers of the Early Republic,* edited by Emory Elliott (1985)

38: *Afro-American Writers After 1955: Dramatists and Prose Writers,* edited by Thadious M. Davis and Trudier Harris (1985)

39: *British Novelists, 1660-1800,* 2 parts, edited by Martin C. Battestin (1985)

40: *Poets of Great Britain and Ireland Since 1960,* 2 parts, edited by Vincent B. Sherry, Jr. (1985)

41: *Afro-American Poets Since 1955,* edited by Trudier Harris and Thadious M. Davis (1985)

42: *American Writers for Children Before 1900,* edited by Glenn E. Estes (1985)

43: *American Newspaper Journalists, 1690-1872,* edited by Perry J. Ashley (1986)

44: *American Screenwriters,* Second Series, edited by Randall Clark, Robert E. Morsberger, and Stephen O. Lesser (1986)

45: *American Poets, 1880-1945,* First Series, edited by Peter Quartermain (1986)

46: *American Literary Publishing Houses, 1900-1980: Trade and Paperback,* edited by Peter Dzwonkoski (1986)

47: *American Historians, 1866-1912,* edited by Clyde N. Wilson (1986)

48: *American Poets, 1880-1945,* Second Series, edited by Peter Quartermain (1986)

49: *American Literary Publishing Houses, 1638-1899,* 2 parts, edited by Peter Dzwonkoski (1986)

50: *Afro-American Writers Before the Harlem Renaissance,* edited by Trudier Harris (1986)

51: *Afro-American Writers from the Harlem Renaissance to 1940,* edited by Trudier Harris (1987)

52: *American Writers for Children Since 1960: Fiction,* edited by Glenn E. Estes (1986)

53: *Canadian Writers Since 1960,* First Series, edited by W. H. New (1986)

54: *American Poets, 1880-1945,* Third Series, 2 parts, edited by Peter Quartermain (1987)

55: *Victorian Prose Writers Before 1867,* edited by William B. Thesing (1987)

56: *German Fiction Writers, 1914-1945,* edited by James Hardin (1987)

57: *Victorian Prose Writers After 1867,* edited by William B. Thesing (1987)

58: *Jacobean and Caroline Dramatists,* edited by Fredson Bowers (1987)

59: *American Literary Critics and Scholars, 1800-1850,* edited by John W. Rathbun and Monica M. Grecu (1987)

60: *Canadian Writers Since 1960,* Second Series, edited by W. H. New (1987)

61: *American Writers for Children Since 1960: Poets, Illustrators, and Nonfiction Authors,* edited by Glenn E. Estes (1987)

62: *Elizabethan Dramatists,* edited by Fredson Bowers (1987)

63: *Modern American Critics, 1920-1955,* edited by Gregory S. Jay (1988)

64: *American Literary Critics and Scholars, 1850-1880,* edited by John W. Rathbun and Monica M. Grecu (1988)

65: *French Novelists, 1900-1930,* edited by Catharine Savage Brosman (1988)

66: *German Fiction Writers, 1885-1913,* 2 parts, edited by James Hardin (1988)

67: *Modern American Critics Since 1955,* edited by Gregory S. Jay (1988)

68: *Canadian Writers, 1920-1959,* First Series, edited by W. H. New (1988)

69: *Contemporary German Fiction Writers,* First Series, edited by Wolfgang D. Elfe and James Hardin (1988)

70: *British Mystery Writers, 1860-1919,* edited by Bernard Benstock and Thomas F. Staley (1988)

(Continued on back endsheets)

Dictionary of Literary Biography • Volume Eighty-four

Restoration and Eighteenth-Century Dramatists
Second Series

Dictionary of Literary Biography • Volume Eighty-four

Restoration and Eighteenth-Century Dramatists
Second Series

Edited by
Paula R. Backscheider
University of Rochester

8063

A Bruccoli Clark Layman Book
Gale Research Inc. • Book Tower • Detroit, Michigan 48226

Manufactured by Edwards Brothers, Inc.
Ann Arbor, Michigan
Printed in the United States of America

Library of Congress Cataloging-in-Publication Data

Restoration and eighteenth-century dramatists.
    Second series / edited by Paula R. Backscheider.
    p. cm.–(Dictionary of literary biography; v. 84)
    "A Bruccoli Clark Layman book."
    Includes index.
    ISBN 0-8103-4562-5
    1. English drama–18th century–Dictionaries. 2. English
drama–Restoration, 1660-1700–Dictionaries. 3. English
drama–18th century–Bio-bibliography. 4. English drama–
Restoration, 1660-1700–Bio-bibliography. 5. Dramatists,
English–18th century–Biography–Dictionaries. 6. Dramatists, English–Early modern, 1500-1700–Biography–Dictionaries. I. Backscheider, Paula R. II. Series.
PR701.R4 1989
822.009–dc20
[B]
                                                    89-11870
                                                         CIP

To Jacob H. Adler in the year of his retirement

Contents

Plan of the Series...ix

Foreword...xi

Acknowledgments..xix

Henry Carey (circa 1687-1689-1743) 3
   Charles Michael Carroll

Susanna Centlivre (1669?-1723) 15
   Jean Gagen

Colley Cibber (1671-1757) 42
   Linda E. Merians

William Congreve (1670-1729) 61
   Peter Holland

George Farquhar (circa 1677-1707)....................91
   Shirley Strum Kenny

Henry Fielding (1707-1754).............................117
   Paula R. Backscheider

David Garrick (1717-1779)...............................146
   Douglas H. White

John Gay (1685-1732) 181
   Calhoun Winton

Aaron Hill (1685-1750).....................................200
   Sophia B. Blaydes

John Home (1722-1808).....................................219
   Barbara M. Benedict

John Hughes (1677-1720)..................................227
   William J. Burling

Charles Johnson (1679-1748)...........................234
   William J. Burling

George Lillo (1691-1739) 243
   William J. Burling

Nicholas Rowe (1674-1718)..............................262
   J. Douglas Canfield and Alfred W. Hesse

Frances Sheridan (1724-1766) 289
   Ann Messenger

Richard Steele (1672-1729)..............................300
   Calhoun Winton

Catharine Trotter (1679-1749).........................317
   Sophia B. Blaydes

William Whitehead (1715-1785) 334
   Martin J. Wood

Appendix I: The Licensing Act of 1737.........343

Appendix II: Plays, Playwrights, and Play-
goers...349

Checklist of Further Readings........................385

Contributors...389

Cumulative Index...393

Plan of the Series

. . . Almost the most prodigious asset of a country, and perhaps its most precious possession, is its native literary product—when that product is fine and noble and enduring.

Mark Twain*

The advisory board, the editors, and the publisher of the *Dictionary of Literary Biography* are joined in endorsing Mark Twain's declaration. The literature of a nation provides an inexhaustible resource of permanent worth. We intend to make literature and its creators better understood and more accessible to students and the reading public, while satisfying the standards of teachers and scholars.

To meet these requirements, *literary biography* has been construed in terms of the author's achievement. The most important thing about a writer is his writing. Accordingly, the entries in *DLB* are career biographies, tracing the development of the author's canon and the evolution of his reputation.

The purpose of *DLB* is not only to provide reliable information in a convenient format but also to place the figures in the larger perspective of literary history and to offer appraisals of their accomplishments by qualified scholars.

The publication plan for *DLB* resulted from two years of preparation. The project was proposed to Bruccoli Clark by Frederick G. Ruffner, president of the Gale Research Company, in November 1975. After specimen entries were prepared and typeset, an advisory board was formed to refine the entry format and develop the series rationale. In meetings held during 1976, the publisher, series editors, and advisory board approved the scheme for a comprehensive biographical dictionary of persons who contributed to North American literature. Editorial work on the first volume began in January 1977, and it was published in 1978. In order to make *DLB* more than a reference tool and to compile volumes that individually have claim to status as literary history, it was decided to organize volumes by topic, period, or genre. Each of these freestanding volumes provides a biographical-bibliographical guide and overview for a particular area of literature. We are convinced that this organization—as opposed to a single alphabet method—constitutes a valuable innovation in the presentation of reference material. The volume plan necessarily requires many decisions for the placement and treatment of authors who might properly be included in two or three volumes. In some instances a major figure will be included in separate volumes, but with different entries emphasizing the aspect of his career appropriate to each volume. Ernest Hemingway, for example, is represented in *American Writers in Paris, 1920-1939* by an entry focusing on his expatriate apprenticeship; he is also in *American Novelists, 1910-1945* with an entry surveying his entire career. Each volume includes a cumulative index of subject authors and articles. Comprehensive indexes to the entire series are planned.

With volume ten in 1982 it was decided to enlarge the scope of *DLB*. By the end of 1986 twenty-one volumes treating British literature had been published, and volumes for Commonwealth and Modern European literature were in progress. The series has been further augmented by the *DLB Yearbooks* (since 1981) which update published entries and add new entries to keep the *DLB* current with contemporary activity. There have also been *DLB Documentary Series* volumes which provide biographical and critical source materials for figures whose work is judged to have particular interest for students. One of these companion volumes is entirely devoted to Tennessee Williams.

We define literature as the *intellectual commerce of a nation:* not merely as belles lettres but as that ample and complex process by which ideas are generated, shaped, and transmitted. *DLB* entries are not limited to "creative writers" but extend to other figures who in their time and in their way influenced the mind of a people. Thus the series encompasses historians, journalists, publishers, and screenwriters. By this means readers of *DLB* may be aided to perceive litera-

*From an unpublished section of Mark Twain's autobiography, copyright © by the Mark Twain Company.

ture not as cult scripture in the keeping of intellectual high priests but firmly positioned at the center of a nation's life.

DLB includes the major writers appropriate to each volume and those standing in the ranks immediately behind them. Scholarly and critical counsel has been sought in deciding which minor figures to include and how full their entries should be. Wherever possible, useful references are made to figures who do not warrant separate entries.

Each DLB volume has a volume editor responsible for planning the volume, selecting the figures for inclusion, and assigning the entries. Volume editors are also responsible for preparing, where appropriate, appendices surveying the major periodicals and literary and intellectual movements for their volumes, as well as lists of further readings. Work on the series as a whole is coordinated at the Bruccoli Clark Layman editorial center in Columbia, South Carolina, where the editorial staff is responsible for accuracy of the published volumes.

One feature that distinguishes DLB is the illustration policy—its concern with the iconography of literature. Just as an author is influenced by his surroundings, so is the reader's understanding of the author enhanced by a knowledge of his environment. Therefore DLB volumes include not only drawings, paintings, and photographs of authors, often depicting them at various stages in their careers, but also illustrations of their families and places where they lived. Title pages are regularly reproduced in facsimile along with dust jackets for modern authors. The dust jackets are a special feature of DLB because they often document better than anything else the way in which an author's work was perceived in its own time. Specimens of the writers' manuscripts are included when feasible.

Samuel Johnson rightly decreed that "The chief glory of every people arises from its authors." The purpose of the *Dictionary of Literary Biography* is to compile literary history in the surest way available to us—by accurate and comprehensive treatment of the lives and work of those who contributed to it.

The *DLB* Advisory Board

Foreword

This volume of the *Dictionary of Literary Biography: Restoration and Eighteenth-Century Dramatists*, Second Series, includes some of the most brilliant and distinguished writers of the eighteenth century. Born between 1670 and 1727, several of these eighteen playwrights put their first plays on in the 1690s, and David Garrick, the next to youngest of them, his last in the 1770s. Among them were Henry Fielding, the great novelist, and Richard Steele, the journalistic pioneer who founded the *Tatler*.

During their lifetimes the theater changed enormously, and they enjoyed one of the golden eras of British theater. In the decade when William Congreve's *Double Dealer* (1693), Colley Cibber's *Love's Last Shift* (1696), and George Farquhar's *Constant Couple* (1699) were performed, a successful run would be eight or nine nights and numerous performances in repertory. They and their contemporaries represented in this volume would come to judge success quite differently, and several would count the initial runs of their plays in scores of performances. The change was in the air by February 1723 when Elijah Fenton's *Mariamne* drew audiences that attracted widespread notice. A later commentator said that this histrionic blank-verse tragedy "seemed to show the town the way to the Theatre, to which they were averse before." An eyewitness said that the play drew "the greatest audience ever known at either theatre." Although the play's receipts on the author's first benefit night were two hundred pounds, it ran only thirteen nights before one of the principal actresses refused to perform her part, and *Mariamne* played but four more times that season.[1] Yet theater managers had seen a glimmer of the future.

In the remarkable 1727-1728 season Colley Cibber's revision and completion of John Vanbrugh's *Journey to London* was performed as *The Provok'd Husband* thirty-seven times and John Gay's *The Beggar's Opera* sixty-two. Gay's play has become the most continuously performed English play other than some of Shakespeare's, and, helped by Nigel Playfair's 1920 revival and Bertolt Brecht's *Threepenny Opera* (1928), it is familiar

to most twentieth-century high-school graduates. Within a few years of that 1727-1728 season, the theatrical world was very different. The Little Theatre in the Haymarket opened in May 1728, and Thomas Odell opened the Goodman's Fields theater. By 12 November 1729, four companies were giving daily performances. On 29 November, five plays were performed on the same day for the first time in one hundred years.[2] Plays like Fielding's *Author's Farce* (1730) and George Lillo's *London Merchant* (1731) brought huge, new audiences into the theaters. In 1732, John Rich opened the new Covent Garden Theatre, which held an audience of more than 1,300, as did one other London playhouse, Lincoln's Inn Fields. Success continued, and even now-forgotten plays like Henry Carey's *Dragon of Wantley* (1737) enjoyed phenomenal runs, as this play did of sixty-seven nights.

Although Farquhar wrote in his preface to *The Twin-Rivals* (1702) that the theater audience "take all Innovations for Grievances," it was a period of great change and innovation. Moreover, theatergoers enjoyed a large variety of existing kinds of plays and soon would enjoy more. In a typical nine-month season in the 1690s they could see six to ten new plays and revivals of another one hundred plays from the rich archives of English theater—Elizabethan, Caroline, and Restoration. Their theater had spectacle, stunning scenery, elaborate costumes, dancing, music, action, merriment, and soundly plotted plays, and it would come to develop new forms in order to consider a variety of realistic problems of great contemporary interest.

The most popular plays throughout this period were comedies, and comedy especially benefited from the receptive atmosphere. Although the comedy of manners remained the most popular form, and farces and comedies of intrigue continued to be performed and written, early century plays often had strong sentimental elements and, unlike Restoration comedy, tended to focus on domestic situations rather than the beau monde and the war between the sexes during courtship. Especially after the retirements of Van-

The Laughing Audience *(1733), by William Hogarth*

brugh and Congreve, comedy, except for a group of highly topical satires, slanted decidedly toward the domestic, and many tended toward good nature. The middle class now attended the theater regularly, and they could see people more like themselves coping with extravagant spouses, conflicting duties to loved ones, and complications caused by the intrusion of an outsider. Rather than hoping to outwit their parents or guardians, children depicted in these plays wanted both to obey their parents and to marry the lover of their choice. Wives and husbands found fidelity or the quiet life happier than the fashionable social whirl that characters like William Wycherley's and Sir George Etherege's could not bear to give up. As John Loftis has pointed out in *Comedy and Society from Congreve to Fielding* (1959) merchants and country families came to be sympathetically portrayed.

Drawing upon a rich comic tradition, play-

wrights produced a host of crowd-pleasing plays. Even those now largely forgotten contributed excellent plays. Susanna Centlivre, for instance, wrote two of the four non-Shakespearean comedies performed before 1750 that remained in the theatrical repertory through the beginning of the twentieth century: *The Busy Body* (1709) and *The Wonder* (1714). One of the other two, Colley Cibber's *She Wou'd and She Wou'd Not* (1702) also came from this era.[3] Centlivre's plays often follow the pattern of intrigue comedy with elements drawn from the strategies of Ben Jonson, Molière, Pierre Corneille, and other seventeenth-century comic dramatists. Dramatists had quickly learned to combine popular forms in order to satisfy diverse tastes. Subplots were common, one for the middle and upper classes and another allegedly for the lower-class, rowdier crowd. Playwrights like Vanbrugh had routinely provided a witty and a sentimental couple with their respective plots, and these authors expanded the kinds of comedies brought together within one work. In Steele's *Conscious Lovers* (1721), for example, the Tom and Phillis commentary contrasts with the seriousness of the Indiana-Bevil Junior plot. Cibber's *Careless Husband* (1704) has four acts of intrigue and then reformations and reconciliations that are in harmony with sentimental comedies, like his own *Love's Last Shift*. Moreover, the *Careless Husband* offers the audience two plots, both concluding with reforms. In the main plot Lady Easy brings her husband to give up his adulterous dalliances, and in the subplot Lady Betty Modish ends her flirtatious ways.

Yet another kind of comedy gained in popularity: the topical satire. Some of them, like John Gay's *The What D'Ye Call It* (1715) cheerfully recognized audience tastes for what they were. In it, Sir Roger asks his steward: "And is this the play as I order'd it, both a Tragedy and Comedy? I would have it a Pastoral too; and if you could make it a Farce, so much the better–and what if you crown'd all with a spice of your Opera?" This play was an "afterpiece," the kind of shorter, often farcical or musical play that had become increasingly popular during the period. The fact that it was frequently paired with Nicholas Rowe's *Tragedy of Jane Shore* (1714) reinforces the impression that the early eighteenth-century theater audience definitely preferred a mixed bill of entertainment, for it burlesqued pathetic tragedy. Fielding's *Covent-Garden Tragedy* (1732), his very popular *Tragedy of Tragedies* (1731), and *Pasquin* (1736) turn the same kinds of characters, themes, and conventions into hilarious burlesques of their originals.

Other literary burlesques turned the plight of playwrights into delightful comedies. Luckless in Fielding's *Author's Farce* must turn his play into a puppet show in order to sell it, both authors in his *Pasquin* see their plays mutilated by unsympathetic players and the manager, and Gay's Phoebe Clinket, silenced by the pretense that a man wrote her play, must endure the revision of her *Universal Deluge* in his *Three Hours after Marriage* (1717). Such plays included much topical satire, and in the decade before the Licensing Act of 1737 playwrights wrote burlesque plays that were as much social and political criticism as literary. Fielding came to be a master with the form, as *The Historical Register for the Year 1736* (1737) demonstrates. Since actors could mimic the speech, gestures, and characteristic stances of liv-

ing people and at that time felt rather free to ad-lib, when provided with a suitable vehicle the stage could engage in a running commentary on public events. Fielding's *Eurydice Hiss'd* (1737), with its portrayal of Walpole as Pillage, who suffers the defeat of the Excise Bill and notes his friends' reactions, is such a play.

In fact, concern about social issues and institutions appears often in the plays of this time. A number of playwrights satirized the corruption that was increasing at each election. Susanna Centlivre's *Gotham Election* (1715) was never performed because its content was considered too explosive for the year of a Jacobite rebellion, but Fielding's *Rape upon Rape* (1730) and *Pasquin* have exposés of contemporary election abuses. *The Fall of Mortimer* (1733) satirized court favorites and, in the same year, Walpole and his cronies were recognizable in *Love Runs All Dangers*. Farquhar's *The Recruiting Officer* (1706) and Gay's *The What D'Ye Call It* comment on the impressment of rural men into the military. A number of plays, including *Exchange-Alley; or the Stock-Jobber Turned Gentleman* (1720) and Colley Cibber's *The Refusal* (1721) dramatize the South Sea Bubble behavior, the actions of people who speculated wildly on investments in the South Sea and other stock companies only to experience the rapid decrease in stock value somewhat similar to our 1929 stock-market crash. Crime and the legal structure received generous attention. The popular publications of short criminal biographies with titles like *The Newgate Calendar* provided material; Gay's Timothy Peascod in *The What D'Ye Call It* makes a dying speech that mocks the formulaic repentances in the criminal biographies. He says, "I play'd at Nine-pins first in Sermon time: / I robb'd the Parson's Orchard next; and then / (For which I pray Forgiveness) stole–a Hen." A number of plays and pantomimes often appeared at the time of the capture, trial, and execution of particularly notorious criminals. For instance, Jack Sheppard, the thief who became famous for his escapes from England's stoutest prisons, had been dead only twelve days when *Harlequin Sheppard* (1724) opened at Drury Lane, and another playwright was at work on *The Prison Breaker*.[4] Corrupt judges, avaricious bailiffs, and dishonest informers populate more plays than the well-known *Beggar's Opera*.

Marriage, of course, was the social institution most commonly scrutinized on the stage. Increasingly playwrights engaged the most serious problems in realistic ways; by doing so, these

The execution of the notorious criminal Jack Sheppard in 1724 provided inspiration for popular plays.

plays point toward the "problem plays" of the late eighteenth and nineteenth centuries. Poverty, domestic disharmony, illegitimacy, men ruined in business, and grief joined the traditional obstacles to a happy marriage as complications in plots. Many of these plays might remind a modern reader of soap operas, for some are full of melodrama, sentimentality, and coincidence. They are not, however, formulaic, and at their best can still entertain and move an audience. Farquhar's *Beaux Stratagem* (1707), for example, depicts Mrs. Sullen in a sterile, unhappy marriage. Her good nature shows that she deserves better, and, when Archer comes to the country and they get to know each other, the audience has a painful glimpse of what might have been. Here, and in other plays, the need for more humane divorce

laws received open comment. Fielding's *Modern Husband* (1732) shows a spendthrift couple reduced to cutthroat behavior and fraud.

Just as comedy flourished and developed in variety, so did the use of music in plays. As moderns, we often forget that music was always an important part of a sizable number of Restoration and eighteenth-century plays. In fact, masques might be staged within plays as "The Loves of Dido and Aeneas" was in Gildon's *Measure for Measure* (1700). Acts often ended with songs, dances, or both, and many characters, like the ingenues Kitty Raftor Clive played, had several songs to sing in a five-act play. Between 1670 and 1710 English "dramatick operas" of high quality, like the Drury Lane *Tempest* (1712) and especially the productions of Thomas Betterton, enjoyed great pop-

Thomas Betterton, who led the 1695 revolt of actors against Christopher Rich and managed their new company until 1710

ularity.[5] A combination of spoken dialogue, music, dance, and spectacle, they finally succumbed to the trained voices of Italian singers and to Handel's oratorios, but another distinctive English form, the ballad opera, developed.

The name of John Gay, of course, will always be synonymous with the ballad opera because of the singular success of his *Beggar's Opera*. However, Colley Cibber, Henry Carey, Charles Johnson, and Henry Fielding all wrote good ballad operas, and many, like Carey's *Dragon of Wantley* and Fielding's *Author's Farce*, were enormously popular. A host of plays with titles like *The Quaker's Opera* (Thomas Walker, 1728), *The Beggar's Wedding* (Charles Coffey, 1729), *The Cobler's Opera* (Lacy Ryan, 1729), *The Village Opera* (Charles Johnson, 1729), and *The Prisoner's Opera* (Edward Ward, 1730) suggest Gay's important influence.[6] These plays had be-

tween twenty and sixty songs, most set to familiar English airs such as "Chevy Chase," "Over the Hills and Far Away," or "Lillibullero," which sometimes provided commentary but always helped audiences learn them more easily. Among the songs made famous by these plays were "Fill Ev'ry Glass," "The Roast Beef of Old England," and "Rule, Britannia."

Playwrights of every age aspire toward writing great tragedy, and these turn-of-the-century playwrights were not exceptions, and in this form, too, they wrote experimental and innovative plays. Both Congreve (*The Mourning Bride*, 1697) and Gay (*The Captives*, 1724), for instance, tried the blank-verse form that John Dryden had used so effectively in *All for Love* (1677). The number of playwrights who conformed to the old joke of coming to London with a tragedy in their pockets is very large. Susanna Centlivre, for example, began her career with *The Perjur'd Husband*

(1700), and Aaron Hill with *Elfrid: or the Fair Inconstant* (1710).

No matter how successful at comedy, the playwright was tantalized by the tragic muse. John Gay tried repeatedly; in addition to *The Captives*, there was even a "pastoral tragedy" in heroic couplets: *Dione* (1720). After her spectacular success with *The Gamester* (1705), *The Busy Body*, and *The Wonder*, Susanna Centlivre tried a second tragedy, *The Cruel Gift* (1716), but it had only seven performances. Aaron Hill's *Fatal Extravagance* (1721) and especially Osborne Wandesford's *Fatal Love* (1730) showed the possibilities of "fate tragedy," in which circumstances rather than any fault in the hero motivate plot. Some of these plays, like John Home's *Douglas* (1756) were among the best written in the century. Others, like George Lillo's *London Merchant*, were also among the most popular. This story of the corruption and hanging of a promising apprentice was considered so instructive that merchants bought up blocks of tickets for their apprentices, closed their shops, and filled both theaters on 26 December, an apprentice's holiday. These plays, and especially Hill's play and Lillo's *Fatal Curiosity* (1736), which was carefully staged and rehearsed by Fielding, also had great influence on the problem plays of the next 150 years.

Among the most popular tragedies were some of a very different kind from these domestic ones. The "Roman tragedy" with its exemplary hero who sacrificed for the public good with courage, nobility, and dignity seemed to be sustained on Lady Mary Wortley Montagu's alleged advice to Joseph Addison—she had recommended that he double the number of times that the actors used the word "liberty" in his *Cato* (1713), and the audience had approved. William Whitehead's *The Roman Father* (1750), John Home's *The Siege of Aquileia* (1760), and Richard Cumberland's *Sibyl* (1813) were but three of the attempts to take advantage of a fad. As Calhoun Winton points out, even "American Indian Roman plays" appeared.[7] The Roman plays often reminded the audience of the Roman presence in pre-Norman Britain, and the audience saw the exemplary virtues as those of their own country. No wonder, then, that the theaters also produced a group of historical tragedies set in early Britain.

By far, the most popular tragedies had a strong female part, and many featured a woman. Nicholas Rowe, the only really first-rate trage-

dian in this group, produced two classics of the type: *The Fair Penitent* (1703) and *The Tragedy of Jane Shore*. Women in these plays and others were both repentant and suffering. They had usually committed some indiscretion, sinned in youth, or been placed in a situation in which any choice would be wrong. Jane Shore, for instance, has been taken to court by King Edward VI, a man she could hardly have refused; when she does refuse Hastings, she brings about her death. Isabella in Southerne's *Fatal Marriage* (1694), impoverished and thinking her first husband dead, inadvertently becomes a bigamist. Although pathos was far more common than horror in these plays, some included shocking acts of violence. Aaron Hill's Zara in the play of that name (1735) stabs herself rather than marry the sultan Osman (whom she loves but must renounce because he is not Christian).

These plays had exotic settings and elaborate costumes and show that the audience still had a strong taste for spectacle. In fact, the 1727-1728 season produced a number of coronation plays, each more elaborate than its predecessor. Inspired by the coronation of George II, Drury Lane staged *Henry VIII*, and when interest began to wane the managers would substitute *Vertue Betray'd: or, Anna Bullen* (1703), then would add new historical figures to Anne Bullen's coronation procession or to Queen Elizabeth's christening regardless of which play was being performed. Next they added a coronation scene to *Jane Shore*. Before the season ended, the company performed at least three other plays with such scenes.[8]

Unlike the periods immediately before or after it, this era was marked by two intervals of intense competition for audiences. The first came when the leading actors in Christopher Rich's United Company revolted and formed a new company to perform in the tennis court at Lincoln's Inn Fields in 1695. As Shirley Strum Kenny has shown, this event encouraged playwrights like Congreve, Vanbrugh, Cibber, Farquhar, and Steele, who responded by writing twenty of the twenty-five comedies from the fifteen seasons during which the rival company survived that became "staples in the theatrical repertory." Between 1715 when this company ceased to exist and 1775, the performances of the plays of these five men totaled 1,244, consistently providing more than thirty percent of the comic repertory and rising to fifty percent in the years immediately after the Licensing Act.[9] In the second peri-

The Stage Mutiny *(1733), by John Laguerre. In March 1733 Colley Cibber sold his share in the Theatre Royal in Drury Lane to John Highmore rather than granting it to his actor son, Theophilus, who then led a revolt of discontented actors against Highmore and his partner, John Ellis. In Laguerre's satiric print Theophilus Cibber, dressed as Pistol in* Henry IV, part 2 *(his best-known role) confronts Highmore. Colley Cibber, seated at right, holds his profits from the sale.*

od of great competition, the decade before the passage of the Licensing Act in 1737 when awareness of the size of the potential audience for theater was at its height, playwrights and theatergoers came to be able to choose among five playhouses. In this milieu John Gay, Henry Carey, Henry Fielding, and George Lillo wrote some of the most innovative plays ever produced on the British stage.

At the moment when the Licensing Act passed, the theater seemed to be at the beginning of a new Golden Age. Part of its rise had been based upon playwrights' increasing interest in turning political and social problems and issues into drama–serious, comic, and satiric. Such theater attracts the best minds of a generation; theater confined to the innocuous does not. Plays like Rowe's propagandistic *Tragedy of the Lady Jane Gray* (1715), Colley Cibber's troubling *The Non-Juror* (1717), Fielding's brilliant *Historical Register*, and Gay's immortal *Beggar's Opera* would have no immediate successors, and the best young writers turned to poetry, journalism, and the novel. The

theater, however, was far from dead. In the years after the Licensing Act, Cibber, Garrick, and a rich repertory, one unequaled by any period between the closing of the theaters and the fin de siècle plays, kept memory alive. A brilliant group of players remained as well, and they included the most brilliant of all, David Garrick. The intensity and emotion he brought to parts long played by the greatest British actors set the stage for players whose names are still familiar to us–Sarah Siddons, Frances Abington, and John Kemble. They and others, like Mary Ann Yates and Henry Mossup, brought new passion to performance.

                                        –Paula R. Backscheider

1. Leo Hughes, *The Drama's Patrons* (Austin: University of Texas Press, 1971), p. 98.

2. Arthur H. Scouten, Introduction to *The London Stage, 1660-1800, Part 3: 1729-1747,* 2 volumes, edited by

Scouten (Carbondale: Southern Illinois University Press, 1961), I: cxxxix.

3. Richard Bevis, *The Laughing Tradition* (Athens: University of Georgia Press, 1980), p. 8.

4. See Horace Bleackley, "Epilogue: Jack Sheppard in Literature and Drama," in his *Jack Sheppard* (Edinburgh: Hodge, 1933), pp. 64-136.

5. Richard Luckett, "Exotick but Rational Entertainments: The English Dramatick Operas," in *English Drama: Forms and Development* (Cambridge: Cambridge University Press, 1977), pp. 124-139.

6. See William Eben Schultz, *Gay's Beggar's Opera: Its Content, History, and Influence* (New Haven: Yale University Press, 1923; New York: Russell & Russell, 1967), appendix: 285-306.

7. Calhoun Winton, "The Tragic Muse in Enlightened England," in *Greene Centennial Studies*, edited by Paul J. Korshin and Robert R. Allen (Charlottesville: University Press of Virginia, 1984), pp. 128-132.

8. Hughes, pp. 112-115.

9. Shirley Strum Kenny, "Perennial Favorites: Congreve, Vanbrugh, Cibber, Farquhar, and Steele," *Modern Philology*, 73, part 2 (1976): S4-S7.

Acknowledgments

This book was produced by Bruccoli Clark Layman, Inc. Karen L. Rood, senior editor for the *Dictionary of Literary Biography* series, was the in-house editor.

Production coordinator is James W. Hipp. Systems manager is Charles D. Brower. Art supervisor is Susan Todd. Penney L. Haughton is responsible for layout and graphics. Copyediting supervisor is Joan M. Prince. Typesetting supervisor is Kathleen M. Flanagan. William Adams, Laura Ingram, and Michael D. Senecal are editorial associates. The production staff includes Rowena Betts, Joseph M. Bruccoli, Teresa Chaney, Patricia Coate, Mary Colborn, Sarah A. Estes, Brian A. Glassman, Cynthia Hallman, Susan C. Heath, Kathy S. Merlette, Laura Garren Moore, and Sheri Beckett Neal. Jean W. Ross is permissions editor.

Walter W. Ross and Jennifer Toth did the library research with the assistance of the reference staff at the Thomas Cooper Library of the University of South Carolina: Lisa Antley, Daniel Boice, Faye Chadwell, Cathy Eckman, Gary Geer, Cathie Gottlieb, David L. Haggard, Jens Holley, Jackie Kinder, Marcia Martin, Jean Rhyne, Beverly Steele, Ellen Tillett, Carol Tobin, and Virginia Weathers.

Dictionary of Literary Biography • Volume Eighty-four

Restoration and Eighteenth-Century Dramatists
Second Series

Dictionary of Literary Biography

Henry Carey

(circa 1687-1689 - 4 October 1743)

Charles Michael Carroll
St. Petersburg Junior College

PLAY PRODUCTIONS: *The Contrivances; or More Ways than One,* London, Theatre Royal in Drury Lane, 9 August 1715; revived, with music by Carey, 20 June 1729;

Hanging and Marriage; or The Dead Man's Wedding, London, Lincoln's Inn Fields, 15 March 1722;

Harlequin Dr. Faustus, pantomime by John Thurmond and Barton Booth, with music by Carey, London, Theatre Royal in Drury Lane, 26 November 1723;

Harlequin Sheppard, pantomime by Thurmond, with music by Carey, London, Theatre Royal in Drury Lane, 28 November 1724;

Apollo and Daphne; or Harlequin Mercury, pantomime by Thurmond, with music by Carey and probably Richard Jones, London, Theatre Royal in Drury Lane, 20 February 1725;

The Quaker's Opera, ballad opera by Thomas Walker, with musical contributions by Carey, London, Bartholomew Fair, 28 September 1728;

Love in a Riddle, ballad opera by Colley Cibber, with musical contributions by Carey, London, Theatre Royal in Drury Lane, 7 January 1729;

The Generous Freemason, ballad opera by William Chetwood, with musical contributions by Carey, London, Bartholomew Fair, 20 August 1730;

Cephalus and Procris, London, Theatre Royal in Drury Lane, 28 October 1730;

Amelia, libretto by Carey and music by John Frederick Lampe, London, Little Theatre in the Hay-Market, 13 March 1732;

Teraminta, libretto by Carey and music by John Christopher Smith, Jr., London, Lincoln's Inn Fields, 20 November 1732;

Betty; or The Country Bumpkins, London, Theatre Royal in Drury Lane, 1 December 1732;

The Happy Nuptials, London, New Theatre in Ayliffe Street, Goodman's Fields, 12 November 1733; revised as *Britannia; or The Royal Lovers,* London, New Theatre in Ayliffe Street, Goodman's Fields, 11 February 1734;

The Festival; or The Impromptu Revels, music, and possibly the libretto, by Carey, London, Little Theatre in the Hay-Market, 24 November 1733;

The most Tragical Tragedy that ever was Tragedized by a Company of Tragedians, called Chrononhotonthologos, London, Little Theatre in the Hay-Market, 22 February 1734;

The Honest Yorkshireman, London, Little Theatre in the Hay-Market, 15 July 1735;

The Dragon of Wantley, libretto by Carey, music by Lampe, London, Little Theatre in the Hay-Market, 10 May 1737;

The Coffee House, ballad opera by James Miller, with musical contributions by Carey, London, Theatre Royal in Drury Lane, 26 January 1738;

Margery; or A Worse Plague than the Dragon, libretto by Carey, music by Lampe, London,

3

Henry Carey, 1729 (portrait by Worsdale; by permission of the Bodleian Library)

Theatre Royal in Covent Garden, 9 December 1738;

Nancy; or The Parting Lovers, London, Theatre Royal in Covent Garden, 1 December 1739, and produced again, 18 March 1740 (later revived as *The Press Gang* and *True Blue*).

BOOKS: *The Records of Love: or weekly amusements for the fair sex*, no. 1-2 (London: Printed by J. Grantham & sold by D. Brown & J. Milner, 7 January-25 March 1710);

Poems on Several Occasions (London: Printed & sold by J. Kent and J. Brown, 1713; enlarged, London, 1720; enlarged again, London: Printed by E. Say, 1729);

The Contrivances; or, More Ways than One. As it is Acted at the Theatre-Royal in Drury-Lane (London: Printed for W. Mears & J. Brown,

1715); revised as *The Contrivances: With Songs and Other Additions, As now Acted at the Theatre-Royal in Drury-Lane. By His Majesty's Servants* (London: Printed for W. Mears & sold by J. Roberts, 1729);

Sally in Our Alley [single sheet] (London, circa 1715);

Sweet William's Farewell to Black Ey'd Susan. The tune by Mr. Carey, words by John Gay [single sheet] (London, circa 1720);

Hanging and Marriage; or, The Dead-man's Wedding. A Farce. As it is Acted at the Theatre-Royal in Lincoln's-Inn-Fields (London: Printed for W. Chetwood, J. Shuckburg & W. Meadows, 1722);

Cantatas for a Voice with Accompanyment; Together with Songs on Various Subjects, for one, two and three voices, a through bass to the whole and all the songs transposed for the flute. The words &

musick by H. Carey (London: Printed for the author, 1724);

Namby Pamby. Or, a Panegyric on the New Versification address'd to A--- P--- [broadside] (London, 1725);

The Works of Mr. Henry Carey. The Second Edition (London, 1726);

A Learned Dissertation on Dumpling; Its Dignity, Antiquity, and Excellence. With a Word upon Pudding. And Many other Useful Discoveries, of Great Benefit to the Publick (London: Printed for J. Roberts & sold by the booksellers of London and Westminster, 1726); facsimile, with introduction and notes by Samuel L. Macey (Los Angeles: William Andrews Clark Memorial Library, University of California, 1970);

Pudding and Dumpling Burnt to Pot. Or, A Compleat Key to the Dissertation on Dumpling. Wherein All the Mystery of that dark Treatise is brought to Light; in such a Manner and Method, that the meanest Capacity may know who and who's together. Published for the general information of Mankind. By J. W. Author of 684 Treatises (London: Printed & sold by A. Dodd and H. Whitridge, 1727); facsimile, with introduction and notes by Macey (Los Angeles: William Andrews Clark Memorial Library, University of California, 1970);

Away, Away. The hunting song, in Apollo and Daphne, probably by Carey [single sheet] (London, circa 1730);

All the songs in the new entertainment of Cephalus and Procris, with their symphonies & basses (London: T. Cobb, 1731);

Amelia. A New English Opera, As it is Perform'd at the New Theatre in the Hay-market, After the Italian Manner. Set to musick by Mr. John Frederick Lampe (London: Printed for J. Watts, 1732);

Six Cantatas . . . The words & music by H. Carey (London, 1732);

Teraminta. An Opera. As it is perform'd at the Theatre Royal in Lincoln's-Inn-Fields. Written by Mr. Carey, and set to musick by John Christopher Smith (London: Printed by J. Watts & sold by John Shuckburgh, 1732);

The Songs, as they are Sung in Betty, or The Country-Bumpkins. At the Theatre-Royal in Drury-Lane [single sheet] (London, 1732);

The Tragedy of Chrononhotonthologos; Being The most Tragical Tragedy that ever was Tragediz'd by any Company of Tragedians (London: Printed for J. Shuckburgh, L. Gilliver & J. Jackson, sold by A. Dodd & E. Nutt, 1734);

Of Stage Tyrants. An Epistle to the Right Honourable Philip Earl of Chesterfield. Occasion'd by the Honest Yorkshire-man being rejected at Drury-Lane Play-house, and Since Acted at Other Theatres with Universal Applause (London: J. Shuckburgh & L. Gilliver, 1735);

A Wonder; or, An Honest Yorkshire-man; A Ballad Opera (London: Printed for Ed. Cook, 1736 [i.e. 1735]); republished as *The Honest Yorkshire-man; A Ballad Farce. Refus'd to be Acted at Drury-Lane Playhouse, but now Perform'd at the New Theatre in Goodman's Fields, with Great Applause* (London: L. Gilliver, 1736);

The Dragon of Wantley. A Burlesque Opera. As perform'd at the Theatres with Universal Applause. Set to musick by Mr. John Frederick Lampe (London: Printed for the proprietors, 1737);

The Musical Century, in One Hundred English Ballads, on Various Subjects and Occasions; Adapted to Several Characters and Incidents in Human Life, and Calculated for Innocent Conversation, Mirth, and Instruction. The Words and Musick of the Whole, by Henry Carey, 2 volumes (London: Printed for the author, 1737, 1740); facsimile, volume 22 of *Monuments of Music and Music Literature in Facsimile* (New York: Broude, 1976);

Margery; or, A Worse Plague than the Dragon: A Burlesque Opera. As it is perform'd at the Theatre-Royal in Covent-Garden. Altered from the original Italian of Signor Carini. Set to musick by Mr. John-Frederick Lampe (London: Printed for J. Shuckburgh, 1738);

Nancy or The Parting Lovers. A Musical Interlude as Performed at ye Theatre-Royal in Covent Garden (London: Printed for the author, 1740?);

Three Burlesque Cantata's, viz. The New Year's Ode (for 1736-7), The Mare that lost her shooe, The Medley, or Musical Hodge Podge. With their symphonies and basses . . . by Sig^r Carini (London: Printed for the author, 1741 [i.e., 1740]).

Collections: *The Dramatick Works of Henry Carey* (London: Printed by S. Gilbert, 1743)—comprises *Amelia, Teraminta, The Dragon of Wantley, The Dragoness* [*Margery*], *Chrononhotonthologos, The Contrivances, The Honest Yorkshire Man,* and *Nancy*;

The Poems of Henry Carey, edited by Frederick T. Wood (London: Scholartis Press, 1930);

The Plays of Henry Carey, edited by Samuel L. Macey (New York & London: Garland, 1980).

Set design for scene 1 of Harlequin Dr. Faustus *(1723), a pantomime for which Carey composed music (by permission of the Victoria and Albert Museum)*

OTHER: Extracts from *The Happy Nuptials, The Gentleman's Magazine* (November 1733).

Nothing is known definitely of Henry Carey's origins. He was born before the end of 1689, perhaps as early as 1687, probably in Yorkshire. The date is deduced from his probable age at later stages in his life; his birthplace from locales, turns of phrase, and similar evidence of Yorkshire in his writings. During his lifetime he was said to be an illegitimate son of George Savile, the first marquis of Halifax (1633-1695), the Whig politician who was largely responsible for putting William III and Mary on the throne. Frederick T. Wood, who edited Carey's poems in 1930, suggested that Carey was more likely the son of the marquis's fourth child, George (born 1667), who died in either 1688 or 1689. During his lifetime Carey neither confirmed nor denied any of these rumors, although he did include Savile in the names of two sons, and his widow named their fifth or sixth child, born after Carey's death, George Savile Carey, pointing in no uncertain manner to a family connection with the first marquis.

In 1713 Carey published his first volume of poetry, *Poems on Several Occasions* (enlarged in 1720 and further expanded in 1729). One of the poems in the first edition is characterized as "A Pastoral Eclogue on the Divine Power of God, spoken by two young ladies, in the habits of shepherdesses, at an entertainment performed at Mrs. Carey's school, by several of her scholars." It is generally conceded that this was Carey's way of acknowledging that his mother was a schoolmistress named Carey. Of more than this there is no record.

On 4 April 1708 a Henry Savile was married to Sarah Dobson at Rothwell, near Rotherham in West Yorkshire. Carey's wife was named Sarah, but whether the Henry Savile in Yorkshire in 1708 became Henry Carey in London in 1713, one can only speculate. However, it is probably not a coincidence that Carey's early career in the city was assisted by prominent Whigs, who would have had little incentive to assist a simple Yorkshireman.

On 9 August 1715 Carey's brief comedy *The Contrivances; or More Ways than One* was acted at the Theatre Royal in Drury Lane. At about the same time he published what was to become one of his best-known poems, *Sally in Our Alley*. Carey wrote the original music accompanying the poem, but, though Carey's tune still exists, the words were later sung to different tunes. Since about 1790 Carey's poem has been sung to a traditional English tune, "What though I am a country lass." The original Sally is reputed to have been Sally Salisbury, really Sarah Priddon, a famous courtesan and inhabitant of Mother Whyburn's bawdy house, but it is also possible that the poem recounts a personal experience, since Carey's wife was also named Sarah. Whomever the name may have belonged to, she has been famous ever since. Early in the twentieth century a musical comedy entitled *Sally in Our Alley* was produced in London. In 1920 *Sally* (originally entitled *Sally in Our Alley*) by Jerome Kern was produced in New York City by Florenz Ziegfeld. The show, which starred Marilyn Miller, ran for sixteen months; in 1929 it was made into a successful film. Both musicals were based on Carey's poem:

> Of all the girls that are so smart
>   There's none like pretty Sally;
> She is the darling of my heart,
>   And she lives in our alley.
>
> There is no lady in the land
>   Is half so sweet as Sally,
> She is the darling of my heart;
>   And she lives in our alley.
>
> Her father he makes cabbage-nets
>   And through the streets does cry 'em;
> Her mother she sells laces long
>   To such as please to buy 'em:
> But sure such folks could ne'er beget
>   So sweet a girl as Sally!
> She is the darling of my heart;
>   And she lives in our alley.
>
> When she is by, I leave my work;
>   I love her so sincerely;
> My master comes like any Turk;
>   And bangs me most severely—
> But let him bang his bellyful,
>   I'll bear it all for Sally;
> She is the darling of my heart,
>   And she lives in our alley.
> ....
> My master and the neighbors all
>   Make game of me and Sally,

> And, but for her, I'd better be
>   A slave and row a galley;
> But when my seven long years are out
>   O then I'll marry Sally,—
> O then we'll wed, and then we'll bed . . .
>   But not in our alley!

The poem has been characterized as combining grace, tenderness, simplicity, and humor. One might add naiveté, sentimentality, even bathos—and yet it must be said that the poem does have a certain charm, as if the simplicity of Fontenelle's shepherds were transposed into the brittle milieu of the city. According to Carey, the poem was written "to set forth the Beauty of a chaste and disinterested Passion, even in the lowest Class of Human Life." He goes on to say, "The real Occasion was this: A Shoemaker's 'Prentice making Holiday with his Sweetheart, treated her with a sight of Bedlam, the Puppet-shows, the Flying Chairs, and all the Elegancies of Moorfields. From whence proceeding to the Farthing Pye-House, he gave her a Collation of Buns, Cheesecakes, Gammon of Bacon, Stuff'd Beef and Bottled Ale. Through all these scenes, the Author dodged them, charmed with the Simplicity of their Courtship: from whence he drew this little Sketch of Nature."

Whether based on observation or drawn from his personal experience as a wooer, *Sally in Our Alley* serves as a dependable guide to Carey's later literary production. Simplicity remains a hallmark throughout his career, in plot, expression, and realization. His language is never complex, his expression never turgid or mysterious. His characters, if not drawn literally from life, are closely modeled on it. Most important, in this poem Carey breaks with tradition by offering his reader not the imaginary classical world where his contemporaries were setting poems, but the real world of poverty and exploitation around him; and he makes it palatable. Instead of Phyllis and Strephon in a make-believe Arcadia, he presents a girl-child of the working class, wooed not with the language of Christopher Marlowe's passionate shepherd but with cheesecakes, stuffed beef, bacon, and ale. Instead of chaste love unrequited, the author holds out the virtual certainty of wedded bliss, once the term of apprenticeship has been served to its onerous end. Carey never tired of reminding his peers, when they disparaged the poem's simplistic nature, that "the divine Addison" spoke favorably of it.

Carey's claim to fame lies in his literary works, but in the early part of his career he

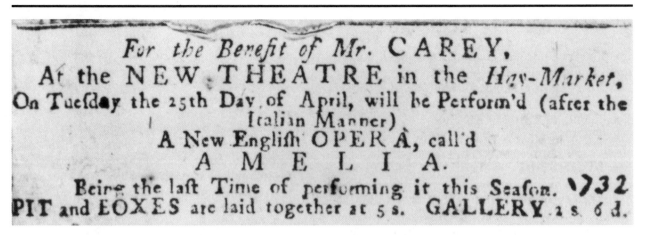

Announcement for an author's benefit performance of Amelia, *which premiered on 13 March 1732*

thought of himself primarily as a musician, and after these early successes, he set about to increase his musical skills. He took lessons from Olaus Westeinson Linnert, about whom little is known, then from two better-known masters, Francesco Geminiani, the renowned violinist and composer, and Thomas Roseingrave (1688-1766). Roseingrave was the son of an English musician of some repute and later established a reputation of his own. In 1709 his father sent him to Italy to study, and on his return to England in 1715 he became known as a supporter of the works of Domenico Scarlatti, with whom he had formed a friendship while in Italy. Probably Carey knew his teachers in this order, with Roseingrave coming last and exerting the most decisive influence. With two such Italianate influences in his background, it is not surprising that Carey's musical works display the characteristic Italian style of the early eighteenth century. Melody was his forte. Sprightly tunes, usually simple but rarely trite, are to be found in all his works. Counterpoint is almost nonexistent, and orchestration was beyond his powers. He never wrote an instrumental overture for any of his stage works.

The two major music historians of the period, Sir John Hawkins and Charles Burney, have left testimonies to Carey's skill in melodics. Hawkins says of Carey, "though he had little skill in music, he had a prolific invention, and very early in his life distinguished himself by the composition of songs, being the author both of the words and the music." However, Hawkins also notes that "the extent of his abilities seems to have been the composition of a ballad air, or at most a little cantata, to which he was just able to set a bass. Being thus slenderly accomplished in his art, his chief employment was teaching at

boarding-schools, and among people of middling rank in private families."

Burney's praise is not so precise in technical terms but in view of his strongly held opinions about the state of the theater in his day constitutes a remarkable encomium: "Poetry and Music, in high antiquity, formed but one profession, and many have been the lamentations of the learned that these sister arts were ever separated. Honest Harry Carey and Jean Jaques Rousseau are the only bards in modern times who have had the address to reconcile and unite them.... Carey, without musical learning, invented many very pleasing and natural melodies, which neither obscured the sense of the words, nor required much science to hear."

During the 1720s Carey worked irregularly for Colley Cibber at Drury Lane, adding songs to old productions and providing music for the ballad operas which proved successful with the public after *The Beggar's Opera* (1728). In 1729 his own work *The Contrivances* was revived with songs by Carey himself and played for the next two decades. But it was as librettist that Carey made his principal contribution to the theater of his era. He supplied the text for John Frederick Lampe's *Amelia* (1732) and for John Christopher Smith's *Teraminta* (1732). (Smith was the son of Handel's amanuensis J. C. Smith and, like Carey, a pupil of Roseingrave.) Neither work was a success, partly because of Carey's strained attempts to be pretentious. Gentle satire and burlesque were his natural elements, and it was Carey working on his own who finally showed the possibilities latent in burlesquing the Italian operatic style rather than imitating it.

On 22 February 1734 Carey (under the pseudonym Benjamin Bounce) produced at the

The SONGS, as they are Sung in

BETTY, or The COUNTRY-BUMPKINS.

At the THEATRE-ROYAL in *Drury-Lane*.

[*Given Gratis at the* THEATRE.]

AIR I.

HOW hard is the Fortune of all Womankind,
For ever subjected, for ever confin'd.
The Parent controuls us until we are Wives,
The Husband enslaves us the rest of our Lives.
If fondly we love, yet we dare not reveal,
But secretly languish, compell'd to conceal.
Deny'd e'ry Freedom, of Life to enjoy,
We're sham'd if we're kind, we're blam'd if we're coy.

AIR II.

Pr'ythee Fellow take Denial,
Go at once thy way,
Vain is any farther Trial,
Han't I said thee nay?
Needless 'tis to tarry here,
For thou shalt never marry here.
Then make no pother,
Get another,
For I'm not thy Lot,
Go try thy Fortune,
And importune
Those that know thee not.
But I've more Wit
Than to be bit
By such a hairbrain'd Sot.

AIR III.

False Jade tho' you bubble me,
Tho' you make me your Scoff and your Jeer.
Don't think that shall trouble me,
I can get me another, ne'er fear.
There's *Molly*, there's *Nanny*, and *Sue*,
Are all of 'em better than you,
And I'm resolv'd to marry one of 'em,
Tho' you make Fun of 'em,
Do your worst,
And fret till you burst,
For the Devil a bit will I care.

AIR IV.

Bet.   Audacious Intruder
If thus you grow ruder
I'll raise all the House.   [*Very softly.*]

Rich.   And where's the Man shall curb me,
If any dares disturb me.
I'll ha————sh him as small as a Mouse.

AIR V.

When a Virgin's so prest,
That she must be possest,
And the Lover grows sweetly uncivil,
If Assistance draws near
'Tis the height of her Fear,
And she wishes 'em all at the Devil.

AIR VI.

This Love makes all Men Asses,
We're dangl'd about
With a Smile or a Pout,
By soft deluding Lasses,
Who bubble us o'er and o'er.
Like Flies around a Honey-pot,
We hover about, till our Bane we have got,
Tho' Danger's before our Faces,
Poor Fools we plunge in the more.

When Fortune does enrich us
With Honour and Wealth,
With Vigour and Health,
These Angels so bewitch us;
Much more we esteem their Charms.
What Risques do we run for a Woman's sake?
What Stratagems use, and what Toils undertake,
To barter our Treasure
For Pleasure,
Within the Fair One's Arms?

AIR VII.

Leave me, leave me, thou troublesome Elf,
I scorn thy Person, I scorn thy Pelf,
My Heart is not to be sold.
Why shou'd I marry so silly a Sot,
When a cleverer Fellow's my Choice, my Lot?
Content is better than Gold.
What shou'd a Woman do with such a Spouse,
But squander his Money, and branch out his Brows?
Then cease to teaze
You ne'er can please,
Your Absence only will give me Ease.
You really are too old.

AIR VIII.

Courtiers Words are nothing but Wind,
They vary their Hearts with their Fashions,
They make a Bubble of all Mankind,
And nothing consult but their Passions.
Wou'd you be wise
And endeavour to rise,
You must pimp to their Interest or Pleasure,
That's a sure way
All your Toils to repay,
And to get you a Snack of their Treasure.

AIR IX.

Spare, O spare, my dearest Lover,
See my Tears and bended Knee,
And by them you may discover,
Hurting him, you punish me.

AIR X.

Why shou'd I my Passion smother,
And the Man I love torment,
Scorn may dri————ve him to another,
Then too late,
Hapless Fate,
Then too late may I repent.

Sweet Endearments shall allure him,
Never will I be at rest,
Till for e————ver I secure him,
Then, O then!
Of all Men
He alone can make me blest.

AIR XI.

What tho' they call me Country Clown;
If ever I live to see *London*'s fine Town,
I'll make a hard Push for a Chain and a Gown
Oh, cou'd I see the Day!
I'll rake, I'll scrape, I'll push, I'll strive;
Wherever the Nail will go, there I'll drive;
And one way or other, depend on't, I'll thrive
With a *Stand by, clear the way!*

Recto of song sheet distributed at performances of Betty *during the 1732-1733 theater season*

Little Theatre in the Hay-Market the musical burlesque entitled *The most Tragical Tragedy that ever was Tragedized by a Company of Tragedians, called Chrononhotonthologos*. Carey was doubtless inspired by Henry Fielding's *Tragedy of Tragedies, or the Life and Death of Tom Thumb the Great*, which had been very successful in 1730; but Carey goes to greater lengths to satirize the dramatic conventions, complicated plots, and inane dialogue of the contemporary stage, especially the operatic stage. The plot concerns an invasion of the kingdom of Queerummania, the realm of King Chrononhotonthologos, by the king of the Antipodes (whose kingdom is aptly named, for he walks with his head where his feet should be). The king of the Antipodes is captured by Bombardinian, leader of Queerummania's army, and brought to the royal palace, where Queen Fadladinida falls in love with him. At a dinner attended by the principals King Chrononhotonthologos, who feels that the cook has insulted him, kills the unfortunate servant. A fight ensues in which Bombardinian kills Chrononhotonthologos, the physician who has come to treat Chrononhotonthologos, and finally himself, as the surviving company *"All Groan, a Tragedy Groan."* A few quotations will show the level of the dialogue. When Chrononhotonthologos strikes him, Bombardinian says:

> A Blow! Shall Bombardinian take a Blow?
> Blush, Blush, thou Sun! Start back, thou
>   rapid Ocean!
> Hills! Vales! Seas! Mountains! all commixing
>   crumble,
> And into *Chaos* pulverize the World.
> For *Bombardinian* has receiv'd a Blow,
> And *Chrononhotonthologos* shall die.

He kills his king and then realizes the possible consequences:

> Ha! What have I done?
> Go, call a Coach, and let a Coach be call'd,
> And let the Man that calls it be the Caller;
> And in his Calling, let him nothing call
> But Coach! Coach! Coach! Oh, for a Coach, ye
>   Gods!

The doctor explains the futility of the case: "My Lord, he's far beyond the Power of Physick;/His Soul has left His Body and this World." Bombardinian replies:

> Then go to to'ther [*sic*] World and fetch it back
>   [*Kills him*]

> And, if I find thou triflest with me there,
> I'll chase thy Shade through Myriads of Orbs,
> And drive thee far beyond the Verge of Nature.
> Ha!---call'st thou, *Chrononhotonthologos?*
> I come! Your Faithful *Bombardinian* comes!
> He comes in Worlds unknown to make new Wars,
> And gain thee Empires num'rous as the Stars.

Of the music for *Chrononhotonthologos*, only one page of airs survives, printed with the libretto; they are all popular tunes, indicating that Carey probably did not compose any original music for this work.

Carey enjoyed two great successes as librettist for works with music composed by his friend and colleague John Frederick Lampe, *The Dragon of Wantley* (1737) and a sequel, *Margery; or A Worse Plague than the Dragon* (1738). *The Dragon of Wantley* achieved a remarkable first run of sixty-seven performances, more than *The Beggar's Opera*. Hawkins states that *The Dragon of Wantley* "may be said to be the truest burlesque of the Italian opera that was ever represented, at least in this country." *Margery* was, like many sequels, not quite the same overwhelming success, leading many contemporary critics to rate it a failure; but Hawkins calls it "in no respect inferior to the Dragon of Wantley."

The Dragon of Wantley is full of topical references, not only to Italian opera, which is burlesqued, but also to Carey's native Yorkshire. Carey especially liked to poke fun at castrato singers; "Senesino," Francesco Bernardi (d. 1759), who was one of Handel's favorite singers, was one of Carey's favorite targets. Wantley is really Wharncliffe Cragge, near Sheffield (which in turn is near Rotherham). There is near Wharncliffe a cave known as the Dragon's Den, and a well in the middle of Wharncliffe golf links is still called the Dragon's Well. According to a local tradition, this well never freezes.

Yorkshire is also the locale for what was probably Carey's best work among those of which he was both author and composer: *The Honest Yorkshireman* (1735). Toward the end of his life Carey looked on himself as a musician by profession and regarded poetry as only a hobby. But like Richard Wagner—who regarded himself as primarily a dramatist—Carey was mistaken. *The Honest Yorkshireman* reveals an accomplished wit and dramatist, but a limited musical talent. These qualities are also to be found in *Nancy; or The Parting Lovers* (1739), the last and one of the longest-lived of Carey's dramatic works. It is also one of the briefest, originally lasting only ten minutes.

Frontispiece and music from the 1734 edition of Chrononhotonthologos

(Of Carey's theatrical pieces only the two *Dragon* burlesque operas could be termed full-length works. Even *Chrononhotonthologos* takes only half an hour to present. Carey called it a work in half an act.) *Nancy* is based on an incident the author had witnessed: a young man torn from the arms of his sweetheart by a press-gang. The possibility for pathos and sentiment made it one of Carey's most successful works. In 1739 the text referred to the political situation resulting from the Spanish war (often called the War of Jenkins' Ear), but in 1756 *Nancy* was revived as *The Press Gang* with textual changes referring to what became the Seven Years War.

In 1740 Carey published three burlesque cantatas under the pseudonym Signor Carini, a nom de plume he had used previously. Only one of the three works was new; the other two had been published previously; perhaps that is an indication of the low state of his muse and his fortunes. These were his last works. In the ensuing three years nothing further came from his pen,

and on 4 October 1743 Carey died in mysterious and ambiguous circumstances.

The contemporary records say only that he rose in good health and died soon after. The *Daily Post* for 5 October is typical: "Yesterday morning, Mr. H. Carey, well known to the musical world for his droll compositions, got out of bed from his wife, in perfect health, and was soon after found dead. He has left six children behind him." (The *Post* was slightly mistaken; four or five children survived Carey, and another was to be born shortly.) Yet Hawkins states in his history, "About the year 1744, in a fit of desperation he laid violent hands on himself, and at his house in Warner-street, Coldbath Fields, put a period to a life which had been led without reproach." It is true that Carey had enjoyed no commissions from the theater for more than three years; on the other hand, there are contemporary reports—not to be discounted—that he enjoyed a pension from the Savile family throughout his life, which if true would have eased the "desperation" of imminent or real poverty. Death came suddenly, that much is certain. All else is speculation.

Carey made his principal contribution to the cultural life of his era in the theater, either as musician or librettist or both. His works outside the theatrical milieu are important in filling out his portrait as an artist in both literature and music. His principal poetic works are contained in his *Poems on Several Occasions,* first published in 1713, republished in an enlarged volume in 1720, and further expanded in 1729. Each edition contains poems not found in the other two, but the final version, which comprises ninety-one poems, is the most important. While Carey's poetry is (to make a pun on his title) eminently "occasional," two of his poems have survived into the twentieth century. In addition to *Sally in Our Alley* the other candidate for immortality is *Namby Pamby. Or, a Panegyric on the New Versification,* if only for the fact that it added a word to the English vocabulary. *Namby Pamby* is a satire on the verse of Ambrose Philips (1675?-1749), much of it of such studied simplicity and hackneyed rhyme that it was ripe for flaying. Simplicity was, of course, one of Carey's trademarks, but Philips's poems were so mawkish and inviting that Carey could not refuse the opportunity:

> All ye poets of the age!
> All ye witlings of the stage!
> Learn your jingles to reform,
> Crop your numbers and conform;
> Let your little verses flow
> Gently, sweetly, row by row,
> Let the verse the subject fit,
> Little subject, little wit,
> Namby-Pamby is your guide,
> Albion's joy, Hibernia's pride. . . .
> Now the venal poet sings
> Baby clouts and baby things,
> Baby dolls and baby houses,
> Little misses, little spouses,
> Little playthings, little toys,
> Little girls and little boys.

Carey's other major literary achievement is a contribution to the kind of political satire which became a specialty of the eighteenth century. *A Learned Dissertation on Dumpling* appeared in 1726, followed the next year by *Pudding and Dumpling Burnt to Pot. Or, A Compleat Key to the Dissertation on Dumpling.* Although both were published anonymously, there is little doubt that they are the product of Carey's agile sense of wit.

Carey does not waste words; *A Learned Dissertation on Dumpling* is only twenty-five pages long, the key only thirty-one. *Dumpling* is apparently a history of English dumpling making and eating, from Julius Caesar through King John to the present. Allegorically, it is an attack on Sir Robert Walpole and Charles Spencer, later duke of Marlborough, and their appetite for dumpling and pudding, that is, bribery and perquisites. *Pudding and Dumpling Burnt to Pot* is somewhat more openly an attack on Jonathan Swift and the possibility (which Carey obviously considered real, even imminent) of an entente between Swift and Walpole that he felt was dangerous if not disastrous. Samuel Macey, in his introduction to the Augustan Reprint Society facsimile, states, "The pamphlets are distinguished by the fact that the author's level of imagination and writing makes them delightful reading even today. In *Dumpling* the author displays a considerable knowledge of cooks and cookery in London; by insinuating that to love dumpling is to love corruption, he effectively and amusingly achieves a satiric indirection against a number of political and social targets, including Walpole. The *Key* is in many ways a separate pamphlet in which Swift is the central figure under attack after his two secret visits to Walpole during 1726. *Dumpling* had a long life for an eighteenth-century pamphlet and was published as late as 1770. Dr. F. T. Wood has even suggested that it may have influenced Lamb's *Dissertation on Roast Pig;* readers might wish to test this for themselves."

Carey's authorship of *Dumpling* and *Key* are accepted by most scholars today; the same cannot be said of "God Save the King." Speculation about the origin of the words and the music has been surrounded by controversy. William Chappell gives several possible sources for the words and music, from a song, "Grand Dieu, sauve le Roi," sung by the nuns of Saint-Cyr to a melody ascribed to Jean Baptiste Lully during the reign of Louis XIV, to several somewhat more credible possibilities. The first public performance of what came to be called the English national anthem (although music historians have pointed out that the work under discussion is a hymn or song but definitely not an anthem) seems to have been given in 1745; the first of these is noted in the *Daily Advertiser* for Monday, 30 September 1745: "On Saturday night last, the audience at the Theatre Royal, Drury Lane, were agreeably surprised by the gentlemen belonging to that house performing the anthem of *God save our noble King.*

The universal applause it met with–being encored with repeated huzzas–sufficiently denoted in how just an abhorrence they hold the arbitrary schemes of our insidious enemies, and detest the despotick attempts of Papal power." The *General Advertiser* for 2 October 1745 noted, "At the Theatre in Goodman's Fields, by desire, *God save the King,* as it was performed at the Theatre Royal in Drury Lane, with great applause." Among the letters of Benjamin Victor is one addressed to David Garrick (dated October 1745), in which he says, "The stage [at both houses] is the most pious, as well as the most loyal place in the three kingdoms. Twenty men appear at the end of every play; and one, stepping forward from the rest, with uplifted hands and eyes, begins singing, to an old anthem tune, the following words:

> O Lord, our God, arise,
> Confound the enemies
>   Of George our King!
> Send him victorious,
> Happy and glorious,
> Long to reign over us,
>   God save the King!

which are the very words, and music, of an old anthem that was sung at St. James's Chapel, for King James the Second, when the Prince of Orange landed to deliver us from popery and slavery; which God Almighty, in his goodness, was pleased *not* to grant."

There is room for much controversy here: whether such a song would have been sung supporting James II, whether at a later date it would have supported the efforts of James III (as his supporters called him), whether a hymn sung in support of James II would have had Latin words. What is incontrovertible is that after a flurry of use around 1745, "God save the King" disappeared for nearly half a century. Charles Burney, who is supposed to have arranged it for use at Covent Garden, was not sufficiently impressed to mention it in his 1789 history of music. Sir John Hawkins makes no mention of the tune in his 1776 work. It seems not to have been sung again till the mid 1790s, when the uncertainties brought on by the health of George III and the aftermath of the French Revolution caused a resurgence of patriotic feeling. About 1795 George Savile Carey, Henry's son, applied to the king for a pension on the grounds that his father had received nothing for the composition of the words and music of "God save the King." His claim was based on a report that Henry Carey had sung both words and tune at a tavern in Cornhill on the occasion of Adm. Edward Vernon's capture of Portobello (November 1739). According to another report, J. C. Smith, the younger, Carey's colleague and collaborator, is supposed to have said once that Carey had brought him such a song in order for Smith to correct the bass and harmony. None of these claims was ever established, and George Savile Carey found no success with his requests for the pension that would have acknowledged his father as the creator.

It is possible that Henry Carey wrote the words and music of "God save the King." (It should be noted that some of the text has been changed with the passing of the years, and today even Englishmen deplore the lines "Confound their politics, frustrate their knavish tricks.") But few authorities today are willing to support his case. The lack of mention by Burney and Hawkins and the lack of its use for nearly fifty years after its appearance weigh against it. The fact that Carey himself did not include the song in his collection *The Musical Century* (1737, 1740) removes what might have been a conclusive argument for his claim to authorship. While Carey's claim may be more compelling than that of Jean-Baptiste Lully, John Bull, Thomas Arne, or Henry Purcell, it is not sufficient; the attribution must be anonymous.

Henry Carey enjoyed a career which brought him many successes; considering the politics and jealousies that are a part of the theatrical milieu, Hawkins's opinion that he led a life without reproach is a noteworthy tribute. But Carey himself put the best postscript to his career; in the preface to *The Musical Century* he states: "As the Entertainment of the Publick has been the chief Pleasure and Study of my Life, and as I have had the good Fortune to succeed, I thought it incumbent on me to offer this Testimony of my Gratitude, in return of the Encouragement I have found from the Generous and good Natured, which has supported me against the Injuries of Stage Tyrants, whom I now have the Pleasure to despise.... there are several Songs contained in this Work, which I hope will never be the worse esteemed, for being Composed many Years ago; they have pleased the Predecessors of many Persons now living, and may do the same to their Successors."

References:
Charles Burney, "Carey, Henry," in Rees's *Cyclo-*

paedia, or Universal Dictionary of the Arts, Sciences, and Literature (London, 1819);

Burney, *A General History of Music from the Earliest Ages to the Present Period (1789)*, 2 volumes, edited by Frank Mercer (New York: Harcourt, Brace, 1935);

William Chappell, *Popular Music of the Olden Time; a Collection of Ancient Songs, Ballads, and Dance Tunes, illustrative of the National Music of England*, 2 volumes (London: Cramer, Beale & Chappell, 1855-1859);

H. J. Dane, "The Life and Work of Henry Carey," Ph.D. dissertation, University of Pennsylvania, 1967;

Roger Fiske, *English Theatre Music of the Eighteenth Century* (London & New York: Oxford University Press, 1973);

Sir John Hawkins, *A General History of the Science and Practice of Music,* 5 volumes (London: Printed for T. Payne & son, 1776); new edition, "with the author's posthumous notes," 2 volumes, edited by J. Alfred Novello (London & New York: Novello, 1853);

William Henry Hudson, *A Quiet Corner in a Library* (Chicago: Rand, McNally, 1915), pp. 59-91;

E. L. Oldfield, "The Achievement of Henry Carey," Ph.D. dissertation, University of Washington, 1969;

Richard Baily Price, "A Textual, Dramatic and Musical Analysis of two Burlesque Operas: *The Dragon of Wantley* and *Margery, or A Worse Plague than the Dragon*," Ph.D. dissertation, University of Texas at Austin, 1975.

Susanna Centlivre
(1669?-1 December 1723)

Jean Gagen
University of Kansas

PLAY PRODUCTIONS: *The Perjur'd Husband, or, The Adventures of Venice*, London, Theatre Royal in Drury Lane, September or early October 1700;

The Beau's Duel: or, A Soldier for the Ladies, London, Lincoln's Inn Fields, June 1702;

The Heiress; or, The Salamanca Doctor Out Plotted (published as *The Stolen Heiress or The Salamanca Doctor Outplotted*), London, Lincoln's Inn Fields, 31 December 1702;

Love's Contrivance, or, Le Médecin Malgré Lui, London, Theatre Royal in Drury Lane, 4 June 1703;

The Gamester, London, Lincoln's Inn Fields, January 1705;

The Basset-Table, London, Theatre Royal in Drury Lane, 20 November 1705;

Love at a Venture, Bath, New Theatre, probably 1706;

The Platonic Lady, London, Queen's Theatre, 25 November 1706;

The Busy Body, London, Theatre Royal in Drury Lane, 12 May 1709;

The Man's Bewitched: or, The Devil to Do about Her, London, Queen's Theatre, 12 December 1709;

A Bickerstaff's Burying: or, Work for the Upholders, London, Theatre Royal in Drury Lane, 27 March 1710;

Marplot: or, The Second Part of The Busy Body, London, Theatre Royal in Drury Lane, 30 December 1710;

The Perplexed Lovers, London, Theatre Royal in Drury Lane, 19 January 1712;

The Wonder: A Woman Keeps a Secret, London, Theatre Royal in Drury Lane, 27 April 1714;

The Cruel Gift: or The Royal Resentment, London, Theatre Royal in Drury Lane, 17 December 1716;

A Bold Stroke for a Wife, London, Lincoln's Inn Fields, 3 February 1718;

The Artifice, London, Theatre Royal in Drury Lane, 2 October 1722;

A Wife Well Manag'd. A Farce, London, New Theatre at Hay-Market, 2 March 1724.

BOOKS: *The Perjur'd Husband: or, The Adventures of Venice. A Tragedy. As 'twas Acted at the Theatre-Royal in Drury-Lane, By His Majesty's Servants* (London: Printed for Bennet Banbury, 1700);

The Beau's Duel: or A Soldier for the Ladies. A Comedy, As it is Acted at the New Theater in Lincoln's-Inn-Fields, By Her Majesties Servants (London: Printed for D. Brown & N. Cox, 1702);

The Stolen Heiress or The Salamanca Doctor Outplotted. A Comedy. As it is Acted at the New Theatre in Lincoln's-Inn-Fields. By Her Majesties Servants (London: Printed for William Turner & John Nutt, 1703);

Love's Contrivance, or, Le Medecin malgré Lui. A Comedy. As it is Acted at the Theatre Royal in Drury-Lane (London: Printed for Bernard Lintott, 1703);

The Gamester: A Comedy. As it is Acted at the New-Theatre in Lincolns-Inn-Fields, By Her Majesty's Servants (London: Printed for William Turner & William Davis, 1705);

The Basset-Table. A Comedy. As it is Acted at the Theatre-Royal in Drury-Lane (London: Printed for William Turner & sold by J. Nutt, 1706 [i.e. 1705]);

Love at a Venture. A Comedy. As it is Acted By his Grace, the Duke of Grafton's Servants, at the New Theatre in Bath (London: Printed for John Chantry, 1706);

The Platonick Lady. A Comedy. As it is Acted at the Queens Theatre in the Hay-Market (London: Printed for James Knapton & Egbert Sanger, 1707);

The Busie Body: A Comedy. As it is Acted at the Theater-Royal in Drury-Lane, By Her Majesty's Servants (London: Printed for Bernard Lintott, 1709);

The Man's bewitch'd; or, The Devil to do about Her. A Comedy, As it is Acted at the New-Theatre in the

15

Susanna Centlivre (mezzotint by P. Pelham, based on a painting by D. Fermin)

Hay-Market; By Her Majesty's Servants (London: Printed for Bernard Lintott, 1709);

A Bickerstaff's Burying; or, Work for the Upholders, A Farce; As it was Acted at the Theatre in the Hay-market, By Her Majesty's Sworn Servants (London: Printed for Bernard Lintott, 1710);

Mar-Plot; Or, The Second Part of the Busie-Body. A Comedy. As it is Acted at the Theatre-Royal in Drury-Lane, By Her Majesty's Servants (London: Printed for Jacob Tonson, 1711);

The Perplex'd Lovers. A Comedy. As it is Acted at the Theatre-Royal in Drury Lane, By Her Majesty's Servants (London: Printed for Owen Lloyd, William Lewis, John Graves & Tho. Harbin, 1712)–includes "To his Illustrious Highness Prince Eugene of Savoy";

The Masquerade. A Poem. Humbly Inscribed to his

Grace the Duke d'Aumont (London: Printed for Bernard Lintott, 1712);

The Wonder: A Woman keeps a Secret. A Comedy. As it is Acted at the Theatre Royal in Drury-Lane. By Her Majesty's Servants (London: Printed for E. Curll, 1714);

An Epistle to Mrs. Wallup Now in the Train of Her Royal Highness, The Princess of Wales. As it was sent to her in the Hague (London: Printed & sold by R. Burleigh & A. Boulter, 1715);

A Poem. Humbly Presented to His most Sacred Majesty, George, King of Great Britain, France, and Ireland. Upon His Accession to the Throne (London: Printed for T. Woodward, 1715);

The Humours of Elections. And A Cure for Cuckoldom: or, The Wife Well Manag'd. Two Farces (London: Printed for J. Roberts, 1715); the two farces were also published separately as *A Wife Well Manag'd. A Farce* (London: Printed & sold by S. Keimer, 1715) and *The Gotham Election. A Farce* (London: Printed & sold by S. Keimer, 1715);

The Cruel Gift: A Tragedy. As it is Acted at the Theatre Royal in Drury-Lane, By His Majesty's Servants (London: Printed for E. Curl & A. Bettesworth, 1717);

An Epistle to the King of Sweden From a Lady of Great Britain (London: Andrew & William Bell . . . and J. Baker and J. Warner, 1717);

A Bold Stroke for a Wife: A Comedy; As it is Acted at the Theatre in Little Lincoln's-Inn-Fields (London: Printed for W. Mears, J. Browne & F. Clay, 1718); modern edition, edited by Thalia Stathas, Regents Restoration Drama Series (Lincoln: University of Nebraska Press, 1968);

A Woman's Case: In An Epistle to Charles Joye, Esq; Deputy Governor of the South-Sea (London: Printed for E. Curll, 1720);

The Artifice. A Comedy. As It Is Acted At the Theatre-Royal in Drury-Lane. By his Majesty's Company of Comedians (London: Printed for T. Payne, 1722).

Collections: *Four Celebrated Comedies* (London: Printed for W. Mears, 1735);

The Works of the Celebrated Mrs. Centlivre, 3 volumes (London: Printed for J. Knapton, C. Hitch & L. Hawes, 1760-1761);

The Dramatic Works of the Celebrated Mrs. Centlivre with a new Account of her Life (London: J. Pearson, 1872);

The Plays of Susanna Centlivre, edited by Richard C. Frushell, 3 volumes (New York & London: Garland, 1982).

OTHER: "On the Death of John Dryden," signed Polimnia, in *The Nine Muses, Or, Poems Upon the Death of the late Famous John Dryden, Esq.*, possibly compiled by Delarivière Manley (London: Printed for Richard Basset, 1700);

Letters, in *Familiar & Courtly Letters Written by Monsieur Voiture. . .* , 2 volumes (London: Printed for Sam. Briscoe, 1700), I: 236-237, 239-240, 251-253; II: "A Pacquet from Wills," 36-37, 40-42, 44-46;

Letters, signed Astraea, in *Letters of Wit, Politicks and Morality*, edited by Abel Boyer (London: Printed for J. Harley, W. Turner & Tho. Hodgson, 1701);

"To Mrs. S. F. on her Incomparable Poems," signed S. C., in *Poems on Several Occasions, Together with a Pastoral. By Mrs. S. F.*, by Sarah Fyge (London: Printed & sold by J. Nutt, 1703);

"On the Right Hon. Charles Earl of Halifax Being Made Knight of the Garter," *The Patriot*, no. 97 (16-18 November 1714);

"To the Army," in *Political Merriment: or Truths Told to Some Tune*, supplement to part 3 (London: Printed for A. Boulter & sold by S. Keimer, 1714);

"To Her Royal Highness the Princess of Wales at her Toylet on New Year's Day," *The Patriot*, no. 123 (15-18 January 1715);

"Invocation to Juno Lucina for the Safe Delivery of Her Royal Highness the Princess of Wales," *Protestant Packet*, 2 (21 January 1716);

"Upon the Bells Ringing at St. Martins in the Fields on St. George's Day 1716, being the Anniversary of Queen Anne's Coronation," *The Flying Post*, no. 3800 (10-12 May 1716);

"Ode to Hygeia," in *State Poems* (London: Printed for J. Roberts, 1716);

"These Verses Were writ on King George's Birth-Day," in *A Collection of State Songs, Poems, &c. that have been published since the Rebellion* (London: Printed for Andrew & William Bell . . . and J. Baker & T. Warner, 1716);

"A Pastoral to the Honoured Memory of Mr. Rowe," in *Musarum Lachrymae: or Poems to the Memory of Nicholas Rowe* (London: Printed for E. Curll, 1719);

"To the Dutchess of Bolton upon Seeing Her Picture Drawn Unlike Her"; "To the Earl of Warwick on his Birthday"; "From the Country to Mr. Rowe in Town, MDCCXVIII," in *A New Miscellany of Original Poems, Translations and Imitations*, edited by Anthony Hammond (London: Printed for T. Jauncey, 1720);

"Letter on the Receipt of a Present of Cyder," in *Miscellaneous Collection of Poems, Songs, and Epigrams, By Several Hands* (Dublin: Published by T. M. Gent, printed by A. Rhames, 1721);

Untitled poem on the anniversary of George I's coronation, *The Weekly Journal*, 20 October 1722, p. 2373;

Untitled poem addressed to Isaac Bickerstaff (Richard Steele), in *Original & Genuine Letters Sent to the Tatler and Spectator*, edited by Charles Lillie, 2 volumes (London: Printed

by R. Harbin for Charles Lillie, 1725)–
Centlivre's poem is in volume 1;

Untitled poem, originally written on the flyleaf
of Anne Oldfield's copy of Fontenelle's *Plurality of Worlds,* published in *Faithful Memoirs
of the Life, Amours and Performances of . . .
Mrs. Anne Oldfield,* by William Egerton (probably a pseudonym for Edmund Curll) (London, 1731);

Untitled poem addressed to a Whig, asking him
to attend a benefit performance of one of
her plays, *Carribeana,* 6 September 1732.

Susanna Centlivre became a minor celebrity
in the literary world of London in the early eighteenth century because of her success as a dramatist. She wrote nineteen plays, three of which
were farces. Her most popular plays, which had
long runs not merely during her lifetime but for
many years afterward, were *The Gamester* (1705),
The Busy Body (1709), *The Wonder: A Woman Keeps
a Secret* (1714), and *A Bold Stroke for a Wife*
(1718). Many famous actors and actresses played
roles in her plays, which are noted for being su-
perbly actable. Her plots are lively; she handles
dramatic action effectively; and she presents a
wide range of characters from a variety of back-
grounds. Though she bowed to the increasing emphasis on morality in the theater, her comedies
do not easily fit into any one category. She was
skilled in writing romantic comedies of intrigue,
which often include a large measure of comedy
of manners and also, at times, comedy of humours. She likewise had a strong attraction to
farce. Of her three one-act farces, one satirizes corrupt Tory electioneering, one burial customs in
England, and the other a lustful and hypocritical
Catholic priest. She became an ardent Whig and
supporter of the House of Hanover but rarely allowed political issues to appear directly in her
plays. She had many friends in the theatrical
world, notably Nicholas Rowe, George Farquhar,
and Richard Steele.

No complete biography of Susanna Centlivre has ever been written, although the critical
studies by John Wilson Bowyer and F. P. Lock
contain biographical information. Several early
works contain biographical material based at least
in part on firsthand knowledge. An incomplete biography of Centlivre by Giles Jacob appeared in
The Poetical Register in 1719. At the time of her
death, Abel Boyer, who had known her personally, wrote a brief obituary which was printed in
The Political State of Great Britain (December

1723). John Mottley, who knew her in the latter
part of her life, wrote an account of her life and
works which appeared in *A Compleat List of all the
English Dramatic Poets* (1747). William Rufus
Chetwood likewise has a short account of
Centlivre's life in *The British Theatre* (1750).

Neither the names of her parents nor the
date and place of her birth are known with certainty. Jacob, Mottley, and Chetwood all agree
that she was the daughter of a Mr. Freeman of
Holbeach in Lincolnshire. Jacob says that her
mother was the daughter of Mr. Marham of
Lynn Regis, Norfolk. None of these three biographers specifies the Christian name of the dramatist's father. Bowyer suggests that Edward Freeman may well have been the father of the
dramatist since an *Edward* Freeman of Holbeach,
in his will dated 4 March 1673 and proved 23
June 1674, left twenty shillings to Susanna, the
youngest of his children. Lock, however, considers it more likely that *William* Freeman was the father of the dramatist. William Freeman and his
wife, Anne, also had a daughter Susanna, and
for this Susanna a baptismal record exists in the
parish church of Whaplode, which is near
Holbeach. The date of the baptism was 20 November 1669. Lock considers William rather than
Edward Freeman the father of the dramatist because the terms of Edward's will suggest that his
daughter Susanna was not at that time a child,
and if that assumption is correct, it would place
Susanna's birth date earlier than other evidence
suggests, 1669 or 1670 being the probable dates
usually listed for her birth.

Mottley says that the dramatist left home at
the age of fifteen after the death of her father because she was ill-treated by her father's second
wife, her own mother having died when Susanna
was a child. Mottley is also the source of the account of the "gay adventures" of her youth, one
of them being a sojourn of several months at Cambridge, where, disguised as a boy, she lived with
a student who called her his cousin Jack. After
some months, gossip about their relationship and
the identity of cousin Jack persuaded this student
(Anthony Hammond) to send Susanna to London, though with a generous gift of money and arrangements for her to live with a gentlewoman.
In London, according to Mottley, she learned
French, read poetry, and "studied Men as well as
Books."

According to Mottley, at age sixteen Susanna "was married, or something like it" to Mr.
Fox, nephew of the late Sir Stephen Fox, and

lived with him one year. Whether Mr. Fox died–
or what happened to him–Mottley does not claim
to know. No record of this "marriage" has ever
been found. Nor is there any record of her marriage to a Mr. Carroll, a young gentleman in the
army who, Mottley says, was killed a year later in
a duel. The dramatist's first plays were published
under the name of Carroll and are often so
listed in catalogues today.

On 23 April 1707 Susanna married Joseph
Centlivre, one of the royal cooks with the title Yeo-
man of the Mouth. This marriage apparently
brought Susanna a financial security new to her
life and, according to Lock, provided her with
more time and freedom to devote to writing her
plays. Susanna Centlivre died on 1 December
1723; she was survived by her husband for about
one year.

As far as we know, Centlivre's motives for becoming a playwright were, at least in part, financial, though it was not easy to earn an adequate living in this way. Moreover, in her early years as a
playwright she blamed her lack of success on prejudice against women playwrights. Later when she
had assured successes, she dropped this complaint.

Mrs. Centlivre's first play, *The Perjur'd Husband,* premiered at the Theatre Royal in Drury
Lane in the fall of 1700. In her preface to the
printed edition that appeared shortly afterward,
Centlivre claimed that this play "went off with general Applause," though its failure to be performed a sixth night she attributed to poor acting and to the fact that it was performed too
early in the season, before there was a "full
Town."

Later critics, however, have attributed its failure to the weaknesses of the play itself. It follows
the pattern of George Etherege's *The Comical Revenge,* for example, and a number of Dryden's
tragicomedies in being a multiple-plot play with a
serious main plot in verse and a comic plot in
prose. This type of play was subject to much criticism in the seventeenth and eighteenth centuries
on the basis of its disunity in action, theme, and
style.

Centlivre's two plots are connected only by
the facts that they take place in Venice during
the carnival season and that the main characters
from both plots are aristocrats and appear at the
entertainments at the beginning and ending of
the play. The main plot deals with conflicts between love and honor. Surrendering to love
rather than to honor results in tragedy for every-

one concerned. The perjured husband is Bassino, who, in spite of being married to Placentia,
is determined to contract a bigamous marriage
with Aurelia, who is betrothed to Alonzo. So determined is Bassino to win Aurelia that he listens
only in a perfunctory way to the voice of honor.
Aurelia also knows that she is honor bound to
marry Alonzo, but she too is willing, without
much soul-searching, to violate her honor for the
sake of her love of Bassino. To her credit, however, Aurelia does not know that Bassino is married until his wife, Placentia, disguised as a man,
discloses her true sex to Aurelia and reveals that
she is the wife of Bassanio. Aurelia, however, is
so passionately in love with Bassino that she
claims that she would not credit Placentia's story
even if an angel from heaven descended to confirm it and then insults Placentia as a "common
Thing."

Enraged over Aurelia's lack of virtue, Placentia draws her sword and stabs Aurelia, only to be
stabbed herself in revenge by Bassino, who does
not recognize his wife in men's clothing. After
Bassino learns that he has stabbed his loving
wife, he expresses his remorse and repentance in
the sentimentally inflated and extravagant manner that was becoming increasingly popular in
tragedy. Aurelia likewise repents her faithlessness
to Alonzo. There are magnanimous exchanges of
forgiveness among the three. Bassino is then
killed by the wronged Alonzo, and Bassino's
friend Armando pronounces the final moralistic
lines affirming that "Vengeance always treads on
Perjury." The suddenness of the catastrophes has
been criticized, as well as the length of time it
takes for Aurelia, Placentia, and Bassino to die,
though without this delay the orgy of repentances and forgiveness would have had to be omitted. The blank verse of this plot is without distinction, and the characters are relatively flat and
colorless.

The subplot, in prose, likewise deals with il-
licit love but in a markedly different way. The infidelity of a young wife, Lady Pizalta, is treated in
a comic manner throughout. She actually succeeds in cuckolding her old but lecherous husband with Ludovico, a visiting Frenchman with a
penchant for amorous intrigues. Though Lady
Pizalta's husband, Pizalto, discovers that he has
been cuckolded, he himself has been unfaithful
to his wife and has been plotting to seduce the
maid Lucy, who is the principal intriguer in this
comic plot. Although Lucy guards her chastity,
she extorts money from Pizalto by promising him

sexual favors that she refuses to grant. Centlivre is obviously objecting to the tiresome equation of a woman's virtue or honor with her chastity, for Lucy is chaste but guilty of dishonor in her avarice and deception of Pizalto. Moreover, though Lucy offers herself in marriage to Ludovico, who has resolved to "leave this wenching-Trade," he resists Lucy's offer to marry him even when he learns that she has a considerable fortune, for he scorns to marry a mere chambermaid. The prose of the subplot has vigor and the characters vitality, but its ending is scarcely moral, and in this respect it contrasts with the ending of the serious plot.

Although the modest reception of *The Perjur'd Husband* was a disappointment to Centlivre, she was not deterred in her attempt to succeed as a playwright. Her second play, *The Beau's Duel,* is generally conceded to be a much better play. It was originally presented at Lincoln's Inn Fields in June 1702, and Bowyer notes that it was repeated at Lincoln's Inn in the autumn, then revived many years later at Drury Lane, in April 1785, when it was presented for the benefit of the actor Robert Baddeley, who took the part of Careful in the performance. Otherwise, however, the play was not revived in spite of its undeniable merits.

The play is a comedy with one principal plot, though with many strands which Centlivre integrates reasonably well into the main design. Although the play attacks parental tyranny in the person of Careful, who tries to force his daughter Clarinda, who is in love with Captain Manly, into a marriage with a wealthy fop, much of the satire appropriately centers on the follies of fops, beaux, and cowards. Sir William Mode, whom Careful has selected to be Clarinda's husband, is both a wealthy fop and a coward. Modeled in part on Sir Novelty Fashion, he does not rival his original in the humor he excites, but he does have some good comic scenes. One of the best is the opening scene of the second act, where, in his nightclothes, he carries on an imaginary conversation before his mirror with a lord who has noticed him at a playhouse, flown into his arms as amorously as a mistress, and suggested that they go together to another playhouse so that the ladies *there* will also have a chance to see him. Toper, a drunkard who is another object of satire, is nevertheless a sympathetic character because he proves a help to the lovers in overcoming the obstacles to their marriage. For example, he teases Sir William and Ogle, a conceited fortune hunter who

considers himself a poet and an irresistible beau, into a duel. In private, however, Sir William and Ogle agree to fight their duel with foils.

Clarinda and her lively cousin Emilia go to the duel disguised as men in the hope of getting proof of Sir William's cowardice. When they approach Sir William and Ogle with swords drawn, they discover that the two men are indeed fighting only with foils. Before leaving them, Clarinda kicks Sir William, and Emilia pulls Ogle by the ears. But when the two girls inform Careful of Sir William's cowardice, Careful cynically remarks that Sir William will agree to a "swinging jointure," and, if Clarinda finds that she does not like him, she may live apart from him. In fact, he issues an ultimatum that if Clarinda does not marry Sir William the next day by six, *he* will marry before twelve.

As Sir William and Clarinda are apparently on their way to church on foot to be married, Captain Manly kidnaps Clarinda and marries her immediately. When her father discovers that he has been tricked, he is relatively indifferent because he now has matrimonial designs on Mrs. Plotwell, who has disguised herself as a Quaker lady of such piety that she has even converted her parrot, who now "talks of nothing but the Light of the Spirit." Careful is enchanted by her because she professes to regard handsome garments as sin, inveighs against jewelry and fashionable clothing, claims to detest visits, tea talk, and card playing. So delighted is he with her that he claims to be willing to marry her without a fortune. In fact, he settles his whole estate on her.

Immediately after the ceremony, however, his Quaker bride refuses to be kissed by him because of his sour breath, calls for servants to go to the exchange to fetch her a French nightgown, and then sets her dressing table in order with paint, powder, and patches. After admitting that her sanctity was only a trap to catch him, she demands separate beds, separate chambers, and separate tables because she cannot endure Careful's conversation. This mock marriage frequently has been said to be taken from Jasper Mayne's *The City Match* (1637), though in the bride's metamorphosis after her marriage, there are certainly reminiscences of Ben Jonson's *Epicoene* (1609).

Clarinda and her cousin Emilia, as well as Manly and his friend Bellmein, are all in on the plot and delighted to learn that Plotwell has nearly driven Careful out of his mind. When Careful is at a high point of desperation, Bellmein offers to free him from this marriage but on certain conditions: he must forgive Clarinda and Manly and give her the same fortune she would have received had she married Sir William. Careful not only agrees to these terms but offers even more. In the midst of Clarinda and Manly's romance and its vicissitudes, Emilia and Bellmein have fallen in love but more lightheartedly and wittily than Clarinda and Manly, probably because they have faced fewer obstacles. After Careful has made the necessary promises, Colonel Manly and Clarinda come in to receive Careful's blessing. Plotwell enters also and surrenders to him the marriage settlement. She then explains why she posed as the sanctimonious Quaker—namely, to reduce him to reason and to force him to receive a "Man of Sense and Honour" as his son-in-law instead of a blockhead.

As Bellmein has asserted, Plotwell has indeed formerly been Bellmein's mistress. But she has informed Bellmein that she is now a woman of virtue and requires nothing of him but his respect. Though Bellmein is surprised that his still-beautiful former mistress is "setting up for Virtue," she emphasizes that she is now a mistress of a fortune that, had she possessed it sooner, would have prevented her from straying from virtue. Now she expects to enjoy "all innocent Diversions" and to "keep the best Company, pay and receive Visits from the highest Quality, People who are better bred than to examine into past Conduct." At the close of the play Mrs. Plotwell accepts the thanks of Clarinda and promises henceforth to devote herself to virtue and good causes. Hoping for pardon from heaven for the follies of her past life, she warns women of the precious jewel of their virtue, which men only have the power of betraying, and then delivers the last lines of the play:

> O happy she, that can securely say
> Folly be gone, I have no Mind to Play.
> My Fame is Clear, I have not sinn'd to-day.

Though it is possible to interpret the final lines ambiguously, it is reasonable to assume that Plotwell is Centlivre's portrait of a fundamentally good woman who has genuinely repented of her past behavior to which she had succumbed out of fear of poverty. In fact, Plotwell is the most unusual character in the play, the rest of whom, though adequate, are unremarkable and are clearly derivative from earlier dramas. As a fallen woman, she is unlike her many ancestresses in drama in the sympathy directed to her. True, Aphra Behn had

shown marked sympathy for fallen women, but not in so thoroughly moral a context. This comedy is worth reading for many reasons, but one of the main ones is certainly the portrait of Plotwell.

Centlivre's third play, *The Stolen Heiress,* which was presented in December 1702 at Lincoln's Inn Fields, ran only a few nights. Though she had acknowledged authorship of her first two plays, she made an attempt to conceal the sex and name of the author of this play in the hope of avoiding prejudice against women playwrights. In the prologue the author is referred to as *he,* and the printed version was published anonymously in January 1703. The anonymity of the author, however, did nothing to increase the popularity of the play.

Set in Palermo, the play is called a comedy on the title page but might better be considered a tragicomedy since, like Centlivre's first play, it has two plots, one serious and one comic, both dealing with parental tyranny. In the serious plot Gravello insists that his daughter, Lucasia, marry the wealthy Pirro, who himself wishes to marry only for money. In order to bring off the marriage Gravello even stoops to deception, claiming that his son, Eugenio, who is traveling, has died and that Lucasia is now his only heir. Lucasia, however, runs away with the man she loves, Palante, and secretly marries him. Gravello, enraged at this defiance of his authority, attempts to invoke the death penalty on Palante for stealing an heiress. However, on Eugenio's return, very much alive, Lucasia is no longer an heiress, and Palante thus escapes the death penalty. Moreover, Palante learns that he is not a foundling but the son of a wealthy lord. Once Gravello learns of Palante's wealth, he eagerly accepts him as a son-in-law. Potential tragedy is thus averted, and the plot ends happily for the lovers.

The comic subplot is a lively comedy of intrigue, much more entertaining than the serious plot. Its theme parallels that of the main plot in that it too deals with a tyrannical father, Larich, who is the brother of Gravello. Although Larich is not so despicable as Gravello, he too is motivated by greed in his choice of a husband for his daughter, Lavinia. But in addition to his greed, Larich has an intense but uncritical love of learning and has for this reason picked a pedant from Salamanca as Lavinia's prospective husband.

Fortunately, Francisco, the man whom Lavinia loves, has once known at Salamanca the pedant chosen to be Lavinia's husband and thus wins his confidence. The pedant, Sancho, again fortunately for the lovers, is a learned fool who believes Francisco when he assures him that the only way to win Lavinia is to throw off his physics and metaphysics and acquire the arts of the fine gentleman. After some instruction from Francisco, Sancho appears as an impudent gentleman, well versed in foolish fopperies and claiming that he never saw a book but the chronicle chained in his father's hall. Eventually, however, this deception is discovered, and Lavinia is again threatened with marriage to Sancho, who has rewon her father's good opinion when he realizes the trick that has been pulled on Sancho. But Sancho is not merely a fool but a good-natured fool. Lavinia's outcries of grief over being forced to marry him touch his heart, and he begs her father to listen to her. Finally, when Larich remains unmoved by either her pleas or Sancho's, she claims that she is expecting a child. But when Larich, in Sicilian fashion, threatens to stab her, Sancho comes to the rescue and claims the child as his own. The somewhat unusual complications of this plot are resolved when Francisco claims to be the father of Lavinia's child and offers to marry Lavinia even though Larich says that he will disinherit her. Poor old Sancho is saddened over losing his mistress (he considered fathering another man's child "the least Thing in a thousand"), but when news comes that Francisco has inherited a fortune from his uncle even Larich now rejoices. The audience has already been informed in an aside that Lavinia is not really pregnant, and in the final scene Larich also learns that Lavinia is still a pure virgin. Only Sancho is sad at the close over the loss of his intended bride and worried over what he will tell his father.

The source of the play is considered to be Thomas May's *The Heir* (1620). Although Centlivre made many changes with the intention of strengthening the play, it apparently was never revived, though to readers with a tolerance for even second- or third-rate plays, this play is not a trial to read.

Centlivre continued to disguise her identity when *Love's Contrivance* opened at Drury Lane in June 1703. This play had a greater success than any of her previous plays, not only running for six nights when first performed but being revived the next season and occasionally thereafter, the last two revivals in 1726. Not until the dedication of *The Platonic Lady* (1707) did she acknowledge her authorship of *Love's Contrivance* with the

comment that being considered the work of a man, *Love's Contrivance* enjoyed a great success.

Centlivre borrows not merely from Molière's *Le Médecin malgré lui* (1666), as the subtitle indicates, but from other plays by Molière—*Le Mariage forcé* (1664) and *Sganarelle, ou le cocu imaginaire* (1660). She cleverly combines, alters, and adds to material from these three plays so that her finished play focuses on the outwitting of the tyrannical father Selfwill, who is determined to marry his daughter Lucinda to Sir Toby Doubtful, a wealthy old city knight of sixty-one. In the preface to the first edition of the play, Centlivre claims that whatever she has borrowed, she has touched with "the Colours" of "an English Pencil" and adapted to English manners. Though she professes to consider the three unities "the greatest Beauties of a Dramatick Poem," she justifies violating them because "the other way of writing pleases full as well and gives the Poet a larger Scope of Fancy, and with less Trouble, Care, and Pains." She implies that the main purpose of plays is to entertain, but, probably in deference to the increased popularity of stricter morality in drama, she claims that she took "peculiar Care to dress" her thoughts in "such a modest Stile, that it might not give Offence to any." The latter comment did not, however, prevent her from allowing Sir Toby, exuberant at the prospect of wedding Lucinda, to exclaim that once she is his, he will do as he pleases with her—caress, toy, play, and kiss her from head to foot, suck her "pretty Ears . . . to a Vermillion Colour, her Alabaster Neck, and those two pretty Bubbies," for all of her person will be his to caress at his discretion. Such graphic and sensual comments would have been deleted from dramas more thoroughly influenced by the moralistic emphasis spearheaded by Jeremy Collier and popularized in part by Richard Steele. Much later in the century, Richard Brinsley Sheridan's Sir Anthony Absolute in rapturously describing the charms of the girl he has chosen to be his son's wife discreetly stops the catalogue of her beauties with her neck.

Lucinda and her lover Bellmein are, of course, determined to prevent Lucinda's marriage to Sir Toby. The way in which Lucinda herself, aided by Bellmein, his former servant Martin, and Bellmein's friend Octavio, discourage Sir Toby from pursuing the marriage results in delightfully comic scenes. The love that is conducted by Octavio and Lucinda's cousin Belliza during the many frantic attempts to prevent the threatened marriage of Lucinda and Sir Toby has both lively and witty moments, though they are not to be compared with the best of the love games in Restoration comedy. The attempt to outwit Selfwill succeeds. Bellmein and Lucinda are happily married, and apparently Octavio and Belliza soon will be. The popularity of the play is certainly understandable today, for it is lively and entertaining throughout. Centlivre has skillfully adapted the material borrowed from Molière's plays into the framework of her comedy of romantic intrigue. She was fortunate that her play was performed by a strong group of actors and actresses. In her preface she mentions with gratitude Robert Wilks, who played the part of Bellmein, and Benjamin Johnson, who played Sir Toby Doubtful.

Influenced by the emerging emphasis on comedy that had a purpose beyond making the audience or readers laugh, Centlivre next attempted two comedies in which she attacks the fashionable social vice of gambling–*The Gamester* (1705) and *The Basset-Table* (1705). In her dedication to the earl of Huntingdon in the first edition of *The Gamester* she states that "The Design of this Piece were to divert, without that Vicious Strain which usually attends the Comick Muse; and according to the first Intent of Plays, recommend Morality, and I hope I have in some measure, perform'd it; I dare affirm there is nothing Immodest, nor immoral in it. . . ." She admits that she is obliged to the French for the character of the Gamester but has "reclaim'd him" from the "ill Consequence of Gaming." The play to which she is referring is Jean-François Regnard's *Le Jouer* (1696), though Centlivre made other important changes beyond the one to which she refers. Again she did not admit authorship of the play, and her authorship of it was not widely known.

The play was remarkably successful and was revived on a number of occasions, not only in the years closely following 1705 but throughout the century, with many distinguished actors and actresses taking the major roles. Its initial success was undoubtedly due in part to an excellent cast with Thomas Betterton in the role of Lovewell, Mrs. Anne Bracegirdle as Angelica, Mrs. Elizabeth Barry as Lady Wealthy, and John Vanbruggen as Valere. The main plot centers on Angelica and Valere, who are in love; but Valere is addicted to gambling, and Angelica refuses to marry him until he overcomes this addiction. It is a relief to find something other than a tyrannical father blocking the marriage of a young couple.

Though Valere often vows to give up gambling, he repeatedly breaks his vows. Valere's father becomes so thoroughly disgusted with him that he refuses to cover any more of his debts. Reduced to desperation, Valere turns once more to Angelica, who again forgives him but gives him a valuable miniature of herself and warns him that if he loses it, he will also lose her love. Then Angelica, disguised as a man, seeks out Valere where he has already broken his promise not to gamble. When she challenges him to play, he loses all his money (he has previously had a winning streak) and surrenders the miniature of Angelica to the victor. Even before he discovers that Angelica is the man to whom he reluctantly surrendered Angelica's miniature, he is shaken by remorse and vows never to enter a gambling house again. The apparent sincerity of his remorse and self-accusation help to render more plausible his later promise of reformation. His penitence is increased when Angelica produces the miniature and when his father in a fit of rage disinherits him. Angelica, however, is so shocked by the harshness of Valere's father that she is moved to generosity and eventual forgiveness of her abused lover.

The subplot deals with Lady Wealthy, a widow who is Angelica's sister and who is as addicted to coquetry as Valere is to gambling. She trifles with the affections of her honorable suitor, Lovewell, and to satisfy her vanity she flirts with other men, even Valere. When Lovewell confronts her with her latest folly involving Valere, he does so with such understanding and restraint that she repents. Because of Lovewell's "noble usage" of her, she resolves to banish from her house "the senseless train of Fop Admirers" whom she has kept to feed her vanity. Lovewell so thoroughly forgives her that he urges her not to dash his transports by delay and to marry him immediately. He is certain that in spite of the liberties she has taken, "Honour is center'd" in her soul, and a husband will frighten all foolish pretenders from approaching.

Discussions about whether or not *The Gamester* is a sentimental play are inevitably involved in the question of what a sentimental play is. Certainly the play shows the influence of one of the characteristics of what has been called sentimental comedy, a belief in the fundamental goodness of human nature and in the possibility of genuine repentance and forgiveness. It can also be called "sentimental" in the excessively emotive use of language in speeches where individuals repent, exhibit remorse, and are forgiven. Yet there are many purely comic scenes in the play, and the gambling scenes have often been praised for their verisimilitude.

The Basset-Table, first produced 20 November 1705 at Drury Lane, ran only four nights and was never revived. Modern readers, however, often prefer it to *The Gamester.* Its well-designed plot is more complex, and it presents a variety of colorful characters with various "humours" or eccentricities.

In the unsigned dedication to the 1706 edition Centlivre continues her theorizing about the function of drama that she had introduced into the dedication of *The Gamester.* The theater of Greece and Rome, she points out, accepted the thesis that the principal design of poetry is "to Correct, and rectify Manners." For this reason tragic writers "inspired their Audiences with *Noble* and *Heroick Sentiments,* and the *Comick* laugh'd and diverted them out of their *Vices;* and by ridiculing *Folly, Intemperence,* and *Debauchery,* gave them an Indignation for those Irregularities, and made them pursue the opposite of *Virtues.*" Although she admits that in the present degenerate age writers have failed to follow in the footsteps of their predecessors, she asserts that in her play "the main Drift" is "to Redicule and Correct one of the most reigning Vices of the Age."

That vice is, of course, gambling. The main plot centers on this fashionable vice as it is pursued by a variety of people who nightly congregate about the basset table of Lady Reveller, a young widow who makes her home with her uncle Sir Richard Plainman. Lady Reveller is cured of her addiction to gambling by a fellow gambler, Sir James Courtly. He shocks her into reformation by pretending to demand that she surrender her virtue to him in payment for the money he has lent her. Her protests over his insolent attack on her honor are met by ridicule of the idea that she can lay claim to virtue when she does not scruple to lure all sorts of people to her basset table, where they regularly lose their money. She is rescued from what she believes is an imminent rape by Lord Worthy, who has conveniently been placed in an adjoining room, ready to rush to her defense. Suddenly Lady Reveller sees the purity of Lord Worthy, whom she has repeatedly slighted, and professes now to hate herself and her folly. When she begs Lord Worthy for forgiveness, he is more than eager to grant it.

Another gambler who is cured is Mrs. Sago, wife of a shopkeeper. Her social aspirations draw her nightly to the basset table, where she may associate with wealthier and more socially prominent people. Her addiction, however, has plunged her husband in debt, for she has stolen from him and invariably lost what she has stolen. Sir James, whose mistress she has been, effects *her* reformation too, though not from entirely disinterested motives. Tired of her and eager to be free from her, Sir James bails out her husband, Sago, when he is about to be imprisoned for debt and offers to help pay his debts. In gratitude for this rescue, Mrs. Sago vows never to gamble again, and there is a tearful reconciliation between her and her husband.

There is a possibility that Sir James may also reform although this reformation has not taken place by the end of the play. But he is in love with the sensible and very moral Lady Lucy and knows that he can win her only if he can genuinely change his own ways. In the meantime he plays a helpful role in the subplot involving Valeria, the daughter of Sir Richard Plainman and the cousin of Lady Reveller.

Unlike her frivolous cousin, Valeria is addicted to the laboratory rather than the basset table. Earlier learned ladies in drama boasted of their knowledge of ancient languages, but Valeria is fascinated with science or natural philosophy. Ensconced in her laboratory, she performs experiments on frogs, fish, and flies. Even her pet dove has been sacrificed in the interests of science and is now being studied under the lens of her microscope. One of Lady Reveller's crew of gamesters, however, has fallen in love with the little "She Philosopher," who, unlike most of her learned predecessors, is extremely attractive in spite of her scientific ardor. To humor Valeria and just to be in her presence, Ensign Lovely pretends to an interest in natural philosophy, brings her fish and flesh flies for dissection, and patiently listens to her disquisitions on substance, material being, and the like.

In her absorption in science and philosophy she fails to pay much attention to Ensign Lovely's attempts to woo her and does not realize that her father is determined to see her married to a sea captain, for he has a special passion for rugged men of the sea, whom he regards as men of "honour, Probity and Courage." The hearty sea captain who is introduced to her as her prospective husband lights no fire in her heart since he has no interest in discussing whether or not the stars are inhabited and obviously has no concern whatsoever for improving and cultivating her mind.

In a short time it becomes apparent that no sensible conversation between them is possible. Valeria considers him an irrational beast, while he is convinced that her interest in natural philosophy is a serious distemper that fits her better for Moorfields (the location of Bethlehem Hospital for the insane) than for matrimony. This crisis, however, provides Ensign Lovely with the opportunity he needs to win Valeria. With the cooperation of the captain and Sir James, Ensign Lovely is carefully tutored into appearing as a plain-dealing seaman who has never lived more than two months ashore. Captivated by him in this guise, Sir Richard offers him his daughter and a portion large enough to make him an admiral.

Valeria, who is wise in the ways of natural philosophy but untutored in the ways of the world, never even considers a stratagem to escape this marriage. Instead she accepts her father's decree with docility and consoles herself with the thought that she will remain spiritually united with Ensign Lovely, however her body is disposed. Moreover, she does not even recognize her suitor Lovely in this "rough and Storm-like" tar whom she marries. Lovely has to reveal his identity to her after the ceremony. Of course, she is relieved that she is not married to a bluff and utterly uncongenial sea captain but to Lovely, although she is surprised and perhaps chagrined that her training in natural philosophy has not sharpened her senses enough to detect him under his disguise. As for her father, he is pacified to learn that Lovely is a gentleman, although a younger brother, and that he genuinely loves Valeria.

In spite of Valeria's excesses and limitations, her passion for the laboratory and natural philosophy is treated with gentle amusement rather than harsh ridicule, and her desire to be educated beyond the frivolities that engage the attention of the revelers who cluster around the basset table arouses genuine sympathy. To present-day readers Valeria's hunger for knowledge is considerably more interesting and relevant than the vices of Lady Reveller and her cohorts. Only Aphra Behn had previously treated a learned lady with anything approaching the sympathetic understanding that Centlivre has shown in her portrayal of Valeria. The play is lively, the plots well integrated, and the characters more than ordinarily interesting. The play's lack of success continues to remain a mystery.

Love at a Venture (1706) was not presented in London but at the New Theatre in Bath by the Duke of Grafton's Servants, and Centlivre herself is said to have acted in it. According to Mottley, Colley Cibber had rejected it as "silly" although he stole from it in writing *The Double Gallant* (1707). Though Cibber tried to deny the accusation, his plagiarism is now generally accepted by scholars who have studied the two plays.

Centlivre made no claim to have incorporated incentives to moral reformation in the play, which is full of laughter from beginning to end, but there is no question that the play shows the influence of the contemporary emphasis on a more edifying type of drama. Her main plot was borrowed from Thomas Corneille's *Le Galant doublé* (1660), although she introduced many changes in the central character and added characters and episodes not present in the Corneille play. The main plot centers on the young Belair, who has returned to London without his father's knowledge because he has learned that his father is determined that he marry. Belair is willing to marry but wants to choose the woman for himself. Meanwhile he tells his friends that he is going to enjoy his love and liberty as long as he can and "like the Bee, kiss every Plant, and gather Sweetness from every Flower." But, if by chance he meets someone who can attract and hold his love, he will marry her.

As he embarks on his career of seduction and possible marriage, he assumes two identities–Constant and Colonel Revel–but also functions at times in his actual identity. He pursues a woman, Camilla, whom he (as Constant) has saved from drowning and whom he seriously wishes to know better. In a more lighthearted vein, as Colonel Revel, he pursues the witty Beliza, whom he does not know is the cousin of Camilla, who lives with her. Probably the most amusing scene in the play is the one in which he has to face Camilla and Beliza at the same time without divulging his double identity.

Under his own name, Belair also pursues Lady Cautious, a "warm and wishing" young wife unhappily married to Sir Paul, a man who is old, jealous, and suspicious. Both characters are, of course, time-honored types, though Sir Paul is given a touch of individuality by his hypochondria (he has a physician living with him) and his terror of death. In his concern with himself he neglects his young wife, who is more than willing to be seduced by Belair, though she is prevented by the intervention of her brother Sir William Freelove, who, in spite of his name, is a bastion of morality and constancy.

Sir William is not only Belair's friend but a sensible gentleman of fashion. Incidental comedy is created by the presence of Wou'd-be, a fop who tries desperately to imitate the fashionable clothing of Sir William. Wou'd-be is also a projector in the Jonsonian tradition. Among his projects is the establishment of an office for poetry which would supply poets with "all Sorts of refin'd Words adapted to their several Characters" and a plan to build streets that would move by clockwork. Wou'd-be is also a descendant of a long line of linguistic fools who frantically use and misuse learned or impressive words to elevate their sense of self-importance. The result of his various follies is bankruptcy and a reluctant decision to return to the country.

Belair has points of similarity with Restoration rakes, such as Dorimant, but he is singularly unsuccessful in his attempts at seduction. Not realizing that Beliza is the woman with whom his friend Sir William is in love, Belair finds himself threatened with a drawn sword by Sir William for traitorously pursuing both his sister, Lady Cautious, and his love, Beliza. In fact, Sir William becomes half mad with jealousy when he realizes that Belair is wooing Beliza. Belair's relationship with Camilla is more fortunate. He falls so sincerely in love with her that he is willing to defy his father openly in order to marry her. But at this very moment his father, Sir Thomas, recognizes that Camilla is the very girl he has chosen for Belair and throws her into his arms.

The play thus ends with a series of reconciliations. Lady Cautious vows to Sir William that her aborted affair with Belair was the only slip she has ever made and that if Sir William will forgive her she will shun in the future even the resemblance of such a crime. She also apologizes to Sir Paul for her "foolish Passion" and promises that henceforth her behavior will give Sir Paul no cause for complaint. After Sir William has promised to engage his honor for the performance of this promise, Sir Paul agrees to pardon and trust his wife. Beliza realizes that in accepting Sir William as her husband she is risking the dangerous venture of having a jealous husband, but she agrees to accept him, though with the warning not to suspect her conduct. The more he watches her, she insists, the more she will study to deceive him, for the only way to have a virtuous wife is to put aside "Spanish Airs" and behave like a "true English Husband." Agreeing that this advice is reasonable, Sir William promises to allow her to be mistress of herself and him.

The moralistic note which has been struck in Lady Cautious's repentance reappears in a somewhat surprising context when Belair, the unsuccessful seducer, applauds reason and sound judgment rather than the ungoverned, loose liberty of youths who fear the marriage knot until reason and sound judgment convince them that "The truest Joy that waits on human Life / Is a constant Temper—and a virtuous Wife."

When Centlivre's next play was produced in 1706 at the Queen's Theatre in the Haymarket, she no longer hid her authorship of the play as she had since the appearance of her first two plays. Two of her "anonymous" plays had had striking successes—*Love's Contrivance* and *The Gamester*. In spite of a brilliant cast, *The Platonic Lady* ran only four nights and was never revived. In her dedication in the first edition of the play (1707), "To all the Generous Encouragers of *Female Ingenuity*," Centlivre appeals for an unbiased consideration of plays on the basis of their merits, not the sex of the author. She insists that plays known to be written by women are condemned or ignored simply because they are the work of a woman. There is no doubt that women writers faced prejudices, but the failure of *The Platonic Lady* was due to more than the sexual identity of its author.

The play has a number of refreshing and interesting characters and situations but has far more improbabilities in plot than are usually tolerated in comedies. Most of these improbabilities center on Belvil, who is introduced at the beginning of the play as a soldier of unknown parentage (although told that he was English by birth) who had been taken to Spain by his foster father to be raised. On returning to England, he "happens" to find shelter in the home of the kindly Sir Thomas Beaumont, who listens with intense interest to Belvil's account of his past. Sir Thomas forces money on Belvil, allows him the freedom of his home, but insists that Belvil never attempt to marry his niece, Lucinda. Sir Thomas also tells Belvil to procure from the widow Mrs. Dowdy some papers concerning an estate which her husband had dishonestly acquired from a relative of Sir Thomas. In neither case does Sir Thomas explain the reason for his demands.

Not surprisingly, Belvil and Lucinda fall in love with each other. Sir Thomas's insistence that Belvil never entertain any matrimonial hopes as far as Lucinda is concerned is reinforced by the fact that Lucinda claims to be a lady "devoted to Platonick Notions" and personally requires Belvil to show to the world that his relationship with her is one of only friendship and that he admires the beauties of her mind without regard to her person. At the same time she demands that during Belvil's league with her he must not address any other woman, her reason being that her pride will not permit it to be said that a man esteemed worthy of her friendship would be acknowledged as the conquest of another woman. When Lucinda believes that Belvil has been false to this agreement, she rages as indignantly as any woman who believes that her love has been false to her. The fact is that she is in love with Belvil and later openly admits before her uncle that she has "a real Passion" for Belvil that "cannot be disguised." At last the situation involving Belvil and Lucinda is critical enough for Sir Thomas to reveal the secrets of Belvil's parentage and upbringing. Belvil is the son of Sir Thomas's deceased brother. Lucinda and Belvil are therefore sister and brother. As Belvil's father was dying he decided to entrust his son and the management of his estate to his steward Dowdy, who took the boy to Spain, changed his name to Belvil, boarded him there, and then came back pretending that the boy had died. Dowdy brings with him a forged will, according to which he is the heir to Belvil's estate. Sir Thomas never explains adequately why Belvil was not entrusted to him as his sister was, or why he was not able to get the boy back from Spain or settle legally the injustices of which he was aware.

Even more improbabilities involve the attempt of a girl with whom Belvil had fallen in love in France, though without ever knowing her name, to win his affections in various unbelievable disguises that she adopts in the hope of attracting his attention. The girl is Isabella, an English heiress, who on her return to England pursues Belvil with matrimonial ambitions but without revealing until late in the play that she was the beautiful unknown with whom he had fallen in love in Paris. When Lucinda realizes the impossibility of marrying Belvil, she recommends Isabella to him. Isabella had been contracted as a child to Sir Charles Richley, but she had no love for him. With the loss of her to Belvil, Sir Charles apparently has a chance to win Lucinda, with whom he has already fallen in love.

During the time when his parentage was still a mystery to him, Belvil had indeed followed Sir Thomas's instructions and procured from Mrs. Dowdy the papers that revealed how her husband had cheated Belvil of his estate. She makes no attempt to fight the matter for she has enough honestly acquired money to suit her purposes. When she had been widowed, she had come to London from Somerset with two purposes–to become a lady of fashion and to win a husband. She is amusing because of her farcical dialectical speech and her conflict between a basic dislike of the inconveniences of being remade as a woman of fashion and her pride in her new appearance. Because of her naiveté, she is unable to detect deceit in her wooers and ends up married to Sharper, who has pretended to be a knight and has married her only for her money. Later, Sharper openly admits that he wishes he had never married her because the loss of Belvil's estate makes her a much less desirable marital catch. Yet Dowdy, very aware that she has paid dearly for learning London fashions, orders her new spouse to go down to the country with her because she still has enough money to maintain him and make him a gentleman.

Dowdy's uninhibited frankness and preference for the simpler life in the country is refreshing, as is Sir Thomas, who–unlike typical father figures in Centlivre's plays and plays by other playwrights of the time–has nothing of the tyrant in him. The play is something of a hodgepodge, however, in spite of a few redeeming features. Centlivre's genuine abilities, displayed on occasion in earlier plays, have been poorly realized in this one, although in Mrs. Dowdy there is some amusing social comedy. The most severe criticism leveled against the play in Centlivre's day was directed toward the theme of incest. In spite of the fact that no actual lovemaking ever takes place between Belvil and Lucinda, there is no question that the two are incestuously attracted to each other, though without knowing that they are brother and sister.

The Busy Body, first produced two years after Centlivre's marriage in 1707, is often considered her finest play. It premiered at the Theatre Royal in Drury Lane on 12 May 1709 and ran initially for thirteen performances. Soon it became a fixture in the repertoire of Drury Lane. It was acted at Lincoln's Inn Fields and other theaters as well. In fact Bowyer declares that *The Busy Body* was performed more than two hundred fifty times before 1750 and more than two hundred additional times before 1800. It became a favorite for benefits and royal command performances at court. Moreover, it continued to be performed throughout the nineteenth century.

Act III. BUSY BODY. *Scene 1.*

M.ʳ WOODWARD *in the Character of* MARPLOT
"There he goes."

Henry Woodward, who played Marplot in The Busy Body *for the first time on 3 December 1736, has been called the greatest interpreter of the part.*

It was fortunate in opening with a fine cast of actors and actresses, Robert Wilks turning in a delightful performance as Sir George Airy even though Mottley reported that during rehearsals Wilks had so mean an opinion of his part that once he threw it off the stage swearing "that no body would bear to sit to hear such Stuff." Mottley also said that the Town had been told that the play was "a silly thing wrote by a Woman that the Players had no opinion of." But although the first-night audience was prejudiced against the play in advance, they were soon "agree-

ably surprized; more and more every Act, till at last the House rung with as much applause as was possible to be given by so thin an Audience." When word of the delightfulness of the play was bruited about, crowds began to flock to see the performances.

Most of the critical attention given the play has centered on the structure of the plot and the character of Marplot, both of which have been highly praised and discussed with unusual thoroughness. The plot, which skillfully blends comedy of intrigue with comedy of humours and judicious doses of farce, is extraordinarily well structured. It deals, as usual, with two pairs of lovers, each trying to escape the tyranny of a parent or guardian; the dilemmas of the two sets of lovers are so neatly woven together that the transitions from situations involving one set of lovers to those involving the other seem easy and natural. The play has more than Centlivre's usual "business." In fact, the schemes by which the young lovers outwit the "blocking" by the older generation are full of unexpected crises and heightened tension, followed by clever resolutions brought about by a character's clever thinking.

The two pairs of lovers are Sir George Airy and Miranda, and Charles Gripe and Isabinda. Since Sir George and Charles are friends, they confide in each other the difficulties each faces in the pursuit of his love. Isabinda is the daughter of Sir Jealous Traffick, whose humour is his passion for all things Spanish, a passion acquired when he lived in Spain, where he came to admire many Spanish customs, especially the strictness with which the honor of young women was guarded. He has therefore imposed a virtual house arrest on Isabinda and has negotiated a marriage between her and a Spanish gentleman who is traveling to England for the wedding. Perhaps because Isabinda is so closely guarded she seems unable to help herself and creates the impression of being rather colorless. Disguised as the Spanish merchant, Charles Gripe eventually wins her in marriage, but it is Isabinda's maid Patch, a witty, wise, and skillful intriguer, who suggests and explains the entire stratagem to him. Moreover, Sir George, who disguises himself as Seignior Babinetto's friend, saves the day at awkward moments when Charles is being introduced to Sir Jealous and is faltering in his new role. It is Sir George too who prevents Sir Jealous from entering the chamber where Isabinda is being married by Mr. Tackum to Charles. When Sir Jealous realizes that he has been outwitted, he good-naturedly accepts the inevitable and even blesses the newly married couple.

Sir Francis Gripe, however, is an object of both ridicule and contempt and is truly despicable rather than merely foolish like Sir Jealous. Gripe's chief humour is his avarice. He refuses to turn over to his son, Charles, the money left to him by his uncle, which has been rightfully his for several years. He also forces his ward Marplot to pay interest on the money he lends Marplot out of Marplot's own fortune, still held in the grip of Sir Francis. Moreover, although he is sensually attracted to Miranda, who is also his ward, her fortune of thirty thousand pounds is also a major attraction in his determination to marry her himself.

The character of Miranda is much more fully and delightfully developed than that of Isabinda. Miranda is clever enough to realize that only by pretending to dislike the young gentleman and to be as eager to marry Sir Francis as he is to marry her has she a chance to win his trust and then devise a way both to marry a man of her own choosing and also to save her fortune from Gripe. She consequently pretends to deep affection for him so convincingly (calling him her pet name "Gardy" while he responds by calling her "Chargy") that he surrenders her fortune to her before their marriage and allows her to take all the "writings" bearing on her inheritance and give them to a lawyer who, she claims, will look after Sir Francis's interests in the marriage competently. Admittedly this ruse is improbable but understandable only on the basis of Sir Francis's egotistic and besotted conviction of Miranda's deep devotion to him.

In the meantime, incognito and with her face veiled, she has talked to Sir George to find out if this gentleman is the sort she can trust. Their conversations are sprightly and amusing, and, once Sir George knows her identity, they even have a brief proviso scene. Satisfied that marriage to Sir George, though a gamble, is infinitely preferable to marriage to Sir Francis, Miranda finally asks Sir George if they can agree "on the same terrible Bugbear, Matrimony," without heartily repenting later, and Sir George replies that this has been his wish since he first beheld her. Among the most frequently praised scenes in their courtship are the dumb scene (in which Miranda refuses to say a word to Sir George, who has bought an hour with her for one hundred guineas) and the monkey scene, in which Marplot, whose curiosity has revealed Sir George's hiding place, covers up his blunder by claiming that the china which Sir George broke in his hasty exit was actually broken by a pet monkey that has whisked out the window.

Marplot, of course, is the busybody who, because of his insatiable curiosity, is continually prying into the affairs of his friends Charles and Sir George and usually disrupting or threatening to disrupt whatever intrigues they have carefully devised to pursue their loves in spite of the opposition they face. But Marplot's motive is more than mere curiosity. Amiable and eager to be of service, his intentions are often good even if the results are not. Though he is the butt of ridicule, he is never contemptible because there is not a trace of malice in him as he rushes about marring the "best laid" plans of his friends in what he frequently believes are their best interests. Moreover, instead of existing merely as a focal point of laughter because of his humour of curiosity, he is involved in some way in all the major intrigues of the play. The part of Marplot was taken by a succession of famous actors, including David Garrick, who played the role thirteen times during the 1758-1759 season. Though Marplot is often compared to Dryden's Sir Martin Mar-all, there are many differences between them, Marplot being far more likeable and intelligent.

In the study of characters in the play Marplot has naturally received the lion's share of attention, but Miranda deserves more than has been directed to her. Not only is she clever and witty but resourceful, daring, and gifted with unusual self-control in not betraying to Sir Francis her contempt for him. Moreover, she displays a fundamental decency in refusing to cooperate with Sir Francis when he offers to disinherit his son, Charles, in her favor. Instead she gives Charles the papers to his estate so that he can receive his long-overdue inheritance. Miranda's virtue obviously encompasses far more than her chastity and may be Centlivre's attempt to demonstrate again her idea of what virtue in a woman really is.

The play which followed *The Busy Body, The Man's Bewitched: or, The Devil to Do about Her* (1709) is far inferior to *The Busy Body*. It ran only three nights, though in her preface to the first printed edition, Centlivre claims that the play "met with a kind Reception in general." She also compliments the players by asserting that had she searched all the theaters in the world, she "could not have selected a better Company." She blames the failure of the play in part to raising the prices on the first day and to the nearness of Christmas. But the principal reason for the closing of the play she attributes to the "Pique" of the actors, who were annoyed at a paragraph in the 14 December issue of *The Female Tatler*, which she was accused of having written. Centlivre vigorously denied having written this piece, in which she supposedly complained of factions and divisions among the actors. A great deal of scholarship has attempted to prove whether or not Centlivre wrote the offending paragraph, but there is no conclusive evidence either way.

Apart from the fracas with the actors, it is unlikely that this farcical comedy would have had a long run. Its two main plots are taken from two French comedies, *Le Deuil* (1672), by Noël le Breton, sieur de Hauteroche, and Jean-François Regnard's *Les Folies amoureuses* (1704). As usual, Centlivre introduces changes and gives her play an authentic English setting and flavor. Each plot has to do with complications in love and ends with the pairing of the lovers who overcome many hindrances. It is generally admitted that the plots are not well integrated. The title and subtitle are drawn from the second plot dealing with the struggles of Laura and Faithful to marry in spite of the opposition of her guardian, who wishes to marry her himself. Sir David Watchum, her guardian, is ridiculed for keeping Laura closely confined and for suspiciously rambling about the house all night locking one door, opening another, spitting, yawning, stamping, and muttering as he repeatedly surveys his house from door to door and gate to gate to insure that no one intrudes. Of course, Laura's lover, Faithful, not only succeeds in gaining entrance but in escaping with Laura after a scene in which Laura pretends to be bewitched. After Faithful's servant exorcises the devil from Laura, it supposedly enters Faithful, and in the confusion the two lovers escape. This scene is lively, and one would expect it to have been successful on stage. It is, of course, one of the most farcical scenes in the play. The ghost scene, which Centlivre claims was especially popular, occurs in the first plot, involving the efforts of Constant, the son of Sir Jeffrey, to marry Belinda, the daughter of Trusty, the steward of Sir Jeffrey. His plot consists of a hurried trip to Peterborough, where Trusty lives. Constant announces the sudden death of his father, claims that he has inherited his father's estate, extracts some money from the steward, and marries Belinda. When Sir Jeffrey arrives unexpectedly, he is taken at first for a ghost in an amusing scene of comic confusion. Sir Jeffrey is reconciled to Constant's marriage, however, when he learns that Belinda is actually not Trusty's child but the daughter of a lord by a secret marriage and the inheritor of a fortune of one thousand pounds a year.

The most successful parts of the play, according to Lock, are the scenes in Peterborough, where Centlivre effectively creates local color, especially in the persons of two rustics–Num, a landowner with pretensions to Belinda's hand, and his servant Slouch. Lock compares them favorably with George Farquhar's rustic characters in *The Recruiting Officer* (1706) and *The Beaux Stratagem* (1707). In spite of the popular appeal of the farcical scenes, the play was never revived, but these scenes were reprinted later by compilers of collections of farces.

A Bickerstaff's Burying: or, Work for the Upholders is a one-act farce, the first of three farces which Centlivre wrote as afterpieces. Produced at Drury Lane on 27 March 1710, it ran for three nights, and was revived on 5 May 1715 under the title *The Custom of the Country* as a benefit for Centlivre. There were a few more performances in 1715-1716, but the farce did not become a standard part of the repertory.

The use of the name *Bickerstaff* in the original title of the farce is derived ultimately from the persona introduced by Jonathan Swift in his satire on the astrologer John Partridge (1708-1709), though Richard Steele developed the persona of Bickerstaff further by publishing *The Tatler* under his name and attributing to Bickerstaff a campaign to see that the "walking dead"–or people who are good for nothing–be decently buried.

The dedication, which satirizes the ostentation and insincerity of funeral customs in England–"Rooms clad in Sable . . . Tapers burning in their Silver Sockets, the weeping Virgins fixt like Statues round"–foreshadows the subject matter of the farce itself. In fact, the burial customs of the island of Cosgar function as a kind of metaphor for burial customs in England. In Cosgar, when one spouse dies, the other must be buried alive with him or her. This custom quite naturally results in extreme grief whenever a husband or wife seems to be on the point of death, not because of the loss of the spouse but because of the dread of being buried alive. In her dedication, however, Centlivre alludes to the fact that young women who marry old men for wealth are "inter'd with Misery, from the first Day of their Marriage." That the grief of a surviving spouse in England is often as insincere in its way as is the grief displayed in Cosgar is underscored when Lady Mezro, a former Englishwoman married to the lord of the island but eager to escape in order to avoid the horrid burial custom of Cosgar, remarks that what England demands of a widow is "Widow's Weeds" and "the civil Ceremonies of Shedding Tears at the Grave," the implication being that these insincere expressions of grief are infinitely preferable to the barbarous custom of Cosgar.

Lady Mezro and her niece do indeed escape through the good fortune of a storm which strands an English ship near the island. While the damage to the ship is being repaired, Lady Mezro has an opportunity to enlist the help of the hearty, plain-dealing, and decent English sailors, who sympathize entirely with her dilemma. The storm, the shipwreck, and the curiosity of the sailors in finding themselves on a strange island have obvious parallels to *The Tempest*. But there is general agreement that Centlivre's plot is drawn from Sinbad's fourth voyage in the *Arabian Nights,* in which he visits a country where the surviving partner in a marriage must be buried alive with his or her deceased spouse. In spite of the gruesomeness of the subject matter, there is a great deal of farcical humor aroused by the pretended expressions of grief over the approaching death of a spouse–grief which ill conceals the panic of the spouse facing the prospect of being interred alive.

Marplot: or, The Second Part of The Busy Body, which was produced on 30 December 1710, is the sequel to Centlivre's popular success, *The Busy Body.* Though *Marplot* initially had a successful run and was repeated on several later occasions, the last one apparently in 1772, it failed to match the popularity of *The Busy Body.* One of the major reasons for its inferiority is the degeneration of the character of Marplot. He has lost what was amiable and attractive about him in *The Busy Body,* his curiosity is more compulsive, and his exploits more farcical and less well motivated.

The comedy is set in Lisbon. Lock explains that because England was at war with Spain, while Portugal was an important English ally, Portugal rather than Spain was thus a more probable place for English merchants to visit on business than Spain. The play deals with two amorous intrigues, in both of which Marplot becomes farcically involved, though without really influencing seriously the outcome of either. Charles has come to Lisbon to settle some of the affairs of his deceased father-in-law, Sir Jealous Traffick, and has brought Marplot with him to see the sights. Now as bored with his wife, Isabinda, as a Restoration husband, Charles promptly begins an intrigue with a beautiful young wife, Doña Perriera. In compliance with the moral emphasis of the age, Centlivre does not allow the cuckolding actually to take place, though not because of any lack of desire either on Charles's or Doña Perriera's part. Again in compliance with the "new morality," Charles's wife,

Isabinda, proves to be heroically loyal to her wavering husband. In this respect she is reminiscent of Amanda in Colley Cibber's *Love's Last Shift* (1696). Isabinda follows her husband to Lisbon, determines to reclaim him, and even saves his life by bribing the priests engaged by Doña Perriera's husband to kill Charles when he is with Doña Perriera. Isabinda not only saves her husband's life but allays Don Perriera's suspicions of his wife's fidelity. In gratitude, Doña Perriera regards Isabinda as an angel in disguise, while Charles begs Isabinda to forgive him and declares that she has more virtue in her breast than her whole sex can boast.

Colonel Ravelin is another Englishman in Lisbon who becomes acquainted with Charles and, like him, plans to enjoy an amorous intrigue. In fact, he pursues two women, not realizing for a time that they are sisters. Ravelin's intrigues are less well developed and less interesting than Charles's, and they end abruptly with one of the sisters deciding to enter a convent and the colonel willing to settle for marriage with the other sister. Throughout the play there are incidental references to the freedom which English women enjoy in contrast to the strict confinement of women in Portugal. Centlivre also vents her anti-Catholicism in her portraits of the two priests who were commissioned to kill Charles but whom Isabinda was able to corrupt for her own purposes.

The Perplexed Lovers (1712) has the dubious distinction of being considered Centlivre's weakest play. She herself attempts no defense of the play, about which she admits in her preface that she "took very little pains." She declares that most of the plot was taken from a Spanish source, but that source has not been identified. Realizing that the fact that four of the acts of the play took place in the dark (a proper time for intrigue but a cause of perplexity to the audience) was a problem, she promised to "take Care to avoid such Absurdities for the future" and to "endeavour to make . . . amends" in her next play.

What is of more interest than the two love intrigues is the fact that for the first time Centlivre openly declared her political preference. For the next few years she tried to be of service to the Whigs and the House of Hanover, especially in her poetry but also in her plays. The epilogue, which was originally intended to be delivered by Mrs. Oldfield, was not licensed in time for the first performance and was not spoken at the next two performances because of the furor aroused over the rumor that it was a "notorious whiggish Epilogue." Her firmest expression of her Whiggish sympathies appears, however, in her preface to the play, where she first professes not to know the difference between Whigs and Tories when patriotism is the issue. Then she adds that "if the Desire to see my Country secur'd from the Romish Yoke, and flourish by a Firm, Lasting, Honourable Peace, to the Glory of the best of Queens, who deservedly holds the Ballance of all Europe, be a Whig, then I am one, else not."

The Wonder: A Woman Keeps a Secret (1714) is often considered one of Centlivre's best plays. Her political convictions are expressed only indirectly in this play, through her hatred of absolutism in family, church, or state. It ran initially for six nights but was frequently revived. According to Bowyer, it was presented in London fifty times before 1750 and nearly two hundred times between 1750 and 1800. It is a lively comedy of intrigue set in Lisbon and dealing with the vicissitudes and final triumph of two pairs of lovers—Don Felix and Violante, and Colonel Britton and Isabella. The principal hindrances to the love of Violante and Don Felix are her father's determination that she become a nun so that he can retain control of the major portion of her fortune left her by her grandfather; and Don Felix's recurrent bouts of jealousy and suspicion of her fidelity. Don Felix and his sister, Isabella, are the children of Don Lopez, a Grandee of Portugal, who threatens Isabella with marriage to Don Guzman, a rich and well-born fool.

Don Lopez happens to be on friendly terms with a much-respected merchant, Frederick, who openly protests the injustice of sacrificing Isabella to "Age, Avarice, and a Fool" only to have Lopez retort that being a fool is no "Blot in a Husband, who is already posses'd of a good Estate," though a "Poor Fool indeed is a very Scandalous thing." The liveliness and flashes of wit in this opening conversation between Lopez and Frederick are typical of the skill in repartée which this play often exhibits. Frederick, of course, is stamped immediately as a virtuous man of decency and good sense in spite of his "want of noble Birth." Although his role in the play is minor, he is a friend of the major characters and is occasionally a mouthpiece for sentiments of which Centlivre obviously approves, such as his praise of hardy, courageous Englishmen and their love of liberty and his protests against parental tyranny. Frederick also recognizes that the ex-

WONDER.

M.ʳ GARRICK as DON FELIX.

My passion choaks me I cannot speak:
Oh I shall burst! Act V.

David Garrick first played Don Felix in The Wonder *on 6 November 1756 and acted in that role more than sixty-five times, ending his career with a performance of* The Wonder *on 10 June 1776.*

cessive love of money is a potent destroyer of "the comforts of Matrimony."

The dilemmas involving the two sets of lovers are interwoven by the fact that Isabella is the sister of Don Felix, whom Violante loves. Moreover, when Isabella, desperate to escape marriage to the loathsome Don Guzman, jumps out of the window of the room where she has been imprisoned, she is caught in the arms of a very surprised Scotchman, Colonel Britton, who brings her by chance to Violante's home for safekeeping. Out of compassion and friendship for Isa-

bella, Violante agrees to keep Isabella's presence a secret from both Isabella's father and her brother, who, according to Isabella, has an even more scrupulous sense of honor than her father. Isabella uses this situation to investigate for herself the character of Colonel Britton, who has appealed to her as a matrimonial prospect. This intrigue causes difficulties for Violante especially when the colonel taps on a window in Violante's home because he is searching for the veiled beauty whom he rescued and in whom he now is taking an interest. Don Felix, however, flies into a fit of jealousy because he is convinced that the man at the window is one of Violante's lovers. In fact, Violante's loyalty to her promise to keep secret Isabella's presence in her home leads to a number of crises in which Violante's reputation is imperiled, and Felix is given what seems to him irrefutable evidence of Violante's infidelity.

Violante, however, is not crushed by her lover's frenzied accusations. She is able to confront him and defend herself intelligently and convincingly even though she is not free until the end of the play to reveal the cause of the compromising situations into which Isabella has placed her. The full-bodied quarrels between her and Don Felix have an impressive ring of truth in spite of the improbabilities of the circumstances that fuel Felix's jealousy. Violante is clearly a woman with unusual strength of character, for her ability to keep a secret and to remain loyal to a friend under great stress were virtues generally considered "manly" at that time and beyond the reach of the "weaker sex."

The liveliness of the plot, with its many crises and narrow escapes, keeps interest in the play at a high pitch throughout. Don Felix's fits of jealousy, followed by his repentances and then renewed outbursts of suspicion and indignation, are both amusing and convincing if one understands that Felix is represented as a hot-blooded "Spaniard." The part of Don Felix was taken during the play's long period of popularity by a succession of famous actors, originally by Wilks and later in the century by David Garrick, who particularly distinguished himself in this role.

That *The Wonder* can still appeal to modern audiences was demonstrated when it was revived at the Festival Theatre in Pitlochry, Scotland, in May 1959. Its first-rate comic situations were widely praised along with its lively pace, its vitality, and humor. The play is considered largely original, Centlivre's most specific borrowings coming from Edward Ravenscroft's *The Wrangling Lovers* (1677). Bowyer presents a history of performances of the play throughout the eighteenth and even the nineteenth centuries. It was played in America as well as in Great Britain and deservedly earned its reputation for being among the most popular and highly regarded of Centlivre's works.

Centlivre's two farces *The Humours of Elections* and *A Cure for Cuckoldom: or, The Wife Well Manag'd* were published together in London in 1715 by J. Roberts. They were also published separately in the same year by S. Keimer, who brought out *The Humours of Elections* as *The Gotham Election*. In the preface to the joint edition of the two farces, Centlivre expresses her disappointment over the fact that the Master of the Revels did not license *The Humours of Elections* because of its subject matter. She claims that the play was read by a number of persons of distinction and taste who believed that the play would be entertaining on the stage. Centlivre's stated intention was to "show their Royal Highnesses the manner of our Elections, and entertain the Town with a Subject entirely new . . . ," but her intention was also satiric, and the object of her satire was the electioneering methods of the Tories in Gotham.

Centlivre was correct in realizing that no previous play had attempted to deal so directly with a contemporary political issue. The failure of this play to be licensed was undoubtedly due to the inflammable political atmosphere of the time. Bowyer has pointed out that since the election in January of 1715 had provoked some violence, the government understandably wished to avoid encouraging anything that would fan the flames of dissension. In fact, clergymen had been ordered to refrain from expressing political opinions in their sermons.

Gotham, which, of course, is an actual town in England, is the scene of an election for two seats at Westminster. There are three candidates. Two are local gentlemen who are Whigs and whose names indicate that they are men of impeccable integrity–Sir John Worthy and Sir Roger Trusty. They are lovers of England and the English church and opposed to France and the "popish" religion. The Tory candidate is Tickup, a Londoner with pro-French and Jacobite sympathies. He is also deeply in debt and hopes to recoup his finances after his election. Throughout his campaign, he shows himself guilty of gross deception and dishonesty in his attempts to garner votes. His two chief supporters are both presented unsympathetically. One is the mayor of Gotham, who hopes to send his daughter Lucy to a nunnery in France so that he can keep the major portion of her fortune. Tickup's other chief supporter, Lady Worthy, though married to Sir John Worthy, considers Whigs so despicable that she throws herself and all her own money into Tickup's campaign. She follows the lead of Tickup himself in the exorbitant pre-election promises she makes to local simpletons such as Goody Shallow and Goody Gabble. For example, she promises Goody Shallow that her husband will be the tailor of a "great Prince" who has a great kindness for Tickup. The Tory sympathizers among the common people of Gotham are presented as politically ignorant and credulous.

All the honest and upright characters in the play are Whig, including Lucy, the sensible daughter of the Tory mayor. Near the end of the play, she gives herself in marriage to Friendly, an agent of Sir Roger Trusty, because he loves her and rescues her from her father's attempt to put her in the nunnery. When the Whigs win the election, the Tory mayor loudly protests that the election was unfair, but within the play itself only Tory electioneering was shown to be dishonest.

That the farce is politically biased is perfectly obvious; yet it has a number of amusing scenes. Undoubtedly it would have been entertaining on the stage if political tempers at the time had been sufficiently calm and detached to permit the audience to laugh rather than riot over Centlivre's robust satire of the Tories. Centlivre's knowledge of rural characters and regional dialects is put to good use in this farce. It is unfortunate that Centlivre did not more often exploit this facet of her talent.

A Wife Well Manag'd was not produced until 2 March 1724. Revised as a ballad opera, it was acted at the New Theatre in the Hay-Market in 1732 as *The Disappointment*. According to Bowyer, it was produced again with its original title at the Bartholomew Fair in 1747 and at the Hay-Market in August 1789. Richard Frushell, however, questions whether the play revived in 1747 was actually the one written by Centlivre. Centlivre assumed that the reason for the initial refusal to license the play was the Lord Chamberlain's fear of offending people who would object to a play exposing the vices of a Catholic priest. The farce does indeed expose the vices of a "popish" priest, Father Bernard. In fact, it deals with the clever way in which the wronged husband exposes and punishes the lechery and hypocrisy of both his lascivious wife and the lustful and hypocritical priest, who is eager to have an assignation with her. Don Pisalto, her clever husband, procures by chance the letter Lady Pisalto has written to invite Father Bernard to an assignation with her. With the information provided by this letter, Don Pisalto plots a delicious revenge. First he visits and procures from Father Bernard the habit of a priest, which he says he wants to use for just an hour or two. Then he tells his wife that legal business requires him to be away for several hours. Thinking the coast is clear now for Father

Bernard, Lady Pisalto joyfully prepares for the coming of her lover-priest, whom she had instructed to come at twilight. At the appropriate time, Don Pisalto, disguised as Father Bernard, goes to his wife's room, pretends to embrace her, but just as he is promising to cool the raging fever in her blood, he beats her soundly—as a penance, he claims. He leaves without Lady Pisalto's learning his true identity.

Returning in his own person, Don Pisalto tells his wife that Father Bernard has come to sup with them. Pretending to be indisposed, she tells her husband that she has no appetite for supper and will remain in her room. On Father Bernard's arrival Don Pisalto informs him that his lady is possessed with evil spirits and beats everyone who comes near her. He urges Bernard to administer spiritual counsel to her and to do what he can for her to rid her of unclean spirits. When Father Bernard enters the room and sees Lady Pisalto presumably lying asleep, he comments on the "delicious Morsel" that "this old sapless *Log*" has "every Night to snoar over." Ravished by the sight of her, he kneels beside the bed and feasts his eyes on her loveliness. But when he wakens her with a kiss, she berates him as a traitor, a monster, pulls off his hood and beats him, aided by her maid, Inis. In desperation he throws holy water on her but soon is convinced that the devil is so strong in both women that he cannot help. After Bernard has left, Don Pisalto then shows his wife her letter to the priest and threatens to kill her. When she repents in a frenzy of fear, Don Pisalto accepts her repentance on the condition that she never see her "ghostly Father" again.

Partisan politics aside, the farce is uproariously funny and could undoubtedly be acted successfully today. Though the Irish servant Teague does not have a prominent role in the plot, his broad Irish dialect is a source of additional amusement, as is Lady Pisalto's hypocritical pretense of deep affection for her husband, whom she calls her "Pudsey," while he calls her his "little Figgup." This is an old comic device, but it is used effectively.

The Cruel Gift (1716) is Centlivre's second attempt at writing tragedy, her first having been the main plot of her first play, *The Perjur'd Husband*. Possibly the admiration of Nicholas Rowe's tragedies, her friendship with him, and her realization that tragedy was considered a higher art form than comedy may have tempted her to try her hand at writing a full-length tragedy after

Frontispiece to the 1717 edition of The Cruel Gift

many years of success as a comic writer. The play initially had what was considered a successful run—six nights. It was revived once the next season by royal command for Centlivre's benefit (3 May 1717). It has been suggested that what limited success the play may have had was due in part to Whig support. Though Centlivre was indeed enlisting her plays in support of the Whig cause, and *The Cruel Gift* supposedly has a number of political allusions to Whig-Tory conflicts, the references are not explicit or integral to an understanding of the play. For example, the authoritarian king of Lombardy is thought to represent a

"would-be" absolute monarch, while the idealized Learchus, son of the prime minister, represents Whig sentiments in his refusal to participate in any attempt to suppress liberty. Nevertheless, the conflicts between love and duty that engage the two sets of lovers are clearly in the forefront of interest.

About the best that can be said for this tragedy is that it is a "respectable" performance; even that may be an overstatement. It has many affinities with heroic drama, though it is written in blank verse rather than heroic verse. The verse achieves a modest degree of fluency and in general avoids the inflated excesses and bombast of some heroic drama, the most notable exception being Leonora's speech when what she is told is the heart of her lover is brought to her in a goblet. She also has a brief mad scene in typical heroic style. Yet the characters in the play are somewhat more believable than those often found in heroic dramas, and neither villains nor heroes are inflated much beyond life size. The fact that the play does not generate much genuine feeling either of pathos or passion again links it with the heroic mode.

Leonora, daughter of the king of Lombardy, has married Lorenzo, the general of Lombardy, secretly because she knows that her father would never consent to her marriage to someone not of royal blood. When her father learns of their love affair, the anticipated explosion does occur. He throws Lorenzo in prison and plans to execute him. Learchus, keeper of the Royal Fort and a man of impeccable honor, is appointed Lorenzo's guardian. Lorenzo's sister, Antimora, is in love with Learchus and he with her. Because of her sense of duty to her brother, Antimora pleads with Learchus to free Lorenzo and save his life. But Learchus's duty to his country and his king obliges him to deny Antimora's request, prompting her to swear eternal enmity to him.

These love conflicts are quickly resolved, however, when a hermit appears and reveals that he is the duke of Milan, whose throne was usurped many years ago, and that Lorenzo is in fact his son, though he had been given to Alcanor, father of Antimora, to be raised. The king is now filled with guilt because Lorenzo's royal blood would have made him a suitable son-in-law. But the king believes that Lorenzo has been executed, and, by the king's own command, his heart brought in a cup to Leonora. A heart had indeed been brought to Leonora, who was told that it was the heart of the dead Lorenzo, and her frenzied reaction had quickly led to madness. But Leonora quickly regains her wits when she learns that Learchus had secretly saved Lorenzo's life and had substituted for Lorenzo's heart the heart of another man who had died. Leonora is reunited happily with Lorenzo, whom the king now declares the heir apparent to the crown of Lombardy. Antimora and Learchus are also happily reconciled. This play adds nothing positive to Centlivre's reputation as a dramatist. But it is a pardonable "experiment" in a genre to which her talents are obviously not suited.

A Bold Stroke for a Wife, first performed in February 1718 at Lincoln's Inn Fields, had an initial run of six nights, which meant it was a success. But its success grew throughout the century. Although it was not revived in London until 1728, its popularity increased thereafter. Bowyer has noted that it was performed in London more than eighty times before 1750 and one hundred fifty times between 1750 and 1800. In fact, it continued to please audiences well into the nineteenth century and attracted a succession of great actors.

Nevertheless, early critics belittled the play as a mere farce and refrained from devoting serious attention to it. There were even objections to it on moral grounds. Now it is commonly considered one of the finest of Centlivre's plays. The plot is much simpler than Centlivre's usual plots. It is well constructed in that it is perfectly unified in action and theme; all of the incidents involve the efforts of one man, Fainwell, to trick each of the four guardians of the woman he loves–Anne Lovely–into consenting to allow him to marry her. The four guardians, each of whom is an example of a stock humours character, were deliberately chosen by Anne Lovely's father, who was himself a humours character. Because he "hated posterity" and "wished the world were to expire with himself" he tried at least to prevent his daughter from marrying and reproducing. By choosing four eccentric guardians with widely diverse interests and inclinations, he hoped that no man could win the consent of all four to marrying Anne.

Although there is nothing new in their eccentricities, each of these four guardians is an amusing butt of satire. Sir Philip Modelove is "an old beau," or fop, loosely in the Fopling Flutter tradition. He delights in all things French and fashionable. Periwinkle is a virtuoso who is fascinated with antiquity and natural history and uncritical and credulous about both. Tradelove, a stock jobber, is zealously alert to acquire every bit of information about stock prices because of his desire to make a quick fortune. In addition to his delight in his own gains, he rejoices in the ruin of his competitors, to which he contributes whenever possible. The last guardian is Obadiah Prim, a Quaker. In spite of their plain style of dress and their pretense to virtue, Obadiah and his wife, Sarah, are in secret unashamedly licentious. Their son, Tobias, has seduced their maid, Tabatha; not because of lust, Mrs. Prim declares, but because the buffeting of Satan was too strong for him.

When Fainwell sets out to win the consent of all four guardians, his disguises are as amusing and preposterous as the humours of the men he is attempting to outwit. His schemes to cater to the humour of each of the guardians demand ingenuity, skill, and steadiness of nerve. The successful deception of Periwinkle requires two attempts on Fainwell's part, but Periwinkle finally succumbs as do the other three. These episodes are lively and full of sheer fun. The satire on the vices and foibles of the four eccentrics had a special relevance to eighteenth-century audiences, but the satire is amiable and laughable rather than sternly indignant.

Centlivre's claim in the prologue that the plot is new "without one borrowed line" is frequently disputed. Yet it is likely that she is speaking the simple truth in not having drawn directly from any one source. She has undeniably drawn on her wide knowledge of stock themes and characters but made them her own by the skill with which she has revitalized them and fit them into the structure of her comedy.

Mrs. Centlivre's last play, *The Artifice*, produced at Drury Lane in early October 1722, ran for only three nights. Although there are many lively scenes and characters in the play, the most obvious reason for its failure is its extreme length (it is by far the longest of Centlivre's plays) and its overloaded plot. The four strands of the plot are structurally interwoven, with certain characters appearing in more than one subplot, but these strands are not integrated into a coherent pattern of thematic parallels and contrasts. Lock has also complained of the lack of a consistent moral perspective from which to view the play as a whole and its mixture of serious and comic actions. Shirley Markel, however, rightly emphasizes that artifice itself functions as the principal unifying factor in the play. To Markel the play's disunity should be attributed to its unwieldly plot, not to a lack of a consistent moral perspective. There is no question that artifice is an important factor in each of the plots, though the attitude toward it varies from plot to plot according to the circumstances and the motives of the persons involved in artifice. Greed—often closely associated with self-interest—is typically, but not invariably, the chief motive.

If any one character is central in the play, it is Ned Freeman, who is involved significantly in three of the plots—one involving his conflict with his brother, Sir John, over the inheritance of their father's estate; one involving the Dutch woman Louisa, who considers herself Ned's lawful wife; and one describing his farcical attempts to seduce the very willing Mrs. Watchit.

Although he is a younger son, Ned has had the good fortune to inherit his father's fortune but at the expense of his older brother, Sir John, who was disinherited because of a political prank which he committed seven years previously and for which his father never forgave him. Sir John has expected to marry Olivia, the daughter of Sir Philip Moneylove. But after Sir John has been disinherited, Sir Philip withdraws his consent to the marriage and wants Olivia to marry Ned instead. On hearing that he is heir to his father's estate, the surprised and delighted Ned ungraciously refuses to give Sir John even enough money to buy a colonel's commission. Though Ned does not seem eager to marry Olivia nor she him, Sir John nevertheless worries that he may lose Olivia to Ned.

Sir John knows that Ned has been betrothed to a Dutch girl, Louisa, and that she has given birth to Ned's child. Sir John also knows that Louisa regards Ned as her husband because, according to Dutch custom, a betrothal is the virtual equivalent of marriage. Sir John has accordingly arranged for Louisa to come to England in the hope of persuading Ned to acknowledge her as his wife. Although Sir John is not without sympathy for Louisa, his principal motive for bringing Louisa to England is to prevent Ned from marrying Olivia.

In the meantime Ned has been attracted to Mrs. Watchit, a beautiful young wife who is virtually imprisoned in her home by a pathologically jealous husband determined that his wife shall give birth to no child that is not his own. This segment of the plot is amusing in a farcically immoral way for one's sympathies can scarcely avoid being with Mrs. Watchit and Ned. Her husband's barbaric treatment of Mrs. Watchit naturally provokes her into trying to outwit him and to do in fact what he is always suspecting her of trying. Ned, of course, finds a way into Mrs. Watchit's home and once is even discovered by her husband after he has been hiding behind a screen. Yet Ned is so quick-thinking that he is able to persuade Watchit that he had just entered the room by himself because no servant had answered when he had rung the bell. Perhaps as a concession to the "new morality," Centlivre does not permit Mrs. Watchit and Ned to succeed in their attempted assignations, though Watchit is invariably outwitted and outmaneuvered.

When Louisa finally confronts Ned with her claims on him, he still refuses to accept her as his wife. In fact, he is coldly cynical in what he suggests as a solution to her dilemma: he promises to arrange for her to become a mistress of an English lord with a particular liking for Dutch women. The witty, engagingly charming Ned, who wins our sympathies in his encounters with Mrs. Watchit and her husband, seems contemptible in his treatment of Louisa. Furious at Ned's rejection of her, Louisa is angry enough to kill him but instead resorts to artifice to persuade him to accept his responsibilities as her husband. With the help of Sir John, she gives Ned a potion that will make him ill but will not be fatal. When Ned begins to feel the effect of the potion, he readily believes Louisa, who tells him that she has poisoned him and that he is going to die. Now presumably repentant and eager to make amends for his bad behavior, he agrees to an immediate marriage to Louisa and even deeds his estate to Sir John. But when Ned learns that his sickness is not mortal, he flies into a rage over having been tricked. Although Sir John generously agrees to give him one-half of the inheritance, Louisa assures Sir John that if Ned will forgive the artifice by means of which she induced him to marry her, he will be beyond the reach of want. Then she reveals that at her father's death, she became the mistress of forty thousand pounds a year. On hearing this astonishing news, Ned exclaims that there is no need for her to ask his forgiveness. No woman, he asserts, can be guilty of any fault or need forgiveness if she has forty thousand pounds, and he admits that few women could boast of Louisa's constancy. The comic (happy) ending of the conflict between Louisa and Ned softens the impact of Ned's earlier treatment of Louisa, and his outspoken delight in her fortune is wreathed in laughter. This resolution proves happy for Olivia and Sir John also, for now Sir Philip Moneylove is perfectly content to have Olivia marry Sir John.

When Mrs. Watchit learns that her lover Ned is married, she remarks that she is glad they were no better acquainted. This is hardly a sign of repentance. She has, however, so thoroughly shamed and outwitted her husband that he is willing to be reconciled to her and she to him if he consents to certain provisos. She insists that he must cease to be jealous, that he must not try to expose her unless she gives him real cause, and

that he must allow her to enjoy "the Liberties of an English Wife." The comic ambiguity of this statement could not be lost entirely on Watchit, but he agrees nevertheless to banish not only his suspicions but his locks, bolts, and iron bars.

The plot focusing on the Widow Heedless also emphasizes artifice since both of the men who are pursuing her and her fortune resort to deception in the hope of winning her. Ensign Fainwell, who is the more clever and less culpable of the two matrimonial intriguers, succeeds in tricking the widow into marrying him and defeating the crassly unscrupulous Tally, who has been masquerading as a lord. Though the widow has insisted that she would marry no one beneath a lord, Fainwell, in spite of the deceptions by which he has tricked her into marrying him, has really done her a service in saving her from the rapacious Tally. Moreover, Fainwell seems sincere in his promises to love her, and he consoles her by assuring her that he is at least a gentleman. At the conclusion, the widow is considering the possibility that for a thousand pounds Fainwell might be knighted.

The play is clearly a tissue of artifices, all of them tainted morally, though some are much less deplorable than others. In fact, the artifice by means of which Louisa traps Ned into marrying her seems justifiable, even though, in an exemplary comedy, Louisa probably would have won Ned by a display of magnanimity so overpowering that it would have softened even Ned's stony heart.

Centlivre's attitude toward artifice is set in a fundamentally comic context in spite of serious elements in the plot as a whole. This attitude is not inconsistent but worldly wise in recognizing the varieties of artifice and viewing them in accordance with the particular dramatic and moral context in which they appear. Lock has said that Centlivre could have made two good plays out of the material crowded injudiciously into this one play. One may wish that Centlivre had ended her long career with a better play. Yet in spite of its failure on the stage, one can still recognize in it many instances of Centlivre's many-faceted talents, not at their zenith, but not in absolute decay either. Moreover, the play testifies to what an assiduous reader of her plays may have long suspected, namely, that Centlivre was most at home not with the new morality being foisted increasingly on dramatists but on the witty amorality of Restoration comedy or the uproarious immorality of farce.

Centlivre's long and successful career in the theatrical world, in spite of the prejudice against women playwrights in the early eighteenth century, is worthy of note. The successful revival of several of her best comedies in this century is proof of their enduring appeal. *A Bold Stroke for a Wife,* for example, was successfully revived as recently as the summer of 1988 at the Alabama Shakespeare Festival in Montgomery, Alabama.

Centlivre's comedies have long been recognized as unusually "actable," entertaining, and lively, though earlier critics tended to deny them any solid literary merit. Later critics, however, have recognized much more fully the artistry of these plays. It is true that Centlivre used stock characters and stock situations, but she was capable of infusing them with vitality. In fact, at times, especially in the cases of Valeria in *The Basset-Table* and Mrs. Plotwell in *The Platonic Lady,* stock characters are given individual qualities that lift them far above the stereotypes from which they are derived. Unlike Margaret Cavendish, duchess of Newcastle, who pioneered as a professional writer in the mid seventeenth century with the hope of winning for herself eternal fame, Centlivre apparently had in mind more immediate rewards. But as long as eighteenth-century dramatists are read and remembered, Susanna Centlivre will enjoy her modest share of "eternal fame."

Bibliography:

J. E. Norton, "Some Uncollected Authors XIV: Susanna Centlivre," *Book Collector,* 6 (Summer 1957): 172-178; (Autumn 1957): 280-285.

Biographies:

Giles Jacob, "Mrs. Susanna Centlivre," in *The Poetical Register: or, The Lives and Characters of the English Dramatic Poets,* 2 volumes (London: E. Curll, 1719);

Abel Boyer, Obituary of Centlivre, *The Political State of Great Britain,* 26 (December 1723): 670-671;

John Mottley, "Mrs. Susanna Centlivre," in *A Compleat List of all the English Dramatic Poets,* appended to Thomas Whincop's, *Scanderbeg* (London: W. Reeve, 1747), pp. 185-192;

William Rufus Chetwood, "Mrs. Susanna Centlivre," in *The British Theatre, Containing the Lives of English Dramatic Poets* (Dublin: Peter Wilson, 1750);

John Wilson Bowyer, *The Celebrated Mrs. Centlivre* (Durham, N.C.: Duke University Press, 1952);

Nancy Cotton, Entry on Susanna Centlivre, in *A Dictionary of British and American Women Writers 1660-1800* (Totowa, N.J.: Rowman & Allanheld, 1985), pp. 77-79.

References:

Paul Bunyan Anderson, "Innocence and Artifice: or Mrs. Centlivre and the Female Tatler," *Philological Quarterly,* 16 (October 1937): 358-375;

F. W. Bateson, *English Comic Drama 1700-1750* (Oxford: Clarendon Press, 1929);

Ernest Bernbaum, *The Drama of Sensibility* (Boston: Ginn, 1915);

Terence William Burke, "Susanna Centlivre's 'A Bold Stroke for a Wife': A Re-evaluation," Ph.D. dissertation, Case Western Reserve University, 1971;

Nancy Cotton, *Women Playwrights in England 1363-1750* (Lewisburg, Pa.: Bucknell University Press, 1980);

Richard C. Frushell, "Marriage and Marrying in Susanna Centlivre's Plays," *Papers on Language and Literature,* 22 (Winter 1986): 16-38;

Henry Ten Hoor, "A Re-examination of Susanna Centlivre as a Comic Dramatist," Ph.D. dissertation, University of Michigan, 1963;

Robert D. Hume, *The Development of English Drama in the Late Seventeenth Century* (Oxford: Clarendon Press, 1976);

F. P. Lock, "Astraea's 'Vacant Throne': The Successors of Aphra Behn," in *Women in the Eighteenth Century,* edited by Paul Fritz and Richard Norton (Toronto: Samuel Stevens Hakkert, 1976), pp. 25-36;

Lock, *Susanna Centlivre* (Boston: Twayne, 1979);

John Loftis, *Comedy and Society from Congreve to Fielding* (Stanford: Stanford University Press, 1959);

Loftis, *The Politics of Drama in Augustan England* (Oxford: Clarendon Press, 1963);

Loftis, *The Spanish Plays of Neoclassical England* (New Haven: Yale University Press, 1973);

John Mackenzie, "Susan Centlivre," *Notes and Queries,* 198 (September 1953): 386-390;

Shirley A. Markel, "'The Cook's Wife' Reconsidered: An Evaluation of the Comedies of Susanna Centlivre," Ph.D. dissertation, University of Kansas, 1982;

Eleanor Mattes, "The 'Female Virtuso' in Early Eighteenth-Century English Drama," *Women and Literature*, 3 (1975): 3-9;

Ezre Kempton Maxfield, "The Quakers in English Stage Plays Before 1800," *PMLA*, 45 (March 1930): 256-273;

Allardyce Nicoll, *A History of Early Eighteenth Century Drama* (Cambridge: Cambridge University Press, 1925); republished as *Early Eighteenth-Century Drama*, volume 2 of *A History of English Drama, 1660-1900* (Cambridge: Cambridge University Press, 1965);

Robert Seibt, "Die Komodien der Mrs. Centlivre," *Anglia*, 33 (1910): 77-119;

Arthur Sherbo, *English Sentimental Drama* (East Lansing: Michigan State University Press, 1957);

George Sherburn, "The Fortunes and Misfortunes of Three Hours After Marriage," *Modern Philology*, 24 (August 1926): 91-109;

Robert Strozier, "A Short View of Some of Mrs. Centlivre's Celebrat'd Plays," *Discourse*, 7 (Winter 1964): 62-80;

Frederick T. Wood, "The Celebrated Mrs. Centlivre," *Neophilologus*, 16 (1931): 268-278.

Papers:
Harleian Ms. 7649(2) in the British Library is an unpublished poem by Mrs. Centlivre, "A Poem on the Recovery of the Lady Henrietta Holles from the Small Pox."

Colley Cibber

(6 November 1671-11 December 1757)

Linda E. Merians
La Salle University

PLAY PRODUCTIONS: *Love's Last Shift, or the Fool in Fashion,* London, Theatre Royal in Drury Lane, January 1696;

Woman's Wit, or the Lady in Fashion, London, Theatre Royal in Drury Lane, January or February 1697;

Xerxes, London, Lincoln's Inn Fields, February or March 1699;

The Tragical History of King Richard III, adapted from William Shakespeare's *The Tragedy of Richard The Third,* London, Theatre Royal in Drury Lane, late December 1699 or January 1700;

Love Makes a Man, or the Fop's Fortune, derived from John Fletcher and Philip Massinger's *The Elder Brother* and *The Custom of the Country,* London, Theatre Royal in Drury Lane, 9 December 1700;

The School Boy, or the Comical Rivals, afterpiece based on the last three acts of *Woman's Wit, or the Lady in Fashion,* London, Theatre Royal in Drury Lane, 24 October 1702;

She Wou'd and She Wou'd Not, or the Kind Imposter, derived from John Leanerd's *The Counterfeits,* London, Theatre Royal in Drury Lane, 26 November 1702;

The Rival Queans, with the Humours of Alexander the Great, burlesque of Nathaniel Lee's *The Rival Queens, or, the Death of Alexander the Great* (unrecorded performances by 1703), London, Queen's Theatre, 29 June 1710;

The Careless Husband, London, Theatre Royal in Drury Lane, 7 December 1704;

Perolla and Izadora, derived from Roger Boyle's *Parthenissa,* London, Theatre Royal in Drury Lane, 3 December 1705;

The Comical Lovers, or Marriage a la Mode, based on John Dryden's *Secret Love* and *Marriage A la Mode,* London, Queen's Theatre, 4 February 1707;

The Double Gallant, or the Sick Lady's Cure, adapted from William Burnaby's *The Reformed Wife* and *The Lady's Visiting Day* and Susanna

Centlivre's *Love at a Venture,* London, Queen's Theatre, 1 November 1707;

The Lady's Last Stake, or the Wife's Resentment, London, Queen's Theatre, 13 December 1707;

The Rival Fools, based on Fletcher's *Wit at Several Weapons,* London, Theatre Royal in Drury Lane, 11 January 1709;

Ximena, or the Heroick Daughter, adapted from Pierre Corneille's *Le Cid,* London, Theatre Royal in Drury Lane, 28 November 1712;

Cinna's Conspiracy, translation of Corneille's *Cinna,* attributed on very tenuous evidence to Cibber, London, Theatre Royal in Drury Lane, 19 February 1713;

Venus and Adonis, by Cibber, set to music by Christopher Pepusch, London, Theatre Royal in Drury Lane, 12 March 1715;

Myrtillo. A Pastoral Interlude, by Cibber, set to music by Pepusch, London, Theatre Royal in Drury Lane, 5 November 1715;

The Bulls and Bears, attributed to Cibber, London, Theatre Royal in Drury Lane, 2 December 1715;

The Non-Juror, derived from Molière's *Tartuffe,* London, Theatre Royal in Drury Lane, 6 December 1717;

The Refusal; or, The Ladies Philosophy, derived from Molière's *Les Femmes Savantes,* London, Theatre Royal in Drury Lane, 14 February 1721;

Caesar in Egypt, London, Theatre Royal in Drury Lane, 9 December 1724;

The Provoked Husband; or, A Journey to London, by Cibber and John Vanbrugh, London, Theatre Royal in Drury Lane, 10 January 1728;

Love in a Riddle, London, Theatre Royal in Drury Lane, 7 January 1729;

Damon and Phillida. A Ballad Opera, musical afterpiece based on the subplot of *Love in a Riddle,* tenuously attributed to Cibber but never acknowledged by him, London, Little Theatre in the Hay-Market, 16 August 1729;

Colley Cibber as Novelty Fashion, lord Foppington, in John Vanbrugh's The Relapse, *the sequel to Cibber's*
Love's Last Shift *(engraving based on a painting by G. Grisoni; courtesy of the Folger Shakespeare Library)*

Polypheme, Paul Rolli's libretto translated into English by Cibber, music by Nicholas Porpora, London, Queen's Theatre, February 1735;

Papal Tyranny in the Reign of King John, adapted from Shakespeare's *King John,* London, Theatre Royal in Covent Garden, 15 February 1745.

BOOKS: *A Poem on the Death of Our Late Sovereign Lady Queen Mary* (London: Printed for J. Whitlock, 1695);

Love's Last Shift; Or the Fool in Fashion. A Comedy. As it is Acted at the Theatre Royal, By His Majestys Servants (London: Printed for H. Rhodes, R. Parker, & S. Briscoe, 1696);

Woman's Wit; Or, the Lady in Fashion. A Comedy. Acted at the Theatre Royal. By His Majesty's Servants (London: Printed for J. Sturton, 1697);

Xerxes, A Tragedy, As it is Acted at the New Theatre in Little Lincoln's Inn Field (London: Printed & sold by J. Nutt, 1699);

The Tragical History of King Richard III. As it is Acted at the Theatre Royal (London: Printed for B. Lintott & A. Bettesworth, 1700); modern edition, in *Five Restoration Adaptations of Shakespeare,* edited by Christopher Spencer (Urbana: University of Illinois Press, 1965); facsimile of 1700 and 1718 editions (London: Cornmarket Press, 1969);

Love Makes a Man: Or, the Fop's Fortune. A Comedy. Acted at the Theatre Royal in Drury Lane, By His Majesty's Servants (London: Printed for Richard Parker, Hugh Newman, E. Rumbal, 1701);

She Wou'd and She Wou'd Not: or, The Kind Imposter. A comedy, as it is now acted at the Theatre-Royal in Drury-Lane, by Her Majesties Servants (London: Printed by W. Turner, 1703);

The Careless Husband. A comedy. As it is acted at the Theatre royal, by Her Majesty's servants (London: Printed for W. Davis, 1705); modern edition, edited by William Appleton (Lincoln: University of Nebraska Press, 1966; London: Arnold, 1967);

A Prologue in the opera call'd Camilla. Written and spoke by Mr. Cibber at the Theatre Royal in Drury-Lane, July the 5th 1706 [broadside] (London: Printed for B. Lintott, 1706);

Perolla and Izadora. A tragedy, as it was acted at the Theatre Royal, By Her Majesty's Servants (London: Printed for Bernard Lintott, 1706);

The School Boy: or, The Comical Rivals. A Comedy. As it has been often acted at the Theatre-Royal in Drury-Lane, with great applause (London: Printed for Ben. Bragg, 1707);

The Comical Lovers. A Comedy. Acted by Subscription at the Queen's Theatre in the Hay-Market (London: Printed for Bernard Lintott, 1707);

The Double Gallant: Or, The Sick Lady's Cure. A Comedy. As it is Acted at the Queen's Theatre in The Hay-Market (London: Printed for Bernard Lintott & sold by John Phillips, 1707); modern edition, edited by John W. Brunton (New York: Garland, 1987);

The Lady's Last Stake, or, the Wife's Resentment. A Comedy. As it is Acted at the Queen's Theatre in the Hay-market, By Her Majesty's Servants (London: Printed for Bernard Lintott, 1707);

The Rival Fools. A comedy. As it is acted at the Theatre-Royal in Drury Lane. By Her Majesty's sworn comedians (London: Printed for Bernard Lintott, 1709);

Cinna's Conspiracy. A tragedy. As it is acted at the Theatre-Royal in Drury-Lane by Her Majesty's Servants (London: Printed for B. Lintott, 1713);

Venus and Adonis, a masque: as it is presented at the Theatre-Royal (London: Printed for B. Lintott, 1715);

Myrtillo. A Pastoral Interlude, as it is perform'd at the Theatre Royal (London: Printed for B. Lintott, 1716);

The Non-Juror. A Comedy. As it is acted at the Theatre-Royal, by His Majesty's servants (London: Printed for B. Lintot, 1718);

Ximena; or the Heroick Daughter. A tragedy. As it is acted at the Theatre-Royal by His Majesty's servants (London: Printed for B. Lintot, A. Bettesworth & W. Chetwood, 1719);

The refusal; or, The ladies philosophy: a comedy. Acted at the Theatre-Royal, by His Majesty's Servants (London: Printed for B. Lintot, W. Mears, and W. Chetwood, 1721);

Caesar in Aegypt. A tragedy. As it is acted at the Theatre-Royal in Drury-Lane by His Majesty's Servants (London: Printed for J. Watts, 1725);

The provok'd husband; or, A journey to London. A comedy, as it is acted at the Theatre-Royal, by His Majesty's Servants, by Cibber and John Vanbrugh (London: Printed for J. Watts, 1728); modern edition, edited by Peter Dixon (Lincoln: University of Nebraska Press, 1974);

Love in a riddle. A pastoral. As it is acted at the Theatre-Royal, By His Majesty's servants (London: Printed for J. Watts, 1729);

The Rival Queans, with the Humours of Alexander the Great. A Comical-Tragedy. As it was Acted at the Theatre-Royal, in Drury Lane (Dublin: Printed by Ja. Carson for Thomas Benson, 1729); modern edition, edited by William H. Peterson, Lake Erie College Studies, volume 5 (Painesville, Ohio: Lake Erie College, 1965);

Damon and Phillida: A Ballad Opera of one act. As it is performed at the Theatre-Royal in Drury-Lane by His Majesty's Servants. With the musick prefix'd to each song (London: Printed for J. Watts, 1729);

An Ode to His Majesty, for the New-Year 1730/31 (London: Printed for John Watts, 1730);

An Ode for His Majesty's Birth-Day, October 30, 1731 (London: Printed for John Watts, 1731);

Polypheme. An Opera. By Paul Rolli, F.R.S. Composed by Nicholas Porpora, for the English Nobility (London: Printed by Charles Bennet, 1734);

The Blind Boy [broadside] (London, 1735);

An Apology for the Life of Mr. Colley Cibber, Comedian, and Late Patentee of the Theatre-Royal. With an Historical View of the Stage during His Own Time (London: Printed by J. Watts for the author, 1740); modern edition, edited by B. R. S. Fone (Ann Arbor: University of Michigan Press, 1968); critical edition, edited by John Maurice Evans (New York: Garland, 1987);

A Letter from Mr. Cibber to Mr. Pope, Inquiring into the Motives that Might Induce Him in His Satyrical Works, to be so Frequently Fond of Mr. Cibber's Name (London: Printed by W. Lewis, 1742);

The Egoist, or Colley upon Cibber. Being His Own Picture Retouch'd to so Plain a Likeness That No One Now Would Have the Face to Own it but Himself (London: Printed & sold by W. Lewis, 1743);

A Second Letter from Mr. Cibber to Mr. Pope. In Reply to Some Additional Verses in His Dunciad, Which He Has not yet Published (London: Printed for A. Dodd, 1743);

Another Occasional Letter from Mr. Cibber to Mr. Pope. Wherein the New Hero's Preferment to His Throne in the Dunciad Seems not to be Accepted. And the Author of That Poem His More Rightful Claim to it is Asserted. With an Expostulatory Address to the Reverend Mr. W[arburto]n, Author of the New Preface and Adviser in the Curious Improvements of That Satire (London: Printed & sold by W. Lewis, 1744);

Papal tyranny in the reign of King John. A tragedy. As it is acted at the Theatre-Royal in Covent-Garden. By His Majesty's servants (London: Printed for J. Watts and sold by B. Dod, 1745);

The Character and Conduct of Cicero, Considered from the History of His Life by the Reverend Dr. Middleton. With Occasional Essays and Observations upon the Most Memorable Facts and Persons during that Period (London: Printed by John Watts for the author, 1747);

The Lady's Lecture, a Theatrical Dialogue between Sir Charles Easy and His Marriageable Daughter. Being an Attempt to Engage Obedience by Filial Liberty, and to Give the Maiden Conduct of Virtue, Chearfulness (London: Printed & sold by W. Lewis, 1748);

A Rhapsody upon the Marvellous, Arising from the First Odes of Horace and Pindar. Being a Scrutiny into Ancient Poetical Fame Demanded by Modern Common Sense (London: Printed for W. Lewis, 1751);

Verses to the Memory of Mr. Pelham. Addressed to His Grace the Duke of Newcastle (London: Printed for J. Jolliffe, 1754).

Collections: *Plays Written by Mr. Cibber*, 2 volumes (London: Printed for J. Tonson, B. Lintot, W. Mears, & W. Chetwood, 1721);

The Dramatic Works of Colley Cibber, 4 volumes (London: Printed for J. Clarke, C. Hitch & L. Hawes, D. Browne, J. & R. Tonson, J. Rivington, R. Baldwin, T. Caslon, C. Bathurst, S. Crowder & co., T. Longman, H. Woodgate & S. Brooks, C. Corbet, G. Kearsly, J. & T. King, & T. Lownds, 1760);

The Dramatic Works of Colley Cibber, Esq., 5 volumes (London: Printed for J. Rivington & sons, 1777);

Colley Cibber: Three Sentimental Comedies, edited by Maureen Sullivan (New Haven: Yale University Press, 1973).

OTHER: *Prologue spoken at Her Majesty's theatre in the Haymarket, on Saturday the 8th of November*, in *The Muses Mercury, or the Monthly Miscellany* (October 1707);

Epilogue to *The Man's bewitch'd, or, The Devil to do about Her*, by Susanna Centlivre (London: Printed for Bernard Lintott, 1709);

Epilogue to *The Victim*, by Charles Johnson (London: Printed & sold by Ferd. Burleigh, 1714);

Epilogue to *The Invader of his Country, or the Fatal Resentment*, by John Dennis (London: Printed for J. Pemberton, 1720);

Epilogue to *The Lover*, by Theophilus Cibber (London: Printed for J. Watts, 1730);

Epilogue to *The London Merchant; or the History of George Barnwell*, by George Lillo (London: Printed for John Gray, 1731);

Epilogue to *The Modern Husband*, by Henry Fielding (London: Printed for J. Watts, 1732);

Epilogue to *The Miser*, by Fielding (London: Printed for J. Watts, 1733);

Prologue to *The Tragedy of Zara*, by Aaron Hill (London: Printed for J. Watts, 1736).

Actor, playwright, and theater manager, Colley Cibber was a leading figure in the eighteenth-century London theater world. As an actor, Cibber specialized in playing the fop, the man of fashion whose affectations make him a deserving candidate for ridicule. Original works as well as adaptations, Cibber's plays cross the genres: he wrote twelve comedies, six tragedies, one tragicomedy, one farce, and several musical entertainments. Although Cibber is regarded as a professional rather than an artful playwright, his original comedies are representative of the new wave of reform and humane comedies that grew in popularity during the century. Finally, from 1710 to 1732, Cibber served as one of the actor-managers of the Theatre Royal in Drury Lane, where his considerable acumen as a businessman helped to promote his own as well as his company's interests. Cibber's autobiography, *An Apology for the Life of Mr. Colley Cibber* (1740), is an example of his great talent at self-promotion. The work recounts his entire career, and as such it contains much valuable information, but his self-serving memory undermines the text's reliability for theater historians. The general success Cibber enjoyed throughout his fifty-five-year career highlights three essential characteristics of the eighteenth-century theater world: the institution

Caius Gabriel Cibber, the playwright's father (engraving by A. Bannerman)

of the actor-manager; the burgeoning "business" of the stage; the social power of fame or even infamy.

Cibber was born in London on 6 November 1671. His mother, Jane Colley (1645-1696), came from a family that hailed from Rutland as early as the fifteenth century; her father moved the family to London. Cibber's father, Caius Gabriel Cibber (1635-1700), was an accomplished sculptor who would later win appointment as William III's "Sculptor in Ordinary." Caius Cibber's two most famous works, the figures of Raving and Melancholy commissioned for Bethlehem Hospital, were executed while he was held for debt (1673-1678) in Marshalsea Prison. In 1682 Colley Cibber was sent to the free school of Grantham in Lincolnshire. His father hoped that his son would have a career in the church, but in 1687

Colley Cibber was unsuccessful in his bid to win election to Winchester College. In his *Apology* he relates that after this failure he timed his return to London so that he might enjoy an evening's entertainment at the theater before he returned to his family's house. Cibber's father was then working at the earl of Devonshire's estate at Chatsworth, and his son soon joined him there. When the Glorious Revolution occurred, father and son found themselves under Devonshire's command. Colley Cibber took his father's place in Devonshire's troop and stayed with the nobleman when he returned to London in 1689. He was a member of the household for a few months, but in February 1690 he joined the United Company of actors at the Theatre Royal in Drury Lane. His *Apology* relates his desire for a stage career:

The song sung in act 4, scene 3, of Love's Last Shift, *as it was printed in* Deliciae
Musicae: A Collection of the newest and best Songs *(1696)*

But, Alas! in my Intervals of Leisure, frequently seeing Plays, my Wise head was turn'd to higher Views, I saw no Joy in any other Life than that of an Actor, so that (as before, when a Candidate at *Winchester*) I was even afraid of succeeding to the Preferment I sought for. 'Twas on the Stage alone I had form'd a Happiness preferable to all that Camps or Courts could offer me! and there I was determin'd, let Father and Mother take it as they pleas'd, to fix my *non ultra*.

With no theatrical training or experience, Cibber initially had a probationary role in the company. His first recorded acting part was in late September 1690, as a servant in Thomas Southerne's *Sir Anthony Love*. He won notice on 9 February 1692 when he played the Chaplain in Thomas Otway's *The Orphan*. In his *Apology* Cibber remembers how these early years helped him to perceive his own limitations as an actor: "The first Thing that enters into the Head of a young Actor, is that of being a Heroe: In this Ambition I was soon snubb'd, by the Insufficiency of my Voice; to which might be added, an uninform'd meagre Person (tho' then not ill made) with a dismal pale Complexion. Under these Disadvantages, I had but a melancholy Prospect of ever playing a Lover, with Mrs. *Bracegirdle,* which I had flatter'd my Hopes that my Youth might one Day, have recommended me to. What was most promising in me, then, was the Aptness of my Ear; for I was soon allow'd to speak justly, tho' what was grave and serious did not equally become me." Although his *Apology* makes clear that Cibber recognized he was better suited for comic rather than tragic roles, he insisted on playing tragic roles throughout his career. Cibber's first major success as an actor, however, occurred in January 1694, when he substituted for Edward Kynaston as Lord Touchwood in a revival of William Congreve's comedy *The Double Dealer*.

In 1695, when Thomas Betterton and some of the other leading actors severed their relationship with Christopher Rich and formed their own company at Lincoln's Inn Fields, Cibber remained at Drury Lane. Cibber made himself useful during the spring of 1695. He wrote two important prologues: for the reopening of the theater (25 March 1695) and a new one to Aphra Behn's *Abdelazer* (April 1695). Moreover this season marked his acting triumph as Fondlewife in Congreve's *The Old Bachelor*. When lead parts did not come his way after his success in 1695, Cibber created one for himself by writing *Love's Last Shift* (1696). Cibber's portrayal of Sir Novelty Fashion, a part intended to be a "portrait of the foppery then in fashion," was instrumental in establishing his "line" as an actor. Moreover, this play marked the first, but certainly not the last, time Cibber would cast himself in a role that was sure to bring him to the attention of the London audience.

The action in *Love's Last Shift* centers on the reformation of Ned Loveless, a Restoration-style rake, who deserts his wife in London in order to lead a dissolute life abroad. At the start of the play he has returned to London, hungry and penniless, but generally unrepentant about his absence. He meets an old acquaintance, Young Worthy, whose virtue leads him to sympathize with the sad plight of Loveless's angelic wife, Amanda. Worthy and Amanda essentially plan a Restoration-style bed trick, to which Loveless succumbs, and by the end of the fifth act the reformed rake presents himself as a sincere advocate of marriage: "By my example taught let every man, whose fate has bound him to a married life, beware of letting lose his wild desires: for if experience may be allowed to judge, I must proclaim the folly of a wandering passion: the greatest happiness we can hope on earth, And sure the nearest to the joys above/Is the chaste rapture of a virtuous love." The moral lesson embedded in the play, which advocates marriage rather than rakery and marital reconciliation rather than revenge, makes this play a prototypical example of reform comedy.

Cibber's second play, *Woman's Wit, or the Lady in Fashion* (1697), attempted to present a female counterpart (Leonora) to Sir Novelty Fashion, but it was a total failure. In his *Apology* Cibber explains that he wrote the play too quickly; whatever the case, it played for only one night and was never revived. Cibber spent the next two years acting in a variety of roles and writing his next work, *Xerxes*, a tragedy that was rejected by Christopher Rich, the manager of the Drury Lane theater. Betterton's company at Lincoln's Inn Fields performed the play only once in February or March 1699.

After the failures of two of his first three original plays, Cibber began to write adaptations of earlier works. Great controversy surrounded his adaptation of Shakespeare's *Richard III* in December 1699. Lord chamberlain Robert Spencer, earl of Sunderland, ordered Cibber to cut the first act because he was afraid that Cibber's characterization of Henry VI would remind the audience of James II. Adding to the furor as well was Cibber's own playing of Richard III, a role unsuited to him but one that he continued to play until almost the end of his career.

Notwithstanding the failure of the first production, Cibber's skills as a playwright-adapter are evident in this work. In fact, after the play was revived in 1710, it became the standard acting version for the next 150 years. Critics now acknowledge that Cibber's decision to focus on Richard simplifies and sharpens the play. Cibber deleted the characters Margaret, Edward IV, Clarence, and Hastings; consequently, Richard appears in far more scenes in Cibber's adaptation than in Shakespeare's original (fifteen of twenty rather than fifteen of twenty-five). Cibber's Richard is more evil and, with the help of new soliloquies, more talkative than Shakespeare's. A characteristic example of the style of Cibber's version can be seen by a comparison of the end of III. i. In Shakespeare's original (circa 1591-1592) Buckingham, Gloster (Richard III), and Catesby plan their approach to Lord Hastings; the scene ends when Gloster promises Buckingham the earldom of Hereford. In Cibber's play Richard dismisses his accomplices and ends the scene by delivering a new soliloquy:

> Come; this Conscience is a convenient Scarecrow,
> It Guards the fruit which Priests and Wisemen tast,
> Who never set it up to fright themselves:

Painted bust of Colley Cibber, probably by L. F. Roubiliac (by permission of the National Portrait Gallery, London)

They know 'tis rags, and gather in the face on't,
While half-starv'd shallow Daws thro Fear are hon-
    est.
Why were Laws made, but that we're Rogues by Na-
    ture?
Conscience! 'tis our Coin, we live by parting with it,
And he thrives best that has the most to spare:
The protesting Lover buys hope with it,
And the deluded Virgin shortliv'd pleasure.
Old gray beards cram their Avarice with it,
Your Lank-jaw'd hungry Judge will dine upon't,
And hang the Guiltless rather than eat his Mutton
    cold.
The Crown'd Head quits it for Despotick sway,
The stubborn People for unaw'd Rebellion:
There's not a Slave but has his share of Villain;
Why then shall after Ages think my deeds
Inhumane? Since my worst are but Ambition:
Ev'n all Mankind to some lov'd Ills incline,
Great Men chuse Greater Sins—Ambition's mine.

Cibber's second adaptation, *Love Makes a*

Man, or the Fop's Fortune (1700), derives from John Fletcher and Philip Massinger's *The Elder Brother* (circa 1625) and *The Custom of the Country* (circa 1619). Cibber's play was performed eight times in its first season and found its way into the standard repertory. As Arthur H. Scouten and Robert D. Hume have shown, the success of this work is remarkable because it was achieved during an era when there were many more failures than successes of new plays on the London stage. In fact, the longevity of *Love Makes a Man* is staggering; it was performed at least once a season every year during the eighteenth century except for the following years: 1756, 1770, 1773, 1777, 1781-1783, 1789, 1791, 1793, 1796.

Cibber retains the original plot line from *The Elder Brother:* how love transforms a studious young man who is scornful of romance into a pas-

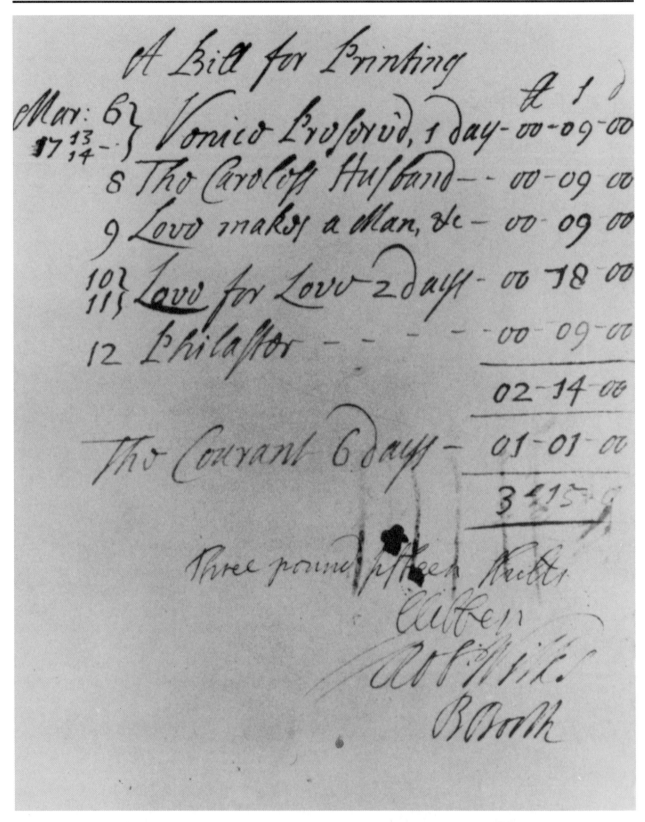

Costs for play notices in the Daily Courant *(1714) and for renting stage properties (circa 1715), signed by Cibber, Robert Wilks, and Barton Booth, proprietors of the Theatre Royal in Drury Lane (MS. Collection of Wardrobe and Property Bills, Drury Lane; by permission of the Folger Shakespeare Library)*

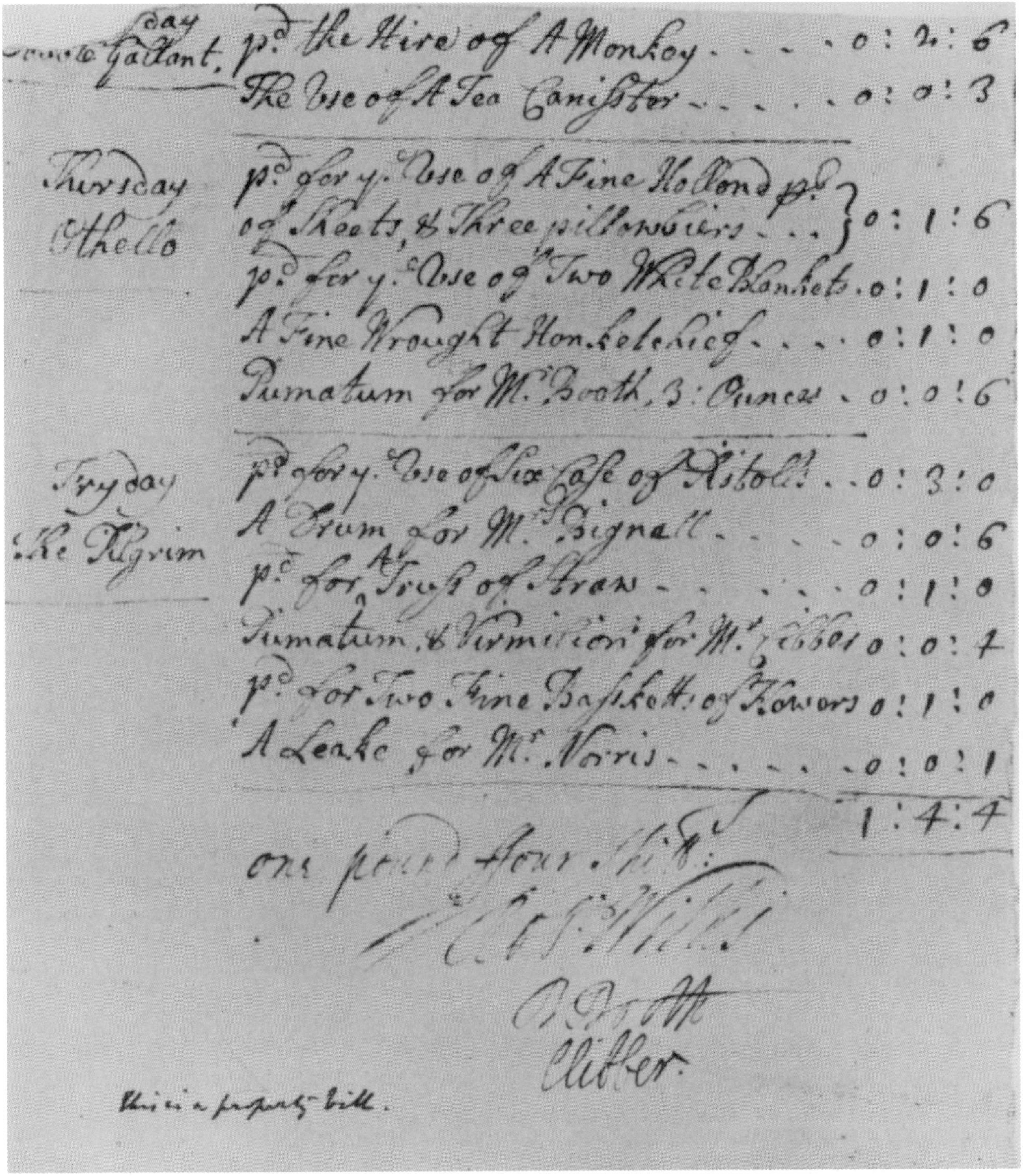

...nate Gallant.   pd the Hire of A Monkey - - - - - - .0: 2: 6
The Use of A Tea Canister - - - - . .0: 0: 3

Thursday   pd for ye Use of A Fine Holland pr ⎞
Othello   of Sheets, & Three pillowbiers - . . ⎠ 0: 1: 6
pd for ye Use of Two White Blankets .0: 1: 0
A Fine Wrought Hon.kekeief - - - .0: 1: 0
Pumatum for Mr Booth, 3: Ounces - .0: 0: 6

Fryday   pd for ye Use of Six Case of Pistols . .0: 3: 0
The Pilgrim   A Drum for Mr Bignall - - - - - .0: 0: 6
pd for A Truss of Straw - - 0: 1: 0
Pumatum, & Vermilion for Mrs Cibber 0: 0: 4
pd for Two Fine Baskets of Flowers 0: 1: 0
A Leake for Mr Norris - - - - - .0: 0: 1
                                    ‾‾‾‾‾‾‾
                                    1: 4: 4

one pound four shill.

[signatures]
Wilks
Booth
Cibber.

this is a property bill.

On 28 November 1724, a few days after the hanging of the notorious criminal Jack Sheppard, Robert Wilks, Barton Booth, and Colley Cibber staged a pantomime called Harlequin Sheppard, *an attempt to capitalize on public interest in the execution. In A Just View of the British Stage (above) William Hogarth attacked them for descending to sensationalism.*

sionate and heroic lover. Cibber's tendency to moralize is what makes this play notable. The sincere love that Carlos and Angelina come to share not only shows them to be exemplary characters, but it also serves to inspire Louisa, a lady of pleasure, to renounce her evil life-style at the end of the fifth act: "O! you have given me such an Image of the contentful Peace, th'unshaken Quiet of an honest Mind, that now I taste more solid Joy, being but the Instrument of your united virtuous Love, than all my late false Hopes propos'd, even in the last Indulgence of blind Desire: Now love long and happily; forgive my Follies past, and

you have overpaid me." Thus does Cibber preach the positive social value of sincere love and courtship.

Cibber's next comedy, *She Wou'd and She Wou'd Not, or the Kind Imposter* (1702), failed to pay the house charges on the sixth night of its first run. Yet after its revival in 1714, it too became one of the century's most-popular plays. Modern scholars recognize it as one of Cibber's best-constructed works. Fundamentally, the play presents a familiar Restoration comedy of intrigue. Cibber uses the plot to stress a moral message familiar to his audience: sincere love makes for happy marriages. The action focuses on the adventures and misadventures of two couples, Don Philip and Hypolita and Octavio and Rosara. Disguises, duels, and a witty servant (Trappanti) ensure that the ending will teach the intended lesson.

Cibber's next play, an original comedy, *The Careless Husband* (1704), was a great success. It played for ten nights in December and immediately became a part of the standard repertory. Although modern critics have complained about the play's heavy-handed morality, the characterizations and the easy interaction between the two plot lines make it a stage-worthy work. Cibber's contemporaries generally praised the play, and its reputation grew during the century. It came to be regarded as an exemplary genteel comedy and, like *Love Makes a Man*, had an enviable performance history, with more than three hundred recorded performances from 1704 to 1800.

Set in Windsor, the action chronicles Sir Charles Easy's indiscretions with Lady Graveairs and with Mrs. Edging, his wife's maid. Lady Easy discovers her husband's infidelity, but rather than cause a public scandal, she works and schemes to reform him. The subplot features the repentance of Lady Betty Modish, who flirts incessantly with Lord Foppington (the role Cibber wrote for himself), although she really loves Lord Morelove. At the play's end both couples are reconciled and are happy with their lives.

Curiously, Cibber next wrote a tragedy, *Perolla and Izadora*, which was performed seven times between 3 December 1705 and 2 January 1706. Why he switched genres at this point remains a mystery. *The London Stage* records more successful comedies than tragedies during this season; thus, appealing to the current taste of the audience does not account for the change. Whatever the reason, Cibber found his source in Roger Boyle's *Parthenissa* (1651-1669), but tragic romance was not what the London audience wanted to see. The addition of singers and dancers on the fourth night probably helped to carry the play until its last performance.

Fierce competition between the two legitimate companies in London existed throughout the first decade of the century. In April 1705 the Haymarket theater opened (called the Queen's or the King's, depending on the sex of the reigning monarch), and Thomas Betterton's company moved in. At this time Betterton and John Vanbrugh shared managerial responsibilities for the company. The rivalry between the two companies

was heightened when both began to offer operas, but Rich's company fared better. On 5 July 1706 Cibber wrote and delivered a new prologue for Owen Swiney's translation of *Camilla*, a very successful opera that was performed by the largely English members of Rich's company at Drury Lane. Vanbrugh's company had only one moderate success (George Granville's *The British Enchanters*) and two failures (Peter Motteux's *The Temple of Love* and Thomas Durfey's *Wonders in the Sun*). The expensive salaries demanded by the imported Italian singers and the other exorbitant costs of producing operas threatened the interests of both theater managers. Vanbrugh proposed a merger of the two companies into one new United Company, with himself in control, but Rich refused to entertain the notion.

The competition between the Haymarket and Drury Lane theaters touched Cibber in the fall of 1706. The theaters were reorganized so that the Haymarket company (by then managed by Owen Swiney, who hired many of Rich's best actors) would not offer any musical entertainments, and the Drury Lane company could perform whatever it wished. In October 1706 Swiney promised Cibber a larger salary than the one he earned at Drury Lane. Until this time (except for a brief period in 1696), Cibber had benefited from his loyalty to Rich. As early as 1700 Rich had given Cibber some managerial responsibilities in the company, most likely reading scripts and overseeing rehearsals. The thirty shillings per week Cibber earned as a result of these duties made him the highest-paid actor in the company in 1704, but Rich's refusal to raise Cibber's salary inspired him to join Swiney's company at the Haymarket. In his *Apology* Cibber credits his defection with the greatest possible significance: "To conclude, I agreed, in two Words, to act with *Swiney;* and from this time, every Change that happen'd in the Theatrical Government, was a nearer Step to that twenty Years of Prosperity, which Actors, under the Menagement of Acts, not long afterwards enjoy'd." The 1706-1707 season proved to be a successful one for Swiney and his players.

Cibber wrote three comedies (two adaptations, one original) for his new company, but none was very successful. He completed his first, *The Comical Lovers, or Marriage a la Mode* (based on John Dryden's *Secret Love*, 1667, and *Marriage A la Mode*, 1671), in six days. The play was performed only three times (4, 5, and 8 February 1707) in its first run. Cibber's next adaptation, *The Double Gallant, or the Sick Lady's Cure*, from Wil-

THEOPHILUS CIBBER, *COMEDIAN*,
In the Character of a Fine Gentleman.

Colley Cibber's actor-son (engraving by R. Clamp)

liam Burnaby's *The Reformed Wife* (1700) and *The Lady's Visiting Day* (1701) and Susanna Centlivre's *Love at a Venture* (1706), fared a little better with four recorded performances in November 1707. Cibber's original comedy, *The Lady's Last Stake, or the Wife's Resentment* (1707), was performed only six times in its first season. The preface that Cibber wrote for the published version of the play unconvincingly blamed the play's failure to become a town favorite on its strong moral message: "If I would have been less instructive, I might easily have had a louder, tho' not a more valuable Applause." The preface and the epilogue present a discussion of the theatrical warfare then raging, as well as a prose encomium to the lord chamberlain, to whom the edition is dedicated. Evidently, Cibber could be politic and didactic at the same time.

The characters are named as if they were in a morality play (Lady and Lord Wronglove, Sir Friendly Moral, Lady Gentle, Lord George Brilliant, Mrs. Conquest, and Miss Notable). The main plot features the marital reconciliation of the Wrongloves, whose marriage is threatened because Lord Wronglove is unfaithful to his wife and because Lady Wronglove refuses to be a friend and conjugal companion to her husband. With the help of Sir Friendly Moral, the two erring partners learn how to love correctly. The subplot tells the potentially sad story of Lady Gentle, a basically virtuous woman who has become addicted to the gaming table. She loses two thousand pounds to George Brilliant, who schemes to have her pay him back in bed. Money miraculously comes her way, allowing her to escape from her dangerous situation.

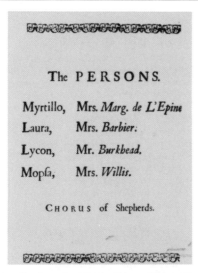

The PERSONS.

Myrtillo,   Mrs. *Marg. de L'Epine*
Laura,   Mrs. *Barbier*.
Lycon,   Mr. *Burkhead*.
Mopſa,   Mrs. *Willis*.

CHORUS of Shepherds.

Cast list from the 1716 edition of Myrtillo

In January 1708 Vanbrugh finally persuaded the lord chamberlain to order a genre split, effectively ending the free competition between the houses. Operas were to be performed only at the Haymarket, and drama became the province of the company at the Drury Lane theater. That company was now comanaged by Henry Brett and Owen Swiney because Christopher Rich had been silenced very temporarily by the lord chamberlain in March 1707. In March 1708 Brett assigned his powers as manager to Cibber, Robert Wilks, and Richard Estcourt. Rich, however, was scheming to regain full management of the company. He soon had control of the theater, but the actors were in a rebellious mood. They grew angry at Rich because he deducted more than the forty pounds in house charges from their benefit-night earnings, and so they appealed to the lord chamberlain for help. Rich's greed caused his own downfall; the lord chamberlain silenced him again on 6 June 1709, an action that ended his involvement with the London stage.

Before that final stroke, however, on 10 March 1709 Cibber, Wilks, and Thomas Doggett entered into a partnership with Swiney, promising to return to the Haymarket at the end of the season. During a short summer season Cibber's burlesque of Nathaniel Lee's *The Rival Queens* (1677), wittily titled *The Rival Queans,* was revived for one performance on 29 June 1710. The partnership between Swiney and the three actors was quickly beset with misunderstandings and acrimonious disputes. In the summer of 1710 the three took some cash they said Swiney owed them, and he responded by closing the theater in the fall. Although Swiney and the three actors were given a license to operate the Haymarket theater in November 1710, they hesitated to accept it because performances were limited to only four nights per week. When William Collier assigned a lease he had obtained for the Drury Lane theater to Swiney, Cibber, Wilks, and Doggett, the triumvirate management with Swiney as a silent partner began.

Management duties demanded Cibber's full attention over the next few years. Vice-chamberlain Thomas Coke's papers document that as a comanager Cibber was involved in every aspect of running the company. There were constant struggles between Doggett and Wilks, but the three met at least once a week to pay the bills, to decide matters of casting and repertory, and to see to the legal and technical concerns of the company and the house. With no competition from a rival house, the early years of the triumvirate management proved to be very successful ones. In the 1712-1713 season the company earned a profit of four thousand pounds, and the 1713-1714 season brought in thirty-six hundred pounds. Throughout his management career, which lasted until 1732, Cibber had the reputation of a greedy, hardheaded, and abrasive man. He was not generally liked by his players or the playwrights whose works he read and often rejected, but he had the ability to help run a company in an efficient way.

Cibber became less active as a playwright and actor during his first years as a comanager. He continued to act in his favorite roles, but from 1710 to 1717 he played only one to three new roles a year, compared to the five to nine new roles a year he had undertaken between 1700 and 1707. The only play he wrote during this time was *Ximena, or the Heroick Daughter* (first performed on 28 November 1712), an adaptation of Pierre Corneille's *Le Cid* (1637). The play was performed seven times in its first season and a few times in the next season, but Cibber had little interest in it, and he did not publish the work until 1719. *Cinna's Conspiracy,* first performed on 19 February 1713, presents a translation of Corneille's *Cinna* (1640). In 1713 Daniel Defoe ascribed the work to Cibber, who spoke the prologue, but Cibber himself never acknowledged the play as his own. Richard Hindry Barker, Cibber's most reliable modern biographer, maintains that the play is not Cibber's.

In 1714 John Rich, the son of Christopher Rich, reopened the Lincoln's Inn Fields theater;

PROLOGUE.

Spoke by the AUTHOR.

THE hardy Wretch, that gives the Stage a Play,
Sails, in a Cockboat, on a tumbling Sea!
Shakespear, whose Works no Play-wright could excel,
Has lanch'd us Fleets of Plays, and built them well:
Strength, Beauty, Greatness were his constant Care;
And all his Tragedies were Men of War!
Such tow'ring Barks the Rage of Seas defy'd,
The Storms of Criticks, adverse Winds, or Tide!
Yet Fame, nor Favour ever deign'd to say,
King John was station'd as a first rate Play;
Though strong and sound the Hulk, yet ev'ry Part
Reach'd not the Merit of his usual Art!
To cure what seem'd amiss——a Modern Muse,
Warm'd by the Subject, lets his Rashness loose;
Takes on himself the Errors of to Day,
And, thus refitted, trusts it to the Sea!
The Purpose of his Voyage this——to shew,
How England groan'd——five hundred Years ago!
When, veil'd with Sanctity, the Papal Sway
To wolvish Pastors made our Folds a Prey!
When Roman Prelates here, like Princes reign'd,
Yet scarce e'er visited the Land they drain'd!
And while the Bigots Neck this Yoke endures,
Our Souls were sav'd by foreign Sine-cures!
Thus while each Pontiff, like the Sun, from hence
Exhal'd the Vapours——of his Peter-pence;
Their lock'd-up Heav'n they promis'd (such the Grace is!)
That Popes, like Box-keepers, secur'd you Places:

But

PROLOGUE.

But not as here, their Laws more firm were made,
None were admitted there, before they paid.
As if the Right divine of Roman Pow'r,
Were first to blind their Flocks, and then devour!
This carnal Discipline the fi'ry John,
Determin'd to suppress, asserts his Throne!
Defiance to the lordly Pontiff flings,
And spurns his Legates that would cope with Kings!
Hence! roar'd the holy Thunder through the Land!
Aghast! the People hear the dread Command!
Terror, Confusion, Rage and civil War,
At once the Bowels of the Nation tear;
'Till the lost Monarch vanquish'd and alone,
His Subjects to regain resigns his Throne;
With vassal Homage at her Feet lays down,
To hold, from Rome, his Tributary-Crown!
These dire Disasters, this religious Rage,
That shames our Annals, may become the Stage:
Where the wild Passions, which these Contests raise,
If well presented, may deserve your Praise;
At least this Pleasure from the View may flow,
That long! long distant were those Scenes of Woe!
And as such Chains no more these Realms annoy,
Applaud the Liberty you now enjoy.

D R A-

Prologue to Cibber's Papal Tyranny in the Reign of King John, *in the 1745 edition of the play Cibber adapted from William Shakespeare's* King John

his company was composed largely of young actors who had defected from Cibber's company at Drury Lane. With renewed competition between the houses, musical entertainments became increasingly popular. Cibber wrote libretti for two afterpieces with music by Christopher Pepusch, *Venus and Adonis* (first performed on 12 March 1715) and *Myrtillo* (first performed on 5 November 1715); both proved to be reasonably successful. Recent scholarship by William Burling suggests that Cibber was also responsible for *The Bulls and Bears,* an afterpiece farce, which had only three performances at the Drury Lane theater (2, 3, and 5 December 1715) and was never published.

The two companies did not benefit from

their competition. By 1717 neither house was doing particularly well, although the fortunes of the Drury Lane company were helped considerably by *The Non-Juror* (1717), Cibber's first mainpiece comedy in more than seven years. Cibber's extremely political adaptation of Molière's *Tartuffe* (1664) aroused great controversy, and not coincidentally, filled the Drury Lane theater for sixteen successive nights in December 1717. Not surprisingly, Cibber cast himself as Dr. Wolf, the papist priest disguised as a non-juror. Tories with Jacobite sympathies decried the play; it would earn Cibber their enmity for the rest of his life and beyond. Whigs and Hanoverian Tories applauded the play; from this time on, Cibber would be regarded by them as a loyal servant of the Hanoverian monarchy.

Besides helping to restore the financial health of the company, Cibber himself profited from the play. Lintot paid him one hundred pounds for the copyright, and five editions were published in 1718. Cibber dedicated *The Non-Juror* to the king, who eventually gave him two hundred pounds. A letter Cibber wrote to the earl of Sunderland on 10 March 1718 reveals that he indeed expected some reward for the dedication: "I have been inform'd by several Persons of Credit, that some mark of his Majestys Favour was intended for the Play of the Nonjuror, But I consider, that my Humble Pretensions may be very undesignedly forgot in the Hurry of Greater business: If your Lo^d thinks my Endeavours were of any use to the Publick, I know, on that acc't, you will forgive my reminding you of them."

The politics of *The Non-Juror,* however, worked to the disadvantage of Cibber's next two plays. Cibber's enemies disrupted the first performance of *The Refusal; or, The Ladies Philosophy* on 14 February 1721. *The London Stage* records Whincop's contemporary account: "Mr. Cibber's Enemies shew'd themselves very warmly at the Representation of this Piece, and I think without much Discretion; for they began to hiss it before they had heard it, and I remember very well, began their Uproar, on the first Night, as soon as he appeared to speak the Prologue." Cibber and/ or his friends tried to prepare the town for *Caesar in Egypt* (9 December 1724). An anonymous volume entitled *The Life and Actions of Caius Julius Caesar in Aegypt &c. Collected from the Best Historians. Illustrating the History of Caesar and Cleopatra; From Whence the Plot of Mr. Cibber's New Tragedy is Taken* was printed while the play was in rehearsal, and it advertised that the play would have new scenes and that the actors would perform in "new and magnificent Cloaths." Unruly and disrespectful members of the audience jeered Cibber when he made his entrance as Achoreus, and the show was performed only six times.

It was not, in fact, until 10 January 1728, when *The Provoked Husband* premiered, that Cibber would once again enjoy success as a playwright. This comedy presents Cibber's reworking of the late John Vanbrugh's unfinished play *A Journey to London,* about an incompatible marriage. Cibber altered the main plot so that, although it would chronicle how Lady Townly's nocturnal lifestyle threatens her marriage with Lord Townly, the resolution would be their reconciliation. In his dedicatory epistle addressed to the queen, Cibber explains that he hoped his play would "expose and reform the licentious irregularities that too often break in upon the peace and happiness of the married state." By the end of the play Lady Townly learns that "married happiness is never found from home."

The play's subplot focuses on the dangers faced by the family of Sir Francis Wronghead when they journey to London for the first time. The members of this country-bumpkin clan do not act appropriately, and the play's action shows how their inexperience puts them in peril. Interestingly, Cibber does not resolve this plot, perhaps emphasizing to his middle-class audience that the potentially dismal fate of the various Wrongheads could befall them if they are not true to themselves.

John Rich, the manager of the Lincoln's Inn Fields theater, tried to counter the work's popularity by staging a John Vanbrugh miniseason, but the public filled the Drury Lane theater for twenty-eight consecutive nights in order to see Cibber's play. Cibber himself was not too proud to use the same sort of copycat strategy the following year when John Rich and his company were enjoying their successful production of John Gay's *The Beggar's Opera,* a work Cibber had rejected for his own company. Cibber wrote a ballad opera himself, *Love in a Riddle,* but it had only two performances (on 7 and 8 January 1729). *Damon and Phillida* (16 August 1729, at the Little Theatre in the Hay-Market) has been attributed to Cibber, although he never acknowledged it as his own. William Burling argues convincingly that Henry Carey should be credited with the work.

Cibber began the 1730s as the subject of much controversy. He was named poet laureate in November, and his enemies responded by denouncing him and his poetry in satiric attacks. In 1732, with his comanagers retiring and dying, Cibber rented his shares for one season to his son, Theophilus, a dissolute actor-playwright with pretensions to theater management. In March 1733 Cibber finally sold his shares for three thousand guineas to John Highmore, then the majority stockholder of the Drury Lane theater. At this time Cibber announced that he would retire from the stage at the end of the season, although he acted and wrote sporadically throughout this and part of the next decade. He badly translated into English, *Polypheme* (1735), an opera composed by Nicholas Porpora, with words by Paul

Colley Cibber and his granddaughter Jenny, daughter of Theophilus Cibber, circa 1740
(engraving by Edward Fisher, based on an engraving by J. B. Vanloo)

Rolli. He also wrote several epilogues. In 1734 Cibber and John Fleetwood, the manager of Drury Lane, agreed on a contract that would allow Cibber to play his favorite comic roles (Bayes, Lord Foppington, Sir John Brute, Sir Courtly Nice, Sir Fopling Flutter, and Fondlewife), which he did for the next two seasons.

Cibber briefly retired from the stage in 1736 but returned two years later to play Shallow in *Henry IV*, part 2, and Richard III in his own adaptation of the play. Cibber's decision to play Richard at this time of his career (he was sixty-seven) caused a flurry of negative comments: *The Laureat* (1740) says that "He screamed through four acts without dignity or decency. The audience, ill-pleased with the farce, accompanied him with a smile of contempt; but in the fifth act he degenerated all at once into Sir Novelty; and when in the heat of the battle at Bosworth Field the King is dismounted, our comic-tragedian came on stage, really breathless, and in a seeming panic screaming out this line thus—'A harse, a harse, my kingdom for a harse.' This highly delighted some and disgusted others of his auditors; and when he was killed by Richmond, one might plainly perceive that the good people were not better pleased that so *execrable a tyrant* was destroyed than so *execrable* an actor was silent."

Cibber was also attacked for his final play, an adaptation of Shakespeare's *King John* (circa 1594-1596), titled *Papal Tyranny in the Reign of King John* (1745), which had been in rehearsal at

Drury Lane as early as 1737, only to be withdrawn. In his dedicatory epistle to Chesterfield, Cibber puffed his own play, stating that his design was to "inspirit his King *John* with a Resentment that justly might become an *English* Monarch, and to paint the intoxicated Tyranny of *Rome* in its proper Colours. And so far, at least, my Labour has succeeded, that the additional sentiments which King *John* throws out upon so flagrant a Provocation, were receiv'd with those honest cordial Applauses, which *English* Auditors I foresaw would be naturally warm'd to." An anonymous address to Cibber, *A Letter to Colley Cibber, Esq.; on His Transformation of King John*, published after the first edition of *Papal Tyranny* was available in 1745, argues that Cibber never achieved his goal. The ironic-voiced critic ends his attack with a populist flair: "In short, dear *Colley*, (for I know you love quaint Expressions) give me a *Dram of Shakespear's* Spirit by itself, and deal about, as largely as you please, of your own Mixture: People's Tastes will distinguish sufficiently between." Cibber played Pandulph, the Pope's envoy. *Papal Tyranny* was never revived after its last performance on 26 February 1745, which also marked Cibber's final appearance on the stage.

Cibber's retirement did not signal his retreat from public life. He led an active social life, wrote minor pieces of prose and poetry, and defended himself against his enemies, most notably Alexander Pope, in numerous publications. This was a career unto itself, culminating in his *Apology* (1740) and in his famous letters to Pope (1742, 1743, 1744). Pope would immortalize Cibber as Dulness's appointed one in the 1742 *Dunciad:*

> Dulness with transport eyes the lively Dunce,
> Remembering she herself was Pertness once.
> Now (shame to Fortune!) an ill Run at Play
> Blank'd his bold visage, and a thin Third day:
> Swearing and supperless the Hero sate,
> Blasphem'd his Gods, the Dice, and damn'd his
>   Fate.
> Then gnaw'd his pen, then dash'd it on the ground,
> Sinking from thought to thought, a vast profound!

Cibber's private life was almost as stormy as his public life. He married Katherine Shore, a singer and actress, on 6 May 1693. Cibber's father-in-law refused to acknowledge the match, leaving his daughter a third of his estate but calling her Shore, not Cibber, in his will. Like his father, Cibber once went to prison (in 1697 for a number of

months), probably for an inability to pay his gambling debts. According to Helene Koon's genealogy of the Cibber family, Katherine Shore Cibber carried twelve children to term; of these, five survived into adulthood. Catherine Cibber Brown (1694-1760) had a close relationship with her father, and was the chief beneficiary of his estate. Anne Cibber Boultby (1699-?) was a shopkeeper until her marriage. Elizabeth Cibber Brett Marples (1701-?) had a stage career. Two other children, Theophilus (1703-1758) and Charlotte (1713-1761), failed miserably in their attempts at theatrical careers; both were known for their debauched and eccentric life-styles. When Katherine Shore Cibber died on 17 January 1734, she and Cibber had not lived together for many years. Cibber's death on 11 December 1757 received little notice.

Although Cibber was not a major talent, he must be considered a major figure. When he was correctly cast, his skills as an actor were formidable. He acted in more than 130 roles during his career. A number of his own compositions became favorites and held the stage during the eighteenth century and beyond. Moreover, Cibber's power and influence as a manager determined careers as well as repertory in his own time and well into the next era of English stage history. The controversy attending him throughout much of his career underscores his influence and his importance in all the aspects of his professional and personal life. As befits a man of the stage, his was a most public life.

Bibliographies:

L. R. N. Ashley, "Colley Cibber: A Bibliography," *Restoration and Eighteenth-Century Theater Research*, 6 (May 1967): 14-27, 51-57;

Ashley, "Colley Cibber: A Supplement," *Restoration and Eighteenth-Century Theater Research*, 7 (May 1968): 17.

Biographies:

Richard Hindry Barker, *Mr. Cibber of Drury Lane* (New York: Columbia University Press, 1939);

Helene Koon, *Colley Cibber: A Biography* (Lexington: University Press of Kentucky, 1986).

References:

William Burling, "New Light on the Colley Cibber Canon: *The Bulls and Bears* and *Damon and Phillida*," *Philological Quarterly*, 67 (Winter 1988): 117-123;

Robert D. Hume, *The Development of English Drama in the Late Seventeenth Century* (Oxford: Clarendon Press, 1976);

Hume, "Marital Discord in English Comedy from Dryden to Fielding," *Modern Philology,* 74 (February 1977): 248-272;

Hume, "The Multifarious Forms of Eighteenth-Century Comedy," in *The Stage and the Page: London's "Whole Show" in the Eighteenth-Century Theatre,* edited by George Winchester Stone (Berkeley: University of California Press, 1981), pp. 3-32;

Hume, *The Rakish Stage: Studies in English Drama, 1660-1800* (Carbondale: Southern Illinois University Press, 1983);

Hume, "The Sponsorship of Opera in London, 1704-1720," *Modern Philology,* 85 (May 1988): 420-432;

Shirley Strum Kenny, "Humane Comedy," *Modern Philology,* 75 (August 1977): 29-43;

Kenny, "Perennial Favorites," *Modern Philology,* 73 (May 1976): S4-S11;

John Loftis, *The Politics of Drama in Augustan England* (Oxford: Clarendon Press, 1963);

Judith Milhous, *Thomas Betterton and the Management of Lincoln's Inn Fields, 1695-1708* (Carbondale: Southern Illinois University Press, 1979);

Milhous and Robert Hume, "The Silencing of Drury Lane in 1709," *Theatre Journal,* 32 (December 1980): 427-447;

Milhous and Hume, *Vice Chamberlain Coke's Theatrical Papers, 1706-1715* (Carbondale: Southern Illinois University Press, 1982);

Allardyce Nicoll, *A History of English Drama, 1660-1900,* revised edition, volume 2 (Cambridge: Cambridge University Press, 1955);

Arthur H. Scouten and Hume, " 'Restoration Comedy' and its Audiences, 1660-1776," *Yearbook of English Studies,* 10 (1980): 45-69.

Papers:

Although there is no indication that any manuscripts of Cibber's plays are extant, other Cibber materials can be found in libraries and record offices in Great Britain and the United States. Cibber's will can be found at Somerset House, London. The Middlesex Record Office (WJ/SR/2192) holds papers relating to the troubles resulting from Cibber's fathering of a bastard child. Financial information about Cibber's parents can be found at the British Library (Add. MS. 23,067). Papers relating to Cibber's role in theater management can be found at major collections in America: the Harvard Theatre Collection; the Folger Shakespeare Library (Drury Lane MSS.); the Huntington Library; the New York Public Library (Berg Collection). In England documents relating to the management of the Drury Lane theater may be found at the Public Record Office (L.C. 5/154-157; L.C. 7/3) and the British Library (Add. MS. 32,607; 38,607). All documents relating to Cibber's career as a manager are catalogued in L. R. N. Ashley's "The Management of The Theatre-Royal in Drury Lane under Cibber, Booth and Wilks," Ph.D. dissertation, Princeton University, 1956.

William Congreve

(24 January 1670-19 January 1729)

Peter Holland
Cambridge University

PLAY PRODUCTIONS: *The Old Bachelor*, London, Theatre Royal in Drury Lane, 9 March 1693;

The Double Dealer, London, Theatre Royal in Drury Lane, October 1693;

Love for Love, London, Lincoln's Inn Fields, 30 April 1695;

The Mourning Bride, London, Lincoln's Inn Fields, February 1697;

The Way of the World, London, Lincoln's Inn Fields, March 1700;

The Judgment of Paris, London, Dorset Garden Theatre, 21 March 1701 (with music by John Eccles); 28 March 1701 (with music by Godfrey Finger); April 1701 (with music by Daniel Purcell); 6 May 1701 (with music by John Weldon);

Squire Trelooby, adapted from Molière's *Monsieur de Pourceaugnac*, by Congreve, John Vanbrugh, and William Walsh, London, Lincoln's Inn Fields, 30 March 1704.

BOOKS: *Incognita: or, Love and Duty Reconcil'd. A Novel* (London: Printed for Peter Buck, 1692);

The Old Batchelour, A Comedy. As it is Acted at the Theatre Royal, by Their Majesties Servants (London: Printed for Peter Buck, 1693);

The Double-Dealer, A Comedy. Acted at the Theatre Royal, by their Majesties Servants (London: Printed for Jacob Tonson, 1694);

The Mourning Muse of Alexis. A Pastoral. Lamenting the Death of our late Gracious Queen Mary of ever Blessed Memory (London: Printed for Jacob Tonson, 1695);

Love for Love: A Comedy. Acted at the Theatre in Little Lincoln's-Inn Fields, By His Majesty's Servants (London: Printed for Jacob Tonson, 1695);

A Pindarique Ode, Humbly Offer'd to the King on his Taking Namure (London: Printed for Jacob Tonson, 1695);

The Mourning Bride, A Tragedy. As it is Acted at the Theatre in Lincoln's-Inn-Fields, By His Majesty's Servants (London: Printed for Jacob Tonson, 1697);

The Birth of the Muse. A Poem. To the Right Honourable Charles Montague, Chancellour of the Exchequer, &c. (London: Printed for Jacob Tonson, 1698);

Amendments of Mr. Collier's False and Imperfect Citations &c., from the Old Batchelour, Double Dealer, Love for Love, Mourning Bride (London: Printed for Jacob Tonson, 1698);

The Way of the World, A Comedy. As it is Acted at the Theatre in Lincoln's-Inn-Fields, By His Majesty's Servants (London: Printed for Jacob Tonson, 1700);

The Judgment of Paris: A Masque (London: Printed for Jacob Tonson, 1701);

A Hymn to Harmony, Written in Honour of St. Cecilia's Day (London: Printed for Jacob Tonson, 1703);

The Tears of Amaryllis for Amyntas. A Pastoral. Lamenting the Death of the late Lord Marquis of Blandford (London: Printed for Jacob Tonson, 1703);

A Pindarique Ode, Humbly Offer'd to the Queen, on the Victorious Progress of her Majesty's Arms, Under the Conduct of the Duke of Marlborough. To which is Prefixed a Discourse on the Pindarique Ode (London: Printed for Jacob Tonson, 1706);

An Impossible Thing. A Tale (London: Printed for J. Roberts, 1720);

A Letter from Mr Congreve to the Right Honourable the Lord Viscount Cobham (London: Printed for A. Dodd & E. Nutt, 1729);

Mr Congreve's Last Will and Testament, with Characters of his Writings (London: Printed for E. Curll, 1729).

Collections: *The Works of Mr William Congreve*, 3 volumes (London: Printed for Jacob Tonson, 1710);

The Complete Works of William Congreve, 4 volumes, edited by Montague Summers (London: Nonesuch Press, 1923);

John C. Hodges, William Congreve
The Man, *1941*

The Comedies; The Mourning Bride, Poems and Miscellanies, 2 volumes, edited by Bonamy Dobrée (London: Oxford University Press, 1925, 1928);

The Complete Plays of William Congreve, edited by Herbert Davies (Chicago & London: University of Chicago Press, 1967);

The Complete Works, 3 volumes, edited by D. F. McKenzie (Oxford: Clarendon Press, forthcoming 1990).

OTHER: Satire XI and "To Mr Dryden," in *The Satires of Decimus Junius Juvenalis. Translated into English Verse. By Mr Dryden, and Several other Eminent Hands. Together with the Satires of Aulus Persius Flaccus. Made English by Mr. Dryden* (London: Printed for Jacob Tonson, 1693);

"An Essay Concerning Humour in Comedy," in *Letters upon Several Occasions*, edited by John Dennis (London: Printed for Sam. Briscoe, 1696);

Book III, in *Ovid's Art of Love*, translated by Congreve and others (London: Printed for Jacob Tonson, 1709);

"Dedication," in *The Dramatick Works of John Dryden, Esq.*, 6 volumes (London: Printed for Jacob Tonson, 1717);

"The Story of Orpheus and Eurydice" and "The Fable of Cyparissus," in Book III of *Ovid's Metamorphoses in Fifteen Books. Translated by the most Eminent Hands* (London: Printed for Jacob Tonson, 1717).

William Congreve is, by common consent, the greatest writer of comedies in the late seventeenth century. *The Way of the World*, above all, has come to represent the standard against which all other comedies of the period have to be measured, the crowning glory of Restoration comedy and of "the comedy of manners," whatever that title may be supposed to represent. His dialogue, usually praised in ecstatic terms for its dazzling or even coruscating wit, and the comedy of his fools who pretend to wit, have been the prime qualities which have secured his preeminence. Yet every revival, especially of *The Way of the World*, is greeted by theater reviewers with an automatic response of incomprehension at the daunting complexities of Congreve's plots, the price the audience supposedly has to pay to be allowed to listen to the subtlety and sophistication of his lovers' speeches. Recent academic criticism has taken the brilliance of the dramatic language for granted and has set itself to puzzle out the extraordinarily individualistic way Congreve turns the materials of his plays into complete and coherent actions. On rare occasions when directors have been prepared to take the plots seriously, as, for example, in John Barton's excellent production of *The Way of the World* for the Royal Shakespeare Company in London in 1978, the seriousness of Congreve's concerns, of which the wit is only a small part, has been revealed with startling clarity. For Congreve is a serious writer who uses comedy to examine the potentialities of human behavior in ways that the audience comes to respect. As Horace commented, in a phrase from his *Ars Poetica* that Congreve put as a motto on the title page of *The Double Dealer*, "sometimes however even comedy raises its voice."

Congreve was born at Bardsey in Yorkshire. His father, William, came from a staunchly Royalist family while his mother, Mary Browning Congreve, was connected to the Lewis family whose wealth derived from trade with India and Persia.

His parents lived in a house on the Lewis estate, but his father, as a younger brother, had little expectation from his family. By 1672, the Congreves were in London, where his elder sister, Elizabeth, was buried. In 1674 his father joined the army in Ireland as a lieutenant and moved the family to Youghal, an Irish seaport. Congreve lived in Ireland until 1691, leading many contemporaries to assume him to be Irish, in spite of his protestations, and allowing Dr. Johnson to assume that Congreve's claim to an English birth was a "falsehood of convenience or vanity." In Youghal the family established a friendship with the Boyle family, including Charles, eldest son of the second earl of Cork and the dedicatee of Congreve's first play. In 1678 the family moved to Carrickfergus and then, in 1681, to Kilkenny. Congreve may have gone to school in Youghal, but he was certainly at Kilkenny College, one of the greatest schools in Ireland, from 1682 to 1686. Jonathan Swift, a few years his senior, was at the same school, and there Congreve also began his enduring friendship with Joseph Keally, the recipient of many of his best letters. His time at Kilkenny College was the beginning of many other significant recurrent events in his life: his nearsightedness, which led to a number of operations in later life; his interest in Greek; his writing poetry (his earliest known composition is on the death of a master's magpie); and, above all, his contact with drama. The school had a long tradition of performing plays, but Congreve may also have seen the Smock Alley Players, the professional theater company from Dublin, on one of their visits to perform at the Castle in Kilkenny.

In 1686 Congreve entered Trinity College, Dublin, where he pursued his study in Greek and his interest in eating well and drinking substantially, practices he never gave up. His regular absences from college on Saturday afternoons were probably spent at the Smock Alley Theatre, run by Joseph Ashbury, who had been, like Congreve's father, a lieutenant in the regiment of the duke of Ormond. The Smock Alley company included players such as Thomas Doggett, Joseph Trefusis, and William Bowen, who later moved to London and for whom Congreve wrote parts. At Smock Alley Congreve could have seen plays which had recently been successful on the London stage. But, alongside this introduction to contemporary drama by Thomas Shadwell, Thomas Southerne, Thomas Otway, or John Dryden, Congreve began to read in literary and

William Congreve during his attendance at Kilkenny College (portrait by W. D. Clarea; John C. Hodges, William Congreve The Man, *1941)*

dramatic theory. The catalogue of his library indicates that he had probably already purchased copies of Dryden's *Essay on Dramatic Poesy* (1668), Wentworth Dillon, earl of Roscommon's 1680 translation of Horace's *Ars Poetica*, and such French theorists as René Rapin and François Hédelin, author of *The Whole Art of the Stage* (1684).

Congreve left Trinity College in 1689 and was soon in London. In March 1691 he entered the Middle Temple, one of the Inns of Court, using the opportunity, as did so many other young men, less to study law than to join fashionable London society, particularly, in Congreve's case, the literary circles centered on Will's Coffeehouse.

Though he had probably already completed *The Old Bachelor*, Congreve's first published work was a short novel, *Incognita* (1692). Its action is an intricate maze of disguisings and mistakings, set against the background of carnival in Florence and following the adventures of two young men, Aurelian and Hippolito, as they fall in love with Incognita and Leonora. Entangled by Aurelian's father's intention to marry his son to Juliana in order to resolve a long-standing family feud, the two men take each other's names with inevitable confusions. Equally inevitable is the final discovery, long anticipated by the reader, that Incognita's real name is Juliana, the intended bride of Aurelian, and hence that his attempts to avoid being found by his father prove to have been totally unnecessary since his love for Incognita and his duty to his father are not in opposition (as the novel's subtitle forewarns: *"Love and Duty Reconcil'd"*). The twistings and turnings of the narrative, complete with masked balls, wedding tournaments, duels, attempted rape, letters, and dozens of chance meetings, sound irredeemably trivial, and *Incognita* has usually been written off as a youthful foray enlivened only by its own energetic exuberance, its delight in its own wit, and its pleasure in the amused observation of the contortions forced on its characters.

But while it undoubtedly possesses those qualities it also has an extraordinary and unprecedented self-consciousness, revealing itself as thoughtfully concerned with its own procedures. No sooner has the narrative indulged in an elaborate set-piece description of dusk, couched in flowery language of painful pretentiousness, than the narrator intervenes to apologize for such "impertinent digressions" and to differentiate sharply between the author's pleasure and the reader's:

> I think it fit to acquaint him, that when I degress, I am at that time writing to please my self, when I continue the Thread of the Story, I write to please him; supposing him a reasonable Man, I conclude him satisfied to allow me this liberty, and so I proceed.

This wry control over the reader's irritations extends into the narrative itself in its consideration of the characters' psychology. If on the one hand the maneuverings of the plot treat the characters as puppets at the behest of the author's will, on the other their reactions are offered from a sophisticated perception of individual motive. Don Fabio's concern for Aurelian's education is complexly self-directed, a consequence of seeing his son as "the Type of himself," so that his sustained gazing on his son at dinner is offered by the narrator as the result either of "regret, at the Recollection of his former self, or for the Joy he conceiv'd in being, as it were, reviv'd in the Person of his Son."

There is nothing heavy-handed about this concern with the novel's own progress. Throughout there is a deft lightness that anticipates the brilliance of Congreve's dramatic dialogue. Congreve's serious consideration of the methods of the novel does not induce in him an awkward and uncharacteristic ponderousness. The thoughtful games Congreve plays through the interventions of the narrator's voice are balanced by the other major innovation Congreve is determined to explore: the interrelationship of the two genres, novel and drama. The action of *Incognita* owes its matter far more strongly to the traditions of late-seventeeth-century comedy than to anything in the recent development of prose narrative. If, in its brevity and skittishness, the action is in conscious opposition to the extreme length and weighty moralism of French-style prose romance, it clearly also derives its incidents by carefully transposing into the novel the kinds of scenes that fill plays such as Dryden's *An Evening's Love* (1668). Aurelian and Juliana are, ad-

mittedly, far more serious lovers than Restoration comedy had been prepared to tolerate, but the formal balance provided by the two couples is reminiscent of the basic structure of countless comedies. Even at this early stage, however, Congreve's perception of drama is a combination of innovation and tradition as well as a predisposition to respect the genre for its emphasis both on action and structure. In an important passage in the preface, Congreve defines the originality of *Incognita* by reference to drama:

> Since all traditions must indisputably give place to the *Drama*, and since there is no possibility of giving that life to the Writing or Repetition of a Story which it has in Action, I resolved in another beauty to imitate *Dramatick* Writing, namely, in the Design, Contexture and Result of the Plot. I have not observed it before in a Novel.

The basic design of *Incognita* has the dramatic form of slow and steady growth, through a number of incidental scenes, toward a climatic scene of discovery and resolution. Everything, as Congreve is at pains to stress, is directed toward that end; all the minor catastrophes combine to make the end both postponed until the required moment of unraveling and at the same time inevitable at that point at which the emotions of the characters and the complications of event have been satisfactorily wound up to an extreme of tension. The "Thread of the Story" is never abandoned, and the digressions are never digressions of narrative, only of circumstantial description.

Hence Congreve is able to claim for his novel what he will repeatedly claim for his plays: "In a Comedy this would be called the Unity of Action; here it may pretend to no more than an Unity of Contrivance." It is appropriate that Congreve should go on in the preface to call attention to his adherence, at least comparatively so, to the other two virtues of neoclassical dramatic theory, the unity of place (Florence) and the unity of time (two or three days). The novelist's skill lies as much in the accomplishment of the action within the terms of such critical orthodoxy as in the local effects of the narrative style: "the difficulty is in bringing it to pass, maugre all apparent obstacles, within the compass of two days."

Congreve's pride in the achievement *Incognita* represents is based, then, on the technical originality of its form. There is a combination here of what Dr. Johnson might have seen in Congreve as a natural inclination to witty dialogue and an obligation to critical awareness; it is per-

Letter from Congreve to Joseph Keally (28 September 1697), Congreve's Kilkenny College schoolmate and lifelong friend. This letter was written soon after Keally had traveled to Ireland from London, where he had been studying law. The opening sentences refer to French privateers who were seizing English ships and to the soon-to-be signed Treaty of Ryswick (Henry W. and Albert A. Berg Collection, by permission of the New York Public Library, Astor, Lenox and Tilden Foundations).

books at that time I have no want of any kind
to send you I have not seen bottom since Ireceivd
yo.r letter but Amory I just now parted with
who is yours. Jory Marsh is here. as for Luther
I find him told by yo.r account & his own proceeding
unalterable and I hope Champs & you will come
over together. pray give my hearty service to my
Cosen Congreve tell the Good Bishop I must have
very good fortune before I am reconciled to the necessity
of my staying in England at a time when I promisd
my selfe the Happinesse of seeing him at Kilkenny
I would say something very devout to the Dutchesse
but you are a prophane dog & would spoil it. if
the Bishop would sanctifie my Duty to her I would
require him in my way. prithee heartily distribute
my service in a most particular manner & make me
popular amongst those acquaintance whom I have forgott
let me hear when I may expect you & make haste to your
                                                    W. Congreve

Congreve in his early twenties (portrait by Henry Tilson; William Congreve: Letters and Documents, *edited by John C. Hodges, 1964)*

haps a central part of Congreve's debt to Ben Jonson. It also represents in embryo what would be the recurrent critical problem of responding to Congreve's work: the balance between the celebration of the dazzling local effects of brilliantly polished language and a recognition of the deliberate and innovative peculiarities of Congreve's dramatic forms. In *Incognita*, at least, the harmony between the delightful energy of the one and the provocative sophistication of the other has not received its critical due.

Incognita, published anonymously, made, unsurprisingly, comparatively little impact. Congreve's literary career was immeasurably helped at this time by his remarkable warm friendship with Dryden, still the greatest literary figure in

London. Dryden had begun work in 1691 on a translation of Juvenal and Persius, parceling out the satires among a number of different translators. Congreve's translation of Juvenal's Satire XI appeared in the volume when it was published in October 1692 (with 1693 on its title page), together with his poem "To Mr Dryden" prefacing the Persius translations. Dryden's high opinion of Congreve as translator was expressed in the preface to another collection of Dryden's translations, *Examen Poeticum* (1693), where he wishes Congreve had the leisure and encouragement to produce a complete Homer. By the time *Examen Poeticum* was published Congreve was on the verge of his triumphant debut as playwright, but the easy stylishness and scholarly worth of his early translations under Dryden's aegis was much more than an adroit use of the skills learned at university for other larger ends. Throughout his life Congreve returned periodically to the art of translation, contributing, for instance, to the translation of Ovid's *Ars Amatoria* in 1709 and his *Metamorphoses* in 1717. Some of his weightiest poetry was written as a series of public and politic celebrations of military successes, the victory at Namur in 1695 or Marlborough's campaign in 1706, all based on the Pindaric ode. Congreve's essay on the form of the Pindaric ode, published in 1706, was the first attempt in English to define the nature of the apparently formless form, establishing its rules and prescribing its use. It is a typically Congrevean combination of scholarship and contemporary application, of theory and practice.

Congreve began writing *The Old Bachelor* during his stay at his grandfather's home, Stretton Manor in Staffordshire, in 1689, a visit which also resulted in meeting Katherine Leveson, the dedicatee of *Incognita*. He worked on the play again in the Derbyshire Peaks in 1692. In London he showed it to Thomas Southerne, already an established dramatist and a friend of cousins of Congreve, as well as being an Irishman educated, like Congreve, at Trinity College, Dublin. Southerne in turn showed it to Dryden, who, recognizing the play's extraordinary promise, determined to help it along by giving it what Southerne later described as "the fashionable cutt of the town." With help from Dryden, Southerne, and Arthur Mainwaring, the play was polished, Dryden reordering the scenes. Southerne secured its performance at the Theatre Royal in Drury Lane, where it was first produced on 9 March 1693, and Congreve was given the author's privilege of free admission to the playhouse an unprecedented six months before the premiere. Well-worn theatrical clichés about overnight successes are for once fully justified. The theater was full and the play was, as the earl of Burlington wrote to Congreve's father, "by all the Hearers applauded to bee the best that has been Acted for many yeares."

Some part of *The Old Bachelor*'s success must have derived from its brilliant and vital re-creation of familiar, almost conventional, characters and situations from the tradition of Restoration comedy. Most critical judgments of the play have simply been subtle expansions of Dr. Johnson's opinion: "it will be found to be one of those comedies which may be made by a mind vigorous and

acute, and furnished with comick characters by the perusal of other poets, without much actual commerce with mankind." If much seemed to Johnson to be borrowed material, his praise of the energy in Congreve's handling is crucial. There is a dramatic impetus to the play created by the combination of conventional expectation, stock situations, and a new and dazzling way with words, an impetus largely unprecedented. If the affectations of Belinda, for instance, derive largely from a character such as Melantha in Dryden's *Marriage A la Mode* (1671), there are, in her inventiveness of description and breathlessness of wit, things that had been missed in Restoration drama for many years. When she narrates to Araminta her meeting with a country family shopping at the Exchange, she easily reaches out for an unexpected image to describe the two girls: "fat as Barn-door-Fowl: But so bedeck'd, you would have taken 'em for *Friezland*-Hens, with their Feathers growing the wrong way." In the same way her rejoinder to her lover Bellmour is crushing as its picks up his image and reshapes it:

BELLMOUR. . . . Courtship to Marriage, is but as the Musick in the Play-house, till the Curtain's drawn; but that once up, then opens the Scene of Pleasure.

BELINDA. Oh, foh,—no: Rather, Courtship to Marriage, as a very witty Prologue to a very dull Play.

Congreve's teasing delight in the poise and subtlety of his lovers' wit depends on a remarkable degree of attentiveness on the part of the characters, the actors, and the audience. The image has to be heard, held, and then turned. There is the beginnings, throughout *The Old Bachelor*, of that intensity of shared dialogue that Congreve makes peculiarly his own in his later comedies. It is, above all, a spoken wit, a language sensitively aware and alive to the especial qualities of voice in the theater.

Some of the multiple, interlacing plots of *The Old Bachelor* betray their dramatic ancestry only too clearly. Sharper's gulling of Sir Joseph Wittoll and Captain Bluffe is a neat strand showing Congreve at his most Jonsonian. Captain Bluffe himself is a braggart soldier plainly derived from Bobadill in Ben Jonson's *Every Man In His Humour* (1598), prepared to be cuffed and kicked and to find any possible excuse to avoid drawing his sword. Heartwell, the old bachelor of the title, escapes from his marriage to Sylvia, represented in the play rather unconvincingly as a whore, when the parson who marries them turns

Actress Anne Bracegirdle, who created the parts of Araminta in The Old Bachelor, *Cynthia in* The Double Dealer, *Angelica in* Love for Love, *Almeria in* The Mourning Bride, *Millamant in* The Way of the World, *Venus in* The Judgment of Paris, *and Julia in* Squire Trelooby. *According to Colley Cibber, Mellefont's feelings for Cynthia in* The Double Dealer *reflect Congreve's love for Bracegirdle.*

out to be Bellmour in disguise, a trick borrowed in part from William Wycherley's *The Country Wife* (1675). But if such moments in the action serve only to corroborate Dr. Johnson's criticism, the central action of the play, the relationships of Bellmour and Belinda and of Vainlove and Araminta, is a disturbing reconsideration of the activities of the rake, feeding on a perception of individual anxiety and neurosis that in its peculiarities is both daringly innovative and creatively based on a genuine "commerce with mankind." Restoration comedy thrived on the balance between two men and two women, with one pair embodying the comic and ethical norm of the plays in their greater wit. But both couples convention-

ally ended the plays with parallel commitments to love and impending matrimony. *The Old Bachelor* cannot simply adopt such a pattern unquestioned. Taking the conventional characteristics of the rake, Congreve redistributes them between Vainlove and Bellmour in an unexpected way. Vainlove's pleasure lies wholly in the pursuit of an apparently unattainable prey. Using all the rake's wit and charm, he seeks to persuade women to fall for him. But once a woman has committed herself, once she has admitted to being in love with him or being prepared to have sex with him, his interest is immediately terminated. What Vainlove describes as the tedium of the mechanics of sex, frequently covered in the play by the

THE

Old Batchelour,

A

COMEDY.

As it is ACTED at the

Theatre Royal,

BY

Their MAJESTIES Servants.

Written by Mr. *Congreve*.

Quem tulit ad Scenam ventoso gloria Curru,
Exanimat lentus Spectator ; sedulus inflat.
Sic leve, sic parvum est, animum quod laudis avarum
Subruit, aut reficit——
                Horat. Epist. I. Lib. II.

LONDON,
Printed for *Peter Buck*, at the Sign of the *Temple*
near the *Temple-gate* in *Fleet-street*, 1693.

To the Right Honourable, Charles *Lord* Clifford
of Lanesborough, &c.

My Lord,

IT is with a great deal of Pleasure, that I lay hold on this first Occasion, which, the Accidents of my Life have given me of writing to your Lordship : For since at the same time I write to all the World, it will be a means of publishing, (what I would have every Body know) the Respect and Duty which I owe and pay to you. I have so much Inclination to be yours, that I need no other Engagement : But the particular Ties, by which I am bound to your Lordship and Family, have put it out of my power to make you any Complement ; since all Offers of my self, will amount to no more than an honest Acknowledgment, and only shew a willingness in me to be grateful.

I am very near wishing, That it were not so much my Interest to be your Lordships Servant, that it might be more my Merit ; not that I would avoid being obliged to you, but I would have my own Choice to run me into the Debt ; that I might have it to boast, I had distinguished a Man, to whom I would be glad to be obliged, even without the hopes of having it in my Power, ever to make him a return.

It is impossible for me to come near your Lordship, in any kind, and not to receive some Favour ; and while in appearance I am only making an Acknowledgment (with the usual underhand dealing of the World) I am at the same time, insinuating my own Interest. I cannot give your Lordship your due, without tacking a Bill of my own Priviledges. 'Tis true, if a Man never committed a Folly, he would never stand in need of a Protection : But then Power would have nothing to do, and good Nature no occasion to shew it self ; and where those Vertues are, 'tis pity they should want Objects to shine upon. I must confess this is no reason, why a Man should do an idle thing, nor indeed any good Excuse for it, when done ; yet it reconciles the uses of such Authority and Goodness, to the necessities of our Follies ; and is a sort of Poetical Logick, which, at this time I would make use of, to argue your Lordship into a Protection of this Play. It is the first

       A 2   Of

The Epistle Dedicatory.

Offence I have committed in this kind, or indeed, in any kind of Poetry, tho' not the first made publick ; and, therefore, I hope will the more easily be pardoned : But had it been Acted, when it was first written, more might have been said in its behalf ; Ignorance of the Town and Stage, would then, have been Excuses in a young Writer, which now, almost four Years experience, will scarce allow of. Yet I must declare my self sensible of the good Nature of the Town, in receiving this Play so kindly, with all its Faults, which I must own were, for the most part, very industriously covered by the care of the Players ; for, I think, scarce a Character but received all the Advantage it would admit of, from the justness of Action.

As for the Criticks, my Lord, I have nothing to say, to, or against any of them of any kind ; from those who make just Exceptions, to those who find fault in the wrong place. I will only make this general Answer in behalf of my Play (an Answer, which Epictetus advises every Man to make for himself, to his Censurers) viz. That if they who find some Faults in it, were as intimate with it as I am, they would find a great many more. This is a Confession, which I need not to have made ; but however, I can draw this use from it, to my own Advantage, that I think there are no Faults in it, but what I do know ; which, as I take it, is the first step to an amendment.

Thus I may live in hopes (sometime or other) of making the Town amends ; but you, my Lord, I never can, tho' I am ever

        Your Lordships

           most obedient and

           most humble Servant,

             Will. Congreve.

                     To

To Mr. CONGREVE.

WHEN *Vertue in pursuit of Fame appears,*
   And forward shoots the growth beyond the Years :
We timely court the rising Hero's Cause ;
And on his side, the Poet wisely draws ;
Bespeaking him hereafter, by Applause.
The days will come, when we shall all receive,
Returning Interest from what now we give :
Instructed, and supported by that Praise,
And Reputation, which we strive to raise.
Nature so coy, so hardly to be Woo'd
Flies, like a Mistress, but to be pursu'd.
O CONGREVE! *boldly follow on the Chase ;*
She looks behind, and wants thy strong Embrace :
She yields, she yields, surrenders all her Charms,
Do you but force her gently to your Arms :
Such Nerves, such Graces, in your Lines appear,
As you were made to be her Ravisher.
DRYDEN *has long extended his Command,*
By Right divine, quite through the Muses Land,
Absolute Lord ; and holding now from none,
But great Apollo, his undoubted Crown :
(That Empire settled, and grown old in Pow'r)
Can wish for nothing, but a Successor :
Not to enlarge his Limits, but maintain
Those Provinces, which he alone could gain.
His eldest Wicherly, in wise Retreat,
Thought it not worth his quiet to be great.
Loose, wandring, Etherege, in wild Pleasures tost,
And foreign Int'rests, to his hopes long lost :
Poor Lee and Otway dead ! CONGREVE *appears ;*
The Darling, and last Comfort of his Years :
May'st thou live long in thy great Masters smiles,
And growing under him, adorn these Isles :
But when——when part of him (be that Fat late)
His Body yielding must submit to Fate,
Leaving his deathless Works, and thee behind,
(The natural Successor of his Mind)
Then may'st thou finish what he has begun :
Heir to his Merit, be in Fame his Son.
What thou hast done, shews all is in thy Power ;
And to Write better, only must Write more.
'Tis something to be willing to commend ;
But my best Praise, is, that I am your Friend.

                    THO. SOUTHERNE.

Title page, dedicatory epistle, and commendatory verse by Thomas Southerne, from the first edition of Congreve's first play. Southerne had helped to polish the play and had convinced the management of the Theatre Royal in Drury Lane to stage it.

word *business*, is demonstrably a fear both of commitment and of sex itself. Hence he can assert of Laetitia, the wife of the foolish Alderman Fondlewife, that "I hate Love when 'tis forced upon a Man," though he has evidently been pursuing her for some time. As far as Bellmour is concerned, Vainlove displays extraordinary friendship in his willingness to hand over his victims, once raised to a pitch of sexual readiness:

> BELLMOUR. . . . Dear *Frank* thou art the truest Friend in the World.
> VAINLOVE. Ay, am I not? To be continually starting of Hares for you to Course. We were certainly cut out for one another; for my Temper quits an Amour, just where thine takes it up.

The action of the play, then, is the consequence of the difference between the squeamishness and fastidiousness of Vainlove and Bellmour's readiness to be, as he puts it, "a Cormorant in Love." Hence, Bellmour visits Laetitia in the disguise of Parson Spintext that Laetitia had suggested to Vainlove, while Vainlove's obsessions mean that there is no way his love for Araminta can reach marriage. His refusal to "marry *Araminta* till I merit her" meets an exasperated response from Bellmour:

> BELLMOUR. But how the Devil dost thou expect to get her if she never yield?
> VAINLOVE. That's true; but I would–
> BELLMOUR. Marry her without her Consent; thou'rt a Riddle beyond Woman–

Sylvia need only send Vainlove a letter purporting to come from Araminta and apparently indicating her love for Vainlove for Vainlove to announce "she has miscarried of her Love" and to insult her when they next meet. At the end of the play, as Bellmour and Belinda agree to marry, Vainlove's plea to Araminta for a comparable conclusion, "May I presume to hope so great a Blessing?," secures from her only a nervous withdrawal, frightened at the risk of an end to love that agreeing might produce in him: "We had better take the Advantage of a little of our Frends Experience first." Vainlove's blindness comes, through Congreve's careful juxtaposition of scenes, to appear dangerously close to the blindness of Fondlewife. It disturbs the action of the play throughout and renders the ending necessarily inconclusive.

Congreve's reading in dramatic theory has one further significant effect on the play, an unusual care in the interaction and interconnection of the scenes within each act. Each entrance and exit is highlighted, marked by a character's observation of others' movements. The result, given how many elements of plot go to making up the play as a whole, is integrated and cohesive in a way that multiple-plot Restoration comedy had rarely managed.

In its quirkily individualist characterization and in its brilliant sense of the possibilities of the theater, *The Old Bachelor* deservedly marked an auspicious debut. But its qualities of dramatic skill and unusually perceptive psychology were placed in a context sufficiently familiar not to trouble the audience.

It was hardly surprising after the success of *The Old Bachelor* that Congreve's next play should have been eagerly anticipated and, as so often in such circumstances, hardly surprising that it should have disappointed. The savagery of the satire in *The Double Dealer*, first produced in October 1693, was unexpected, and, as Dryden noted in a letter to William Walsh on 12 December 1693, it was "much censur'd by the greater part of the Town. . . . The women think he has exposed their Bitchery too much; and the Gentlemen, are offended with him; for the discovery of their follies: and the way of their Intrigues, under the notion of Friendship to their Ladyes Husbands." Dryden contributed magnificently to the defense of the play by writing his generous poem "To my dear friend Mr Congreve," printed in the first edition of the play (1694), while Congreve used the preface to defend the play against some of its critics' charges. The town's antagonism or at best hesitancy over the play was, however, a natural response to its experimentation both in matter and manner.

The Old Bachelor set its action of love and sex in the normal urban locales of Restoration comedy. The rooms, streets, and parks of London provide the setting for the flow of the action across the city of the audience. For *The Double Dealer* Congreve establishes something like a theatrical laboratory in which the action can move precipitately under the vigilant gaze of the audience at its scientific demonstration of human activity. The entire action of the play takes place in Lord Touchwood's house; indeed, every scene takes place in the gallery, except for a single scene set in a bedroom opening off it. The house has a garden into which characters can wander, but, be-

To my Dear Friend

Mr. Congreve,

On His COMEDY, call'd,

The Double-Dealer.

WELL then; the promis'd hour is come
    at last ;
        The present Age of Wit obscures the past :
Strong were our Syres; and as they Fought they Writ,
Conqu'ring with force of Arms, and dint of Wit ;
Theirs was the Gyant Race, before the Flood ;
And thus, when Charles Return'd, our Empire stood.
Like Janus he the stubborn Soil manur'd,
With Rules of Husbandry the rankness cur'd :
Tam'd us to manners, when the Stage was rude ;
And boistrous English Wit, with Art indu'd.
Our Age was cultivated thus at length ;
But what we gain'd in skill we lost in strength.
Our Builders were, with want of Genius, curst ;
The second Temple was not like the first :

a 2   Till

On the Double-Dealer.

The Father had descended for the Son ;
For only You are lineal to the Throne.
Thus when the State one Edward did depose ;
A Greater Edward in his room arose.
But now, not I, but Poetry is curs'd ;
For Tom the Second reigns like Tom the first.
But let 'em not mistake my Patron's part ;
Nor call his Charity their own desert.
Yet this I Prophecy ; Thou shalt be seen,
(Tho' with some short Parenthesis between :)
High on the Throne of Wit ; and seated there,
Not mine (that's little) but thy Lawrel wear.
Thy first attempt an early promise made ;
That early promise this has more than paid.
So bold, yet so judiciously you dare,
That Your least Praise, is to be Regular.
Time, Place, and Action, may with pains be wrought,
But Genius must be born ; and never can be taught.
This is Your Portion ; this Your Native Store ;
Heav'n that but once was Prodigal before,
To Shakespeare gave as much ; she cou'd not give
    him more.

Maintain Your Post : That's all the Fame You need;
For 'tis impossible you shou'd proceed.
Already I am worn with Cares and Age ;
And just abandoning th'Ungrateful Stage :
Unprofitably kept at Heav'ns expence,
I live a Rent-charge on his Providence :

But

To Mr. CONGREVE,

Till You, the best Vitruvius, come at length;
Our Beauties equal ; but excel our strength.
Firm Dorique Pillars found Your solid Base :
The Fair Corinthian Crowns the higher Space ;
Thus all below is Strength, and all above is Grace.
In easie Dialogue is Fletcher's Praise :
He mov'd the mind, but had not power to raise.
Great Johnson did by strength of Judgment please :
Yet doubling Fletcher's Force, he wants his Ease.
In differing Tallents both adorn'd their Age ;
One for the Study, t'other for the Stage.
But both to Congreve justly shall submit,
One match'd in Judgment, both o'er-match'd in Wit.
In Him all Beauties of this Age we see ;
Etherege his Courtship, Southern's Purity ;
The Satire,Wit,and Strength of Manly Witcherly.
All this in blooming Youth you have Atchiev'd ;
Now are your foil'd Contemporaries griev'd ;
So much the sweetness of your manners move,
We cannot envy you because we Love.
Fabius might joy in Scipio, when he saw
A Beardless Consul made against the Law,
And joyn his Suffrage to the Votes of Rome ;
Though He with Hannibal was overcome.
Thus old Romano bow'd to Raphel's Fame ;
And Scholar to the Youth he taught, became.

Oh that your Brows my Lawrel had sustain'd,
Well had I been Depos'd, if You had reign'd!

The

To Mr. CONGREVE, &c.

But You, whom ev'ry Muse and Grace adorn,
Whom I foresee to better Fortune born,
Be kind to my Remains ; and oh defend,
Against Your Judgment Your departed Friend !
Let not the Insulting Foe my Fame pursue ;
But shade those Lawrels which descend to You :
And take for Tribute what these Lines express :
You merit more ; nor cou'd my Love do less.

John Dryden.

Prologue

John Dryden's response to the public's criticism of Congreve's second play (from the 1694 edition of The Double Dealer). *As Dryden explained to a friend, "The women think he has exposed their Bitchery too much; and the Gentlemen, are offended with him; for the discovery of their follies; and the way of their Intrigues, under the notion of Friendship to their Ladyes Husbands."*

yond the fact that it must be within moderately easy reach of the town of St. Albans, there are no precise clues to the house's geographical location. It functions both as a perfect example of the neoclassical unity of place that Restoration comedies had consistently ignored and, at the same time, as a dramatic limbo, a dreamlike world into which the characters have been drawn and kept for the duration of the action.

Even the precision of the location in the gallery has its own function, the action unfolding in a space through which characters must pass from one unseen room to another, a space in which chance meetings are paradoxically inevitable as the characters perform their own private routines of courtship and adultery, bumping into others similarly self-obsessed. The stage is simultaneously emphatically real and intensely theatrical, a normal room and a performance space in which the action is played out.

As if to increase the audience's awe at the virtuoso skills needed to contain the action within such a small compass of space, Congreve exacerbates the difficulty by demanding a similarly restricted time. Congreve takes the neoclassical notion of the unity of time to its logical extreme, the entire action taking place between "Five a Clock to Eight in the Evening." Not only does the time of performance exactly match the time of the action but the play insistently watches the clock, reminding the audience more than a dozen times of the interconnection between the time and the action. Even more tightly than its only predecessor in Restoration comedy, Sir Samuel Tuke's *The Adventure of Five Hours* (1663), *The Double Dealer* observes the unity of time to produce a nightmarish, fantastical compression on the action, a nervous and excitable energy onstage–and in the audience–as the plots blossom and wither at breakneck speed. The rapidity of the action in the hours after dinner on the eve of the wedding of Mellefont and Cynthia is both a threat (will the marriage be prevented?) and a promise of release (if the lovers can survive this evening their future happiness will be assured).

This tension is both a fear of the detailed plotting that threatens to stop the match and an equally disturbing fear for the examples of matrimony that cluster around them. Mellefont and Cynthia are innocent, virtuous, passive, and consequentially fearful. That Mellefont is not foolish for failing to perceive the plots ranged against him is one of the claims Congreve is at pains to make in the preface: "Is every Man a Gull and a Fool that is deceiv'd? . . . If this Man be deceived by the Treachery of the other; must he of necessity commence Fool immediately, only because the other has proved a Villain?" Cynthia's wry comment in act 2 on the knowledge gained by looking around her at the other married couples was a view Congreve would later have to defend against Jeremy Collier: "I'm thinking, that tho' Marriage makes Man and Wife One Flesh, it leaves 'em still Two Fools"–hence her following question to Mellefont: "What think you of drawing Stakes, and giving over in time?"

The parallel actions of *The Double Dealer* follow three comparable triangles of adultery. The most foolish are Lord and Lady Froth with their attendant cuckolder, the fop Brisk. Mellefont sets his friend Careless to intervene in the marriage of Cynthia's parents, Sir Paul and Lady Plyant, in order to head off the threat posed by Lady Plyant's assumption that Mellefont is really in love with her, not Cynthia, her stepdaughter. Both of these are comic actions of a comfortable form; both contain moments of exuberant oddity that set them apart from their forebears. Lady Froth's endless disquisitions on her verse-epic, *The Sillibub*, or the wonderfully deflating line with which she punctures the hysteria and tension of the end of the play, "You know I told you *Saturn* look'd a little more angry than usual," provide an untroubling comic underpinning of the rest of the play. The Plyants' bizarre bedtime habits are offset by the touching simplicity of Sir Paul's yearning for a son, a son he is unlikely to have when his wife will allow sex only once a year: "But if I had a Son, ah, that's my affliction, and my only affliction; indeed I cannot refrain Tears when it comes in my mind."

The crisscrossing of these plots is contrasted in the play by the rigid separation of the other triangle from the rest of the action. Lord Touchwood may begin as foolish cuckold but the intensity of the action that surrounds him leads him to acquire a remarkable and distinctly uncomic dignity. His wife, Lady Touchwood, has a power that in its passionate extremes has much more to do with the angry women of Restoration tragedy. Her outbursts to her lover, Maskwell, her desperation at Mellefont's lack of interest in her, and her fury when her plots are themselves thwarted create a scale of emotion far beyond the compass of the comic world. Where the anger of, for example, Mrs. Loveit in George Etherege's *The Man of Mode* (1676) produces only mockery in response from other characters and audience alike, Lady

Thomas Doggett, the comedian for whom Congreve wrote the parts of Fondlewife in The Old Bachelor,
Sir Paul Plyant in The Double Dealer, *Ben in* Love for Love, *and the title role in* Squire Trelooby

Touchwood's language has a frightening energy which takes it well beyond ridicule: "Death, do you dally with my Passion? Insolent Devil! But have a care,–provoke me not." Indeed the plotting against Mellefont and Cynthia is finally overcome only because Lady Touchwood *has* been provoked beyond endurance by the discovery of the ramifications of Maskwell's plotting and because her offstage screaming at him is overheard by Cynthia and Lord Touchwood, who happen to be passing through the gallery at the critically right moment. Most critical attention has been focused on the strange mixture of styles that Congreve has chosen to bring together in the play. The alienness of Lady Touchwood–it is impossible to imagine her as a character in *The Old Bachelor*–seems to upset critics as readers in a way that it never does theater audiences. On stage the grand scope of the play is entirely coherent, and the intrigues that emanate from Maskwell–frequently expounded in soliloquies that in their directness of address to the audience recall Shakespeare's Iago–generate a fascinated and troubled attentiveness.

For there is no doubt that Maskwell is troubling. His status in the Touchwood household, somewhere between servant and friend, fuels his ambitions. If the three triangles of characters is a pattern that seems to isolate the duo of Mellefont and Cynthia, that is only because as the play develops it becomes clear that Maskwell plans to create a different sort of triangle for them, aiming to marry Cynthia himself, with the help of a tame chaplain, a disguise with the armholes stitched up, and a coach to take him and Cynthia to St. Albans. There is a hideous fascination in Maskwell's brilliant machinations that lures the audience toward a sympathy with the energies and attractiveness of villainous evil. *The Double Dealer* goes far beyond comedy's normal concerns with folly and instead, in Maskwell, presents viciousness and malevolence in its most tempting form. It also makes clear that such evil cannot be controlled by the actions of the good characters. In the end the play relies on Cynthia's agreement in act 4 to an escape clause if Mellefont should fail to defeat his aunt and her accomplices:

> CYNTHIA. Well, if the Devil should assist her, and your Plot miscarry—
> MELLEFONT. Ay, what am I to trust to then?
> CYNTHIA. Why if you give me very clear demonstration that it was the Devil, I'll allow for irresistable odds.

Maskwell's diabolic cunning excuses Mellefont. It is plainly inadequate to argue, as Aubrey Williams has, that the play is an orthodox demonstration of the workings of providence. Rather it shows how the power of evil is self-defeating in the intensely theatrical world Congreve has created in which to demonstrate the extent of its threatening power. On a comic stage with its hidings, overhearings, and disguisings, even the devilish ingenuity of a Maskwell is bound to fail.

Love for Love, Congreve's next comedy, was written in 1694 and scheduled for production by the United Company. When the senior actors of the company, led by Thomas Betterton and Mrs. Elizabeth Barry, decided they could no longer put up with the dictatorial mismanagement of the theater by Christopher Rich and petitioned for the right to establish a new company, Congreve had no hesitation in allowing them to take with them his new comedy. *Love for Love* was the opening production for the secessionists in their hastily refurbished theater in Lincoln's Inn Fields, with Congreve supplying a prologue specially written for "the opening of the New House" on 30 April 1695.

After the deliberate experimentation of *The Double Dealer*, *Love for Love* marks a conscious decision to return to the more conventional concerns of Restoration comedy, avoiding the problem of outright evil in favor of a new investigation of generous love. Its title reformulates the concerns of so much of the comedy of the 1690s, epitomized in Thomas Durfey's play *Love for Money*, which premiered in 1691. Durfey's title–and the action of his play–suggests an undeviatingly satiric view of the place of love in contemporary society: love, as sexual desire or as marriage, is bought and sold, exchanged for money. In Congreve's comedy the buying and selling of love is a tenet which the central character, Valentine, must learn to revalue, coming in the course of the play to understand that the only commodity for which love can be exchanged is love.

The action opens in a conventional situation, the rake penned up in his room to avoid the demands of his creditors. From Dryden's *The Wild Gallant* (1663) onward, the position of the penniless young man who has run through his inheritance and now finds himself unable to approach the woman he loves was a familiar starting point for comedy. Valentine's attempts to evade his creditors and to shed his responsibilities, to escape the consequences of his actions, veer between a comic sequence of ploys and a more brutal, more desperate note. At its most vicious, Valentine's attempt to avoid the legacy of his past behavior is seen in his apparently lighthearted exasperation that the wet nurse who appears at the door seeking money for the upkeep of one of his bastards "knows my Condition well enough, and might have overlaid the Child a Fortnight ago, if she had any forecast in her." It is entirely characteristic of the play's continual redefinition of expected reactions that such a suggestion should be stoutly resisted by Valentine's cynical friend Scandal, who sends money to "Bouncing *Margery*, and my Godson."

Margery's lack of "forecast" anticipates the play's multiple consideration of foresight. At its most comic, there is Foresight himself, uncle to Valentine's beloved Angelica, superstitiously unable to act without checking on the omens and prophecies of late-seventeenth-century astrology. Foresight's obsessions with pseudo-scholarship, a sure subject for satire, are contrasted at the opposite end of the scale by the naiveté of Valentine's younger brother Ben, a sailor unable to find his land legs in the play's society, where his forthright honesty is mystified by the indirectness and

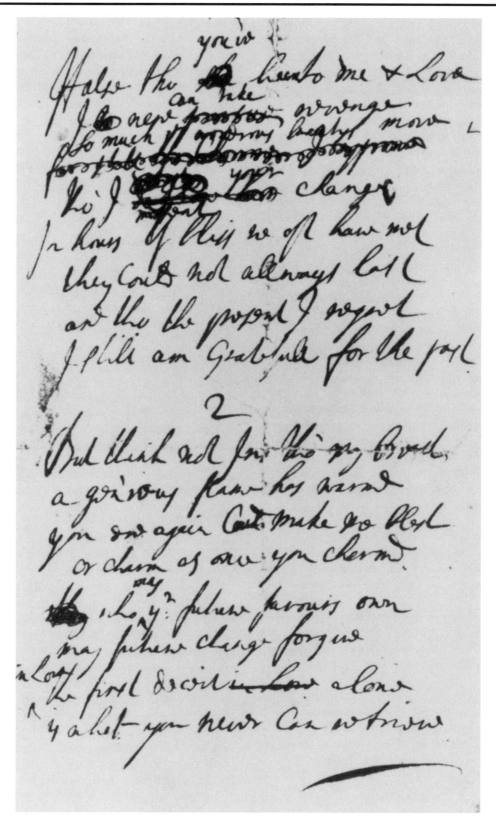

Draft for a poem that Congreve is believed to have addressed to Anne Bracegirdle. A somewhat different version of the first eight lines was published as "A Complaint to Pious Selinda" in 1710 (John C. Hodges, William Congreve The Man, 1941).

deviousness of social behavior. Ben and Miss Prue, Foresight's daughter, are the ideal social prey for Mrs. Frail and Tattle, adept in the way of this comic world and pragmatic enough to seize the opportunities for wealthy marriage offered by the two innocents. But their foresight is insufficient and a series of disguisings and maskings result in Tattle and Mrs. Frail marrying each other, with mockery rather than social success the consequence of their plans.

The play's central concern, however, is with the escape route from financial ruin that is dangled temptingly in front of Valentine, a substantial sum from his father, Sir Sampson Legend, to clear his debts in return for his signature to a deed of disinheritance. The action provides an immediate solution but poses a problem of foresight for him, not only in terms of his future financial prospects but also in terms of his future prospects with Angelica. Much of the action of the play is taken up with Valentine's attempts to avoid the final decision. Having signed a note of intent and received his cash advance, Valentine feigns madness, since insanity will prevent his executing a binding contract. But Valentine's machinations cannot begin to constitute an adequate response to Angelica. Her response to his feigned madness is to play along with it, to treat his protestations of love as yet more ravings, and to propose, in apparent seriousness, to marry the outrageous and unfatherly Sir Sampson. The play awaits the moment at which Valentine, finally trapped, is forced to act with honesty but also through love. Angelica's forthright statement of her demand for control over her destiny is the final indication of Valentine's need to accept responsibility for his actions; as she sums it up, "you must pardon me, if I think my own Inclinations have a better Right to dispose of my Person, than yours." Valentine's speech of understanding is unlike anything Congreve had written before:

> I have been disappointed of my only Hope; and he that loses hope may part with any thing. I never valu'd Fortune, but as it was subservient to my Pleasure; and my only Pleasure was to please this Lady: I have made many vain Attempts, and find at last, that nothing but my Ruine can effect it: Which, for that Reason, I will sign to—Give me the Paper.

Angelica's response, "Generous *Valentine!*" and her immediate agreement to marry him defines the nature of the love test through which she has put him. Her refusal to be passive in the world, waiting on male decisions about love and marriage, is both a remarkable reformulation of the place of the virtuous woman in Restoration drama and a perceptive recognition on Congreve's part of the extent of male construction of the female. As Angelica says in the last speech of the play,

> You tax us with Injustice, only to cover your own want of Merit. You would have all the Reward of Love; but few have the Constancy to stay till it becomes your due.

Yet Angelica's attempt to act with proper foresight and self-determination, her refusal to be as simply angelic as her name suggests, has puzzled critics. An exchange on the play between Mrs. Mirvan and Lord Orville in Fanny Burney's novel *Evelina* (1778; volume 1, letter 20), typifies later responses:

> "Yet, in a trial so long, . . . there seems rather too much consciousness of her power."
> ". . . I will venture to say, that Angelica bestows her hand rather with the air of a benefactress, than with the tenderness of a mistress. Generosity without delicacy, like wit without judgment, generally gives as much pain as pleasure."

The audiences' and critics' natural sympathies with the comic energies of Valentine are inevitably confused by Angelica's far more subtle perception of the inadequacies of his love. Intelligently, though without recourse to the conventional wit of Restoration heroines, Angelica presents the need for a transparent honesty. When Valentine announces in act 3 that he knows "no effectual Difference between continued Affectation and Reality," he is accurate about everyone else's behavior but wrong in assuming that this is a necessary state of social existence. The flatness of his eventual speech of acceptance is an eschewal of the theatricality that had been the key characteristic of his own and others' language in the play. When he realizes he can choose, he does so without the extravagant heroics or linguistic affectation that such moments had usually summoned forth in earlier plays. A simplicity and purity of language seems in itself almost enough to convince Angelica that he has come to differentiate between affectation and reality.

In February 1696, Trinity College, Dublin, awarded Congreve and his fellow dramatist, Thomas Southerne, honorary M.A.'s. In the summer after the success of *Love for Love* Congreve received his first government office, being appointed one of the five commissioners for licensing hackney coaches at a salary, recently halved, of one hundred pounds a year. In 1697 he became one of the managers of the Malt Lottery and from 1700 to 1703 the Customer at Poole, sharing the fees with the deputy who did the work. In 1705 he became a commissioner for wines. But none of these offices provided him with anything like the income of a gentleman, and, while their insignificance meant they survived the changes of party in government, Congreve's search for a lucrative post, sufficient to live on in comfort, was a constant source of anxiety in these years. His friends frequently commented on his poverty.

Encouraged by John Dennis, Congreve took the opportunity in July 1695 of setting down some thoughts on humor in comedy in the form of a letter, "An Essay concerning Humour in Comedy." This, Congreve's only attempt outside his prefaces and the Collier controversy to outline any theory of comedy, is a remarkably careful and benign attempt to distinguish the types of dramatic character, discriminating between humor, habit, and affectation:

> *Humour* is from Nature, *Habit* from Custom; and *Affectation* from Industry.
> *Humour*, shews us as we *are*.
> *Habit*, shews us, as we appear, under a forcible Impression.
> *Affectation*, shews us what we would be, under a Voluntary Disguise.

For Congreve the comedy in a character is not a product of natural deformity but instead of an untroubling individuality, something "peculiar and Natural to one Man only." While he recognizes that habit and affectation are appropriate forms of characterization for comedy, they are qualitatively less worthwhile than humor, which is prized for its consonance with nature. Like Dryden in *An Essay of Dramatic Poesy*, Congreve singles out for praise Morose in Jonson's *Epicoene* (1609), recognizing how Morose's intolerance for noise is only an exacerbated form of most people's dislike of knives scratched on plates or the sound of a cork being cut. There is, throughout his analysis, a geniality and a genuine fascination with the variety of real people, the only proper study for a writer of comedies.

Congreve was now beginning to be sought by new writers as a patron, critic, and advisor. New plays were regularly submitted to him for ap-

proval by writers such as Catharine Trotter and Charles Hopkins. When, in 1697, Mary Pix found the plot of her new play had been stolen by George Powell for his *The Imposture Defeated*, Congreve accompanied his protégé to the premiere to hiss the thief.

Catharine Trotter introduced herself to Congreve by writing a poem to him that she hoped he would publish with the text of *The Mourning Bride* (1697). If the twentieth-century history of Congreve's critical and theatrical fortunes has been a steadily increasing valuation of the comedies, little has been found to say in favor of this play, Congreve's only tragedy. The play's initial success and its continued popularity throughout the eighteenth century–it was by far the most often performed of his plays–has seemed to be nothing more than an aberration of previous audiences' taste. Dr. Johnson announced authoritatively "if I were required to select from the whole mass of English poetry the most poetical paragraph, I know not what I could prefer to an exclamation in *The Mourning Bride*," quoting Almeria's description of a temple in act 2:

> No, all is hush'd, and still as Death–'Tis dreadful!
> How rev'rend is the Face of this tall Pile,
> Whose antient Pillars rear their Marble Heads,
> To bear aloft its arch'd and pond'rous Roof,
> By its own Weight, made stedfast, and immoveable,
> Looking Tranquility.

But Johnson's praise has puzzled Johnson's critics and seems embarrassing hyperbole to anyone who has read *The Mourning Bride* through. Even the rapidly growing recent understanding of the considerable merits of other Restoration tragedies, such as Dryden's late plays, has not significantly affected opinions of Congreve's. Recognition that a speech such as the following by Zara in act 2 is deeply affected or infected by Congreve's reading of Shakespeare cannot persuade readers that the language does not collapse into bathetic excess as it strives for effect:

> who knows
> What racking Cares disease a Monarch's Bed?
> Or Love, that late at Night still lights his Camp,
> And strikes his Rays thro' dusk, and folded Lids,
> Forbidding rest; may stretch his Eyes awake
> And force their Balls abroad, at this dead Hour.

Tracing the lineage and descendants of Zara's passion and anger in the rest of Congreve's work back to Lady Touchwood and forward to Mrs.

Elizabeth Barry as Zara in the first production of The Mourning Bride

Marwood in *The Way of the World*, both also played by Elizabeth Barry, only reveals the comparative poverty of intelligent characterization here, in the same way that the passivity of the virtuous heroine Almeria is infuriating when located between Anne Bracegirdle's other roles as Angelica in *Love for Love* and Millamant in *The Way of the World*. It is as if the subtlety of Congreve's perception of the social position of women in comic society deserts him under the dead weight of heavy grandeur appropriate to heroic tragedy.

Equally well, the complexity of plotting, which in the comedies is part both of the indecipherability of social activity and a major part of the moral argument the plays are designed to investigate, here becomes sensationalistic, a pretext for moments of high emotion. Congreve, in a letter in 1703, advised Catharine Trotter that in her new play *The Revolution in Sweden* (1706),

> One thing would have a very beautiful effect in the catastrophe, if it were possible to manage it

> thro' the play; and that is to have the audience kept in ignorance, as long as the husband ... who *Fredage* really is, till her death.

The action of *The Mourning Bride* depends on who knows that Osmyn, captured by Manuel, is really Alphonso, son of Manuel's enemy and husband of his daughter Almeria. Yet the audience is in the know from act 2 onward, and the only moment at which the information is handled with subtlety is when, at the end of act 4, Almeria half reveals Osmyn's identity to her father and his counsellor Gonsalez under the misapprehension that they know already. As Gonsalez comments in soliloquy after her exit, "Osmyn Alphonso! no; she over-rates/My Policy, I ne'er suspected it." Not the least of the problems Congreve's plot poses is the essential passivity of both Almeria and Osmyn. Osmyn moves from captivity to freedom and back to captivity, from safety to danger to eventual safety, purely as a result of the everchanging moods and passions of Zara, who

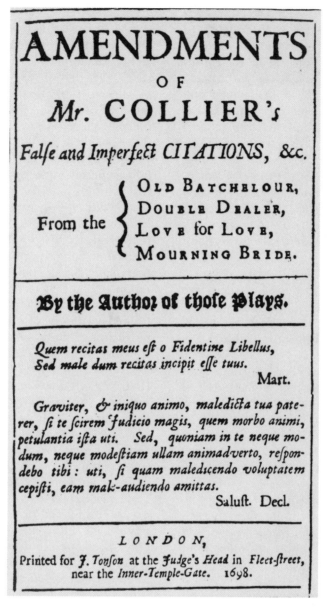

AMENDMENTS

OF

Mr. COLLIER's

False and Imperfect CITATIONS, &c.

From the { OLD BATCHELOUR,
DOUBLE DEALER,
LOVE for LOVE,
MOURNING BRIDE.

By the Author of those Plays.

Quem recitas meus est o Fidentine Libellus,
Sed male dum recitas incipit esse tuus.

Mart.

Graviter, & iniquo animo, maledicta tua pate-
rer, si te scirem judicio magis, quem morbo animi,
petulantia ista uti. Sed, quoniam in te neque mo-
dum, neque modestiam ullam animadverto, respon-
debo tibi: uti, si quam maledicendo voluptatem
cepisti, eam male-audiendo amittas.

Salust. Decl.

LONDON,

Printed for *J. Tonson* at the *Judge's Head* in *Fleet-street,*
near the *Inner-Temple-Gate.* 1698.

Title page for Congreve's response to Jeremy Collier's A Short View of the Immorality and Profaneness of the English Stage. *Congreve argues in part that, by taking lines out of context, Collier "first commits a Rape upon my Words, and then arraigns 'em of Immodesty; he has Barbarity enough to accuse the very Virgins that he has deflowr'd. . . ."*

loves him and is loved by Manuel. There seems to be virtually nothing an honorable man such as Osmyn can do to affect his own or others' fate. Energy and the handling of the action is at the mercy of those who are passionate without a concomitant virtue. While that has often been problematic for writers of tragedy, in *The Mourning Bride* it becomes a serious hampering of the balance between the good, who, as Oscar Wilde's Miss Prism recommends, "end happily" and the bad, who end "unhappily."

For all its obvious shortcomings the play has a series of moments of fully achieved and highly

successful theatricality where Congreve's inability to find an adequate tragic language is offset by the assuredness with which the stage image is created. Almeria first meets Osmyn, for instance, when she enters the vault to grieve at the grave of Anselmo, Osmyn-Alphonso's father. Kneeling, she calls on her husband, whom she assumes to have drowned in a shipwreck which Congreve seems to have borrowed from *Twelfth Night* (circa 1601): "To thee, to thee I call, to thee *Alphonso.* /O *Alphonso.*" Her cry is answered by Osmyn, "ascending from the Tomb": "Who calls that wretched thing, that was *Alphonso*?" The use of "was" is mannered and overweighted, but the effect of Osmyn's calling as he ascends the steps from his father's tomb is self-evidently powerful and effectively dramatic. The echo of *Hamlet* (circa 1600-1601) in Almeria's reply ("Angels, and all the Host of heaven support me!") and the succeeding action, in which each thinks the other is an apparition, with Almeria fainting, inevitably demeans the effect. Zara's death scene, accompanied by her servant Selim and two mutes bearing bowls of poison, has a ritualized solemnity, particularly as the "mutes kneel and mourn over her"; here silence is a valid antidote to the outpouring of poor verse that Congreve feels obliged to give Zara as she dies. Given the number of better Restoration tragedies unrevived, it will be a long time until *The Mourning Bride* receives a professional production, but there are enough signs in the play to suggest that its revival might be more than an act of piety and reveal a work as dramatically and melodramatically successful as Congreve's comedies.

In April 1698 Jeremy Collier launched his attack on contemporary drama in *A Short View of the Immorality and Profaneness of the English Stage*, and it was inevitable that Congreve should be one of his prime targets, his plays picked apart for details to substantiate Collier's charges. Congreve delayed replying but realized that his work had to be defended. His *Amendments of Mr. Collier's False and Imperfect Citations* was published in July. Congreve's defense was, in its turn, attacked both by Collier himself in the *Defence of the Short View* (published late in 1698) and by anonymous supporters of Collier's campaign in *A Letter to Mr Congreve on his Pretended Amendments, etc of Mr Collier's Short View* and *Animadversions on Mr Congreve's Late Answer to Mr Collier*, both published in the autumn of 1698. The later pamphlets added little to the main charges while finding Congreve's defense, particularly the few places where he was prepared to give ground and admit the justice of Collier's attack on particular words and phrases, vulnerable for its inconsistencies and special pleadings. Congreve outlines four crucial grounds for his defense: that comedy has a moral purpose in laughing the audience out of vice by delighting as well as instructing; that comedies must contain vicious and foolish characters if they are to achieve this moral aim; that passages must be considered in the scene in which they appear, not wrenched out of context as Collier consistently does; and that words have a "diversity of subject" which

gives a "diversity of signification" and, hence, that a word used in one sense in a sacred context need not carry that religious meaning over when "otherwise apply'd." The criteria, except for the last, which deliberately underplays the resonance of biblical usage that Congreve frequently plays on, are, of course, entirely reasonable, however unlikely they were to satisfy Collier. In carrying them over into the detailed defense of speeches, Congreve concentrates on the third, emphasizing how a speech is placed in a scene, fixed and constricted in its meaning by its surroundings.

While the genuine threat of prosecution and the change in the temper of the times had their local effects in the detailed changes to the dialogue that Congreve introduced in the second edition of *The Double Dealer* in 1706 and in his preparation of the text of all his plays for the edition of his works in 1710, the major response to Collierism that he offered is in the form and matter of the only comedy he wrote after the Collier controversy began, *The Way of the World*.

On 12 March 1700 Lady Marow wrote to a friend, "Congreve's new play, doth not answer expectation, there being no plot in it but many witty things." Lady Marow was the first reviewer of *The Way of the World;* she is also the last one to complain that the play lacked plot. Congreve's statement in the dedication to the published text, "That it succeeded on the Stage, was almost beyond my Expectation," is not simply an author's excuse for a failed play: *The Way of the World* deliberately sets out to make life difficult for the audience. Even the family relationships that bind the characters together are both complex and presented in ways that make it virtually impossible for an audience to follow, even a Restoration audience highly attuned to family trees. When Fainall describes Sir Wilfull Witwoud to Mirabell in act 1, he identifies him as "half Brother to this *Witwoud* by a former Wife, who was Sister to my Lady *Wishfort*, my Wife's Mother. If you marry *Millamant* you must call Cousins too." Like Shakespeare's history plays, *The Way of the World* seems to need genealogical tables in the program.

The whole action of the play, its series of plots and counterplots in the quest for control of Lady Wishfort's fortune and her control over that of her niece Millamant, moves forward by hint and innuendo. Only at the end of the play, for instance, does the audience discover what on earth Mirabell meant in act 2 when he said to the unhappy Mrs. Fainall about her husband, "When

THE

Way of the World,

A

COMEDY.

As it is ACTED

AT THE

Theatre in *Lincoln's-Inn-Fields*,

BY

His Majesty's Servants.

Written by Mr. *CONGREVE.*

Audire est Operæ pretium, procedere recte
Qui machis non vultis——   Hor. Sat. 2. l. 1.
——Metuat doti deprensa.——   Ibid.

LONDON:

Printed for *Jacob Tonson,* within *Gray's-Inn-Gate* next
Gray's-Inn-Lane. 1700.

Title page for the first edition of Congreve's most complex comedy. After the mediocre reception accorded its first production, Congreve wrote, "That it succeeded on the stage, was almost beyond my Expectation; for but little of it was prepared for that general Taste which seems now to be predominant in the Palates of our Audience."

you are weary of him, you know your Remedy." Only then do we learn that Fainall's plots, increasingly violent and vicious as the play proceeds, have been entirely pointless since, as he reads on a piece of legal parchment handed to him by Mirabell, there is "*A deed of Conveyance of the whole Estate real of* Arabella Languish *Widdow in trust to* Edward Mirabell." If Mirabell controls Mrs. Fainall's estate, Fainall's activities are foredoomed, though it takes the whole play for this crucial piece of evidence to be revealed.

Congreve, having digested so brilliantly the tenets of neoclassical theory, seems to have decided to ignore its instructions and to create a drama whose plot is mystifyingly opaque. The deed of trust is, as Mirabell tells Fainall, "*the way of the World,* Sir: of the Widdows of the World." It constitutes a solution in itself, by virtue of its immutability and its legality. Such documents, summoned up in *Love for Love* only to be rejected, are necessary in a society deeply affected by the

malevolence of Fainall and his mistress, Mrs. Marwood. The deed is an example of Mirabell's prescience, of his combination of virtue, at least in the play's terms, and social cunning. He is, as Mrs. Fainall says in her last words in the play, "a Cautious Friend, to whose advice all is owing."

Yet Mirabell's actions have increasingly troubled the play's critics. Within the time span of the play there is perhaps little to worry us, but the play is uneasy about a crucial piece of its past. Mirabell and Mrs. Fainall (then Arabella Languish) ended their affair when she thought she was pregnant, and Mirabell was instrumental in her marrying Fainall. There is something too coldly rational in Mirabell's answer to her question in act 2: "Why did you make me marry this Man?" As Ian Donaldson has emphasized, the answer is unpalatably evasive for the most part: "A better Man ought not to have been sacrific'd to the Occasion; a worse had not answer'd to the Purpose." The play never contemplates why Mirabell

William Congreve, 1709 (portrait by Sir Godfrey Kneller; by permission of the National Portrait Gallery, London)

and Mrs. Fainall did not marry. Instead Mrs. Fainall's extraordinary generosity toward Mirabell, apart from this one moment of complaint, leads her to aid his plans to win Millamant. It is significant and moving that, at the end of the proviso scene, in which Millamant and Mirabell set out the conditions under which they are prepared to marry, Millamant's agreement is only secured when Mrs. Fainall enters and gives her opinion:

> MILLAMANT. *Fainall*, what shall I do? shall I have him? I think I must have him.
> MRS. FAINALL. Ay, ay, take him, take him, what shou'd you do?

While it is never quite clear whether Millamant knows of Mirabell's affair with Mrs. Fainall, there is no comparable example in Restoration comedy of a cast mistress so generously assenting to her former lover's marriage.

The Way of the World is full of such revaluations of apparently stereotypical characters. Indeed the opening section of the play, a long dialogue between Mirabell and Fainall, establishes a tone in which the two rakes, cautiously and delicately probing each other's motives, are indistinguishable. That the play will go on to show Mirabell's generosity and thoughtfulness and Fainall's passionate viciousness is impossible to predict from their fencing exchanges at the start. Typically, though, where plays such as *The Old Bachelor* open with conversation between two friends, addressing each other as Ned and Frank, *The Way of the World* opens with Mirabell calling the other "Mr. *Fainall*"; the formality of address is disconcerting. No wonder that the "hasty Judges," of whom Congreve complains in the dedication, did not "distinguish betwixt the Character of a *Witwoud* and *Truewit*," since it is no longer simply a matter of identifying the fools in the play but of discriminating between those who are apparently wits.

Even the glib labeling of certain characters as fools proves increasingly inadequate. Sir Wilfull Witwoud, the country cousin arriving in town with mud on his boots and a rustic incomprehension of town manners, comes at the end of the play to be valued for his generosity and his humane compassion, so that Mirabell can say of him without the slightest trace of irony "Sir *Wilfull* is my Friend." Nothing will make Sir Wilfull more intelligent, but his good nature matters far more. No wit has ever been prepared to consider a man like Sir Wilfull as his friend before. The moment is the culmination of the play's intense examination of the word "friend," from Mirabell's early description of Mrs. Marwood to Fainall as "your Friend, or your Wife's Friend" (that is, mistress or friend) onward. Friendship, in the ways of this world, is a valuable but also a dangerous commodity, an identification of an individual's perception of value.

In response to a society of such complexity, characters such as Fainall or Mirabell can choose to control it or, at least, to attempt to control it. But for many the only course is to blunder through it with an undeviating belief in themselves. For Lady Wishfort, whose folly in believing herself younger and more attractive than she is leads her to come close to marrying Mirabell's servant Waitwell, disguised as his nonexistent uncle Sir Rowland, the recognition of her own foolishness can lead to its own form of generosity in giving Millamant to Mirabell: "Well Sir, take her, and with her all the Joy I can give you." It is characteristic of the care of Mirabell's plotting, however, that he ensures that Waitwell marries Lady Wishfort's maid Foible before he will allow the plot to go forward.

For Millamant the acuity of perception of the nature of her society leads her to need a defense. Her language, mesmerizing in its profusion and the sheer inventiveness of its wit, is a self-protective device to bemuse others with her surface and keep her inner self hidden. The performance is done with such skill that, as Mirabell says after their first encounter in the play, "To think of a Whirlwind, tho' 'twere in a Whirlwind, were a Case of more steady Contemplation." Her avowal of love to Mirabell at the end of the proviso scene–"Well, you ridiculous thing you, I'll have you"–is as close as she dare come to a direct statement of love to him. Millamant's hesitancy at this point comes about not least because the play

is nowhere near its resolution. Where earlier proviso scenes in Restoration comedy had been placed in act 5, Congreve puts his in act 4. Not until the threat by Fainall has been fully revealed and overcome can the lovers actually commit themselves in an exchange that contrasts the fixity of their earlier legalisms with the fluidity that is the hallmark of Millamant:

> MILLAMANT. . . . wou'd you have me give my self to you over again?
> MIRABELL. Ay, and over and over again; for I wou'd have you as often as possibly I can.

If Mirabell is "sententious," as Millamant calls him, and cautiously analytic, he is still able to find the imaginative and emotional response Millamant needs, a firm recognition of the vulnerability she understands only too well: "Well, heav'n grant I love you not too well, that's all my fear," as he says, adopting her language style for the only time in the play. Millamant is never able to say to Mirabell, only to Mrs. Fainall, that "I find I love him violently."

The Way of the World is not a comforting play. Its society is terrifying in its secrecy and only marginally less threatening when Fainall finally resorts to drawing his sword and tries to run his wife through. Audiences who indulgently enjoy the sophistication of the witty dialogue of Millamant and Mirabell miss the equivalent sophistication in the play's view of a society barely able to contain Fainall's aggression and heavily reliant on trusting Mirabell. Trust, even more than love, comes in the play to be a value society has to have, provided it knows where to place it. Arabella Languish's deed of trust is the play's final symbol of the rules by which society can be effectively and fairly run. *The Way of the World* is a serious and intensely moral comedy, the culmination of Congreve's recurrent fascination with the moral comedy of Terence and, as Congreve knew, like Terence's plays, his masterpiece was hardly likely to please most of the audience.

If *The Way of the World* was by no means the failure that tradition would have us believe, it was by no means the success that it deserved. In the following few years Congreve wrote three more pieces for the stage but no more full-length plays. His libretto on the subject of the judgment of Paris was written as the text for a music competition. The masque was set by four different composers, John Eccles, John Weldon, Godfrey Finger, and Daniel Purcell, and the four versions were performed successively in the spring of

Henrietta, duchess of Marlborough, the mother of Congreve's daughter, Mary (engraving by F. Kyte, based on a portrait by Sir Godfrey Kneller; courtesy of the National Portrait Gallery, London)

1701 at Dorset Garden Theatre with eighty-five performers and a specially constructed stage. Finally all four were given on the same night and the prize money of two hundred pounds distributed, with Weldon unexpectedly the winner. The text is adequate but unremarkable. Far more substantial is Congreve's opera libretto *Semele*, set by John Eccles but probably not performed and later set again brilliantly by Handel. Congreve's exploration of Juno's revenge on the ambitions of Semele for immortality, a present she seeks from Jupiter, who has set her up in her own palace, veers with great confidence from high heroic seriousness to teasing comedy. Juno's aria of triumph, for instance, sung as she ascends to heaven in a chariot, contrasts the evanescent joys of love with the enduring pleasures of revenge:

With what Joy shall I mount to my Heav'n again,
    At once from my Rival and Jealousie freed!

The Sweets of Revenge make it worth while to
    reign,
    And Heav'n will hereafter be Heav'n indeed.

Even Semele, first seen as a virtuous lover of the ruler of heaven, finds when set up as a mistress that love soon palls:

I love and am lov'd, yet more I desire;
Ah, how foolish a Thing is Fruition!
As one Passion cools, some other takes Fire,
And I'm still in a longing Condition.
    Whate'er I possess
    Soon seems an Excess,
For something untry'd I petition;
    Tho' daily I prove
    The Pleasures of Love,
I die for the Joys of Ambition.

At such moments Congreve demonstrates the consequences of applying the virtuosic skills of the songs in his comedies to a subject apparently less amenable to such ironic treatment. *Semele* is the outcome of the embedding of songs into plays in, for example, Sylvia's song to Heartwell in act 3 of *The Old Bachelor* or Millamant's use of a song, "Love's but the frailty of the Mind," to seal her triumph over Mrs. Marwood for Mirabell's love in act 3 of *The Way of the World*.

In 1704 Congreve contributed one act to a version of Molière's *Monsieur de Pourceaugnac* (1669), with one act each from Vanbrugh and Walsh. The completed play, called *Squire Trelooby*, was performed a few times, beginning on 30 March 1704, but never published. The play was a prelude to the much more substantial collaboration between Congreve and Vanbrugh in the establishment of a new theater in the Haymarket. The company was licensed in December 1704 with the money for the building of the Queen's Theatre coming primarily from a subscription from members of the Kit-Cat Club of 100 guineas each. The theater opened with Italian opera in April 1705 but, in spite of Congreve's energetic work, little could compensate for the deficiencies of the theater's design, and by the end of the year Congreve bought his way out of the partnership.

For the rest of his life Congreve lived in comparative retirement, remaining a member of the Kit-Cat Club, writing occasional poems and translations, and seeking cures for the cataracts in his eyes and the gout he suffered because of his taste for good wine. Voltaire, visiting Congreve in 1726, reported angrily (in his *Letters Concerning the English Nation* [1733]) that Congreve spoke disparagingly of his plays as trifles and asked that Voltaire "should visit him upon no other Foot than that of a Gentleman, who led a Life of Plainness and Simplicity." Voltaire found such a notion proof of exceptional vanity, but for Congreve it was the logical outcome of his family and his current status.

It was in the context of gentlemanly retirement that Congreve prepared his works for publication in three octavo volumes in 1710. *The Works* was the greatest product of his long friendship with Jacob Tonson, the finest Restoration publisher and founder of the Kit-Cat Club. Tonson and Congreve had become acquainted soon after Congreve's arrival in London. By 1695 Congreve had lodgings in Tonson's house in Fleet Street, above the publisher's shop, and may have begun living in the Tonson household from as early as 1693. From the publication of *The Double Dealer* onward all Congreve's works were published by Tonson.

The collected edition was one of a series of Restoration writers that Tonson published in the first years of the eighteenth century, uniform with Nicholas Rowe's octavo edition of Shakespeare (1709). Without the portentousness and size of the great folio editions of Renaissance dramatists such as Jonson (1616), Shakespeare (1623), or Beaumont and Fletcher (1647), Tonson's editions were designed to be read by gentlemen, and Congreve responded to the challenge of preparing reading editions. Apart from revising the texts of the plays, Congreve took the chance of presenting the plays with acts and scenes divided in the neoclassical manner, a new scene being marked with a type ornament and a list of characters onstage at each entrance or exit. With great sensitivity Congreve and Tonson devised a typographic format that would reflect the plays' structures and Congreve's achievement. As Don McKenzie has argued in a preparatory study for his own edition of Congreve, the central volume of *The Works* was designed to state emblematically on its title page the comprehensive nature of Congreve's oeuvre, incorporating one example each of tragedy, comedy, masque, and opera: *The Mourning Bride, The Way of the World, The Judgment of Paris*, and *Semele*. Throughout his work Congreve thought of a scene as a unit of dialogue altered by the arrival or departure of a character. Only in *The Works* was he able to demonstrate that definition in print, allowing the careful specification of *liaison de scènes*, the linking between characters' movements that he had learned from his reading of Hédelin, to have its full effect. At moments such as Mirabell's soliloquy in act 2 of *The Way of the World*, when Millamant sweeps out while he has "something more" to say, *The Works* creates a combination of dramatic form and typographical layout that is as beautiful as it is effective. The transition of the plays from the theater to the new form of "polite literature" is brilliantly accomplished.

In 1714 Congreve finally secured the government office he needed to give him financial security. Appointed secretary to the Island of Jamaica, he drew a salary of more than seven hundred pounds a year and could begin saving and investing. In 1719 he was at last able to repay Southerne's help with *The Old Bachelor* when he was able to secure production of *The Spartan Dame*, a long-banned tragedy. His friendship with Alexander Pope, mirroring his own friendship with Dryden, resulted in his being the

Monument to Congreve in Westminster Abbey

dedicatee of Pope's translation of *The Illiad* in 1715.

Congreve's close friendship with the actress Anne Bracegirdle had begun to dwindle by 1710. If they were lovers, Congreve gave way before the money and power of the earl of Scarsdale, who wooed her for years. His friendship with the Godolphin family, however, resulted in his only true love affair, with Godolphin's wife, Henrietta, duchess of Marlborough. When she gave birth to a daughter, Mary, in 1723, nearly twenty years after the birth of her last child, Congreve and Henrietta deflected the town's suspicions. In his

will Congreve left her his fortune, now amounting to more than ten thousand pounds, with her husband appointed executor. Henrietta spent more than seven thousand pounds of the money on a diamond necklace and earrings, bequeathing them in turn to their daughter.

Severely ill after an accident in a carriage in Bath, Congreve died in London and was buried in Westminster Abbey. Nearby Henrietta erected a monument to "so worthy and Honest a Man, Whose virtue Candour and Witt gained him the love and Esteem of the present Age and whose writings will be the Admiration of the Future."

Letters:

William Congreve: Letters and Documents, edited by John C. Hodges (London: Macmillan, 1964).

Bibliograhies:

Albert M. Lyles and John Dobson, *The John C. Hodges Collection of William Congreve in the University of Tennessee Library: A Bibliographical Catalog* (Knoxville: University of Tennessee Libraries, 1970);

Laurence Bartlett, *William Congreve: A Reference Guide* (Boston: G. K. Hall, 1979).

Biographies:

Charles Wilson, *Memoirs of the Life, Writings, and Amours of William Congreve* (London, 1730);

Samuel Johnson, "Congreve," in his *Prefaces, Biographical and Critical, to the Works of the English Poets*, 10 volumes (London: Printed by J. Nichols, for C. Bathurst, etc., 1779-1781); republished in *Lives of Poets*, 3 volumes, edited by G. B. Hill (Oxford: Clarendon Press, 1905), II: 212-234;

John C. Hodges, *William Congreve The Man* (New York: Modern Language Association of America/London: Oxford University Press, 1941);

Kathleen Lynch, *A Congreve Gallery* (Cambridge, Mass.: Harvard Univerity Press, 1951).

References:

E. L. Avery, *Congreve's Plays on the Eighteenth-Century Stage* (New York: Modern Language Association of America, 1951);

F. W. Bateson, "Second Thoughts: II. L. C. Knights and Restoration Comedy," *Essays in Criticism*, 7 (January 1957): 56-67;

Richard Braverman, "Capital Relations and *The Way of the World*," *ELH*, 52 (Spring 1985): 133-158;

H. F. B. Brett-Smith, ed., *William Congreve: Incognita* (Oxford: Blackwell, 1922);

Brian Corman, " 'The Mixed Way of Comedy': Congreve's *The Double Dealer*," *Modern Philology*, 71 (May 1974): 356-365;

Corman, "*The Way of the World* and Morally Serious Comedy," *Univerity of Toronto Quarterly*, 44 (Spring 1975): 199-212;

T. W. Craik, "Congreve as a Shakespearean," in *Poetry and Drama 1570-1700: Essays in Honour of Harold F. Brooks*, edited by Antony Coleman and Antony Hammond (London: Methuen, 1981), pp. 186-199;

Ian Donaldson, " 'Dear Liberty': *The Way of the World*," in his *The World Upside-Down* (Oxford: Clarendon Press, 1970), pp. 119-158;

Jean Gagen, "Congreve's Mirabell and the Ideal of a Gentleman," *PMLA*, 79 (September 1964): 422-427;

Brian Gibbons, ed., *Congreve: The Way of the World* (London: Benn, 1971);

Harriett Hawkins, *Likenesses of Truth in Elizabethan and Restoration Drama* (Oxford: Clarendon Press, 1972);

John C. Hodges, "The Composition of Congreve's First Play," *PMLA*, 58 (December 1943): 971-976;

Hodges, *The Library of William Congreve* (New York: New York Public Library, 1955);

Norman Holland, *The First Modern Comedies* (Cambridge, Mass.: Harvard University Press, 1959);

Peter Holland, *The Ornament of Action* (Cambridge: Cambridge University Press, 1979);

Paul J. Hurley, "Law and Dramatic Rhetoric in *The Way of the World*," *South Atlantic Quarterly*, 70 (Spring 1971): 191-202;

Anthony Kaufman, "Language and Character in Congreve's *The Way of the World*," *Texas Studies in Language and Literature*, 15 (Fall 1973): 411-427;

Malcolm Kelsall, *Congreve: The Way of the World* (London: Arnold, 1981);

Kelsall, ed., *Congreve: Love for Love* (London: Benn, 1969);

L. C. Knights, "Restoration Comedy: The Reality and the Myth," in his *Explorations* (London: Chatto & Windus, 1946);

Clifford Leech, "Congreve and the Century's End," *Philological Quarterly*, 41 (January 1962): 275-293;

John Loftis, *Comedy and Society from Congreve to Fielding* (Stanford: Stanford University Press, 1958);

Harold Love, *Congreve* (Oxford: Blackwell, 1974);

Charles Lyons, "Congreve's Miracle of Love," *Criticism*, 6 (Fall 1964): 331-348;

Patrick Lyons, ed., *Congreve: Comedies: A Casebook* (London: Macmillan, 1982);

David D. Mann, ed., *A Concordance to the Plays of William Congreve* (Ithaca & London: Cornell University Press, 1973);

Mann, "Congreve's Revisions of *The Mourning Bride*," *Papers of the Bibliographical Society of America*, 69 (1975): 526-546;

D. F. McKenzie, "Typography and Meaning: The Case of William Congreve," *Wolfenbütteler Schriften zur Geschichte des Buchwesens*, 4 (1981): 81-126;

McKenzie, "When Congreve Made a Scene," *Transactions of the Cambridge Bibliographical Society*, 7 (1979): 338-342;

Brian Morris, ed., *William Congreve* (London: Benn, 1972);

Paul and Miriam Mueschke, *A New View of Congreve's Way of the World* (Ann Arbor: University of Michigan Press, 1958);

Kenneth Muir, "The Comedies of William Congreve," in *Restoration Theatre*, edited by J. R. Brown and B. Harris (London: Arnold, 1965), pp. 221-237;

Maximillian Novak, *William Congreve* (New York: Twayne, 1971);

Elmer B. Potter, "The Paradox of Congreve's

Mourning Bride," *PMLA*, 58 (December 1943): 977-1001;

Alan Roper, "Language and Action in *The Way of the World, Love's Last Shift* and *The Relapse*," *ELH*, 40 (Spring 1973): 44-69;

J. C. Ross, ed., *Congreve: The Double-Dealer* (London: Benn, 1981);

John Harrington Smith, *The Gay Couple in Restoration Comedy* (Cambridge, Mass.: Harvard University Press, 1948);

H. T. Swedenberg, ed., *Congreve Consider'd* (Los Angeles: William Andrews Clark Memorial Library, 1971);

William Van Voris, *The Cultivated Stance* (Dublin: Dolmen, 1965);

Gerald Weales, "The Shadow on Congreve's Surface," *Educational Theatre Journal*, 19 (March 1967): 30-32;

Aubrey L. Williams, *An Approach to Congreve* (New Haven: Yale University Press, 1974).

George Farquhar

(circa 1677-May 1707)

Shirley Strum Kenny

Queens College, City University of New York

PLAY PRODUCTIONS: *Love and a Bottle,* London, Theatre Royal in Drury Lane, circa December 1698;

The Constant Couple; or a Trip to the Jubilee, London, Theatre Royal in Drury Lane, circa 28 November 1699;

Sir Harry Wildair: Being the Sequel of the Trip to the Jubilee, London, Theatre Royal in Drury Lane, circa April 1701;

The Stage-Coach, adapted from Jean de la Chapelle's *Les Carrosses d'Orléans,* by Farquhar, with contributions by Peter Anthony Motteux, London, Lincoln's Inn Fields, circa December 1701-February 1702;

The Inconstant: or, The Way to Win Him, a modernization of John Fletcher's *Wild Goose Chase,* London, Theatre Royal in Drury Lane, circa February 1702;

The Twin-Rivals, London, Theatre Royal in Drury Lane, 14 December 1702;

The Recruiting Officer, London, Theatre Royal in Drury Lane, 8 April 1706;

The Beaux Stratagem, London, Queen's Theatre, 8 March 1707.

BOOKS: *The Adventures of Covent-Garden, In Imitation of Scarron's City Romance* (London: Printed by H. Hills for R. Standfast, 1699);

Love and a Bottle. A Comedy, As it is Acted at the Theatre-Royal in Drury Lane by His Majesty's Servants (London: Printed for Richard Standfast & Francis Coggen, 1699);

The Constant Couple; or a Trip to the Jubilee. A Comedy Acted at the Theatre-Royal in Drury-Lane, by His Majesty's Servants (London: Printed for Ralph Smith & Bennet Banbury, 1700); second edition, "with a New Scene added to the part of Wildair" (London: Printed for Ralph Smith & Bennet Banbury, 1700); third edition, "With a New Scene Added to the Part of Wildair; and a New Prologue" (London: Printed for Ralph Smith [variant imprint: London: Printed for Ralph Smith & sold by Bennet Banbury], 1701);

Sir Harry Wildair: Being the Sequel of the Trip to the Jubilee. A Comedy. As it is Acted at the Theatre-Royal in Drury-Lane, by His Majesty's Servants (London: Printed for James Knapton, 1701);

Love and Business: in a Collection of Occasionary Verse, and Eipistolary Prose, Not hitherto Publish'd. A Discourse likewise upon Comedy in Reference to the English Stage. In a Familiar Letter (London: Printed for B. Lintott, 1702);

The Inconstant: or, The way to win him. A Comedy, As it is Acted at the Theatre Royal in Drury-lane. By his Majesty's Servants (London: Printed for J. Knapton, G. Strahan & B. Lintott, 1702);

The Twin-Rivals. A Comedy. Acted at the Theatre Royal By Her Majesty's Servants (London: Printed for Bernard Lintott, 1703);

The Stage-Coach. A Farce. As it was Acted at the Theatre in Lincolns-Inn-Fields. By Her Majesties Servants, by Farquhar and Peter Anthony Motteux (Dublin: Printed & sold by the booksellers, 1704); republished from a second manuscript as *The Stage-Coach A Comedy: As it was Acted at the New Theatre in Lincolns-Inn-Fields. By Her Majesties Servants* (London: Printed & sold by Benjamin Bragg, 1705); republished, from a third manuscript, as *The Stage-Coach. A Farce. As it is Acted at the Theatre-Royal in Drury-Lane* (London: Printed for W. Feales, 1735);

The Recruiting Officer. A Comedy. As it was Acted at the Theatre Royal in Drury-Lane By Her Majesty's Servants (London: Printed for Bernard Lintott, 1706); second edition, corrected (London: Printed for Bernard Lintott, 1706);

The Prologue Spoken by Mr. Wilks, At the Opening of the Theatre in the Hay-Market, October the 15th, 1706 [broadside] (London: Printed for Benjamin Bragg, 1706);

The Beaux Stratagem. A Comedy. As it is Acted at the Queen's Theatre in the Hay-Market. By Her

George Farquhar (engraving by R. Clamp)

Majesty's Sworn Comedians (London: Printed for Bernard Lintott, 1707);

Love's Catechism. Compiled by the Author of the Recruiting Officer, for the Use and Benefit of all Young Batchelors, Maids, and Widows, that are inclinable to change their Condition, attributed to Farquhar (London, 1707);

Barcellona. A Poem. Or, The Spanish Expedition, Under the Command of Charles Earl of Peterborough. Until The Reduction of the City of Barcellona to the Obedience of Charles III. King of Spain (London: Printed for John Smith & Richard Standfast, [variant imprint: London: Publish'd for the Benefit of the Author's Widow & Children], 1710).

Collections: *The Comedies of Mr. George Farquhar: Viz. Love and a Bottle, Constant Couple: Or a Trip to the Jubilee, Sir Harry Wildair, Inconstant: Or, The Way to win Him, Twin-Rivals, Recruiting Officer, Beaux Stratagem* (London: Printed for Bernard Lintott [variant imprint: London: Printed for James Knapton, Ralph Smith & George Strahan, and Bernard Lintott], 1708);

The Works Of the late Ingenious Mr. George Farquhar: Containing all his Letters, Poems, Essays, and Comedies Publish'd in his Life-time. The Comedies are Illustrated with Cuts representing the principal Scenes in each Play [text of *Love and Business,* bound with the second edition of the *Comedies*] (London: Printed for Bernard Lintott, 1711);

The Works of the late Ingenious Mr. George Farquhar: Containing all his poems, Letters, Essays and Comedies, Publish'd in his Life-time. In Two Volumes. The Sixth Edition. Corrected from the Errors of former Impressions. To which are added some Memoirs of the Author, never before Publish'd (London: Printed for J. & J. Knapton, B. Lintott, G. Strahan, and J. Clark, 1728);

The Dramatick Works of Mr. George Farquhar. In Two Volumes, seventh edition (London: Printed for B. Lintott, J. J. & P. Knapton, G. Strahan, & J. Clarke; and sold by W.

Feales, 1736)–the first edition of the *Works* to include *The Stage-Coach;*

The Works of George Farquhar, 3 volumes (Dublin: Thomas Ewing, 1775);

The Dramatic Works of Wycherley, Congreve, Vanbrugh, and Farquhar. With Biographical and Critical Notices, edited by Leigh Hunt (London: Moxon, 1840);

The Dramatic Works of George Farquhar, edited by A. C. Ewald, 2 volumes (London: Nimmo, 1892);

George Farquhar, edited by William Archer, Mermaid Series (London: Unwin / New York: Scribners, 1906)–comprises *The Constant Couple, The Twin-Rivals, The Recruiting Officer,* and *The Beaux Stratagem;*

The Complete Works of George Farquhar, edited by Charles Stonehill, 2 volumes (London: Nonesuch Press, 1930);

The Works of George Farquhar, edited by Shirley Strum Kenny, 2 volumes (Oxford: Clarendon Press, 1988).

OTHER: "Epilogue. Writ by Mr. Farquhar," in *The Grove, Or, Love's Paradise,* by John Oldmixon (London: Printed for Richard Parker, 1700);

Familiar and Courtly Letters, Written by Monsieur Voiture To Persons of the greatest Honour, Wit, and Quality of both Sexes in the Court of France, includes letters by Farquhar (London: Printed for Sam Briscoe & sold by J. Nutt, 1700);

"Prologue, Written by Mr. Farquhar, and spoken by Mr. Powell," in *Courtship A-la-Mode,* by David Crauford (London: Printed for J. Barnes & E. Rumbal, 1700);

A Pacquet from Will's: Or a New Collection of Original Letters on Several Subjects, includes letters by Farquhar (London: Printed for Sam. Briscoe & sold by John Nutt, 1701); published in volume 2 of *Familiar and Courtly Letters Written to Persons of Honour and Quality, by Mons. Voiture . . .* (London: Printed for Sam. Briscoe & sold by John Nutt, 1701);

Letters of Wit, Politicks and Morality. Written Originally in Italian, By the Famous Cardinal Bentivoglio; Also Select Letters of Gallantry out of the Greek. . . . To which is added a large Collection of Original Letters of Love and Friendship, includes letters of Farquhar (London: Printed for J. Hartley, W. Turner & Tho. Hodgson, 1701);

"Prologue. By Mr. Farquhar. Spoke by Mr. Wilks," in *All for the Better,* by Francis Manning (London: Printed & sold by B. Bragg, 1703 [i.e., 1702]);

Epilogue, *The Patriot: or, The Italian Conspiracy,* by Charles Gildon (London: W. Davis, 1702);

"To a Gentleman who had his Picket Pick'd of a Watch and Money by a Mistress," in *The Poetical Courant,* no. 2 (2 February 1706);

"Prologue. By Captain Farquhar. Spoken by Mr. Betterton," in *The Platonick Lady,* by Susanna Centlivre (London: Printed for James Knapton & Egbert Sanger, 1707).

In comparing the work of William Wycherley, William Congreve, John Vanbrugh, and George Farquhar, Leigh Hunt concluded that, of the four, "Farquhar had the highest animal spirits, with fits of the deepest sympathy, the greatest wish to please rather than to strike, the most agreeable diversity of character, the best instinct in avoiding revolting extravagances of the time, and the happiest invention in plot and situation; and, therefore, is to be pronounced, upon the whole, the truest dramatic genius, and the most likely to be of lasting popularity." Indeed Farquhar was the most popular and perhaps the best playwright producing plays for the London stage at the turn of the eighteenth century. He was certainly the most original; in an era in which authors borrowed from earlier English drama or translated plots or scenes from Greek, Latin, French, or Spanish models (as they mixed several sources together in a single play), Farquhar created original plots in all of his plays except *The Stage-Coach,* a translation of a French farce, and *The Inconstant,* a modernization of John Fletcher's *Wild Goose Chase* (circa 1621). During the course of the first half of the eighteenth century, his plays were favorites on the London stage; year after year they continued to play well; they have remained in the repertory even in the twentieth century.

Farquhar was born in 1677 or 1678 in Londonderry. His father, William Farquhar, was an Anglican clergyman with seven children and a living of one hundred fifty pounds a year. Biographers claim that young George's penchant for poetry and the polite arts brought him early attention from his mother's relative Dr. Capell Wiseman, the bishop of Dromore, who promised to provide for him in the Church. William Farquhar, according to tradition, was plundered and burned out of all his possessions by Jacobites dur-

Tantum de medio Sumptis accedit honoris.

Ben Jonson, wearing a laurel wreath and holding a copy of his Bartholomew Fair, *presents Farquhar to Apollo and the Nine Muses. The lines beneath the engraving are from Horace's* Ars Poetica *and may be translated "So great the charm that can crown the most ordinary words" (frontispiece to the 1711 edition of Farquhar's works).*

ing the violence in Ireland which followed the Glorious Revolution of 1688; he died soon after.

James Sutherland claims that Farquhar served in the Battle of the Boyne in 1690; he would have been twelve or thirteen at the time. *Love and Business* includes a Pindaric ode, "On the Death of General Schomberg kill'd at the Boyne"; perhaps it derives from firsthand experience. Farquhar entered Trinity College, Dublin, as a sizar (a student who worked in exchange for expenses) on 17 July 1694 at age seventeen. He

won an exhibition (scholarship), was suspended from it, and had it reinstated in February 1696. His formal education, however, did not last long. According to one story, perhaps apochryphal, he was expelled for answering an assignment about Christ's walking on water with the explanation that "He that is born to be hanged need fear no drowning."

By 1696 Farquhar had left Trinity without a degree and become an actor in Joseph Ashbury's troupe in Dublin's Smock Alley Theatre. There he struck up a lasting friendship with the actor Robert Wilks, whose life became inextricably connected with Farquhar's. Accounts seem to agree that Farquhar was an attractive and amiable actor, but his weak voice was a distinct disadvantage on stage. He played many roles, including Lenox in *Macbeth,* Lord Dion in Francis Beaumont and John Fletcher's *Philaster,* Rochford in John Banks's *Virtue Betrayed,* Guyomar in John Dryden's *The Indian Emperor,* Young Bellair in William Congreve's *The Man of Mode,* Careless in Sir Robert Howard's *The Committee,* and Young Loveless in Beaumont and Fletcher's *The Scornful Lady.* Then one night when he played the role of Guyomar, he forgot to exchange his sword for a foil and consequently wounded the actor playing Vasquez; although the wound did not prove dangerous, Farquhar swore off acting.

Before the accident had even occurred, Wilks had supposedly encouraged Farquhar to give up acting for writing comedy. Farquhar took his advice. He left for London in 1697 or 1698, with or without a draft of his first comedy in hand (early biographers disagree on the details). In December 1698 his first play, *Love and a Bottle,* opened at Drury Lane. He was twenty or twenty-one at the time.

Love and a Bottle is the work of a young man, brash and naively enamored of brisk wit, the social graces, and machismo. In the play the poet Lyrick says that the hero of comedy "is always the Poet's Character," and critics have assumed that George Roebuck is a barely disguised George Farquhar. Like Farquhar, Roebuck has just come from Ireland to London; he has not a farthing in his pocket. He left Ireland to escape his old mistress, Trudge, who is pursuing him, baby in tow. He has also left Leanthe, who truly loves him. Strolling in Lincoln's Inn Fields, he spies Lucinda exchanging witticisms with her maid, Pindress, and experiences instant desire for her. Then he meets his friend and Leanthe's brother, Lovewell, who truly loves Lucinda; they hatch a plot to test her virtue by having Roebuck court her and attempt to seduce her. Lovewell provides him money and a young page sent to London by Leanthe (actually, Leanthe in disguise). The plot proceeds by tricks and disguises, in a highly complex, highly imitative fashion; Leanthe disguises herself as a page, a device that has reminded critics of Viola in *Twelfth Night* (1602), Fidelia in William Wycherley's *The Plain Dealer* (1676), Olivia in Aphra Behn's *The Younger Brother* (1696), and Helena in Behn's *The Rover* (1677).

The plots and counterplots are exemplified by Leanthe's explanation to Lovewell toward the end of act 5: "The fear she [Lucinda] lay under of being discover'd by you, gave me an opportunity of imposing *Pindress'* Night-Gown as a Disguise. To make the Cheat more current, she disguis'd her self in my Cloaths, which has made her pass on her Maid for me; and I by that opportunity putting on a Suit of hers, past upon this Gentleman for *Lucinda,* my next business is to find her out, and beg her pardon, endeavour her reconcilement to you, which the discovery of the mistakes between both will easily effect." A plot with trickery and disguise so complicated that it must be solved through such a complicated set of offstage machinations was merely a tentative step on the way to Farquhar's mature dramaturgy. He filled out the subplot with a set of beau makers, who redesigned the university beau Mockmode, in scenes reminiscent of Molière's *Le Bourgeois gentilhomme* (1670).

Farquhar brought to his first play his actor's knowledge of stock characters, including the two contrasting sets of lovers, witty and slow servants, the cast mistress, and minor characters such as the poet and the dancing master, as well as echoes of many lines from other playwrights from Shakespeare to John Dryden and Nathaniel Lee. He reused trite plot devices of mistaken identity, multiple disguises, and tricked marriages. He was deft at incorporating wit, particularly bawdy double entendres, perhaps trying too hard and yet effecting a pleasing energy and exuberance. Five songs as well as some comic dancing added color, and the shortcomings of the denouement were masked by an Irish "Fingalian" dance with six performers.

Early audiences and most critics have treated the play with good humor and good-natured praise. Compared to Farquhar's other comedies, *Love and a Bottle* seems old-fashioned in its determination to be bawdy, its reliance on stock characters and plot devices, its harsh treatment of the cast mistress, and its focus on sexual pursuit. Farquhar tested his theatrical skills, but he created little that was new or influential in his initial foray into play writing.

He was obviously not yet wed to drama as a vocation, for his novella, *The Adventures of Covent-Garden,* appeared anonymously in mid December, a few weeks after *Love and a Bottle* opened and a couple of weeks before it was published. *The Adventures of Covent-Garden* was supposedly based on Antoine Furetière's *Le Roman bourgeois*

Sir Harry Wildair beating Smuggler at Lady Lurewell's house, illustration by E. Knight for
act 2 of The Constant Couple *(from the 1711 edition of Farquhar's works)*

(1666), translated as *Scarron's City Romance, Made English* (1671). None of Farquhar's early biographers attributed the novella to him. Isaac Reed reproachfully noted in his copy in 1795 that Farquhar plagiarized a bit from it for *The Constant Couple*. Leigh Hunt, who had acquired Reed's copy, was the first to recognize that Farquhar himself was the author of the novella. Hunt said Farquhar was the author described in the novella as "a young gentleman somewhat addicted to poetry and the diversions of the stage"; he also noted a precursor to Lady Lurewell, and most conclusively identified a poem later printed with the addition of six lines as "The Lovers Night" in *Love and Business*. In fact, Farquhar, who often reused his own materials but seldom borrowed from others, also repeated lines from *Love and a Bottle* in *The Adventures of Covent-Garden*. In his novella he introduced the plot of the lover's escape in the porter's clothes, which he recycled for *The Constant Couple*, and he first explored the dramatic theory that he later elaborated in *A Discourse upon Comedy*.

In *The Adventures of Covent-Garden* the hero, Peregrine, happens upon Emilia, who had shunned his courtship in order to marry Richly; he is enamored again, and prefers misuse at Emilia's hands to the affection of the likable and intelligent Selinda. The novella records his escapades in the world of redcoats, beaux, fashionable ladies, wits, and sharpers; the slight work is interesting almost entirely for its relations to other Farquharian efforts. Oddly enough, it ends abruptly with his discovery of Emilia's perfidy but without the reconciliation with Selinda that one would expect. *The Adventures of Covent-Garden* had no noticeable impact on English reading habits.

The actor Robert Wilks followed his young friend to London, probably in 1699. A player at Smock Alley from 1691, he had previously performed in London during the 1693-1694 season, then returned to Smock Alley, where he remained through the 1698-1699 season. For his friend's return to London Farquhar wrote "An Epilogue, spoken by Mr. Wilks at his first Appearance upon the English Stage," first published in *Love and Business*. Although Joseph Williams had played Roebuck in *Love and a Bottle*, Wilks became available for *The Constant Couple*. From that time on, he created all Farquhar's heroes in full-length comedies.

The Constant Couple; or a Trip to the Jubilee (1699) made Farquhar's reputation. An instant success and long-time favorite, it broke all performance records in its first season, playing fifty-three nights in London and twenty-three in Dublin, a record unmatched until 1728 when *The Beggar's Opera* ran sixty-two nights in London. Its success infuriated the competing playwrights and actors at Lincoln's Inn Fields.

Although critics have looked for sources and suggested some, the play is highly original except for Farquhar's reuse of materials from *The Adventures of Covent-Garden*. The events in London in the spring and summer of 1699 provided the setting. On 26 March 1699 the army had been disbanded by Act of Parliament, except for seven thousand men and the force in Ireland. The act had resounding social and economic effects; many former officers found themselves impoverished and unemployed. Meanwhile, news had reached London of the Papal Jubilee in Rome, which was to begin at Christmas 1699, a month after the premiere of *The Constant Couple*. The play's action unfolds against a backdrop of these two public events.

The hero, Sir Harry Wildair, has just returned from Paris, a war hero and fine fellow, who proves that bravery and "humorous Gaiety" are not inconsistent. He is introduced as "a Gentleman of most happy Circumstances, [who was] born to a plentiful Estate, has had a genteel and easy Education, free from the rigidness of Teach-

ers, and Pedantry of Schools. His florid Constitution being never ruffled by misfortune, nor stinted in its Pleasures, has render'd him entertaining to others, and easy to himself—Turning all Passion into Gaiety of Humour, by which he chuses rather to rejoice his Friends, than be hated by any." Like the rakes of the Restoration, Wildair is charged with intense sexual energy; he pursues women enthusiastically, with both joie de vivre and common sense. Although only he would laugh at his war experiences, his romantic ones are quite another matter. He returns from Paris to court Lady Lurewell until someone mentions Angelica, a beautiful, rich virgin of sixteen. He fully pursues "the Business of Pleasure," as he calls it, and embraces virtue only for the sake of Angelica. Throughout all, he maintains his common sense, never glorifying war or the pursuit of honor even though he has earned badges of courage.

In a more serious and brittle second love plot Colonel Standard, recently disbanded, finds himself without riches or the woman he loves. He also courts Lurewell, who has vowed cruelty to all men because she believed herself abandoned by the one she truly loved (actually Standard, who has in fact sought her faithfully). In the end, having uncovered her unfaithfulness through a ring trick, Standard discovers that she is his lost love of twelve years earlier, and they reunite emotionally. The farcical subplot focuses on an apprentice turned beau who longs to go to Rome for the Jubilee.

The extraordinary success of *The Constant Couple* can be attributed in part to clever plotting, good pacing, and witty lines, but to judge from the critics, it was the character of Sir Harry Wildair that hit the public fancy and guaranteed the success of the play. Hostile critics claimed that Wilks's interpretation of Wildair carried the play, and Farquhar himself cheerily agreed; in the preface to the printed play (first published 11 December 1699, with 1700 on the title page) he praised Wilks's performance and added, "That he made the Part, will appear from hence, that whenever the Stage has the misfortune to lose him, Sir *Harry Wildair* may go to the Jubilee."

Shortly after the opening of the play, Farquhar revised the confrontation between Wildair and Angelica in V.i, perhaps to preserve consistency in Sir Harry's character as Wilks interpreted him. The first version poses a highly emotional and conventionally sentimental scene in which Wildair exclaims in speeches such as,

"Ha! . . . I feel her piercing Words turn the wild Current of my Blood; and thrill through all my Veins." In the revision (published in the second edition, 1 February 1700) he continues in his mistaken belief that she is "the first Whore in *Heroicks*" that he has ever met. Instead of concluding that her "Presence, like a Guardian Angel shall fright away all Vice," when he finally realizes his mistake, he concludes he must either "commit Murder, or commit Matrimony," and chooses the latter because "Cowards dare fight, I'll marry, that is the most daring Action of the two. . . ."

The Constant Couple not only made Farquhar the most successful playwright in London and Wilks the most successful actor but also had a major impact on the theatrical warfare between Christopher Rich's company at Drury Lane and the best actors in London, who had broken from Rich's heavy-handed management of the United Company in 1695 and set up at Lincoln's Inn Fields. All the leading actors had fled—Thomas Betterton, Anne Bracegirdle, Ann Barry, and others. Drury Lane was left with mostly neophytes, although some established performers such as George Powell stayed on, and the comedians William Pinkethman, William Bullock, and Joe Haines gave Drury Lane a certain edge for comedy. Both houses competed for audiences by mounting extravagant performances, importing musical artists, staging novelty acts, spending heavily on scenery and machinery, and staging operas. They also attempted to mount as many new plays as possible. A hit like *The Constant Couple* propelled Drury Lane into a far more competitive position; in fact, it proved the turning point in Drury Lane's struggle to compete.

Understandably the Lincoln's Inn Fields company was furious. They ridiculed the play and its Irish author with cruel malice. Farquhar had felt the sting of harsh criticism even by the time he wrote the preface to the published play, which appeared less than two weeks after the opening. He addressed two points, that he had ignored the rules and that the subtitle was a misnomer. He also acknowledged "The Beauties of this Play, especially those of the third Night," that is, the profits of his benefit performance. Undoubtedly the critics' contempt was fueled by their unrelenting envy. They condemned *The Constant Couple* as irregular farce and complained that audiences seemed to prefer such trash to their plays. They ridiculed Farquhar as an Irishman, a son of Flecknoe, who fattened by farce and thrived by

nonsense. And they continued complaining for several years. As late as 1703 both Charles Boyle, earl of Orrery, and Mary Pix caviled in prologues to their new plays; in 1704 the author of *The Tryal of Skill* continued to carp. Farquhar forever after had a reputation as a lightweight—and almost without exception his later plays were successful.

As good natured as was his response in the preface to the first edition, he felt compelled to address at least one of his critics, John Oldmixon. He had contributed the epilogue to Oldmixon's *The Grove* (1700) and might have expected appreciation; nevertheless, Oldmixon attacked him viciously in the prologue to Charles Gildon's adaptation of *Measure for Measure* (1700). Farquhar responded with a new prologue to *The Constant Couple*, first spoken on 13 July 1700 and published in the third edition on 20 August 1700 (with 1701 on the title page). In it he summarized the nature of most of the criticism: "Our Plays are Farce, because our House is Cram'd; / Their Plays all Good: For What?—because they'r Damn'd." Farquhar never adopted the stance of a serious dramatic poet. He was a writer of comedy, probably the most popular—and arguably the best—writer of comedy in his lifetime. He attracted audiences, and he did not take himself terribly seriously. He was, after all, when he struck theatrical gold, a mere twenty-two or twenty-three years old. He must have enjoyed his success enormously, and with the exception of the faithless attack of Oldmixon, he did not seem to let the hysterical critics bother him.

The Constant Couple was not only an instant success; it was one of the most popular plays in the eighteenth-century theater. *The London Stage,* which lists only 4 of the estimated 53 performances for the first season and is extremely sketchy until 1703, lists a total of 365 performances in the eighteenth century; it is likely that the total approaches 450. In the period from 1730 to 1750, 170 London performances occurred, and the last performance recorded in *The London Stage* was in 1795. Of course the play continued to run in the next century and occasionally in the twentieth century as well.

For thirty years Farquhar was right about the part of Wildair belonging to Wilks. Wilks played Wildair more than 150 times; when he retired, Henry Giffard continued with it for 68 performances and Lacy Ryan for 32, and 23 other actors from Theophilus Cibber to David Garrick to Samuel Foote played the role. Oddly enough,

Robert Wilks as Sir Harry Wildair, a role he played more than one hundred and fifty times, while also creating
the parts of Young Mirabel in The Inconstant, *Elder Wou'dbe in* The Twin-Rivals, *Plume in*
The Recruiting Officer, *and Archer in* The Beaux Stratagem.

after Wilks, the most famous performer of Wildair was by Peg Woffington, who played Sir Harry 73 times from 1740 to 1757, and nine other actresses portrayed him before the end of the century. Why? Woffington played the role straight, not touching directly on the ambiguity of a woman's portraying a rakish young man. Although she naturally evoked interest by assuming a transvestite role, she played it as seriously as any male actor would have done.

The triumphant season of 1699-1700 had established Farquhar as a leading playwright, popular enough to precipitate the flood of attacks from his less successful colleagues at Lincoln's Inn Fields. He dabbled in other kinds of writing, and we may assume most of his efforts were easily peddled. He wrote at least two additional prologues and two epilogues for Drury Lane. He drank with the actors at the Rose Tavern. He

had several amours and published some letters allegedly resulting from them in an epistolary collection that spring. His name was linked with those of two prominent playwrights, Susanna Centlivre and Catharine Trotter (later Cockburn), both of whom wrote plays that opened at Drury Lane in fall 1700. He perhaps even started work on his next play.

On 7 August 1700, less than a month after his prologue attacking Oldmixon was performed, Farquhar sailed for Holland. The purpose of the voyage is not known, but the trip must have been less than pleasurable, for Farquhar was again stricken with a terrible bout of illness which almost sent him "on a longer Journey than he was willing to undertake at present," as he said in a letter reprinted in *Love and Business*. He remained in Holland at least until 23 October, when he wrote to a woman he was courting, perhaps his future wife, Margaret Pemell. As it happened, King William, who was suffering from various illnesses including swelling in his legs, had arrived in Holland on 27 July and was at The Hague when Farquhar sailed. The young playwright obviously made contact with the courtiers abroad; in fact, he sailed with Martin Lister (or Lyster), who had been dispatched to inform the king of the death of the young duke of Gloucester, Queen Anne's only surviving child. The three published letters from his trip, included in *Love and Business*, give ample factual evidence of his journey but no clue about why he decided to travel.

Nor is there any evidence on when he began to write his third play, *Sir Harry Wildair: Being the Sequel of the Trip to the Jubilee*. The play did not open until April 1701, unusually late in the season for the premiere of a major money-maker, and presumably the Drury Lane troupe, ever eager for success, would have rushed it on stage at the first opportunity. Internal evidence also suggests that Farquhar did not complete the play before late autumn or winter 1700, perhaps even later. It was first published on 13 May 1701.

He reused the characters that had made *The Constant Couple* (called *The Trip to the Jubilee* at the time) so popular. Sir Harry, Jubilee Dicky, Standard, Lurewell, Angelica, Parly, and Clincher all reappear. So popular were Wilks as Sir Harry and Henry Norris as Jubilee Dicky (he earned the nickname "Dicky" Norris from the role) that they alone should have assured success for the new piece. The sequel focused once again on Wildair's rakishness and Lurewell's cynical flirtatiousness, but of necessity the action had to take place within a context of marriage, since *The Constant Couple* had ended with the promise of wedding vows.

When *Sir Harry Wildair* opens, Angelica has presumably been dead for more than a year. After Sir Harry's wandering eye had sparked a lover's quarrel, he had abruptly departed for Italy. She then vanished to France, where she took ill, supposedly died, and, not being a Catholic, could not be buried in a public cemetery but was interred in private grounds through the goodness of a kind gentlewoman. Now, more than a year later, Sir Harry has returned to London and to his rakish ways. He flirts with Lurewell, who has meanwhile both taken up gambling and returned to coquetry not only with Sir Harry but with a French marquis as well. Sir Harry's younger brother, Beau Banter, whom he has not seen for seven years (actually Angelica in disguise), arrives in London. Complications arise when Lurewell accrues gambling debts and begins flirtations with both Monsieur Marquis and Sir Harry; Standard discovers that her virtue is both fragile and endangered; and Sir Harry's roving eye threatens to betray his friendship. Angelica assumes yet another disguise, that of her own ghost, to shock Lurewell, Standard, and finally Wildair. But unlike other stage heroes stricken by sorrow or remorse at the sight of a ghost, Sir Harry grasps the absurdity of the situation, grabs the ghost, and finds her to be altogether substantial. Unlike other stage characters who find their lost loves alive, he does not react in rhetorical ecstasy when he discovers she is indeed alive. Rather than emoting in iambic pentameter, as was the fashion for greeting ghosts on stage, he proposes that Angelica and he eat, drink, listen to music, then "hurl off our Cloaths, leap into Bed," and there engage in "Raptures more natural and more moving than all the Plays in *Christendom*." In the end, both couples recommit to their vows.

The plot is creaky and poorly executed, and as is often true in sequels the brilliance of the original has dimmed. Still, the views of marriage that inform the dialogue are remarkable for the time. Sir Harry outlines for Lurewell his sense of the ideal wife when he taunts her with a description of his former marital bliss:

WILDAIR. Sirrah!

DICKY. Sir, Sir! shall I order your Chair to the back-door by Five a Clock in the Morning!

WILDAIR. The Devil's in the Fellow. Get you gone.

> Dicky *runs out.*

Now, dear Madam, I have secur'd my Brother, you have dispos'd the Colonel, and we may rail at Love till we han't a Word more to say.

LUREWELL. Ay, Sir *Harry*.—Please to sit a little, Sir.— You must know I'm in a strange Humour of asking you some Questions.—How do you like your Lady, pray Sir?

WILDAIR. Like her!—Ha, ha, ha.—So very well faith, that for her very sake I'm in love with every Woman I meet.

LUREWELL. And did Matrimony please you extremely?

WILDAIR. So very much, that if Polygamy were allow'd, I wou'd have a new Wife every day.

LUREWELL. Oh, Sir *Harry*! This is Raillery. But your serious Thoughts upon the Matter pray.

WILDAIR. Why then, Madam, to give you my true Sentiments of Wedlock: I had a Lady that I marry'd by chance, she was Vertuous by

Sir Harry discovers that Angelica's "ghost" is alive, illustration by E. Knight for act 5 of
Sir Harry Wildair (from the 1711 edition of Farquhar's works)

chance, and I lov'd her by great chance. Nature gave her Beauty, Education an Air, and Fortune threw a young Fellow of Five and Twenty in her Lap.–I courted her all Day, lov'd her all Night; she was my Mistress one Day, my Wife another: I found in One the variety of a Thousand, and the very confinement of Marriage gave me the Pleasure of Change.

LUREWELL. And she was very Vertuous?

WILDAIR. Look ye, Madam, you know she was Beautiful. She had good Nature about her Mouth, the Smile of Beauty in her Cheeks, sparkling Wit in her Forehead, and Sprightly Love in her Eyes.

LUREWELL. Pshaw! I knew her very well; the Woman was well enough. But you don't answer my Question, Sir.

WILDAIR. So Madam, as I told you before, she was Young and Beautiful, I was Rich and Vigorous; my Estate gave a Lustre to my Love, and a Swing to our Enjoyment; round, like the Ring that made us one, our golden Pleasures circl'd without end.

At the end of the play, both male and female ideal partners are described by the principals:

STANDARD. Now, Sir, *Harry,* we have retriev'd our Wives; Yours from Death, and mine from the Devil; and they are at present very honest. But how shall we keep 'em so?

ANGELICA. . . . the great Secret for keeping Matters right in Wedlock, is never to quarrel with your Wives for Trifles. . . .

LUREWELL. And another Rule, Gentlemen, let me advise you to observe, Never to be Jealous; or if you shou'd, be sure never to let your Wife think you suspect her; . . . .

WILDAIR. We're oblig'd to you, Ladies, for your Advice; and in return, give me leave to give you the definition of a good Wife, in the Character of my own.

The Wit of her Conversation never outstrips the Conduct of her Behaviour: She's affable to all Men, free with no Man, and only kind to me: Often chearful, sometimes gay, and always pleas'd, but when I am angry; then sorry, not sullen: The Park, Play-house, and Cards, she frequents in compliance with Custom; but her Diversions of Inclination are at home. She's more cautious of a remarkable Woman, than of a noted Wit, well knowing that the Infection of her own Sex is more catching than the Temptation of ours: To all this, she is beautiful to a Wonder, scorns all Devices that engage a Gallant, and uses all Arts to please her Husband.

So, spite of Satyr 'gainst a marry'd Life,
A Man is truly blest with such a Wife.

Despite the fact that the two marriages have faltered before the play opened, the audience must believe that both couples, now wiser, will find prolonged marital bliss as the curtain falls.

The play is unusually short, a fact that led W. J. Lawrence to speculate on whether *The Stage-Coach* originally ran as its afterpiece, but clearly that farce opened at Lincoln's Inn Fields. Perhaps the brevity of *Sir Harry Wildair* was a result of Farquhar's failure to develop a well-integrated plot. The characters, popular as they were, could not continue to enchant audiences without a strong vehicle. The marital dimension, which evoked significant and original social commentary, failed to sustain the plot of farfetched trickery and disguises. Married rakes and coquets were quite a different matter from unmarried ones; the stakes in the battle of the sexes had become too high for lighthearted levity.

The play proved to be the least successful of Farquhar's efforts. Although we do not know the length of the first run because performances were not yet recorded daily in advertisements, Farquhar's tormentors jeered at the "Explosion" or disappointing failure of the sequel. Farquhar did not bother to write a preface for the printed play, and he never referred to *Sir Harry Wildair* in later works. There is no proof that the first season was not successful—at least three performances were recorded in April and May—but there is no evidence of an extended run either. Although most of Farquhar's plays were performed numerous times during the century, *Sir Harry Wildair* next appeared for five nights at Lincoln's Inn Fields in 1737 and then disappeared from the repertoire forever.

Farquhar published some more letters, in the second volume of *Familiar and Courtly Letters*, in May 1701, and in *Letters of Wit, Politicks and Morality*, in July. He wrote "A Prologue on the propos'd Union of the Two Houses," first published in *Love and Business*. On 3 July 1701 he signed an agreement with Bernard Lintot to publish a miscellany and "A Discourse upon Comedy In Fourteen Letters." The miscellany of poems, letters, and a critical essay on comedy (not in fourteen letters) was assembled and published by Lintot under the title *Love and Business* on 22 November 1701 (with 1702 on the title page). Characteristic of miscellanies published at the turn of the century, *Love and Business* contains poetry and prose, much of it seemingly written for earlier occasions. One poem, for example, "On the Death of the late Queen," must have been written by a teenaged Farquhar when Queen Mary died in 1694. Another, "On the Death of General Schomberg," probably dated from his school years, unless he actually fought at the Battle of the Boyne as a teenager. Others were clearly written after his arrival in London. The travel letters can be dated by his trip to Holland, and the love letters undoubtedly were a product of his time in London. Whether the love letters were fictitious or actual letters sent to young ladies and either requested back or copied on the chance of publication, one cannot say. On the one hand they seem highly artificial, more witty than passionate. On the other the author frequently complained in them of illness, particularly his debilitating bouts of fever and painful inflammation of the joints, a state of being that does not often find its way into fictionalized romantic letters.

A Discourse upon Comedy was, however, unquestionably written specifically for publication. Farquhar took a daring and unpopular line: that, as Samuel Johnson was to say forty-six years later, "The Drama's laws the Drama's Patrons give." He rejected Aristotle and other revered critics, saying that regularity and adherence to the Unities do not make a good comedy; rather a comedy is to be judged by its effectiveness in the theater. Predictably the common sense of *A Discourse upon Comedy*, a precursor to Johnson's dramatic criticism, sent Farquhar's detractors into paroxysms of anger. The appreciation of the moderns at the expense of the ancients, particularly by a playwright who was remarkably successful on stage despite his refusal to pay obeisance to conventional critical views, inevitably aroused rule-

William Bullock, the comic actor who played Mockmode in Love and a Bottle, *Clincher Jr. in* The Constant Couple, *Duretete in* The Inconstant, *a bumpkin recruit in* The Recruiting Officer, *and Bonniface in* The Beaux Stratagem

bound and inept neoclassical dramatists to condemn his impudence and call him a hack.

Farquhar next tried a collaboration with Peter Anthony Motteux, a Frenchman turned English playwright. The project, translating a French farce as a frivolous afterpiece, proved far from easy. Although Farquhar bragged in *Love and Business* that ordinarily he worked quickly ("I can by Three hours Study live One and Twenty with Satisfaction my self, and contribute to the Maintenance of more Families than some who have Thousands a Year"), the afterpiece proved to be a struggle. It was an adaptation of *Les Carrosses d'Orléans* (1680) by Jean de la Chapelle. This was Farquhar's first attempt at translation, his first three plays having been highly original; it proved to be unbearable drudgery. In one of

the letters in *Love and Business*, he complained that: "The Angry Fates and dire Stage-Coach / Upon my liberty incroach, . . ." The Stage-Coach of the poem was, of course, the farce with which he struggled. Sometime between late 1701 and early 1702, however, the farce was ready for the stage.

The action takes place at an inn at which a stagecoach full of diverse passengers, a kind of ship of fools, arrives. The main love plot unites Isabella and Captain Basil after the requisite number of scrapes, mistaken identities, disguises, and nighttime bedroom hopping. Isabella's old uncle Micher, the sympathetic Irishman Macahone, the country booby Squire Somebody, the coachman Tim Jolt, and other stock characters round out the cast.

Unlike Farquhar's other plays, *The Stage-Coach* was first performed at Lincoln's Inn Fields. Oddly enough, it was first published in 1704 in Dublin, where Farquhar had a brother who was a publisher and where Farquhar was serving in the army at the time. The London edition came later, on 3 or 4 May 1705, at least three years after the premiere. Farces used as afterpieces were, of course, quite new at the time, and publication was rare. Farquhar might well have felt there was no market. Moreover, there were clearly problems about co-authoring a play, a mode Farquhar never tried before or after. Motteux certainly contributed "The Stage-Coach Song," and there are other details characteristic of him, but Farquhar was probably the primary author (see Kenny's "The Mystery of *The Stage-Coach* Reconsidered"). The Dublin and London editions come from two totally separate manuscripts, and the edition published in 1735 derives from a third.

The Stage-Coach was a success on stage and remained in the repertory as late as 1787. In 1704 a new prologue and epilogue by Samuel Philips were added and then published with later editions. In 1730 the farce was turned into a ballad opera, following the success of *The Beggar's Opera* in 1728. Its seventeen airs were probably a creation of William Rufus Chetwood, the prompter at Drury Lane. As both farce and opera, the afterpiece proved a great success. Farquhar may have displeased the critics, but he had an unflagging instinct for what the paying customers wanted.

The farce was an early example of the genre. Emmett L. Avery estimates that only ten of 225 programs in 1704-1705 were double bills. The success of *The Stage-Coach* encouraged other writers to try the genre. But Farquhar himself never felt called upon to suffer through either another farce or another collaboration with Motteux.

He was working on his next play, *The Inconstant*, at the same time that he patched together the miscellany in 1701. The comedy was based loosely on Fletcher's *Wild Goose Chase*, published posthumously in 1652. In the preface Farquhar claimed he "took the hint" from Fletcher's play; some of his detractors claimed he plagiarized it and did even that poorly. As Arthur Colby Sprague says, Farquhar's borrowings did not constitute plagiarism "in its coarser or burglarious forms," but even a free adaptation was unusual for Farquhar. In fact, although there are specific

borrowed passages, Farquhar diverged from Fletcher's play quite liberally. He reduced the cast from twelve characters to eight by omitting some characters and combining others; the characters' names, other than Mirabel, Oriana, and Dugard (based on de Gard), are also different. After the first two acts, the play takes on its own shape. In a period when adaptations and translations were the norm, Farquhar tried only one of each, and these two plays in very rapid succession. Farquhar was apparently unable to rein in his creativity; the final two acts are highly original.

The plot centers on Oriana's pursuit of Mirabel. The rakish young man, skittish after contracting to marry her, has fled the country and left her faithfully waiting for his return. His doting father has become the guardian of both Oriana and her madcap friend Bisarre. As the play opens, Mirabel has just returned to Paris, to his father's delight and Oriana's keen anticipation. However, he prefers to remain single and profligate and to avoid marriage as though it were the noose. Oriana executes a variety of tricks to win him over, but in each instance her ruse is discovered before she succeeds. First she pretends to have a Spanish lover (Old Mirabel in disguise) in order to stir his jealousy. Next she claims to have taken vows as a nun; just as Mirabel kneels to her in adoration mixed with awe, Old Mirabel comes looking for the "Counterfeit Nun"; after that she pretends madness, but once she reveals her plot to Mirabel, he reneges yet again on his vows. Finally, Oriana poses as a servant boy sent to Mirabel by his uncle in Picardy, and in that disguise she watches him succumb to the fatal charms of the wicked Lamorce. When Lamorce lures him to her lodgings to be robbed and murdered by four bravoes, Oriana attends him, pretends she will fetch wine, and runs for help, thus rescuing him and winning his everlasting gratitude–and his hand in marriage. Farquhar claimed this incident was based on an adventure of Alexis Henri, chevalier de Chastillon, but scholars have conjectured that he himself was the hero of the original. Actually, he probably invented it. The romance between Mirabel and the determined Oriana progresses through clever and often witty dialogue; Oriana's inventiveness and enthusiasm prove quite engaging; far from a sentimental heroine to be rescued by the man she loves, she rescues him.

In the subplot Mirabel's friend Duretete, whose "plaguey bashfulness" makes him painfully awkward at courtship, suffers at the hand of the playful Bisarre. She leads him a merry chase—making him act foolish and in general dance to her tune until he learns to enjoy the game and give as well as take. They do not speak of love, but throughout their quirky, playful courtship, they discover genuine affection, and by play's end, they as well as Oriana and Mirabel are headed for matrimony—although they have not yet admitted it.

In this play as in most of his others, Farquhar created flesh-and-blood men and women. The superhuman rakes and heroines of earlier Restoration playwrights had been replaced by characters who actually displayed some interest in marriage as a permanent context for love, although they seldom directly admitted it in dialogue. Farquhar excelled at creating men and women who seem real and even familiar. With Robert Wilks, his Sir Harry, taking the role of Mirabel and Jane Rogers performing Oriana, the fondness for lovably extravagant characters, who could be brave at war but silly at courtship, continued.

The play probably opened in February 1702; the second edition of *Love and Business* was advertised at the end of the month as the work of the author of *The Inconstant*, so it had certainly opened before then. The premiere was disrupted when the prologuist made some shocking impromptu additions and was greeted by noisy contempt from the audience. Nevertheless, *The Inconstant* must have been received favorably, because it played at least six nights. It might well have run longer during its first season had not King William died on 8 March; the theaters remained dark until after Queen Anne's coronation on 23 April. The theater tunes were published 5 March, and the quarto of the play on 11 March.

After the first season, the comedy remained dormant for fourteen years; Lincoln's Inn Fields then revived it for three nights; after another seven years, Drury Lane picked it up for three nights. Later, in the 1730s, the popularity of *The Inconstant* accelerated; at least 123 more performances occurred in London by the end of the century, and the comedy remained in the repertory throughout the nineteenth century. The German playwright Karl Lessing based his play *Der Wildfang* on it. Its durability proved extraordinary, given its modest beginning.

Predictably, critics damned the play even before opening night, carping both that Farquhar borrowed from Fletcher and that he did not borrow carefully enough. Throughout the nineteenth century, critics either praised *The Inconstant* (William Hazlitt) or scorned it as inferior to Fletcher (Leigh Hunt). Twentieth-century critics have tended to look at it primarily as an adaptation, despite the fact that the last acts were decidedly original. In the twentieth century, it has not been considered one of Farquhar's major plays.

The following fall Farquhar was back at Drury Lane, writing *The Twin-Rivals*, which opened on 14 December 1702. During the course of the fall, he also wrote a prologue for Francis Manning's *All for the Better* and an epilogue for Charles Gildon's *The Patriot: or, The Italian Conspiracy*. There is no evidence that Manning had any connection with Farquhar, and Gildon could be considered an antagonist. The prologues of two of Gildon's plays had attacked *The Constant Couple*, and he was probably the author of *A Comparison Between the Two Stages* (1702), which also condemned Farquhar's work. Farquhar obviously agreed to write the prologue and epilogue because of his loyalty to the Drury Lane company and particularly his friend Wilks, who performed in both plays.

But his primary attention was focused on a new comedy, in which he veered in a totally different direction from his earlier work. Perhaps influenced by the success of Richard Steele's impressively successful humane comedy *The Funeral* the previous season, he created a melodramatic main plot of a young hero blocked from his inheritance by a genuinely wicked person who poses a serious threat to the well-being of the hero. In both *The Funeral* and *The Twin-Rivals* shoddy lawyers attempt to misrepresent the will of a deceased person for personal gain. Each play has two love plots, one involving the threatened hero and a chaste and serious-minded lady and the other his comrade in arms and a lighthearted girl. Each play also contains an attempted rape masterminded by a greedy woman. Although no debt to Steele can be proved, clearly the theater had felt the first effects of a new kind of sententious and sometimes sentimental comedy for which Steele was largely responsible. Nevertheless, Charles A. Stonehill was right to recognize *The Twin-Rivals* as "a play of great originality," despite the comparisons that critics over the years have made to a vast variety of earlier plays from Ben Jonson's *Volpone* (1606) to Howard's *The Committee* (1662) to Shakespeare's *Richard III* (circa 1601-1602).

Trueman rescuing Aurelia, while Constance–saved from the younger, hunchbacked Wou'dbe twin–
is reunited with his elder brother; illustration by E. Knight for the conclusion of The Twin-Rivals
(from the 1711 edition of Farquhar's works)

The play pits the good, noble, handsome natural heir Elder Wou'dbe against his churlish, evil, hunchbacked but somewhat humorous twin, Young Wou'dbe, who is determined to usurp his brother's rightful inheritance. When their father dies, the wicked brother plots, buys the compliance of scoundrels, then takes physical possession of his father's estate. His friend Richmore, equally duplicitous, got the fair Clelia pregnant, but then grew determined to escape responsibility for the child. Despite the fact that only four years earlier Roebuck in *Love and a Bottle* had suffered no authorial wrath for his treatment of his cast mistress, Trudge, Richmore seems despicable

for taking advantage of a young girl's adoration and then abandoning her to the ministrations of the shady midwife / bawd Midnight. Young Wou'dbe, having taken over his father's estate, affects the role of beau, with the help of grasping accomplices such as his father's steward, Clearaccount, and Midnight, who had presided at the twins' births and later served as his bawd. She will abet Young Wou'dbe's scheme by helping him forge a letter describing his brother's death in a German duel, then by lying about the order of the twins' births. She will also serve as midwife for Clelia and Richmore's baby, and help Richmore seduce Aurelia. Midnight, incidentally, was played by the comedian William Bullock and must have been an altogether unsavory–but funny–character on stage.

Constance and her cousin Aurelia are enamored of Elder Wou'dbe and his faithful friend Trueman, who aspires to marry Clelia. In act 3 Elder Wou'dbe arrives home from his travels, eager to find Constance. He brings with him his simple but loyal Irish servant, Teague. Upon arrival he discovers he has lost both his father and his birthright. He happens upon Constance weeping over his supposed death, and in this discovery scene the emotion at finding a supposedly dead lover alive (unlike the comparable scene in *Sir Harry Wildair*) evokes exclamations about virtue that could attract the listening angels, and passion that would bear the lovers like whirlwinds into each other's arms. When the elder twin attempts to claim his rightful inheritance, he is temporarily bested by his wicked brother, with the help of Clearaccount and Midnight, both of whom expect exorbitant recompense for their lies. When Elder Wou'dbe draws his sword to protect Teague, he is hauled off to jail. Trueman, disguised as a constable, rushes to Midnight's house, where he rescues Aurelia from Richmore's plot to seduce her there. By play's end all the wrongs are righted: Elder Wou'dbe has both his patrimony and his bride, Constance; Trueman has forced Richmore to marry the pregnant Clelia; Trueman and Aurelia have decided to marry; and all the perfidy has been discovered.

The Twin-Rivals, Farquhar's one foray into serious and sententious comedy, differs from all his other works. Although the plot still pivots on mistaken identity, trickery, and disguises, it centers on fraternal jealousy, threat of miscarried inheritance, cruel seduction, desertion, and rape. The characters face real dangers, and the perpetrators of the various crimes against them are truly despicable, although some are also still amusing. The stakes are very high; the possibility for miscarriage of justice strong. The play points to real and important social issues, with detachment that never belies the seriousness of the work. The play is far more closely related to Steele's *The Funeral* or *The Conscious Lovers* (1722) or to Colley Cibber's *Love's Last Shift* (1696) than to *Love and a Bottle. The Twin-Rivals* must be considered experimental, an attempt to deal with the new comedy created by Steele and Cibber, burdened with morally ideal characters and real villains, and filled with rhetorically moralistic dialogue. Farquhar, aware of the impact of Jeremy

Collier's *Short View of the Immorality and Prophaneness of the English Stage* (1699), intentionally tried to write a play according to its moralistic strictures.

Even so, the comedy met immediate criticism for immorality. In the preface to the printed work, Farquhar said that the "most material Objection against this Play, is the importance of the Subject, which necessarily leads into Sentiments too grave for Diversion, and supposes Vices too great for Comedy to Punish." The prevailing view was that comedy should ridicule folly and leave the punishment of vice for tragedy. But what, asks Farquhar, "if there be a middle sort of Wickedness, too high for the *Sock,* and too low for the *Buskin,* is there any reason that it shou'd go unpunish'd?" If, according to Farquhar, the characters are not elevated enough in stature for the heroic, "they must of necessity drop into Comedy." As well as Farquhar defended his play, he did not continue to write sentimental comedies after this one. Perhaps it was because the critics treated it so harshly.

There is no clear evidence of the length of the first run. Most critics and biographers indicate the play had a substantial run. Thomas Wilkes claimed it ran thirteen nights, but Farquhar complained that the galleries were thin. This time the premiere was disrupted by a duel on stage between two members of the audience, one of whom was wounded. Whether this affected the first run is hard to say. First published on 29 December 1702, the play disappeared from the stage for fourteen years, but was revived in 1716-1717, and ran regularly thereafter. Regardless of what critics thought, Farquhar continued to have the knack for holding an audience.

From the time Bernard Lintot bought the copyright for *The Twin-Rivals* on 22 December 1702 until he purchased the copyright for *The Recruiting Officer* on 12 February 1706, Farquhar disappeared from the theatrical scene. A fourth edition of the farce *The Constant Couple* and the Dublin edition of *The Stage-Coach* appeared in 1704; the London edition of the farce was published in 1705; but no new plays, prologues, or epilogues by Farquhar were advertised in London. What we know about these years is limited to information about his marriage and his military career.

Farquhar by all accounts had numerous amatory adventures while successfully avoiding the altar. He listed among his conquests some of the most interesting women of his time, including the famous actress Anne Oldfield and the playwrights Catharine Trotter (later Cockburn) and Susanna Carroll (later Centlivre). The time-honored tradition is that Farquhar first heard Oldfield read Beaumont and Fletcher's *The Scornful Lady* (circa 1615) behind the bar in her aunt's Mitre Tavern in St. James's Market and declared she should be an actress; this chance encounter allegedly led to Sir John Vanbrugh's signing her to act. Biographers have inferred broadly from Farquhar's extant published letters that he wrote of Oldfield as Penelope in *Love and Business* and Chloe in *Letters of Wit, Politicks and Morality;* that he himself often used the pseudonym Damon, as in the series of letters to Susanna Carroll, the Astraea of *Letters of Wit, Politicks and Morality;* and that the published letters were genuine expressions of fact and feelings in his various affairs. The letters are, in fact, highly artificial and carefully sequenced for publication, but at least some autobiographical detail can be found in them, for example, the references to his bouts of fever and the painful swelling in his extremities. If the biographer's catalogue of his amours is far from complete and by no means reliable, the general conviction that he was prodigiously successful with women can be found in many contemporary sources. His good looks, his wit, his flair and dash, and his success in the theater must have contributed to his amours, particularly with actresses and playwrights.

Knowing of his conquests, people were astounded when he chose to marry Margaret Pemell, an army widow with three children. He was about twenty-five; she had a son who was old enough to join the army a few years later. The unproved but persistent story is that he hoped to salvage his fortune by marrying a wealthy woman, and she wanted so desperately to marry him that she pretended to riches until after the ceremony. However, if the widow Pemell was the recipient of the letter in *Love and Business* dated 23 October 1700 from The Hague, as seems possible, Farquhar was at that point arguing her case for a royal pension with the king's men in Holland and, therefore, could scarce have believed her wealthy. Whatever the reasons, to everyone's amazement and his detractors' amusement, Farquhar married her, probably in 1703 but at least by 1704. Scholars and wits have agreed that he remained a faithful husband and cared for her children until his death in 1707. He also apparently fathered two daughters. One of his great

worries at death was leaving "two helpless girls," whom his friend Wilks helped and for whose support Margaret Farquhar petitioned the queen. These daughters later received the profits from benefits of *The Recruiting Officer, The Beaux Stratagem,* and other plays, the two of them until 1737 and a single daughter as late as 1750. Margaret Farquhar was preoccupied with her financial situation; she constantly sought reparation for her first husband's death in the army, and when Farquhar also died, she redoubled her efforts to receive patronage.

Perhaps the necessity of supporting his new bride and her three children encouraged Farquhar to leave the stage for military pursuits. He acquired a lieutenant's commission, probably in March 1704, through either James Butler, duke of Ormonde, or Charles Boyle, earl of Orrery, according to Robert John Jordan. Since the Irish treasury was out of funds, he probably began his work as a recruiting officer in mid June. Jordan believes that his service in Shrewsbury, the setting of *The Recruiting Officer,* may well have occurred before he was garrisoned in Dublin in spring 1705.

The early recruiting days hurt rather than helped Farquhar's financial condition, although recruiting might have been a lucrative assignment. The army was notoriously negligent in providing sufficient levy money; subsistence funds were either late or nonexistent. If recruits defected, the officers had to recompence the levy money. Therefore, many of the officers ended up paying out of their own pockets rather than profiting. Farquhar must have been one of these unfortunates. After his death Orrery, arguing for a pension for Margaret, wrote of Farquhar's having recruited "to the great prejudice of his family."

When the regiment was sent to Dublin in spring 1705, Farquhar may well have stayed with his brother, a bookseller, since no barracks were provided. The regiment moved on to an encampment in Kildare in June, and Farquhar probably left to recruit in Lichfield, the site of *The Beaux Stratagem,* after 23 October.

Little is known of his military career. There is some confusion about whether he gave up his commission with the understanding that Ormonde would shortly give him a captaincy; some rather ambiguous evidence sustains that tale. Some say he actually died of a broken heart after the captaincy did not materialize. Whether he actually relinquished his commission before he was ready to leave the army and return to play writ-

Serjeant Kite in the marketplace at Shrewsbury, illustration by E. Knight for act 1, scene 1, of The Recruiting Officer *(from the 1711 edition of Farquhar's works)*

ing is by no means clear. Nevertheless, we can assume that the military stint did little to improve his financial situation.

Sometime between November and March, Farquhar got permission from Ormonde to return to his old theater, Smock Alley, to perform Sir Harry Wildair in *The Constant Couple*. The interest in his performance was intense enough to yield one hundred pounds rather than the usual fifty pounds one might expect at Smock Alley. Despite the financial success, Farquhar's acting was poor enough that "his friends blushed to see him act it."

He was back in London by 12 February 1706, when he signed an agreement for Lintot to publish *The Recruiting Officer*, which appeared in print on or before 25 April. Whether he had drafted the new comedy during his military service is unknown, but it is striking that the play contains no references to public events later than the victory at Blenheim in August 1704. Both the military satire and the characters clearly date from his service. The models for Ballance, Silvia, Kite, and perhaps Worthy and Melinda were acquaintances during his time in Shrewsbury. The satirical commentary on the cheats of recruiting and other aspects of military life are blended with good-natured courtship comedy; critics have perceived a freshness and energy that they attribute to the country air of Farquhar's military sojourn outside London.

The play opens on the humorous low scene in which the hilariously duplicitous Serjeant Kite tricks and cajoles country louts to join Her Majesty's Service. Kite serves the hero, Captain Plume, who relies on Kite not only for successful recruiting but for marrying the local wenches the captain has seduced and impregnated. Meanwhile Plume courts Silvia, the daughter of a local justice of the peace, proclaiming clearly dishonorable intentions to protect his reputation as a rake; his friend Worthy similarly tries to seduce Melinda. When, however, Melinda inherits twenty thousand pounds and Silvia's brother dies, leaving her the heir to her father's estate, the young philanderers confront a suddenly changed situation. Melinda, angered by Worthy's eager willingness to set her up as a mistress, flirts with everyone. Justice Ballance ships Silvia off to the country to hide her from Plume, who meanwhile dallies with Rose, sister of one of his loutish recruits. Plume also decides, on a jesting wager with Worthy, to vie with the miles gloriosus Captain Brazen for Melinda's affections. The plots interweave through disguise, trickery, and energetic action; Silvia poses as young Jack Wilfull, recruited by Plume, and she sleeps with Rose to prevent his doing so; Kite turns fortune teller for potential recruits, and Melinda makes predictions to influence their behavior; Plume and Brazen have an off-handed duel over Melinda. "Wilfull" is brought before the justice (her father), and when he detects her ruse, she is sentenced to matrimony with Plume. Melinda agrees to marry Worthy, and Brazen is consoled with Plume's twenty recruits, since now Plume will resign his commission to stay with his wife and "raise Recruits the Matrimonial Way."

The comedy opened at Drury Lane on 8 April 1706. Oddly enough, the advertisements for that season did not mention that Farquhar was the author; his name clearly no longer had the power that followed his success with *The Constant Couple*. The casting was predictable, with Wilks playing Plume, as he had played Sir Harry, Mirabel, and Elder Wou'dbe; Cibber played Brazen; Oldfield was Silvia; and the comedians Bullock and Norris played bumpkin recruits to Richard Estcourt's exceedingly popular Kite. The comedy was an immediate hit. It ran ten times the first season; had it opened in October rather

than April, it might well have broken performance records.

By the next season, 1706-1707, most of the original cast had moved to the Queen's Theatre at the Haymarket; the play ran nine times at that house, with Pack substituting for Estcourt. Drury Lane countered with twelve performances, almost totally recast but with the original Estcourt as Kite.

Throughout the century, *The Recruiting Officer* remained one of the most popular English plays, with 512 performances in London and many more in England, Ireland, and the Colonies. It reached its greatest popularity at mid century, with more than 100 London performances in 1740-1750. If critics were unwilling to praise *The Recruiting Officer*, at least they grudgingly admitted that it played well on stage. Steele tended to attribute Farquhar's success to the acting, but some critics believed that Farquhar created a pleasurable naturalness in his characters and ease in dialogue. People flocked to the theater, and critics and playwrights continued to regret the poor taste of audiences that ignored Farquhar's disrespect for the tenets of classicism.

Farquhar returned from military service to the theater with no new concepts of drama, but rather with a surer artistry in fashioning old-style materials into a comedy of unusual quality. No revolutionary, he re-energized familiar patterns: two love plots plus a comic echo; a heroine disguised as a boy, a device he had used three times before; a rakish hero finally domesticated by a lively and spirited girl; a witty and crafty comic servant; a group of buffoons; intricate and unbelievable plots merged with sensitive and believable dialogue. Farquhar had learned to create lovers who were friends, comrades in the absurdities of sexual pursuit, equally well armed with wit, good humor, a certain toughness, and zestful determination to win at the game of life. He may have gotten his first hint of how to create believable heroines from Shakespeare, but he added his own contemporary touch, and in so doing, he created women who spoke of the issues of their day, the pains and pleasures of the matrimonial game. His heroines perhaps made possible the kind of flawed, humane heroes that Wilks played so well—men who play at the game of irresponsible sexuality but who adjust to the prospect of marriage as though they are more than willing to be trapped into it. Farquhar did not break new ground in *The Recruiting Officer*, but he provided a splendid example of the genre that he had so greatly influenced with *The Constant Couple*.

He wrote a prologue for Wilks for the opening of the new Queen's Theatre in the Haymarket in October and another for Susanna Centlivre's new play *The Platonick Lady,* which opened at the new theater the following month. Second and third editions of *The Recruiting Officer,* the second bearing very distinctive variants from the April edition, were published in October and December.

He may have been working on his final masterpiece, *The Beaux Stratagem,* during the summer, fall, and winter, but tradition has held the poignantly romantic view that he wrote the comedy within a mere six weeks, "with a settled Sickness upon him all the time; nay, he even perceiv'd the Approaches of Death, e'er he had finish'd the second Act" ("Memoirs," published with *The Stage-Coach* in 1735). Thomas Wilkes gives an even more dramatic account: Robert Wilks, having missed seeing Farquhar at the theater for a couple of months, discovered he had left his lodgings in York Buildings and found him at a new address in St. Martin's Lane, living miserably in a back garret, greatly distressed over his lost commission. Wilks urged him to write a play and left some money to tide his friend over. Farquhar, ill as he was, finished the play in six weeks, writing most of it in bed. Wilks, according to the account, visited Farquhar on the night of the premiere and reported the play's success, jestingly adding that Mrs. Oldfield, who played Mrs. Sullen, complained that he had used her character too loosely by giving her to the hero without a proper divorce. Farquhar replied that he would get a divorce and marry her and then "she shall be a real Widow in less than a fortnight."

The tale is, of course, romanticized and inaccurate in detail. But Farquhar's perennially fragile health was declining, and his best and brightest, most good-natured comedy may well have been written in whole or in part during feverish weeks in bed. Farquhar sold the copyright to Lintot on 27 January 1707, and the *Muses Mercury* for that month, actually published in February, announced that Farquhar had finished a new comedy. On 7 February the *Daily Courant* announced that his comedy, "The Broken Beaux," would speedily be acted and then published by Lintot. The play could have been written in six weeks, but the story is probably exaggerated.

Once again Farquhar created a highly original play from the traditional materials of British comedy. Although there are analogues for certain characters and actions in other plays, one cannot label them borrowings. A motif here, a character trait there, but the mixture is that of a mind at work on the materials of contemporary culture. Perhaps the most striking similarity is to Steele's *The Lying Lover* (1703), in which two buddies pose as master and servant while searching for a wife. W. J. Lawrence and Peter Kavanagh have looked toward living models for some of the comic characters, but their suggestions are incapable of proof.

Clearly two literary sources did influence Farquhar. First is a succession of witty catechisms such as *The Beaux Catechism* and *The Ladies Catechism* (both 1703), published as pamphlets, that prefigure Cherry's catechism scene. Second and far more important, Farquhar obviously knew Milton's *Doctrine and Discipline of Divorce* (1643), for his dialogue on divorce clearly reflects Milton's views. One might speculate on why the topic of divorce interested the playwright, but there is no indication that he had personal reasons to study the subject. Rather, it was a subject of great topical interest in London, fed by the sensational divorce trial of Charles Gerard, earl of Macclesfield, whose divorced wife married Henry Brett, to whom Farquhar dedicated *The Twin-Rivals.* Moreover, Farquhar's final play rounded out the complex and comprehensive set of observations on courtship and marriage that inform his entire canon.

The Beaux Stratagem introduces two very attractive "Gentlemen of broken Fortunes," who firmly believe that "there is no Scandal like Rags, nor any Crime so shameful as Poverty." Having frittered away their money, they must now look to marriage and security. They are scouring the countryside for rich brides, posing as master and servant, reversing their roles at each new town. They arrive in Bonniface's inn in Lichfield, headquarters not only for coach passengers looking for lodging but also for the local highwaymen. Archer, playing servant, immediately begins seducing the innkeeper's daughter Cherry, who is dazzled by his witty lovemaking but never forgetful of her own need to escape the inn for a better life. The two adventurers go to church to look over the local ladies, and Aimwell immediately spots Dorinda, the daughter of Lady Bountiful, a gentlewoman who generously aids and ministers to all the poor and sick of the county. Dorinda's sister-in-law, Mrs. Sullen, is a beautiful and intelligent sophisticate from London, sen-

Aimwell pretending to be ill at Lady Bountiful's house, illustration by E. Knight for act 4, scene 1, of The Beaux Stratagem *(from the 1711 edition of Farquhar's works)*

tenced to the miseries of marriage with a dull, drunken country lout.

Aimwell feigns a swoon near Lady Bountiful's house as a ruse to gain entrance; as the good old woman fusses about with hartshorn drops and cordials, Aimwell makes advances to Dorinda, and his supposed valet, Archer, begins his eloquently literary courtship of Mrs. Sullen.

Mrs. Sullen, the most complex and interesting of all Farquhar's heroines, is a mixture of good instincts and human foibles. She loves Dorinda, and when she learns Dorinda loves Aimwell, she is joyous–and bursts into tears over her own unhappiness. She experiences a power-

ful sexual attraction to Archer, despite her marital vows and her belief that he is a mere servant; even though she has strength of character, she is in real danger of seduction until his onslaught is interrupted by the arrival of a gang of highwaymen. If Aimwell and Dorinda feel simple puppy love, marred only by his fortune-hunting motivation, Archer and Mrs. Sullen exemplify the real difficulties of a social world in which marriage is a matter of financial arrangements, and escape from a bad marriage almost impossible.

The denouement is suitably happy if far from verisimilitudinous. Cherry reveals to Aimwell the highwaymen's plans to rob Lady Bountiful's house, and the two adventurers rush to the ladies' defense. During the scuffle with the highwaymen, Archer is wounded, giving Lady Bountiful someone else to cluck over with her lint and plaster while Aimwell completes his courtship of Dorinda. Mrs. Sullen's brother, Sir Charles Freeman, who happens to be Archer's friend, arrives; Archer believes their ruse will be discovered and all lost. But Sir Charles brings word that Aimwell's brother has died (yet another brother conveniently dispatched by Farquhar), and the impecunious wanderer is now the wealthy Viscount Aimwell, obviously sufficiently well endowed to marry Dorinda. The Sullens decide to divorce by a ceremony of common consent, avowing their incompatibility before all. Such a divorce was, of course, impossible since only parliamentary divorce or annulment could end a marriage, but Farquhar's audience seemed to accept the unrealistic separation as though it could happen. Since Sullen refuses to return his wife's dowry, Aimwell gives Archer ten thousand pounds, with which he pays Mrs. Sullen's portion. Dorinda will take care of Cherry, who can leave her loathsome employment at her father's inn, and life in the country will settle down as the happy couples return to London. The impossibility of the ending is covered by a dance, and the final tag lines conjecture on who is happiest, the couples who have joined or those who have separated. The play ends with the legally inaccurate Miltonic sentiment that "Consent, if mutual, saves the Lawyer's Fee, / Consent is Law enough to set you free."

Once the working title "The Broken Beaux" was dropped, the play was consistently called *The Stratagem* in the theater although it was published as *The Beaux Stratagem*. An unusually strong advertising campaign was mounted for the first run; the *Daily Courant* contained twenty-nine advertisements for the twelve performances from 8 March 1707 until the end of the season. The play opened amid a flurry of performances of Farquhar's plays in March 1707; thirteen of the thirty-three comedies performed in London that month were his, including four performances of *The Recruiting Officer* at Drury Lane and one of *The Constant Couple* at the Queen's Theatre. Farquhar received three benefits, money he must have desperately needed given the state of his health; the third preceded his death by only a month.

The Beaux Stratagem was not only immediately successful but perennially popular. It ran 632 times in London during the eighteenth century, including 220 performances in 1730-1750.

Of those performances, 194 were benefits, including two for his daughters. Since popular plays were selected to increase the take at benefits, the large number indicates how successfully *The Stratagem* continued to attract audiences. Moreover, it played every single season except one, 1795-1796. Its popularity lasted in the nineteenth century, and even now it is probably Farquhar's most frequently performed play.

From the beginning, critics liked Farquhar's final play; the jealousy and spitefulness that filled the commentary on his earlier plays was muted, perhaps by knowledge of his illness. In his final comedy Farquhar achieved his finest work. The play is lively, good natured, and brisk yet sensitively underlaid with a perceptive exploration of the most important of human passions and pains. The characters are drawn with exquisite precision, from the comic servant Scrub to the complex Mrs. Sullen. The plot was Farquhar's best. The interweaving of the two love plots and the robbery attempt in act 5 unites the plot strands as adeptly as any play of the period; in that final act, Farquhar balances broadly humorous and somewhat frivolous action with actual danger—Archer is, after all, wounded. But in this comedy even the robbery seems inconsequential compared to the risks of ordinary married life. The play maintains an extraordinary tone which blends the irresponsibility of courtship with full awareness of the seriousness of married life.

It is hard to believe that this genuinely amusing and touching play was written by a twenty-nine or thirty-year-old man, so ill that he died only two and a half months after it opened. The cheerful tone, the careful consideration of the plot, the telling characterizations and witty dialogue bespeak vitality, not the approach of death. But on 23 May, George Farquhar was buried at St. Martin's-in-the-Fields. *The Muses Mercury* (May 1707) lamented,

> All that love Comedy will be sorry to hear of the Death of Mr. Farquhar, whose two last Plays had something in them that was truly humorous and diverting. 'Tis true that Criticks will not allow any Part of them to be regular; but Mr. Farquhar had a Genius for Comedy, of which one may say, that it was rather above Rules than below them.... In a word, his Plays have in them the *toute ensemble*, as the Painters phrase it, a certain Air of Novelty and Mirth, which pleas'd the Audience every time they were represented: And such as love to laugh at the Theatre, will probably miss him more than they now imagine.

AN

EPILOGUE,

Defign'd to be fpoke in the Beaux Stratagem.

IF to our Play Your Judgment can't be kind,
    Let its expiring Author Pity find.
Survey his mournful Cafe with melting Eyes,
Nor let the Bard be dam'd before he dies.
Forbear you Fair on his laft Scene to frown,
But his true Exit with a Plaudit Crown;
Then fhall the dying Poet ceafe to Fear,
The dreadful Knell, while your Applaufe he hears.
At Leuctra *fo, the Conqu'ring* Theban *dy'd,*
Claim'd his Friend's Praifes, but their Tears deny'd:
Pleas'd in the Pangs of Death he greatly Thought
Conqueft with lofs of Life but cheaply bought.
The Difference this, the Greek was one wou'd fight
As brave, tho' not fo gay as Serjeant Kite;
Ye Sons of Will's *what's that to thofe who write?*
To Thebes *alone the Grecian ow'd his Bays,*
You may the Bard above the Hero raife,
Since yours is greater than Athenian *Praife.*

Dramatis

The epilogue published in the first edition of The Beaux Stratagem *refers to Farquhar's imminent death.*

Wilks presumably helped his friend's widow and two daughters, and the theater did not forget them. Performances benefited Farquhar's daughters on various occasions, as late as 1750. The thirty pounds he got from Lintot for the copyright in January 1707 may well have been used up before the edition appeared on 27 March; although at least fifty editions were published in England, Ireland, and Scotland during the century, Farquhar's family would not have profited beyond the original payment.

His widow, Margaret, continued to petition the queen for patronage, but she also chose to make money on what may have been the last bit of his writing she could find. Farquhar supposedly burned all his manuscripts before he died, but at least one escaped. He had written an epic on the Battle of Barcellona, in which he praised Charles Mordaunt, earl of Peterborough, com-

mander-in-chief of the expeditionary force that went to Spain in spring 1705 to support the claim of the throne of Spain. Unfortunately, the allied military commanders squabbled among themselves and bumbled through less than glorious maneuvers. Farquhar knew an extraordinary amount about the expedition; his description of the leaders' quarrels and the battles matches not only published accounts but also private letters dispatched home to the war office from the front. Unfortunately, Mordaunt fell from Queen Anne's favor, and Farquhar never published the epic; had he chosen to have it printed before he died, he probably would have received no patronage. But after Farquhar's death Peterborough's fortunes rose again, and Margaret Farquhar seized the opportunity to publish *Barcellona* posthumously. Peterborough may have rewarded her, and perhaps the queen did, too, for Margaret wrote to Robert Harley that "her Majesty was pleased to give me ten guineas for the book which you did me the honor to receive." Critics do not even bother to comment on this embarrassing work.

Throughout the century Farquhar's plays were performed and republished. Even today *The Recruiting Officer* and *The Beaux Stratagem* appear with relative frequency. Farquhar produced, in only eight and a half years, eight plays, a miscellany, a novella, an essay on comedy, poems, songs, prologues, epilogues, and an epic. He became the most popular playwright on the English stage, and his comedies still play as well or better than those of his contemporaries. As spectacularly successful as he was on stage, he was never financially comfortable, and he died full of worry about money to support his children. Yet, during his few theatrical years in London, he created plays of extraordinary appeal. He was not a daring innovator—nor were his contemporaries—and yet he broke new ground in creating humanly believable characters, including flawed and often funny heroes and heroines and comic characters that have exuberance, vitality, and individuality. Moreover, his plays remained the most popular on the London stage for decade after decade. As *Pasquin*, no. 75, phrased it in 1723, "Had this Gentleman been as happy in his Fortune as he was in his Genius, he might perhaps have been thought one of those Poetick Comets which are seen scarce in an Age."

Bibliography:

Eugene Nelson James, *George Farquhar, A Reference Guide* (Boston: G. K. Hall, 1986).

Biographies:

William Rufus Chetwood, *The British Theatre, Containing the Lives of the English Dramatic Poets* (Dublin: Peter Wilson, 1750);

Theophilus Cibber, *The Lives of the Poets of Great Britain and Ireland to the Time of Dean Swift*, 5 volumes (London: R. Griffiths, 1753);

David Erskine Baker, *The Companion to the Play-House*, 2 volumes (London: T. Becket & P. A. Dehondt, 1764); augmented and revised by Isaac Reed as *Biographia Dramatica*, 2 volumes (London: Printed for Rivingtons, 1782); augmented and revised again by Stephen Jones, 3 volumes (London: Hurst, Rees, Orme & Brown, 1812);

James R. Sutherland, "New Light on George Farquhar," letter, *Times Literary Supplement*, 6 March 1937, p. 171;

Peter Kavanagh, "George Farquhar," letter, *Times Literary Supplement*, 10 February 1945, p. 72;

Willard Connely, *Young George Farquhar, The Restoration Drama at Twilight* (London: Cassell, 1949);

Robert John Jordan, "George Farquhar's Military Career," *Huntington Library Quarterly*, 37 (May 1974): 251-264.

References:

Jackson Cope, "*The Constant Couple:* Farquhar's Four-Plays-in-One," *ELH*, 41 (Winter 1974): 477-493;

Michael Cordner, Introduction to *The Beaux' Stratagem*, edited by Cordner, The New Mermaids (London: Benn, 1976; New York: Norton, 1976);

Peter Dixon, Introduction to *The Recruiting Officer*, edited by Dixon, The Revels Plays (Manchester: Manchester University Press, 1986);

A. J. Farmer, *George Farquhar* (London: Longmans, Green, 1966);

Charles N. Fifer, Introduction to *The Beaux' Stratagem*, edited by Fifer, Regents Restoration Drama Series (Lincoln: University of Nebraska Press, 1977);

Verlyn Flieger, "Notes on the Titling of George Farquhar's 'The Beaux Stratagem,'" *Notes & Queries*, new series 26 (February 1979): 21-23;

W. Heldt, "Fletcher's *Wild-Goose Chase* and Farquhar's *Inconstant*," *Neophilogus*, 3 (1917): 144-148;

Robert D. Hume, *The Rakish Stage: Studies in English Drama, 1660-1800* (Carbondale: Southern Illinois University Press, 1983);

Eugene Nelson James, "The Burlesque of Restoration Comedy in *Love and a Bottle*," *Studies in English Literature, 1500-1900*, 5 (Summer 1965): 469-490;

James, *The Development of George Farquhar as a Comic Dramatist* (The Hague: Mouton, 1972);

Shirley Strum Kenny, "A Broadside Prologue by Farquhar," *Studies in Bibliography*, 25 (1972): 179-185;

Kenny, "Farquhar, Wilks, and Wildair; or, the Metamorphosis of the 'Fine Gentleman,'" *Philological Quarterly*, 57 (Winter 1978): 46-65;

Kenny, "George Farquhar and 'The Bus'ness of a Prologue,'" *Theatre Survey*, 19 (November 1978): 139-154;

Kenny, "The Mystery of Farquhar's *Stage-Coach* Reconsidered," *Studies in Bibliography,* 32 (1979): 219-236;

Kenny, "Perennial Favorites: Congreve, Vanbrugh, Cibber, Farquhar, and Steele," *Modern Philology,* 74 (1976): S4-S11 (Friedman Festschrift);

Kenny, "Songs in *Love and a Bottle,*" *Scriblerian,* 17 (Autumn 1984): 1-7;

Kenny, "Theatrical Warfare, 1695-1710," *Theatre Notebook,* 27 (Summer 1973): 130-145;

Martin A. Larson, "The Influence of Milton's Divorce Tracts on Farquhar's *Beaux' Stratagem,*" *PMLA,* 39 (March 1924): 174-178;

W. J. Lawrence, "Foigard in 'The Beaux' Stratagem,'" *Notes & Queries,* 9th series 11 (17 January 1903): 46-47;

Lawrence, "The Mystery of 'The Stage Coach,'" *Modern Language Review,* 27 (October 1932): 392-397;

Judith Milhous and Robert D. Hume, *Producible Interpretation: Eight English Plays 1675-1707* (Carbondale: Southern Illinois University Press, 1985), pp. 289-316;

Richard Morton and William M. Peterson, "The Jubilee of 1700 and Farquhar's 'The Constant Couple,'" *Notes & Queries,* 200 (1955): 521-525;

W. F. Prideaux, "The Recruiting Officer," *Notes & Queries,* 9th series 1 (26 March 1898): 241-242;

J. G. Robertson, "Lessing and Farquhar," *Modern Language Review,* 2 (October 1906): 56-59;

Sybil Rosenfeld, "Notes on *The Recruiting Officer,*" *Theatre Notebook,* 18 (Winter 1963-1964): 47-48;

John Ross, Introduction to *The Recruiting Officer,* edited by Ross, The New Mermaids (London: Benn, 1977; New York: Norton, 1977);

Eric Rothstein, "Farquhar's *Twin-Rivals* and the Reform of Comedy," *PMLA,* 79 (March 1964): 33-41;

Rothstein, *George Farquhar* (New York: Twayne, 1967);

D. Schmid, *George Farquhar, Sein Leben und Seine Original Dramen* (Vienna & Leipzig: Wilhelm Braumüller, 1904);

Michael Shugrue, Introduction to *The Recruiting Officer,* edited by Shugrue, Regents Restoration Drama Series (Lincoln: University of Nebraska Press, 1965);

Kaspar Spinner, *George Farquhar als Dramatiker* (Bern: Francke, 1956);

Louis A. Strauss, Preface to *A Discourse upon Comedy, The Recruiting Officer, and The Beaux Stratagem,* edited by Strauss (Boston & London: D. C. Heath, 1914).

Henry Fielding

(22 April 1707- 8 October 1754)

Paula R. Backscheider

University of Rochester

See also the Fielding entry in *DLB 39: British Novelists, 1660-1800.*

PLAY PRODUCTIONS: *Love in Several Masques,* London, Theatre Royal in Drury Lane, 16 February 1728;

The Temple Beau, or The Intriguing Sisters, London, Odell's Theatre in Ayliffe St., Goodman's Fields, 26 January 1730;

The Author's Farce, London, Little Theatre in the Hay-Market, 30 March 1730;

The Pleasures of the Town, London, Little Theatre in the Hay-Market, 20 April 1730;

Tom Thumb, London, Little Theatre in the Hay-Market, 24 April 1730;

Rape upon Rape, or The Justice Caught in his own Trap, London, Little Theatre in the Hay-Market, 23 June 1730; revived as *The Coffee-House Politician,* London, Little Theatre in the Hay-Market, 30 November 1730;

The Letter-Writers, or A New Way to Keep a Wife at Home, London, Little Theatre in the Hay-Market, 24 March 1731;

The Tragedy of Tragedies; or, The Life and Death of Tom Thumb the Great, London, Little Theatre in the Hay-Market, 24 March 1731;

The Welsh Opera, or the Grey Mare the Better Horse, London, Little Theatre in the Hay-Market, 22 April 1731; revised as *The Genuine Grub-Street Opera;* later revised as *The Grub-Street Opera* (neither version staged in Fielding's lifetime);

The Lottery, London, Theatre Royal in Drury Lane, 1 January 1732;

The Modern Husband, London, Theatre Royal in Drury Lane, 14 February 1732;

The Covent Garden Tragedy (Honours of Covent Garden), London, Theatre Royal in Drury Lane, 1 June 1732;

The Old Debauchees (also known as *The Debauchees, or The Jesuit Caught in his own Trap*), London, Theatre Royal in Drury Lane, 1 June 1732;

The Mock Doctor, or the Dumb Lady Cured, London, Theatre Royal in Drury Lane, 23 June 1732;

The Miser, London, Theatre Royal in Drury Lane, 17 February 1733;

Deborah, or A Wife for You All, London, Theatre Royal in Drury Lane, 6 April 1733;

The Intriguing Chambermaid, London, Theatre Royal in Drury Lane, 15 January 1734;

Don Quixote in England, London, Little Theatre in the Hay-Market, 5 April 1734;

An Old Man Taught Wisdom, or The Virgin Unmask'd, London, Theatre Royal in Drury Lane, 6 January 1735;

The Universal Gallant, or The Different Husbands, London, Theatre Royal in Drury Lane, 10 February 1735;

Pasquin, London, Little Theatre in the Hay-Market, 5 March 1736;

Tumble-Down Dick: or, Phaeton in the Suds, London, Little Theatre in the Hay-Market, 29 April 1736;

Eurydice, or The Devil Henpecked, London, Theatre Royal in Drury Lane, 19 February 1737;

The Historical Register for the Year 1736, London, Little Theatre in the Hay-Market, 21 March 1737;

Eurydice Hiss'd, or A Word to the Wise, London, Little Theatre in the Hay-Market, 13 April 1737;

Miss Lucy in Town, a Sequel to The Virgin Unmasked, revised by Garrick and perhaps others, London, Theatre Royal in Drury Lane, 6 May 1742;

The Wedding-Day, London, Theatre Royal in Drury Lane, 17 February 1743;

The Election, or Bribes on Both Sides, London, Theatre Royal in Covent Garden, 29 March 1749;

The Fathers; or, The Good Natured Man, reworked by David Garrick and Richard Sheridan, London, Theatre Royal in Drury Lane, 30 November 1778.

Henry Fielding (engraving by James Basire, based on a drawing by William Hogarth)

SELECTED BOOKS: *The Masquerade, A Poem. Inscribed to C---t H--d--g--r.... By Lemuel Gulliver, Poet Laureat to the King of Lilliput* (London: Printed & sold by J. Roberts & A. Dodd, 1728); modern edition, in *The Female Husband and Other Writings,* edited by Claude E. Jones, Liverpool University English Reprint Series (Liverpool: Liverpool University Press, 1960);

Love in Several Masques. A Comedy, as it is acted at the Theatre-Royal, by His Majesty's Servants (London: Printed for John Watts, 1728);

The Temple Beau. A Comedy. As it is Acted at the Theatre in Goodman's-Fields (London: Printed for J. Watts, 1730);

The Author's Farce; and The Pleasures of the Town. As Acted at the theatre in the Hay-Market, as Scriblerus Secundus (London: Printed for J. Roberts, 1730; revised edition, London: Printed for Watts, 1750);

Tom Thumb. A Tragedy. As it is Acted at the theatre in the theatre in Hay-Market (London: Printed & sold by J. Roberts, 1730);

Rape upon Rape; or, The Justice Caught in his own Trap A Comedy. As it is Acted at the Theatre in the Hay-Market (London: Printed for J. Watts, 1730); republished as *The Coffee-House Politician; or, The Justice Caught in his own Trap. A Comedy. As it is Acted at the Theatre Royal in Lincoln's Inn-Fields* (London: Printed for J. Watts, 1730);

The Letter-Writers; Or, a New Way to Keep a Wife at Home. A Farce, in Three Acts. As it is Acted at the Theatre in the Hay-Market, as Scriblerus Secundus (London: Printed & sold by J. Roberts, 1731);

The Tragedy of Tragedies; or The Life and Death of Tom Thumb the Great. As it is Acted at the Theatre in the Hay-Market. With the Annotations of H. Scriblerus Secundus (London: Printed & sold by J. Roberts, 1731);

The Welsh Opera: or, The Grey Mare the better Horse As it is Acted at the New Theatre in the Hay-Market, as Scriblerus Secundus (London: Printed for E. Rayner & sold by H. Cook, 1731); republished as *The Genuine Grub-Street Opera* (London: Printed & sold for the benefit of the Haymarket Comedians, 1731); republished as *The Grub-Street Opera* (London: Printed & sold by Roberts, 1731 [most likely printed by Andrew Millar in 1755]);

The Lottery: A Farce (London: Printed for J. Watts, 1732);

The Modern Husband. A Comedy. As it is Acted at the Theatre-Royal in Drury-Lane. By His Majesty's Servants (London: Printed for J. Watts, 1732);

The Old Debauchees. A Comedy. As it is Acted at the Theatre-Royal in Drury-Lane. By His Majesty's Servants. By the Author of The Modern Husband (London: Printed for J. W. & sold by J. Roberts, 1732);

The Covent-Garden Tragedy. As it is Acted at the Theatre-Royal in Drury-Lane. By His Majesty's Servants (London: Printed for J. Watts & sold by J. Roberts, 1732);

The Mock Doctor. or The Dumb Lady Cur'd. A Comedy. Done from Molière. As it is Acted at the Theatre-Royal in Drury-Lane, By His Majesty's Servants. With the Musick prefix'd to each Song (London: Printed for J. Watts, 1732);

The Miser. A Comedy. Taken from Platus and Molière. As it is Acted at the Theatre Royal in Drury-Lane, by His Majesty's Servants (London: Printed for J. Watts, 1733);

The Intriguing Chambermaid. A Comedy of Two Acts. As it is Acted at the Theatre-Royal in Drury-Lane, By His Majesty's Servants. Taken from the French of Regnard (London: Printed for J. Watts, 1734);

Don Quixote in England. A Comedy. As it is Acted at the New Theatre in the Hay-Market (London: Printed for J. Watts, 1734);

An Old Man taught Wisdom; or, The Virgin Unmask'd. A Farce. As it is Perform'd By His Majesty's Company of Comedians at the Theatre-Royal in Drury-Lane. With the musick prefix'd to each song (London: Printed for John Watts, 1735);

The Universal Gallant: or, The Different Husbands: A Comedy. As it is acted at the Theatre-Royal in Drury-Lane. By His Majesty's Servants (London: Printed for John Watts, 1735);

Pasquin. A Dramatick Satire on the Times: Being the Rehearsal of Two Plays, viz. a Comedy call'd, The Election; And a Tragedy call'd The Life and Death of Common-Sense. As it is Acted at the Theatre in the Hay-Market (London: Printed for J. Watts, 1736);

Tumble-Down Dick: or, Phaeton in the Suds. A Dramatick Entertainment of Walking, in Serious and Foolish Characters: Interlarded with Burlesque, Grotesque, Comick Interludes Call'd, Harlequin a Pick-Pocket. As it is Perform'd at the New Theatre in the Hay-Market. Being ('tis hop'd) the last Entertainment that will ever be exhibited on any Stage. Invented by the Ingenious Monsieur Sans Espirit. The Musick compos'd by the Harmonious Signior Warblerini. And the Scenes painted by the Prodigious Mynheer Van Bottom-Flat (London: Printed for J. Watts, 1736);

The Historical Register for the Year 1736. As it is Acted at the New Theatre in the Hay-Market. To which is added a very merry Tragedy, called Eurydice Hiss'd, or, A Word to the Wise (London: Printed & sold by J. Roberts, 1737);

The Champion: or, British Mercury, by Capt. Hercules Vinegar, nos. 1-158 by Fielding and James Ralph (London, 15 November 1739-15 November 1740); essays of nos. 1-94 (15 November 1739-19 June 1740); republished as *The Champion: Containing a Series of Papers, Humourous, Moral, Political, and Critical,* 2 volumes (London: Printed for J. Huggonson, 1741);

The Military History of Charles XII. King of Sweden, Written by the express Order of His Majesty, By M. Gustavus Adlerfeld. . . . Translated into English, translated by Fielding, 3 volumes (London: Printed for J. & P. Knapton, J. Hodges, A. Millar & J. Nourse, 1740);

Of True Greatness. An Epistle to the Right Honourable George Dodington Esq. (London: Printed for C. Corbett, 1741);

The Vernon-iad. Done into English, From the Original Greek of Homer. Lately found at Constantinople.

With Notes in usum, &c. Book the first (London: Printed for Charles Corbett, 1741);

An Apology for the Life of Mrs. Shamela Andrews. In which, the many notorious Falshoods and Misrepresentations of a Book called Pamela, are exposed and refuted; ... By Mr. Conny Keyber (London: Printed for A. Dodd, 1741);

The Crisis: A Sermon, on Revel. XIV. 9, 10, 11. Necessary to be preached in all the Churches in England, Wales, and Berwick upon Tweed, at or before the next General Election. Humbly inscribed to the Right Reverend the Bench of Bishops. By a Lover of his Country (London: Printed for A. Dodd, E. Nutt & H. Chappelle, 1741);

The History of Our Own Times, by a Society of Gentlemen, nos. 1-4 (15 January-5 March 1741; attributed to Fielding but not certainly his); modern edition, with an introduction by Thomas Lockwood (Delmar, N.Y.: Scholars' Facsimiles & Reprints, 1986);

The Opposition. A Vision (London: Printed for T. Cooper, 1742 [i.e. 1741]);

The History of the Adventures of Joseph Andrews, and of his Friend Mr. Abraham Adams. Written in Imitation of The Manner of Cervantes, Author of Don Quixote, 2 volumes (London: Printed for A. Millar, 1742);

A Full Vindication of the Dutchess Dowager of Marlborough: Both With regard to the Account Lately Published by Her Grace, and to Her Character in general; against The base and malicious Invectives contained in a late scurrilous Pamphlet, entitled Remarks on the Account, &c. . . . (London: Printed for J. Roberts, 1742);

Miss Lucy in Town. A Sequel to The Virgin Unmasqued. A Farce; With Songs. As it is Acted at the Theatre-Royal in Drury-Lane, by His Majesty's Servants (London: Printed for A. Millar, 1742);

Plutus, the God of Riches. A Comedy. Translated from the Original Greek of Aristophanes: With Large Notes Explanatory and Critical, translated by Fielding and William Young (London: Printed for T. Waller, 1742);

Some Papers to Be Read before the R---l Society Concerning the Terrestrial Chysipus, Golden-Foot or Guinea; an insect or vegetable, resembling the polypus, which has this surprising property, that being cut into several pieces, each piece becomes a perfect animal, or vegetable, as complete as that of which it was originally only a part. Collected by Petrus Gualterus, but Not Published till After His Death (London: Printed for A. Millar, 1743);

The Wedding-Day. A Comedy, As it is Acted at the Theatre-Royal in Drury-Lane. By His Majesty's Servants (London: Printed for A. Millar, 1743);

Miscellanies, 3 volumes (London: Printed for the author & sold by A. Millar, 1743)–includes first printings of *A Journey from This World to the Next* (in volume 2) and *The Life of Mr. Jonathan Wild* (volume 3); modern edition of *A Journey from This World to the Next,* introduction by A. R. Humphreys, notes by Douglas Brooks (London: Dent/New York: Dutton, 1973);

An Attempt towards a Natural History of the Hanover Rat (London: Printed for M. Cooper, 1744);

The Charge to the Jury: or, The Sum of the Evidence on the Trial of A.B.C.D. and E.F. All M.D. for the Death of One Robert at Orfud, at the special commission of oyer and terminer ... before Sir Asculapius Dosem, Dr. Timberhead, and others . . . (London: Printed for M. Cooper, 1745);

The History of the Present Rebellion in Scotland. . . . Taken from the Relation of Mr. James Macpherson, Who Was an Eyewitness of the Whole (London: Printed for M. Cooper, 1745);

A Serious Address to the People of Great Britain. In which the Certain Consequences of the Present Rebellion, Are fully demonstrated (London: Printed for M. Cooper, 1745);

A Dialogue between the Devil, the Pope, and the Pretender (London: Printed for M. Cooper, 1745);

The True Patriot; and The History of Our Own Times, nos. 1-33 (London: Printed for M. Cooper, 5 November 1745-17 June 1746);

The Female Husband: or, The Surprising History of Mrs. Mary, Alias Mr. George Hamilton, who was convicted of having married a young woman of Wells and lived with her as her husband. Taken from Her Own Mouth since Her Confinement (London: Printed for M. Cooper, 1746); modern edition, in *The Female Husband and Other Writings* (1960);

The Jacobite's Journal, by John Trott-Plaid, Esq., nos. 1-49 (London, 5 December 1747-5 November 1748);

Ovid's Art of Love Paraphrased, and Adapted to the Present Time. With Notes. And a most correct Edition of the Original. Book I (London: Printed for M. Cooper, A. Dodd & G. Woodfall, 1747);

A Dialogue between a Gentleman of London, Agent for Two Court Candidates, and an Honest Alderman Of the Country Party. Wherein the Grievances under which the Nation at present groans are fairly and impartially laid open and considered. Earnestly address'd to the Electors of Great-Britain (London: Printed for M. Cooper, 1747);

A Proper Answer To a Late Scurrilous Libel, Entitled, An Apology for the Conduct of a late celebrated Second-rate Minister. By the Author of the Jacobites' Journal (London: Printed for M. Cooper, 1747);

The History of Tom Jones, a Foundling, 6 volumes (London: Printed for A. Millar, 1749);

A Charge Delivered to the Grand Jury, at the Sessions of the Peace Held for the City and Liberty of Westminster, &c. On Thursday the 29th of June, 1749 (London: Printed for A. Millar, 1749);

A True State of the Case of Bosavern Penlez, Who Suffered on Account of the late Riot in the Strand. In which The Law regarding these Offences, and the Statute of George the First, commonly called the Riot Act, are fully considered (London: Printed for A. Millar, 1749);

An Enquiry Into the Causes for the late Increase of Robbers, &c. with Some Proposals for Remedying this Growing Evil (London: Printed for A. Millar, 1751);

A Plan of the Universal Register Office (London, 1751);

Amelia, 4 volumes (London: Printed for A. Millar, 1751);

The Covent-Garden Journal. By Sir Alexander Drawcansir, Knt. Censor of Great Britain, nos. 1-72 (London, 4 January 1752-25 November 1752); modern edition, edited by Gerard Edward Jensen, 2 volumes (New Haven: Yale University Press/London: Oxford University Press, 1915);

Examples of the Interposition of Providence in the Detection and Punishment of Murder . . . With an introduction and conclusion, both written by Henry Fielding, Esq. (London: Printed for A. Millar, 1752);

A Proposal for Making an Effectual Provision for the Poor, for Amending their Morals and for Rendering them useful Members of the Society (London: Printed for A. Millar, 1753);

A Clear State of the Case of Elizabeth Canning, who hath sworn that she was robbed and almost starved to Death by a Gang of Gipsies and other Villains in January last, for which One Mary Squires now lies under Sentence of Death (London: Printed for A. Millar, 1753);

The Life of Mr. Jonathan Wild the Great. A New Edition with considerable Corrections and Additions

(London: Printed for A. Millar, 1754); modern edition, published with *The Journal of a Voyage to Lisbon*, introduction by A. R. Humphreys, notes by Douglas Brooks (London: Dent/New York: Dutton, 1973);

The Journal of a Voyage to Lisbon (London: Printed for A. Millar, 1755); modern edition, edited by Harold Pagliaro (New York: Nardon, 1963);

The Fathers; or, The Good-Natur'd Man. A Comedy. As it is Acted at the Theatre-Royal, in Drury-Lane (London: Printed for T. Cadell, 1778).

Collections: *The Works of Henry Fielding, Esq.; with the Life of the Author*, edited by Arthur Murphy, 4 volumes (London: Printed for A. Millar, 1762);

The Shakespeare Head Edition of Fielding's Novels, 10 volumes (Oxford: Blackwell, 1926);

The Wesleyan Edition of the Works of Henry Fielding, edited by W. B. Coley and others, 16 volumes to date (Oxford: Clarendon Press/ Middletown, Conn.: Wesleyan University Press, 1967-   ).

OTHER: Epilogue to *Orestes: A Dramatic Opera as it is Acted at the Theatre-Royal in Lincoln's Inn Fields*, by Lewis Theobald (London: Printed for J. Watts, 1731); epilogue republished in *The Female Husband and Other Writings*, edited by Claude E. Jones, Liverpool University Reprint Series (Liverpool: Liverpool University Press, 1960);

Epilogue to *The Modish Couple. As it is acted at the Theatre-Royal in Drury-Lane. By His Majesty's Servants*, by Charles Bodens (London: J. Watts, 1732); epilogue republished in *The Female Husband and Other Writings*;

Epilogue to *Fatal Curiosity: A True Tragedy of Three Acts. As it is Acted at the New Theatre in the Haymarket*, by George Lillo (London: Printed for John Gray, 1737); epilogue republished in *The Female Husband and Other Writings*;

Sarah Fielding, *The Adventures of David Simple*, second edition, 2 volumes, preface by Henry Fielding (London: Printed for A. Millar, 1744);

Sarah Fielding, *Familiar Letters between the Principal Characters in David Simple, and some Others . . . To Which is Added, A Vision*, preface and letters 40-44 by Henry Fielding (London: Printed for the author & sold by A. Millar, 1747);

"An Original Song written on the first Appearance of the Beggars Opera," in *Country Maga-*

Sharpham Park, Somerset, Fielding's birthplace

zine for 1786-1787 (Salisbury & London, 1788).

Although we usually think of Henry Fielding as a novelist, he was a prolific and innovative playwright who published twenty-one plays before his first novel, *Joseph Andrews* (1742). His plays capture the excitement, creativity, and upheaval of the London theatrical world of the 1730s, and they range from conventional types to outrageous experiments. The theater was Fielding's choice of occupation; he worked at it seriously and diligently. He had successful plays at the Theatres Royal in Drury Lane and Covent Garden, and he made the Little Theatre in the Hay-Market famous. He invented several new forms of drama, and in 1737, the year of his highly successful *Historical Register For the Year 1736* and the year after his *Pasquin* ran sixty nights, managers and the public expected him to continue to produce hits and to dominate the profession for another twenty-five years. Fielding's plans to build a theater for a company of his own were published in the *Daily Advertiser* for 4 February 1737.

When he was forced from drama by the Licensing Act of 24 June 1737, he himself said that he had "left off writing for the stage when he ought to have begun." George Bernard Shaw called him the most important dramatist between Shakespeare and Ibsen, and the description is not unwarranted.

Henry Fielding, born a gentleman at Sharpham Park, near Glastonbury, Somersetshire, was the eldest child of Edmund and Sarah Gould Fielding, and grew up on a large farm in beautiful East Stour, Dorset. His mother died in April 1718, a few days before Henry's eleventh birthday. His father was a career military man who had often been away; he put his children in the care of his wife's mother, Lady Gould, and aunt, Mrs. Cottington, and quickly married a Catholic widow. Martin Battestin, Fielding's modern biographer, has described Henry's early life as resembling in broadest outline that of his hero Tom Jones. Henry became an unruly, mercurial boy, and his father sent him to Eton in 1719, at age twelve. There he made lifelong friends with men such as William Pitt and George Lyttelton

The house at East Stour, Dorset, where Fielding spent his childhood

and began a solid classical education. His father and his maternal relatives engaged in a long legal battle over custody of the children and the estate. The Goulds won, and, in addition to the estate, Edmund was ordered to account for the rents and profits he had received since Sarah's death and, soon after, to repay seven hundred pounds he had borrowed from Mrs. Cottington to pay a gambling debt. Henry, however, appears to have remained on good terms with both sides of the family throughout these years. Soon after he left Eton in 1724, he fell in love with Sarah Andrew, a young Lyme Regis woman who once attempted to elope with him, but in 1726 she married another man.

In 1728, like so many country boys, Henry Fielding went to London with a play in his luggage, no trade, and no inheritance. At that time London was the most exciting city in the world, and drama was still the prestige genre. A novelist could hope for little more than twenty pounds for his book, but a dramatist could realize a thousand pounds for a single play. The poet laureateship was still routinely given to a playwright, and the twelve thousand or so regular London theatergoers delighted in the gossip about the players that appeared in the daily and weekly periodicals. Moreover, he arrived in the season that produced the stunningly successful *Beggar's Opera*

and the highly profitable *Provok'd Husband*. With some help from his well-connected second cousin, Lady Mary Wortley Montagu, the woman who had offered editorial suggestions concerning works no less prestigious than Addison's *Cato* (1713), Fielding succeeded in his first season in getting *Love in Several Masques* produced at the Theatre Royal in Drury Lane.

In that year, too, Fielding published *The Masquerade, A Poem. Inscribed to C---t H--d--g--r.... By Lemuel Gulliver, Poet Laureat to the King of Lilliput.* Although Fielding soon left London and the theater to study at the University of Leyden for a year and a half, that first year marked his later dramatic career in significant ways and pointed to directions his art would take. Just as many of his plays would do, the poem held up for ridicule fashionable people and entertainments. He wrote, "O muse, some simile indite,/To shew the oddness of the sight.... " and feigned amazement at seeing "Here, running footmen guzzle tea;/There, milk-maids flasks of Burgundy..../A lady in a velvet hood,/(Her mein [*sic*] St. James's seem'd t' explain,/ But her assurance–Drury-lane,/Not Hercules was ever bolder." The poem has a sturdy plot that serves as effective vehicle for the satire, and Fielding's fondness for episodic, topical writing is evident. The final verse begins, "These are the scenes–wherein engage/The numbers now upon this stage." The writer who would sign his preface to the expanded version of his fourth play H. Scriblerus Secundus showed his fascination with the satiric objects and techniques of Jonathan Swift, Alexander Pope, and the other Scriblerians. When the narrator sees Heidegger he exclaims, "Monstrous! that human nature can/Have form'd so strange burlesque a man." With the emphasis on man's perversions of natural order, processes, and forms and with his alertness to language misused, Fielding ranged himself beside the older satirists.

In that year John Gay, one of the Scriblerians, showed the possibilities for literary and political satire within the framework of an enjoyable and unified play with his *Beggar's Opera*. And it was effective satire. Fielding must have heard the play discussed, people chuckling over Sir Robert Walpole's humiliation, and the songs sung and hummed in coffeehouses and music rooms. In the caricatures of actual people, including the mimicry of opera singers, he saw the opportunities for satire most often associated with the formal verse satire.

In the Vanbrugh-Cibber comedy, *The Provok'd Husband*, he recognized the vitality of Restoration comic conventions and dialogue and the possibilities for the exploration of serious domestic and social situations. Colley Cibber's combination of sentimental and farcical elements suggested different ways for Fielding to depict the licentiousness of London recreations and the miseries of unhappy marriages. Fielding's own first play, *Love in Several Masques,* is closer to Cibber's than to Gay's and has elements drawn from the Restoration wits and from Colley Cibber, Thomas Shadwell, Susanna Centlivre, and Molière. It combines characteristics of the comedy of manners with the comedy of intrigue and shows early promise in characterization, satire, and irony.

Fielding assembles the best stock characters and constructs a conventional comic plot, but the play is mediocre. His mistake appears to be his unwillingness to sacrifice any of the age's most successful dramatic ploys. The plot involves three couples, each with different obstacles to marriage and each concerned with a slightly different set of eccentric characters. The primary plot revolves around Lady Matchless, a widow who has vowed "never to run a second hazard," who believes men to be gullible fools, and who delights in outwitting them. Her suitors make up a gallery of originals: Wisemore, a country squire who

unfashionably praises philosophy, constancy, and the rural life; Lord Formal, a descendant of George Etherege's Sir Fopling Flutter; Sir Apish Simple, a fortune hunter; and Rattle, modeled after William Congreve's Tattle in *Love for Love* (1695). When Lady Matchless seems unaccountably attracted to Formal, Wisemore disguises himself and announces that her fortune is being threatened by a court suit in order to expose the avarice of the other suitors. The second plot combines elements of Thomas Shadwell's comedies, especially *The Virtuoso* (1676), and of Susanna Centlivre's *Bold Stroke for a Wife* (1718). Helena has as guardians an old-fashioned Puritan, Sir Positive Trap, and his lascivious wife. He, like Centlivre's Obadiah Prim, utters platitudes such as "Dancing begets warmth, which is the parent of wantonness." This humor is amusing, but touches like his foolish claim to a distinguished ancestry including Julius Caesar seem superfluous. When Lady Trap tricks Helena's Merital into meeting her in the dining room, she sounds like Shadwell's Mrs. Gimcrack; Helena, like the nieces in *The Virtuoso*, transfers her guardianship to her fiance. The third couple, Malvil and Vermillia, add little to the play. Malvil becomes jealous of his friend Merital, challenges him to a duel, and then repents in the manner of Myrtle in Steele's *Conscious Lovers* (1721).

The conclusion of *Love in Several Masques* becomes a scrapbook of popular endings. All of the couples are reconciled, and the worst of the characters are suitably rebuked. Fielding even provides a nationalistic song for Lady Matchless. The derivative nature of the play does not mean that it is unskillful. Fielding's humours characters are highly entertaining, strongly drawn, and good satiric vehicles. Formal, for example, laments the necessity of memorizing title pages "for since the ladies have divided their time between cards and reading, a man, to be agreeable to them, must understand something of books. . . . " and fears that eyestrain will destroy his "direct ogle." Fielding's satires of fops, of the education of gentlemen, and of fashionable flirtation rituals have originality and moral bite. The scene when Helena comes upon Lady Trap and Merital in the darkness is one of the most effective uses of dramatic irony in the decade. The ways Fielding has characters expose their baser natures point to the principle incorporated in his novels that people will "discover" themselves, that is reveal their true characters. Greed, affectation, lasciviousness, and generosity, all finally emerge and reveal the characters' true natures.

Fielding's play came on the stage when Drury Lane was managed by Robert Wilks, Barton Booth, and Colley Cibber. Booth is reputed to have declared that "he and his partners lost money by new plays; and that, if he were not obliged to it, he would seldom give his consent to perform one of them." In that season of 1727-1728, the only original plays besides Fielding's produced there were *The Provok'd Husband* (Cibber's revision and completion of Vanburgh's *A Journey to London*) and Lewis Theobald's *Double Falsehood*. Thus Fielding's was the only one by a living, unestablished dramatist. His play opened on 16 February and played a respectable four nights. It benefited from the strong Drury Lane company, which specialized in the comedy of manners. John Mills played Wisemore, Robert Wilks Merital, Colley Cibber Rattle, Benjamin Griffin Formal, and Anne Oldfield Lady Matchless. Anne Oldfield had saved *The Provok'd Husband* on opening night when the enemies Cibber had made with the *Non-Juror* (1717) packed the theater, and Fielding compliments her in the preface to the published edition of his play. Mrs. Oldfield was forty-five years old and described as "tall, genteel, and well-shaped" with "large speaking eyes." Because "in sprightliness of air and elegance of manner she excelled all actresses," she was ideal for Fielding's Lady Matchless. Without liveliness and grace, this character could appear embittered, competitive, and even malicious. Fielding may have written the part with her in mind and gave her a more challenging and suitable vehicle than Cibber had when he cast her as his Lady Townly. Lady Townly lacks Lady Matchless's wit, intelligence, and emotional depth.

A month after the opening of his play, Fielding was in Leyden enrolled as a "student of letters," that is of Latin and Greek literature. About a year and a half later, he returned to England and to the theatrical world. The 1729-1730 season was a spectacular success for him: *The Temple Beau* opened with a run of nine consecutive nights at Goodman's Fields; both *The Author's Farce* and *Tom Thumb* played more than forty nights; and *Rape upon Rape* opened late in the season and, in spite of being plagued by the bad health of the leading actor, ran at the Little Theatre in the Hay-Market for eight nights in the summer, one more in November of 1730, and played four times at Lincoln's Inn Fields in the

1730-1731 season. Moreover, according to Robert D. Hume, Fielding brought *Don Quixote in England* and *The Wedding-Day* back with him from Leyden.

Fielding undoubtedly wrote *The Temple Beau* with the intention of seeing it performed at Drury Lane. The sophisticated comedy of manners and the number of good parts for men and women suggest that Fielding imagined that company performing it. Neither patent house took the play, however, and Fielding went to Thomas Odell's theater at Goodman's Fields. This theater had opened in October 1729 and proved that an audience for theater existed in a part of London distant from the two Theatres Royal. *The Temple Beau* is Fielding's first imaginative use of pairing characters. The best of the pairs are Lady Pedant/Lady Gravely and Wilding/Pedant, although Veromil/Valentine, Sir Avarice Pedant/Sir Harry Wilding, and Bellaria/Clarissa provide additional thematic interest. These characters possess the embryonic signs of Fielding's distinctive theory of characterization, for they are strongly individual and "probable" yet obviously descended from the humours characters of Ben Jonson and other seventeenth-century playwrights. Fielding constructs scene after scene to reveal the underlying motives in these apparently dissimilar character types.

Fielding's second play that season, *The Author's Farce*, has autobiographical elements. As such it touches more serious subjects and, in spite of its burlesque form, more personal emotions. The simultaneous narrative of the struggling writer's life and the ridicule of the circumstances of the theater give the work unusual texture and meaning. The opening scenes firmly establish the technique of juxtaposing a satiric attack upon an allegorical exposé.

Fielding borrows excerpts from plays such as George Farquhar's *Love and a Bottle* (1698) to place his play in a familiar comic mode. At this time Farquhar's seven plays were a sturdy part of every season's repertoire. Fielding needed such an opening in order to set the audience's expectations and to begin to make the comparisons between *The Author's Farce* and other plays, both earlier and contemporary. Fielding quickly uses his own obviously derivative opening to mock the parasitic formula plays of his time, to evoke a strong surviving strain in comedy, and to begin to comment wryly on his own ambitions as a playwright. Act 1 is full of sentimental dialogue between the lovers and songs in the manner of *The Beggar's*

Opera. Luckless and Harriot create a pastoral world in which their love resists Moneywood's demands for money and sex and Witmore's and Jack's pessimistic reports on the chances for the performance of Luckless's play. Like Gay's *Polly,* Harriot somehow sheds the soil of the city in which she lives. In Farquhar's play the Widow Bullfinch duns Lyric with the lines,

> Mr. Lyric, what do you mean by all this? Here you have lodged two years in my house, promised me eighteen-pence a week for your lodging, and I have never received eighteen farthings, not the value of that, Mr. Lyric. You always put me off with telling me of your play, your play! Sir, you shall play no more with me; I'm in earnest (III.ii).

Fielding begins *The Author's Farce* with Mrs. Moneywood giving a revised version of the speech: "Never tell me, Mr. Luckless, of your play, and your play. I say, I must be paid. I would no more depend on a benefit night of an unacted play than I would on a benefit ticket of an undrawn lottery." Farquhar's speech depends more on puns and Fielding's on the kind of wit most often associated with Wycherley and Congreve. Bullfinch is a thorough scold and Lyric entirely on the defensive; Moneywood claims to have a passion for Luckless that led her to extend so much credit, and Luckless's speeches are longer than Lyric's and more sentimental. Luckless, like Lyric, has sent a friend to sell some writings to a bookseller, and there are similarities between these scenes as well.

As Fielding's plot follows the familiar path of lovers thwarted by poverty and an authoritarian guardian, the satire of the contemporary theater unfolds through three characters: Luckless, who is learning that he must surrender his artistic integrity in order to succeed; Bookweight, who keeps the stable of hacks and feeds the taste of the town; and Witmore, who is the direct voice criticizing the depravity of society's taste. Witmore tells Luckless,

> But now, when party and prejudice carry all before them, when learning is decried, wit not understood, when fools lead the town, would a man think to thrive by his wit? If you must write, write nonsense, write operas, write entertainments, write *Hurlothrumbos,* set up an *Oratory* and preach nonsense, and you may meet with encouragement enough.

Here Witmore summarizes one way of seeing 1730. The popularity of Samuel Johnson of Cheshire's *Hurlothrumbo* (1729) and *The Humours of Harlequin* (1732) testifies to the town's taste for nonsense and variety at the expense of plot and theme. Ironically, no one serves as a better example of the power party prejudice had over theatrical production than the major, individual object of Fielding's play, Colley Cibber. Ever since his *Non-Juror,* a faction had tried to close every play written by the poet laureate. Fielding, however, attacks Cibber by casting him as Marplay, as Mr. Keyber, and as Sir Farcical Comic and by holding up his plays, particularly *Caesar in Egypt* (1724) and *Love in a Riddle* (1729), for ridicule. Cibber as Marplay joins with Wilks as Sparkish in commenting cruelly and desultorily upon Luckless's play. Fielding portrays Cibber as perversely silent or pretentiously critical and given to low, nonsensical utterances (most, such as the famous "Stap my breath" and "I did produce one bone," taken from Cibber's plays). Just as Gay had attacked Walpole through several characters in *The Beggar's Opera,* so Fielding sees the advantages of portraying Cibber through several single-dimension characters. Fielding points out the undeserved respect and influence that Cibber has in society. His debased, simple art pleases, and he can legislate the taste of the town. Furthermore, Cibber does it without principles: "Interest sways as much in the theater as at court," he says in Fielding's play.

When Luckless turns his play into a puppet show, *The Pleasures of the Town,* he demonstrates that his own understanding of the town's taste is now as good as Bookweight's. He tells a player, "since everyone has not time or opportunity to visit all the diversions of the town, I have brought most of them together in one." Luckless's adapted play begins with a cynical prologue that doubles as musical overture. It concludes, "Critics, whilst you smile on madness; / And more stupid, solemn sadness, / Sure you will not frown on Punch." Here, as in several places in the puppet show, Fielding uses one of the stock strategies of the comic burlesque, compression, and shows a firm grasp of his contemporaries' favorite plots and conflicts. He decorates the basic line of the plot (a love-interest comedy) with Punch and Judy, songs, dances, and all of the other stock devices of the debased stage spectacular. Fielding's age had reduced the Restoration procession to outrageous costumes, jugglers, tumblers, and bizarre creatures, and the parade of authors to Charon's boat in *The Pleasures of the Town* would be great theater any time.

Beside the marvelous spectacle of *The Pleasures of the Town,* Fielding makes a number of serious and perceptive comments. First, he uses act 2 of *The Author's Farce* to show the change in Luckless. In lines heavy with irony, Luckless flatters Bookweight: "Who can form to himself an idea more amiable than of a man at the head of so many patriots working for the benefit of their country?" Fresh in the mind's eye is the scene in which Dash, Blotpage, Quibble, Index, and Scarecrow ply their degrading trade. When Harriot commends Luckless for succeeding in the world "by his merit and virtuous industry," the luster is gone from their love, and ideals have become illusion. Witmore, who seems to speak Fielding's opinions most directly, stands above the competitiveness of the theater and rains cynical contempt upon his age, an age in which he finds merit and "true politeness" useless. He equates the scoundrels sentenced at the Old Bailey with the nobility and, by analogy, with the successful playwrights of his time. He advises Luckless to find a patron or marry a rich widow—only by prostituting himself, he implies, can Luckless put money in his purse. Witmore becomes a vehicle for Fielding's equations of politics, literary taste, manners, and even religion—all gravitating toward nonsense and ease. Bookweight and his stable of writers provide Fielding with another means of attack on the state of the theatrical world. He compares writers to stockjobbers, translators to shoplifters, and booksellers to lawyers for "there are as many tricks in the one as the other."

In this play, too, Fielding shows his consistent skill at satirizing the abuses of language. The character Pantomime, of course, has no language, and Tragedio's every speech is inflated. Farcical Comedy's confused babbling shows that he understands no language at all, and Opera uses words as mere vehicles for sound. When Opera decisively defeats Tragedio, Fielding underscores the barrenness of contemporary tragedy with its rants, bombast, and euphuistic verse. Another character, Murdertext, defends Nonsense: "Shall you abuse Nonsense when the whole town supports it?" Significantly, Murdertext, an enthusiastic Nonconformist, marries Mrs. Novel, thereby associating the new literary form with bad English, troublemakers, and the lower classes, tradesmen at best.

In the manner of *The Beggar's Opera,* the ending of *The Author's Farce* gives the audience a con-

ventional, crowd-pleasing conclusion, one so obviously contrived and improbable that the satire cannot be ignored. The dance at the end of the puppet show is interrupted by the standard recognition scene. Luckless is hailed as the King of Bantam, and the Bantomite tells an incredible tale of shipwreck and rescue. Harriot is discovered to be the Princess of Old Brentford, and Luckless makes the puppet characters members of his court, thereby merging the world of the puppet show with the world of the play, much as Luigi Pirandello does at the end of *Six Characters in Search of an Author* (1921). The group that surrounded the Goddess of Nonsense only a moment earlier now surrounds Luckless, King of Bantam. Moneywood discovers herself to be both Harriot's mother and the mother of the puppet Joan. Fielding self-consciously relates the ending to a series of earlier plays including George Villiers, duke of Buckingham's *The Rehearsal* (1671), Thomas Durfey's *The Two Queens of Brentford: or, Bayes No Poetaster* (1721), and Ben Jonson's *Alchemist* (1610) and *Bartholomew Fair* (1614). *The Rehearsal* had two kings of Brentford, and Jonson's Sir Epicure Mammon was promised the throne of Bantam. What began as an apparently straightforward mid-century comedy concludes as a burlesque of opera, tragicomedy, and domestic comedy. Luckless and Harriot have become as ridiculous and unrealistic as Novel and the other passengers on Charon's boat.

On 24 April Fielding's *Tom Thumb* was performed as an afterpiece and was an overwhelming success. Dispensing with the play-within-a-play frame, Fielding simply presented *Tom Thumb* as a satire upon heroic tragedy. Since heroic tragedy often dealt with the most significant aspects of political ethics and routinely included a conflict between love and duty, the form suited Fielding's larger purposes ideally. King Arthur's court reeks of envy, scheming, betrayal, and ambition. Blind conformity to the court opinion is portrayed as lamentable and dangerous. The motives of the courtiers are as shallow as their perception, and the viciousness of poisoning the monkey dressed as Thumb and the naked jealously revealed in Grizzle's murder of Thumb's ghost are elements almost too dark for farcical comedy. However, *Tom Thumb* is still a hilarious play and one rich in original verbal effects. Fielding parodies the way Shakespeare's imitators have plundered the Bard's plays by transplanting lines, as his contemporaries often did, and putting them, as he saw the eighteenth-century writers doing,

Glumdalca and Huncamunca arguing over Tom Thumb; William Hogarth's frontispiece, engraved by Vandergucht, for the 1731 edition of The Tragedy of Tragedies

in thoroughly inappropriate places. Thumb tells Noodle that he loves Huncamunca: "Whole Days, and Nights, and Years shall be too short/For our Enjoyment; ev'ry Sun shall rise/Blushing, to see us in our Bed together." He and Huncamunca, however, are not Dryden's Antony and Cleopatra. Fielding follows this line with one distinctly his own: In spite of this physical image, Noodle says, "Oh, Sir! this Purpose of your Soul pursue." Thus, Fielding draws attention to the discrepancy between the word chosen and the implications of the lines, for it is surely the purpose of Thumb's body, not his soul, that is the topic of discussion.

This afterpiece was a romp for Fielding and, with its mention of Bantam and Brentford, probably specifically written to accompany *The Au-*

thor's Farce when it became clear that Charles Coffey's *The Female Parson* (1730) was not a satisfactory afterpiece. More obviously in the tradition of *The Rehearsal, Tom Thumb* relied more upon plot than had *The Pleasures of the Town*. Both plays, however, depended upon Fielding's critical eye and his vigorous, representational characters. On the surface, his plays might seem as light and pointless as *Hurlothrumbo*, but Fielding's satire and verbal virtuosity set him apart from Johnson of Cheshire. In his play, Fielding's Arthur, named after the legendary king whose Round Table personified virtue, courage, and patriotism, is old and as irrelevant as England's glorious past was becoming. The implied contrast between a time of glory and achievement with his of mediocrity and corruption reminds us of his debt to

Pope.

Fielding followed *The Author's Farce* and *Tom Thumb* with the more traditional satiric comedy, *Rape upon Rape*. The play is more tightly plotted than his first two comedies, but the thematic use of false accusations of rape makes the play both incredible and unpleasant. The first incident, when Hilaret cries "rape" in order to scare Ramble into leaving her alone, turns into a nice comedy of errors with both Hilaret and Ramble amusingly and suitably embarrassed. The other two incidents, when Constant is accused of rape when he rescues Isabella and when Hilaret maneuvers the crooked justice of the peace Squeezum into a compromising situation in order to accuse him of rape, are less funny and, because of their redundancy, less interesting. These three incidents, like the two sets of lovers and the humours character Politick, exist to expose the crooked magistrate and provide the means for Fielding to trace the path of legal injustice and profiteering from the moment of arrest until the release of Constant, Ramble, and Hilaret and the arrest of Squeezum.

In spite of its weak dramatic power, *Rape upon Rape* is an interesting play. Unlike Gay's *Beggar's Opera*, it does not use the legal system as metaphor nor does it make the hackneyed point that poverty had become a crime in England. Although the influence of earlier plays is clear, *Rape upon Rape* is more a harbinger of the domestic melodramas of the late eighteenth and early nineteenth centuries. The seeds of his novel, *Amelia* (1751), may also be seen in this play. Fielding's point is probably more appropriate for an essay than a play, and he does satirize many of the attitudes he will attack later in his periodicals and novels. For example, Squeezum says, "It is better for the publick that ten innocent people should suffer, than that one guilty should escape; and it becomes every person to sacrifice their conscience to the benefit of the publick." A number of speeches approach the editorial. Worthy says, "golden sands too often clog the wheels of justice, and obstruct her course: the very riches which were the greatest evidence of his villainy, have too often declared the guilty innocent; and gold hath been found to cut a halter surer than the sharpest steel." Throughout Fielding points out the discrepancy between the law and its execution. He sees money as the "sand" clogging the wheels of justice and develops the idea through Squeezum's actions and Worthy's didactic speeches. At every point in the judicial sys-

tem, Fielding shows the unfortunate influence of money.

Rape upon Rape was revived as *The Coffee-House Politician* at Lincoln's Inn Fields on 4 December 1730, and John Rich even gave Fielding a benefit night. The Little Theatre in the Hay-Market company had performed the play under its new title with *Tom Thumb* as afterpiece on 30 November; this kind of competitive attempt to steal another playhouse's thunder was fairly common throughout the eighteenth century. Robert D. Hume has used contemporary periodical advertisements to demonstrate that Fielding had nothing to do with the Haymarket production. In 1959 Bernard Miles's adaptation of *Rape upon Rape*, called *Lock Up Your Daughters* (published 1967), was produced and was good enough to be revived in 1962, 1969, and 1978.

On 24 March 1731 Fielding's *Tragedy of Tragedies* and *The Letter-Writers* opened together at the Little Theatre in the Hay-Market. Often described as an expanded revision of *Tom Thumb*, *The Tragedy of Tragedies* is really a very different play. *Tom Thumb* had been largely general political satire and concentrated on jealousy, revenge, and corruption; *The Tragedy of Tragedies* satirized the theater, its conventions, language, machinery, and, through the Scriblerian-style commentary, its professional critics. This brilliant play, the most frequently anthologized of all of Fielding's plays, ran fifteen nights and was revived year after year. In an astonishing display of familiarity with English plays, Fielding managed to jest at more than forty plays by borrowing single lines or more from them and to make a travesty of Lewis Theobald's, John Dennis's, and John Dryden's works. By shaping his play as a burlesque of heroic tragedy, Fielding could produce a hilarious play (heroic tragedy is wonderfully suited to parody and burlesque) and, at the same time, point out how many of its conventions hid in contemporary plays. In fact, Nancy Mace has pointed out how specific the satire is to the plays of Lewis Theobald. In the 1730-1731 season, Theobald's plays saw sixty-eight performances (only plays by Shakespeare, Cibber, and Fielding himself rivaled his), and Fielding used these familiar plays to make Theobald the prototype of the kind of Shakespearian adapter he deplored. In the preface Fielding perceptively described many of Theobald's borrowings as "transplanted flowers": "they being of a very nice Nature, which will flourish in no soil but their own. . . . " Puns, doggerel, mixed metaphors, wit, gross meta-

Air 39. (The King's old Courtier.)
When mighty roast Beef was the Englishman's Food,
It ennobled our Hearts, and enriched our Blood,
Our Soldiers were brave, and our Courtiers were good.
Oh! the roast Beef of England,
And old England's roast Beef.
But since we have learnt from all-conquering France
To eat their Ragouts, as well as to dance;
Oh! What a fine Figure we make in Romance.
Oh! The roast Beef of England,
And old England's roast Beef.

The words to Fielding's Roast Beef of Old England *as they appear in* The Genuine Grub-Street Opera *(1731)*

William Hogarth's The Gates of Calais, or O the Roast Beef of Old England *(1748), which, like Fielding's nationalistic song, satirizes the French while praising the English (by permission of the Tate Gallery)*

phors, clichés, nonsensical statements, and mangled, parodied lines make the satire of the misuses of language an unending delight. Marvelously theatrical, *Tragedy of Tragedies* provides songs, sound effects, bizarre characters, fantastic costumes, dances, farcical scenes, and a final ludicrous parody of Senecan tragedy's stacks of dead bodies.

The afterpiece for *Tragedy of Tragedies* was Fielding's *The Letter-Writers,* a farcical comedy. In it Rakel wants to have affairs with Mrs. Softly and Mrs. Wisdom, whose considerably older husbands have written them anonymous, threatening letters in an attempt to keep them at home. Rakel is frustrated repeatedly in both houses and finally arrested. Here, too, Fielding satirizes the law; Risque asks to be paid for swearing, and Commons gets Rakel off and says to him, "Thou art such a dear wicked dog, I cannot leave thee in the lurch." The play had but four performances, and on 22 April 1731 Fielding's *The Welsh Opera* became the afterpiece for *Tragedy of Tragedies.* Billed as "Written by Scriblerus Secundus, Author of the *Tragedy of Tragedies,*" it returns to the kinds of ridicule of the court begun in *Tom Thumb.* Lady Apshinken (Queen Caroline) wants Puzzletext to help her marry off all of the maids so that her son Owen (Frederick, prince of Wales) will not be tempted. Owen mischievously leaves false notes around to make Sweetissa and Robin too jealous to marry. A happy ending is brought about by the witch, Goody Scratch, who reveals that all of the servants are the children of gentry and, as such, entitled to fortunes and that she is a widow with five hundred pounds a year, who can escape the spell that made her a witch by marrying a parson. Puzzletext eagerly agrees to help her.

The company performed the play a total of four times in April and, according to Edgar V. Roberts, six times in slightly altered form beginning on 19 May. On 21 May the *Daily Post* announced that *The Grub-Street Opera* (a revised version of *The Welsh Opera*) "which was to have been postponed till next Season" would be performed within two weeks. *The Welsh Opera* was performed on 26 May as the afterpiece for *The Fall of Mortimer,* the play that in late July would lead to the warrants for the arrest of the principal actors and the closing of the Little Hay-Market; an edition of it came out on 26 June. A notice in the *Daily Post,* printed by Hume in *Henry Fielding and the London Theatre, 1728-1737,* called the book "a strange Medley of Nonsense" and "a very incorrect and spurious Edition of the Welsh Opera." In early August *The Genuine Grub-Street Opera* was published, and the *Daily Journal* announced that the play had been suppressed but was printed for the benefit of the company. The next day, however, in a retraction also printed in Hume's *Henry Fielding and the London Theatre,* the *Daily Journal* said it had been "imposed on" and that the play had not been suppressed and the actors were not involved in the play's publication. Hume concludes that the editions of *The Welsh Opera* and *The Genuine Grub-Street Opera* were pirated; collations of *The Genuine Grub-Street Opera* and the earlier *Welsh Opera* and later *Grub-Street Opera* show that *The Genuine Grub-Street Opera* may have been a transition piece.

The third published version, *The Grub-Street Opera,* which is surely one of the best ballad operas written in the century, was not performed. As L. J. Morrissey has proved, it was not published until the 1750s, although the date on its title page is 1731. What we discover is that the number of songs had been increased from thirty-one in *The Welsh Opera* to sixty-five in *The Grub-Street Opera* and the plot considerably strengthened. All of the Apshinken family members' parts have been enhanced and better motivated. Owen, for instance, now writes his notes in order to take Sweetissa from Robin. Molly loves Owen in the sentimental manner of Polly in *The Beggar's Opera.* Owen tries to seduce her; when he fails and each servant girl rebuffs him, he marries her. Goody Scratch has been eliminated, and the ending now results from the action. The political satire is also developed, although as most critics now agree, this satire is more cynical and general than it is antiministerial. A number of extremely vicious lines are directed at Prince Frederick; Queen Caroline is portrayed throughout as a shrew and the king as henpecked and weak. At that time, the divisions in the royal family were well known, and Fielding's primary aim was to ridicule abuses of power and corruption.

With the Little Theatre in the Hay-Market closed, Fielding had to find a new home. His *Lottery* premiered at Drury Lane, now managed by Robert Wilks and Colley Cibber, on 1 January 1732, and they produced four more of his plays that season and two the next. Fielding's plays had often included jokes and witty remarks about the lottery, and the controlling metaphor for this play was that life was a lottery. Like his other plays, it satirizes the contemporary theater, "the quality," and public corruption, but the conjugal

Kitty Raftor Clive, for whom Fielding wrote several parts including those of Isabel in The Old Debauchees *and Kissinda in* The Covent Garden Tragedy

idealist of *Love in Several Masques* and the plays to come is much in evidence. A ballad-opera afterpiece, the play has little plot but nineteen effective songs, twenty-two (seven new) in the second printed edition. Kitty Clive, then Miss Raftor, the rising star of comedy and ballad operas, played the romantic heroine Chloe, and the play ran thirty nights that season. Chloe is a frivolous, rather giddy girl who puts her faith in winning the lottery and, therefore, prematurely presents herself as a rich marriage prospect. She is so confident because she has seen "in a coffeedish" that she will win and dreamed of it every

night. Disguised as Lord Lace, Jack Stocks tricks her into marriage, and as Wisemore has bought Lady Matchless in *Love in Several Masques*, Lovemore purchases all rights to Chloe from Stocks for one thousand pounds. This play was performed regularly until the 1780s.

On 14 February, Fielding's *Modern Husband* opened. *The Modern Husband* was as dark as *The Lottery* had been light. Long an admirer of Molière and the serious satiric plays of the Continent, Fielding hoped that the Drury Lane stage and its company would allow him to realize some of the ambitions of his youth. In the prologue he announces that he now "In virtue's just defence aspires to fame," returns to "nature and to truth," and repents the "frolic flights of youth" that created *Tom Thumb*. These statements cannot be dismissed as conventional prologue sentiments, for Fielding's art always had high moral seriousness, and he was happiest when he could, in the words of one of his critics, turn the stage into the courtroom and try offenders. His plays had always exposed corruption relentlessly, and the list of their subjects cover most of the private, social, and institutional vices of the 1730s. In addition he was as sensitive to language as Beaumont and Fletcher, Congreve, Swift, and Pope. He could use it to strip the vicious bare, to turn the affected into buffoons, and to express the solid virtues of Old England. He had the quick discrimination that lets a satirist see the analogy of leaping and creeping contests to politicians jockeying for favor or the similarity of a would-be hero creating giants in order to kill them to the actions of people caught up in the politics of undiscriminating reward and punishment.

He called his *Modern Husband* characters "monsters," as Molière's were, and shows them largely to be so. Mr. Modern has encouraged Mrs. Modern to have profitable affairs with Richly and Bellamant. When Modern needs five hundred pounds, he tries to persuade her to allow him to sue Richly for compensatory damages for their adultery, a familiar provision in eighteenth-century law based upon the idea that the husband, as his wife's "owner" had had his "property" damaged by the affair. Mrs. Modern refuses, because she fears for her reputation. The scene between the Moderns that follows lays bare all of their pretenses. Mr. Modern, for instance, chides her, "Very strange! that a woman who made so little scruple of sacrificing the substance of her virtue, should make so much of parting with the shadow of it." She answers that "the shadow only" is what has value, thereby making the familiar distinction between true virtue and mere reputation. These lines are followed by a vicious argument in which they reveal their vanity, callousness, and parasitic lives. They blame each other for Mrs. Modern's adultery, and the play is full of lines such as Modern's: "In short, Madam, you shall not drive a separate trade at my expense. Your person is mine: I bought it lawfully in the church; and unless I am to profit by the disposal, I shall keep it all for my own use." Modern bribes a servant and tricks Mrs. Modern and Bellamant in order to sue Bellamant for criminal

conversation. In an improbable and hasty ending, the sentimental couple, Mr. Gaywit and Emilia, bring about the exposure of the Moderns and the rescue of the Bellamants.

Among the pessimistic ideas reiterated in the play are that favors "as seldom fall to those who really want [meaning "lack"] them, as to those who really deserve them." In the treatment of the military man and of Bellamant when they need positions, characters make it clear that self-interest, not merit, motivates appointments. The cleverest and most manipulative, Richly becomes the greatest villain. As Mrs. Modern says, he does not catch fools like "fish in the water by a bait, but like the dog in the water by a shadow." Money becomes the supreme means of manipulation. In a line typical of Fielding's moral bite and witty insight, Mr. Modern says "gold in this world covers as many sins, as charity in the next." Richly describes how he has often left money in a woman's hands, because she will be unable to resist spending it, cannot pay it back, and "by virtue of my mortgage, immediately enter upon the premises." Such economic language is characteristic of the play. Women especially are objects to be bought, sold, traded, used, pawned, and cast off. Beneath the surface, however, Fielding's basic sentimentality and idealism lurk. Mrs. Bellamant is a virtuous, forgiving woman; even Mrs. Modern can say, "thou wilt find, though a woman often sells her person, she always gives her heart." By the end of the play we can believe that she regrets the direction her life has taken and that Bellamant is repentant.

The Modern Husband ran thirteen nights, but it did not become a repertory piece. In fact, it shows the flaws of all of Fielding's full-length comedies. There are too many characters, and some of them immediately remind the viewer of better, more fully developed characters from other plays (Sir Charles and Lady Easy in Colley Cibber's *Careless Husband*, 1704, for instance, come to mind). The plot and especially the tempo are ragged and move by fits and starts; the play moves very slowly toward the entrapment of Bellamant in Modern's scheme to make money from the discovery of his wife's adultery, and then the reforms and marriages come in a rush. At their deepest Fielding's characters seem to have sentiments rather than psychology, and many are nearly one-dimensional. Although this technique may work to make Richly more repulsive, it makes Mrs. Modern less interesting and, perhaps, finally unbelievable; Bellamant is downright puzzling in his appar-

Plate 1 in William Hogarth's A Harlot's Progress *(April 1732). The notorious bawd Mother Needham, shown above greeting a young girl from the country, is said to have been the inspiration for Mother Punchbowl in Fielding's*
The Covent Garden Tragedy.

ently motiveless betrayal of the wife whom he always avows he loves. Where Sheridan could write sustained, devastatingly revealing dialogue in similar plays, Fielding's language wavers, and he often falls back on direct statement to reveal character and to make his didactic points. The fullness and detail of the predatory world also work against comedy, but here they point to what some critics find the unforgettable texture and genius of *Amelia*.

He followed *The Modern Husband* with a farce, *The Old Debauchees,* and an afterpiece, *The Covent Garden Tragedy,* written to open together. *The Covent Garden Tragedy* died after its opening night, 1 June 1732, and *The Old Debauchees* managed only six performances. The rather French farce includes many anti-Catholic touches in addition to the lascivious Father Martin. Kitty Clive's performance as the heroine, Isabel, helped the play considerably, but its predictable and contrived intrigue plot and its unpleasant tone surely doomed it. Although Fielding tried to place *The Covent Garden Tragedy* in the company of *Tom Thumb* and again effectively burlesques the out-

worn conventions of tragedy, the play shares the dark tone of *The Old Debauchees*. Wives and whores are compared throughout, and not in a jolly way. Jests like those suggesting that drunkenness distinguishes men from beasts hardly left the audience lighthearted and diverted. The burlesque plot is, perhaps, too close to plays then on the stage. Except for the fact that the play takes place in a whorehouse and the characters have old-fashioned farcical names, the story of the mother pairing off her girls and Captain Bilkum's duel with Lovegirlo over Stormandra might be the stuff of a number of mediocre plays.

On 23 June, Fielding's *Mock Doctor* opened. It was advertised as "Done from *Molière*," and Fielding followed the French play closely. He added nine songs, changed the setting, and made a solid, idiomatic translation. The clever double plot is Molière's, and Kitty Clive, who played Dorcas, deserved the compliment Fielding paid her in his preface. The next February, his adaptation of Molière's *The Miser* appeared at Drury Lane. Rather than an afterpiece, he made it a full-length, five-act play and added no music. In his

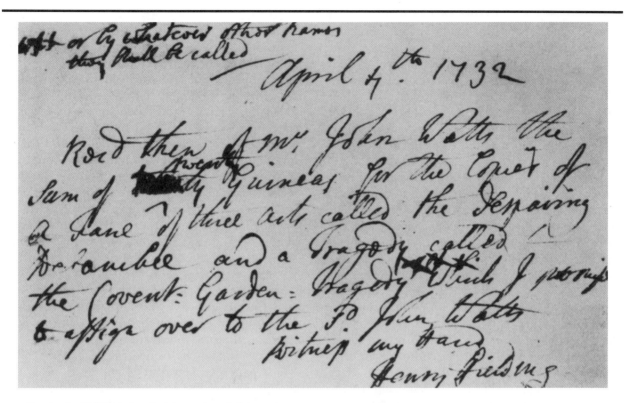

Receipt in Fielding's handwriting acknowledging John Watts's payment of twenty guineas for the copyrights to The Old Debauchees *and* The Covent Garden Tragedy *(Wilbur L. Cross,* The History of Henry Fielding, *1918)*

Miser, Fielding has Frederick in love with the basically good but frivolous Mariana and Clermont in love with the sensible but romantic Harriet. Lovegold, the miser, decides to marry Mariana. Lappet and Mariana put on a vast theatrical show of extravagance–a great comic farce–and Lovegold pays Mariana £10,000 to break their engagement. The lovers are united, and the play ends with a dance. Fielding's belief in sentimental love softened Molière's characters. An immediate success, the play ran until the theater closed on 28 May and was revived throughout the century. On Kitty Raftor Clive's benefit night, 6 April 1733, Fielding's afterpiece *Deborah* had its only performance. Probably a satire of some aspect of Handel's works, no copy of it has been found.

Fielding dedicated his next play, *The Intriguing Chambermaid,* to Kitty Clive. "It is your misfortune to bring the greatest genius for acting on the stage at a time when the factions and divisions among the players have conspired with the folly, injustice, and barbarity of the town, to finish the ruin of the stage. . . ," he wrote. Fielding's entire dramatic career was plagued by the unsettled state of the theatrical world, but his reference here was to the actors' rebellion led by Theophilus Cibber. The efficient management of Wilks, Booth, and Colley Cibber had come to an abrupt end in 1732. First Barton Booth sold one-half of his share of the theater to John Highmore; then Colley Cibber turned his authority and share over to his son Theophilus in September 1732. Wilks died on 27 September, and his wife, Mary, gave one-half of her share to John Ellys on 31 October. The new managers argued constantly, and Covent Garden and Goodman's Fields theaters began to compete vigorously. Booth died on 10 May 1733, and Colley Cibber sold his share, regardless of his promises to Theophilus, to Highmore. In an absurd act the patentees, now Mary Wilks, Hester Booth, John Ellys, and John Highmore, locked the actors out of the theater on 26 May. They had learned that Theophilus and the players were trying to rent the theater. In September 1733 Hester Booth sold her share to Henry Giffard, manager of the New Theatre, Leman Street, Goodman's Fields, and Highmore sold his shares to Charles Fleetwood in the winter of 1734. It would be more than a decade until David Garrick took over the management of Drury Lane and made it a creative place to work again. The apathy of John Rich at Covent Garden and the number of wealthy amateur theater owners who appointed stage managers led to more instability and erratic decisions in the London theaters. In the fall of 1733 Fielding's options were all bad. The skeleton company left at Drury Lane promised a poor season, yet the rebels who had moved into the Little Theatre in the Hay-Market might fail economically, and the courts might rule that they had no right to perform without a patent.

One of Fielding's great strengths as a dramatist was his ability to write parts designed to exploit the strengths of a particular company. His most recent hits showed that he could use the Drury Lane company like a virtuoso instrument. His alterations in the part of Mariana in *The Miser* for Mrs. Christiana Horton, the expansions of the parts of Lappet and Ramilie for Clive and Theophilus Cibber, and uses for William Mullart like James in *The Mock Doctor* and Bubbleboy in *The Miser* demonstrate his ability to use all members of the company well. He chose to stay with Drury Lane, revised *The Author's Farce* to attack Theophilus Cibber, and, in the dedication to *The Intriguing Chambermaid*, praised Kitty Clive for her decision to stay there, too. Fielding augmented her part in three scenes and gave her six solos and five duets, including a funny, deliberately muddleheaded air as Mrs. Novel. *The Intriguing Chambermaid* must have given the struggling remnants of the company a chance. A perfect vehicle for Clive, it has humor, action, sentimentality, and many good songs. In it, Valentine, who has squandered his money, loves Charlotte whom Mrs. Highman intends for Oldcastle. Goodall, Valentine's father, returns unexpectedly and almost disinherits him. Valentine apologizes, Charlotte remains faithful to him, and sentimental songs and speeches close the play. The theatricality comes from the bustling action and Lettice, the maid played by Clive, rather than from the plot and the lovers. Lettice's outrageous, pert speeches, the blundering Colonel Bluff–and scenes such as the one in which the colonel insists that Valentine sold his father's pictures because of their indecent exposure of the women portrayed–promised entertainment, and the play ran eight nights.

Fielding had written *Don Quixote in England* in 1728, and he asserts in the preface that he was encouraged to revise it for performance by the Drury Lane company. In the dedication to Philip Dormer, earl of Chesterfield, he alluded several times to the general corruption of the times that he had portrayed on the stage throughout his career and said that he had added the scenes satirizing election abuses. In a strikingly prescient statement, he said, "The freedom of the stage is, perhaps, as well worth contending for as that of the press." In the play Quixote disturbs an inn where Dorothea is waiting to run away with Fairlove. Her father arrives; Squire Badger, the man her father intends for her, gets drunk and reveals himself to be a rude, coarse man, and Dorothea is allowed to marry Fairlove. Quixote explains that knights-errant foster true love, and Sir Thomas makes peace at the inn. Most of Fielding's favorite satiric objects come in for a few hits: lawyers, opera, inequities in the laws, elections, and abuses of language. The use of the inn has some similarities to the masterful development of its possibilities in *Tom Jones*. By February, however, Theophilus Cibber and the rebel players had won their court case, the Drury Lane company was ousted in early March, and his *Don Quixote in England*, then in rehearsal, was postponed. The company finally performed the play at the Little Theatre in the Hay-Market in April 1734. Although he lost Kitty Clive, who would have been Dorothea, Charles Macklin, one of the premier comic actors of the age, played Squire Badger; he and the fantastic Don Quixote, played by John Roberts, and fine songs sustained a run of nine nights.

On 28 November 1734, Fielding had married Charlotte Cradock of Salisbury. From the hometown of his grandmother and sisters, she was reputed to be beautiful and intelligent. Fielding had courted her for four years, admired and loved her, and found in her the idealistic qualities he had touted in his plays and would give his novel's heroines, Sophia Western and Amelia Booth. They were married at Charlcombe, near Bath, and moved to Buckingham Street, London. They had two children, Charlotte and Harriot.

Like all successful playwrights of the eighteenth century, Fielding took advantage of what worked. *An Old Man Taught Wisdom*, which opened 6 January 1735, was the fifth ballad-farce written as a vehicle for Kitty Clive. In it Goodwill intends to marry his sheltered, giddy daughter Lucy to a relative in order to keep his fortune in the family. Lucy is both innocent and corrupted, and her lines must have brought down the house time after time. In typical lines she tells her father, "I never dreamt of a husband in my whole life, that I did not dream of a coach," and goes on to promise him that if he will give her the coach, she will get her own husband. She quotes "Miss Jenny Flantit's" dubious advice at every

Author's benefit ticket for Pasquin *illustrating the end of act 5, in which Firebrand stabs Queen Common-Sense while Queen Ignorance indicates her support for Italian Opera (Farinelli) and pantomime (Harlequin Rich). Behind them the "Theatrical Barometer" shows Folly ascendant. This ticket is often attributed to William Hogarth, but it may be a forgery (Royal Library, Windsor Castle; by permission of Her Majesty Queen Elizabeth II).*

Queen Common-Sense rewarding Fielding (kneeling) for Pasquin, *as William Shakespeare (seated at left) looks on approvingly and characters from the play cavort*

The Little Theatre in the Hay-Market, which Fielding managed in 1736 and 1737

turn and drives her father into rages. The foolish relatives, Bookish (soon eliminated), Blister, Coupee, Quaver, and Wormwood arrive, and Lucy agrees to marry them all. As though the plot were borrowed from Swift's *Phillis, or, The Progress of Love* (1719), Lucy falls in love with Thomas, the well-dressed footman, and slips out and marries him. She has been most impressed, she says, by his hair, "so prettily drest, done all down upon the top with sugar, like a frosted cake, with three little curles on each side, that you may see his ears as plain!" Such a play must have a happy ending, and Thomas turns out to be a sensible, hardworking man.

In the revision Fielding dropped some songs, the character Bookish, a scene in which Blister planned to get money from Lucy's favorite, and the relatives' plan to marry Lucy without her father's consent. These changes made it a more good-natured, happier, faster-paced play and eliminated the implausible idea that the suitors would risk losing Lucy's fortune by marrying without permission. Robert Hume tells us that the play, often called *The Virgin Unmask'd*, saw nearly

three hundred performances by 1750.

Even this play shows Fielding's longing for serious statement. Lucy's father has the last spoken lines: "'tis less difficult to raise a fortune, than to find one worthy to inherit it." Fielding had dedicated *Don Quixote in England* to Philip Dormer, fourth earl of Chesterfield, and praised him for distinguishing himself "in the cause of liberty," and he dedicated his next play, *The Universal Gallant*, to Charles Spencer, duke of Marlborough, whom he complimented for relieving poverty. Fielding again used contrasting pairs. A jealous man is married to a prude, and a trusting one to a woman who has had an affair with Mondish. Some clever intrigue scenes, including a very good one with a screen, hardly make up for the unpleasant characters and the fact that nothing has changed at the end except that the sentimental young couple, Clarinda and Gaylove, are to marry. The play opened on 10 February 1735 and survived three nights.

The two patent houses had never had much taste for performing new plays, and two or three a year had been the average. In December 1735 Charles Fleetwood and John Rich agreed to share their profits and protect each other from losses; one result of the drastically reduced competition was that Drury Lane mounted but one new play in each of the 1735-1736 and 1736-1737 seasons and Covent Garden none in either. Robert Hume speculates that Fielding had offered Rich his *Good Natur'd Man,* and that the refusal and Fielding's subsequent understanding that he was, once again, without a theater, led to his assembling a company to perform at the Little Theatre in the Hay-Market. Fielding's *Pasquin* opened on 5 March 1736 and enjoyed an unprecedented sixty-eight-night run. Its cast, as Hume rightly describes it, was "scratch." Only fourteen of the forty-four identifiable members of the company were veteran (but fringe) performers; three more were established junior actors. More telling is the fact that none would ever become a star performer. Aaron Hill captured the essence of Fielding's achievement in a complimentary paragraph in *The Prompter* for 2 April 1736: "under the Disadvantage of a very bad House, with scarce an Actor, and at very little Expence, by the single Power of *Satire, Wit,* and *Common Sense,* has been able to run a Play on for 24 Nights, which is now, *but* begining [*sic*] to *rise* in the Opinion of the Town."

With *Pasquin* Fielding returned to the play-within-a-play rehearsal structure. The players are to decide whether to perform Trapwit's comedy, *The Election,* or Fustian's tragedy, *The Life and Death of Common-Sense.* At one point, Fustian gloats that his play is sure to please, for it is "so cram'd with Drums and Trumpets, Thunder and Lightning, Battles and Ghosts, that I believe an Audience will want no Entertainment after it; it is as full of Shew as *Merlin's* Cave itself, and for Wit—no Rope-Dancing or Tumbling can come near it." The play is indeed full of stage effects, of strange characters, of processions (Queen Ignorance and her band of singers, fiddlers, rope dancers, tumblers, and contortionists, for instance, enter to a march), and of farcical scenes. The play is also what Fielding called it in his subtitle, "A Dramatick Satire on the Times." Modern readers can recognize scores of satiric objects, and eighteenth-century playgoers surely found dozens of other lines topically apt and hilarious. We can laugh at the parody of a comic plot with its obligatory marriage and at the jokes leveled at lawyers, but they would immediately have applauded the philosophy of the Card-Box and at

lines such as Fustian's complaint that the manager had hired the actors who played the armies of Queen Ignorance and Queen Common-Sense "out of the Train'd-Bands, they are afraid to fight even in jest." Much of the satire is literary, especially of plays and play performance. The final lines, for instance, are about Sneerwell's relief that Common-Sense has defeated Ignorance: "I was under terrible Apprehensions for your Moral," he says. Fustian replies, "Sir, this is almost the only Play where she has got the better lately."

There is more to this play than good fun and lighthearted topical satire, however. Fielding had often commented on the corruption of his time, and, taken together, the plots within *Pasquin* present a dark picture indeed. As Thomas Cleary has noticed, the tragedy extends many of the accusations about political corruption in *The Election.* When Trapwit describes his play as "an Exact Representation of Nature" as the actors rehearse "direct" and "indirect" election bribery and even Trapwit's rival and denigrator, Fustian, exclaims in approval that Trapwit has depicted the dishonest mayor "quite in the Character of a Courtier," Fielding's seriousness cannot be mistaken. His audiences' delighted approval shows that they, too, recognized the truth of this portrait. The fantastic orders for goods that the country candidates use as bribes extend the satire to several social classes and appeal to the prejudices against "sordid" trade. Cumulatively, the play does suggest a satire of Walpole's policies and ways of doing business. Early on, the play has lines such as "How can you expect that Great Men should do any thing to serve you, if you stick at any thing to serve them." The tragedy is open to the interpretation that Fielding is choosing Henry St. John, viscount Bolingbroke's precepts over Walpole's practices. Certainly Cleary's argument that the play dramatizes the position of the Broad-Bottom opposition (a coalition of "Old Whigs" and the "Patriots") recently formed in Parliament is convincing. The epilogue reinforces the underlying, sober morality and opposes the spread of corruption and ignorance. This variation on the patriotic epilogue asks the audience what nation has produced the equals of Locke, Newton, Boyle, Shakespeare, and Ben Jonson and calls them away from "the Tumbling-Scum of every Nation."

Many modern critics see *Pasquin* as the evidence that Fielding had finally found his own special métier, and the plays that followed—*Tumble-*

Canvassing for Votes, *the second of four pictures in a series titled* An Election, *painted by William Hogarth in 1753-1754 (by permission of Sir John Soane's Museum). Fielding satirized the same sort of corruption in* Pasquin *(1736),* The Historical Register for the Year 1736, *and* Eurydice Hiss'd *(1737).*

Down Dick, Eurydice, The Historical Register, and *Eurydice Hiss'd*–depend upon topical satire and the burlesque form. Fielding had, in fact, brought together the most successful subjects and methods of his earlier plays. A character in *The Historical Register* explains how he would write a successful play, and Fielding's self-conscious art shines through: He would have no subject at all "but I would have a humming deal of satire, and I would repeat in every page that courtiers are cheats and don't pay their debts, that lawyers are rogues, physicians blockheads, soldiers cowards, and ministers. . . ." Episodic, ridiculous plots, music, spectacle, characters that seem to exist partly to wear outrageous costumes, and numerous opportunities for topical ad libs characterize all of these plays.

Tumble-Down Dick: or, Phaeton in the Suds, a detailed parody of a Drury Lane pantomime, *The Fall of Phaeton,* paid Rich back for many slights and ran thirty-five nights as the afterpiece for *Pasquin.* Because it included some of the satiric objects (such as bribery and the theater), characters

(Fustian and Sneerwell, for instance), and formal characteristics from *Pasquin,* it made a smooth continuation of the evening's fun. *Eurydice* is a strong, unified satire of London society and more similar to some of Pope's work than to contemporary plays. In it two pairs of commentators–an author and a critic, and two beaux–watch Orpheus, an opera singer, attempt to lead his wife out of hell. She prefers the fashionable life in hell, however, and tricks Orpheus into looking back. As if this were not unpleasant enough, the play is further darkened by Fielding's usual criticism of the inequities of the law and some of his didactic opinions about marriage. Performed as an afterpiece at Drury Lane for Addison's *Cato* on the night a riot among footmen occurred, it had but one performance.

The Historical Register for the Year 1736 opened on 21 March 1737 and ran twenty-one nights. Fielding called it a dramatic satire, thereby linking it specifically to *Pasquin,* and it is one of the "mock" pieces. As a mock-periodical in the manner of *Mercurius Britannicus,* it has unrelated items on fashionable amusements, politics, and other subjects. Colley Cibber's odes and his production of *King John* are the objects of telling satire. The auction, a scene used by dozens of later playwrights, shows such items as a clear conscience attracting no bidders while interest at court goes for one thousand pounds. Some items, such as modesty ("out of fashion") and the cardinal virtues ("I thought you had said a *cardinal's* virtues."), come in for brief discussion.

On 13 April, Fielding added *Eurydice Hiss'd* as the afterpiece. Although the allusion is to the treatment his *Eurydice* received at Drury Lane, the play is really a farcical political allegory. Spatter, the playwright, talks to a character from *The Historical Register*, Sourwit, as the play for which he has worked so hard to assure success fails. The opening scene of the play-within-the-play shows Pillage, the hero and a playwright-manager, at his levee, for he is, as Spatter explains, a Great Man. As the actors vie for parts, their language and Pillage's replies clearly point to Walpole and his attempts to control Parliament. In this piece and *The Historical Register* Fielding explicitly stated the relationship between the playhouse and the Parliament. Medley says,

> I told you that there was a strict resemblance between the states political and theatrical. There is a ministry in the latter as well as the former. . . . Parts are given in the latter to actors with much the same regard to capacity as places in the former have sometimes been. . . .

He goes on to say that "Lying, Flattering, Dissembling, Promising, Deceiving, and Undermining" are rampant in both. People immediately recognized *Eurydice Hiss'd* as a satire of Walpole and a thinly veiled jest at the loss of the Excise Bill. Bribery, a prominent feature in *Pasquin* and *The Historical Register*, was again an important subject, and Fielding was obviously accusing Walpole of purchasing M.P.'s votes. *Eurydice Hiss'd* ran twenty-one nights, and the ministry was outraged.

What part the economic success of Fielding's plays had in inspiring other political satires cannot be gauged, but the London stage abounded with them. *The King and Titi*, Robert Dodsley's *The King and the Miller of Mansfield*, William Havard's *King Charles the First*, and especially the anonymous *The Golden Rump* were but a few of the objectionable plays performed or planned in 1737. In any event, the Licensing Act passed both houses of Parliament easily, and Fielding's career at the Little Theatre in the Hay-

Market was over. Both Thomas Lockwood and Robert Hume speculate that Walpole paid him generously to give up his theatrical career immediately and quietly, and certainly Walpole purchased his share of journalists during his career. The conservatism of the remaining playhouse managers (surely to be made easier by the lack of competition assured by the Licensing Act) and Fielding's past experiences with them could hardly have left him optimistic about developing his career. In what Wilbur Cross takes to be a moving tribute to Fielding's art, an audience–faced with two justices of the peace ready to read copies of the Riot Act, two files of Grenadiers with fixed bayonets, and a full company of the Guards–prevented a troop of French players from performing in what had become Fielding's theater by, among other things, rising and singing Fielding's own "Roast Beef of Old England," a song written for *The Grub-Street Opera*.

In November 1737 Fielding entered the Middle Temple and was admitted to the bar in June 1740. Poverty forced him into selling the East Stour farm in order to get his one-sixth share, and he wrote periodical essays, translated, and collaborated in the *Champion*. These Grub Street activities did not keep him out of a sponging house for debt, but his commitment to writing and his originality remained undiminished. In 1741 he published a satire of Samuel Richardson's sensationally popular *Pamela* (1740), *An Apology for the Life of Mrs. Shamela Andrews*. By recalling Colley Cibber's autobiography, *An Apology for the Life of Mr. Colley Cibber* (1740), Fielding allied himself with Swift's *Tale of a Tub* (1704) and those works that objected to the radical individualism evident in recent prose fiction and autobiographical forms. This delightful work accused Pamela of dishonest scheming, renamed "Mr. B." "Squire Booby," and ridiculed Richardson's style and chosen form mercilessly.

The History of the Adventures of Joseph Andrews, and of his Friend Mr. Abraham Adams followed the next year. That satiric novel and the three-volume *Miscellanies* published in 1743 gave him a measure of economic security, but his adored wife, Charlotte, died in his arms in 1744, and his grief was described by some who knew him as near madness and a "frenzy." He moved back to London with his daughter Harriot, and his wife's maid, Mary Daniel, whom he made his housekeeper. On 27 November 1747, he married Mary, and went on to write his great novel *Tom Jones* (1749) and to father five more children: William, Mary Amelia, Sophia, Louisa, and Allen. Throughout this time, Fielding practiced law and wrote and contributed to London periodicals, including *The Covent-Garden Journal* and *The Jacobite's Journal.* By all accounts he attended Westminster and the Western Circuit Assizes conscientiously. In April 1746 he had been appointed High Steward of the New Forest, Hampshire, for his support of the government during and immediately after the 1745 Jacobite rebellion, and this position carried a modest grant. In 1748 he was appointed principal magistrate of the Justice Court in Bow Street, Covent Garden, and, on 11 January 1749, for Middlesex. The ground floor of his home served as his court, and his wife, children–including the baby Mary Amelia baptized on 6 January 1749–and blind half-brother, John Fielding, lived with him above. Fielding began a tireless struggle against the violent crime and drunken gambling all around him; fifty commitments a week were not unusual.

His last novel, *Amelia,* appeared in 1751 and has disappointed those who hoped for the bright comedy of *Tom Jones* ever since its publication. *Amelia,* however, is a fine novel and surely one of the best and most searching social and domestic critiques of the age.

Five years after the last performance of *Eurydice Hiss'd,* David Garrick staged *Miss Lucy in Town: A Sequel to The Virgin Unmasked,* a play Charles B. Woods says Fielding had "a very small share" in writing. Fielding's *An Old Man Taught Wisdom* had remained a popular piece, and *Miss Lucy in Town* is a sequel. In it Lucy and her Thomas come to London and inadvertently take lodgings in a bawdy house where the madam offers Lucy to some of her best clients. Three of these clients are singers, and that allows Fielding to satirize Italian opera again and to set up some effective songs. Kitty Clive played Lucy to good effect, and Lucy's attempts to become a fine lady gave Fielding a vehicle for continued satire of fashionable behavior. The play had six performances in May 1742 and twelve more in the 1742-1743 season.

In that same 1742-1743 season Drury Lane staged Fielding's *The Wedding-Day,* a play he had written in 1729. Garrick played Millamour and the cast tried to sustain it through six performances, but it has all of the displeasing aspects of Fielding's early comedies. The plot is contrived and extremely complex. Millamour has betrayed Clarinda, who has married Stedfast in desperation. Heartfort loves Charlotte Stedfast, who

is promised to Young Mutable. Clarinda is Stedfast's illegitimate daughter by Mrs. Plotwell. Finally everything is sorted out, and Millamour marries Clarinda, but the obviously unsatisfactory nature of a happy ending based upon the discovery of an incestuous marriage, and the inclusion of two ruined women as major characters predictably displeased the audience.

Fielding's next venture into the theatrical world was as "Madame de la Nash," proprietor of a puppet theater on Panton Street. As Martin Battestin points out, Fielding had to resort to the subterfuge Samuel Foote had introduced the year before to evade the Licensing Act: "guests" paid for tea, chocolate, or coffee and were entertained "free" by dramatic performances. In 1748 Fielding advertised Madame de la Nash's "Breakfasting Room" and produced his own political satire, *The Covent-Garden Tragedy* and three tried-and-true "fairground drolls," as George Speaight calls them. Advertisements published by Battestin show that Fielding embellished such pieces as *Fair Rosamond* with satires of fashionable amusements. He advertised it as including "the Comical Humours of the Town, as Drums, Routs, Riots, Hurricanes, Hoops . . . Whisk-Learning, Muffle-Boxing, Mimicking, &c." "Mimicking" aimed at Samuel Foote's popular practice of "taking off" well-known people–politicians, players, and socialites–that he had called "indecent, immoral, and even illegal. . . ." Immediately Foote advertised one of his famous "auctions," a parade of caricatures, and the two companies' actors began to mimic the principals and each other. Ad hominem exchanges ensued on stage and in the press. On 9 May Fielding featured "Mr. Puppet Fut" in *The Covent-Garden Tragedy* as Captain Bilkum. By May Fielding seems to have turned back to other kinds of writing, profits dropped, and the enterprise ended on 2 June.

Fielding wrote one other play, *The Fathers: or, The Good-Natur'd Man,* which was not performed until 30 November 1778. Robert Hume believes that Fielding wrote the play in 1735 and could not place it. In any event Fielding had promised it to Garrick in 1743, showed it to him, saw Fleetwood accept it and begin to cast it, but Fielding substituted *The Wedding-Day.* The manuscript was lost for many years after he gave it to his friend Sir Charles Williams for revision suggestions. Williams was sent abroad as a diplomat, returned to England to die, and Fielding died soon after. When Thomas Johnes, who had received the play as a gift from his brother-in-law John Williams, sent it to Garrick in 1776, Garrick allegedly cried out, " 'The Lost sheep is found! This is Harry Fielding's Comedy!' . . . in a *manner* that evinced the most friendly regard for the memory of the author" ("Advertisement," 1778 edition). The play was returned to the Fielding family, but Sir John did not allow Garrick to produce the play until some time later.

Garrick and Richard Sheridan worked over the play that the advertisement to the 1778 edition called "the fragment," and Garrick contributed a delightful prologue and an epilogue. In the prologue Fielding's most-famous characters–Tom Jones, Sophia, Partridge, Blifil, Twackum, Parson Adams, Slip Slop, Western, Mrs. Western, and Allworthy–plead for and against the play. The play itself has amusing satires of the law, of absentee landlords, of extremes in behavior in relationships, and of the Grand Tour and sentimental scenes, like Young Boncour ready to give his fortune to his father, that must have pleased the audience. The play, however, is too wordy and too preachy for good comedy–or, perhaps, for the stage at all.

It is appropriate that Sheridan had a hand in preparing *The Fathers* for the stage, for he, like the best of the playwrights of the late eighteenth and early nineteenth century, showed more of Fielding's influence than is generally acknowledged. Sheridan's *The Critic* (1779), for instance, shows direct borrowing and even uses a number of Fielding's jokes, including the silent politician. Sheridan's marriage comedies and his couples' dialogue improve upon many of Fielding's.

Fielding had suffered from cirrhosis of the liver for years, and, in the summer of 1754, he sailed to Lisbon in hopes of regaining some measure of health in the gentler climate. At age forty-seven, he died in Lisbon on 8 October of that year, and his wife buried him in the British cemetery there, the property of the English Factory.

Fielding's reputation as a playwright has risen in the last ten years, but a good assessment of his contribution to drama remains to be done. Today *The Author's Farce, Pasquin,* and especially *The Tragedy of Tragedies* are offered as the best of his dramatic works, but his three most-often performed plays in order are *The Mock Doctor, An Old Man Taught Wisdom,* and *The Lottery.* In truth, Fielding may be the most original dramatist of the eighteenth century. He wrote in many forms, adapted and transformed them imaginatively, and created a number of highly original plays. The fact that all five of his last performed plays

are rehearsal plays illustrates how intense was his experimental drive. Like so many playwrights of his time, his plays show the influence of Ben Jonson and Beaumont and Fletcher. His humours characters are obviously common and derivative, but he also used inductions and intermeans in ways that Jonson but few others did. He brought both back to the minds of playwrights and demonstrated their potential. His debts to William Congreve and John Vanbrugh are also great. He attempted Congreve's kinds of plots, characters, and wit, and he made frequent use of Vanbrugh's pairings of couples. Like Vanbrugh, too, he put his racy, idiomatic translations of Molière's plays on stage. Another strain in his drama harks back to William Davenant's *Play-House to be Let* (1663), to Buckingham's *Rehearsal* (1671), and to John Gay's *The What D'Ye Call It* (1715).

Fielding's influence on others is so widespread and varied that it is hard to document. Moreover, the number and great variety of plays that he wrote complicate discussion. On the one hand, he wrote burlesque, farce, and dramatic satire, and, on the other, comedies of manners and of humours and sentimental comedies. Nine of his plays are usually classified as ballad operas. His distinctive combination of satire, comedy, and music-hall review held the stage for decades. Dramatic satire came to be associated with his name, and playwrights like Sheridan understood the significance of what he had done and its potential for increasing the seriousness and importance of plays. His *Modern Husband* and *Universal Gallant* anticipated the problem play of the late nineteenth century, and that combined with his continual striving to comment on the actions and themes in his own plays relate him to George Bernard Shaw. As Paul Hunter has said in *Occasional Form,* Fielding–as Shaw would be–was intensely aware of the fact that interpretation depends upon perception, and he wanted to be sure that certain things were noticed and that he was interpreted aright. Peter Lewis points out that, after Buckingham, only *Tumble-Down Dick* and Sheridan's *The Critic* are first-class, true burlesques.

Fielding's contributions are not easily accessible to us. Stagecraft–his masterful use of a company's players and of special effects–can never be fully recovered, and any understanding of it requires much research of a particularly difficult kind and acts of great imagination. His satires are highly topical, and it is no negligible tribute to him that those are his most familiar plays. Specific elections, individual people, long-forgotten plays in performance, practices of a much-changed publishing industry–he puts all of these on the stage, and yet we can laugh. Even his great parodies of the abuses of Shakespeare go unrecognized by all but a few. His most innovative plays, the ones he probably took most seriously, are almost entirely neglected. Of these comedies, only *The Modern Husband* has received much attention, and that has most often been directed toward its similarities to *Amelia*. The great subject of comedy is love, and Fielding had an abiding interest in it. With wit, irony, sentiment, and well-conceived plots and characters he explores it from many angles. These plays deserve to be set within the tradition of the *drame* and evaluated as such.

Fielding's lasting appeal comes from his sophisticated alertness to language and his commitment to the highest purposes of art. His plays satirize the misuses of language by parading clichés, irrational metaphors, euphemisms, evasions, self-deceptions, lies, puns, and doggerel. In devastating lines, he can capture his age as he does in the preface to *The Tragedy of Tragedies* when he explains that "the greatest Perfection of the Language of Tragedy is, that it is not to be understood" and to assure that is to be always "too high or too low for the Understanding." Of his own play, he happily remarks that his language is "rarely within sight through the whole Play, either rising higher than the Eye of Understanding can soar, or sinking lower than it careth to stoop." In comedies like *The Modern Husband* the awareness of the chasm that has opened between the ideal, the theory, or a law's intention and the practice depends on the characters' use of language and their own recognition of how they abuse "virtue," "honor," and "reputation."

Fielding put the theater on stage, transformed it into a symbol of his age, and developed reflexive drama into a flexible, effective satiric instrument. In his work the playwright came to speak in as well as through the play, and no one has ever done it so brilliantly. That he would hone this technique underscores the high seriousness that informs even his most comic plays. The march of corrupt lawyers, theater managers, judges, politicians, guardians, quacks, hack writers, and "modern" couples are both particular examples and general signs of the corruption of the time. Time after time he displays humankind's perversions of natural order, processes,

and forms, and calls for common sense. With characters such as Luckless and Witmore in the early *Author's Farce* to Bellamant in *The Modern Husband*, he shows that interest more often than merit secures position and advantages, and the differences between the theater and the court are negligible. King Arthur's court in *Tom Thumb* vibrates with jealousy, ambition, bribery, and lamentable frailty. Just so are the auditions and readings in Cibber's and Rich's playhouses, and by the time he writes *The Historical Register*, the playwright manager is a Walpole figure and named "Pillage." In *Pasquin*, "The Election" and "The Death of Common-Sense" are analogical constructions. When he retired from the stage, he had moved close to devising ways to return the playwright to the venerable position of moral censor and public "poet," a place honored since classical times.

Bibliographies:

H. George Hahn, *Henry Fielding: An Annotated Bibliography* (Metuchen, N.J.: Scarecrow Press, 1979);

John A. Stoler and Richard D. Fulton, *Henry Fielding: An Annotated Bibliography of Twentieth-Century Criticism, 1900-1977* (New York: Garland, 1980).

Biographies:

Wilbur L. Cross, *The History of Henry Fielding*, 3 volumes (New Haven: Yale University Press, 1918);

Pat Rogers, *Henry Fielding: A Biography* (New York: Scribners, 1979).

References:

Martin C. Battestin, "Fielding and 'Master Punch' in Panton Street," *Philological Quarterly*, 45 (January 1966): 191-208;

Battestin, "Pictures of Fielding," *Eighteenth-Century Studies*, 17 (Fall 1983): 1-13;

Thomas R. Cleary, *Henry Fielding: Political Writer* (Waterloo, Ont.: Wilfrid Laurier University Press, 1984);

L. P. Goggin, "Fielding and the Select Comedies of Mr. de Molière," *Philological Quarterly*, 31 (July 1952): 344-350;

Bertrand A. Goldgar, "The Politics of Fielding's Coffee-House Politician," *Philological Quarterly*, 49 (July 1970): 424-429;

Robert D. Hume, *Henry Fielding and the London Theatre, 1728-1737* (Oxford: Clarendon Press, 1988);

J. Paul Hunter, *Occasional Form: Henry Fielding and the Chains of Circumstance* (Baltimore: Johns Hopkins University Press, 1975);

Michael Irwin, *Henry Fielding: The Tentative Realist* (Oxford: Clarendon Press, 1967);

Peter Lewis, *Fielding's Burlesque Drama: Its Place in the Tradition* (Edinburgh: Edinburgh University Press, 1987);

Thomas Lockwood, "Fielding and the Licensing Act," *Huntington Library Quarterly*, 50 (Autumn 1987): 379-393;

John Loftis, *Comedy and Society from Congreve to Fielding* (Stanford: Stanford University Press, 1959);

Loftis, *Politics of Drama in Augustan England* (Oxford: Clarendon Press, 1963);

Nancy A. Mace, "Fielding, Theobald, and *The Tragedy of Tragedies*," *Philological Quarterly*, 66 (Fall 1987): 457-472;

Brian McCrea, *Henry Fielding and the Politics of Mid-Eighteenth-Century England* (Athens: University of Georgia Press, 1981);

L. J. Morrissey, Critical Introduction to *The Grub-Street Opera* (Edinburgh: Oliver & Boyd, 1973);

Morrissey, "Henry Fielding and the Ballad Opera," *Eighteenth-Century Studies*, 4 (Summer 1971): 386-402;

Ronald Paulson and Thomas Lockwood, *Henry Fielding: The Critical Heritage* (London: Routledge & Kegan Paul, 1969);

Edgar V. Roberts, "Eighteenth-Century Ballad Opera: The Contributions of Fielding," *Drama Survey*, 1 (1961): 71-85;

Roberts, "The Songs and Tunes in Henry Fielding's Ballad Operas," in *Essays on the Eighteenth-Century English Stage*, edited by Kenneth Richards and Peter Thomson (London: Methuen, 1972), pp. 29-49;

George Bernard Shaw, Preface to *First Volume of Plays: Pleasant and Unpleasant* (London: Constable, 1931);

Dane F. Smith, *Plays about the Theatre in England from "The Rehearsal" in 1671 to the Licensing Act of 1737* (London: Oxford University Press, 1936);

Charles B. Woods, "The 'Miss Lucy' Plays of Fielding and Garrick," *Philological Quarterly*, 41 (January 1962): 294-310;

Woods, "Notes on Three of Fielding's Plays," *PMLA*, 52 (June 1937): 359-373.

Papers:
Manuscripts for some of Fielding's poetry survive in the Harrowby MSS Trust, Sandon Hall, Stafford. Some of his letters are at the Bedford Office, London; others and some miscellaneous documents are in various libraries including the British Library, the Houghton Library at Harvard University, the Huntington Library, the Princeton University Library, and the Victoria and Albert Museum. The printer's copy for one of the *Common Sense* essays is at the Public Record Office, Chancery Lane, London.

David Garrick

(19 February 1717-20 January 1779)

Douglas H. White
Loyola University of Chicago

PLAY PRODUCTIONS: *Lethe; or Esop in the Shades*, London, Theatre Royal in Drury Lane, 15 April 1740;

The Lying Valet, London, New Theatre, Ayliffe St., Goodman's Fields, 30 November 1741;

Macbeth, adapted from William Shakespeare's play, London, Theatre Royal in Drury Lane, 7 January 1744;

The Provok'd Wife, alteration of John Vanbrugh's play, with various changes between 1744 and 1777, London, Theatre Royal in Drury Lane, 16 November 1744;

Miss in Her Teens; or, The Medley of Lovers, London, Theatre Royal in Covent Garden, 17 January 1747;

Romeo and Juliet, adapted from Shakespeare's play, London, Theatre Royal in Drury Lane, 29 November 1748;

Every Man in His Humour, altered but mostly edited version of Ben Jonson's play, London, Theatre Royal in Drury Lane, 29 November 1751;

Catharine and Petruchio, afterpiece altered from Shakespeare's *The Taming of the Shrew*, London, Theatre Royal in Drury Lane, 18 March 1754;

The Chances, altered from George Villiers, second duke of Buckingham's adaptation of John Fletcher's play (Garrick continued to alter), London, Theatre Royal in Drury Lane, 7 November 1754;

The Fairies, opera based on Shakespeare's *A Midsummer Night's Dream*, libretto by Garrick and music by John Christopher Smith, London, Theatre Royal in Drury Lane, 3 February 1755;

Florizel and Perdita, afterpiece altered from Shakespeare's *The Winter's Tale*, London, Theatre Royal in Drury Lane, 21 January 1756;

The Tempest, An Opera, adapted from Shakespeare's play, libretto probably by Garrick and music by Smith, London, Theatre Royal in Drury Lane, 11 February 1756;

King Lear, adapted from Nahum Tate's adaptation of Shakespeare's play (Garrick probably continued to alter the text), London, Theatre Royal in Drury Lane, 28 October 1756;

Lilliput, London, Theatre Royal in Drury Lane, 3 December 1756;

The Male Coquette; or, Seventeen Hundred Fifty-Seven (originally titled *The Modern Fine Gentleman*), London, Theatre Royal in Drury Lane, 24 March 1757;

Isabella; or, The Fatal Marriage (or *The Fatal Marriage; or, The Innocent Adultery*), alteration of Thomas Southerne's *The Fatal Marriage*, London, Theatre Royal in Drury Lane, 2 December 1757;

The Gamesters, alteration of James Shirley's play, London, Theatre Royal in Drury Lane, 22 December 1757;

The Guardian, London, Theatre Royal in Drury Lane, 3 February 1759;

Harlequin's Invasion; or, A Christmas Gambol, London, Theatre Royal in Drury Lane, 31 December 1759;

The Enchanter; or, Love and Magic, libretto by Garrick and music by Smith, London, Theatre Royal in Drury Lane, 13 December 1760;

Cymbeline, altered and adapted version of Shakespeare's play, London, Theatre Royal in Drury Lane, 28 November 1761;

The Farmer's Return from London, London, Theatre Royal in Drury Lane, 20 March 1762;

The Clandestine Marriage, by Garrick and George Colman the Elder, London, Theatre Royal in Drury Lane, 20 February 1766;

The Country Girl, alteration of William Wycherley's *The Country Wife*, London, Theatre Royal in Drury Lane, 25 October 1766;

Neck or Nothing, London, Theatre Royal in Drury Lane, 18 November 1766;

Cymon, London, Theatre Royal in Drury Lane, 2 January 1767;

Linco's Travels, London, Theatre Royal in Drury Lane, 6 April 1767;

David Garrick (portrait by Thomas Gainsborough, circa 1770; by permission of the National Portrait Gallery, London)

A Peep Behind the Curtain; or, The New Rehearsal, London, Theatre Royal in Drury Lane, 23 October 1767;

The Jubilee, London, Theatre Royal in Drury Lane, 14 October 1769;

The Institution of the Garter; or, Arthur's Roundtable Restored, London, Theatre Royal in Drury Lane, 28 October 1771;

The Irish Widow, London, Theatre Royal in Drury Lane, 23 October 1772;

Hamlet (last of Garrick's acted versions and the one most representative of his interpretation), London, Theatre Royal in Drury Lane, 18 December 1772;

A Christmas Tale, by Garrick, with music by Charles Dibdin, London, Theatre Royal in Drury Lane, 27 December 1773;

The Meeting of the Company, London, Theatre Royal in Drury Lane, 17 September 1774;

Bon Ton; or, High Life above Stairs, London, Theatre Royal in Drury Lane, 18 March 1775;

The Theatrical Candidates, by Garrick, with music by William Bates, London, Theatre Royal in Drury Lane, 23 September 1775;

May Day; or, The Little Gipsy, libretto by Garrick and music by Thomas Arne, London, Theatre Royal in Drury Lane, 28 October 1775.

BOOKS: *The Lying Valet; In Two Acts. As it is performed Gratis, At the Theatre in Goodman's-*

Fields (London: Printed for & sold by Paul Vaillant & J. Roberts, 1742);

Mr. Garrick's Answer to Mr. Macklin's Case (London, 1743);

An Essay on Acting, in which will be consider'd the Mimical Behavior of a certain fashionable faulty actor, and the laudableness of such unmannerly as well as inhumane proceedings. To which will be added a short criticism on his acting Macbeth (London: W. Bickerton, 1744);

Lethe or, Esop in the Shades. As acted at the Theatres in London, with Universal Applause [unauthorized edition] (London: Printed by J. Cooke, 1745); republished as *Lethe. A Dramatic Satire. By David Garrick. As it is Performed at the Theatre-Royal in Drury-Lane, By His Majesty's Servants* [authorized edition] (London: Printed for & sold by Paul Vaillant, 1749);

Miss in her Teens: or, The Medley of Lovers. A Farce. In Two Acts. As it is Perform'd at the Theatre-Royal in Covent-Garden (London: Printed for J. & R. Tonson & S. Draper, 1747);

Romeo and Juliet. By Shakespear. With Alterations, and an additional Scene: By D. Garrick. As it is Perform'd at the Theatre-Royal in Drury-Lane (London: Printed for J. & R. Tonson & S. Draper, 1750, 1753);

Every Man in his Humour. A Comedy. Written by Ben Jonson. With Alterations and Additions As it is Perform'd at the Theatre-Royal in Drury-Lane (London: Printed for J. & R. Tonson & S. Draper, 1752);

An Ode on the Death of Mr. Pelham (London, 1754);

The Fairies. An Opera. Taken from A Midsummer Night's Dream, Written by Shakespear. As it is Perform'd at the Theatre-Royal in Drury-Lane. The Songs from Shakespear, Milton, Waller, Dryden, Lansdown, Hammond, &c. The Music composed by Mr. Smith (London: Printed for J. & R. Tonson & S. Draper, 1755);

Catharine and Petruchio. A Comedy, In Three Acts. As it is Perform'd at the Theatre-Royal in Drury-Lane. Alter'd from Shakespear's Taming of the Shrew (London: Printed for J. & R. Tonson & S. Draper, 1756);

The Tempest. An Opera. Taken from Shakespear. As it is Performed at the Theatre-Royal in Drury-Lane. The Songs from Shakespear, Dryden, &c. The Music composed by Mr. Smith (London: Printed for J. & R. Tonson, 1756);

Lilliput. A Dramatic Entertainment. As it is performed at the Theatre-Royal in Drury-Lane (London: Printed for Paul Vaillant, 1757);

The Male-Coquette: or, Seventeen Hundred Fifty-Seven. In Two Acts. As it is Performed at the Theatre-Royal in Drury-Lane (London: Printed for P. Vaillant, 1757);

Isabella: or, The Fatal Marriage. A Play. Alter'd from Southern. As it is Now performing at the Theatre-Royal in Drury-Lane (London: Printed for J. & R. Tonson, 1757);

Florizel and Perdita. A Dramatic Pastoral, In Three Acts. Alter'd from The Winter's Tale of Shakespear. By David Garrick. As it is performed at the Theatre Royal in Drury-Lane (London: Printed for J. & R. Tonson, 1758);

The Gamesters: A Comedy. Alter'd from Shirley. As it is Perform'd, By His Majesty's Servants, at the Theatre-Royal in Drury-Lane (London: Printed for J. & R. Tonson, 1758);

The Guardian. A Comedy of Two Acts. As it is perform'd at the Theatre-Royal in Drury-Lane (London: Printed for J. Newberry & sold by R. Bailye at Litchfield, J. Leake & W. Frederick at Bath, B. Collins at Salisbury, & S. Stabler at York, 1759);

Enchanter; Or Love and Magic. A Musical Drama. As it is performed at the Theatre-Royal in Drury-Lane. The Music composed by Mr. Smith (London: Printed for J. & R. Tonson, 1760);

The Fribbleriad (London: J. Coots, 1761);

The Provok'd Wife. A Comedy. As it was acted at the Theatre-Royal in Drury-Lane (London: Printed for J. Brindley, 1761);

Cymbeline. A Tragedy. By Shakespear. With Alterations (London: Printed for J. & R. Tonson, 1762);

The Farmer's Return From London. An Interlude. As it is Performed at the Theatre-Royal in Drury-Lane (London: Printed by Dryden Leach, for J. & R. Tonson, 1762);

Hamlet, Prince of Denmark: A Tragedy. As it is now acted At the Theatres Royal in Drury-Lane, and Covent-Garden (London: Printed for Mess. Hawes & Co., B. Dodd, J. Rivington, S. Crowder, T. Longman, B. Law, T. Caslon, T. Lownds & C. Corbett, 1763);

The Sick Monkey, A Fable (London: Printed for J. Fletcher, 1765);

The Clandestine Marriage, A Comedy. As it is Acted at the Theatre-Royal in Drury-Lane, by Garrick and George Colman the Elder (London: Printed for T. Becket & P. A. De Hondt, R. Baldwin, R. Davis & T. Davis, 1766);

Neck or Nothing, A Farce. In Two Acts. As It Is Performed At The Theatre Royal in Drury-Lane (London: Printed for T. Becket, 1766);

The Country Girl, A Comedy, (Altered from Wycherley) As it is Acted at the Theatre-Royal in Drury-Lane (London: Printed for T. Becket & P. A. De Hondt, L. Davis & C. Reymers, and T. Davies, 1767);

Cymon. A Dramatic Romance. As it is Performed at the Theatre-Royal, in Drury-Lane (London: Printed for T. Becket & P. A. De Hondt, 1767);

A Peep Behind the Curtain; or, The New Rehearsal. As it is Now Performed at the Theatre Royal in Drury-Lane (London: T. Becket & P. A. De Hondt, 1767);

An Ode upon Dedicating a Building, and Erecting a Statue, to Shakespeare, at Stratford upon Avon. By D. G. (London: T. Becket & P. A. De Hondt, 1769);

Songs, Chorusses, &c. Which are Introduced in the New Entertainment of The Jubilee. At the Theatre Royal in Drury-Lane (London: Printed for T. Becket & P. A. De Hondt, 1769);

The Songs, Choruses, and Serious Dialogue of the Masque Called The Institution of the Garter, or, Arthur's Round Table restored (London: Printed for T. Becket & P. A. De Hondt, 1771);

The Irish Widow. In Two Acts. As it is Performed at the Theatre Royal in Drury-Lane (London: Printed for T. Becket, 1772);

The Chances. A Comedy. With Alterations (London: Printed for the proprietors & sold by T. Becket, 1773);

King Lear, A Tragedy, by Shakespeare, as performed at the Theatre-Royal, Drury-Lane (London: Printed for John Bell & C. Etherington at York, 1773); revised edition: *King Lear, A Tragedy: Altered from Shakespeare by David Garrick, Esq. Marked with the Variations in the Manager's Book; at the Theatre-Royal in Drury-Lane* (London: Printed for C. Bathurst, J. F. & C. Rivington, L. Davis, W. Owen & Son, B. White & Son, T. Longman, B. Law, C. Dilly, T. Payne & Son, J. Nicholls, T. Cadell, J. Robson, G. G. J. & J. Robinson, T. Bowles, R. Baldwin, H. L. Gardner, J. Bew, J. Murray, W. Stuart, S. Hayes, W. Lowndes, S. Bladon, G. & T. Wilkie, W. Fox, Scatcherd & Whitaker, R. Faulder, J. Barker, T. & J. Egerton, D. Ogilvy & E. Newbery, 1786);

Macbeth, A Tragedy, by Shakespeare, as performed at the Theatre-Royal, Drury-Lane (London: Printed for John Bell & C. Etherington at York, 1774);

A New Dramatic Entertainment, Called a Christmas Tale. In Five Parts. As it is Performed at the Theatre-Royal, in Drury-Lane (London: Printed for T. Becket, 1774);

Bon Ton: or, High Life above Stairs. A Comedy. In Two Acts. As it is performed at the Theatre Royal, in Drury-Lane (London: Printed for T. Becket, 1775);

May-Day: or, The Little Gipsy. A Musical Farce, of One Act. To Which is added the Theatrical Candidates. A Musical Prelude. As They are both performed at the Theatre-Royal, in Drury-Lane (London: Printed for T. Becket, 1775);

Three Plays by David Garrick, Printed from hitherto unpublished mss., edited by Elizabeth P. Stein (New York: William Edwin Rudge, 1926)—comprises *Harlequin's Invasion, The Jubilee,* and *The Meeting of the Company; or, Bayes Art of Acting*;

The Diary of David Garrick, Being a Record of His Memorable Trip to Paris in 1751, Now First Printed from the Original Ms., edited by Ryliss Clair Alexander (New York: Oxford University Press, 1928);

The Journal of David Garrick, Describing His Visit to France and Italy in 1763, Now First Printed from the Original Manuscript in the Folger Shakespeare Library, edited by George Winchester Stone, Jr. (New York: Modern Language Association of America, 1939).

Collections: *The Poetical Works of David Garrick, Esq.*, 2 volumes, edited by George Kearsley (London: Kearsley, 1785);

The Dramatic Works of David Garrick, Esq., 3 volumes (London: Printed for A. Millar, 1798; facsimile, Gregg International Publishers, 1969);

The Plays of David Garrick, 7 volumes, edited by Harry William Pedicord and Frederick Louis Bergmann (Carbondale & Edwardsville: Southern Illinois University Press, 1980);

The Plays of David Garrick, 4 volumes, edited by Gerald M. Berkowitz (New York & London: Garland, 1981).

Two hundred years after his death what we know of David Garrick confirms that he was one of the true theatrical geniuses of all time. He was an actor of astonishing power and popularity, a manager-entrepreneur of extreme skill and insight, and a writer and adapter of great conse-

David Garrick, 1741 (portrait by Jean Baptiste Vanloo, Somerset Maugham Collection in the National Theatre; by permission of the National Theatre and the Victoria and Albert Museum)

quence for the theater of his era. He raised the status of his profession to a point well beyond that accorded to even the most successful of his forerunners and left it in a state of security and respectability that could hardly have been anticipated before he flashed like a meteor through the theatrical world in the second half of the eighteenth century. His achievements in acting (an area of endeavor that at least before the advent of the motion picture was almost literally "writ in water") have remained the subject of interest and debate well into the twentieth century and provided him with a place in the history of his profession that has seldom if ever been matched.

David Garrick was born in Hereford on 19 February 1717. Though the family home was in Lichfield, his father, Peter Garrick (a lieutenant

in the army), was in Hereford on a recruiting mission, and his wife, Arabella Clough Garrick, had accompanied him. Soon after David's birth they returned to Lichfield, and it was in that cathedral town, where Mrs. Garrick was allied to clerical circles through her father, Anthony Clough, vicar-choral of the cathedral, that David lived into early manhood, with the exception of a one-year sojourn to Lisbon as a sort of apprentice to his uncle David Garrick, a wine merchant in the Portuguese capital. David's formal education included some years at the Lichfield Grammar School, as well as a year under the tutelage of Samuel Johnson at his ill-fated school at Edial from the time of its opening in late autumn 1735 until it closed before the end of January 1737. Despite the quite genuine poverty of the family, they belonged to respectable circles, and David was able to profit from the example and stimulation of the town's leading cultural scion, Gilbert Walmesley, who lived in the Palace of the Bishop and was active in encouraging the endeavors of the talented local inhabitants–his two most impressive successes being Garrick and Samuel Johnson.

It is apparently true, though sparsely documented, that Garrick showed an early interest in the theater and organized a production of George Farquhar's *The Recruiting Officer* in Lichfield when he was in early adolescence; he took the role of Sergeant Kite. Nevertheless, if he harbored an intention of becoming an actor, he kept it well hidden from his family.

In 1737 David set out for London in the company of his former teacher Johnson, the two of them seeking their fortunes in a larger world than Lichfield offered, and both of them quite without funds. David was at least overtly intending to pursue the respectable route of law (Walmesley having provided him with a reference to a tutor in Rochester). He went through the motions so far as to enter himself at Lincoln's Inn, but when he inherited one thousand pounds from the Lisbon uncle in his twenty-first year, he went instead into the wholesale wine business with his brother Peter. David's inching into his theatrical career while at the same time functioning (at least minimally) as a wine merchant is largely undocumented, but it is clear that he made and cultivated theatrical connections, the two most important being the actors and theater managers Henry Giffard and Charles Macklin. He was more serious about the theatrical connection than any of his family knew, for on 15 April 1740, on the night of Giffard's benefit, his afterpiece called *Lethe* appeared at the Theatre Royal in Drury Lane.

The title page of Garrick's *Lethe* classifies it as a "dramatic satire." Today we would call it a skit. If the word *satire* can be applied to the work, its implication must be quite gentle. Garrick's "satire" would never be particularly deep or indignant. The objects of his attack are usually far more nearly comic characters than they are satiric targets, and the attack itself is amusing, diverting, geared to amiable laughter rather than to penetrating analysis of the source of corruption. The characters he makes fun of are all conventional comic butts, with the laughs guaranteed, quite innocent of any sense of revelation or exposé or discrediting. Because they are the usual fops and rakes and bumpkins (either male or female), they have little capacity to engage a viewer into much sense of outrage resulting from discovery. A situation is set up in *Lethe* into which any folly-ridden character can be placed to have his absurdity displayed and then displaced to make room for the next. In fact Garrick did continue to add and subtract characters through most of the theatrical career of this very successful piece. Garrick borrowed the structural pattern from James Miller's *An Hospital for Fools* (1739; itself based on a French source) and on John Vanbrugh's *Aesop* (1696-1697). Garrick's plays are practically never original material. His usual method is, as with his *Lying Valet*, to engage in a process by which a work by someone else is altered to fit what Garrick understands the needs of his theater and the taste of his audience to be.

In *Lethe* Aesop interviews various characters to find out what they want to forget by drinking the waters of Lethe. He finds each complacent, and at the end he leaves no doubt about the message: "Now, mortals, attend! I have perceived from your examinations, that you have mistaken the effect of your distempers for the cause. You would willingly be relieved from many things which interfere with your passions and affections, while your vices, from which all your cares and misfortunes arise, are totally forgotten and neglected. Then follow me and drink to the forgetfulness of vice.

> 'Tis vice alone disturbs the human breast;
> Care dies with guilt; be virtuous and be blest.' "

In order to put this sort of performance into a proper context we must acknowledge that it is extremely gentle. If it is moral, it is jocularly moral–utterly conventional morality handled with lightness of touch. The objects of ridicule are all long-tried and relatively harmless. It is highly performance oriented. Certainly it makes thin reading, though it is amusing. As the occasion for deft comic acting it shows definite promise. In summary, as Harry William Pedicord and Frederick Louis Bergmann note in their edition of Garrick's plays, "The writer of the farce afterpiece aimed no higher than to construct or adapt pieces which would prop up mainpieces and delight the galleries as well as pit and boxes and bring money to the box-office.

"The longevity of Garrick's *Lethe* attests the measure of Garrick's art and predicts his lifelong success as a writer of afterpieces for his theatre–263 performances in 26 seasons." However,

GOODMAN's-FIELDS.

AT the *Late Theatre* in *Goodman's-Fields*, this Day, will be perform'd a CONCERT of VOCAL and INSTRUMENTAL MUSICK. Divided into TWO PARTS.

Tickets at *Three*, *Two*, and *One Shilling*.

Places for the Boxes to be taken at the Fleece-Tavern near the Theatre.

N.B. Between the Two Parts of the Concert will be presented an Historical Play, call'd The LIFE and DEATH of

King RICHARD the Third.

Containing, The Distresses and Death of King Henry VI. The Artful Acquisition of the Crown by King Richard. The Murder of young K. Edward V. and his Brother, in the Tower. The Landing of the Earl of Richmond. And the Death of King Richard, in the memorable Battle of Bosworth-Field ; being the last that was fought between the Houses of York and Lancaster.

With many other True Historical Passages. The Part of King Richard by a GENTLEMAN; (*Who never appear'd on any Stage;*)

King Henry, by Mr. Giffard; Richmond, Mr. Marshall; Prince Edward, by Miss Hippisley ; Duke of York, Miss Naylor; Duke of Buckingham, Mr. Peterson ; Duke of Norfolk, Mr. Blakes; Lord Stanley, Mr. Paget ; Oxford, Mr. Vaughan ; Tressel, Mr. W. Giffard ; Catesby, Mr. Marr ; Ratcliff, Mr. Crofts ; Blunt, Mr. Naylor; Tyrrel, by Mr. Pattenden ; Lord-Mayor, Mr. Dunstall. The Queen, Mrs. Steel; Dutchess of York, Mrs. Yates ; And the Part of Lady Anne, by Mrs. Giffard.

With Entertainments of Dancing by Monf. FROMENT, Madem. DUVALL, and the two Masters and Miss GRANIER.

To which will be added a Ballad-Opera of One Act, call'd The VIRGIN UNMASK'D.

The Part of Miss Lucy by Miss Hippisley.

Both which will be perform'd gratis, by Persons for their Diversion. The Concert will begin exactly at Six o'Clock.

Announcement of Garrick's first appearance as Richard III, 19 October 1741

Garrick as Richard III, 1745 (painting by William Hogarth; by permission of the Walker Art Gallery, Liverpool)

this is an analysis of its *success*, not its excellence, and the assessment is governed by the initial observation that the work's *aim* is not very high. Garrick understood himself to be a writer for the active, performing theater, and he confined himself to what, in the world of literature, are understood to be minor forms, to the middle flight, emotionally, intellectually, artistically; and his success can be determined only by estimating his achievement within that flight. The chief difficulty in getting Garrick into exact focus is that commentators on his work have tended either to overestimate him (that is, to try to push him into a higher flight, to which he did not aspire) or underestimate him (that is, to denigrate his flight merely because it is not higher). It should be remembered that every type of genre requires a performance within its confines to be exactly accommodated to its specific demands, and a misplacement either above or below will be equally destructive. Garrick's artistry allowed him to do precisely what his purpose dictated. He is usually correct in his understanding of what is required and how it is to be achieved, but he never aims at the highest or most exalted effects.

It should also be noticed that Garrick's aim directed him toward types of composition and performance that were popular at the time but grew obsolete. Throughout Garrick's stage career an evening in the theater normally consisted of at least two pieces of entertainment—a full-length or five-act play and a one- or two-act afterpiece—and could include in various combinations entr'acte music or dancing, pantomimes of various lengths, short operettas or burlettas, prologues, epilogues, ballets, pageants, and spectacles. With two possible exceptions Garrick wrote entirely in these forms that were supplementary to the main piece of the evening, and which, when theatrical conventions changed, became obsolete. At the same time not much is gained by suggesting that Garrick or anybody else aimed "merely" at entertaining the gallery. No matter how light the particular form may be, it is not and cannot be seen to function as or in a vacuum. It will have a plot, it will have dialogue, and it will have characters, and one light piece will work better than another light piece because its plot (though light) is better, because its dialogue (though light) is brighter and livelier, because its characters are more engaging and amusing. In other words, Garrick's forms probably were usually selected for audience-pleasing or box-office-filling reasons, but the success of the

piece is the result of his artistry and vivacity and craftsmanship.

When Garrick first appeared as an actor at the New Theatre in Goodman's Fields, on 19 October 1741, the advertisement claimed that the part of Richard III was to be acted by "a gentleman who never appear'd on any Stage," but we now know that Garrick had been serving a surreptitious apprenticeship between his hours in the Durham Yard wine cellar. In fact it was far more than an apprenticeship. Garrick was not only memorizing roles. He was also inventing what would seem to his contemporaries to be a new method of acting. In this he may well have been encouraged and even instructed by Macklin and Giffard, but the result, whatever assistance he may have had from his mentors (Giffard was twenty-three years older than Garrick, and Macklin was eighteen years older), was something that everybody responded to as new and original when they saw it in performance. Garrick's first essays on the stage, however, took place some months before his deceptively advertised debut in Ipswich (if we discount a short appearance in disguise as Harlequin at Goodman's Fields theater) under the name of Mr. Lyddall. At that time he already had in his repertory Aboan in Thomas Southerne's *Oroonoko*, Lord Foppington in Colley Cibber's *The Careless Husband*, Sir Harry Wildair in George Farquhar's *The Constant Couple*, and Chamont in Thomas Otway's *The Orphan*.

It was fairly common at the time to advertise a performance by an actor who had never been on a stage before. Still, when he appeared as Richard III (in the usual adaptation of Shakespeare's play by Colley Cibber), the unknown, anonymous, twenty-four-year-old actor gave his less-than-full-house audience something it had never seen before, and he was an overnight sensation. Fellow actors commented in stunned jealousy, "If he is right, then we have all been wrong." *The Daily Post and General Advertiser* reported the next day that the stranger's "Reception was the most extraordinary and great that was ever known upon such an Occasion." Word spread, and shortly the theater audience was crowding the roads to the out-of-the-way theater to see the new phenomenon. Among them was the great Alexander Pope, who pronounced, as reported by Thomas Davies, that "he was afraid the young man would be spoiled, for he would have no competitor."

Garrick's style was regarded as "natural," but that is not much help in our attempt to visual-

Letter from Garrick to his cousin Peter Fermignac, written the morning after Garrick's first appearance as Richard III
(by permission of the Folger Shakespeare Library)

The only thing that gives me pain upon y.e
occasion is that My Friends I suppose
will look very cool upon Me particular[l]y
y.e Chief of 'em, those at Carshalton — But w.t
can I do, I am wholly bent upon y.e Thing
~~year make very near 300 £ annum~~
of It — as My Brother will settle at
Litchfield I design to throw up y.e wine
Business as soon as I can conveniently.
& I desire you'll let My Uncle know — if
you should want to Speak with Me y.e Stage
door will be always Open to You — or
~~any other~~ part of y.e house, for I am
manager with M.r Giffard & You may
always command
                              Y.r most hum.le Servant
                                        D Garrick
                                        &c

ize it or hear it, for new acting styles–that is, breaks from contemporary conventions–are always called "natural," and it is not very likely that a twentieth-century audience would favor Garrick's style with that word. However, such distinctions must be understood as matters of degree, and his audience was seeing him in comparison with Colley Cibber and James Quin, perhaps even Thomas Betterton, not Laurence Olivier or Marlon Brando. Garrick did not rant and intone and orate. He worked for a delivery that would approximate the way of speaking in everyday life. He internalized and searched for individual characteristics. He paused; he hesitated; he put his hands in his pockets. His audience was amazed that he displayed no sign of the actor at work. He *became* the character. Henry Fielding in his ironic way gives, through the naiveté of Partridge, a delightful summary of the effect of Garrick's acting in *Tom Jones* (1749; book 16, chapter 5):

> "He the best Player!" cries *Partridge* with a contemptuous Sneer, "Why I could act as well as he myself. I am sure if I had seen a Ghost, I should have looked in the very same Manner, and done just as he did. And then, to be sure, in that Scene, as you called it, between him and his Mother, where you told me he acted so fine, why, Lord help me, any Man, that is, any good Man, that had such a Mother, would have done exactly the same. I know you are only joking with me; but, indeed, Madam, though I was never at a Play in *London*, yet I have seen acting before in the Country; and the King for my Money; he speaks all his Words distinctly, half as loud again as the other.–Any Body may see he is an Actor."

No one doubts, whatever Partridge's mistakes, that Fielding is saying that Garrick is such a good actor that one forgets that he is acting.

Clearly, though, Garrick's theater was much more orational than ours, although it was apparently less so than Cibber's. The audience was prepared to interrupt the performance with applause frequently, for certain speeches, for certain reactions, even for certain pieces of business, and the success of the performance was, according to contemporary descriptions, gauged by the number of such interruptions. In other words, the audience was much involved with the performance dimension of the evening, very ready to react to what the actor was doing, rather than what the character intended. Students of eighteenth-century audiences are often reminded of opera rather than theater audiences of today. The vociferous expression of approval and disapproval, the "fan" mentality, the willingness to see the same performance over and over or the same work with different casts, the wild applause for the arias, the dancers, the scenery, or whatever else asserts itself, the fascination with stars and with their particular style and delivery, even audible expressions of disapproval like hissing or booing, all were part of the daily theater experience. If we are a little puzzled that Garrick could play Benedick or Ranger when he was in his middle twenties and continue to play them into his retirement year when he was nearing sixty, or that he could play Lear at twenty-five, we need only remember any number of opera singers whom, at least to the fans, age could not wither. Nor is it a matter merely of curiosity. Such audiences are fascinated and moved by the stars' inimitable ways of doing their roles. The rest, in a performance-oriented medium, can, if need be, be supplied by other means, especially as one's seat gets farther from the stage and the lighting gets dimmer.

What a thrill for young David Garrick from Lichfield to have all of his work and aspiration and hesitation received with such wild approval and how he must have basked in the triumph when he wrote to his brother Peter. After a discussion of the wine business–the surprise:

> Last Night I play'd Richard the Third to the Surprize of Every Body & as I shall make very near £300 p Annum by It & as it is really what I doat upon I am resolv'd to pursue it– . . .
> I am D^r bro[ther]
> Yrs Sincerely
> D Garrick
> I have a farce [*The Lying Valet*] coming out of Drury Lane.

Thus, in addition to his diligent preparations for acting, he had written two theater pieces, both of which had been accepted for performance, though *The Lying Valet* came out of Goodman's Fields rather than Drury Lane.

The Lying Valet, which Garrick in his postscript calls a farce, is a short, two-act comedy, written as an afterpiece and adapted from Peter Motteux's *All Without Money*. It is airy, amusing, playable; and it would make an entertaining episode (or maybe two) in a television sitcom, and it is cleverly conceived and artfully crafted for its purpose. It is the first of Garrick's compositions that comes under the head of an *imitation*, that is, a work translated from another language or period, in which the translator changes the context and milieu as well as the words. The end product is somewhere between the original composition and a translation. Pope and Dryden produced great poetic works in this medium by writing imitations of great Roman writers, notably Horace.

In *The Lying Valet*, Gayless is a young man who formerly had a fortune of his own. He squandered it in high living. As a consequence, his father disowned him, and he became engaged to Melissa, herself possessed of the fortune necessary for their subsistence. However, while on the one hand he is a fortune hunter, on the other he is a true sentimental (or good-natured) hero, loves Melissa, and is ashamed of deceiving her. The comic incidents of the plot involve Gayless's attempts (with Sharp, the mendacious valet in question, as the chief instigator) to hide his poverty. When his true condition is discovered, Gayless falls back on his sentiments: "to endeavor to vindicate my crimes would show a greater want of virtue than even the commission of 'em." And Melissa, not to be outdone in the sententious, replies, "Your necessities, Mr. Gayless, with such real contrition, are too powerful motives not to affect the breast already prejudiced in your favor. You have suffered too much already for your extravagance; and as I take part in your sufferings, 'tis easing myself to relieve you. Know, therefore, all that's past I freely forgive." Melissa also gives him a letter from his father that reinstates him into the family's good graces, a letter that she has known about during the most urgent action. In a nonsentimental comedy one might wonder what to make of the fact that Melissa knew of the reinstatement and his improved financial condition before she gave his virtue its ultimate test, but here we find instead joy in another piece of conventional morality: "So virtuous love affords us springing joy,/Whilst vicious passions, as they burn, destroy."

Despite all the apparent success of his theatrical ventures, David Garrick's attempts in the fall of 1741 to convince his brother that he was behaving responsibly were not successful in assuaging Peter's fear for the family name. Nevertheless, there was no turning back, especially (David Garrick supplicated), "as My Genius that Way (by the best Judges) is thought Wonderful. . . ." As he continues to win his brother over he engages in some impressive name dropping, for from the very beginning he showed the additional talent

of attracting the friendship of the wealthy, the titled, the important.

The endeavor at the Goodman's Fields theater was from the start one of doubtful legality. The Licensing Act of 1737 had been instituted in order to bring the potential propagandistic power of the theater under government control, and it left only two patent theaters in London. Goodman's Fields was not one of them. Giffard had, however, set out to circumvent the law by taking literally its stipulation of staging plays *for money*. He, therefore, advertised the activities at his theater as "A Concert of Vocal and Instrumental Music" with a sly note announcing (in much larger letters) that *King Richard the Third* would be performed gratis during the intermission. Either because Giffard had friends at court or because the authorities were not much interested, he was able to carry this ruse on for a while, but, it is generally believed, after the patent houses began to feel at the box office the competition of Garrick's success, Goodman's Fields was closed on 24 May 1742. For Garrick, Goodman's Fields had certainly served its purpose. By the end of the season he had become a genuine force in the London theater world. For about a month after the opening of *Richard III* his anonymity had continued, but by 28 November the name David Garrick appeared in a playbill. And as the season went on he added role after role to his repertory: Clodio in Colley Cibber's *Loves Makes a Man*, Chamont in Otway's *The Orphan*, Jack Smatter in James Dance's adaptation of Richardson's *Pamela*, Sharp in his own new afterpiece *The Lying Valet*, Lothario in Nicholas Rowe's *The Fair Penitent*, the Ghost in *Hamlet*, Fondlewife in William Congreve's *The Old Bachelor*, Costar Pearman in Farquhar's *The Recruiting Officer*, Witwoud in Congreve's *The Way of the World*, Bayes in George Villiers, duke of Buckingham's *The Rehearsal*, King Lear, Lord Foppington in Cibber's *The Careless Husband*, Pierre in Otway's *Venice Preserved*, and Brazen in Farquhar's *The Recruiting Officer*.

One notices immediately from this list that Garrick had the rare capacity of acting with equal skill in both comic and tragic roles. He had, of course, followers who preferred him in one or the other, but the disputes themselves serve largely to show how effective he was in both. In the tragic roles he personalized and humanized the heroes and was particularly expert at the pathetic dimension of the roles. A constant in descriptions of Garrick's tragic performances was praise for his ability to reduce the audience

Edmund Burton as Subtle, John Palmer as Face, and Garrick as Abel Drugger in The Alchymist *(engraving by J. Dixon, 1771; based on a painting by Johann Zoffany)*

(including the often sophisticated reporters) to tears. In comic roles his power was in *acting* them (when they had been mugged, danced, and strutted for years) so that in his hands the characters became funny; in contrast, the laughter had often in recent years stemmed more directly from the comedian's style. With Garrick the audience laughed at the character; with Colley Cibber or Samuel Foote they laughed at the actor. By the end of his first season Garrick had played 133 performances including a successful benefit, and in June he was in Dublin playing with the summer company of the theater in Smock Alley. He had another triumphant success in that city, playing most of the repertory from his London successes and adding the title role in *Hamlet.*

For the fall season of 1742 he was engaged at the Drury Lane theater, then under the management of Charles Fleetwood. He also shared an apartment with the Irish actress Margaret (Peg) Woffington. They had a relationship that evidently went to the brink of marriage but never crossed it. They did, however, remain friends.

Garrick joined a large company of experienced actors, and his sudden stardom and his youth must have caused some dissension. In fact he did remarkably well in winning them over. Judith Milhous and Robert D. Hume have shown that, because of the recent death of William Milward and the defection of Theophilus Cibber to Covent Garden, Garrick did not have to displace the actors who had claim to his roles in more than four cases; however, Dennis Delane's career was destroyed by the competition. Hume and Milhous have also supplied the figures to show that the box-office response to the phenomenon of Garrick was astonishing: "We may ask, for example, how many times the theatre grossed more than £100 during the season (excluding benefits). At performances without Garrick, it did so just twice: £102 on 9 October and £105 on 12 October. With Garrick acting, it did so 57 times, and on 23 nights the receipts were above £140. Only 21 times when Garrick acted did the theatre gross less than £100, and only four times during the entire season did the company take less than

£60 with Garrick acting." During that season Garrick added Hamlet to his London repertory as well as Hastings in Rowe's *Jane Shore*, Sir Harry Wildair in Farquhar's *The Constant Couple*, and Abel Drugger in Ben Jonson's *The Alchemist*.

That first season at Drury Lane, despite Garrick's artistic successes, collapsed around his ears when it became clear that Fleetwood's finances were in serious disarray. There were alarming signs of impending bankruptcy, and the actors had not been paid for some time. An actors' rebellion that included Charles Macklin, William Havard, Edward Berry, Mrs. Hannah Pritchard, Mrs. Kitty Raftor Clive, with Garrick acting as spokesman, resulted in something very like a strike. The strikers signed an agreement of solidarity, presented Fleetwood with their ultimatum, and drew up a petition for permission to operate a licensed theater at the Haymarket. A comic twist was added by Charles Fitz Roy, duke of Grafton, then lord chamberlain, who was so scandalized that a mere group of players could claim salaries as high as five hundred pounds a year that he refused to accept the petition. The duke knew men, including his own son, who risked their lives in the military service of their country and received less than half that amount. The actors' plight fell on deaf ears.

Fleetwood, in order to break the strike, hired some additional actors and prepared to open the fall season. The rebellious actors had little recourse but to accept whatever terms Fleetwood would give, but their pledge of solidarity proved a serious problem because Fleetwood refused to reinstate Macklin (who had also acted as a sort of assistant manager some of the time and whom Fleetwood accused of disloyalty bordering on treachery). Garrick would be reinstated, but he was trapped by his agreement with Macklin. Garrick was only twenty-four and was in the second year of his professional career. Macklin was forty-five and had been a professional performer for nineteen years or maybe even longer (and had himself acted as a strikebreaker for John Highmore after Theophilus Cibber's revolt to the Haymarket in 1733). Garrick clearly tried to come at an honorable solution short of self-destruction, but Macklin was adamant that he abide by the agreement that they sink or swim together. After trying everything within his power (including offering to pay Macklin a salary and get his wife a contract at Covent Garden), Garrick decided to return to Drury Lane. Never known for coolness and reason,

Macklin declared war and set out to destroy him professionally.

The first volley was a pamphlet, *The Case of Charles Macklin, Comedian* (1743), and in addition he organized a group of hecklers to interrupt Garrick's first night performance after his return. In his 1801 biography Arthur Murphy explained that Garrick:

> was not suffered to speak. Off! off! resounded from all parts of the house. The play went on in dumb shew, scene by scene, from the beginning to the end; Garrick, during the whole, standing aloof, at the upper part of the stage, to avoid the rotten eggs and apples, which showered down in great plenty.

Garrick wrote his own pamphlet in reply and explanation, but the deciding factor was meeting force with force. For Garrick's next performance Fleetwood hired his own set of ruffians, armed with clubs, and chased Macklin's thugs into retreat. Things returned to normal at Drury Lane, but Macklin did not act there again until late in 1744, after Fleetwood had sold his part of the patent.

In the season of 1743-1744 Garrick added the role of Macbeth to his repertory and so began an important and extremely controversial part of his literary career. He "adapted" the play. In doing so he brought down on his head the full wrath of a couple of centuries of purists and enlisted a group of defenders who have written pages, indeed tomes, of justification. Garrick is the foremost artist in history in whom the exigencies of drama and theater are inseparable. He never claimed that he was producing definitive study texts of Shakespeare. He made acting texts for the purpose of producing what he deemed to be the most effective staged performances for the conditions that prevailed in the theater of his time, with attention to its style, its actors, and its audience. Few of us have ever seen an unadapted (or at least unedited) performance of a play by Shakespeare. The practice of adapting or editing in order to put a printed text on the stage is still with us. Success in this endeavor is varied and extremely subject to taste. In the case of *Macbeth* Garrick did not really go back to Shakespeare, although he did readapt Sir William Davenant's version and bring the play text closer to the various scholarly texts that had been published in the first half of the eighteenth century, notably those of Alexander Pope and Lewis Theobald, and he may have consulted Samuel Johnson and William

Warburton personally. In future years, as he adapted this and other plays by Shakespeare, Garrick added much authentic material to plays that had a long stage history in adaptation; he rescued scenes, lines, speeches that had not been heard on the stage for decades, so that his acting versions of Shakespeare were closer to the original text than any seen within the lifetimes of most of his auditors. Also, however, a great deal of what Shakespeare wrote was omitted; important scenes were rewritten, augmented, cropped; important elements of complexity and moral ambiguity were simplified and robbed of some of their chief beauties. It must not be supposed, however, that there was no opposition to adaptation. Voices of reason who, like Addison, warned that the adaptations were inferior to their originals were heard if not heeded. Garrick's twentieth-century defenders resort to some degree of damning with faint praise as they conclude that Garrick's version of *Macbeth* was "the most accurate stage version of a Shakespeare play which had appeared since 1671."

We would probably do well to notice that Garrick adapted with a variety of purposes in mind. Some changes or deletions probably had to do with the differences between the physical makeup of the stage in his theater and the somewhat different stage in the theaters of Shakespeare's time. Some editing may have had to do with the necessity to end before midnight, especially since Garrick's theater produced more than one work in an evening. As long as the spirit of the play is not transgressed, these motivations are easily understood and accommodated. But there is another that was certain to be less acceptable after the reasons for following it vanished, and that is the bowdlerization stemming from the wave of narrow, middle-class sensibility that had become a powerful influence, and tolerated only a simplified moral view and a shallow awareness of the complexity of human life, that could respond, or even understand, only overt moralizing and conventional sentiments. This sensibility dictated that a villain must repent, a rake must reform, a good hero must return to his throne, and that a Horner must be omitted from *The Country Wife*. A consequence (although it is difficult to determine cause and effect) of such sentimental morality was Garrick's attraction to the pathetic, which guided the plays in that direction rather than toward some of the more complex and profound alternatives of interpretation. In a twentieth-century view, Shakespeare tends to transcend tears rather than settle (or even strive) for them.

With his production of *Macbeth* Garrick also engaged in another practice that would play a role in his future professional activities. He had already written a pamphlet defending himself against Macklin's attack; in fact actors and actresses fairly often made appeals to the public through the press; indeed it was a form of publicity. At various times in his career Garrick advertised himself or protected himself by attacking himself anonymously in print so that he could come to his own defense or let somebody else come to his defense. In this case the pamphlet was titled *An Essay on Acting, in which will be consider'd the Mimical Behavior of a certain fashionable faulty actor. . . . To which will be added a short criticism on his acting Macbeth* (1744). Evidently on the principle that a good offense is the best defense, Garrick, in the pamphlet, questioned whether a man of his stature should play heroic characters. It was an area where he was vulnerable since Garrick was only five feet four inches tall, and, in fact, later in his career his physical height probably did interfere with his playing more heroic roles such as Othello. Garrick must have felt that if he could get the matter out in the open he could disarm it forever.

In the 1744-1745 season Garrick continued to add new roles to his repertory, both successfully and unsuccessfully. The management of the theater changed when Fleetwood sold his patent; thus Garrick began his relationship with James Lacy, one of the new patentees. The beginning was not auspicious, for there were immediate arguments over money. The result was that Garrick accepted an offer from Thomas Sheridan to share with him the management of the Dublin United Company, which was then performing both in Smock Alley and Aungier Street. Before leaving London, however, he contracted to act in the following season (1746-1747) at Covent Garden rather than Drury Lane.

The season in Dublin was very successful, with Garrick playing a large repertory of the roles he had already mastered. He returned to London in May and ratified his intention to act the next season at Covent Garden. Perhaps he began to see an opportunity in the fact that conditions at Drury Lane under Lacy had gotten, if anything, worse, but his own financial prospects were bright. At Covent Garden he shared the stage successfully with James Quin, and it is particularly interesting to note that neither adapted his

David and Eva Maria Garrick (portrait by William Hogarth, 1757; Royal Collection, Windsor Castle; by permission of Her Majesty Queen Elizabeth II. Copyright reserved)

style to the other, in case we should assume that once Garrick's acting revolution took place everything fell in line. An eyewitness, the playwright Richard Cumberland, gave the following account:

> Quin presented himself upon the rising of the curtain in a green velvet coat embroidered down the seams, in a enormous full bottomed periwig, rolled stockings and high-heeled square-toed shoes: with very little variation of cadence and in a deep full tone, accompanied by a sawing kind of action, which had more of the senate than of the stage in it, he rolled out his heroics with an air of dignified indifference, that seemed to disdain plaudits, that were bestowed upon him. . . . after long and eager expectation I first beheld little Garrick, then young and light and alive in every muscle and in every feature, come bound-

ing on the stage, and pointing at the wittol Altamont and heavy-paced Horatio–heavens what a transition!–it seemed as if a whole century had been stept over in the transition of a single scene; old things were done away, and a new order at once brought forward, bright and luminous, and clearly destined to dispel the barbarisms and bigotry of a tasteless age.

Garrick's successes during the year at Covent Garden included the production of a new work of his own composing, the farce *Miss in Her Teens*. He played the comic role of Fribble. He also added the role of Ranger in the new play by Benjamin and John Hoadly, *The Suspicious Husband*. The latter became one of his greatest impersonations and remained in his repertory through his last season.

Miss in Her Teens was an extremely successful afterpiece, and it shows Garrick's impressive artistic growth. Again it is an adaptation of a French original, *La Parisienne* by Florent Carton Dancourt, and is even closer to the original than his other two afterpieces. As Pedicord and Bergmann explain, "By following Dancourt's text literally in most instances, by paraphrasing occasionally, transposing scenes, and cutting bits of the French original, he arrived at a more sparkling and vigorous English comedy. . . ." Whether or not Garrick's imitation of Dancourt was better than the original need not be debated, but it is a more delightful play than *The Lying Valet*. The dialogue is much faster, livelier, and more individualized than that in the earlier play. It must be evaluated in its own category, but in that category it has few rivals. All the characters are sprightly and funny. The situation is on the comic target, and the total effect is quite delightful. The play involves a clever girl who contrives to get rid of unwanted suitors and marry her true love. The farcical scenes with characters hidden behind doors and the supposed duel between two reluctant and cowardly combatants are deft and witty, and the little play is an inspired piece of fluff.

Garrick, despite his success, was not satisfied at Covent Garden, perhaps because John Rich was always more interested in extraliterary elements in the theater; in addition, a splendid opportunity presented itself. To revive the faltering Drury Lane, James Lacy offered in 1747 to sell Garrick half of the patent for eight thousand pounds. Garrick was to be artistic director, and Lacy was to be in charge of finances. The advantage of having Garrick perform the double role of leading actor (with proven and extraordinary drawing power) and manager was not lost on his partner. The two men had little temperamental compatibility, but for the most part Lacy minded his business and let Garrick mind his. The partnership lasted until Lacy's death in 1774.

Garrick gathered together an excellent company–taking some away from Covent Garden and adding some from other sources–and had a successful first season, despite some ill health. In the second season there were some changes in the acting roster, both losses and additions. Garrick staged *Much Ado About Nothing* on 14 November 1748 and played Benedick. It became one of his signature roles. He staged Samuel Johnson's *Irene* with moderate success and added his adaptation of *Romeo and Juliet* to the repertory on 29 No-

vember, increasing the pathos of the last act by having Juliet awaken before Romeo dies in order to supply a touching farewell scene. Spranger Barry played Romeo during that run of the play.

It was apparently during 1747 that Garrick started his assault on the heart of the Viennese dancer Eva Maria Veigel, a protegé of Dorothy Saville Boyle, countess of Burlington. The two lovers were in agreement, but the countess had to be won over, for she had more exalted plans for Eva Maria than marriage to an actor. Eventually she gave her consent, and the lovers were married on 22 June 1749. It proved an ideal marriage for both. They rarely, if ever, spent a night apart.

Garrick lost both Spranger Barry and Susannah Arne Cibber to Covent Garden for the season of 1750-1751, and the immediate result was the famous war of the Romeos. Covent Garden advertised *Romeo and Juliet* with Barry and Cibber, and Drury Lane countered with the same play with Garrick (who had not played Romeo before) and his new leading lady George Anne Bellamy. Beginning 28 September 1750, for twelve nights both theaters played *Romeo and Juliet*, but Covent Garden blinked first, and Garrick won the contest with the longer run.

In May of 1751 the Garricks took the first of two tours to the Continent, staying about two months in Paris. He went to the theater, saw most of the tourist attractions, was unimpressed with much of what he saw on the stage but showed an active, enthusiastic interest in a different life-style. He met some members of the theatrical community and attended some evening soirees. At one of them he performed the dagger scene from *Macbeth* to great approval.

For the 1755 season Garrick arranged to import a ballet extravaganza that had been the rage of Paris, *The Chinese Festival* (*Les Fêtes Chinoises*), to serve as an afterpiece. What he did not take into account was an unusual degree of xenophobia resulting from the current threatenings of war between France and England. When Garrick heard that there might be some resistance, he ran a piece in the *Public Advertiser* explaining that the ballet was the work of Jean-Georges Noverre, who was Swiss, not French, and that most of the dancers were not French. (A pamphlet on the subject that was published on 15 November quoted a reply from the audience to this reasoning: "Swiss! What the devil do we know of Swiss! a Swiss is a foreigner, and all foreigners are Frenchmen; and so damn you all!") During the first

George Anne Bellamy and Garrick in Romeo and Juliet *(engraving by T. Stayner, based on a 1753 painting by Benjamin Wilson)*

three performances (8, 12, and 13 November) there was hissing from the audience, even though the king was present at two of them; at the fourth (14 November) there was a small riot, and some of the benches were pulled up. However, at the sixth, 18 November, a battle broke out which could not be quelled even by the presence of Justice Henry Fielding and a battery of constables. The mob stormed out of the theater and broke the windows of Garrick's house in Southampton Street. *The Chinese Festival* did not play again. The whole affair was said to have cost Garrick four thousand pounds, not counting the extra revenue he had anticipated from a successful run.

In the 1756-1757 season Garrick pushed his acting text for *King Lear* closer to the original, but he did not, nor did he ever, abandon all of Nahum Tate's adaptation. He also staged two of his own pieces during the season. *Lilliput* is a curious expansion of a paragraph from Jonathan Swift's *Gulliver's Travels* regarding a supposed romance between Gulliver and Flimnap's wife. The comic point is centered on Gulliver's solemn de-

nial of any impropriety while apparently being oblivious to the impossibility of the alliance because of the disparity in their sizes, the lady being but five inches tall. Garrick elects (with a mock pedantic letter from a friend of Gulliver's contrived to change Gulliver's story) to make the lady actually lust after Gulliver. Most of the lines in the resultant play make some reference to the utter amorality, not to say depravity, of the nobility.

Garrick's second new piece of that season is best weighed against his own disclaimer:

The following scenes were written with no other view than to serve Mr. Woodward last year at his benefit; and to expose a set of people (the Daffodils) whom the author thinks more prejudicial to the community, than the various characters of Bucks, Bloods, Flashes, and Fribbles, which have by turns infested the town, and been justly ridiculed upon the stage. He expects no mercy from the critics: But the more indulgent public, perhaps, will excuse his endeavors to please them, when they shall know, that the performance was planned, written, and acted in less than a month.

Garrick as Kitely in Every Man in His Humour, *1768 (painting by Sir Joshua Reynolds; Royal Collection, Windsor Castle; by permission of Her Majesty Queen Elizabeth II. Copyright reserved)*

The Modern Fine Gentleman, later known as *The Male Coquette*, hardly warrants Pedicord and Bergmann's comparison of it with the comic plays of the Restoration. Daffodil has no claim to being a Restoration rake, being, indeed, a contrary type of character. This particular flirt wants the reputation of a womanizer without the exertion. It would certainly be curious if a character with the obviously allegorical name of Daffodil were to be equated with characters with the equally allegorical names of Dorimant, Horner, and Mirabel. His effeminacy is clearly under scrutiny:

> RUFFLE. Pray, Sir, with submission, for what end do you write to so many ladies and make such a rout about 'em? There are now upon the list half a dozen maids, a leash of wives, and the Widow Damply. I know your honor don't intend mischief, but what pleasure can you have in deceiving them and the world? For you are thought a terrible gentleman.
> DAFFODIL. Why, that pleasure, Booby.
> RUFFLE. I don't understand it. What do you intend to do with 'em all? Ruin 'em?
> DAFFODIL. Not I, faith.
> RUFFLE. But you'll ruin their reputations.
> DAFFODIL. That's their business, not mine.
> RUFFLE. Will you marry any one of 'em?
> DAFFODIL. Oh, no. That would be finishing the game at once. If I preferred one, the rest would take it ill; so, because I won't be particular, I give 'em all hopes without going a step further.

Daffodil is exposed and the play ends, but not without the moral, and one should note that it is addressed to the women rather than to Daffodil:

> In you coquettry is a loss of fame;
> But in our sex 'tis that detested name

> That marks the want of manhood, virtue, sense,
> and shame.

Despite the indignation in the advertisement toward the Daffodils and despite these lines which attack male coquettes (or perhaps the "detested name" is supposed to be *homosexual*), the attack, if any, is really on the women who are so foolish as to be attracted by Daffodil rather than on the "coquette" himself.

A 1759 afterpiece, *The Guardian*, like *Miss in Her Teens*, is another imitation. Garrick's critics have decided that he forsook the spirit of the original and elected to satirize the "excessive" sentiment of the two main characters rather than to sympathize with it. From the text itself this is a fairly arbitrary conclusion for there is no need to interpret the characters unsympathetically, there being no clear line where the right amount of sensibility becomes the wrong amount. The situation upon which the plot is constructed demands that the characters be unusually delicate in their perceptions. There is no adequate way to decide what extra adjective or interjection becomes excessive and renders the speaker an object of ridicule rather than delight. Heartly and Harriet are characters in a comedy, but a gentle comedy of sentiment. They are too good for this world rather than not good enough for it. The situation of Heartly and Harriet is quite delicate (for example, in its basic nature it is that of Emma and Mr. Knightley in Jane Austen's *Emma*). Although their social and legal relationship is one of guardian and ward (that is, pseudo parent and child), they have come to love one another romantically. The greatest constraint is on Heartly, who, it is fairly clear, has repressed his feelings for two important reasons. One is that he is her guardian and is, therefore, required to think of her welfare in the way a father would–to find her a suitable match and to make sure she is satisfied with it. The other is that he is old enough to be her father and is acutely aware of the disparity in their ages and modestly sensitive to the probability that she would not be romantically interested in somebody of his vintage. She is the stronger of the two because she has to be, since the apparent inappropriateness is all on his side. She knows she loves him, but she cannot tell him because women are not supposed to be the aggressors in relationships, and because, in this particular relationship, his extreme delicacy and decency (his main attraction to her) might be shocked by the thought of violating his position as her guardian. Still, she loves him enough to be unwilling to let

him go by default, although he can give her to a suitor of appropriate age if one comes along–and if she loves him.

There is nothing in the play to suggest that either character is a silly, muddleheaded sentimentalist, blundering through the world crying at every opportunity. In general both seem sound, intelligent people, but in this particular situation, where great tact is required, they are so cognizant of the real problems that they almost miss their opportunity for love, since neither is likely to find his or her equal in refined perceptions elsewhere. This is a comic situation but hardly a satiric one. They certainly are no danger to anyone but themselves. Their sensitivity is right and is undoubtedly a part of their suitability for one another, but (the comic world can and often does observe) in this world it is not just faults and foibles that can get one into trouble but one's best qualities as well. We would not wish them, either of them, to be less "delicate." They would be less worthy of one another if they were. The character of the maid supplies all the necessary cynicism, but the maid reflects the way the world thinks and the way the world acts. The world, however, is drastically unattuned to people of genuine refinement. The treatment of the two chief characters is too gentle to warrant our being critical of them. They are too good for this world, but they find one another, and they do not sacrifice their true gentility in the process. In his advertisement at the beginning of the printed edition of the play Garrick says that Fagan's play, in the opinion of Voltaire and other French writers, is "the most complete *Petite-Piece* upon their stage." Garrick's "imitation" does it reasonable justice. It is lighthanded and quite charming.

In the 1757-1758 season Drury Lane produced Shakespeare's *The Tempest, Henry IV, Part II*, and *Anthony and Cleopatra* in versions essentially true to Shakespeare's texts. In the next season Garrick introduced a pantomime of his composing: *Harlequin's Invasion*. He had struggled with both inclination and conscience to keep pantomime out of the Drury Lane repertory. He wanted the house to be devoted to higher forms, but the success of Rich's pantomimes at Covent Garden made it financially imprudent to ignore their popularity, especially during the Christmas season, which was the traditional time for presenting holiday material for a holiday audience. Henry Woodward had considerable success with his pantomimes at Drury Lane between 1750 and 1756, but he left the company in 1756. When Gar-

Act 3d Scene continues.
Enter Dolly Snip OP

Was there ever any thing so unlucky. I was this
Morning out of my Senses, and thought my Father
a great Man, and myself a fine Lady — and now
my Dreams out — My Father has lost his Head;
My Mother is breaking her Heart, and what is
worse than all, I must work for my Living — it is
a sad Thing, a terrible thing to be oblig'd to work
when one has set ones mind upon lying a Bed
and thinking of nothing. then there's Abram too.
I wish I had not turn'd him of — I must not let
him go, I know he can't help loving me — and he
knows his Interest — So I will e'en marry him; —
Make my Mother give up the Shop to him —
Allow her a trifle to maintain her, and take
the Business into my own Hands — I can't (3)
think of any thing better at present.   Abram
          Enter Sukey Chitterlin. PS
              Sukey
Cousin Dolly! — Cousin Dolly — Cousin Dolly.
              Dolly
Lord what a Noise you make; always Roaring
and Romping.
          Sukey.

Page from the manuscript for Harlequin's Invasion *(Barton-Ticknor Collection; by permission of the Boston Public Library)*

rick tried his hand, he added speech to his version–presumably because he had no mime of Woodward's excellence to call on. There is, of course, no evaluating such a piece from the printed page. It was tailored to special effects (transparencies, sudden appearances through trap doors, floating heads) and to music and singing. In the final song glorifying Shakespeare, Garrick allowed himself to stand his ground in loyalty to the bard but at the same time profit from the popularity of sensational material. It was introduced on New Year's Eve as an afterpiece for *The London Merchant*. It played many times during the next decade.

The next year (1760) his Christmas spectacle was a short opera libretto called *The Enchanter; or, Love and Magic*. It too is an ephemeral piece and does not reveal itself in print, for it was heavily dependent upon spectacular effects and music. Garrick was evidently interested in improving the stageworthiness of opera by reducing the amount of recitative. In the advertisement he notes that he "has endeavored to carry on what fable there is, chiefly by the songs." Its music may have been its chief attraction, but *The Enchanter* did have a successful run.

In January of 1763 the second most serious riot of Garrick's tenure at Drury Lane occurred. It was the custom at this time to admit spectators after the third act of the main piece for half price, and the managers of the two theaters evidently elected to end the practice and the consequent diminution of revenue. A troublemaker named Fitzpatrick decided to head a revolt against this incursion into the rights of the "public," and riots were initiated in both theaters. Drury Lane, which fell first, advertised a performance of *Two Gentlemen of Verona* for the benefit of the author of the alterations with the announcement that "Nothing under Full Price will be taken." The rioters demanded that no such policy be instituted except at the run of a new pantomime (apparently acknowledging that the elaborate stage machinery cost enough to warrant reimbursement). The management did not agree, and "the Mob broke Chandeliers, &c." The next night the same demand was made by the rioters, and this time Garrick came out and agreed to their demands. They then changed their attack to Covent Garden. There the damages were estimated at two thousand pounds, and the theater was closed for repairs until 2 March.

Obviously it was a trying season for Garrick, and at the end of it he seems to have been seri-

ously considering retiring. At any rate, in September 1763 he and his wife left for their second sojourn on the Continent, this one to last until April of 1765. On his second arrival in Paris he was much more of a celebrity, his fame having preceded him, and he was quite lionized by the theatrical and intellectual circles of the French capital. He and his wife continued their tour, stopping at Lyons and Turin, where he found the audiences even ruder than those in London: "the People in ye Pitt & Boxes talk all ye while as in a Coffee house, & ye Performers are Even with 'Em, for they are very little attentive, laugh & talk to one another, pick their Noses, & while they are unEngag'd in Singing, they walk up to ye Stage Boxes, (in which the other Actors & dancers sit dress'd in Sight of ye Audience) turn their backs, & join in ye laugh & Conversation of their Brethren, without ye least decency or regard to ye Audience. . . ."

The Garricks continued on to Florence, Rome, Naples, Bologna, Venice. Eva Maria Garrick came down with a rheumatic condition that quite crippled her and that was finally relieved by the mud baths of Abano. Then, in Munich David Garrick was rendered invalid by something in the eighteenth century called a fever (possibly typhoid), which left him extremely thin and exhausted. In November they returned to Paris, where he recuperated, and they entered again into the social activities of their recently acquired Parisian friends. As their return to London drew nearer, Garrick became a little apprehensive about how he would be received. Although he may earlier have been talking about retiring and was now appearing reluctant to return, he was becoming worried about his replaceability. He had left some of his chief roles to William Powell, a new young actor whom he had trained and encouraged and who had been very well received in Garrick's absence. He decided to presage his return with one of his self-deprecating squibs, and he sent a poem and an accompanying print titled *The Sick Monkey* to George Colman the Elder. It did not do much toward an achievement of its purpose, but he need not have worried, for his audience greeted him with rapture, and he was able to settle back into the routine of management and the performance of his favorite and most popular roles.

The season of 1765-1766 brought the premiere of *The Clandestine Marriage*, the five-act play on which he had collaborated with Colman. Through the years there has been some contro-

Garrick as the title character in The Farmer's Return from London *(frontispiece to the 1762 edition)*

versy over how much of the final play is to be attributed to Colman and how much to Garrick, with a tendency to minimize Garrick's contribution. Recent discoveries, however, have altered that assessment, and the current wisdom is that Garrick contributed at least half of both the writing and the inspiration.

In dealing with the play itself it is fortunate that we are no longer required to become befuddled over the supposed triumph of sentimental comedy over laughing comedy. Recent studies have provided useful information and analysis upon which to base a conclusion that laughing comedy never disappeared and that sentimental comedy never took over the stage to anything like the extent that had formerly been taken for granted, largely because of Oliver Goldsmith's *An Essay on the Theatre; or, A Comparison Between Laugh-*

ing and Sentimental Comedy (1773). *The Clandestine Marriage* is, in its primary direction, more akin to *The Conscious Lovers* than to *The Way of the World*. It is sentimental (perhaps only *good natured*) in the conception of its main characters. The danger the plot puts them in is not the result of any serious flaw or limitation in their psychological or moral makeup. It stems rather from the likelihood of misunderstanding and hostile reaction from the people surrounding them, who operate on a standard that is far less delicate and ethical than theirs. These characters tend to speak in sentiments (especially Lovewell), but the sentiments are not hypocritical and do represent both the standard by which they reason ethically and that by which they act.

The possibility that the audience will notice the gentle and ambiguous irony involved in a situation where the characters have a sensibility that exceeds what the world can manage is inherent in such a work, but good-natured comedy is based on the ability of the characters to succeed while being true to their beliefs when it would be easier and more conventionally effective to sell out in order to achieve what the world means by success. Such a play is a refutation of the philosophy of "If you can't beat 'em, join 'em."

Fanny is not a purse-mouthed holier-than-thou. She is, in fact, without even trying, so good-natured and attractive that most of the men in the play are in love with her, and it is around her genuine attractiveness that the chief episodes in the play revolve, for the male characters, preferring her to her social-climbing sister, create much of the play's tension by pressing her to marry them when she cannot accept and cannot explain her refusal–her clandestine marriage. Lovewell's true relationship to Fanny is finally revealed, and her father's fury is mitigated by Lord Ogleby, although why he should suddenly become the source of reason and charity is not very clear. A light and amusing play, it fits the description (if not definition) of comedy that Garrick wrote to Mrs. Victor (when discussing another work): "I said indeed that the Comedy wanted interest, but not of the *Passions*–I meant a Comic interest, resulting from the various humours of the Characters thrown into spirited action & brought into interesting Situations, naturally arising from a well-constructed fable or Plot–This, with a good Moral, deduc'd from the whole, is all I wish or look for in a *Comedy*." Garrick's humors are never at the level of intensity or brilliant realization of the truly great ones of Ben Jonson or William Wycherley, but they are charming and actable.

In the season of 1766-1767 four of Garrick's own pieces were produced. One of them was *The Country Girl*, a bowdlerization of Wycherley's *The Country Wife* (1675), for which he gives the following explanation in his advertisement to the printed edition:

Though near half of the following play is new written, the alterer claims no merit but his endeavor to clear one of our most celebrated comedies from immorality and obscenity. He thought himself bound to preserve as much of the original as could be presented to an audience of these times without offence; and if this wanton of Charles's days is now so reclaimed as to become innocent without being insipid, the present editor will not think his time ill employed, which has enabled him to add some little variety to the entertainments of the public. There seems, indeed, an absolute necessity for reforming many plays of our most eminent writers. For no kind of wit ought to be received as an excuse for immorality; nay, it becomes still more dangerous in proportion as it is more witty.

The Country Girl is not nearly as good a play as Wycherley's and the best parts of it are the earlier playwright's, but as it came from Garrick's hand, it is lively and entertaining. The battle between authors and director-manager-actors is clearly never ending. Garrick is neither better nor worse than his equivalents in the twentieth century who want to make movies or stage productions out of earlier works but wish to produce their own statement rather than that of the original author and who appeal to public taste as a defense. Authors and their adherents are always offended at having the original defaced. The adapter is always satisfied with the new work, and most of the audience is unaware of or uninterested in the issue as long as they get what they want for their money–what they call entertainment. And the adaptor is usually richer than the original author ever thought of being.

In the 1766-1767 season Garrick also introduced his afterpiece *Neck or Nothing*, an imitation of Alain-René Lesage's *Crispin rival de son maître* (1707). This time in the advertisement he calls his play an *imitation*. Two servants, who are confidence men at heart, try to cheat their masters out of both love and money but are apprehended at the last moment. It was not one of Garrick's more popular pieces, but his rendering of the material into English language and milieu is up to his usual standard.

Garrick called *Cymon*, which premiered during the Christmas season (2 January 1767), "A Dramatic Romance." It is another work that relies heavily on extravagant stage effects as well as music. It also participates in the mock-pastoral tradition á la John Gay's *Shepherd's Week* (1714). Its chief maxim is that there is "no magic like virtue." Two simple and virtuous characters, Cymon (he once calls himself simple Cymon) and Sylvia, are set upon by forces of evil and magic but triumph in the end. There are many magic transformations of scenery and other startling stage effects. The play never takes itself very seriously, as most of the characters speak in unpastoral strains and fall into song at will. A magic opera, it is akin to the masque, especially in its elaborate staging. It had no capacity to survive its century since much of its appeal was the result of the theatrical fashions, not to say fads, of its own decade. Nobody ever claimed it to be high art, but if readers can supply the requisite enchanting stage pictures out of their imaginations, they can see that it could make an evening of beguiling amusement. It was quite popular into the 1790s.

One of the most popular characters in *Cymon* was the Papageno-like Linco, and Garrick quickly capitalized on that character's audience appeal with an interlude called *Linco's Travels*. It is a rhymed set of about 160 lines of couplets on the foibles of the English–the same form as *The Farmer's Return from London* (1762). It was designed to be performed between a main piece and an afterpiece.

Yet another of Garrick's pieces was given its premiere on 23 October 1767, his rehearsal farce *A Peep Behind the Curtain*, containing a burletta on Orpheus. It is much slighter than either Buckingham's *The Rehearsal* or Richard Brinsley Sheridan's later *The Critic* (1779), but it is a funny enough little piece, fragmentary as it is in nature. Garrick's health was fairly troublesome for the next few years, although he often applied himself to his theater with great energy, both as actor and as manager. In the summer of 1768 he did a series of command performances for the king of Denmark, who was visiting London.

In the summer of 1769 he embarked on an adventure that was either a major triumph or the largest debacle of his career. The Great Shakespeare Jubilee started out with the town burgesses of Stratford-upon-Avon wanting to obtain financing for a memorial to Shakespeare that they decided to put into the new town hall. They sent a request to Garrick for a statue or picture of the bard and himself "that the memory of both may be perpetually together." The seed thus planted in Garrick's mind grew into a far more elaborate scheme than the burgesses of Stratford anticipated, for he decided to couple the dedication of the statue with a "Jubilee" to the memory of Shakespeare, replete with extravagant attractions. Garrick did not make plans for a Shakespeare festival, with high-quality productions of his best plays; in fact what he did settle on contained not a single play that Shakespeare wrote. Stratford was a small town with few accommodations for tourists, but Garrick's name attracted a numerous following. He had a rotunda constructed on the banks of the Avon to house some of the main attractions (formal dinners and balls and the performance of an ode of Garrick's composing with music by Thomas Arne). He planned a costumed procession or pageant of Shakespeare's characters through the streets, a horse race, and a large display of fireworks. On the first day, 6 September, the Jubilee started with a breakfast in the assembly room of the town hall fitted out with transparencies executed by Drury Lane's scene designers. The events that followed were a performance in the church of an Arne oratorio that had nothing to do with Shakespeare, preceded by the laying of wreaths at Shakespeare's statue, and an elaborate dinner in the rotunda. Throughout the day there were bands and strolling singers in the streets. The event of the evening was a ball, also in the rotunda. The evening was to have ended with fireworks, but as the weather looked threatening, they were postponed. The first day, however, was a success with those who were willing to have a good time (even if there was some indignation expressed at the prices the natives of Stratford were charging for everything), and had the remainder of the festival met with the same luck all would have been well.

On the second day heavy rain began to fall. The pageant of Shakespearean characters, in costumes from Drury Lane, marching down the main street had to be canceled. The rain was so torrential that the streets were awash with mud, and, in fact, the Avon was rising alarmingly. Garrick's chief activity that day was the recitation of his ode, with the orchestral accompaniment of Arne. The ode was to have followed the pageant and been its climax, but now it would have to stand on its own. It could not have been helpful to his frame of mind that in the morning Garrick's barber, while shaving him, had gashed him from the corner of his mouth to his chin, and much of the morning was spent with styptics in the attempt to staunch the blood. The performance that Garrick and Arne had composed was a combination of spoken verse in recitation and choral and solo music. By virtually unanimous testimony, Garrick's recitation was masterful. It is not clear today, reading his text, how it could have been so thrilling, but according to all accounts, he exercised his full skill in bringing an audience to tears. Charles Dibdin, a playwright and song writer who was more inclined to be critical of Garrick than charitable, wrote, "There never was exhibited in England a Performance more pleasing, more grand, or more worthy of Shakespeare, and the Genius and Talents of Garrick."

The fireworks were a debacle as the unending downpour reduced them to mush. The rotunda was on the bank of the Avon, and as the ball progressed the flood waters rendered it hourly more isolated from dry land. Hasty plank drawbridges were thrown together, horses waded in water to their knees to get to them, and many guests were in muddy water over their shoe tops as they struggled to gain entrance. But, for the most part, they rose to the occasion.

Garrick's plans had been entertaining, and what little was realized did not disgrace him, however much it might have annoyed the purists who could not approve of a mere popular celebration of Shakespeare's name. Garrick absorbed the financial loss–in the neighborhood of two thousand pounds.

At the beginning of the 1769-1770 season Colman (now manager of Covent Garden) decided to cash in on Garrick's publicity from the jubilee and on 7 October 1769 introduced his comedy *Man and Wife; or, The Shakespeare Jubilee*, including a version, elaborately costumed and orchestrated, of the aborted pageant of characters from the plays. Garrick, however, was ready, and a week later, as an afterpiece to Elizabeth Griffith's *The School for Rakes*, he introduced his *The Jubilee* with his own pageant, "as it was intended for Stratford-upon-Avon." A framework playlet makes use of his firsthand knowledge of the suspicions that the Stratford natives had directed toward the jubilee. To this complication he adds the discomforts of the tourists. The chief character is an Irishman who cannot find a room and so spends the night trying to sleep in a post chaise. Though he is anxious to see the pageant, he falls asleep and misses it. Throughout, there are songs with music by Dibdin, and there is an inspirational ending with a "magnificent" transparency "in which the capital characters of Shakespeare are exhibited at full length, with Shakespeare's statue in the middle crowned by Tragedy and Comedy, fairies and cupids surrounding him, and all the banners waving at the upper end," followed by a grand chorus in which all the costumed characters from the pageant join, "during which the guns fire, bells ring, etc., etc. and the audience applaud. Bravo Jubilee! Shakespeare forever!" Sheer kitsch, and obviously the audiences had a wonderful time. According to George Winchester Stone, Jr., in *The London Stage* (part 4), "It created the record run for any piece on the London stage for the whole century, by receiving ninety performances during this one season alone. He also capitalized upon his *Ode to the Memory of Shakespeare*, spoken at Strat-

ford, which he used as a specialty recitation at Drury Lane."

On 28 October 1771, also as an afterpiece for *The School for Rakes*, Garrick introduced his *Institution of the Garter*, a masque, the chief occasion for which was an unusually large number of installations into that order during the preceding summer.

Garrick's gout and stone attacks continued during the next years, and he performed less, although he continued active as manager. He was not adding new roles to his acting repertory. In February of 1772 he moved from Southampton Street to one of a new block of houses designed by the Adams brothers–Adelphi Terrace. In the fall of that year he produced his afterpiece *The Irish Widow*. It too is an imitation of a French play (Molière's *Le Mariage forcé*, 1664), though this time somewhat farther from the original. As usual Garrick produced a lively piece on familiar themes. A pair of young lovers are thwarted by an old man, guardian to the lover and with the power over him of having to give consent to his marriage. The old man falls in love with the girl (the Irish widow of the title) and has to be tricked out of his infatuation by a ploy similar to the one in Jonson's *Epicoene, or The Silent Woman* (1609 or 1610). All is conducted within the middle range of comic engagement–the characters, the emotions, and the wit, but that middle range is Garrick's playing field.

In the next years Garrick advanced his interest in improving the artistic quality of the scenes and lighting of Drury Lane as a result of his having hired the important scene designer Philippe Jacques de Loutherbourg. He acted rather infrequently during these seasons, but he was active in staging productions, especially the extravaganzas for the Christmas season.

One might also cite events of the years from 1772 to 1774 as the source for attacks that Garrick suffered throughout his career. For someone who wielded as much power as he did such attacks can probably be regarded as inevitable. He had to turn down plays for production and in doing so engaged the fury of authors scorned. He was in the public eye, seeking public approval (at least at the box office). It appears from the extant material that he handled all such obligations with as much good nature and tact as could be expected. But he was attacked, and he did not like it. An added thorn in his side was inserted when Lacy died and his share of the patent was inherited by his son Willoughby, who decided to chal-

Garrick Standing with the Bust of Shakespeare, *John Hoppner's copy of the painting Thomas Gainsborough made for the Stratford Town Hall in 1769 (by permission of the Folger Shakespeare Library). The original was destroyed by fire in 1946.*

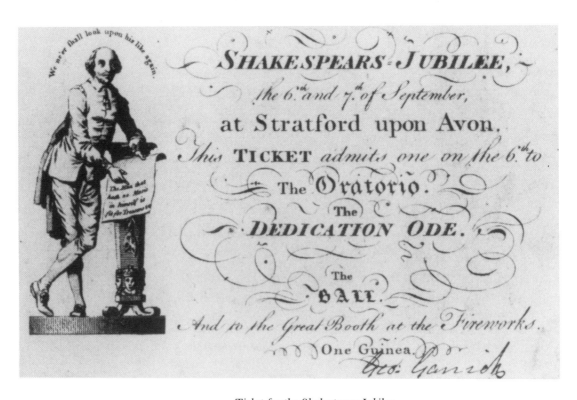

Ticket for the Shakespeare Jubilee

Garrick reciting his ode at the Shakespeare Jubilee

Garrick as steward of the 1769 Shakespeare Jubilee (engraving by J. Saunders, based on a painting by Benjamin van der Gucht)

Enter Weston

Parsons

What little Tom Weston give me your hand Boy.

Weston

As tall as yourself goodman Parsons the Giant.

Parsons.

Come, come, we won't dispute about a quarter of an Inch. — You are a new Man, so sleek so clear, & the end of your Nose as fair, as the rest of your face — what have you been doing Boy?

Weston

Turn'd over a New leaf.

Parsons

In some Tavern book I suppose.

Weston

No, no, the leaves there were quite full I was oblig'd to reform having no Money — I am taking care of my Constitution.

Parsons

Reform! I should be glad to hear what you cale Reformation.

Weston

Why, what other folks call Reformation I live Soberly when I am ill, in order to get well & when I am well, I live a little pleasantly to

Page from the manuscript for The Meeting of the Company or Bayes's Art of Acting *(by permission of the Henry E. Huntington Library and Art Gallery)*

lenge Garrick's position as sole voice in artistic matters and who (quite mistakenly it appears) fancied himself an actor. In addition to various actors in his company who were constantly responding to slights (probably more imaginary than real), Garrick was attacked in print by Francis Gentleman, William Kenrick, Francis Newberry, the Reverend David Williams, and Tom Davies (who later wrote a biography of Garrick), all of whom can be mentioned as examples of people dedicated to making his life less than serene.

In 1773 he was elected to "The Club," a discussion group including Samuel Johnson, Sir Joshua Reynolds, and Edmund Burke, from which he had been excluded during the first eight years of its existence (partly from Johnson's peevishness). Apparently he yearned for membership, although it is hard to imagine anything more self-consciously intellectual, with all its rumors of "brilliant" conversation. His membership did, however, show that he had achieved intellectual, as well as social, eminence.

His holiday-season entertainment for 1773-1774 was *A Christmas Tale*, designed by Loutherberg (in his debut at Drury Lane) with music by Dibdin. It was the main piece and had spectacular stage effects of unusual interest. The play is a free imitation of *La Fee Urgele* (1765) by Charles-Simon Favart. It too is a work that resists being put into any established category of serious composition. While it is true that it was geared to the scenic effects, it would surely be an oversimplification to deny that Garrick was after something that was harmonious with those effects, and in this case the term most readily available would probably be "fairy story." That is, the work takes place in a never-never land peopled by evil spirits, good spirits, and sprites and accomplishes nothing, or tries to accomplish nothing that is too complex in its moral subtlety to be handled in such a context.

For the genre of this piece, the most readily available comparison may be Mozart's *The Magic Flute*, with the same mixture of character types and the same totally symbolic and stylized relationship to whatever moral engagement might be involved, including the music hall comedian level associated with Papageno and the earnest solemnity of Tamino. If Garrick had had Mozart to set his piece, it would have been charming, but there is no need to apologize, for as usual Garrick has an excellent eye for what the occasion requires. Clearly what the text needs is music that is equal to it. Even William Hopkins was aware that

Dibdin's music was not very successful, calling it his worst. As usual, Garrick minimized the piece in the advertisement of the printed edition and allowed it to be known that he had tossed it off as a support for Loutherberg's scenery.

The season of 1774-1775 opened on 17 September 1774 with Addison's *The Drummer*. Garrick supplied, as a substitute for the usual season-opening prologue, a short rehearsal comedy called *The Meeting of the Company; or, Bayes's Art of Acting*. It employs members of the company as themselves and takes as its subject matter bad acting, both in tragedy and comedy:

> Would you in tragedy extort applause,
> Distort *yourselves*–now rage, now start, now pause.
> Beat breast, roll eyes, stretch nose, up brows, down jaws.
> Then strut, stride, stare, goggle, bounce and bawl,
> And when you're out of breath, pant, drag and drawl.
> ....
> Observe in comedy to frisk about.
> Never stand still. Jerk, work; fly in, fly out,
> Your faults conceal in flutter and in hurry;
> And with snip, snap, the poet's meaning worry,
> Like bullies hide your wants in bounce and vapor.
> If mem'ry fails, take snuff, laugh, curse and caper.
> Hey, Jack! what!–damn it! ha, ha! Cloud, dull, sad,
> Cuss it! Hell devil! Woman, wine, drunk, mad!

The piece also directs attention to the audience, saying that if they get bad acting such as that prescribed by Bayes and bad writing such as that produced by Bayes, it is because they allow it.

Garrick's afterpiece *Bon Ton; or, High Life above Stairs* was first performed on 18 March 1775. In the advertisement Garrick says that it "had been thrown aside for many years" (prompter William Hopkins says for fifteen or sixteen years). The chief character, Sir John Trotley, a good, solid Englishman with sound middle-class values, is visiting a dissipated group of higher-class nobles who have adopted the false morals of Europeans learned from their travels abroad and who are acting the roles of what the twentieth century has come to call swingers. The same suspicion of the morals of the upper classes that is belabored in *Lilliput* is the chief subject, and the usual sallies regarding the corruption of the servant class by the bad example of their betters are a part of the business. The immoralists are suitably punished by loss of money, and Sir John's sense of decency carries the day. The piece shares the unripened nature of these short

David Garrick (portrait by Sir Joshua Reynolds, circa 1776; by permission of the Folger Shakespeare Library)

plays. There is not time to develop both the characters and the complexities of the plot, so both have to be drawn from conventional sources in order to do through familiarity what cannot be accomplished through serious attention. Pedicord and Bergmann, editors of Garrick's plays, question the date of composition but putting it, as they do, at about the stage of Garrick's development shown in *Lethe* or *The Lying Valet* would do no violence to credibility.

Garrick's last two staged compositions were introduced early in the 1775-1776 season. The first was a musical prelude, the occasion being that the interior of the theater had been redesigned and redecorated by the Adam brothers, James and Robert. *The Theatrical Candidates* is about 180 lines of verse in dialogue and songs portraying an appeal to the audience for favor by the muse of tragedy, the muse of comedy, and Harlequin. It is a return to the subject of what the theater repertory should be and a reiteration of the charge that the audience is responsible: " 'Tis you must decree,/For your praise is the key,/

To open the temple of Fame."

On 28 October 1775, as an afterpiece to *The Fair Penitant*, Garrick introduced a one-act comic opera, *May Day; or, The Little Gipsy*, with music by Arne. He had written it specifically for the debut of a young singer, a pupil of Arne's, one Miss Abrams. The libretto is another story of a father who is his son's rival in love. Arne's music was much admired, and Garrick's work is certainly adequate for its limited purpose.

It is rather a shock when reading Garrick's correspondence for December of 1775 to come upon the letter to Colman dated 29 December, in which Garrick informs him that he is going to sell his share of the patent and thus retire from the stage. Colman, who had sold his share of the Covent Garden patent at the end of the season in 1774, and who by that time had suffered all he cared to suffer of partnerships, refused to buy Garrick's share, and it went to Richard Brinsley Sheridan and a group of associates. Willoughby Lacy retained his share, and the spring of 1776 be-

Playbill for Garrick's last appearance on the stage

came Garrick's final season on the stage. He bade farewell to one role after another in a season in which ticket buying approached hysteria. In his last month he played Abel Drugger, Benedick, Kitely, Hamlet, Sir John Brute, Leon, Lear, Archer, Ranger, Richard III, and, for his final performance on 10 June 1776, he chose Don Felix in Susanna Centlivre's *The Wonder.* Hopkins wrote, "This being the Last time of Mr G. performing he generously gave the Profits of the Night to the Theatrical Fund, he spoke the Usual prologue & after the play he went forward & address'd the Audience in so pathetic a Manner as draw Tears from the Audience & himself & took his leave of them forever." On 18 June Garrick wrote to Suzanne Necker,

> I flatter myself that you will not be displeased to know, that I departed my theatrical life on Monday the 10th of June–it was indeed a sight very well worth seeing! Though I performed my part with as much, if not more spirit than I ever did, yet when I came to take the last farewell, I not only lost almost the use of my voice, but of my limbs too: it was indeed, as I said, *a most awful moment.* You would not have thought an English audience void of feeling if you had then seen and

heard them. After I had left the stage, and was dead to them, they would not suffer the *petite piece* to go on; nor would the actors perform, they were so affected: in short, the public was very generous, and I am most grateful.

His retirement was short. He frequently visited his wealthy friends at their estates, and he had some contacts with the theater (he did not find it easy to collect the interest owed him by Willoughby Lacy), but his health was deteriorating. While visiting the Spencers at Althorp, he became ill. He died at his home in the Adelphi on 20 January 1779. He had what amounted to a state funeral and was buried in Westminster Abbey. His wife survived him by forty-three years.

Garrick left behind him a name and a reputation unprecedented in the annals of the theater. He touched all areas of theatrical art and left each better than he found it. He was a man of great charm, an actor of great skill, a producer of insight and feeling. As a writer and adapter he displayed deep knowledge of the demands that performance makes on printed texts, and, although he did not always achieve the end prescribed by abstract aesthetics, he consistently realized his own aims with wit and vivacity.

Letters:

The Private Correspondence of David Garrick, 2 volumes, edited by James Boaden (London: H. Colburn & R. Bentley, 1831-1832);

Some Unpublished Correspondence of David Garrick, edited by George Pierce Baker (Boston: Houghton, Mifflin, 1907);

Letters of David Garrick and Georgiana Countess of Spencer, 1759-1779, edited by Earl Spencer and Christopher Dobson (Cambridge: The Roxburghe Club, 1960);

The Letters of David Garrick, 3 volumes, edited by David M. Little and George M. Kahrl, associate editor Phoebe deK. Wilson (Cambridge, Mass.: Harvard University Press, 1963).

Bibliographies:

Mary E. Knapp, *David Garrick: A Checklist of His Verse* (Charlottesville: University Press of Virginia, 1955);

Gerald M. Berkowitz, "David Garrick—An Annotated Bibliography," *Restoration and Eighteenth Century Theatre Research*, 11 (May 1972): 1-18.

Biographies:

Arthur Murphy, *Life of David Garrick*, 2 volumes (London: J. Wright, 1801);

Thomas Davies, *Memoirs of the Life of David Garrick*, 2 volumes (London: Longman, Hurst, Rees & Orme, 1808);

Joseph Knight, *David Garrick* (London: Kegan Paul, Trench, Trübner, 1894);

Percy Fitzgerald, *The Life of David Garrick* (London: Simpkin, Marshall, Hamilton, Kent, 1899);

Margaret Barton, *Garrick* (London: Faber & Faber, 1949);

Carola Oman, *David Garrick* (London: Hodder & Stoughton, 1958);

George Winchester Stone, Jr., and George M. Kahrl, *David Garrick, A Critical Biography* (Carbondale & Edwardsville: Southern Illinois University Press, 1979);

Alan Kendall, *David Garrick: A Biography* (London: Harrap, 1985).

References:

Frederick L. Bergmann, "David Garrick and *The Clandestine Marriage*," *PMLA*, 67 (March 1952): 148-162;

Bergmann, "Garrick's *Zara*," *PMLA*, 74 (June 1959): 225-232;

Lance Bertelson, "David Garrick and English Painting," *Eighteenth-Century Studies*, 11 (Spring 1978): 308-324;

Richard Bevis, *The Laughing Tradition: Stage Comedy in Garrick's Day* (Athens: University of Georgia Press, 1980);

Kalman A. Burnim, *David Garrick, Director* (Pittsburgh: University of Pittsburgh Press, 1961);

Richard Cumberland, *Memoirs of Richard Cumberland* (London: Lackington, Allen, 1806);

Thomas Davies, *Dramatic Miscellanies Consisting of Critical Observations on Several Plays of Shakspeare* [sic]: *With a review of his principal characters, and those of various eminent writers as represented by Mr. Garrick, and other celebrated comedians*, 3 volumes (London: Printed for the author, 1783, 1784);

Christian Deelman, *The Great Shakespeare Jubilee* (New York: Viking, 1964);

Phyllis T. Dirks, *David Garrick* (Boston: Twayne, 1985);

Dirks, "Garrick's Fail-Safe Musical Venture, *A Peep Behind the Curtain*, an English Burletta," in *The Stage and the Page: London's "Whole*

Invitation to Garrick's funeral

Show" in the Eighteenth Century Theatre, edited by George Winchester Stone, Jr. (Berkeley, Los Angeles & London: University of California Press, 1981), pp. 136-148;

Martha W. England, *Garrick and Stratford* (New York: New York Public Library, 1962);

England, *Garrick's Jubilee* (Columbus: Ohio University Press, 1964);

Samuel Foote, *A Treatise on the Passions, So Far As They Regard the Stage, with a Critical Inquiry into the Theatrical Merit of Mr. G—k, Mr. Q—n, and Mr. B—y. The First Considered in the Part of Lear, the two Last Opposed in Othello* (London: C. Corbett, 1747);

John Genest, *Some Account of the English Stage from the Restoration in 1660 to 1830*, 10 volumes (Bath: Printed by H. E. Carrington & sold by T. Rodd, 1832);

Lillian Gottesman, "Garrick's *Institution of the Garter*," *Restoration and Eighteenth Century Theatre Research*, 6 (November 1967): 37-43;

Gottesman, "Garrick's *Lilliput*," *Restoration and Eighteenth Century Theatre Research*, 11 (November 1972): 34-37;

F. A. Hedgcock, *A Cosmopolitan Actor, David Garrick and His French Friends* (London: Paul, 1912);

Leo Hughes, *A Century of English Farce* (Princeton: Princeton University Press, 1956);

Hughes, *The Drama's Patrons* (Austin: University of Texas Press, 1971);

Judith Milhous and Robert D. Hume, "David Garrick and Box-Office Receipts at Drury Lane in 1742-43," *Philological Quarterly*, 67 (Summer 1988): 323-344;

Allardyce Nicoll, *The Garrick Stage: Theatres and Audience in the Eighteenth Century* (Athens: University of Georgia Press, 1980);

George C. D. Odell, *Shakespeare from Betterton to Irving*, 2 volumes (New York: Scribners, 1920);

Florence Mary Wilson Parsons, *Garrick and His Circle* (New York: Putnam's, 1906);

Harry W. Pedicord, *The Theatrical Public in the Time of Garrick* (New York: King's Crown Press, 1954);

Cecil Price, *Theatre in the Age of Garrick* (Totowa, N.J.: Rowman & Littlefield, 1973);

Sir Joshua Reynolds, *Portraits; Character Sketches of Oliver Goldsmith, Samuel Johnson, and David*

Garrick, Together with other Manuscripts of Reynolds Discovered Among the Boswell Papers, edited by Frederick W. Hilles (New York: McGraw-Hill, 1952);

Edward Robins, *Twelve Great Actors* (New York: Putnam's, 1900);

Arthur H. Scouten, "Shakespeare's Plays in the Theatrical Repertory When Garrick Came to London," *University of Texas Studies in English*, 24 (1944): 257-268;

D. Nichol Smith, *Shakespeare in the XVIII Century* (Oxford: Clarendon Press, 1928);

Hazelton Spencer, *Shakespeare Improved* (Cambridge, Mass.: Harvard University Press, 1927);

Arthur Colby Sprague, *Shakespeare and the Actors* (Cambridge, Mass.: Harvard University Press, 1944);

Sprague, *Shakespearean Players and Performances* (Cambridge, Mass.: Harvard University Press, 1953);

Elizabeth P. Stein, *David Garrick, Dramatist* (New York: Modern Language Association of America, 1938);

Johanne M. Stochholm, *Garrick's Folly: The Shakespeare Jubilee of 1769 at Stratford and Drury Lane* (London: Methuen, 1964);

George Winchester Stone, Jr., "Bloody, Bold, and Complex Richard: Garrick's Interpretation," in *On Stage and Off*, edited by John W. Ehrstine and others (Pullman: Washington State University Press, 1968);

Stone, "A Century of *Cymbeline*; or Garrick's Magic Touch," *Philological Quarterly*, 54 (Winter 1975): 138-152;

Stone, "David Garrick's Significance in the History of Shakespearean Criticism," *PMLA*, 65 (March 1950): 183-197;

Stone, "Garrick and an Unknown Operatic Version of *Love's Labour's Lost*," *Review of English Studies*, 15 (July 1939): 323-328;

Stone, "Garrick and Othello," *Philological Quarterly*, 45 (January 1966): 304-320;

Stone, "Garrick's Handling of *Macbeth*," *Studies in Philology*, 38 (October 1941): 609-628;

Stone, "Garrick's Long Lost Alteration of *Hamlet*," *PMLA*, 49 (September 1934): 890-921;

Stone, "Garrick's Presentation of *Anthony and Cleopatra*," *Review of English Studies*, 13 (January 1937): 20-38;

Stone, "Garrick's Production of *King Lear*: A Study in the Temper of the Eighteenth-Century Mind," *Studies in Philology*, 45 (January 1948): 89-103;

Stone, "*A Midsummer Night's Dream* in the Hands of Garrick and Colvan," *PMLA*, 54 (June 1939): 467-482;

Stone, "*Romeo and Juliet*: The Source of Its Modern Career," *Shakespeare Quarterly*, 15 (Spring 1964): 191-206;

Stone, "Shakespeare's *Tempest* at Drury Lane During Garrick's Management," *Shakespeare Quarterly*, 7 (Winter 1956): 1-7;

Hugh Taite, "Garrick, Shakespeare, and Wilkes," *British Museum Quarterly*, 24 (1961): 100-107;

Tate Wilkinson, *Memoirs of His Own Life*, 4 volumes (York: Printed for the author, 1790);

Leigh Woods, *Garrick Claims the Stage: Acting as Social Emblem in Eighteenth Century England* (Westport, Conn.: Greenwood Press, 1984).

Papers:

The Folger Shakespeare Library houses many of Garrick's manuscripts, including letters, one of the two extant journals, promptbooks and other personal material, a working copy of *The Clandestine Marriage*, and much of his verse. Another repository for Garrick's correspondence is the Forster collection of the Victoria and Albert Museum, London. The Huntington Library (especially in the Larpent Collection) has manuscript material for several plays. The Garrick Club in London has, among other material, a manuscript outline of *The Clandestine Marriage*. The Little and Kahrl edition of the letters lists, so far as possible, the location of each letter.

John Gay

(circa 30 June 1685-4 December 1732)

Calhoun Winton
University of Maryland at College Park

PLAY PRODUCTIONS: *The Wife of Bath,* London, Theatre Royal in Drury Lane, 12 May 1713; revised version, London, Theatre Royal, Lincoln's Inn Fields, 19 January 1730;

The What D'Ye Call It, London, Theatre Royal in Drury Lane, 23 February 1715;

Three Hours after Marriage, London, Theatre Royal in Drury Lane, 16 January 1717;

Acis and Galatea, libretto by Gay and music by G. F. Handel, Canons, Middlesex, private performance, circa 1718; London, Theatre Royal, Lincoln's Inn Fields, 26 March 1731;

The Captives, London, Theatre Royal in Drury Lane, 15 January 1724;

The Beggar's Opera, London, Lincoln's Inn Fields, 29 January 1728;

Achilles, London, Theatre Royal in Covent Garden, 10 February 1733;

The Distress'd Wife, London, Theatre Royal in Covent Garden, 5 May 1734.

SELECTED BOOKS: *Wine, A Poem* (London: Printed for William Keble, 1708);

The Present State of Wit, in a Letter to a Friend in the Country (London, 1711);

The Mohocks: A Tragi-Comical Farce. As it was Acted near the Watch-house in Covent Garden. By Her Majesty's Servants (London: Printed for Bernard Lintott, 1712);

Rural Sports. A Poem. Inscribed to Mr. Pope (London: Printed for Jacob Tonson, 1713);

The Wife of Bath. A Comedy. As it is Acted at the Theatre-Royal in Drury-Lane, By Her Majesty's Servants (London: Printed for Bernard Lintott, 1713); revised as *The Wife of Bath. A Comedy. As it is Acted at the Theatre-Royal in Lincoln's Inn Fields* (London: Printed for Bernard Lintott, 1730);

The Fan. A Poem. In Three Books (London: Printed for Jacob Tonson, 1713);

The Shepherd's Week. In Six Pastorals (London: Printed for Ferd. Burleigh, 1714);

The What D'Ye Call It: A Tragi-Comi-Pastoral Farce (London: Printed for Bernard Lintott, 1715);

Trivia: or, The Art of Walking the Streets of London (London: Printed for Bernard Lintott, 1716);

Three Hours after Marriage. A Comedy, As it is Acted at the Theatre-Royal (London: Printed for Bernard Lintot, 1717);

Poems on Several Occasions (London: Printed for Jacob Tonson & Bernard Lintot, 1720)–includes *Dione. A Pastoral Tragedy;*

The Captives. A Tragedy. As it is acted at the Theatre-Royal in Drury-Lane, By His Majesty's Servants (London: Printed for Jacob Tonson, 1724);

Fables (London: Printed for Jacob Tonson & John Watts, 1727);

The Beggar's Opera. As it is Acted at the Theatre-Royal in Lincoln's-Inn-Fields (London: Printed for John Watts, 1728);

Polly: An Opera. Being the Second Part of The Beggar's Opera (London: Printed [by William Bowyer] for the author, 1729);

Acis and Galatea: An English Pastoral Opera. In Three Acts. As it is Perform'd at the New Theatre in the Hay-Market. Set to Musick by Mr. Handel (London: Printed for John Watts, 1732);

Achilles. An Opera. As it is Perform'd at the Theatre-Royal in Covent-Garden (London: Printed for John Watts, 1733);

Fables. By the late Mr. Gay. Volume the Second (London: Printed for J. & P. Knapton & T. Cox, 1738);

The Distress'd Wife. A Comedy (London: Printed for Thomas Astley, 1743);

The Rehearsal at Goatham (London: Printed for Thomas Astley & sold by R. Baldwin, 1754).

Collection: *John Gay: Dramatic Works,* edited by John Fuller, 2 volumes (Oxford: Clarendon Press, 1983).

John Gay's masterpiece, *The Beggar's Opera,* has so dominated the landscape of his subsequent reputation that many theatergoers are not

John Gay (engraving by W. Aikman)

aware he did anything else. *The Beggar's Opera* is a great work, indisputably, and deserves the acclaim it enjoys; everyone knows that it made "Gay rich and Rich [the theater manager] gay," as the wits of his own time said. But Gay's other works for the stage are also interesting, in their own right and for the insights into *The Beggar's Opera* that they provide from an angle, as it were.

One should remember that Gay was a man of the theater, from his entrance onto the literary scene–a few minor poems excepted–with the publication of his first play, *The Mohocks*, in 1712, until his death in 1732, when he left three plays in various stages of completion. *The Beggar's Opera* (1728) was certainly the high point of his career, but it needs to be viewed in the perspective of what came before and what followed it.

Gay was born in Barnstaple, a village on the North Devon coast, about 30 June 1685 and attended the local, excellent grammar school. After the early death of his parents, William and Katherine Hanmer Gay, he was apprenticed to a silk merchant in London. In later life Gay did not choose to speak either of his rural origins or his urban apprenticeship, but they were both important to his development as an artist. Barnstaple gave him a knowledge of the English countryside–with its accents, customs, and folklore–which was unusual among writers of his time and which he was to employ here and there in his plays; and London provided that total understanding of the seamy, even criminal, side of life which is the essence of *The Beggar's Opera*.

Gay negotiated an end to his apprenticeship before he had completed his articles and returned to Barnstaple. Rather soon after that he made his way back to the metropolis; from about 1707 he was essentially a Londoner for the rest of his life. This time he came to London as a member of the gentry, barely. His entrée was provided by Aaron Hill, then just at the beginning of a long career as a projector, miscellaneous writer, and man of the theater. Hill had been a classmate of Gay's at the Barnstaple Grammar

School, and he appears to have taken his old friend on as a private secretary, a job to help him keep body and soul together. Hill had money, and he was generous. This was an appointment of significance because Hill had decided to pursue a career in the theater and was doing so with spectacular initial success, becoming somehow—probably through family influence—the manager of the Theatre Royal in Drury Lane at the age of twenty-four. Although his tenure there was stormy and lasted only through the season of 1709-1710, Hill managed to get two of his own plays produced during that time, the tragedy *Elfrid* and the farce *The Walking Statue*. The farce was the most successful play Hill ever wrote, and it is a fair guess, though only a guess, that his private secretary had something to do with it. At the very least Gay was learning how the London theater world operated.

Hill quarreled with his actors and left Drury Lane, to surface the next season as manager of the Queen's Theatre opera house in the Haymarket. Here he and Gay were involved in an enterprise that was to have lasting consequences for Gay, the production of G. F. Handel's first opera in England, *Rinaldo*. Hill had probably seen productions of Italian opera seria during his earlier travels through the courts of Germany and Austria as part of a diplomatic entourage; there is even the possibility that he met Handel on his travels. When Handel arrived in England, Hill approached his contemporary—Hill, Gay, and Handel were all born in 1685—and proposed that he produce an opera seria in Italian for the London audience. Hill sketched the libretto in English, borrowing the plot line from Tasso's familiar account, and oversaw its translation into Italian. The production of *Rinaldo* in February 1711, though mercilessly satirized by Joseph Addison and Richard Steele in *The Spectator* (nos. 5, 18, and 29), was a triumph for both Hill and Handel. It was the most popular of Handel's operas during his lifetime.

The consequences for Gay were twofold: meeting Handel, for whom he would later write the libretto of *Acis and Galatea*, and becoming immersed in opera seria. Unlike most other writers of his time, Gay approached Italian opera from the inside, knowing what the composers, or at least the greatest of the composers, Handel, had in mind, what they were attempting to do with their music. He learned early, in short, what music in the theater could mean. The concept of integrating words and music, of allowing the words to play against the music and the music against the words, is a difficult one for most writers to accept; it was part of Addison's problem in dealing with opera, for example. Music, he felt strongly, must be subordinated to words. Gay intuited the partnership of music and words, or, perhaps more likely, he learned it from Handel.

By the spring of 1712 Gay had a play of his own ready for production, *The Mohocks*, which he presented to the managers of the Drury Lane theater. It was a one-act farce in three short scenes, to be used as an afterpiece. Audiences were beginning to demand short dramas like this one (and like Hill's *The Walking Statue*) to follow the main production. *The Mohocks* concerns a group of London toughs, the Mohocks of the title, who are ruled over by an "emperor." The Mohocks capture members of the watch (the equivalent of the police), exchange clothes with them, and, thus disguised, bring the watch before the justices of the peace. There they charge the watch with being the street toughs. At the end the truth, or a version of it, emerges, and all join in a concluding dance.

Here, clearly, is the transvaluation of values to be seen again fifteen years later in *The Beggar's Opera*: the world turned upside down, with criminals usurping the customs and prerogatives of the governing classes. Gay handles the farcical crowd scenes effectively; *The Mohocks* is apprentice work but that of an apprentice who knows his craft surprisingly well.

Unfortunately for Gay, his timing was off. London was having trouble with what we would term muggers (the contemporary term was "scowrers"), and rumors abounded that the Mohocks (named for some Iroquois Native Americans who had visited London in 1710) really existed. The issue became politicized, Whigs accusing Tories of "Mohocking" and the reverse, and the cautious Drury Lane management probably decided not to touch Gay's play. The fact that the one-acter required a large cast, with twenty-two speaking parts, may have worked against its chances as well. It was a promising beginning, though, and Steele's *Spectator* no. 324, telling of the Mohocks' misdeeds, was probably part of a preview or "puff" for Gay's play, which Steele had seen in manuscript. To no avail. Gay published the play on 10 April 1712 as a "Tragi-comical Farce" and received two pounds, ten shillings from Bernard Lintot for the copyright.

About this time Gay secured appointment as household steward for Anne Scott, duchess of

John Gay

Monmouth. This post was modestly honorific and probably more remunerative than working for Aaron Hill, but it began a pattern of behavior that lasted the rest of his life and has done Gay's reputation no good: he became known as an amiable hanger-on to the aristocracy. This was a fate that confronted other writers of his time: Addison, Steele, and Pope achieved social and moral independence by means of their writing, Swift by his position in the Church, and in each case by establishing their literary identity. Gay found the process difficult, but he was sensitive, and his activities in 1713 may reflect his efforts to break out of the aristocratic bonds. He was writing poetry for Steele's *Poetical Miscellanies,* and he was working on another play.

This one was not set in contemporary London but in Chaucer's England, or Chaucer's En-

gland as Gay, and probably Pope, imagined it. *The Wife of Bath* uses Alison the Wife, and a franklyn–presumably the Franklyn of the *Canterbury Tales*–as well as Chaucer himself in its first scene. The setting is an inn between London and Canterbury; Chaucer and the others have just left the pilgrims, "certainly the most diverting Company," says the Franklyn, "that ever travell'd the Road. . . ." Gay depicts several of the principals as humours characters in the Jonson/Shadwell comic tradition, especially Doublechin the monk, the Franklyn, and Alison, the lecherous widow of Bath. Steele recognized this technique in his preproduction puff for the play (*Guardian* no. 50), speaking of the actress Margaret Bicknell as Alison: "If the rest of the Actors enter into their several Parts with the same Spirit, the humorous Characters of this Play cannot but appear excellent on the Theatre. . . ."

Gay makes no attempt to reproduce Middle-English language effects or medieval customs; the distancing is between town and country, not between the fourteenth and eighteenth centuries. The folk customs and folk beliefs presented and gently satirized are similar to those he used in *The Shepherd's Week*, which he was composing at this time, and are of course derived from his youth in Devon.

Interestingly, Gay's play has as a central character a young poet, Doggerell, who is as much concerned with his social status as with his inept poetry; through the mistakes of a night he finds himself married to Busie the maid at the play's end, whereas Chaucer, the true poet, has won the hand of the Lady Myrtilla, Busie's employer, and saved Myrtilla from becoming a nun. In another strand of the plot the worthy young man Merit—with such a name could he be unworthy?—seeks the hand of the wealthy Franklyn's daughter Florinda, disguising himself as a waiter, and eventually wins her. True worth, human and poetic, in the persons of Merit and Chaucer thus win over snobbery and bad poetry as embodied by Doggerell.

In truth, Gay has more plot than he quite knows what to do with by the fifth act; the five-act form proved to be more troublesome than he may have supposed it would. Still, the play has merits. Gay thought so, for he worked on a revised version for years. Alison is an interesting character, and so is Chaucer. Florinda, told by the monk Doublechin that her father's wish that she marry Doggerell amounts to a command, a daughter not being a free agent, strikes an early feminist note: "Not a free Agent! How, Father, what, compliment the Sex with Slavery?—marry a Woman to her Aversion, and give her Mortification for Life?" Gay was to return to this question of children versus parents on marriage in *The Beggar's Opera*, as did many other dramatists of his time. It was a burning question, one without any apparent solution.

As in *The Mohocks* Gay used songs throughout the play, giving several to Robert Wilks, who created the role of Chaucer, and three to Margaret Bicknell as Alison, one of which was published separately with music. This song, "There was a Swain full fair," reveals Gay as already an accomplished lyricist.

The Wife of Bath was accepted for production at Drury Lane after Addison's *Cato* in the spring of 1713; when *Cato* proved to be the success of the season Gay found his play delayed and delayed again. It was finally performed on 12 May and again on 15 May, as an author's benefit; then no more. This is distinctly odd and suggests that Gay may have fallen victim to some kind of backstage machinations. Pope had befriended Gay, he was working on his own Chaucerian adaptation *The Temple of Fame* that winter and spring, and he may have contributed the epilogue to *The Wife of Bath*. It is possible that some of the free-floating hostility toward Pope, even at this early date, may have rubbed off in some way on Gay—two years later this would certainly be the case. No contemporary reports of those two early performances exist, so all this must be speculative. At any rate, Bernard Lintot, the publisher, was sufficiently impressed to pay Gay twenty-five pounds for the copyright, a ten-fold increase over that for *The Mohocks*. Gay was not prospering as a dramatist, but the payment was not contemptible, either: an individual could live for a year in the country (frugally) on twenty-five pounds.

Gay's tastes were more refined than frugal, however. His wages from the duchess of Monmouth may have been adequate, but he was turning his hand to various literary forms: he was writing poetry, composing essays for Steele's *Guardian*—no pay for that—and doubtless meditating on his next play. During the winter of 1713-1714 he came publicly over to the Tory side, associating himself with Pope, Swift, Dr. John Arbuthnot, and the Tory lord treasurer, Robert Harley, earl of Oxford, in the Scriblerus Club. For all its subsequent fame, the club did not meet often nor accomplish much in the way of literary productions, but the association was undoubtedly energizing for each member. Their principal project, the *Memoirs* (1741) of the pedant Martin Scriblerus, was probably largely the work of Dr. Arbuthnot, the learned and respectable physician to the queen. Arbuthnot was as facetious as the next man when he thought he could get away with it, as in his John Bull pamphlets of 1712. The *Memoirs* has too many satiric victims to be easily categorized, but primary attacks are made on what the Scriblerians took to be antiquarian and scientific pedantry. Arbuthnot knew more about both science and antiquarian pursuits than any of the other Scriblerians, and he probably led the way, with the others happily joining in. Much of the *Memoirs'* power derives from its successful burlesquing of scientific and antiquarian language, the sort sometimes employed in the *Transactions* of the Royal Society or in the

Alexander Pope
his safe return from
T R O Y
a Congratulatory Poem on
the compleating his Translation of Homer's Ilias.

in the manner of the beginning
of the last Canto of
Ariosto.

1.

Long hast thou, Friend been absent from thy soil
Like patient Ithacus at siege of Troy
I have been witness of thy six years toil
Thy daily Labours and thy night's annoy,
Lost to thy native land; with great turmoil
on the wide Sea, oft threatning to destroy.
Methinks with thee, I've trod Sigæan ground,
And heard hoarse Hellespontic shores resound.

2.

Did I not see thee when thou first set'st sail
To seek Adventures fair in Grecian Land
Did I not see thy sinking Spirits fail
And wish thy Bark had never left the Strand?
Ev'n in mid Ocean often didst thou quail
And oft' lift up thy holy eye & hand,
Praying thy Virgin dear, and Saintly Choir
Back to the Port to speed thy Bark entire.

Page from the manuscript for "Mr. Pope's Welcome from Greece," written by Gay in 1715 (by permission of the British Library)

treatises of historical philologists or literary critics. Swift had earlier tuned his ear to this note, in *A Tale of a Tub* (1704). Gay's next two plays were to make much use of this burlesquing technique.

So did his long poem, *The Shepherd's Week*, which appeared in April 1714. This work was in part a burlesque of Ambrose Philips's pastorals. More interesting than the burlesque is Gay's extensive use of folklore, folk dialect, and folk customs, which he had employed to a certain extent the year before in *The Wife of Bath*. *The Shepherd's Week* secured Gay the literary acclaim he had not so far won with his plays. By that spring he was feeling confident enough of his status to seek and find employment as a diplomat, and he accompanied the earl of Clarendon to Germany as his private secretary. Clarendon was sent by the Tory ministry to ingratiate them with the House of Hanover, as Queen Anne's health continued to decline. Unfortunately for the Tories and for Gay personally, the queen died soon after the mission arrived in Hanover; the reins of government slipped away from the divided Tories; and Gay was without formal employment again. Back in London he found the Scriblerus Club effectively dispersed as a club but Arbuthnot and Pope still available. Looking for a patron or for regular employment, Gay drifted into Pope's orbit and remained there for the rest of his life. He also befriended Henrietta Howard, one of the maids of honor to the Princess of Wales, who became a lifelong supporter. By the end of 1714 he was working on his next play.

The What D'Ye Call It is an afterpiece, a farce burlesque, or as its subtitle terms it, echoing Hamlet's players, "A Tragi-Comi-Pastoral Farce." In two short acts with introductory and closing framing scenes, it is set in the country. Gay once again draws on the knowledge of folklore he had shown earlier. A long mock-learned preface, in which the author gravely discusses the objections to his play's being termed a comedy, a tragedy, or a pastoral, stems directly from the meditations of the Scriblerus Club, and Pope and Arbuthnot may well have had a hand in it.

The setting is the hall of a country justice of the peace, where the host, Sir Roger, and his fellow justices are overseeing the production of a Christmas play, a tragedy in blank verse to be put on by the members of their households. The steward's daughter, Kitty, reveals in an aside that she is pregnant by Sir Roger's son, Squire Thomas. The character she plays in the tragedy is in the same condition by her love, Thomas Filbert, who is of course played by Squire Thomas, art faithfully reflecting life. Filbert is apparently hauled off to war by a sergeant and his press gang, who also prepare to shoot Filbert's companion Thomas Peascod for desertion. Five ghosts arise to condemn the justices for sending Peascod to his death, and one of them sings a song; "dismally," orders Gay in his stage direction. A last-minute reprieve and the sergeant's arrest for stealing Gaffer Gap's gray mare, a mad scene, and attempted suicide by Kitty lead to a final wedding between Filbert and Kitty, which turns out in the framing scene to be the real thing, too: Squire Thomas makes an honest woman of the steward's daughter. The parish clerk pronounces perhaps the shortest epilogue in eighteenth-century drama, and perhaps the best: "Our Stage Play has a Moral–and no doubt/You all have Sense enough to find it out."

The What D'Ye Call It demonstrates that Gay was by now the perfect master of stage farce. It is a burlesque not only of blank-verse tragedy but of all tragedy, of the very spirit of tragedy. A published *Key*, prepared by someone who knew a great deal about Gay and Pope, demonstrates that every scene, almost every line, burlesques some motif or some passage in stage tragedy. If there is a ghost in *Macbeth*, there are five of them here, one singing "Ye Goblins and Fairys/With Frisks and Vagarys." Shakespeare, Jonson, Dryden, Otway, Addison, Rowe, each is laid under contribution, but no one needs a *Key* to enjoy *The What D'Ye Call It*: it is self-contained and self-explanatory, as the best farce must be. For example, the convention of verse tragedy which calls for the filling-out of a pentameter line, no matter how many speakers may be involved, is ludicrous enough as it appears on the printed page. But Gay builds comedy into the lines even as he follows and parodies the convention. Kitty and Filbert bid each other farewell:

KITTY. To part is Death.
FILBERT.   'Tis Death to part.
KITTY.   Ah!
FILBERT.   Oh!

Reasonably competent actors can make a good thing of this scene, and in the first production the Drury Lane managers selected the old comedy hand Benjamin Johnson to play Filbert and Margaret Bicknell, an excellent singer, to play Kitty. Gay provided her a lyric with music by Handel which became one of the most popular songs of the century, " 'Twas when the Seas

Henrietta Howard, Gay's lifelong friend and supporter

were Roaring," a ballad of love, parting, and death. With *The What D'Ye Call It* Gay established himself as a farceur and lyricist of formidable ability.

John Fuller, Gay's most recent editor, has observed that in this play Gay "has lodged as much criticism of social injustice as one's belief in the characters can bear." This adds up to a fair amount. The pregnant Kitty, in both roles, is a victimized female; the justices are revealed to be corrupt by the ghosts of those they have condemned; the last-minute wedding of Kitty and Squire Thomas is a piece of poetic justice like that which ends *The Beggar's Opera*. The implied moral of the epilogue, for those who have the

sense to find it out, might well be seen as the same one the Beggar pronounces for his opera: "that the lower Sort of People have their Vices in a degree as well as the Rich: And that they are punish'd for them."

The What D'Ye Call It opened at Drury Lane on 23 February 1715 as an afterpiece–the perfect afterpiece–to Nicholas Rowe's *Jane Shore*, and won an audience immediately. It was played again the following day, a command performance for the Prince of Wales–surely Henrietta Howard had been at work for Gay. The third night, 25 February, was Gay's first benefit, and by the end of the season *The What D'Ye Call It* had been played fifteen times. It had a similar ex-

Lavinia Fenton, who played Polly in the first production of The Beggar's Opera
(engraving by Faber, based on a portrait by J. Ellys)

cellent run at Penkethman's booth in the fair at Southwark. By then Lintot had published two editions of the play, for which he paid Gay the odd sum of sixteen pounds, two shillings, sixpence. It stayed in the repertory for many years, and in the twentieth century it has twice been adapted as a one-act opera.

Ominously for Gay's fame, rumors began circulating that the work was in part, or even principally, by Pope and Arbuthnot. By this time Pope was being stalked by Addison's followers who gathered at Button's coffeehouse: Addison's "Little Senate," as Pope was to describe the group later. To a certain extent the attacks were on party lines: the Scriblerians were well known to be Tories, and Addison and his flock were Whigs. Even as late as 1714 Gay had not totally severed

the ties of friendship with his Whig friends, however, and there was really nothing in any of his first three plays to indicate a partisan position. The next play would alter that.

Three Hours after Marriage shares several of the satiric targets of *The Memoirs of Martinus Scriblerus*, especially in the attacks on the physician and antiquary Dr. John Woodward. It is reasonable to suppose that Gay, Pope, and Arbuthnot were once more at work on the *Memoirs*. In an advertisement to the printed version, published during the initial run of the play, Gay acknowledges "the Assistance I have receiv'd in this Piece from two of my Friends," and the assumption has always been that he is referring to Arbuthnot and Pope. This association was no doubt good for the play's quality, but it provoked a severe reaction from Pope's enemies and in the long run damaged the play and Gay's reputation for originality.

The play is another version of the December and May theme, already ancient in European literature by Chaucer's time. In this case Dr. Fossile, physician and antiquary, has just married Mrs. Towneley but has not yet consummated the marriage. Mrs. Towneley has apparently distributed her favors to half the London smart set (as her name suggests), and the play consists of Fossile's bungling attempts to prove her infidelity, countered by her machinations to prevent this proof. She is aided by two of her lovers, Plotwell and Underplot; in a famous scene they appear disguised as a mummy and a crocodile. A female poet, Phoebe Clinket, and a literary critic, Sir Tremendous, add comic effects. Phoebe is so enamored of the muse that she employs a maid with a desk strapped to her back, ready to receive Phoebe's latest inspiration. Sir Tremendous denounces a play-within-a-play that she has written. At the end a baby is presented and revealed to be Mrs. Towneley's by someone–the father is uncertain but it is not Fossile, who decides to adopt the child. "What signifies," he says, "whether a Man beget his Child or not?"

A great deal of ink has been spilled in identifying the satiric victims in *Three Hours after Marriage,* much of it spilled in vain. The play is understandable without footnotes. Two identifications, however, would immediately have been made by the London audience; both were longtime antagonists of Pope and the Scriblerians. These were John Dennis, the playwright and literary critic, as Sir Tremendous; and Dr. John Woodward, physician and antiquary, as Dr. Fossile. Woodward is attacked with the sort of sustained, personal animus that one associates with Pope rather than Gay: he is vain, pedantic, suspicious, and impotent; even his curtain line on adopting the child, which demonstrates that he does not know the difference between the genuine and the fake, is meant to sting.

Woodward had many friends in London, most of them Whigs, and one of them was Sir Richard Steele himself, the governor of Drury Lane. Woodward was his personal physician and confidant. When the play opened in January 1717, it had a run of seven consecutive playing days and seemed on the way to becoming a success like *The What D'Ye Call It.* Then–nothing. George Sherburn has traced the "fortunes and misfortunes" of *Three Hours after Marriage* and shown how the anti-Scriblerians organized opposition to the play, focusing on Pope's supposed role in writing it. Sherburn seems mistaken, however, in thinking that Colley Cibber, who played the lead, Plotwell, objected to the mild satiric thrusts at himself; Cibber was a professional actor and delighted in publicity, even unfavorable publicity. More likely is that Steele simply passed the word down to the company to scratch the play.

Pope apparently wrote Gay, relaying complaints about *Three Hours after Marriage* that he had heard. Gay replied, accepting responsibility: "I will (if any Shame there be) take it all to myself, as indeed I ought, the Motion [notion?] being first mine, and never heartily approv'd of by you." It was a good, interesting comedy, a farce of ideas; as John Fuller has noted, the characterization has a Jonsonian ring, and Fossile is reminiscent of Morose in *The Silent Woman.* Gay received some solace for the play's short run by counting his royalty from Lintot of forty-three pounds, two shillings, sixpence–quite the largest copyright payment for any of his plays to that time.

He had other consolation as well. He was much involved with the branch of court society that gathered around the Prince of Wales and Caroline, his vivacious and intelligent wife. Tory and Opposition Whig leaders met at their residence because they knew the prince and his father, George I, were bitter enemies, and they hoped to reap benefits when the prince eventually succeeded to the throne. Gay was there because he liked the ladies-in-waiting to Princess Caroline, especially Henrietta Howard, Mary Bellenden, and Mary Lepell. The Town heard that these ladies had commissioned one or more of the performances of *Three Hours after Marriage.*

A great figure in this society by virtue of his enormous wealth was James Brydges, earl of Carnarvon and later duke of Chandos. Brydges fancied himself a patron of the arts. In September 1717 he wrote Dr. John Arbuthnot proudly that "Mr. Handle has made me two . . . Anthems very noble ones" and invited Arbuthnot to visit him at his seat, Canons. Arbuthnot did so sometime during the following winter, and Gay may have been with him then, because in 1718 or thereabouts he completed his most important collaboration with Handel, the pastoral masque or serenata *Acis and Galatea.*

This little gem, based on the story in the thirteenth book of Ovid's *Metamorphoses,* tells of the love of Acis for the nymph Galatea, a love that is threatened by the giant Polyphemus, who also

Thomas Walker as Macheath in the first production of The Beggar's Opera *(courtesy of the Gabrielle Enthoven Collection, Victoria and Albert Museum)*

longs for the nymph. This is a work that demands to be seen and heard, for Handel's glorious music but also for Gay's witty and subtle libretto. As Bertrand Bronson has observed, here are "words and music inseparably united."

Nevertheless, some of Gay's virtues may be noted by a reader of the text. His lyrics are crystal clear, intelligible at every point, but also poetically interesting. Some of the sight comedy–always present in Gay's comedies–depends on the auditor's imagination: for example, the contrast between the giant Polyphemus, who carries a pine tree for a walking stick, and his Lilliputian lady love, Acis. This is sight comedy waiting for a medium not yet invented, photography.

The serenata apparently did not receive a public performance until 1731, but Chandos no doubt commissioned private presentations at Canons, as he did for other works. Whether Gay received any monetary compensation we do not know, but working with Handel on this small masterpiece must have been enormously stimulating to Gay's artistic imagination. It was further preparation for *The Beggar's Opera*.

Then, like many another artist riding the crest of his success, Gay tried something he could not do. In face of the fact that everything he had ever written well was in the comic mode, Gay turned to tragedy, and pastoral tragedy at that, for his next play. *Dione* relates the story of unre-

Act 3, scene 2, of The Beggar's Opera, *as it was depicted in 1728 or 1729 by William Hogarth (by permission of the National Gallery of Art, Washington, D.C.; Paul Mellon Collection). On the Lincoln's Inn Fields stage, surrounded by members of the audience in boxes, are Jane Giffard Egleton as Lucy Lockitt, John Hall as her father, Thomas Walker as Macheath, Lavinia Fenton as Polly Peachum, and John Hippisley as her father. Behind Hippisley, John Rich, the theater manager, is talking to auctioneer Christopher Cook. Gay is standing behind Cook.*

quited love in Arcadia, in rhymed pentameter couplets. When Laura the shepherdess tells us "Three times the lark has sung his matin lay,/ And rose on dewy wing to meet the day," the reader waits expectantly for the burlesque to come, waits to be drawn back into the world of *The What D'Ye Call It*. But *Dione* plods relentlessly on. Gay even abandons the world of English folklore and folk customs that had served him so well in the past; these are classical shepherds, or rather, to be precise, classical gentry, these Lycidases and Alexises, and Parthenissas. Samuel Johnson once asked, "who will hear of sheep and goats, and myrtle-bowers and purling rivulets, through five acts?" As it turned out, no one had the chance. The lord chamberlain, Thomas

Pelham-Holles, duke of Newcastle, ordered that it be produced at Drury Lane in the late winter of 1720, but his order was either evaded or ignored by the company. Yet, the fact that the lord chamberlain could be persuaded to exercise his authority indicates Gay had powerful friends somewhere, no doubt in the circle of the Prince and Princess of Wales. He had not given up thoughts of royal favor; nor had his friends Pope and Swift, not yet.

Gay had *Dione* included in the handsome *Poems on Several Occasions* that Jacob Tonson and Bernard Lintot brought out in 1720, and significantly the Prince and Princess of Wales lead the distinguished list of subscribers; lords and ladies abound but also old friends such as Matthew

Prior and Alexander Pope. Charles and Catherine Douglas, the duke and duchess of Queensberry, who would be important in Gay's later life, put their names down for five copies.

Gay was much to be seen in fashionable circles now, living in Richard Boyle, earl of Burlington's splendid Burlington House, angling for some sort of preferment. In 1723 he wrote Henrietta Howard, "I know that if one would be agreeable to men of dignity one must study to imitate them, and I know which way they get Money and places." Perhaps he thought a tragedy would more befit a man on the make. In the same letter he compares statesmen to highwaymen and goes on jocularly in this vein, forecasting clearly the satiric basis of *The Beggar's Opera,* but his next play was another tragedy.

The Drury Lane company agreed to present *The Captives* in January 1724. In the dedication to the printed version, published during the initial run of the play, Gay thanks Princess Caroline for "being permitted to read this play to you before it was acted." He was calling on all his resources; newspapers reported that free brandy was distributed in the box seats. Drury Lane put its leading players into the cast: Robert Wilks, Barton Booth, Anne Oldfield; no place for comedians Cibber or William Penkethman in this one.

The play is set in that Never-Never-Land of the East of which tragic authors were fond, in this case called Media. There is a conspiracy afoot against the Median king's life that comes to involve his queen and the two captives of the title, Sophernes the Persian prince and his long-lost wife, Cylene. The queen's complicity in the conspiracy is revealed; she stabs herself, and the loving Persians are reunited and forgiven by the king, they not having participated in the attempt on his life. This is the sort of tragedy that was achieving some success in the eighteenth century: a female character, or in this instance two female characters, are depicted in a stressful situation involving love and marriage. Death, usually by some form of stabbing, is the invariable outcome. In *The Captives* Gay removes some of the tragic sting by having the young couple spared to live, presumably, happily ever after. As is the case in tragedies of this sort, the female characters direct and control the action. *The Captives* is well constructed and is notably sparing of tragic fustian, but tragedies were not doing well at the box office, though literary critics kept calling for more of them and deploring audience taste. Gay's play had a run of seven nights, enough for him to get

two benefit performances. The attention to Princess Caroline may have netted him a substantial gift; Edward Young reported that *The Captives* brought Gay more than a thousand pounds, and he of course would not have done nearly that well from benefits and copyright profits.

He continued to seek his fortune at court, dedicating the first volume of his highly successful *Fables* in 1727 to William, duke of Cumberland, then just six years old. The accession of William's parents, the Prince and Princess of Wales, to the throne that year, however, did not provide Gay with the ample preferment he dreamed of: he felt downright insulted by the offer of becoming a gentleman-usher to Princess Louisa, aged two years. This humiliation, as he felt it, was enough in itself to turn his mind back to satire, comedy, and literary burlesque.

The Beggar's Opera had been a long time in gestation. As early as 1716 Swift had written Pope about what Gay might do: "what think you of a Newgate pastoral, among the whores and thieves there?" Swift knew his man: he knew Gay's wit from the days of the Scriblerus Club, and he knew that Gay understood the world of Newgate from *his* days as a London apprentice, just as he, Swift, understood Dublin because he had lived there off and on since boyhood. Neither Pope nor Swift nor Gay could have known, however, that Gay's knowledge and talents would add up to the creation of a work of genius. It is a Scriblerian kind of genius, furthermore, combining social satire, political satire, and literary burlesque as Pope was combining the same ingredients just at this time in the first version of *The Dunciad* and Swift in *Gulliver's Travels.* The three works are utterly different, but they are recognizably kin, too.

The Beggar's Opera opened at Rich's theater, Lincoln's Inn Fields, on 29 January 1728. There is no way of knowing how long Gay had actually been working on it; he had been perfecting his stagecraft for sixteen years or more and had listened to music of every variety for at least as long. A guess is that he wrote *The Beggar's Opera* rather quickly, in 1727 after his supposed rebuff at Court. He showed the play to Voltaire, who was on his first visit to England, and to William Congreve, who judged that "it would either take greatly, or be damned confoundedly." The Drury Lane managers turned it down; all Whigs, they were picking their way carefully and may have felt that the satire was too strong for the taste of the lord chamberlain (who had the ultimate power of censorship).

Cibber and his partners came to regret this decision. *The Beggar's Opera* had an initial run of sixty-two performances, as far as one knows a record run to that time on the London stage, and one that was not equaled until the production of Fielding's *Pasquin* (1736). The Drury Lane management tried playing everything against it, in the traditional manner of the rival theaters—*Hamlet, The Way of the World*—but nothing worked; everyone wanted to see Gay's opera. Gay wrote Swift with quiet pride and satisfaction: "I think I shall make an addition to my fortune of between six and seven hundred pounds. I know this account will give you pleasure, as I have push'd through this precarious Affair without servility or flattery."

As Bertrand Bronson has observed in the best critical essay on the work, the reasons for "this extraordinary success are not immediately apparent in the fable itself." It is an intentionally simpleminded story, this tale of the handsome highwayman Macheath (that is, son of the heath, dweller on the open road) and his ladyloves, who are no ladies. Gay draws on English and French theatrical traditions, on the commedia dell'arte, on the folklore and argot of the London underworld for his drama, and on popular and formal music wherever he found it for his songs. Tone and theme are both set in the very first musical piece, Peachum's song while he is looking over his accounts:

> THROUGH all the Employments of Life
> 　　Each Neighbour abuses his Brother;
> Whore and rogue they call Husband and Wife:
> 　　All Professions be-rogue one another.
> The Priest calls the Lawyer a Cheat,
> 　　The Lawyer be-knaves the Divine;
> And the Statesman, because he's so great,
> 　　Thinks his Trade as honest as mine.

These lyrics were perhaps written by Swift; the music is from a broadside ballad, one of the popular songs of the day sold on the street in single-sheet broadsides. Theme, tone, satiric thrust, and effective music are combined from the opening: ballad opera, indeed musical comedy, has arrived.

The theme of transvaluation of values—instinctive with Gay since at least *The Mohocks*—is employed with considerable subtlety. To say that *The Beggar's Opera* is primarily a satiric attack on Sir Robert Walpole, as many critics have done, is

to reduce its power; if this had been the case, its stage history would probably have ended with the fall of his administration, and Gay's opera would have gone the way of Barbara Garson's *Macbird* (1966). There are, it goes without saying, satiric thrusts at the pretensions of statesmen, as voiced by Peachum in his song and as exemplified by the names of such characters as "*Robin* of *Bagshot*, alias *Gorgon*, alias *Bluff Bob*, alias *Carbuncle*, alias *Bob Booty*." The audience in Rich's theater would not have required a key or a footnote to figure that one out. Walpole himself led the laughter at an early performance. Gay's satire cuts both ways: at Walpole the politician but also at Peachum the bourgeois entrepreneur; at Macheath the gay blade but also at Polly the misty-eyed romantic. This is a Ship of Fools, this world of ours, and one had better laugh than cry.

The Beggar's Opera is not to everyone's taste, but it has been to the taste of many; it was, for example, George Washington's favorite play. Bertolt Brecht and Kurt Weill's great variation on Gay's theme, *Die Dreigroschenoper* (*The Threepenny Opera*), is certainly one of the most important pieces in twentieth-century musical theater, arguably *the* most important, but it has not at all displaced *The Beggar's Opera*, which is playing in London and probably ten other places around the world as this is written.

The Beggar's Opera and *The Threepenny Opera*, it should be emphasized, are operas, meldings of words and music; without the music they are not what they are. Gay's opera, furthermore, has an important relationship to Handel's "Italian" operas and not merely in the fact that Gay borrowed tunes from Handel. The scene opening act 2, for example, in which Macheath's gang assembles at the tavern and Macheath enters while they sing "Fill ev'ry glass," is not a "satire" on opera, it *is* opera. Yvonne Noble has argued that it represents the rebirth of a specifically English opera tradition.

Gay's next work for the stage, *Polly*, is less of an opera and less of a work of art, it must be admitted, though significant in its own right. It was designed as a sequel to *The Beggar's Opera* and had as subtitle "Being the Second Part of The Beggar's Opera." Naturally buoyed up by the runaway success of *The Beggar's Opera*, Gay wrote *Polly* in 1728 and had it ready for presentation by November of that year. He was living with the duke and duchess of Queensberry then, and their contacts at court may have picked up the fact that the ministry was not favorably disposed

The Beggar's Opera Burlesqued (*1728, questionably attributed to William Hogarth*). *John Rich's Lincoln's Inn Fields theater is at left, and on the right an Italian opera is being performed. On center stage are characters from* The Beggar's Opera *portrayed as animals: Mr. Lockitt (bull), Lucy Lockitt (pig), Macheath (ass), Polly Peachum (cat), Mr. Peachum (dog), and Mrs. Peachum (owl). Apollo and one of the Muses are asleep beneath the stage. Harmony is flying away. The Latin motto above the two stages says "ready to sing and answer verse for verse" (Virgil,* Eclogue VII*).*

toward Gay, even though nothing had been said during the initial run of *The Beggar's Opera*. Gay personally carried a copy of the play, made from the prompt copy, to Charles Fitzroy, duke of Grafton, now lord chamberlain. The lord chamberlain chose to exercise his prerogative and in December ordered *Polly* suppressed. Whether Walpole himself intervened to order the suppression is uncertain, although often asserted. At any rate, the prohibition stuck: *Polly* was not produced for almost half a century, receiving its first performance, in altered form, in 1777.

Gay, meanwhile, had prepared the text for publication and authorized an edition at his own expense (so that he could reap maximum profits), soliciting subscribers at one guinea a copy. This was a huge edition by the standards of the time; 10,500 were printed, and, though pirated copies hurt Gay's sales, he still made hundreds of pounds. In a saucy preface he denied any seditious thoughts or satire against the government, "with the strictest truth affirm[ing], that I am as loyal a subject and as firmly attach'd to the present happy establishment as any of those who have the greatest places or pensions." The implication being that those rich placemen and pensioners are not so very firmly attached.

Preface from the 1729 edition of Polly, *which was suppressed by the lord chamberlain in December 1728, before it went into rehearsal*

Polly in fact has less political bite than *The Beggar's Opera,* and one wonders why the lord chamberlain bothered to suppress it. Gay resumes the story in the West Indies, where Macheath has been transported and where he has assumed the identity of a black pirate, Morano, living bigamously with Jenny Diver. Mrs. Trapes is also in the Indies, acting as a supplier of females to the colonists. When Polly arrives, seeking Macheath, Mrs. Trapes undertakes to supply her to the settler Ducat, over the objections of Ducat's shrewish wife. The pirates under Morano attack, and settlers make common cause in defense with the Native Americans, a group of most noble noble savages. The attack fails; Morano is captured, revealed as Macheath, and executed. At the curtain Polly is left to marry the Indian prince Cawwakee when her grief subsides.

By displacing the action to the West Indies, Gay has given up much of the satiric point, the wealth of local references, with which *The Beggar's Opera* is enriched. The scenes involving the would-be-keeper Ducat, his wife, and the innocent Polly represent good, standard London domestic comedy, and the dialogues between the high-minded Indians and Macheath echo *Gulliver's Travels* with Pohetohee as the Houyhnhnm master and Macheath a cynical Gulliver. As a composer of lyrics Gay was never better, completely in control of meter, varying form and tone to suit the topic, and, interestingly, employing duets, trios, and quartets of voices: he was confident now of the musical resources he could summon.

The duke and duchess of Queensberry did everything they knew how to promote *Polly,* soliciting subscriptions for the printed version at court and elsewhere. One or both of the royal couple took umbrage at this activity, and the duchess was excluded from court. Gay had now given up even a pretense of expecting future royal favor. Financial independence would come only by his pen.

He decided to rewrite *The Wife of Bath* and try it again on the stage. It is a sad comedown. In an attempt, presumably, to improve the stagecraft of the original version, which admittedly did have some joints that showed, Gay takes Chaucer the character right out of his play and replaces him with Sir Harry Gauntlet, a country squire in the vein of Addison and Steele's Sir Roger de Coverley. The exuberant language of the earlier play is pared down and so is the exuberance of Alison, the wife. Rich, the manager of

Lincoln's Inn Fields, may have been nervous about sponsoring Gay after the silencing of *Polly,* or perhaps Gay himself, now older, was more cautious.

Most puzzling is the virtual exclusion of music. Here was an area in which Gay was the unchallenged master of the London stage, but in the rewritten *Wife of Bath* he leaves out the songs of the 1713 version. It was not from want of singing talent: the very players, among others, who had created the roles of Peachum and Lucy Lockitt in *The Beggar's Opera* acted in the revival, but they were not given songs.

The Wife of Bath opened on 19 January 1730 at Lincoln's Inn Fields and made it through three performances, so that Gay collected his author's benefit, and not a bad one, fifty-six pounds, sixpence. Lintot paid him another seventy-five pounds for the copyright–scant reward for all the work, however misguided, that Gay had put into rewriting his play. It was not revived.

Gay's health, which had been uncertain for years, was beginning to fail, but he still kept writing plays. In October 1732 he went back to the west of England where he had come from, to try sea air and exercise as a cure at Orchard Wyndham in Somersetshire, seat of his friend Sir William Wyndham. Neither air nor exercise seemed to help, but he continued to work, writing Swift in November that "I have not been [idle] while I was in the Country." It was the last correspondence between the old friends; Gay died on 4 December 1732 and was buried in Westminster Abbey on 23 December.

He left behind him three plays in various stages of completion, one, *Achilles,* being almost ready for production. It is a work of daring originality. The author of the prologue, perhaps Pope, compares Gay to a rope dancer *"that tries at all." "Why is this Man so obstinate an Elf?/Will he, alone, not imitate himself?"* Gay was dead by the time *Achilles* was first performed, at Covent Garden, in February 1733, but his wit and command of the musical stage survived him.

Achilles is, superficially, a classical ballad opera. The Greek warrior of the title, disguised as "Princess Pyrrha," is placed by his mother, Thetis, in the court of Lycomedes, so that he will escape the Trojan War, which her goddess's "Presentiment" knows is coming. Lycomedes lusts after the charming "princess," much to the displeasure of his consort, Theaspe, while Achilles meanwhile is falling in love with and impregnating their daughter, Deidamia. Lycomedes attempts to rape Achilles but is resisted and indeed overpowered by the potent princess. Ulysses and Diomedes come through, disguised as clothing merchants; Ulysses recognizes "Princess Pyrrha" as the missing son of Thetis and calls him to war. Achilles is eager to join them and does so after marrying Deidamia; then he departs for Troy. Woven into three brief acts are no fewer than fifty-four tunes, drawn as in the earlier ballad operas from music of every description.

The legend of the disguised Achilles is found in Statius and other classical writers, and Gay typically makes it his own. As Yvonne Noble has pointed out, Gay charges a farcical situation with meaning, focusing on the attempted rape of Achilles. If Achilles had indeed been a woman, the rape would have taken place; the "predicament of women represents one mode of the wider condition of dependency, the dynamics and abuses of which Gay knew all too well in his own life...."

Little thought of Gay's former predicament, no doubt, was in the minds of the audiences who attended nineteen performances in the spring of 1733, an excellent run and one that would have pleased the dead playwright. He had left the small estate he had to his sisters, who entrusted the duke of Queensberry with seeing about his literary remains. These included, in addition to *Achilles*, a domestic comedy entitled *The Distress'd Wife* and a political farce, *The Rehearsal at Goatham*.

Because *The Rehearsal at Goatham* concerns the suppression of a play, specifically a puppet show, it probably was composed soon after the silencing of *Polly* and reflects Gay's resentment at his treatment by the lord chamberlain and Walpole. Peter, a somewhat naive puppeteer, comes to the village of Goatham to present his show. Spurred on by the local playwright, Jack Oaf, the town corporation is persuaded that the show's satire is directed at themselves, and Sir Headstrong Bustle closes the performance, asking "To what End hath a Man Riches and Power, if he cannot crush the Wretches who have the Insolence to expose the Ways by which he got them."

The Rehearsal at Goatham is a ten-scene farce, an afterpiece, which Gay may have thought Rich would produce at Lincoln's Inn Fields. Oaf, John Fuller argues persuasively, represents Colley Cibber and Sir Headstrong, Walpole. Like *The Mohocks*, *The Rehearsal at Goatham* has the flaw of requiring many speaking parts, more than two

dozen of them, and the possibility exists that Gay never really expected to see it produced but wrote it for private circulation, perhaps for an amateur show at the Queensberrys'. He evidently planned to publish it, however, for he names his source (*Don Quixote*, part 2, chapters 25-27) and speaks in the first person in the advertisement to the version that was finally printed in 1754.

The Distress'd Wife is more of a play, and more of a problem because of that fact. One wishes that its dating could be established, but so far no external evidence has been found to date it. It is a conventional domestic comedy; many similar to it were produced in the 1720s and 1730s. The distress comes to the wife in question, Lady Willit, when her husband, Sir Thomas Willit, proposes that they quit London and return to their country estate. She has learned to gamble, drink, and flirt fashionably under the tutelage of her friend, Lady Frankair. Two marriageable young kinswomen, Miss Sprightly and Miss Friendless, are in the care of the Willits, and Miss Sprightly, an heiress, receives and rebuffs the attentions of old Lord Courtlove. In the last act she reveals that she is already married, whereupon Courtlove offers his hand to Miss Friendless, who, incredibly, accepts it. The Willits return to the country to pay off the debts Lady Willit has run up in London.

Sir Thomas's uncle and confidant, Barter, is a London merchant, bluff and honest like Sir Andrew Freeport of *The Spectator*'s Club. He and Sir Thomas represent English virtue, as exemplified by the man of business and the country squire, and are contrasted to Lord Courtlove, who seeks his fortune, as his name suggests, by associating with the rich and powerful at court. This is all familiar material in the drama of the time, but the play is strangely flat; it was not the sort of piece, evidently, that Gay felt easy in writing. As Howard Erskine-Hill has noted, *The Distress'd Wife* is the only play in which Gay attempted the comedy of manners, the most successful form of his period. Gay was always drawn to the offbeat, the experimental; the world of realistic comedy is not Gay's world. *The Distress'd Wife* had four performances at Covent Garden in 1734 and has never been revived in its original form, though George Colman the Elder, manager of Covent Garden, tried an anonymous adaptation, as *The Modern Wife*, in 1771.

Gay's three posthumous plays demonstrate that his inventiveness had not left him in the last years of his life. The 1720s, and the 1730s before the guillotine of the Licensing Act descended, were creative and innovative years for the London stage, an atmosphere in which an original talent like Gay's might have flourished. Would he perhaps have collaborated with Handel on an opera in English? Tried more political satire like *The Rehearsal at Goatham?* We will never know. His masterpiece, *The Beggar's Opera,* has insured him a permanent place in dramatic history, and, given Gay's even temperament, he probably died content. Observing the world around him with a most discerning eye, he composed his own epitaph: "Life's a jest; and all things show it./I thought this once; but now I know it."

Letters:

The Letters of John Gay, edited by C. F. Burgess (Oxford: Clarendon Press, 1966).

Biography:

William Henry Irving, *John Gay: Favorite of the Wits* (Durham, N.C.: Duke University Press, 1940).

References:

Bertrand Bronson, "The True Proportions of Gay's *Acis and Galatea*" and "*The Beggar's Opera,*" in his *Facets of the Enlightenment* (Berkeley & Los Angeles: University of California Press, 1968), pp. 45-59, 60-90;

Winton Dean and John Merrill Knapp, *Handel's Operas: 1704-1726* (Oxford: Clarendon Press, 1987), pp. 140-205;

Ian Donaldson, *The World Upside-Down: Comedy from Jonson to Fielding* (Oxford: Clarendon Press, 1970), pp. 159-182;

Howard Erskine-Hill, "The significance of Gay's drama," in *English Drama: Forms and Development,* edited by Marie Axton and Raymond Williams (Cambridge: Cambridge University Press, 1977), pp. 142-163;

John Fuegi, "Most Unpleasant Things with *The Threepenny Opera:* Weill, Brecht, and Money," in *A New Orpheus: Essays on Kurt Weill,* edited by Kim H. Kowalke (New Haven: Yale University Press, 1986), pp. 157-181;

P. E. Lewis, "Another Look at John Gay's *The Mohocks,*" *Modern Language Review,* 53 (October 1968): 790-793;

Yvonne Noble, "Sex and Gender in Gay's *Achilles,*" in *John Gay and the Scriblerians,* edited by Nigel Wood and Peter Lewis (New York: St. Martin's Press, 1988), pp. 184-215;

Noble, ed., *Twentieth Century Interpretations of The Beggar's Opera* (Englewood Cliffs, N.J.: Prentice-Hall, 1975);

William Eben Schultz, *Gay's Beggar's Opera: Its Content, History & Influence* (New Haven: Yale University Press, 1923);

George Sherburn, "The Fortunes and Misfortunes of *Three Hours After Marriage,*" *Modern Philology,* 24 (August 1926): 91-109;

James R. Sutherland, " 'Polly' Among the Pirates," *Modern Language Review,* 37 (July 1942): 291-303;

Calhoun Winton, "The Tragic Muse in Enlightened England," in *Greene Centennial Studies: Essays Presented to Donald Greene in the Centennial Year of the University of Southern California,* edited by Paul J. Korshin and Robert R. Allen (Charlottesville: University Press of Virginia, 1984), pp. 125-142.

Aaron Hill
(10 February 1685 - 8 February 1750)

Sophia B. Blaydes
West Virginia University

PLAY PRODUCTIONS: *Elfrid: or The Fair Inconstant*, London, Theatre Royal in Drury Lane, 3 January 1710; revised as *Athelwold*, London, Theatre Royal in Drury Lane, 10 December 1731;

The Walking Statue: or The Devil in the Wine-Cellar, London, Theatre Royal in Drury Lane, 9 January 1710;

Squire Brainless, or Trick Upon Trick, London, Theatre Royal in Drury Lane, 27 April 1710;

Rinaldo, an Opera, English translation by Hill of Giacomo Rossi's Italian text, music by George Frederick Handel, London, Queen's Theatre, 24 February 1711;

The Fatal Vision; or, The Fall of Siam, London, Lincoln's Inn Fields, 7 February 1716;

The Fatal Extravagance, one-act version, by Hill but attributed by him to Joseph Mitchell, London, Lincoln's Inn Fields, 21 April 1721;

King Henry the Fifth: or The Conquest of France by the English, from Shakespeare's play, London, Theatre Royal in Drury Lane, 5 December 1723;

The Tragedy of Zara, from Voltaire's *Zaire*, London, York Buildings, 29 May 1735;

Alzira, from Voltaire's *Alzire*, London, Lincoln's Inn Fields, 18 June 1736;

Merope, from Voltaire's *Merope*, London, Theatre Royal in Drury Lane, 15 April 1749;

The Roman Revenge, influenced by Voltaire's *La Mort de Cesar*, Bath, circa 1753;

The Insolvent: or, Filial Piety, from Sir William Davenant's *The Man's the Master* and Philip Massinger's *Fatal Dowry*, London, Theatre Royal in the Hay-Market, 6 March 1758.

BOOKS: *Camillus. A Poem, Humbly inscrib'd to the Right Honorable Charles, Earl of Peterborough and Monmouth* (London: Printed for Thomas Bickerton, 1707);

The Invasion: A Poem to the Queen (London: Thomas Bickerton, 1708);

The celebrated Speeches of Ajax and Ulysses, for the Armour of Achilles, in the 13th Book of Ovid's Metamorph. Essay'd in English Verse, by Mr. Tate Poet Laureat; and Aaron Hill, Gent. (London: Printed for William Keble & Thomas Bickerton, 1708);

A full and just Account of the Present State of the Ottoman Empire in all its Branches: with the Government, and Policy, Religion, Customs, and Way of Living of the Turks, in General. Faithfully related from a Serious Observation, taken in many Years Travels thro' those Countries (London: Printed for the author & sold by John Mayo, 1709; second edition, with additions, 1710);

The Walking Statue: or, The Devil in the Wine-Cellar. A farce of one act. As it was acted at the Theatre Royal in Drury-Lane (London?: John Mayo?, 1709);

Elfrid: or The Fair Inconstant. A tragedy: as it is acted at the Theatre royal, by Her Majesty's servants. To which is added the Walking Statue: or, The Devil in the wine cellar. A farce (London: Printed for Bernard Lintott & Egbert Sanger, 1710); revised as *Athelwold: a Tragedy. As it is acted at the Theatre-Royal in Drury-Lane, by His Majesty's Servants* (London: Printed for L. Gilliver, 1731);

Rinaldo, an Opera as it is performed at the Queen's Theatre in London, Italian text by Giacomo Rossi and English verse translation by Hill (London, 1711; London: Printed for J. Tonson, 1717);

The Dedication of the Beech-Tree. To the most honourable the Earl of Oxford, Lord High Treasurer of Great Britain. Occasioned by the late discovery of making Oil from the fruit of that Tree (London: Sold by John Morphew, 1714);

An impartial account of the nature, benefit and design, of a new discovery and undertaking, to make a pure, sweet, and wholesome Oil, from the Fruit of the Beech Tree. By authority of her Majesty's Royal Letters Patents, under the great seal of Great Britain. With particular answers to every

Objection, which has been made, or may reasonably be conceived against it. And proposals for raising a stock not exceeding twenty thousand pounds: wherein every hundred pounds advanc'd, will entitle to an annuity for fourteen years of fifty pounds per annum, and for a less sum proportionably, upon a good and solid security (London, 1714);

Proposals for raising a Stock of one hundred thousand pounds; for laying up great quantities of Beech Mast for two years, at an Interest of Forty-Five Pounds per cent. per Annum, to the Subscribers, and upon a Security whereby they will always have in their own Hands, above Ten Times the Value of the Sum, they Contribute. To which is added, a particular account of the nature, benefit, and design of the undertaking (London, 1714)–includes patent for procedure to extract oil from beech mast, 23 October 1713;

An Account of the Rise and Progress of the Beech-Oil Invention, and All the Steps which have been taken in that Affair, from the first discovery to the present time, as also, what is further design'd in that undertaking (London, 1715);

An impartial state of the case between the Patentee, Annuitants, and Sharers in the Beech-Oil Company. Publish'd by the Patentee as well in Vindication of his own Measures, as for the General Satisfaction of all the concern'd Parties (London: Aaron Hill, 1716);

The Fatal Vision: or, The Fall of Siam. A tragedy: As it is acted at the New theatre in Lincoln's-Inn-Fields, 1716 (London: Edw. Nutt, 1716);

The Northern-Star. A Poem (London: Printed by E. Berington & J. Morphew, 1718); republished as *The Northern Star: A Poem: on the Great and Glorious Actions of the Present Czar of Russia; in English and Latin,* Latin translation by Gilbert Hill (London: Printed for T. Payne, 1724); republished as *The Northern-Star, A Poem Sacred to the Memory of the Immortal Czar of Russia. The third edition* (London: Printed for W. Mears, 1725); revised as *The Northern Star: A Poem. Originally publish'd in the life-time of Peter Alexiovitz, Great Czar of Russia. The fifth edition, revised and corrected by the Author* (London: Printed for T. Cooper, 1739);

The Creation. A pindaric illustration of a poem, originally written by Moses, on that subject. With a preface to Mr. Pope, concerning the sublimity of the ancient Hebrew poetry, and a material and obvious defect in the English (London: Printed for T. Bickerton, 1720); preface republished in Augustan Reprint Society Series Four: *Men, Manners and Critics,* no. 2, edited by Gretchen Graf Pahl (Los Angeles, 1949);

The Fatal Extravagance. A tragedy. As It Is Acted at the Theatre in Lincoln's-Inn-Fields. Written by Mr. Joseph Mitchell, by Hill but attributed by him to Mitchell (London: Printed for T. Jauncy, 1720); two-act version (Dublin, 1721; London, 1726); one-act version (London: Printed for J. Watts, 1730);

The Judgment-Day, a Poem (London: Printed for T. Jauncy, 1721?);

King Henry the Fifth; or, The Conquest of France, by the English. A tragedy. As it is acted at the Theatre-Royal in Drury-Lane, by His Majesty's servants (London: Printed for W. Chetwood & J. Watts, 1723);

The Plain-Dealer, by Hill and William Bond, nos. 1-117 (23 March 1724-7 May 1725); republished as *The Plain-Dealer, being select essays on several curious subjects, relating to friendship, love, and gallantry, marriage, morality, mercantile affairs, painting, history, poetry, and other branches of polite literature. Publish'd originally* in the year 1724. And now first collected into two volumes (London: Printed for S. Richardson & A. Wilde, 1730);

The Progress of Wit: a Caveat. For the use of an eminent writer. By a fellow of All-Souls. To which is prefixed, an explanatory discourse to the reader. By Gamaliel Gunson, professor of Physic and Astrology (London: Printed for J. Wilford, 1730);

Advice to the Poets. A Poem. To which is prefix'd, an Epistle dedicatory to the few Great Spirits of Great Britain (London: Printed for T. Warner, 1731);

See and Seem Blind: Or, A critical Dissertation on the Publick Diversions, &c. of Persons and Things, and Things and Persons, and what not (London: Printed for H. Whitridge, 1732); facsimile, edited by Robert D. Hume, Augustan Reprint Society, no. 235 (Los Angeles: William Andrews Clark Memorial Library, 1986);

The Prompter: A Theatrical Paper, by Hill and William Popple, nos. 1-173 (London, 12 November 1734-2 July 1736); modern edition, selected and edited by William W. Appleton and Kalman A. Burnim (New York: Benjamin Blom, 1966);

The Tragedy of Zara. As it is acted at the Theatre-Royal in Drury-Lane, by His Majesty's Servants, from Voltaire (London: Printed for J. Watts, 1736);

Alzira, a Tragedy. As it is acted at the Theatre-Royal In Lincoln's-Inn-Fields (London: Printed for J. Osborne, 1736);

The Tears of the Muses: in a Conference between Prince Germanicus and a Male-content Party (London: T. Ward, 1737);

An enquiry into the merit of Assassination: with a view to the character of Caesar: and his designs on the Roman republik . . . (London: Printed for T. Cooper, 1738);

The Fanciad. An heroic poem. In six cantos. To His Grace the Duke of Marlborough, on the turn of his genius to arms . . . (London: Printed for J. Osborn, 1743);

The Impartial. An address without flattery. Being a poet's free thoughts on the situation of our public affairs anno 1744 (London: Printed for M. Cooper, 1744);

The Art of Acting. [poem] Part I. Deriving rules from a new principle, for touching the passions in a natural manner. An essay of general use, to those, who hear, or speak in public . . . but adapted, in particular, to the stage . . . (London: Printed for J. Osborn, 1746);

Free Thoughts upon Faith: or, the Religion of Reason. A Poem (London: Printed for J. Osborn, 1746);

Gideon, or the Patriot An Epic Poem in Twelve Books. Upon a Hebrew Plan. In honour of the two chief Virtues of a people: Intrepidity in Foreign War, and spirit of domestic Liberty. With miscellaneous Notes, and large reflections upon different Subjects: Critical, Historical, Political, Geographic, Military, and Commercial (London: Printed for A. Millar, 1749);

Merope: a Tragedy. Acted at the Theatre-Royal in Drury-Lane, by His Majesty's servants, from Voltaire (London: Printed for A. Millar, 1749);

The Roman Reenvge [sic], *a Tragedy,* influenced by Voltaire's *La Mort de Cesar* (London: Sold by M. Mechell, 1753);

The Works of the Late Aaron Hill, Esq; in four volumes Consisting of Letters on Various Subjects, and of Original Poems, Moral and Facetious. With an Essay on the Art of Acting [prose]. *Printed for the Benefit of the Family,* 4 volumes (London, 1753);

The Insolvent: or, Filial Piety. A tragedy. Acted at the theatre in the Hay-market, . . . under the direction of Mr. Cibber . . . Partly on a plan of Sir William D'Avenant's and Mr. Massenger's (London: Printed & sold by W. Reeve, 1758);

The Dramatic Works of Aaron Hill, Esq. In two volumes (London: Printed for T. Lowndes, 1760)—comprises a life of Hill by J. K., previously published plays, and the following short unacted pieces: I. *Merlin in Love* (pantomime opera); II. *Muses in mourning* (opera), *Zara,* to which is added, an interlude, never before printed, *Snake in the grass* (burlesque), *Saul* (unfinished tragedy), *Daraxes* (pastoral opera), *Some love letters,* by the author.

Collections: *The Poetical Works of Aaron Hill* (Edinburgh: Mundell, 1794);

The Plays of Aaron Hill, edited by Calhoun Winton (New York: Garland, 1981).

OTHER: "On making China Ware in England, as good as ever was brought from India," in *Essays, for the month of December, 1716, to be continued monthly. By a Society of Gentlemen. For the Universal Benefit of the People of England. Adorned with Four Beautiful Cuts* (London: J. Roberts, 1718);

Epilogue to *The Fair Captive,* by Eliza Haywood (London: Printed for T. Jauncy & H. Cole, 1721);

Miscellaneous poems and translations. By several hands. Publish'd by Richard Savage, son of the late Earl Rivers, includes poems by Hill (London: S. Chapman, 1726);

Prologue to *The Tuscan Treaty,* by William Bond (London: Printed for J. Watson, 1733);

Prologue and epilogue to *The Lady's Revenge,* by William Popple (London: Printed for J. Brindley & sold by A. Dodd, 1734);

Epilogue to *Fatal Falsehood,* by John Hewitt (London: T. Worrall, 1734);

Prologue to *The Double Deceit,* by Popple (London: Printed for T. Woodward & J. Walthoe & sold by T. Cooper, 1736).

Aaron Hill is usually recognized because of others' achievements, not his own. He is probably better known as one of Alexander Pope's targets in the *Dunciad* than for his own poetry. So, too, his role in the development of the periodical or the critical essay is obscured by the essays of his friend Sir Richard Steele. Similarly, in the history of eighteenth-century drama or theater management, one finds Hill overshadowed by Henry Fielding and David Garrick. Even Dorothy Brewster in her 1913 study of Hill added to the growing list of figures who stand out more clearly than he does. While she increased our understanding of the eighteenth-century impresario, she also offered a valuable perspective when she wrote: "Those who have written in recent years of Richardson and Fielding, of Pope and Thomson and Savage, have found Hill in their path." One might in all fairness ask, if others in the eighteenth century did all that Hill did—and did it better—why bother with him at all?

Brewster has already offered one answer: Hill is worth our attention because he was significant to others who better stood the test of time. Perhaps that is the fate of impresarios: their success depends upon their ability to reflect the tastes of their age. It follows then that their reputations will suffer as tastes change. Like the impresario Sir William Davenant, Hill was influential in his own day, and, like his Restoration predecessor, Hill applied a philosophy of drama that would be important for many years, giving spectacle and reality through scenes and machines that Davenant had introduced so effectively almost a century earlier. Like Davenant, Hill wanted to draw larger audiences and to convey the meaning of his drama. However, like Davenant, Hill was criticized, especially for his treatment of Shakespeare's plays. While Davenant pleased his audiences when he adapted *The Tempest* and *Macbeth* to the tastes and stage of his day, Hill offended when he offered a sympathetic portrait of Julius Caesar and an unsympathetic one of Henry V, arguably England's most revered monarch. Most tellingly, like Davenant, Hill left an enormous volume of published works–occasional verses dedicated to great figures, epic poetry, burlesques, tragedies, comedies, operas, adaptations from Voltaire and Shakespeare, and essays and treatises on the theater and other projects. Just as Davenant's works have gathered dust, so Hill's have had few readers.

After reviewing Hill's life and work, Brewster graphically outlines the quick change in Hill's reputation:

> When, three years after Hill's death, his *Works* were published in four volumes, his reputation was still great enough to attract over fifteen hundred subscribers; but seven years later, only one-fourth that number could be persuaded to subscribe to his *Dramatic Works*. The course of his fame was steadily downward as the impression of his vigorous personality faded away, and only his works were left to speak for him. They spoke very badly. Although seventy years after his death, selections were still made from his poetry and his plays for volumes of the British poets and the British drama, these volumes themselves are now little read.

Hill's works are now judged by literary standards and not by the measures of the popular culture that they originally served. As with Davenant's works, aside from the *Three Centuries of Drama* microprints, little of Hill's work is easily available today.

In part in reaction to the position he enjoyed in his own day, Hill has over the centuries suffered from a critical backlash. In an influential essay for the *Dictionary of National Biography*, Sir Leslie Stephen describes Hill as self-important, pompous, and "terribly long-winded," a friend who "punished Pope sufficiently perhaps by long letters." Seeing Hill as "absurd and a bore of the first water," Stephen adds, "he was apparently a kindly and liberal man, and abandoned the profits of his plays, such as they were, to others." D. C. Tovey goes one better and sees Hill as "a practical joke concocted between the Muses and Momus, to bring the judgments of mortals into contempt" (quoted in Dobson). More decorously, Austin Dobson suggests that writers are tempted by "bigger game than Aaron Hill." Even

Brewster joins in, citing Hill's "vanity, self-confidence, and extravagance." Few critics disagree. As Calhoun Winton wittily notes, "Hill is in little danger of being overvalued by modern criticism. The Hill revival will be a long time coming." Yet many concur with Brewster that Hill is interesting, even inspiring:

> none of those who mention him find it possible to be merely perfunctory. They grow cheerful and witty . . . or in soberer mood, they express a curiosity about other aspects of his life and character than those they touch upon. They all acknowledge the generosity and kindliness of his nature, his humanity and politeness, as Dr. Johnson has it,–a tribute that can be paid without reserve to very few of the greater men of his time.

For Brewster, Winton, and others, Hill is a key to his age. Yet, one may share some of Stephen's doubts when confronted with the texts of Hill's works, where literary standards cannot be affected by the taste of the times or the personality of the writer.

Born in London in Beaufort Buildings in the Strand, Hill had an unusual childhood, in part because of his father's early death. With his younger brother Gilbert, Hill was left to the care of his grandmother, Mrs. Ann Gregory, and his mother. According to Colley Cibber, George Hill, Aaron's father, was an attorney whose "estate of about 2000 l. a year . . . was entailed upon him, and the eldest son, and to his heirs for many descents. But the unhappy misconduct of Mr. George Hill, and the weakness of the trustees . . . has rendered it of no advantage to his family; for, without any legal title so to do, he sold it all at different times for sums greatly beneath the value of it." By his ninth year, Aaron was in a free grammar school at Barnstaple in Devon, where he first met John Gay. Hill went on to Westminster for his classical instruction from Dr. Busby's successor, Dr. Knipe. There he befriended Barton Booth.

By the time he was fourteen, Hill had bypassed an expensive and conventional education at Oxford or Cambridge for an expedition to meet his relative Lord Paget, ambassador to Constantinople. Hill's adventure was supported by his grandmother, who had "uncommon understanding and great good-nature." By 2 March 1700 the boy was sailing for Turkey via Portugal and Italy. Although Hill's arrival surprised Lord Paget, the boy's appearance must have pleased the older man. According to Cibber, Hill "was (in youth) extremely fair and handsome; his eyes were a dark blue, both bright and penetrating; brown hair and visage oval; which was enlivened by a smile the most agreeable in conversation where his address was affably engaging; to which was joined a dignity which rendered him at once respected and admired by those (of either sex) who were acquainted with him. He was tall, genteelly made, and not thin. His voice was sweet, his conversation elegant, and capable of entertaining upon various subjects." Lord Paget gave Hill his friendship and "a very learned ecclesiastic in his own house, and under his tuition sent him to travel, being desirous to improve, so far as possible, the education of a person he found worthy of it." Hill traveled to Greece, Mecca, the Holy Land, Egypt, and returned to Constantinople in 1702. His most harrowing experience occurred when Arab thieves nearly buried his party alive in the catacombs near Memphis. He described the experience vividly seven years later in his first full-length book, *A full and just Account of the Present State of the Ottoman Empire* (1709). In 1702 Hill began his journey home with Lord Paget, through Bulgaria, Rumania, and Germany, reaching Holland in September, when Lord Paget was directed to Vienna. In December they were sent to the court of Bavaria. On the brief sea voyage home they had one last adventure, a sea fight with the French. They landed in England on 12 April 1703.

On his return Hill remained for a time with Lord Paget, who, according to Cibber, "took great pleasure in instructing [Hill] himself." Soon, young Hill became tutor to William Wentworth of Bretton Hall in Yorkshire and held the position until March 1706 when the boy succeeded to the baronetcy. In 1707 Hill published *Camillus*, a poem in heroic couplets dedicated to Charles, earl of Peterborough and Monmouth. As general of the army that supported Charles of Austria's claim to the Spanish throne, Peterborough conducted himself with what might be called "panache." Hill's poem cuts through the criticism and defends the general. Peterborough was so impressed that he hired Hill as his secretary. In 1710 Peterborough went abroad, and Hill married Margaret Morris, the only daughter and heiress of Edmund Morris of Stratford, Essex. While she may have prevented Hill from accepting Peterborough's invitation to go abroad, through their marriage she provided Hill with means to fund projects that were to occupy him for the rest of his life. Evidently, the marriage

was a happy one, producing nine children, four of whom lived beyond infancy: Urania, Astraea, Minerva, and Julius Caesar.

From 1708 to 1710 Hill prospered, in part because of his associations with powerful people. While secretary to Peterborough, for example, he published two poems, *The Invasion: A Poem to the Queen* (1708) and *The celebrated Speeches of Ajax and Ulysses* (1708), a translation from Ovid's *Metamorphoses* in collaboration with the poet laureate Nahum Tate. Hill also helped his former schoolmate Gay publish his first poem, *Wine*, and hired Gay as his secretary when Hill began writing for the weekly *British Apollo,* the paper Austin Dobson called "that curious forerunner of Steele's 'Tatler.'" During the paper's first year, 1708, the *British Apollo* printed more than a dozen unsigned poems that were later attributed to Hill and included in his works. In addition, on 2 July 1708, the periodical announced that the *Ottoman Empire* had gone to press after being "delayed for filling the subscriptions." A folio of fifty-two chapters, the book actually came out in 1709 with a dedication to Queen Anne, a subscription list of 424 names, including the queen's, and seven plates dedicated to seven members of the nobility.

That same year, although he was only twenty-four years old and without theatrical experience, Hill became the manager of London's Theatre Royal in Drury Lane. Responding to complaints from the actors against Christopher Rich, the lord chamberlain had closed the doors of the Drury Lane in June. William Collier, M.P., one of its shareholders, was granted permission to operate the theater, and he appointed Hill as Rich's replacement. Hill's tenure as manager began on 23 November 1709 with a production of John Dryden's *Aureng-Zebe* and lasted until June 1710. During those few months Hill not only offered plays by William Congreve, George Farquhar, Thomas Otway, and William Shakespeare but he also presented his first tragedy, *Elfrid: or The Fair Inconstant,* and two farces, *The Walking Statue: or The Devil in the Wine-Cellar* and *Squire Brainless, or Trick Upon Trick.*

Hill understandably was more concerned with his tragedy that premiered on 3 January 1710. The subject may have been suggested by Barton Booth, Hill's former schoolmate, and it may even have been written for the great tragic actor. Not long after its debut, however, Hill was ashamed of it. Twenty years later he excused *Elfrid* as a hastily written, youthful work, his "first dramatic sally . . . an unpruned wilderness

Hill's school friend Barton Booth, who played Athelwold in the premiere of Elfrid, *Hill's first play (engraving by Evans)*

of fancy, with here and there a flower among the leaves." The original text was printed by "Bernard Lintott and Egbert Sanger" in 1710, and this version was also included in the 1760 *Dramatic Works,* even though Hill tried to correct his errors, as he saw them, by rewriting it. His new version appeared more than twenty years later, on 10 December 1731, at the Drury Lane with the title *Athelwold.*

Elfrid is short and preserves the unities in its presentation of the tragic consequences of Athelwold's lapses in loyalty and honor. Before the play begins, Athelwold has told Edgar the Saxon king of Elfrid's celebrated beauty. Sent by the king to see and woo Elfrid in his behalf,

Athelwold falls in love with her and secretly marries her. He compounds his disloyalty by reporting to the king that Elfrid does not merit attention. The play opens with Edgar's unexpected arrival at Athelwold's castle. Forced to confess his duplicity to Elfrid, Athelwold asks her permission to have his sister, Ordelia, pose as his wife. With misgivings and some mistrust of her husband, Elfrid consents to the lie. All is lost, however, when one of Ordelia's suitors is upset by the king's interest in her and reveals Athelwold's secret. At first the king is angry, but then he sees Elfrid and vows to claim her. Understandably, the king sends Athelwold on a mission. Athelwold, however, is forced home by his father's ghost and returns in time to see Edgar leaving Elfrid's room. As he attempts to kill the king, Athelwold sees his wife and kills her instead. Edgar kills Athelwold and then delivers his eulogy. Even though the play was performed five times between 3 January and 21 February 1710 and at least once more in 1723, most literary historians accept Stephen's verdict that the play "was ridiculed for its bombast."

The Walking Statue fared much better, at least on stage; to John Genest, for instance, it was "more amusing to watch than it is to read." It opened on 9 January 1710 as a companion to *Elfrid.* Performed sixty-seven times by 1786, most often as an afterpiece, the play was among the first farces to become part of the repertory, where it remained for many years. To Hill, however, the success of his farce could not compensate for the comparative failure of his tragedy. Ironically, of the two plays, it is the farce that commands attention today because of its popularity during the eighteenth century and because of its role in the history of the genre. Perhaps the ease with which Hill wrote his comedies made him disdainful of them. On 27 April 1710 Hill produced his second farce, *Squire Brainless,* and David Erskine Baker in *Biographia Dramatica* tells us that it was poorly received by its first audience. Genest, however, in *Some Account of the English Stage* (1832), writes that it had three performances. The play was neither published in 1710 nor included in the collected works after Hill's death.

By June 1710 Hill's tenure as manager of the Drury Lane was in jeopardy. Despite the praise of his managerial skills in the *British Apollo* on 3 April 1710, Hill was unable to control the seven actors who insisted upon sharing the manager's role, Barton Booth among them. Hill's former school chum rebelled when Hill undermined the actors and appointed his brother, Gilbert, to direct rehearsals. During a visit to Essex Hill left his brother in charge but was soon called back. Physical violence, harsh words, and the threat of an actors' strike forced Hill to close the theater. By 14 June 1710 the lord chamberlain upheld Hill, dismissing or suspending five of the culprits; yet, all but Hill returned to Drury Lane for the fall season.

Later that year Hill found himself at the Queen's Theatre in the Haymarket where on 22 November 1710 he became its director of the opera. With his wife's fortune Hill was able to pay Collier annual rent of six hundred pounds for the Wednesday evening performances of the operas. By 24 February 1711 that investment brought Hill lasting fame. After producing three operas of modest success, Hill presented George Frederick Handel's *Rinaldo.* As Dr. Charles Burney reported, "hearing of the arrival of a master, the fame of whose abilities had already penetrated into this country, [Hill] applied to [Handel] to compose an opera." Both Hill and Handel spent two weeks preparing their parts. However, Handel's composition became part of England's celebrated music while Hill's libretto is undistinguished. The combination, nonetheless, produced a success. The opera ran until June, its music enhanced by the spectacle that Hill provided: orange groves, mountains, an enchanted castle, caged and flying sparrows, black clouds filled with monsters, thunder and lightning, fireworks, chariots, and crystal gates that disappear. The descriptions recall the seventeenth-century masques of the Stuart court and the operas that Davenant introduced to the English stage with *The Siege of Rhodes* (1656). Just as *The Rehearsal* burlesqued Davenant's opera along with the heroic dramas, so Addison provided satiric commentary on Handel and Hill's achievement in the *Spectator* (nos. 5, 18, 29). The opera was performed fifteen times during its first season and nineteen more by 1731. It earned superlatives from many in the eighteenth century, including the composer himself, who–according to Brewster–considered Rinaldo's aria "Cara sposa" "the best air he ever wrote."

Like most opera, *Rinaldo* has a plot that is incidental to the music and the spectacle. Hill explains in the play's dedication to the queen that since other English operas were "wanting the Machines and Decorations, which bestow so great Beauty on their Appearance, they have been heard and seen to very considerable Disadvantage." His hope is to "fill the Eye with more delightful Prospects, so at once to give Two Senses equal Pleasure." Hill's production was designed to remedy the problem. As for his libretto, it is in blank verse and has a plot that Hill explains in the "Argument":

> Godfrey, general of the Christian forces . . . against the Saracens, to engage the assistance of Rinaldo, a famous hero . . . , promises to give him his daughter Almirena, when the city of Jerusalem should fall into his hands. The Christians, with Rinaldo at their head, conquer Palestine, and besiege its king Argantes in that city. Armida, an Amazonian enchantress, in love with

and beloved by Argantes, contrives by magic to entrap Rinaldo in an enchanted castle, whence, after much difficulty, being delivered by Godfrey, he returns to the army, takes Jerusalem, converts Argantes and Armida to the Christian faith, and marries Almirena, according to the promise of her father Godfrey.

The success of *Rinaldo* in 1711 depended upon the blend of Handel's music and Hill's spectacle; according to Dr. Burney, it was the best musical composition performed in England to that time.

That Hill was unable to follow his success with another may be attributed to Collier's greed. Collier resumed the management of the opera. Cibber becomes hazy over the details: "upon what occasion, if I could remember, it might not be material to say." Years later Charles Dibdin is more direct, explaining that when Collier saw the profit from the opera, he "found out an informality in the agreement, and took the property back to himself before the season was over; while Hill, who was too wise or too powerless to contend with him, relinquished his right without murmuring." With operatic justice, Handel returned to Hanover the following summer, the opera did not bring Collier the profit he expected, and he was ordered to pay Hill whatever was due him.

Without his theater to manage, Hill turned his attention to the first of many projects he would pursue during his active life. For years he had studied a procedure he had encountered while a boy: the extraction of oil from the beech mast. He believed that he could develop an industry in England that would use the beechnut native to England to provide oil for clothiers, perfumers, and apothecaries. Convinced himself, he convinced others first by taking out a patent on the process in 1713 and then by publishing his proposals in a series of pamphlets. By 1716 he had attracted £120,000 from investors. However, the project suffered the fate of many of his dreams—it worked better on paper than in reality. While the demand for the oil was high in 1714, the crop suffered one bad year, and by the end of 1714 a blight set upon the beeches. Guaranteeing that those who wished could withdraw their money with twenty-five percent interest, Hill followed through with a new set of proposals in *An Account of the Rise and Progress of the Beech-Oil Invention* (1715). However, 1715 brought another bad harvest, and a last pamphlet in November 1716 concluded the project. The bad news was that his scheme suffered because of bad crops and that neither he nor his friends benefited from it; the

good news was that his skilled manipulation of the investments prevented his ruin. For the curious, a series of publications is available that documents Hill's beech-oil activities: his poem *The Dedication of the Beech-Tree* (1714), his two pamphlets of 1714, and his "vindication" in 1716.

Undaunted by his failure, by December 1716 Hill had begun an association that promised to bring forth a new invention or project each month. Hill's purpose, according to the advertisement, is "nothing but the public good." The first essay, "On making China Ware" (*Essays, for the month of December, 1716*, 1718), was dedicated to the manufacture of china in England. As Brewster notes, Hill's scheme was not so farfetched. It predates the birth of Josiah Wedgwood and the manufacture of porcelain in England. When Hill wrote his essay, porcelain was just beginning to be produced in Dresden and Vienna; thus Hill was anticipating an industrial development in England.

The year 1716 also brought Hill back to the stage. Almost a year before Hill's beech-oil project failed and even before he proposed the china industry for the benefit of England, Hill had his second tragedy, *The Fatal Vision; or, The Fall of Siam*, produced at Lincoln's Inn Fields by John Rich. It opened on 7 February, ran seven nights, and was funded by Hill himself. He paid for the production's costumes, decoration, and scenery because he insisted in his dedication to John Dennis and Charles Gildon that "Decoration . . . is a fifth Essential: And without it, 'tis impossible but that the finest Tragedy must be maim'd, and strain on Probability." Hill explained that in the production he strove for "all the necessary strictness" of the French and "the common taste for fullness of design" of the Elizabethans.

The play concerns the emperor of China, his two sons, the captive princess of Siam, and a captive general of Siam who, along with the Chinese princes, loves the princess. Mind-boggling as it may seem, the emperor's eunuch, Selim, is revealed in act 2 to be the empress, who had been banished because of a prophecy that her third son would kill his father. The captive general, it turns out, is that very third son. With campy complexity, the emperor sentences the two princes to death, and the eunuch and the captive general—a. k. a. the empress and her son—plan to rescue them. They free the imprisoned Siamese forces who in turn kill the Chinese royal family. The third son and the princess are left to marry and reign. Little wonder that the play survives only in its original 1716 edition and the 1760 collected works.

Two years later Hill published the first version of his panegyric to Peter the Great of Russia, *The Northern-Star* (1718). In 1724 a Latin-English text, with the Latin version by Gilbert, Hill's brother, was published, and it was this text that came to the czar's attention. A year later, on the death of the czar, the third edition of the poem was published. Before he died, the czar had ordered a medal to be sent to Hill, and on her husband's death the czarina had it sent to Hill. Hill in turn requested papers from the czarina in order to write a biography of the late czar. The czarina died before many could be sent, and Hill did not write the work. A fifth edition of the poem was published in 1739 with Hill's revisions and corrections.

More than as a gesture to a foreign leader, *The Northern-Star* is better known because of the war that it generated between Pope and Hill, who had submitted the poem before its publication to Pope's judgment via their mutual friend and publisher, Bernard Lintot. According to Pope's biographer W. J. Courthope, Lintot surprised Hill with the following report: "Mr. Pope said there were several good things in *The Northern Star*, but it would be taken for an insult on the government, for, though the Czar is King George's ally, yet we are likely to quarrel with Sweden; and Muscovy, whispered Bernard, lies, he says, in the north." In the "Preface to Mr. Pope" that he appended to the published poem, Hill reacts as much to Pope's earlier slight in *An Essay on Criticism* as he does to Lintot's report. He writes: "My esteem for your genius as a poet is so very considerable that it is hardly exceeded by my contempt of your vanity." Then, generally accusing poets of "narrowness of mind," Hill blames their poor judgment on their "precarious subsistence.... A mere poet, that is to say, a wretch who has nothing but the jingle in his brains to ring chimes to his vanity, and whose whole trade is rhyme-jobbing—such a creature is certainly the most worthless incumbrance of his country." Pope ignored the outburst, but Hill did not forget, for in 1720 he sent Pope *The Creation. A Pindaric* with an apology. In his acknowledgment Pope assures Hill that he did like the first poem and had so incumbent on any well-meaning man to acquit himself of an ill-grounded suspicion in another, who perhaps means equally well, and is only too credulous. I am sincerely so far from resenting this mis-

take, that I am more displeased at your thinking it necessary to treat me so much in a style of compliment as you do in your letter." Regretting his impetuous response, Hill answered, "it was passionate and most unjustifiable levity." He printed his humble apology in another preface to Pope in *The Creation*. More letters were exchanged between the two men over the next twenty years or so, and, judging from Brewster's account, one might be led to believe that there was less hostility between the two poets than met the eye.

On 21 April 1721 Hill once again returned to the stage, this time at Lincoln's Inn Fields to help his friend Joseph Mitchell, the Scottish poet. Hill's play, *The Fatal Extravagance*, carried Mitchell's name, and it was even printed in 1720 with Mitchell as author, but in its preface Mitchell revealed his debt to Hill "in the scheme, in the sentiments, and language." Theophilus Cibber, Benjamin Victor, and J. K. all identify Hill as the author, and it is attributed to Hill in Hill's 1760 collected works. In 1721 a two-act version was published in Dublin; then in 1726 another edition was printed, as well as a five-act version by Mitchell himself. J. K. writes: "of a good Tragedy of two acts [Mitchell] made a sort of *Farce* of five; which no one afterwards disputed being his *own*." In 1730 Hill's one-act version was again printed; finally, in 1794 an alteration of Hill's play was published under the title *The Prodigal*.

The preface to the first edition, signed by Mitchell, reveals that the play was inspired by Hill's didacticism, and by *A Yorkshire Tragedy* (1609), at the time attributed to William Shakespeare. In the original prologue Hill emphasizes his purpose: "We teach, to-night,—ah! wou'd 'twere not too late, / How, rash, believing avarice galls a state." In the February 1730 revival, Hill's new prologue refers even more specifically to the topical inspiration—the domestic impact of the South Sea bubble with its "stocks, *like* syrens, *charm'd all ranks to* buy, /*That their* directors *might, of course*, destroy."

The one-act play is swift and forceful. The point is easily understood and the characterizations are credible. According to Cibber, the original one-act play by Hill is one of the writer's best: "I know not if Mr. Hill has anywhere touched the passions with so great a mastery." Bellmour, a gamester, has lost his friend's and his own fortunes. As the play opens, Bellmour hears that his friend has been arrested for debt. Soon, he too is forced to face his creditor, Bargrave, who taunts Bellmour into a duel.

Bellmour kills Bargrave, and, instead of escaping, he resolves to poison his wife and children. Providing them with a drink that he believes to be poisoned, he has his family innocently drink it, and then he kills himself. His family survives, however, because their uncle has witnessed some of the action and has secretly replaced the poison with a harmless drink. Bellmour's last moments are eased by the news that a bequest to his family will save them from poverty.

The success of *The Fatal Extravagance* probably encouraged Hill to return to the theater, especially since the position of manager had been strengthened, the theater monopolies weakened, and new investors attracted to the profitable productions. From 1720 to 1737 London had, among other unlicensed theaters, the Little Theatre in the Hay-Market, where Fielding's farces were produced, and Goodman's Fields, where Garrick would debut in 1741. In 1720, when Hill came on the scene without a patent, he reinforced a trend. By January 1722, however, Hill failed in his negotiations with the duke of Montague for use of the new Little Theatre, even though he had already gathered his actors, invested in new costumes, and completed scenery designed for the new theater.

That scenery may have graced the stage at the patented and protected Drury Lane theater when, a year later, on 5 December 1723, Hill's production of his tragedy *King Henry the Fifth* opened. With a cast that included Barton Booth as King Henry, Robert Wilks as the Dauphin, Jane Thurmond as Harriet, and Anne Oldfield as Princess Catharine, the play had debatable success at the Drury Lane with six recorded performances. In the 1735-1736 season it played nine times at Goodman's Fields and once at Tottenham Court. Its publication history during the eighteenth century, however, suggests interest in the play: it appeared in six separate and two collected editions.

As with most Shakespeare adaptations, Hill's *Henry V* has received little favorable or serious commentary. Yet, Hill was an impresario who understood and perhaps stretched the tastes of his audience, just as Davenant had before him and Laurence Olivier and Joseph Papp would later. Of recent critics Calhoun Winton has smiled on the dilemma of Shakespeare-made-fit. While Hill's "Trying himself in the bow of Shakespeare was going too far," Winton is amused by George C. D. Odell's view that "Compared with Shakespeare's manly play, this thing with its maudlin sentimentality and eighteenth-century affectation, is trifling in the extreme.... Hill has minced the good roast beef of old England." Winton admits that today's audiences "are prepared to accept the thesis, at least for the sake of argument, that Prince Hal may have faults."

Prince Hal's character was only one of the problems. In the preface Hill states he was building on the foundation of "The inimitable, and immortal, Shakespear" with "a *new fabric*" (1723). Disdaining the desires of "the *fashionable!*" audience, Hill appeals to "very discreet judges," who like Henry are able to disregard "*French tricks*." Hill calls for the restoration of "a taste for *Tragedy*." To bring about that change, Hill reduced the total number of characters, expanded the number and impact of the female characters, and ignored the tenets of the history play. Of the female characters, one in particular drew criticism–Harriet. An added character, she is in the style of the fallen women in the she-tragedies of Nicholas Rowe and in the pathetic tragedy of George Lillo's *The London Merchant*. Harriet is too much, however, even for Hill's twentieth-century champion, Brewster:

> nothing can prepare us for the appearance of a lady once betrayed by the king, the revengeful Harriet, who roams about the camp disguised as a page, acts as emissary between the English conspirators and the Dauphin, assumes the role of Viola in an interview with Katherine [sic] . . . and is finally so touched by Henry's platitudes about his undiminished love and his kingly responsibilities that she reveals the conspiracy and then stabs herself.

Brewster is also troubled by the less-than-heroic Henry who has worked "devastation among the maidens of England." So, too, was the eighteenth century. Hill's version disappeared after 1738, when Shakespeare's own play returned to the stage.

While his career as theater manager and adapter of Shakespeare may have been uneven, for most of the 1720s Hill was prominent and influential. Like many others at the time, Hill was an independent writer. His sphere of influence included younger writers who recognized his leadership through *The Plain-Dealer*. With his coeditor, William Bond, Hill encouraged and published the work of Edward Young, John Dennis, Richard Savage, the Scots David Mallet, James Thomson, and Joseph Mitchell, among others. The first number appeared on Monday, 23 March

1724, with a refreshing claim: "I have so many things to say, and am so fond of teaching, that I promise to myself no small fame, from the success of my weekly counsel." From the first, the periodical fulfilled its promise. The original plan was that Hill and Bond would alternate, but, according to Brewster's analysis, such was not the case. She explains, "Hill and Bond wrote by turns six numbers, and the quality of the production was observed so regularly to rise during Hill's weeks and fall during Bond's that Savage nicknamed them 'the contending powers of light and darkness.' " Of the 117 numbers, only 4 of the papers mentioned the theater. The last issue appeared on 7 May 1725, and in 1730 all were printed in two volumes; a second edition dedicated to Bond's relative, Lord Hervey, followed four years later.

During these years Hill published a number of poems, many of them in Savage's *Miscellaneous poems and translations* (1726). Brewster estimates that of the ninety-two poems in the collection more than one-third are by Hill. Hill also wrote an epilogue for the premiere of Eliza Haywood's *The Fair Captive* at Lincoln's Inn Fields, 4 March 1721. Haywood is responsible as well for the deference paid to Hill, to whom she gave the name Hillarius. He also published *The Progress of Wit* (1730), which he directed again to Pope, who had satirized him in *The Dunciad* (1728). Even though Pope apologized a year later in the 1729 edition, Hill was still stung by the attack. Subsequently, the two reached a truce, struck in part by Hill's gesture before he published his poem *Advice to the Poets* (1731). Hill sent the poem to Pope and asked him to star passages that might refer to Pope and not meet with the poet's approval. Pope responded with some starred lines and the assurance that "Our hearts beat just together, in regard to men of power and quality; but a series of infirmities, for my whole life has been but one long disease, had hindered me from following your advice" (14 March 1731). Not long after, in a letter dated 22 December 1731, Pope praised Hill for his new tragedy *Athelwold*, which Pope said he had read six times.

Athelwold, a revision of *Elfrid*, premiered at the Drury Lane on 10 December 1731, and despite Hill's extraordinary efforts, it ran just three nights. To assure its success, Hill asked Wilks to play the title role and sketched historically accurate costumes for the production. Others helped Hill by organizing a reading of the play on 22 November. Even Pope was enlisted to prepare "the expectations of people of the first rank" to encourage its success. The audience for the reading included Lord Bathurst, Lord Burlington, Lord Peterborough, and John Gay. When the play finally opened, Wilks was absent from its cast. Instead, the title role was played by Theophilus Cibber. Whether that alone caused the failure is doubtful; after all, the cast had William Mills, Hester Booth, and Jane Johnson Cibber. Hill himself was "nettled" by London's reception.

Giving new dimension to the idea of cold comfort, Brewster suggests that one may find some good lines in the revised play, but they do not compensate for some of its fatal flaws, including a complicated action with too many episodes. For example, Athelwold is shown to have betrayed a new character, Ethelinda, before he marries Elfrid. Edgar, the king, is even more exalted than before; Elfrid abandons it all for a nunnery; Ethelinda commits suicide offstage; and Athelwold drowns himself with her body in his arms.

During the next year or so Hill tried to form a new theater. He resorted to offering advice on performances at Drury Lane and suggesting some basic principles for establishing a kind of academy for training young people for the stage, much like Davenant's own venture into the nursery that William Legg supervised in 1663. Another two years would pass before Hill would return to the theater, and then it was with a prologue for *The Tuscan Treaty*, Bond's tragedy that premiered at Covent Garden on 20 August 1733. Within six months, on 9 January 1734, Hill provided both the prologue and epilogue for William Popple's comedy *The Lady's Revenge*, also at Covent Garden. On 11 February 1734 Hill supplied the epilogue for John Hewitt's *Fatal Falsehood* at the Drury Lane. Then, on 25 April 1735, with his prologue to the new comedy by Popple, *The Double Deceit,* Hill affirmed an association that had led to their collaboration on the periodical *The Prompter*. Popple's play survived one performance.

Six months before Popple's failure, Hill and the unfortunate playwright produced the first number of *The Prompter: A Theatrical Paper,* the first paper concerned mostly with theater. They began the periodical on 12 November 1734, and it ran for 173 numbers, appearing every Tuesday and Friday until 2 July 1736. In keeping with the subtitle, the periodical devoted about forty percent of its numbers to the London theater. Popple wrote entertaining essays on the opera,

NUM. I.

The Prompter.

To be Continued TUESDAYS and FRIDAYS.

—— All the *World's* a *Stage,*

And all the *Men* and *Women,* merely *Players.*   Shakesp.

—— *When we daily see so many Men* ACT *amiss, can we entertain any Doubt that a good* PROMPTER *is wanting?*

See below.

TUESDAY, NOVEMBER 12. 1734.

CUSTOM has made it necessary for a Writer, who aims at the Entertainment or Instruction of his Readers, (I mean in this humble Half-sheet way) to assume a *Character,* either illustrious or obscure, either heroic or ludicrous ; or, to express the common Intention better, such a Character as is most able to excite Curiosity, raise Mirth, and procure Attention. So that a modern Author, like an ancient Pilgrim, as soon as he sets out, must take up some *Sobriquet,* or mock Name, if he hopes to come quietly to the End of his Journey.

CONVINCED of this, before I sat down to form Lessons for the Publick, I spent some time in Search of a Title to appear under : But so many have travell'd before me in this Road, that I found it almost impossible to fix upon one, which I might properly call my own. I believe it must occur to the Memory of every Reader, that even the Subjects, which furnish these kinds of Essays, are not more exhausted, than the Titles, which adorn them.

I LAY long under this Difficulty; and indeed it was so heavy, that I had for some time almost laid aside my Purpose ; till at length, my Love for Theatrical Entertainments, which frequently led me to the Playhouses, gave me an Opportunity of extricating my self. In one of my Walks behind the Scenes, while I had this Matter full in my Head, I observed, an humble, but useful Officer, standing in a Corner, and attentively perusing a Book, which lay before him ; he never forsook his Post, but, like a General in the Field, had many *Aid de Camps* about him, whom he dispatched with his Orders ; and I could perceive, that tho' he seemed not to command, yet all his Instructions

were punctually complied with, and that in the modest Character of an Adviser, he had the whole Management, and Direction of that little Commonwealth. I enquired into his Name and Office, and was inform'd, that he was THE PROMPTER.

I BLEST my Stars for my fortunate Curiosity. We have had, said I to my self, *Dictators* and *Censors, Monitors* and *Instructors,* Names, that carry Presumption and Arrogance in the Sound of them : But since the Analogy is in all Respects so close between the Stage and the World ; what Character is so proper, so modest, so pertinent, for an humble Adviser, as THE PROMPTER ?

BUT in order to give my Readers a higher Idea of the *Dignity* of this Character, I must take the Liberty of being a little more particular in the Description of his Office ; and when I have shewn them, that he, without ever appearing on the Stage himself, has some Influence over every thing, that is transacted upon it, I doubt not, but they will all agree with *Cato,* that *the Post of Honour is a private Station.*

TO proceed then, He stands in a Corner, unseen and unobserved by the Audience, but diligently attended to by every one, who plays a Part ; yet, tho' he finds them all very observant of him, he presumes nothing upon his own Capacity ; he has a Book before him, from which he delivers his Advice and Instructions. From this Part of his Conduct, a very good Moral is to be drawn, which, I hope, I shall never be so forgetful of, as to be accused of *talking without Book.*

HE takes particular Care, not only to supply those, that are *out* in their Parts, with Hints and Directions, proper to set them right ; but also, by way of Caution, drops Words to those, who are perfect,

B

First issue of Aaron Hill and William Popple's theatrical paper

"the foreign plague," as he called them, and Hill wrote about the audience, theater managers, actors, and acting. By 1735 Hill had formulated a theory of acting that he presented in a twenty-line poem, "The Actor's Epitome":

> He who would act must think, for thought will
>   find
> The art to form the body by the mind.
> ....
> Be what you seem. Each pictured passion weigh.
> Fill first your thoughts with all your words must
>   say.

The natural mode that Hill recommends found a responsive audience. He was encouraged to expand the poem to 416 lines and to retitle it *The Art of Acting*. He published it in 1746, and a prose version, *Essay on the Art of Acting*, was published posthumously in 1753 with his collected works.

In addition to his ideas on natural acting, Hill used *The Prompter* to promote the idea of an academy for actors so that the stage could be transformed into a vehicle of virtue and good taste from its current "effeminacy and corruption." Hill suggests ideas that go as far back as Aristotle and recall the more recent statements of Charles II and the practices of Davenant, one of the first patent holders. Denying that theaters are merely places of "public diversion," Hill asserts "that their influence might, as to their political use, be carried higher even than that of the pulpit." Hill asks for reform and regulation, but through patrons, not the Licensing Act. To Hill, the problems rested with the managers, not the actors and playwrights who were to become the real victims of Parliament's forthcoming action.

Hill's next opportunity to put his theories of acting into practice came with his adaptations of Voltaire's plays. *Zaire* had been produced in the fall of 1732 in Paris, and by the following February the French edition was being sold in London. Within four months Hill's translation of a scene appeared in the *Gentleman's Magazine*. A few months later Hill sent copies of his adaptation to Pope and Thomson, assuring them that the play would be produced soon. However, two more years passed before *Zara* had an amateur production for William Bond's benefit in Sir Richard Steele's Music Room at York Buildings. Despite his serious illnesses, Bond played the part of Lusignan. Then, on 28 May 1735, the play was rehearsed "before a great Appearance of Nobility and other Persons of Distinction." It finally

opened the next night, 29 May 1735. The play's unconventional course continued: a benefit for Bond was scheduled for 31 May, but it was postponed until 2 June so that "several Persons of Quality" could attend. Bond collapsed during Lusignan's final scene and died shortly afterward. Two more performances followed before it was finally, and triumphantly, presented at the Drury Lane theater on 12 January 1736.

The cast included William Milward as Lusignan, Theophilus Cibber as Nerestan. Susannah Arne Cibber, Theophilus's second wife, had her dramatic-acting debut as Zara, and the prologue that was written and presented by Colley Cibber asked the audience's patience for his novice daughter-in-law's performance. Hill had coached her so well that Cibber need not have bothered. Not so successful, however, was the debut of Hill's nephew. His performance as the Sultan was so bad that the audience insisted he abandon the role immediately. The part was read by others for seven performances until another actor could master the lines.

Voltaire was so pleased with Hill's adaptation and its success in London that, in the 1736 second edition of the play, he praised Hill for his close translation of the French text. The text, however, had strong echoes of Shakespeare's plays, a coincidence that did not disturb the English, even after Hill pointed out similarities with *Othello* in *The Prompter*, where he defended the play against charges that Voltaire's plot had too many improbabilities.

The play's basic conflict is between love and religion, a variation of the heroic drama's love and honor. That conflict is within the breast of the Christian Zara, a Saracen captive, who is about to marry her beloved sultan. Happy to find that Lusignan, the captive general, is her father and that Nerestan, the Christian envoy, is her brother, Zara is distressed when they secretly beg her to forsake her adopted Mohammedan faith and her fiancé. The Sultan, meanwhile, not knowing that Nerestan is Zara's brother, becomes jealous. When he learns of their true relationship, the Sultan kills Zara and then himself, but only after he asks the survivors to tell his story. The play has traces of *Othello* with its murder-suicide triggered by unfounded jealousy and with its Iago-like confidant to the Sultan. It also has hints of *King Lear*, especially when the aged Lusignan dies from joy after he is reunited with his children.

Susannah Arne Cibber, circa 1733, the year in which she made her acting debut as Zara in the first production of The Tragedy of Zara *(portrait by Thomas Worlidge)*

The play was probably Hill's most successful theater venture. According to *The London Stage,* *Zara* was performed nine times in 1735 at the Music Room, another fourteen times in 1736 at Drury Lane, once in 1742, and another ninety-nine times from 1751 to 1796. As impressive is its publication history: by 1900 it had been printed in at least twenty-six single editions in London, Dublin, and Edinburgh and in thirty collections and anthologies.

Hill's next enterprise, *Alzira,* was his second adaptation of a play by Voltaire, one produced in Paris in January 1736. Hill's play was presented at Lincoln's Inn Fields on 18 June 1736. The theme again offers the power of religion, this time over natural virtue. Set in Peru, the play opens with Don Alvarez, an exemplary Christian who puts the lie to the notion that all Christians are cruel. His son, Don Carlos, loves and marries Alzira, daughter of the Indian king, after she mis-

takenly assumes her Indian lover, Zamor, is dead. Zamor is captured as he attacks the city, but not until he wounds Don Carlos. Zamor is sentenced to death with Alzira after he rejects the bargain of life as a Christian. When Don Carlos forgives his slayer and dies, Zamor is so impressed with the effects of Christianity that he is converted and marries Alzira. Like *Zara, Alzira* is operatic in its grandness and exoticism. Its success was more modest, however. By 1758 it had had at least eighteen performances, eleven separate publications, and seventeen in collections and anthologies. From the beginning the play had the approval of the Prince of Wales and other royals who graced many of the performances.

Hill's pleasant association with Voltaire was nearing its close. The two began to differ on the character of Julius Caesar. Hill's affinity with Caesar was not new—after all, one of his sons was named after the great Roman. So when Voltaire wrote a tragedy that exalted Brutus, Hill responded angrily, and Voltaire, in turn, attacked both Caesar and English taste. For Voltaire, instead of women or love, the play would exalt the love of liberty. Yet Hill could not accept some of Voltaire's notions. For example in Voltaire's version Caesar is Brutus's father. Hill could accept that, but he could not accept Voltaire's twist that Brutus still plans to kill Caesar, even after he learns that Caesar is his father. To Hill, this is "inhuman and bloody" and a slur upon the English taste. In 1737 Hill wrote his own play, keeping the father-son relationship but having Brutus deny its truth. For Hill, Brutus is bereft of honor, and Caesar is absolutely noble. In his version Hill restores Calpurnia and Portia, both of whom are involved in state matters.

Not surprisingly, neither Voltaire's nor Hill's play drew enthusiastic or great audiences—Voltaire's was coldly received in Paris in 1743, and Hill's was not performed in his lifetime. As Calhoun Winton has noted, "The theatre managers might have lacked taste, but they knew a loser when they saw one." Hill's version may have been performed in Bath around 1753, the year that it was published in London. A year later it was published in a second edition, and then a third appeared in 1759 with the information on the title page that "It Was Acted at the Theatre in Bath."

In 1738 Hill left London for Plaistow, his home in Essex, where he hoped to put into practice another of his favorite ideas: the development of a wine industry in England. Having already failed in a number of enterprises, Hill did not hesitate to plant a hundred thousand French vines the first year. He planned to add more each year. The activities and hopes of the period are documented in Hill's correspondence, especially with Samuel Richardson. By 1740, despite a persistent illness, Hill sent his friend a sample of his wine, and letters from Popple reveal that Hill was contemplating shifting the project to the Bermudas, where Popple's brother was governor. Along with the vineyards, Hill was occupied with cheaper ways to manufacture potash. Neither brought him any profit, just as his project in 1727 to acquire timber near the river Spey in Scotland had brought him none. According to Hill's plan, the lumber would be cut and transported by river for ships' masts. The company formed to bring it all about was fitfully successful—most of the timber was too short and management was wasteful. Hill kept some share in the stock, com-

menting on it even as late as 1740. When Parliament dissolved the company in 1829, its proceeds were divided among the stockholders, the debts having been discharged by the increase in the price of the land. In 1738, however, Hill had stopped all active projects except for his grapes and potash at Plaistow.

While at Plaistow, Hill wrote and published, and for the last few years he lived in expectation that he would return to live in London. Litigation and limited funds kept him from the theater and some of his former associations. In 1737 Hill published his poem *The Tears of the Muses* and in 1738 the essay that resulted from his study of Julius Caesar, *An enquiry into the merit of Assassination.* In 1743 he dedicated his poem *The Fanciad* to the duke of Marlborough. A year later he published *The Impartial,* his "free thoughts on the situation of our public affairs anno 1744." In 1746 he published the revised and extended poem *The Art of Acting* and the poem *Free Thoughts upon Faith.* In 1749 Hill produced two major works: the epic poem *Gideon* and the tragedy *Merope,* his final adaptation of a play by Voltaire. It was presented at Drury Lane on 15 April 1749.

Hill had finished his adaptation in 1745, but Garrick, now manager at Drury Lane, did not bring it out for four years, in part, as Kalman A. Burnim points out, because *Merope* was "a play in which no one was anxious to appear. After promising to accept the title role of Merope Mrs. Cibber decided against it, and Mrs. Pritchard was prevailed upon to play it. Barry turned down Polyphontes, obliging the director to settle for Havard." For the production Hill used oblique rather than lateral flats, especially in the last scene of the play where he suggested a tableau that would be partly live and partly painted on the wings and shutters: "some of the side wings depicted columns and painted people who seemed to stand between the columns. So skillfully were these wings to be painted that the people on them would scarcely be distinguishable from the real life in the forward area and around the altar." After a successful premiere the play had twelve initial performances and fifty-four more between 1749 and 1797. It was separately published in fifteen editions in London, Dublin, and Edinburgh and in six anthologies and collections by 1900. In the advertisement for the first edition of 1749, Hill notes that Voltaire found the English inept in tragedy, music, and painting. Hill then launches a chauvinistic attack on Voltaire, French tragedy, and France in general, ending with the promise that he will soon publish a comparison of the two stages.

The plot of *Merope* has a number of familiar elements. Merope is the widow of Cresphontes, king of Messene, who had been murdered years earlier by General Polyphontes. The play opens with Polyphontes urging Merope to marry him so that his position will be strengthened. However, she awaits the return of the son who escaped and has been raised by a friend. Ignorant of his heritage, the son returns to Messene and is arrested for murdering a man who attacked him on his journey. Merope learns of the incident, fears the dead man is her son, and seeks to avenge his death by killing her actual son. She is stopped by the guardian. Polyphontes is killed by the prince at the sacrificial altar in a scene as skillful as any in the great masques of the seventeenth century, a fitting spectacle to the conclusion of Hill's singular career.

The Prince of Wales commanded a benefit performance for Hill during the play's revival at Drury Lane on 9 February 1750, but Hill had died on the eighth, at the moment of an earthquake. He was buried in the West Cloister of Westminster Abbey on 18 February in the same grave with his wife, who had died in 1731. His four children survived him. His disappointing son, Julius, was the administrator of the estate. Urania married an actor, continued her correspondence with Richardson, and wrote a novel.

In 1753 a four-volume edition of Hill's *Works* was published "for the Benefit of the Family." As Brewster noted, a second edition followed in 1754. His play *The Insolvent*, based on works by Massinger and Davenant, was presented at the Theatre Royal in the Hay-Market on 6 March 1758, and that same year it was published in London. Two years later, it was published in Dublin. Not until 1760 were Hill's plays collected in the two-volume *The Dramatic Works* with its biography by J. K. It included all the separately printed plays and several short unacted pieces. Finally, in 1821, "a re-arrangement of Hill's celebrated essay," *The Actor, or Guide to the Stage* was published.

As Brewster convincingly argues, Hill was a man of many talents, with many friends and many achievements: "one cannot but respect in him qualities admirable in themselves, whether or not they bring success to their possessor,—the tireless energy that cannot endure to rust in idleness, the courage that looks upon failure only as an incentive to further effort." As with other impresarios, Hill was a man of enterprise and vision, a vision that was framed by his age, its ethics, and its tastes. He was prominent in the theater for more than forty years, from 1710 with the production of *Elfrid* to 1758 and the posthumous production of *The Insolvent*. He knew the theater and publishing world, not to mention the world of investments and projects; he knew the many greater and lesser lights of his age; and, above all, he knew the public of his day. What, then, does he have to offer? At the very least, he gives us insight into an age of such complexity that it is still being unraveled today and causing us to look again with greater care. To examine Aaron Hill, especially his career in the theater, is to discover the richness of the impresario who reflected his age through his life and his work.

Letters:

A Collection of Letters never before printed: written by Alexander Pope, Esq; and other ingenious Gentlemen, to the late Aaron Hill, Esq. (London: Printed for W. Owen, 1751);

The Works of the Late Aaron Hill, Esq; in four volumes Consisting of Letters on Various Subjects, and of Original Poems, Moral and Facetious. With an Essay on the Art of Acting. Printed for the Benefit of the Family, 4 volumes (London, 1753);

A. D. McKillop, "Letters [1721-1725] from Aaron Hill to Richard Savage," *Notes and Queries,* 199 (September 1954): 388-391.

Bibliography:

Richard W. Bevis, *English Drama: Restoration and Eighteenth Century 1660-1789,* Longman Literature in English Series (New York: Longman, 1988), pp. 309-310.

Biographies:

Richard Cumberland, Biography of Hill, in *Tragedy of Alzira. With the life of the author and a critique* (London: Printed for C. Cooke, by McDonald & Son 175-?);

Theophilus Cibber and others, *The Lives of the Poets of Great Britain and Ireland,* 5 volumes (London: R. Griffiths, 1753), V: 252-276;

J. K., *The Life of Aaron Hill,* in *The Dramatic Works of Aaron Hill, Esq. In two volumes* (London: Printed for T. Lowndes, 1760), I: i-xx;

David Erskine Baker, *The Companion to the Play-House,* 2 volumes (London: T. Becket & P. A. Dehondt, 1764); augmented and revised by Isaac Reed as *Biographia Dramatica,*

2 volumes (London: Printed for Rivingtons, 1782); augmented and revised again by Stephen Jones, 3 volumes (London: Longman, Hurst, Rees, Orme & Brown, 1812);

Robert Anderson, "Life of Hill," in volume 8 of *British Poets* (Edinburgh, 1794);

R. A. Davenport, "The Life of Aaron Hill," in volume 60 of *The British Poets* (Chiswick: Press of C. Whittingham, 1822);

Hans Ludwig, *The Life and Works of Aaron Hill. A Complementary Study to the Era of Pope* (London, 1911);

Dorothy Brewster, *Aaron Hill, Poet, Dramatist, Projector*, Columbia University Studies in English and Comparative Literature, 45 (New York: Columbia University Press, 1913);

Austin Dobson, "Aaron Hill," review of Dorothy Brewster's *Aaron Hill, National Review*, 63 (May 1914): 443-460; republished in *Rosalba's Journal And Other Papers* (London: Chatto & Windus, 1915), pp. 229-262;

Stanley J. Kunitz and Howard Haycraft, eds., "Aaron Hill," in *British Authors Before 1800: A Biographical Dictionary* (New York: H. W. Wilson, 1952), pp. 269-270.

References:

William W. Appleton and Kalman A. Burnim, Preface to *The Prompter: A Theatrical Paper (1734-1736)*, edited by Appleton and Burnim (New York: Benjamin Blom, 1966), pp. v-xv;

H. Barton Baker, *History of the London Stage and Its Famous Players 1576-1903* (London: Routledge, 1904);

W. F. Belcher, "Aaron Hill Earliest Poems," *Notes and Queries*, 29 (December 1982): 531-532;

Gosta M. Bergman, "Aaron Hill: Ein englischer Regisseur des 18. Jahrhunderts," *Maske und Kothurn*, 8 (1962): 295-340;

Jack R. Brown, "From Aaron Hill to Henry Fielding?" *Philological Quarterly*, 18 (January 1939): 85-88;

H. L. Bruce, "Voltaire on the English Stage," *University of California Publications in Modern Philology*, 8, no. 1 (1918): 1-152;

Charles Burney, *A General History of Music from the Earliest Ages to the Present Period*, volume 4 (London, 1789);

Kalman A. Burnim, "Aaron Hill's *The Prompter*: An Eighteenth-Century Theatrical Paper," *Educational Theatre Journal*, 13 (May 1961): 73-81;

Burnim, "Some Notes on Aaron Hill and Stage Scenery," *Theatre Notebook*, 12 (Autumn 1957): 29-33;

Landon C. Burns, "Three Views of *King Henry V*," *Drama Survey*, 1 (February 1962): 278-300;

Colley Cibber, *An Apology for the Life of Colley Cibber, Comedian, and late Patentee of the Theatre-Royal*, edited by R. W. Lowe, 2 volumes (London, 1889); edited by B. R. S. Fone (Ann Arbor: University of Michigan Press, 1968);

William Cook, *Memoirs of Charles Macklin, Comedian, with the Dramatic Characters, Manners, Anecdotes, etc., of the Age in which he lived* (London: Printed for J. Asperne, 1804);

Thomas Davies, *Memoirs of the Life of David Garrick, Interspersed with Characters and Anecdotes of his Theatrical Contemporaries*, 2 volumes (London, 1780);

Charles Dibdin, *A Complete History of the Stage*, 5 volumes (London: Charles Dibdin, 1800);

Alan Downer, "Nature to Advantage Dressed," *PMLA*, 58 (December 1943): 1002-1037;

Edwin Duerr, *The Length and Depth of Acting* (New York: Holt, Rinehart & Winston, 1962);

Paul S. Dunkin, "The Authorship of *The Fatal Extravagance*," *Modern Language Notes*, 61 (May 1945): 328-330;

Robert Eddison, "Topless in Jerusalem [On Zara]," *Theatre Notebook*, 22 (Autumn 1967): 24-27;

Percy H. Fitzgerald, *A New History of the English Stage, from the Restoration to the Liberty of the Theatres, in Connection with the Patent Houses*, 2 volumes (London: Tinsley, 1882);

John Genest, *Some Account of the English Stage, from the Restoration in 1660 to 1830*, 10 volumes (Bath: H. E. Carrington, 1832);

Charles Gray, *Theatrical Criticism in London to 1795* (New York: Columbia University Press, 1931);

Raymond Dexter Havens, "Aaron Hill's Poem on Blank Verse," *Modern Language Notes*, 36 (April 1921): 247-248;

Andrew Hepburn, "Aaron Hill's Theory of Acting," Ph.D. dissertation, University of Washington, 1970;

Phyllis M. Horsley, "Aaron Hill: An English Translator of Merope," *Comparative Literature Studies*, 12 (1944): 17-23;

Leo Hughes, "The Actor's Epitome," *Review of English Studies*, 20 (October 1944): 306-307;

Robert D. Hume, Introduction and notes to *See and Seem Blind*, facsimile of the 1732 edition, Augustan Reprint Society, no. 235 (Los Angeles: William Andrews Clark Memorial Library, 1986), pp. iii-xii;

Paul Philemon Kies, "The Authorship of *The Fatal Extravagance*," *Washington State University Research Studies*, 13 (June 1945): 155-158;

Kies, "Notes on Millay's *The King's Henchman*," *Washington State University Research Studies*, 14 (September 1946): 247-248;

Thomas R. Lounsbury, *Shakespeare and Voltaire* (New York: Scribners, 1902);

Eric Tessler Mace, "The Development of the Eighteenth-Century Periodical Essay," Ph.D. dissertation, Boston University, 1981;

A. C. McKillop, "Peter the Great in Thomson's *Winter*," *Modern Language Notes*, 67 (January 1952): 28-31;

Watson Nicholson, *The Struggle for a Free Stage in London* (Boston & New York: Houghton, Mifflin, 1906);

Gretchen Graf Pahl, Introduction to *"Of Genius" and Preface to* The Creation, Augustan Reprint Society Series Four: *Men, Manners and Critics*, no. 2 (N.p., 1949), pp. 1-6;

James Ralph, *The Taste of the Town, or a guide to all Publick Diversions* (London, 1731);

Fielding Dillard Russell, "Six Tragedies by Aaron Hill," Ph.D. dissertation, George Washington University, 1948;

W. O. S. Sutherland, Jr., "Essays and Forms in the *Prompter*," in *Studies in the Early English Periodical*, edited by Richmond P. Bond (Chapel Hill: University of North Carolina Press, 1957), pp. 135-149;

Sutherland, "Polonius, Hamlet and Lear in Hill's *Prompter*," *Studies in Philology*, 49 (1952): 605-618;

Sutherland, "A Study of the *Prompter* (1734-1736)," Ph.D. dissertation, University of North Carolina, 1950;

Benjamin Victor, *The History of the Theatres of London and Dublin from the year 1730 to the present Time*, 2 volumes (London: Printed for T. Davies, 1761).

Papers:
The Victoria and Albert Museum's collection of Hill's correspondence is in the Forster Mss. 13.2, 14.1, and 15. The British Library's collections of Hill's correspondence and works are in the Sloane Mss. 4055, f. 347, and 4253 and in the Stowe Mss. 143, f. 128.

John Home

(22 September 1722-5 September 1808)

Barbara M. Benedict
Trinity College, Connecticut

PLAY PRODUCTIONS: *Douglas*, Edinburgh, Canongate Theater, 14 December 1756; London, Theatre Royal in Covent Garden, 14 March 1757;

Agis, London, Theatre Royal in Drury Lane, 21 February 1758;

The Siege of Aquileia, London, Theatre Royal in Drury Lane, 21 February 1760;

The Fatal Discovery, London, Theatre Royal in Drury Lane, 23 February 1769;

Alonzo, London, Theatre Royal in Drury Lane, 27 February 1773;

Alfred, London, Theatre Royal in Covent Garden, 21 January 1778.

BOOKS: *Douglas: A Tragedy. As it is acted at the Theatre-Royal in Covent-Garden. Non ego sum vates, sed prisci conscius aevi* (London: Printed for A. Millar, 1757); republished, with fuller text, as *Douglas: A Tragedy. As it is Acted at the Theatre-Royal in Covent-Garden. Non ego sum vates, sed prisci conscius aevi* (Edinburgh: Printed for G. Hamilton & J. Balfour, W. Gray & W. Peter, 1757); modern edition, edited by Gerald D. Parker (Edinburgh: Oliver & Boyd, 1972);

Agis. A Tragedy. As it is acted at the Theatre-Royal in Drury Lane (London: Printed for A. Millar, 1758);

The Siege of Aquileia. A Tragedy. As it is acted at the Theatre-Royal in Drury-Lane (London: Printed for A. Millar, 1760);

The Fatal Discovery. A Tragedy. As it is performed at the Theatre-Royal in Drury-Lane (London: Printed for T. Becket & P. A. De Hondt, 1769);

Alonzo. A Tragedy. In Five Acts. As it is performed at the Theatre-Royal, Drury-Lane (London: Printed for T. Becket, 1773);

Alfred. A Tragedy. As Performed at the Theatre-Royal in Covent-Garden (London: Printed for T. Becket, 1778);

The History of the Rebellion in the Year 1745 (London: Printed by A. Strahan for T. Cadell, Jun. & W. Davies, 1802).

Collections: *The Dramatic Works of John Home* (London: Printed for A. Millar, 1760);

The Works of John Home now first collected. To which is prefixed an account of his life & writings. By Henry Mackenzie, 3 volumes (Edinburgh: Printed for A. Constable, 1822);

A Sketch of the Character of Mr. Hume and Diary of a Journey from Morpeth to Bath, edited by David Fate Norton (Edinburgh: Tragara Press, 1976);

The Plays of John Home, edited, with an introduction, by James S. Malek (New York & London: Garland, 1980).

OTHER: "The Fate of Caesar," "Verses Upon Inverary," "Epistle to the Earl of Eglintown," "Prologue on the Birthday of the Prince of Wales, 1759," and "Epigrams," in *A Collection of Original Poems by Scottish Gentlemen*, volume 2, edited by Thomas Blacklock (Edinburgh, 1762).

Poet, Presbyterian minister, playwright, and politician, John Home epitomizes the Scottish Enlightenment. Both in his own time and today, Home is best known for his famous friends and his fateful tragedy *Douglas* (1756): the friends made the play, and the play made the man. Backed by the Moderate party of the Scottish church, *Douglas* incited a pamphlet war which thrust Kirk officials out of religious seclusion and into the world of the Enlightenment. With the notoriety of the play fortune, sinecures, and power came to the romantic youth from the Lowlands.

Home, an instinctive flatterer in an age of flattery, rose like his hero in *Douglas* from humble origins. Born in Leith on 22 September 1722 of the town clerk, Alexander Home, and the daughter of a local writer, John attended Leith Grammar School and then the University of Edinburgh. Here he met the loyal friends who

John Home (engraving by Stewart)

would protect and defend him throughout his life: Alexander Carlyle, who characterizes Home in his *Autobiography* as a genius who flatters as a lover flatters and one whose entrance into a room filled it with sunlight; William Robertson, the historian; Hugh Blair, the poet; Adam Ferguson; and his own distant relative David Hume, with whom he wrangled amiably about the spelling of their shared name. These friendships cemented with the call to arms in "the '45." Now, as later, Home's dreams of military valor vied with his religious vocation: he postponed assuming the ministry for which he had been studying to join the student College Company of Edinburgh Volunteers under George Drummond, for he was eager to march on the Jacobite rebels attempting to place Charles Edward Stuart on the British throne. When the principal of the University of Edinburgh, William Wishart, convinced Drummond to spare the untried students, twelve or so of them met in Turnbull's Tavern to resolve to fight against all opposition, the first of many of Home's club gatherings in taverns throughout his life. After an inglorious stint as a night watchman for Sir John Cope following the collapse of Edinburgh to the rebels, Home fought as an officer at the Battle of Falkirk in January of 1746. He was captured with two others and imprisoned in a halfhearted way in the decrepit Doune Castle; by knotting his bedsheets into a rope, he escaped, followed by his companions, one of whom was too heavy for the rope, snapped it, and fell, breaking his leg and needing to be carried away by his young officer,

Margaret (Peg) Woffington, who played Lady Randolph in the first London production of Douglas
(mezzotint by J. Faber, based on a portrait by E. Hayley)

Home. These adventures, recounted in Home's *History of the Rebellion in the Year 1745* (1802), helped to nourish the young man's imaginative thirst for military glory: not only do his dramatic heroes embody the neoclassical ideal of soldierly courage and public duty but his political passion also sparked at notions of a military defense for Scotland and the rejuvenation of a martial spirit in Britons.

After the Jacobites fell at Culloden in April 1746, however, Home returned to religious life for a decade of Church politicking. He succeeded Robert Blair, author of "The Grave," to the apparently melancholy ministry at Athelstaneford, where Home wrote his first play, *Agis*,

based on Plutarch's history and vaunting Spartan heroism. David Garrick rejected it contemptuously in 1749, and so Home, after hearing a recital of the Scottish ballad of a father's unjust revenge on his son "Gil Morrice" one gloomy evening, began *Douglas*. Meanwhile the band of enlightened literati Home had met at Edinburgh University were forming a political party to bid for power in the General Assembly of the Church of Scotland. This party, the Moderates, advocated the interpenetration of religious and social activities, the fusion of Church and Enlightenment, and met in 1751 for the first time, typically in a tavern, to plan their strategy. Home was there, along with six other ministers and a handful of lay elders: Carlyle, Robertson, Blair, John Jardine, Adam Dickson. Opposed to them stood the Evangelicals, led by George Anderson and John Witherspoon, whose satirical *Ecclesiastical Characteristics* attacked the Moderates for heresy, pretentiousness, and pandering in 1752. In a countermove, the Moderates joined the Select Society of Edinburgh, a social club with Enlightenment values and liberal-minded authors, in 1753. Two years later Anderson urged the General Assembly to excommunicate David Hume and Henry Home, lord Kames, for their irreligious writings and their seduction of Kirk ministers to heretical ways. Amid this furor, Home was revising *Douglas* with the extensive help and advice of his Moderate friends, including David Hume. Believing it ready for production, Home posted to London to show it personally to Garrick, so excited that he forgot a saddlebag to hold the manuscript and had to carry it curled in his greatcoat pocket. Garrick, however, remained unimpressed, criticizing the improbability of the plot, the dullness of the characters, and the formality of the language. When a downcast Home returned to Scotland, his friends were only too ready to help: a play written by a minister and produced in Scotland would at once challenge the Evangelicals and demonstrate the literary merit of Scotland to the philosophes of the Enlightenment. They determined to produce it at the Canongate Theater in Edinburgh under West Digges; furthermore, they even rehearsed it themselves in the house of a renowned actress, Sarah Ward. William Robertson played Lord Randolph; David Hume was Glenalvon; Carlyle, who had already laboriously copied the manuscript from Home's illegible print, acted as Old Norval; Adam Ferguson, minister and professor of moral philosophy at the University of Edinburgh, took the part of Lady Randolph; Hugh Blair, who would become extremely powerful in the Church, was assigned Anna, the maid; and Home himself played Douglas. When the play opened on 14 December 1756, the house was full; crowed one chauvinistic spectator, "Whaur's yoor Wally Shakespeare noo?" *Douglas* was a riotous success.

As the Moderates anticipated, the production in Edinburgh of a play written by a minister provoked an instant torrent of controversy. Anderson himself had forced the Edinburgh playhouse to close twenty years earlier, arguing that theater produced iniquity and promoted vice; now, the Evangelicals revived his argument with speeches

from the Glasgow and Edinburgh presbyteries. Carlyle, however, had already prepared an ironic counterblow; within weeks he had published *An Argument to Prove that the Tragedy of Douglas Ought to be Publickly burnt by the Hands of the Hangman*, and Ferguson followed with *The Morality of Stage Plays Seriously Considered*, which championed theater by pointing out the absence of biblical prohibition and by defending the hierarchical employments offered society by the business of producing plays. David Hume also supplied an open letter praising the piece for its pathos and ranking it above those by Thomas Otway and Shakespeare in structure and language, but he withdrew the letter in order to use it as the dedication of his forthcoming *Four Dissertations* and to protect Home from the association with the taint of impiety. More than fifty pamphlets and broadsides appeared in the three months following the play's debut; they attacked Home for profligacy, defended the theater as moral, or argued the role of the clergy, but virtually every one of them tackled the fact of the play rather than the message in it. Three months to the day after it opened in Edinburgh, John Rich produced *Douglas* at Covent Garden. Again, it won instant applause. After attempting to prosecute Carlyle for attending the play, the General Assembly in Scotland confined itself to a gentle injunction to ministers to avoid the theater, so gentle an injunction, indeed, that it seemed almost an invitation. Certainly, in 1776, half of the General Assembly flocked to see Ann Barry play Lady Randolph, and eight years later the Assembly rearranged its schedule to permit members to attend Sarah Siddons's performance of the part. *Douglas* won the battle in the Church for the Moderates and won respect for Scottish belles lettres, playing more than 130 times in the eighteenth century.

Douglas undoubtedly won acclaim partly because of its nationalistic appeal–the Edinburgh prologue deliberately praises the Scots–and partly because of the political and religious controversy surrounding it. It also, however, merits applause for its graceful poetry and for its simple plot: adhering to the unities, replete with highly regular verse speeches, it evokes pity and arouses sentiment in the audience in the fashion of Nicholas Rowe. *Douglas*, however, balances its neoclassical themes of civic duty and private virtue with a proto-romantic atmosphere of melancholy medievalism and immovable fate; its rustic cottages, rugged cliffs, wild nature, and gloomy midnights belong to the "Graveyard School" of poetry, while

Spranger Barry, who played the title role in the first London production of Douglas

its familiar character types evoke the domestic drama of George Lillo. Although *Douglas* cannot be credited with beginning Gothic drama, it can and does point that way with a new combination of tragic elements.

Douglas certainly can be credited with making Home's fortune. In June of 1757 he resigned his ministry, despite his parishioners' support, to become the private secretary of John Stuart, earl of Bute. With the help of his friends he had already won an annual pension of one hundred pounds from the Prince of Wales for *Douglas;* to this he added an additional three hundred pounds per annum in 1763. A repentant Garrick now willingly staged *Agis* in 1758; it ran for eleven nights with Garrick as Lysander playing opposite Susannah Cibber's Euanthe. In fact, the next six years proved the zenith of Home's power and influence. As the trusted intimate of the prime minister's first friend, lord Bute,

Home dispensed favors among his own friends and basked in the favor of the court. Garrick played opposite Susannah Cibber in Home's new play, *The Siege of Aquileia*, in 1760; after nine nights the play was never revived. In the summer of 1761 Home toured the Highlands with James Macpherson. So inspired by the Scottish scenery was he that he wrote *Rivine*, later retitled *The Fatal Discovery;* it was produced with moderate success by Garrick in 1769. Home, typically, believed in the authenticity of Macpherson's Ossian poems and defended him as well as he could; the grateful poet left Home two thousand pounds in his will. In 1763 Home resigned the secretaryship and assumed the post of conservator of Scots Privileges at Compvere in Scotland, a well-paid position with light duties and great power in the General Assembly, but despite the weekly meetings with his friends, and the power, Home resigned this post in 1767 to lease a farm in

Ann Barry, who created the parts of Rivine in The Fatal Discovery *and Orisminda in* Alonzo, *as well as playing Lady Randolph in* Douglas *(engraving by S. Paul [Samuel De Wilde], based on a portrait by T. Kettle)*

Kilduff, marry his plain cousin Mary Home "since no one else would have her," and write several more, unremarkable and unsuccessful plays. In 1773 Garrick produced *Alonzo* but vehemently rejected Home's only comedy, the unpublished *The Surprise.* In 1778 *Alfred* ran for an embarrassing three nights at Covent Garden, with Ann Barry in the lead role.

No more of Home's plays would see production. In 1778 Home accepted a commission in the Mid-Lothian Fencibles, a regiment designed to defend Scotland, and fell from his horse during practice maneuvers. He injured himself so badly that, as his friendly biographer Henry Mackenzie writes, "his mind was never restored to its former vigour, nor regained its former vivacity." Apparently he recovered sufficiently to move to

Edinburgh and regale his friends until he was nearly eighty-six with tales of the Great Rebellion, traditional Scottish feasts, and bottles of the port and claret left to him by his old friend David Hume in his will, on condition that Home finish a bottle of port at one sitting and sign himself "John Hume." In his last years, as in his student days, John Home was beloved and protected by his friends.

Of his six published and two unpublished plays *Douglas* is by far Home's best. Extensively revised with specific criticisms by his friends, it owes its success to its political backing, its timing, and its portrayal of maternal passion, female distress, and military valor supported by strong characters and well-fashioned poetry. "My name is Norval" rightly served as the typical test of elocu-

Sarah Siddons as Lady Randolph, Mrs. Woods as Anna, and Sutherland as Old Norval in the 1784 Edinburgh production of Douglas

tion in Victorian parlors: Home's poetry is compact, aphoristic, simple, affective. Home's influence, nevertheless, remains primarily in the political rather than in the literary arena; his expression of neoclassical values within a romantic framework did not break new ground so much as it recombined familiar elements, and, furthermore, it appears clearly only in *Douglas*, the play revised, backed, and promoted by the most powerful figures in the Scotland of Home's time. Home's play revived Edinburgh theater and represented the Enlightenment values of the Scottish literati.

References:

Paula R. Backscheider, "John Home's *Douglas* and the Theme of the Unfulfilled Life," *Studies in Scottish Literature*, 14 (1978): 90-97;

"Biographical Notice of the Late John Home, Esq., Author of 'Douglas,' and Other Works. By a Near Relative," *New Monthly Magazine*, 57 (November 1839): 289-304; 57 (December 1839): 471-483; 58 (February 1840): 164-176;

Dr. Alexander Carlyle, *The Autobiography of Dr. Alexander Carlyle*, with a supplementary chapter by J. H. Burton (Edinburgh & London: Blackwood, 1860);

Ian D. L. Clark, "From Protest to Reaction: The Moderate Regime in the Church of Scotland 1752-1805," in *Scotland in the Age of Improvement*, edited by N. Y. Phillipson and R. Mitchison (Edinburgh: Edinburgh University Press, 1970), pp. 200-224;

Clark, "Moderation and the Moderate Party in the Church of Scotland, 1752-1805," Ph.D. dissertation, University of Cambridge, 1964;

Alice Edna Gipson, *John Home: A Study of His Life and Works* (Caldwell, Idaho: Caxton Printers, 1916);

Henry Mackenzie, "Account of the Life of Mr. John Home," in *The Works of John Home now first collected*, 3 volumes, edited by Mackenzie (Edinburgh: Constable, 1822), I: 1-184;

James S. Malek, Introduction to *The Plays of John Home,* edited by Malek (New York & London: Garland, 1980), pp. vii-xliii;

Malek, "John Home's Douglas: The Role of Providence," *New Rambler,* 15 (1974): 30-35;

Malek, "John Home's *The Siege of Aquileia*: A Reevaluation," *Studies in Scottish Literature,* 10 (1973): 232-240;

Malek, "The Ossianic Source of John Home's *The Fatal Discovery*," *English Language Notes,* 9 (September 1971): 39-42;

William Mure, ed., *Selections from the Family Papers Preserved at Caldwell 1496-1853,* two parts in 3 volumes (Glasgow: Printed by W. Eadie, 1854);

Gerald D. Parker, Critical introduction to *Douglas,* edited by Parker (Edinburgh: Oliver & Boyd, 1972), pp. 1-18;

Sir Walter Scott, "Life and Works of John Home," in *The Miscellaneous Prose Works of Sir Walter Scott,* 28 volumes (Edinburgh: Cadell, 1834-1835), XIX: 283-367;

Richard B. Sher, *Church and University in the Scottish Enlightenment: The Moderate Literati of Edinburgh* (Princeton: Princeton University Press, 1985);

George R. Thomas, "Lord Bute, John Home and Ossian: Two Letters," *Modern Language Review,* 51 (January 1956): 73-75;

Terence Tobin, *Plays by Scots, 1660-1800* (Iowa City: University of Iowa Press, 1974);

Herbert J. Tunney, *Introduction to Home's "Douglas"* (Lawrence, Kans.: University of Kansas Press, 1924).

John Hughes

(29 January 1677-17 February 1720)

William J. Burling
Auburn University

PLAY PRODUCTIONS: *Amalasont, Queen of the Goths,* London, Theatre Royal in Drury Lane, 1697-1700?;

Calypso and Telemachus, London, Queen's Theatre, 17 May 1712;

Apollo and Daphne, London, Theatre Royal in Drury Lane, 12 January 1716;

The Siege of Damascus, London, Theatre Royal in Drury Lane, 17 February 1720.

BOOKS: *In a grove's foresaken shade. A song in the tragedy call'd Amalasont, Queen of the Goths or, Vice destroys it Self . . . Sung by Mrs. Erwin, and exactly engrav'd by Tho: Cross,* lyrics by Hughes and music by Daniel Purcell [single sheet] (London, circa 1697);

The triumph of peace. A poem (London: J. Tonson, 1698);

Hence ye curst infernal train. A song in the tragedy call'd Amalasont, Queen of the Goths or, Vice destroys it Self . . . Sung by Mrs Lindsey, and exactly engrav'd by Tho: Cross, lyrics by Hughes and music by Daniel Purcell (London, circa 1700);

The court of Neptune, a poem. Address'd to the Right Honourable Charles Montague, Esq. (London: Printed for J. Tonson, 1700);

The House of Nassau. A Pindarick Ode (London: Printed for D. Brown & A. Bell, 1702);

An ode in praise of musick, set for variety of voices and instruments by Mr. Philip Hart (London: Printed for B. Lintot & sold by J. Nutt, 1703);

A complete history of England: with the lives of all the kings and queens thereof; from the earliest account of time, to the death of His late Majesty King William III, 3 volumes (volumes 1 and 2 by Hughes, volume 3 by White Kennett) (London: Printed for B. Aylmer, 1706);

Fontenelle's Dialogues of the Dead, translated by Hughes (London: Printed for J. Tonson, 1708);

Six English Cantatas, humbly inscrib'd to the Marchioness of Kent, words by Hughes and music by

John Christopher Pepusch (London: Printed by J. Walsh, 1710);

An ode, set to musick and sung at the sheriffs feast, before the nobility and gentry, by Mr. Hughes and Mr. Leveridge, at Merchant-taylors-hall, March the 25th, 1712 [broadside] (London, 1712);

Calypso and Telemachus. An opera. Perform'd at the Queen's theatre in the Hay-market (London: Printed for E. Sanger, 1712);

The history of the revolution in Portugal by the Abbot de Vertot, translated from the French by Hughes (London: Sam. Buckley, 1712);

An ode to the creator of the world. Occasion'd by the fragments of Orpheus (London: Printed for J. Tonson, 1713);

The Lay-monk, by Hughes and Sir Richard Blackmore, nos. 1-40 (London: Printed & sold by J. Roberts, 16 November 1713-15 February 1714); republished as *The Lay-monastery, Consisting of essays, discourses, &c. Publish'd singly under the title of The Lay-monk* (London: Printed by Sam. Keimer for Ferdinando Burleigh, 1714);

An ode for the birth-day of Her Royal Highness the Princess of Wales, St. David's day, the first of March, 1715/16 (London: Printed for J. Tonson, 1716);

Apollo and Daphne. A masque. Set to musick, and perform'd at the Theatre Royal in Drury-lane (London: Printed for J. Tonson, 1716);

A layman's thoughts on the late treatment of the Bishop of Bangor (London: Printed for R. Burleigh, 1717);

Charon, or, the ferry-boat a vision (London: Printed & sold by W. Lewis, J. Brotherton, 1719);

Conversations with a lady on the plurality of worlds, translated from the French of Bernard Le Bovier de Fontenelle by Hughes (London: Printed by J. Darby for M. Wellington, 1719);

The ecstasy. An ode. (London: Printed & sold by J. Roberts, 1720);

The history of the siege of Damascus, by the Saracens, in the year 633. As it is Related by Abdo'llah Mo-

John Hughes, as he was depicted in the frontispiece to his Poems on Several Occasions *(engraving by G. Van der Gucht, based on a 1718 portrait by Sir Godfrey Kneller; courtesy of the Folger Shakespeare Library)*

hammed ebn Omar Alwákidi, *the Arabian Historian. Very Useful for the Readers and the Spectators of the Tragedy of The Siege of Damascus* (London: Printed & sold by J. Brotherton & W. Meadows, 1720);

The siege of Damascus. A tragedy. As it is acted at the Theatre-Royal in Drury-lane. (London: J. Watts, 1720);

The letters of Abelard and Heloise, translated by Hughes (London: Printed for J. Watts, 1722);

Poems on several occasions. With some select essays in prose, 2 volumes, edited by William Dun-combe (London: J. Tonson & J. Watts, 1735);

The complicated guilt of the late rebellion. (London: Printed & sold by J. Roberts, 1745);

Cupid and Hymen's holiday. A pastoral masque, The Theatrical Magazine (London), 5 (1781).

OTHER: *Advices from Parnassus, in Two Centuries, with the Political Touchstone, and an Appendix to it. Written by Trajano Boccalini. To which is added a continuation of the Advices by Girolamo Briani. . . . all translated from the Italian by sev-*

eral hands, revis'd and corrected by Mr. Hughes (London, 1706);

Molière, *The Misanthrope,* translated by Hughes, *The Monthly Amusement,* no. 2 (May 1709);

The works of Edmund Spenser. In six volumes. With a glossary explaining the old and obscure words. Publish'd by Mr. Hughes (London: Printed for Jacob Tonson, 1715);

Hamlet, Prince of Denmark; a tragedy, as it is now Acted by His Majesty's Servants. Written by William Shakespear [acting version], edited by Hughes (London: Printed by J. Darby for M. Wellington, 1718).

At the close of the seventeenth century a new generation of dramatists was beginning to emerge in London. Joseph Addison, John Gay, and Richard Steele are surely among the most famous of this group, but a galaxy of minor figures arose as well, and in this second group we find John Hughes. While he began his literary career as a poet, publishing several long poems in honor of William III, Hughes was a playwright early on and contributed solid if undistinguished theatrical entertainments and one tragedy widely acknowledged in his own century as a major dramatic achievement.

Hughes early established and then maintained a respected position in the London theatrical community. Henry Paul reports that Hughes prepared an acting version of *Hamlet* for Robert Wilks "which was the stage version current in London from 1718 to 1763, when it was succeeded by Garrick's first version"; and the *Dictionary of National Biography* relates that Hughes was invited by Addison to complete the final act of *Cato,* although he did not do so. Hughes further is notable for his attempt to change the direction of opera, hoping to popularize those performed entirely in English, but his reputation has finally come to be founded on his nonmusical masterpiece, *The Siege of Damascus.*

A child of modest auspices, Hughes was born at Marlborough, Wiltshire, the *DNB* relates, the "elder son of John Hughes, clerk in the Hand-in-Hand Fire Office, Snow Hill, London, by his wife Anne, daughter of Isaac Burges of Wiltshire." He attended "a dissenting academy apparently in Little Britain, London, under Thomas Rowe, where he was a contemporary of Isaac Watts" but did not matriculate to any university. A staunch supporter of William III and all things Whig, Hughes balanced a career as an author with one in government service. As a minor

bureaucrat, he labored for years, mainly in naval administration, finally receiving a higher and more profitable post in 1717 from his patron, lord chancellor William Cowper. He is not known to have married. After 1698 Hughes was active in many literary endeavors in addition to play writing, including poetry, translation, history writing, and editing. By age twenty or thereabouts he began to publish poetry and probably had a play staged. From 1717 onward Hughes battled consumption, his death taking place on 17 February 1720, the same night as the premiere of his masterpiece, *The Siege of Damascus.*

Scholars for more than two centuries have thought that only three of Hughes's plays were staged, but this writer's research reveals that *Amalasont, Queen of the Goths; or Vice Destroys Itself,* an unpublished (now lost) tragedy and his first play, very likely reached the boards at the Theatre Royal in Drury Lane some time between 1697 and 1700. The existence of this play in manuscript had long been known from an anecdote originating with Hughes's brother-in-law, John Duncombe, but no proof of performance seemed to have survived. Two published songs (with music by Daniel Purcell), however, allow one to state with some certainty that the play was indeed performed: *Hence ye curst infernal train. A song in the tragedy call'd Amalasont . . . Sung by Mrs Lindsey* and *In a grove's foresaken shade. A song in the tragedy call'd Amalasont . . . Sung by Mrs. Erwin.* Mrs. Erwin is known to have performed at Drury Lane only during the years 1695-1700. Both songs were published circa 1697-1700 according to the *British Union Catalogue of Early Printed Music.* We know nothing of the play's content.

Hughes's second attempt was a short, unacted masque, *Cupid and Hymen's Holiday,* which he completed by 1703. First printed in his 1735 *Poems on Several Occasions* and not reprinted until 1781, this didactic piece hammers home the importance of marriage and the joys arising when pleasure is "licensed" by Hymen. The play's closing lines perhaps best express the tenor of the masque:

> how happy are we,
> Where Cupid and Hymen in consort agree!
> We'll revel all day with sports and delight,
> And Hymen and Cupid shall govern the night.

The brevity of the play and the lack of contextual information limit interpretation.

Richard Leveridge, who sang the part of Proteus in Calypso and Telemachus *(engraving by Saunders, based on a portrait by Frye)*

Hughes's next dramatic work was the opera *Calypso and Telemachus*, which was staged at the Queen's Theatre in the Haymarket on 17 May 1712 and played four additional nights during the first run (21 and 24 May; 21 and 25 June). This opera has great significance in Hughes's career, as may be inferred from the extensive critical remarks which preface the published version. Hughes states that he wishes to write a new kind of opera, one which will feature English, a language he believes is worthy of operatic performance. Elaborate musicals that London theatergoers termed operas had been produced in English as early as William Davenant's *The Siege of Rhodes* (2 parts, 1656, 1661), but prior to

Hughes's attempt only one true English opera in the "Italian stile," that is, one in which all of the dialogue is sung in recitatives, had appeared– Addison's *Rosamond* (1707). The rage for Italian opera in London had begun only seven years earlier with the phenomenal success of *Arsinoe* (1705), and recent hits had included *Almahide* (1710) and *Rinaldo* (1711), both revived during the 1711-1712 opera season, along with *Antioco* (1705), which was the season's most popular offering.

Hughes's arguments continue the position he had first outlined in the preface to his and John Christopher Pepusch's *Six English Cantatas* (1710). That operas should be performed only in

Italian, he states, is simply "an Affectation of every thing that is Foreign" and not an argument in itself. And while English "is not so soft and full of Vowels as the *Italian*," still it is not "incapable of Harmony." But the strongest reason he presents, "certainly of much more Consequence in Dramatical Entertainments, is, that they shou'd be perform'd in a Language understood by the Audience." According to Addison in *Spectator* no. 405, even the Italian castrati star Nicolini praised Hughes's *Calypso and Telemachus*. One anecdote reports G. F. Handel as remarking "he would sooner have composed it than any one of his own Operas." Negative criticism was nearly nonexistent, though a remark made by Samuel Johnson in his "Life of Hughes" has been erroneously accepted as fact. Johnson reports that Charles Talbot, duke of Shrewsbury, as lord chamberlain, ordered the Italian "intruders" to run Hughes's play "as to obtain an obstruction of profits, though not an inhibition of performance." All evidence indicates that Johnson was misinformed. There were no Italian "intruders" in the sense Johnson implies. To be sure a number of Italian opera stars were employed by the company that season, but they did not manage the operation, which was, in May 1712, in the hands of Owen Swiney. Having just acquired control of the Queen's opera company in April 1712, Swiney was anxious to increase his ticket sales. Handel was out of the country; because no new foreign operas were offered to him, Swiney took on Hughes's play. The records show that the lord chamberlain, rather than opposing Hughes, in fact, did nothing at all, staying completely out of the day-to-day operations. We know from newspaper advertisements that ticket prices were in effect *raised* for Hughes's play: "Benches in the Pit [are to be] rail'd in at the Price of the Boxes." In other words, the seating was rearranged to produce more higher-priced seats. In summary Johnson's remark, so long accepted as fact even by reputable scholars, simply does not hold up in the face of the facts of theatrical-management history.

Working with composer J. E. Galliard, Hughes chose to base his libretto on an episode from *Les Aventures de Télémaque* (1699), the novel by François Fénelon then beginning to attain the widespread popularity it would ultimately gather during the eighteenth century. The exact episode concerns the near seduction and confinement of Telemachus, the son of Ulysses wandering the seas in search of his father, by the sorceress Ca-

lypso (an elaboration of *Odyssey*, II, 268 ff.). Ulysses himself had barely escaped from the femme fatale who enticed men by offering them the promise of immortality (see *Odyssey*, V, 14-276). With the aid of Mentor, his older male companion, Telemachus barely avoids the snares of Calypso for two acts. In act 3, however, events transpire which cause Mentor to reveal his true identity as the goddess Minerva, who has accompanied Telemachus throughout his journey in order to provide divine protection.

The opera is tightly constructed and moves quickly from incident to incident. Merrill J. Knapp praises the music and remarks that the closing aria is one "of unusual scope and power." Staging and special effects were quite elaborate, as the stage directions indicate: for example, in act 2 Proteus "sinks under the Stage," which is shortly followed by a rising tree which "is suddenly chang'd into Fire and vanishes." And in one section of act 3 "a Machine of Clouds descending fills the Stage," while in another, "The Clouds opening on a sudden, the Stage is illuminated, and in the midst of the Machine *Mentor* now appears as *Minerva*."

The original cast featured several of the principal London opera stars, including Signiora Margarita (Margherita de l'Epine) as Calypso, Jane Barbier as Telemachus, and Richard Leveridge as Proteus. The opera was revived on 27 February 1717 at Lincoln's Inn Fields, with Barbier and Leveridge in their original roles, but it ran for only two more nights (7 and 9 March). The run was apparently cut short by the "indisposition" of Mrs. Barbier.

Again working with music, but this time in a greatly reduced format, Hughes next offered the masque afterpiece *Apollo and Daphne* to Drury Lane by 5 December 1715, and the piece appeared on 12 January 1716. Margarita and Barbier again sang lead roles. This time Barbier played the female role, while Margarita was Apollo. This short but imaginative reworking of the Ovidian myth relies as much as did *Calypso and Telemachus* on special effects. Two of the flashier moments occur, first, when Apollo descends "in the Chariot of the Sun," and later when Daphne "is transform'd into a Laurel-tree" before the audience's eyes. Surviving theater bills for scenery and costumes make clear that the Drury Lane management spent considerable time and money readying this piece for the stage. The audience was lukewarm, however, and the play had only five performances.

Premiering on 17 February 1720 was Hughes's final and greatest play, *The Siege of Damascus,* now recognized as one of the most influential tragedies of the eighteenth century. Hughes lay mortally ill as word reached him of the play's initial success, and he is reported to have been little interested in the acclaim: he died the same evening.

The tragedy revolves around the dilemma faced by Phocyas, a valiant young defender of Damascus in the year 635. As originally noticed by Emmy Weidenmann in 1915 (though later re-reported in 1958 by John Moore, no doubt unaware of Weidenmann's research), Hughes took the original story from Simon Ockley's *History of the Saracens* (1708). Hughes's fascinating and powerful plot, which Edward Gibbon closely followed (historical inaccuracies and all) in his *Decline and Fall of the Roman Empire* (1776-1788), is well worth recalling.

After gaining two victories over the besieging Arabs, Phocyas sues for the hand of Eudocia, daughter of Eumenes, governor of the city. Eumenes had promised Eudocia to another (whom Eudocia does not love) and refuses to grant the boon, becomes annoyed at Phocyas's protest, and finally sends the new hero away in disgrace. Eudocia–angered by her father's insensitivity–and Phocyas attempt to flee together, but he is captured by the Arabs. Instead of executing Phocyas, the Moslems, by promising to save Eudocia from rape and murder, attempt to extort his promise to help their cause and to embrace the Muslim faith. He refuses to change religions, but with his assistance Damascus is taken, and the agreement to spare Eudocia is reluctantly fulfilled. Eudocia, however, is shocked beyond belief that Phocyas had "betrayed" Damascus, and, though she had survived only because of his actions, states that they must separate forever. Later, when the citizens of the city are camped in the Vale of Palms after being forced to abandon their homes, Caled and Daran, two bloodthirsty Arab leaders, concoct a false motive for sweeping down upon the Christians. After killing both of the key Arabs, Phocyas is at last himself a victim in the fray, though he receives Eudocia's forgiveness before his death.

The pathos created by the extraordinary events made no small impression on the London audiences and readers; the combination of Oriental intrigue, conflicts of honor, love, and religion, and extreme emotional duress exploited nearly every aspect of pathetic tragedy a dramatist could employ. The original 1718 plan for the play (published by Duncombe in 1772 in *Letters by several eminent persons deceased*) specified that Phocyas would actually give up his faith, a situation which Hughes felt would create exquisite pathos. But the Drury Lane managers disagreed, arguing that the audience would never accept such a turncoat; Hughes was forced to agree and revise to ensure production of the play.

The original predicament requiring what modern audiences might call situational ethics, may well provide a richer kind of crisis, but Colley Cibber, Robert Wilks, and Barton Booth read audience tastes precisely, for the play went on to popular and critical acclaim. With more than one hundred performances between the premiere and 1785 (sixteen in 1743 alone), *The Siege of Damascus* must be numbered among the most popular tragedies of the eighteenth century and an important index of dramatic taste. Samuel Johnson, always ready to state his view of any literary work, declined to comment on the play in his "Life of Hughes," stating simply that "it is unnecessary to add a private voice to such continuance of approbation."

Hughes is also responsible for a number of complete and partial translations and one unacted original script. The translations include Molière's *The Misanthrope* (1709) and *The Miser* (first act only, published in *Poems,* 1735). The unacted and unpublished play is a tragedy entitled *Sophy Mirza,* of which he completed only two acts. The play is based on the same subject as Sir John Denham's *The Sophy* (1642), according to the *Biographia Dramatica,* which also states that John Duncombe finished the tragedy. The manuscript is said to remain in the hands of the family.

Letters:
Letters by several eminent persons deceased. Including the correspondence of John Hughes ... and several of his friends, published from the originals: with notes explanatory and historical, edited by John Duncombe (2 volumes, London: J. Johnson, 1772; enlarged, 3 volumes, 1773).

Biographies:
David Erskine Baker, *The Companion to the Play-House,* 2 volumes (London: T. Becket & P. A. Dehondt, 1764); augmented and revised by Isaac Reed as *Biographia Dramatica,* 2 volumes (London: Printed for Rivingtons, 1782); augmented and revised again by Stephen Jones, 3 volumes (London: Longman,

Hurst, Rees, Orme & Brown, 1812; reprinted, New York: AMS Press, 1966), I: 378-379; III: 290-291;

Samuel Johnson, "Hughes" (1779), in his *Lives of the English Poets,* edited by G. B. Hill, 3 volumes (Oxford: Clarendon Press, 1905), II: 159-165;

Emmy Weidenmann, *John Hughes: His Life and Works* (Zurich: Ruegg, 1915).

References:

William J. Burling, "British Plays, 1697-1737: Premieres, Dates, Attributions, and Publication Information," *Studies in Bibliography,* 43 (forthcoming 1989);

Merrill J. Knapp, "A Forgotten Chapter in Early Eighteenth-Century Opera," *Music and Letters,* 42 (January 1961): 4-16;

Judith Milhous, "Dates and Redatings for 141 Theatrical Bills from Drury Lane, 1713-1716," *Papers of the Bibliographical Society of America,* 79 (1985): 499-521;

Milhous and Robert D. Hume, *Vice Chamberlain Coke's Theatrical Papers, 1706-1715* (Carbondale: Southern Illinois University Press, 1982);

John Moore, "Hughes' Source for *The Siege of Damascus,*" *Huntington Library Quarterly,* 21 (August 1958): 362-366;

Henry Paul, "Players' Quartos and Duodecimos of *Hamlet,*" *Modern Language Notes,* 49 (June 1934): 369-375.

Charles Johnson

(1679-11 March 1748)

William J. Burling
Auburn University

PLAY PRODUCTIONS: *The Force of Friendship* [tragicomedy], London, Queen's Theatre, 20 April 1710;

The Force of Friendship [tragedy], London, Queen's Theatre, 1 May 1710;

Love in a Chest, London, Queen's Theatre, 1 May 1710;

The Generous Husband, London, Theatre Royal in Drury Lane, 20 January 1711;

The Wife's Relief, London, Theatre Royal in Drury Lane, 12 November 1711;

The Successful Pyrate, adapted from Lodowick Carlell's *Arviragus and Philicia*, London, Theatre Royal in Drury Lane, 7 November 1712;

The Victim, adapted from Jean Racine's *Iphigénie*, London, Theatre Royal in Drury Lane, 5 January 1714;

The Country Lasses, London, Theatre Royal in Drury Lane, 4 February 1715;

The Cobler of Preston, London, Theatre Royal in Drury Lane, 3 February 1716;

The Sultaness, adapted from Jean Racine's *Bajazet*, London, Theatre Royal in Drury Lane, 25 February 1717;

The Masquerade, adapted from Molière's *Dom Garcie* and James Shirley's *The Lady of Pleasure*, London, Theatre Royal in Drury Lane, 16 January 1719;

Love in a Forest, adapted from William Shakespeare's *As You Like It*, London, Theatre Royal in Drury Lane, 9 January 1723;

The Female Fortune-Teller, London, Theatre Royal in Lincoln's Inn Fields, 7 January 1726;

The Village Opera, based on Florent Dancourt's *Le Galant jourdinier* and Alain-René Lesage's *Crispin rival de son maître*, London, Theatre Royal in Drury Lane, 6 February 1729;

Medæa, adapted from classical sources, London, Theatre Royal in Drury Lane, 11 December 1730;

The Ephesian Matron, possibly adapted from Louis Fuzélier's *La Matron d'Ephese*, London, Theatre Royal in Drury Lane, 17 April 1732;

Caelia, London, Theatre Royal in Drury Lane, 11 December 1732.

BOOKS: *A congratulatory verse, to Her Grace, the Dutchess of Marlborough: on the late glorious victory, near Hochstet in Germany. August the 2d 1704* (London: Printed for Robert Battersby, 1704);

The queen: a pindarick ode (London: Printed for Nicholas Cox, 1705);

Love and liberty. A tragedy. As it is to be acted at the Theatre Royal in Drury-lane (London: B. Lintot, 1709);

The force of friendship. A tragedy. As it is acted at the Queen's Theatre in the Hay-market. By Her Majesty's servants. To which is added a farce call'd Love in a chest (London: E. Sanger, 1710);

The generous husband: or, The Coffee House politician. A comedy. As it is acted at the Theatre-royal in Drury Lane. By Her Majesty's Servants (London: Printed for Bernard Lintott & Egbert Sanger, 1711);

The wife's relief: or, The husband's cure. A comedy. As it is acted at the Theatre-Royal in Drury-lane, by Her Majesty's Servants (London: J. Tonson, 1712);

The successful pyrate. A play. As it is acted at the Theatre-Royal in Drury-Lane (London: Printed for B. Lintott, 1713);

The victim. A tragedy. As it is acted at the Theatre Royal in Drury-Lane. By Her Majesty's servants (London: Printed & sold by Ferd. Burleigh, 1714);

The country lasses: or, The custom of the manor. As it is acted at the Theatre-Royal in Drury-lane, by His Majesty's Servants (London: Printed for J. Tonson, 1715);

The cobler of Preston. As it is acted at the Theatre-Royal in Drury-lane (London: Printed by W. Wilkins & sold by W. Hinchcliffe, 1716); modern edition, edited by Leo Hughes and A. H. Scouten, in *Ten English Farces* (Austin: University of Texas Press, 1948);

The sultaness. A tragedy. As it is acted at the Theatre-Royal in Drury-Lane (London: Printed by W. Wilkins for J. Brown, 1717);

The masquerade. A comedy. As it is acted at the Theatre-Royal in Drury-Lane, by His Majesty's Servants (London: B. Lintott, 1719);

Love in a forest. A comedy. As it is acted at the Theatre Royal in Drury-lane, by His Majesty's Servants (London: W. Chetwood, 1723; reprinted, London: Cornmarket Press, 1969);

The female fortune-teller. a comedy. As it is acted at the theatre in Lincoln's-Inn Fields (London: Printed by W. Wilkins & sold by J. Peele & N. Blandford, 1726);

The village opera. As it is acted at the Theatre-Royal, by His Majesty's servants (London: Printed for J. Watts, 1729);

The tragedy of Medæa. As it is acted at the Theatre-Royal in Drury-Lane. With a preface, containing some reflections on the new way of criticism (London: R. Francklin, 1731);

L'étourdi; ou, Les contre-tems, comedie. Par Monsieur de Moliere. The Blunderer: or, The counter-plots. A Comedy. From the French of Moliere, translated by Johnson (London: Printed for J. Watts, 1732);

Cælia: or, The perjur'd lover. A play. As it is acted at the Theatre-Royal in Drury-Lane (London: J. Watts, 1733).

Rightly characterized by Allardyce Nicoll as "one of the most prolific and diversified playwrights of the time," Charles Johnson is the most singularly neglected playwright of the first half of the eighteenth century. Two of his plays were repertory standards throughout the century, and his extensive oeuvre spanned more than two decades; such evidence certainly lends credence to the claim that he deserves to be included in the category of major playwrights of his era, along with George Farquhar, Joseph Addison, Richard Steele, and John Gay. And just as the dramatic career of Thomas Shadwell may be seen as a microcosm of London dramatic tastes and fashions for more than two decades during the late seventeenth century, so may we view Charles Johnson's from 1710 through to the early 1730s. Author of seventeen plays, sixteen of them produced, Johnson had an uncanny sense of what was au courant: his dramatic interests included the pirate story, the ballad opera, and the domestic tragedy, in addition to intrigue and humours comedies, and heroic tragedies. This essay must suffice, then, as a highly selective survey, but

perhaps it will make clear the pleasures and possibilities awaiting future students of Johnson's canon.

Very little is known of Johnson's life. Born in 1679, he entered the Middle Temple in 1701 and trained for the law but was never admitted to the bar. A friend of Robert Wilks, comanager of Drury Lane, and well known for his corpulence, Johnson is immortalized in Pope's *Dunciad*. He wrote for the stage from 1710 until 1732 when the failure of his tragedy *Cælia* led him to retire from authorship. The *Dictionary of National Biography* reports that "after 1733 he is said to have married a young widow with a fortune, and to have set up a tavern in Bow Street, Covent Garden. He quitted business at his wife's death and lived privately upon his savings, which appear to have been considerable, until his death on 11 March 1748."

Johnson's first play was the unacted *Love and Liberty* (published 8 December 1709), though two earlier plays–*The Gentleman-Cully* (1701) and *Fortune in her Wits* (1705)–are often inaccurately ascribed to him. Maurice M. Shudofsky has shown that no evidence exists to suggest that the first is his; the second is an anonymous translation of Abraham Cowley's Latin comedy *Naufragium Joculare*, and attribution to Johnson is without foundation. *Love and Liberty* is a heroic tragedy based on John Fletcher's *The Double Marriage* (circa 1621), and as Johnson later asserted in his prologue to *The Force of Friendship*, the "domestic" drift in the tragedy owes much to the influence of Thomas Otway.

The first produced play of his career, then, was *The Force of Friendship*, which appeared at the Queen's Theatre on 20 April 1710. According to Edward Niles Hooker, this play was originally a tragicomedy, licensed by Charles Killigrew, Master of the Revels, as *The Force of Love* (though the manuscript prompt copy of the tragicomedy, now at the Folger Shakespeare Library, is titled *The Force of Friendship*). After the 20 April performance, because of pressure from the wits of the pit (that is, literary critics who felt the play violated the rules of decorum in mixing comedy and tragedy) the comic scenes were removed from the play and joined together as *Love in a Chest*, produced with *The Force of Friendship*–now a tragedy–on 1 May 1710. It is not known if Johnson himself was responsible for splitting this tragicomedy into a tragedy and a farce. "Whoever was responsible for the operation," Hooker asserts, "*Love in a Chest* was not originally written as

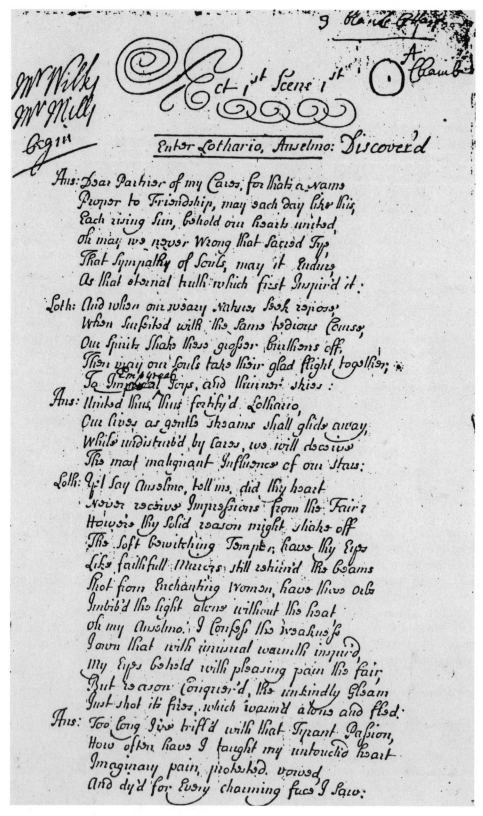

Page from the promptbook used at the first production of Johnson's The Force of Friendship *(by permission of the Folger Shakespeare Library)*

a separate play, and it should not be so listed in a bibliography of Johnson," a dictum ignored by all standard sources. The dedication and preface to *The Force of Friendship* contain important theoretical statements, which reveal Johnson's view that "Tragedy [has] degenerated into Farce" and that "those Gentlemen who have the Management of the Theatres shou'd agree to banish every thing that cou'd be thought the least below the Dignity of the Stage."

Beginning in 1711, through 1719, Johnson produced about a play a year for the Theatre Royal in Drury Lane, entirely through the interests of his important friend actor-manager Robert Wilks. Theatrical historian Benjamin Victor comments that Johnson "was very fortunate in the friendship of Mr. *Wilks*," and Johnson thanked and praised Wilks lavishly in several prefaces. But not so clear are the reactions of the other members of the "Triumvirate" management during this period, Colley Cibber and Thomas Doggett. Helene Koon states that "neither Cibber nor Doggett had much regard" for Johnson's plays, and although this may well have been the case, no citation is offered in support of the assertion, and this writer found no concrete evidence along these lines. What is assuredly true is that Johnson was prolific during the second decade of the eighteenth century. His next play appeared on 20 January 1711.

The Generous Husband, a witty comedy which lasted but three nights (in other words, long enough to secure the author's benefit performance), aroused some controversy during its brief run. As Mary Dias has shown, Johnson satirized noted contemporary critic and playwright John Dennis in the character of Dypthong, a hater of puns and exclaimer of profane oaths, two of Dennis's most recognizable traits. Dennis later attempted to achieve revenge by protesting to the Master of the Revels against Johnson's *The Successful Pyrate* in a letter not republished since the 1721 edition of *Original Letters.*

With his fourth play, *The Wife's Relief* (12 November 1711), Johnson achieved his first major success. This popular comedy was an instant hit the first season, seeing eight performances and two benefits, and went on to play more than forty more times during the next seventy years. This play has received almost no critical attention, however, despite its undeniable success.

The Wife's Relief relies upon three related plots to achieve appeal. The first–and major thread–involves Riot and his wife, Cynthia: he is

tired of her and lusts for his ward and house-guest, Arabella. Cynthia, for reasons not at all clear, has acquiesced to the intentions of her lecherous husband, who has had many sexual conquests. When he casts eyes on Arabella, however, the ladies devise a plan which leads Riot to believe that he has been cuckolded himself, by his best friend, Volatil. In the conclusion Riot sees the errors of his ways and agrees to cease chasing women, hence the play's title.

The other threads are less thematically complex but do portray some entertaining moments. Young Bob Cash, a would-be gentleman, has been set up with an "education" of whoring, drinking, and gambling by his uncle, Sir Tristrum, who believes that money can buy anyone and anything. When matters of honor arise, Bob is amusingly revealed as a coward. Sir Tristrum also ties into the third plot, wherein two friends, Valentine and Horatio, fight with swords, with Horatio believing wrongly that he has killed Valentine. In order to force a marriage between his ward, Teraminta, and Horatio, Sir Tristrum perpetuates the error. The blackmail fails; Valentine appears; and Horatio proceeds to take revenge on Sir Tristrum, a tactic resulting in Sir Tristrum's agreeing to release Teraminta's fortune to her own control.

The play plainly attempts to present everyday ethical problems and answers to the same audience of aspiring but uncultivated cits to whom Addison and Steele directed their lessons in *The Spectator.* Johnson chose to delineate the grounds for proper moral conduct by relying upon the stock convention of the reformed rake, recognizable from Shadwell's *Squire of Alsatia* (1688), Cibber's *Love's Last Shift* (1696), and even Farquhar's *Beaux' Stratagem* (1707), to name only a few of many possible examples. Despite the comment by Pope's friend Henry Cromwell that the play was a "poor Comedy," Johnson made about three hundred pounds from his benefits. Not until four years later, with *The Country Lasses,* would he again achieve such popularity.

Not as successful were his next two plays, *The Successful Pyrate* (7 November 1712) and *The Victim* (5 January 1714). The first, we learn from the prefatory material, was badly received (though it did manage six nights), owing to the audience's belief that Johnson was unduly critical of the legal profession: Johnson rightly pleads that criticism of lawyers was a routine theme of many London comedies and reminds the reader that he respects "the Honourable Profession of the

Robert Wilks, who created the parts of Lothario in The Force of Friendship, *Volatil in* The Wife's Relief, *Aranes in* The Successful Pyrate, *Agamemnon in* The Victim, *Modely in* The Country Lasses, *Sir George Jealous in* The Masquerade, *Orlando in* Love in a Forest, *and Jason in* Medæa *(engraving by I. Faber, based on a portrait by I. Ellys)*

Law; in which I was educated." His appeals apparently went unheeded; the play dropped from sight. A reworking of Carlell's *Arviragus and Philicia* (1635-1636), this presentation of a pirate captain as a tragic hero provoked John Dennis to complain to the Master of the Revels that the play violated all taste in tragedy (slight revenge, no doubt, for Johnson's satire of Dennis in *The Generous Husband*).

Of additional significance is the performance of *The Successful Pyrate* on 16 December, long thought to have been the *fifth* and final appearance of the play. Scholars have failed to take into account that the sixteenth was also Johnson's second benefit night, an arrangement normally

made only for the sixth night. Hence 16 December must have been the sixth, not the fifth, performance. The explanation concerns the brief lacunae in *The London Stage* for 8 and 9 December 1712. The lack of data derives from the cessation of advertising by Drury Lane in *The Spectator*, which ceased publication on 6 December 1712. The theater managers did not begin to advertise in the *Daily Courant* until 10 December, leaving performances on Monday and Tuesday, 8 and 9 December, unrecorded. One of these nights, then, must have featured the fifth performance of Johnson's *The Successful Pyrate* in order for 16 December to have been the sixth staging and his second benefit night.

THE PREFACE.

I At first design'd this Play shou'd have Visited the World without a Godfather, or a Guardian, an Epistle Dedicatory, or a Preface: Not that I Presum'd it did not want both, but I was willing to make a Sacrifice of it to my Good Friends the Critics, as the Indians give one Child in three to the Devil, to save the rest. But an unreasonable Aspersion has been rais'd by some, as if I design'd in the following Scenes to ill Treat, and throw Scandal on the Honourable Profession of the Law; in which I was Educated, and for which I shall always have a dutiful Regard. If those Gentlemen give themselves the Trouble to read the Play, and consider the Characters, and the Place, they will find a wide Difference between the Lawyers at Westminster-Hall, and those toss'd over the Bar, and transported for common Barretry. Pettyfoggers have been always the common Whipstocks of the Drama, and I thought I might innocently enough come in for one Lash in Madagascar. A Foolish Judge is a Foil to a Wise one, and a good Lawyer is distinguish'd by those beneath him in Parts or Probity. As for the Play, I can't without Ingratitude confess; I had Justice done me in the Action; indeed I think those Gentlemen, who are honour'd with their Names in the Royal Licence,

The PREFACE.

cence, behave themselves worthy the Favour they Receive; They have at great Expence given the English Stage a Propriety and Elegance it never knew before, and added to the Beauties of the Poet the just Decorations of the Scene; in order to this they have within themselves Incourag'd the Diligent, and Discountenanc'd the Idle; They have indeavour'd, by the best Copies from the best Authors, to revive in us a Taste for Tragedy; but I doubt we are not reform'd enough, nor they rich enough, yet to purchase it. As to the Incouragement they give those Gentlemen who write, I am an Instance, No body who has the least Claim to Merit can want it; but this City abounds with Dramatic Authors: Were you, my Benevolent Reader, to behold what Reams of Paper are yearly scrawl'd within this Witty Metropolis, in order to produce Scenical Monsters, you wou'd think the whole Town were turn'd Playwrights,

—— Populus calet uno
Scribendi Studio——

'Tis strange! No Body presumes to Curl Wigs, Cut Shoes, or Shape a Coat, but those honest Creatures who are bred to it,

Scribimus indocti doctique Poëmata passim.

Well, 'tis the Vice of the Age; Children write Satyr while the Mothers Milk is on their Lips, and the Citizens ere long must oblige their Apprentices from Playmaking, as well as Gaming, within their Indentures. These must be deny'd the Liberty of abusing the Stage; and none so Angry, none so Noisy, as Children and Fools when they are refus'd doing them-

The PREFACE.

themselves a Mischief; no Wonder then if he who hath the Regulation of the Stage in this Affair does not want Enemies. No Body who has not immediate Opportunity to know it, will imagine the Oeconomy that is requisite in the Management of a Theatre: This Mr. Wilks gives both Life and Being to, and adds to the best Capacity an Unweary'd Application to his Business. But not to detain you any longer, Reader, Now I have had a Word or two with you at the Door, I must desire you to look in, and view the Building; 'tis not design'd from a perfect Model, nor intended to give Pleasure or Pain to any but those who are willing to receive it.

PRO-

Preface to The Successful Pyrate, *from the 1713 edition*

The Victim is an adaptation of Jean Racine's *Iphigénie* (1674), and despite the superb acting efforts of Robert Wilks and Barton Booth, the tragedy could manage only six performances, enough for what must have been two benefits, though only one (11 January 1714) is confirmed by newspaper notices.

On 4 February 1715 appeared Johnson's best-known and most-enduring play, *The Country Lasses*. This comedy held the stage for nearly a century, enjoying well over one hundred performances and spawning at least two adaptations (*The Lady of the Manor* [1778] and *The Farm House* [1789]). Shudofsky, the principal (indeed, almost the only) Johnson scholar, in his useful analysis of this play (though somewhat hampered by his insistence upon the "rise of sentimentalism" in comedy), makes clear that the success apparently stems from the depiction of the country as the seat of virtue: two cit rakes are reformed as a result of meeting virtuous country maids. This plot, of course, reminds one immediately of Farquhar's *The Beaux' Stratagem*.

In the heat of the theatrical competition with Lincoln's Inn Fields, the company at Drury Lane often butted head-on with their rivals. An excellent case in point is Johnson's *The Cobler of Preston* (3 February 1716), an afterpiece inspired by and based loosely upon the preface to Shakespeare's *The Taming of the Shrew*. Both theaters mounted plays of the identical title within a few days of each other. As far as accounts reveal, Johnson's play was in rehearsal when Christopher Bullock, the actor-manager-playwright at Lincoln's Inn Fields, decided to try his own hand at the farce. The Bullock version was the first to appear and no doubt contributed to the shortened run of his competitor's play. As Leo Hughes and A. H. Scouten have shown, Johnson's play contains "numerous references to the stirring political events of the day," the most important being the recent Jacobite invasion. The farce ran for thirteen nights and never again achieved success.

Ironically, one of Johnson's least known plays, *The Sultaness,* earned him his dubious position of fame in Pope's *Dunciad.* In the prologue to *The Sultaness,* a translation of Racine's *Bajazet* (1672) which premiered on 25 February 1717, Johnson took a poke at *Three Hours After Marriage* (1717), a farce by Pope, John Gay, and John Arbuthnot. In retaliation Pope attacks Johnson for his ongoing and tasteless remaking of old plays into new in the 1727 *Dunciad.* Details of this controversy have been usefully summarized by Shudofsky, who further notes that in "A Fragment of a Satire," in lines which ultimately found their final place in the *Epistle to Dr. Arbuthnot* (1734), Pope says of "Johnson, now to sense, now nonsense leaning/Means not but blunders round about a meaning." Once annoyed, Pope seldom forgot a grudge.

Johnson once again garnered considerable attention and financial success with *The Masquerade,* his penultimate commercial success. This adaptation of Molière's *Dom Garcie* (1661) and James Shirley's *The Lady of Pleasure* (1635) opened on 16 January 1719, ran for seven nights, and gained Johnson two author's benefits and considerable notoriety. Along with three other hits of the year, Edward Young's *Busiris,* Thomas Killigrew's *Chit-Chat,* and George Sewell's *Sir Walter Raleigh, The Masquerade* was featured in numerous public accounts, including a popular pamphlet.

Not until four years later did Johnson have another play staged, this time a piece based on Shakespeare's *As You Like It. Love in a Forest* premiered on 9 January 1723 at Drury Lane, and the *London Post* for 14 January 1723 reports that on Johnson's first benefit night (11 January 1723), "there was as numerous an Audience as has for this great while been seen." While the newspaper does not report the fact, the explanation for the excellent turnout probably derives from Johnson's membership in the Order of Masons, to which he dedicated the play. A few nights later, on 15 January, Johnson enjoyed his second and last benefit for this play. Long criticized by commentators as yet another inferior adaptation of Shakespeare, the play has recently been extensively analyzed by Edith Holding, who finds Johnson's version "ingenious; even innovatory," although Holding adheres to the now exploded notion of the contaminating rise and influence of "sentimental" comedy during the eighteenth century.

For reasons that are at present unknown, Johnson's next play, *The Female Fortune-Teller,* premiered at the Theatre Royal in Lincoln's Inn Fields rather than Drury Lane on 7 January 1726. Again achieving a solid if unspectacular seven nights, the play garnered Johnson two benefit performances. Due to the preservation of the Lincoln's Inn Fields account books for that season, we know the proceeds of every performance in the run, including the benefit nights, which allows an accurate analysis of Johnson's popularity

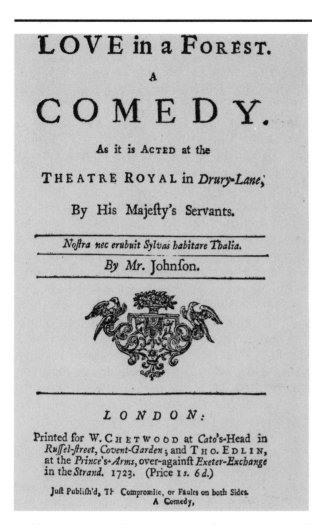

Title page and cast list for the first performance, from the first edition of the play Johnson adapted from William Shakespeare's As You Like It

as realized in ticket sales. Taking his benefit nights as the best examples, we find that on 11 January the house took in £137.8.6, out of which Johnson paid about £40 in house charges, thus netting around £100. On his second night (13 January) he was far from successful; the total was only £38.3, meaning that Johnson made nothing.

Three years later Johnson's *The Village Opera* was staged at Drury Lane. Opening on 6 February 1729, the play encountered severe problems from the outset. *Applebee's* for 15 February 1729 reports that this ballad opera "was perform'd ... with such Hissing and Clapping that the like was never known," and the *Daily Post* of 8 February 1729 reports of the second night's presentation (7 February 1729) that "some Persons in the gallery were so clamorous, that the Play could not go on, but a Constable ... prevail'd on them to walk out." We should not be surprised to learn that under such conditions the

play sank after the third night, although no fewer than three alterations appeared in subsequent seasons, including Isaac Bickerstaffe's *Love in a Village* (1762). The opera is well analyzed by Edmond Gagey, who finds the play "the first and best example" of the village or country opera and second only to *The Beggar's Opera* among all ballad operas. Gagey notes Johnson's sources as Florent Dancourt's *Le Galant jourdinier* (1705) and Alain-René Lesage's *Crispin rival de son maître* (1707).

Johnson's reputation was clearly on the wane following the debacle of *The Village Opera*. With his longtime patron and friend Robert Wilks withdrawing more and more from the day-to-day management of Drury Lane, and with the furor of theatrical activity initiated by the enormous success of Gay's *The Beggar's Opera* (1728), determining the opening of new theaters and the sudden demand for original plays, Johnson was out of step for the most part with the new generation. His translation of Euripides' *Medæa* managed only three nights after its premiere on 11 December 1730. And his feeble ballad opera *The Ephesian Matron* (17 April 1732) faded quickly after the benefit performance on 29 May 1732. This musical may be based on Louis Fuzélier's *La Matron d'Ephese*, but we cannot verify the connection because *The Ephesian Matron* was never published.

On 11 December 1732 Johnson's dramatic career came to an end with the single performance of his tragedy *Cælia*. This play undeservedly failed, as has been noted by many commentators. Following George Lillo's enormously successful *The London Merchant* (1731), *Cælia* is a bourgeois tragedy which explores the plight of the wronged female lover, which, as Shudofsky notes, is one of Johnson's favorite themes, occurring in at least six of his plays. The play features the distresses of a kept mistress; the depiction and circumstances offended the audience. In his advertisement to the printed play, Johnson defends himself, arguing that his tragedy is an exposé of vicious libertinism and thus deserves serious attention. His protests went unheeded, and despite the popularity of other plays which openly presented immoral activity, such as Henry Fielding's *The Modern Husband* had done earlier in 1732 (and Fielding wrote the epilogue for *Cælia*), the play failed. Nicoll and others among modern critics have praised this play, and many obvious parallels with Samuel Richardson's *Clarissa* (1747-1748) have been outlined by Shudofsky, who calls *Cælia* "Johnson's most successful character." After the failure of *Cælia* Johnson retired from theatrical life.

References:

R. C. Boys, "Rural setting in the drama: an early example," *Notes and Queries,* 170 (21 March 1936): 207;

Mary Dias, "A Satire on John Dennis, 1711," *Review of English Studies,* 19 (April 1943): 213-214;

Edmond M. Gagey, *Ballad Opera* (New York: Columbia University Press, 1937);

Edith Holding, "*As You Like It* Adapted: Charles Johnson's *Love in a Forest,*" *Shakespeare Survey,* 32 (1979): 37-48;

E. N. Hooker, "Charles Johnson's *The Force of Friendship* and *Love in a Chest:* A Note on Tragi-comedy and Licensing in 1710," *Studies in Philology,* 34 (July 1937): 407-411;

Leo Hughes and Arthur H. Scouten, Introduction to *The Cobler of Preston* in *Ten English Farces,* edited by Hughes and Scouten (Austin: University of Texas Press, 1948), pp. 145-150;

Helene Koon, *Colley Cibber: A Biography* (Lexington: University of Kentucky Press, 1986);

Allardyce Nicoll, *A History of Early Eighteenth Century Drama* (Cambridge: Cambridge University Press, 1952);

Alexander Pope, *The Correspondence of Alexander Pope,* edited by George Sherburn, volume 1 (Oxford: Clarendon Press, 1956), p. 136;

Maurice M. Shudofsky, "Charles Johnson and Eighteenth Century Drama," *ELH,* 10 (June 1943): 131-158;

Shudofsky, "A Dunce Objects to Pope's Dictatorship," *Huntington Library Quarterly,* 14 (February 1951): 203-207.

Papers:

A manuscript prompt copy of the original version of *The Force of Friendship* is at the Folger Shakespeare Library.

George Lillo

(3 February 1691-3 September 1739)

William J. Burling
Auburn University

PLAY PRODUCTIONS: *Silvia; or, The Country Burial*, London, Theatre Royal, Lincoln's Inn Fields, 10 November 1730;

The London Merchant (also known as *George Barnwell*), London, Theatre Royal in Drury Lane, 22 June 1731;

The Christian Hero, London, Theatre Royal in Drury Lane, 13 January 1735;

Fatal Curiosity, London, Little Theatre in the Hay-Market, 27 May 1736;

Marina, adapted from William Shakespeare's *Pericles*, London, Theatre Royal in Covent Garden, 1 August 1738;

Elmerick, London, Theatre Royal in Drury Lane, 23 February 1740;

Arden of Feversham, adaptation by Lillo, completed by John Hoadly, from an anonymous play of 1591, London, Theatre Royal in Drury Lane, 12 July 1759.

BOOKS: *Silvia; or, The country burial. An opera. As it is performed at the Theatre-Royal in Lincoln's-Inn Fields* (London: J. Watts, 1731);

The London merchant; or, The history of George Barnwell. As it is acted at the Theatre-Royal in Drury Lane. By His Majesty's Servants (London: Printed for J. Gray & sold by J. Roberts, 1731); modern edition, edited, with an introduction, by William H. McBurney (Lincoln: University of Nebraska Press, 1965);

The Christian hero: a tragedy. As it is acted at the Theatre Royal in Drury-Lane (London: J. Gray, 1735);

Fatal curiosity: a true tragedy of three acts. As it is acted at the New theatre in the Haymarket (London: Printed for John Gray, 1737); modern edition, edited, with an introduction, by McBurney (Lincoln: University of Nebraska Press, 1966);

Marina: a play of three acts. As it is acted at the Theatre Royal in Convent [sic] Garden. Taken from Pericles prince of Tyre (London: J. Gray, 1738);

Elmerick, or, Justice Triumphant, a tragedy, as it is acted at the Theatre Royal in Drury-lane (London: J. Gray, 1740);

Britannia and Batavia: a masque. Written on the marriage of the Princess royal with His Highness the Prince of Orange (London: Printed for J. Gray, 1740);

Arden of Feversham. An historical tragedy: taken from Hollingshead's chronicle, in the reign of King Edward VI. Acted at the Theatre-Royal, in Drury-lane (London: Printed for T. Davies, 1762).

Collections: *The Works of Mr. George Lillo; With Some Account of His Life*, 2 volumes, edited, with an account of the author's life, by Thomas Davies (London: Printed for T. Davies, 1775);

Lillo's Dramatic Works with Memoirs of the Author, by Thomas Davies, 2 volumes (London: W. Lowndes, 1810);

The Plays of George Lillo, edited, with an introduction, by Trudy Drucker, 2 volumes (New York & London: Garland, 1979).

In the course of his short but imaginative dramatic career George Lillo created two of the most important tragedies of the eighteenth century. In fact, his *London Merchant* is widely cited as the first modern tragedy, mainly because of Lillo's attention to the "domestic" issues confronting the common man, rather than to the more commonly portrayed affairs and crises of state and honor facing the aristocracy. And although Lillo's name is never mentioned in the company of the greatest of British playwrights, as Isaac Reed states the matter, "Mr. Lillo is far from standing in the lowest rank of merit . . . among our dramatic writers."

Details concerning Lillo's life are limited. Nothing is known of his childhood, schooling, or mature years, even after his success in the theater. A jeweller by trade, Lillo left the world as quietly as had entered it. No correspondence or manuscripts in Lillo's hand are known to exist.

Lillo wrote during the most important decade of eighteenth-century drama–the 1730s. The appearance of *The Beggar's Opera* in January 1728 ushered in unprecedented public interest in theater, an interest that led to a veritable explosion of new theaters and dramatic experimentation. The fast trolley ride came to a sudden halt in June of 1737, however, with the passage of the so-called Licensing Act, a measure that effectively curtailed the theatrical community, reducing it once again to the monopolies at Covent Garden and Drury Lane. The excitement of this decade is exhilarating to contemplate: new theaters springing up, increased production possibilities for aspiring playwrights, new directions in form and content. Lillo, as did his contemporary and eventual friend Henry Fielding to an even greater extent, took advantage of this boom period immediately, and he began as many authors were to do by composing a ballad opera.

Silvia; or, The Country Burial premiered at Lincoln's Inn Fields on 10 November 1730, running for three nights, the last being an author's benefit. The play was the victim of circumstances now impossible to reconstruct. For reasons that we may never know, on the first night the *Daily Courant* (12 November 1730) tells us that "there appeared a Set of People, who seem'd inclined to damn the whole Performance (if it had been in their Power) by their continual Hissing and Cat-Calls; notwithstanding which, the same was perform'd with Applause, by the general Approbation of the Pit and Boxes." And we know from the ledger books of the theater that the play brought in quite respectable sums at the box office: 10 November, £91.9.6; 11 November, £63.4; 12 November (author's benefit night), £100.1. The generally positive audience response and the receipts indicate a healthy opening run that by all rights should have convinced manager John Rich to let the musical continue. But he cut the play off after the third night. We know from a note on the last page of the published play that the opera appeared "in rehearsal too long for one night's entertainment" and was duly shortened to be a manageable length. Even shortened, however, it was apparently too long to make room for the popular afterpiece *The Rape of Proserpine* on the evening's bill; during the fall of 1730 Rich frequently bolstered his mainpieces with such afterpieces. Lillo's play later was reduced to two acts in 1736 (Theatre Royal in Covent Garden, 18 March), so further cuts were possible. Why Rich gave up on this play is a mystery. We

do know from various contemporary and critical responses, however, that the answer does not lie in the play's content.

Thomas Davies, editor of the first collected edition of Lillo's works (1775), states his opinion of the play's merits bluntly: *Silvia* "is one of the best dramatick pieces which had then appeared." He backs up his remark with reasons well worth quoting, as modern critics tend not to see the play in the same terms: the opera "has invention in its fable, simplicity in its manners, gaiety in its incidents, and variety as well as truth of character; but what still more recommends it to the judicious, this . . . Opera was written with a view to inculcate the love of truth and virtue, and a hatred of vice and falsehood." Davies's remarks fall into two groups. First and perhaps most surprising is his assessment that Lillo's play was quite entertaining, even delightful. The dialogue and airs (all sixty-three of them) moved the plot along briskly and provided considerable amusement scene by scene. The main characters of Sir John, Welford, and Silvia are consistent and appealing and were played by (respectively) Thomas Walker, Charles Hulett, and Mrs. Cantrel, all established and talented performers: Walker starred as Macheath in *The Beggar's Opera*, and the other two were members of the original Little Haymarket troupe that had successfully mounted the musical *Damon and Phillida* in 1729.

Davies's second point, concerning the love of truth and the hatred of falsehood, highlights a component of Lillo's artistry that pervades all of his dramatic works. He is always very much concerned that his plays express and confirm clear and powerful moral or social truths. *Silvia* is not a sermon–the play is far from annoyingly didactic; yet it does succeed in driving home a main premise–that marriage is an important and desirable institution, upon which all of society depends. Expectations of moral soundness, such as Davies's, are no longer a part of the critical process, but contemporary commentators also have shown an interest in the moral component.

In his pioneering study of ballad opera, Edmond M. Gagey writes that the character of Silvia "would make an effective and pathetic heroine were it not for her utter perfection and her smug predilection for moralizing, which leads her into aphorisms and into stilted and unnatural language." Gagey's agenda makes clear that for him, Silvia, in order to be "effective," must be imperfect, hence natural, a clear insistence on his part that eighteenth-century ballad opera must conform to what became twentieth-century dramatic and philosophical sensibilities. Gagey concludes that *Silvia* is "a mediocre but very interesting play"; what can he possibly mean by "interesting" after negating the very premises upon which the play is constructed? Allardyce Nicoll, too, finds that the play "presents a number of decidedly interesting features" but neglects to mention any of them in his analysis. He does hypothesize about the play's lack of initial success, however, suggesting that Lillo unwisely attempted to combine "immoral and sentimental motives."

How can *Silvia* be condemned on the one hand as portraying "immoral" motives (Nicoll) and on the other hand be praised for its inculcation of truth and virtue (Davies)? The answer arises from two sources. Both Gagey and Nicoll, writing in the 1920s and 1930s, inherited the moral aspect of critical disposition so vividly championed by their Victorian and Edwardian mentors; that is, they could not discuss a play without making a comparative moral judgment and then arriving at a final estimation of the play's literary "value" by way of that moral evaluation. Simply put, Davies exhibits characteristic eighteenth-century acceptance of artificiality and extreme moral presentations, which included the portrayal of vice in order to highlight virtue (that is, Sir John's seduction of Lettice in *Silvia*). Gagey and Nicoll were apparently charmed by the play's humor and energy but did not like the direct and unquestionable immorality in the characters of Sir John and Lettice. This is the same kind of moral objection voiced so frequently about *Tom Jones* and nearly all of Smollett's works by the same generation of scholars as Gagey and Nicoll.

The second source, difficult to demonstrate but ultimately more revealing, is that the play, as Davies suggested, is as delightful as it is moral. Most entertaining is the burial of Dorothy Stitch in I.viii and following, from which the play's subtitle is derived. Here Lillo shows consummate craftsmanship, especially in a first play, for comic timing and dialogue. Not a spadeful of dirt has been pitched into the grave before Goody Busy attempts to pair off the now eligible widower, Timothy, with Goody Costive (herself a widow). This suggestion initiates discussion by the village ladies concerning the deceased's character: they begin with the assertion that Dorothy was "a very good woman in the main" and then proceed to annihilate her character, revealing, among other faults, that she scolded, swore, stole, and drank

to excess. The tone is decidedly comic and reveals splendid opportunities for mock irony and stage business. The best joke of all, of course, is that Dorothy is not dead but drunk, awakening from her stupor with hiccups. When Dorothy attempts to convince Timothy that she is no ghost, he remarks, "She was always given to lying—I dare not trust her yet." She then launches into a tirade, calling him "a cowardly, cabbaging rogue. . . . What, are you afraid of your own wife, sirrah?" To this outburst Timothy replies "Nay, now I am sure 'tis my Dolly herself." We see, then, that Lillo has successfully presented his version of the henpecked husband and tyrannical wife in good comic taste. In fact this type of humor in the entire Timothy-Dorothy-Lettice subplot is precisely the kind of action that made the play attractive to Davies and, we presume, to the rest of the audience (Rich's cancellation notwithstanding). Nicoll and Gagey failed to discuss, even to mention, the comic vitality of the play, but Davies was sensitive to Lillo's aim and accomplishments.

Lillo's next effort established his reputation among his contemporaries and for posterity. *The London Merchant*, first produced at the Theatre Royal in Drury Lane on 22 June 1731 by the summer company led by Theophilus Cibber, is widely recognized as among the most innovative tragedies of the century. All critics seem to recognize the power of the play, but many admit to feeling little pleasure in it, and few express any understanding of why the play was so enormously popular (it received more than 250 performances during the eighteenth century).

The plot is taken directly from a popular sixteenth-century ballad that tells the story of George Barnwell, a London apprentice who becomes infatuated with a prostitute. Leaving the path of the good life, the young man steals from his employer, forsakes the love of a virtuous young lady and the friendship of all around him, and ultimately murders his uncle in order to get money for his mistress. In the end he is captured, tried, and presumably hanged, but not before recognizing and repenting the evil of his ways and sincerely wishing that his example might deter other apprentices from similar error.

The plot is straightforward; the characterizations are clearly drawn; the dialogue varies from crisp, unadorned prose to didactic passages verging on blank verse. The tone of the play is essentially unambiguous, leaving no doubt as to who is right and wrong, and why. The question then be-

Plates 2 and 3 from William Hogarth's Industry and Idleness *(1747), inspired in part by* The London Merchant

comes, how can such a sharply delineated drama, verging on simplistic, attain any dramatic interest or power? At least four interpretive possibilities have been suggested.

The most obvious approach arises from the title itself, *The London Merchant* (although in its own day the play was commonly known as *George Barnwell*). The play emphasizes the values of a mercantile society in which hard work, truth, control of passions, love of religion, and thirst for profit abide without contradiction. The Puritan work ethic serves as the foundation for this approach, but the implications extend far beyond the individual to all of society. Evidence for this interpretation can be found in virtually every act. The very opening of the play portrays the delivery of news that London merchants, through Italian financial connections, have delayed the assembly and departure of the Spanish Armada. Such powerful influence was indeed in the hands of the emerging mercantile groups who controlled the flow of capital in Europe, especially funds needed by rulers to finance military expeditions and wars. The old world order in which kings collected taxes based on land and crop values to fight their wars was being replaced by a power structure in which merchants had control of finances and hence a significant voice in national and international affairs. The point made by the play's opening would not be lost on the London audience. Throughout the seventeenth century, symbolically culminating in the establishment of the Bank of England in 1694 to finance the wars of William III, the merchant class of London had been gathering riches from the opening of the trade routes to the Far East and the Americas; with that wealth came power through control of finances. The first thirty years of the eighteenth century saw nothing less than continued phenomenal growth along the same lines. Trade and commerce, to be sure, were two different elements in the complex system of eighteenth-century economics, but the pervading mercantile notion–that the export of goods (the balance of trade) should always be greater than the import levels–linked the many branches of the business community.

Various characters in the play allegorize the components of the mercantile philosophy. Thorowgood, Barnwell's master, represents the pinnacle of the London mercantile mentality and serves as its spokesman most clearly in a conversation with Trueman (the good apprentice) in III.i:

Methinks I would not have you only learn the method of merchandise and practice it hereafter merely as a means of getting wealth. 'Twill be well worth your pains to study it as a science, see how it is founded in reason and the nature of things, how it has promoted humanity as it has opened and yet keeps up an intercourse between nations far remote from one another in situation, customs, and religion; promoting arts, industry, peace, and plenty; by mutual benefits diffusing mutual love from pole to pole.

This mercantile portrait, of a world at once serving and being served by the efforts of merchants, bringing peace and civilization to the savage and remote nations and glory to God, stops short, however, of advocating uncontrolled exploitation. As Thorowgood adds in V.ii, "The love of riches and the lust of power he [a "true" merchant] looks on with contempt and detestation, who only counts for wealth the souls he wins and whose ambition is to serve mankind." Moreover, the hard work involved to create this harmonious, sublunary state of affairs is medicine for the soul. As Trueman reminds Barnwell in II.iv, before things have gone too far, "business requires our attendance–business, the youth's best preservative from ill, as idleness his worst of snares." As historian Jeremy Rifkin, among many others, has rightly noticed, this belief that work combats evil can be traced in economic history to the central rule of the sixth-century monk Saint Benedict: "Idleness is the enemy of the soul" (a statement derived, perhaps from Hesiod or Virgil). And it is no coincidence that the Benedictine order was the first group in Europe to emphasize the value of time and of scheduling in order to glorify God in the most efficient and continuous manner–patterns of conduct eminently suited to and adapted by mercantile interests and fostered by the Anglican clergy. Hence profit immediately arose from work (trade) which glorified God.

Lillo was scarcely alone in this view. Virtually every literary figure of the early eighteenth century who wrote on the subject of the influence of trade and commerce on the world agreed on basics with him. Defoe, Addison, Steele, Pope, and Fielding all advocated the civilizing and pacifying of the world through the mercantile philosophy. For examples one need only consult works as diverse as *The Spectator* (1711-1712), *Robinson Crusoe* (1719), and *Windsor Forest* (1713). So when Thorowgood expostulates on the methods and benefits of mercantile attitudes and practices, as in the following lines, he spoke to the heart of an audience receptive to his pronouncements: "On every climate and on every country Heaven has bestowed some good peculiar to itself. It is the industrious merchant's business to collect the various blessings of each soil and climate and, with the product of the whole, to enrich his native country" (III.i). Such points of view served as the rationale, in fact, for most of European imperialistic expansion.

Prosperous, good-hearted, and devout, Thorowgood attempts to save his wayward apprentice from certain doom, but Barnwell's choices have taken him too far for even the best of masters to save. Others try as well, characters who also figure prominently in this mercantile mystery play. Trueman, for example, stands out boldly as the "good" apprentice, the one who follows the system and honors its values. He is the Will Goodfellow of William Hogarth's fascinating engravings entitled *Industry and Idleness* (1747), a series partly inspired by *The London Merchant*. Trueman, like Goodfellow, learns the system from the bottom up, slowly gains the trust of his master, perhaps marries the master's daughter–ironically, as Barnwell could have done–and aspires to becoming a magistrate and then lord mayor of London. As Hogarth maps out this path, one need only stick to the job and success would follow. So, it would seem, is the drift of Trueman's character, for which his name is but the least evidence of his function.

Barnwell himself, of course, is the key figure in the allegory. He is the horrific representative of the evils awaiting young apprentices who drift from their duty. He states directly in IV. xiii:

> Be warn'd ye youths, who see my sad despair,
> Avoid lewd women, false as they are fair;
> By reason guided, honest joys pursue;
> The fair, to honor and to virtue true,
> Just to herself, will ne'er be false to you.
> By my example learn to shun my fate;
> (How wretched is the man who's wise too late!)
> Ere innocence and fame and life be lost,
> Here purchase wisdom cheaply, at my cost.

But the lesson is not merely that one should "avoid lewd women." Implicit is a support of the entire mercantile system, though the actual mention of mercantile matters is broached only in Thorowgood's mention of "the love of riches and the lust of power," a corruption of the proper desire for gain. Barnwell restates his function as

example in V.x, which is then reemphasized in the play's concluding lines by Trueman–again, the "good" apprentice: "In vain / With bleeding hearts and weeping eyes we show / A human gen'rous sense of others' woes / Unless we mark what drew their ruin on, / And, by avoiding that, / prevent our own."

The mercantile interpretation of the play gains considerable support from the fact that the play was supported often and enthusiastically by the London mercantile community, who bought blocks of tickets throughout the eighteenth century. As William H. McBurney notes, Lillo's play became standard fare at traditional holidays for apprentices, Christmas, Easter, and the Lord Mayor's Day, until near the end of the second decade of the nineteenth century. Theophilus Cibber records in his *Lives of the Poets* (1753) that it was "judged a proper entertainment for the apprentices, &c. as being a more instructive, moral, and cautionary drama, than many pieces that had usually been exhibited on those days with little but farce and ribaldry to recommend them." And many nonholiday performances were advertised as "At the particular request of . . . Eminent Merchants." But the play can be interpreted in other ways that do not necessarily exclude the mercantile reading.

A second approach to the play emphasizes the importance of the emerging Masonic movement. Advocated in recent years by Harry W. Pedicord (1974), this interpretation is actually closely related to the mercantile analysis. By highlighting certain key passages which necessarily stress the altruistic motives behind the mercantile philosophy, that is, serving mankind, or preserving "one soul from wandering," as Thorowgood says to Barnwell in V.ii, Pedicord argues that these same motives existed at the core of the Masonic world mission as it existed in eighteenth-century London. He strengthens his case by carefully connecting the new Masonic lodges to the theatrical world: Theophilus Cibber, for example, was a Mason, and every person in the cast of the first production save one was connected to the Masonic movement in one way or another.

Pedicord uses his interpretation to offer an explanation for the play's wild and extended popularity. The tragedy's success derived from its devout advocation of Masonic teachings. Hence Pedicord bluntly states that the play "survived on the strength and appeal of its Masonic teachings and the vigorous fraternal support it received for over sixty years." Again, the point is not necessar-

William Brereton as George Barnwell in a 1776 Drury Lane production of The London Merchant

ily what the play stresses but rather how the message is to be interpreted. Interestingly, Pedicord can find no trace of Masonic leanings in *Fatal Curiosity*.

Nearly all commentators have recognized and remarked upon the considerable religious elements in *The London Merchant*. Lillo was known to be a Dissenter, that is, a Calvinist, but is reported by Davies as "not one of that sour cast which distinguishes some of our sectaries." Bearing Lillo's religious alignments in mind, Stephen Trainor, in a series of articles, has elucidated the ways in which the play seems to rely upon the religious values of Calvinism and has stated the case in no uncertain terms:

While Lillo is often justly cited for his innovations in developing a middle class tragedy, it is often overlooked that he also developed a new and distinctly Protestant tragic theory. . . .
. . . the evidence of his plays clearly identif[ies] him as our first major Calvinist playwright.

According to Trainor, Barnwell's experiences in the play conform to the four-part model established in Calvinistic sermons: 1) apprehension of sin; 2) conviction of conscience; 3) despair; and 4) humiliation of heart. As was true of many such sermons, not only *The London Merchant* but all of Lillo's tragedies "become the dramatic analogue of the spiritual autobiography." The audience's role in the drama is "largely passive" as they view the spiritual conversion of the protagonist, but Lillo by no means intended the play to be merely or only an intellectual experience. Lillo's message, Trainor insists when discussing *Fatal Curiosity* (and he implies as much for *The London Merchant*), "does not specifically seek to inspire or deter through didactic persuasion and rational argument. Rather it seeks an affective conversion of the audience." Hence the play is principally an "affective tragedy" that Lillo meant to stimulate the spiritual passions of the audience.

Opposing the Calvinistic line directly is the sentimental interpretation. This view stresses that the relentless moralizing present in the play derives, not from any specific religious inclination, but rather from Lillo's advocacy of the two cardinal features of that curious eighteenth-century philosophical mode we call sentimentalism: tender feelings and moralizing. Ernest Bernbaum first identified the sentimental tendency of eighteenth-century drama in his *The Drama of Sensibility* (1915), a classic work engendering a series of debates over Lillo's plays. Bernbaum stresses that the hallmark feature of sentimental drama is the insistence upon the goodness of human nature. If so, Lillo's tragedies seem problematic members of this dramatic group: his heroes commit heinous acts and descend to the pits of despair. Hence G. B. Rodman and R. D. Havens exchanged essays in 1945 over the play's alleged sentimentalism, with no advance in our understanding. Roberta F. S. Borkat, however, has recently suggested a way of resolving the contradictions. Noting Erik Erämetsä's seminal linguistic study of sentimentalism (1951), Borkat clarifies the tendency toward moralizing by emphasizing that a character's actions are not the same as his intentions. Thus Lillo places "the responsibility for Barnwell's deeds outside the youth's intentions." His goodness actually becomes his downfall when dealing with the treacherous Millwood. And despite the apparent tendency in *The London Merchant* toward predestination (as inherent in the Calvinistic approach), Borkat sees Lillo reconciling free will and predestination by stressing an important split: "free will is responsible for one's *intentions*; fate causes one's *actions*."

In Borkat's view Barnwell emerges a true tragic hero because his intentions never vary: he is always a good-hearted person. Millwood, too, although not in Barnwell's league, is also not responsible for some of her acts. The meeting between Thorowgood and Millwood late in act 4 thus becomes Lillo's explanation for the apparently irredeemable Millwood. We should not despise her; after all, the world made her the way she is. As F. E. De Boer states the matter, "the implication is clear that to some extent her depravity is the fault of society itself."

Lillo's only unproduced play, the masque of *Britannia and Batavia*, written in late 1733 or early 1734 but not published until 1740, is a blend of nationalistic pride and celebration. Written in honor of the marriage of the Princess of Wales to the Prince of Orange on 14 March 1734, the masque presents in three allegorical, "serious interludes": 1) the protection of Batavia from Tyranny (Spain) and Superstition (the Roman Catholic church) by Britannia; 2) the rescue of Britannia by Liberto and Batavia from these same vile forces of Spain and Rome; 3) the marriage of Princess Anne to William, Prince of Orange, another of the important alliances between the Dutch and the British. The masque is thus best thought of as a compression of Anglo-Dutch relations, with the first interlude approximating the endless assistance provided by the English to the Protestant Dutch during their sixteenth- and seventeenth-century religious wars with Catholic Spain (the "wars" so often mentioned in poems by Edmund Spenser, Sir Philip Sidney, Richard Lovelace, and others); while the second interlude— the rescue of England by Batavia—refers generally to the acceptance of the English throne by William III (of Orange) in 1689, with his subsequent military policy, leading to the defeat of the Spanish and French forces by Marlborough during the first decade of the eighteenth century under Queen Anne. These analogies are, of course, quite general.

Turning to Continental history for his next play, Lillo shaped to his own interests the story of George Castriota, also known as Scanderbeg (pronounced Skan-dur-bay). *The Christian Hero* duly opened on 13 January 1735 at the Theatre Royal in Drury Lane and featured William Milward in the title role and the fast-rising James Quin as Amurath, the Turkish leader. Lasting but four nights, the play was ill received, and a comment in *The Prompter* for 18 February provides a hint of explanation: "the Pulpit seems the properest Theatre for such Representations." Knowing Lillo's tendency toward drama that stresses morality, it can hardly be surprising that his script portrays Scanderbeg as relentlessly advocating and practicing Christianity. But why did not the audience relish such a drama so well in

James Quin, who created the parts of Amurath in The Christian Hero *and the title character in* Elmerick, *which premiered several months after Lillo's death. The prologue spoken by Quin at that first performance said of the playwright, "He knew no art, no rule; but warmly thought / From passion's force, and as he felt he wrote."*

keeping with the strictest and highest Christian precepts?

The story of Scanderbeg the man encapsulated the perfect set of circumstances for Lillo's purposes. As a youth Scanderbeg had been sent, along with his brothers, as hostages to the court of Turkish emperor Amurath to ensure the peace treaty arranged between Albania and the Turkish empire. Scanderbeg was raised publicly as a Moslem but privately practiced Christianity. The sultan's favorite, he was given every advantage of education and training. Upon reaching adulthood Scanderbeg returned to his own country after the death of his father, his brothers having been executed by the sultan, and assumed the throne. In so doing he became to Amurath's surprise and chagrin an active and virtually undefeatable adversary of Turkish interests in Albania, winning battle after battle. In short, Scanderbeg's victorious, militant Christianity stood between the Turks and their aspirations for unlimited conquest in eastern Europe. The Turks had been nearly invincible, and as history reveals but for the naval victory at Lepanto in 1571 might well have overrun Italy and then the rest of Europe; therefore Lillo recognized that in Amurath and the Turkish hordes a formidable and unquestionably threatening pagan challenge lay before the Christian nations of Europe.

The play concerns a final confrontation between Christian forces defending Croia, the capital of Albania, and the besieging Turkish armies. Unable to make headway against the Albanians, the Turks have, in fact, suffered numerous costly and embarrassing defeats, causing Amurath to come out of retirement to attend personally to the siege. Frustrated in his every plan, Amurath's ire increases. At last, Mahomet, the emperor's son, captures Aranthes, a loyal follower of Scanderbeg, and his daughter, Althea, Scanderbeg's beloved.

Scanderbeg is summoned to the Turkish camp to hear the predictable demands of Amurath. To the emperor's great surprise and consternation, the three Christians, while suffering greatly at the adverse turn of circumstances, resign themselves to their respective destinies and refuse to accede to the conqueror's demands. The rest of the play concerns the personal crises in the face of seemingly unavoidable executions. But a series of events involving Helena, the sultan's daughter, turns the tide. The Christians enter the Turkish camp, drive off the guards, and free Aranthes and Althea just as the executioners arrive. In the uplifting conclusion Scanderbeg and Althea are pledged to one another and blessed by the stunned but happy Aranthes.

What, then, is this play about? Trudy Drucker, quoting the prologue ("there's not a theme so dear / As virtuous freedom to the British ear"), claims that "the unmistakable theme . . . is political liberty." If the theme is political, then Drucker should be able to deduce the analogues which Lillo intended; but she makes no such attempt, moving on to comparisons with heroic plays of the late seventeenth century, an interesting but unconnected line of inquiry. If *The Christian Hero* is political, then its allusions would have been immediate and obvious to the audience, and the play would have done for its viewers what *Cato* did in 1713–that is, raised issues relevant to contemporary political problems. Was British liberty threatened in 1735? Not in any sense suggested by *The Christian Hero*. The country had been mostly at peace since the treaty of Utrecht in 1713, and although war with Spain and France would erupt in 1739, no unusual immedi-

ate crisis loomed. As for domestic politics, Sir Robert Walpole was, of course, the regular target of criticism for his irregular personal and public activities, but Lillo's play is no *Beggar's Opera*. No figure in *The Christian Hero* corresponds to a corrupt minister misleading a king. The only ongoing domestic crisis in 1735 was the growing rift between the Prince of Wales and his father, George II. But again Lillo's play scarcely seems to be alluding to that affair, regardless of its seriousness.

The play's theme is stated precisely in the quotation cited by Drucker, but she emphasized the wrong word. "Virtuous freedom" refers not to an elaborate portrayal of freedom but to *virtue*, particularly of the Christian variety. The only piece of surviving contemporary criticism suggests that the audience saw the play in religious rather than political terms. William Popple in *The Prompter* for 18 February 1735 states, "And, indeed, the Pulpit seems the properest Theatre for such Representations, and the Clergy, the properest Actors in the Religious Drama." The unmistakable theme, then, is the emphasis upon Christian acceptance of the vagaries of life and of God's will (a theme which Lillo explores in every serious play) with the holding up of an exemplary set of Christian heroes. What Lillo had in mind was not another *Cato* but rather John Hughes's popular *The Siege of Damascus* (1720), a play about the conflict between religious views and the pragmatic decisions faced during times of extreme duress–the very model noted by Davies in his comments on Lillo's play. Apparently, however, the audience agreed with Popple. Lillo had gone too far in his depiction of Christian virtue and glory: Hughes's treatment was entertaining; Lillo's was not.

Despite the continuing fame of *The London Merchant*, Lillo was not able to get his next play, *Fatal Curiosity*, produced at either of the principal patent theaters, no doubt because of the failure of *The Christian Hero*, the change of management at Drury Lane during the spring of 1734, and John Rich's increased conservatism at Covent Garden. But a new venue managed by Henry Fielding offered a place for Lillo's talents. Hence Lillo's newest tragedy premiered at the Little Theatre in the Hay-Market on 27 May 1736 under the title *Guilt Its Own Punishment; or, Fatal Curiosity*. Running a respectable seven nights, including six in a row with two author's benefits, the play gained the approbation of the contemporary audience and went on to become Lillo's second most

Charlotte Cibber Charke, who created the roles of Lucy in The London Merchant *and Agnes in* Fatal Curiosity

successful play, receiving more than forty performances by 1800.

Fatal Curiosity had a second successful run during March and April 1737, again at the Hay-Market theater. Henry Fielding, Davies tells us, personally directed the production, instructing the actors "how to do justice to their parts." Lillo achieved four benefits during the ten performances. The play managed only a handful of performances from 1737 to 1781, at least two of which were benefits for Charlotte Charke, the eccentric and infamous daughter of Colley Cibber, who played the original role of Agnes (she had been Lucy in the original cast of *The London Merchant*). As William H. McBurney makes clear, critic James Harris was "largely responsible" for a revival of interest in the play, which resulted in adaptations by George Colman in 1782 (under the title of *Fatal Curiosity*) and by Henry Mackenzie in 1784 as *The Shipwreck*. Sarah Siddons also took an interest in the tragedy, reviving the play in 1797.

A strikingly simple and straightforward play, *Fatal Curiosity* is based on an early seventeenth-century Cornish murder story. A son re-

turns home after seeking and finding his fortune to discover that his parents have become impoverished. In order to gain the maximum surprise, in disguise he asks to spend the night with them, intending to reveal his identity a bit later. He wishes, in his curiosity, to see how they live and how much they miss him. But the parents' distresses have become so acute that they plot and then carry out the murder of their visitor-son when they learn of his wealth.

The unambiguous title makes clear that the play's central message concerns the nature of morality, particularly the possibilities for redemption even in the face of such atrocities as murder. Stephen Trainor concludes that *Fatal Curiosity* parallels *The London Merchant* on the key point of being based on the four-part, Calvinistic, spiritual conversion process. Although both Barnwell and Old Wilmot are guilty of murder, the motivations for their actions differ; thus the two plays are not simply copies of each other: whereas Barnwell's motivation was lust, Wilmot's was hubris. The play's opening lines, spoken by Old Wilmot, set up the state of mind and the disintegration of spirit which have overcome him: "To think, and to be wretched. What is life / To him that's born to die? Or what the wisdom / Whose perfection ends in knowing we know nothing? / Mere contradictions all! A tragic farce, / Tedious though short, and without art elab'rate, / Ridiculously sad–." Trainor argues that Old Wilmot's soliloquy is specious and blasphemous because it places "complete faith in himself and the worldly wisdom of Seneca" rather than in God's providence. And after being forced to release Randal, the family servant, Wilmot tells him, "Be a knave, and prosper," cynical and unexpected advice from a man who has been a moral exemplar all of his life. Old Wilmot has lost his faith in God, especially the trust necessary to keep faith when the circumstances of life seem hopeless. Man cannot know the full extent of God's plan, Lillo insists; therefore, to question providence is hubris.

Young Wilmot must also share the blame for the disastrous consequences of his actions. Despite his good heart and genuine love for Charlot and his parents, he is unable to resist the sin of pride: he wishes to know what people think of him, how much they love and esteem him. When first meeting Charlot, he does not reveal his identity to her, but rather pretends to be his own shipmate. He tells Charlot a tale that describes Wilmot's supposed death in a tempest, calling out her name as he died. Further, he goes on to relate that Wilmot's ghost roams the earth at night because Charlot has forgotten her vows to him and "had cast him from her thoughts." The faithful girl–to Wilmot's unspeakable satisfaction (later described as "fierce tumultuous joys")–expresses her "eternal love, and never-failing faith." Finally convinced of her fidelity, he reveals his identity, which rightly shocks the distraught Charlot into stunned silence. To this reaction the insensitive Wilmot remarks, "Why art thou silent?"

When he learns from Charlot that both of his parents are still alive but in the distresses of poverty, Wilmot ejaculates, "My joy's complete!" Clearly he is pleased at hearing that they have not died, but the difficulties they endure, which Charlot terms "worse, much worse, than death," do not enter Wilmot's mind at all. He thinks only of his own satisfaction: "My parents living, and possessed of thee!" (II.i). Wilmot simply cannot comprehend the dimensions of his parents' misfortunes, choosing to wallow in his own pleasure. After inviting Charlot to visit him that evening,

he next meets Randal, the discharged family servant, who, after being subjected to the same recognition game, also wishes to insist upon the family's poverty. The returned son, however, simply shrugs off the urgent pleas with "I've heard it all, and hasten to relieve 'em," and then launches into the plan which sets up the gruesome finale. Wilmot asks Randal, "dost thou think, / My parents not suspecting my return, / That I may visit them and not be known?" Randal is unsure, but Wilmot, recalling the complete lack of recognition in Charlot, decides to try the plan because "My mind at ease grows wanton. I would fain / Refine on my happiness." Randal goes along with the plan at first, but when Wilmot remarks, "ev'ry friend / Who witnesses my happiness tonight / Will, by partaking, multiply my joys!" Randal sagely observes, "You grow luxurious in your mental pleasures / . . . To say true, I ever thought / Your boundless curiosity a weakness," but then goes on to assist the deception.

The importance of the meetings between Wilmot and Charlot and then Randal is central to the play's design. Wilmot is curious in the worst possible sense; he is "luxurious," a word denoting wanton indulgence of personal pleasure through pride. In other words Wilmot is consumed with the supposed importance of his own prosperity, survival, and return, imagining that he alone is responsible for his own accomplishments. Thus the contrast between his success and the abysmal conditions of Wilmot's parents is meant to show that no set of conditions–be they highest joy or lowest despondency and distress– should be dwelt upon to excess, for God's plan is never to be known by mortals, regardless of how much evidence we think we have.

The eventual murder scene is the shocking reversal of fortunes and expectations necessary to further impress the providential message on the audience. Young Wilmot, even upon seeing the indigence and misery of his parents, refuses to reveal his identity for fear "I shall / Defeat my purpose and betray myself," that is, rob himself of the pleasure of the surprise recognition planned for later. Despite all of the warnings from Charlot, Randal, and his own observations, Young Wilmot cannot foresee the possibility of foul play in his own home. As for Old Wilmot, he sees the appearance of the rich, young traveler who claims to have been his now deceased son's friend as a "rare example / Of Fortune's caprice, apter to surprise / Or entertain than comfort or instruct." Continuing thus in his blasphemy, he is led into final temptation when the "stranger" asks the old people to guard a casket of valuables for him while he naps.

Agnes, the mother, first considers the idea of murder, out of "dire necessity." When Old Wilmot revolts at the suggestion, she offers the specious argument that because suicide will soon be their only exit from their financial woes, " 'Tis less impiety, less against nature, / To take another's life than to end our own" (III.i). After only a brief objection, Old Wilmot confesses that he agrees, that his "whole soul [is] infected." When debating the means of "execution," the couple reveals the cause of their financial problems— Old Wilmot's "wasteful riots." The parents incorrectly believe, as all mortals do, that they have control over their destinies. Hence the Wilmots blame themselves for having brought their affairs to the current pitiful condition, just as young Wilmot believes he can alter the lives of his parents, Charlot, and Randal through the force of his own success. All are deluded, however, as Lillo pushes home that humans control *nothing*. Thus Old Wilmot remarks that the sleeping "stranger" is a "Deluded wretch!" for imagining himself the "happiest of mankind," for he is about to feel the "icy hand of grisly Death." His statement implies that while we may never know what is about to happen, mere chance, not God's plan, prevails. Old Wilmot's view, of course, is badly off the mark.

The play's finale highlights Lillo's argument. Immediately following the murder, Charlot, Randal, and Eustace show up and reveal to the Wilmots the identity of the stranger. Upon hearing the ghastly news, Old Wilmot fatally stabs Agnes, who comments "Ever kind, / But most in this!" and later remarks, "Had I ten thousand lives / I'd give them all to speak my penitence, / Deep, and sincere, and equal to my crime." Her penitence, we are to believe, is sincere and effective. Old Wilmot then takes the knife to himself and begins his own expiation:

> This horrid deed that punishes itself
> Was not intended as he was our son;
> For that we knew not, till it was too late.
> Proud and impatient under our afflictions,
> While Heaven was laboring to make us happy,
> We brought this dreadful ruin on ourselves.

The wise Randal then adds the unambiguous message the play intends to deliver:

> Let us at least be wiser, nor complain

> Of Heaven's mysterious ways and awful reign.
> By our bold censures we invade His throne
> Who made mankind and governs but His own.

Circumstances and lack of knowledge, then, absolve the Wilmots of eternal sin, for they never *intended* to kill their own son, nor anyone at all, for that matter. Old Wilmot's suicide and the whole tenor of the play, as Stephen Trainor rightly observes, make clear that man can never know God's plan, and that as long as one has an essentially good heart and never intended to commit sin, then one may rise to heaven regardless of the degree of the sinful act.

Critical opinions have varied wildly on the play. Davies calls the play a "masterpiece" superior to all writers except Shakespeare in depicting "the terrible graces" and "the passions . . . so highly wrought up," and many of his contemporaries, such as James Harris and George Colman, agreed. Charles Lamb later termed the play a "nauseous sermon," but many Continental writers, such as Karl Moritz and Gotthold Ephraim Lessing, were impressed. Some critics and scholars, however, have incorrectly extended Lillo's influence to the twentieth-century existentialist Albert Camus. *L'Etranger* (1942) and *Le Malentendu* (1945) have been supposed to exhibit Lillo's influence, but as Camus's biographer Herbert Lottman points out, the French-Algerian Nobel prize winner actually had in mind a twentieth-century Yugoslavian analogue in which a mother with the aid of her daughter mistakenly killed and robbed her son who had been absent for twenty years. Perhaps the coincidence underscores all the more the fascination the original story held for Lillo.

The next three plays by Lillo—a romance and two tragedies—were unsuccessful, accounting for a cumulative total of only eleven performances, but the plays are interesting for the light they shed on Lillo's aims and methods. The first, *Marina*, was the last play Lillo saw staged, his death coming on 3 September 1739.

An adaptation of *Pericles, King of Tyre, Marina* premiered at the Theatre Royal in Covent Garden on 1 August 1738 and continued for two more performances on 4 and 8 August, the latter being an author's benefit. The play elicited virtually no contemporary critical reactions, and even sympathetic Tom Davies, while mildly praising the uses Lillo made of the corrupt materials, nonetheless adds, "I think Lillo has preserved some characters, and retained some expressions of the

Sarah Siddons, who revived Fatal Curiosity *in 1797 (engraving by Bartolozzi, based on a portrait by Hone)*

old drama, which his judgment should have rejected." His remark stems, however, perhaps more from the eighteenth-century assumption of the crudity of Elizabethan speech and manners then from any technical error on Lillo's part, for "words which might have been spoken without censure in the drawing room of Elizabeth, a swearing and masculine queen, and even in the presence of James, who loved and propagated an obscene jest, would scarce be permitted now in some houses devoted to pleasure. A modern audience rejects with disgust the companions and language of a brothel." We may question the hypocritical assumptions of Davies and his peers concerning their own values and actions, but the fact remains that *Marina* did not please and was never revived. The play's interest, then, comes from an appreciation of the themes and topics of interest to Lillo during his last phase, just when

his dramatic powers were coming to full maturity.

Eighteenth-century editors were reluctant to admit *Pericles* to the Shakespearean canon: Lewis Theobald, Alexander Pope, and Samuel Johnson all excluded the play from their editions: the problems are the corrupt and mangled state of the text and the complications arising from the play being a collaboration. Lillo, whose playwriting sensibilities guided him, discerned correctly that only the last two acts of *Pericles* were in Shakespeare's hand. Thus *Marina* follows only the last thread of a complex and confused set of plots from *Pericles*, that is, the section dealing with the trials of Marina, daughter of Pericles and Thaisa. But the choice of the last two acts did not stem only from their being very likely Shakespeare's; the theme of the closing section of *Pericles* is what captured Lillo's interest. As Shakespeare dealt with his materials, themselves of ancient origin, the theme concerns genuine contrition and penance for sinful acts and, most important, a willingness to follow the path of virtue in the face of temptation and duress. Accompanying these ideas is the notion that one must persevere in life even when all seems lost, in other words, to trust in providence. For Lillo, the Marina section was thus a ready-made scenario for all of his favorite themes.

Lillo makes clear from the prologue forward that he is only adapting Shakespeare's scenes. He fully acknowledges his debts and announces his purpose, that is, to improve upon *Pericles*:

> To glean and clear from chaff his least remains,
> Is just to him, and richly worth our pains.
> ....
> As gold though mix'd with baser matter shines,
> So do his bright inimitable lines.

As recent collations have shown, Lillo used only two scenes from *Pericles,* adding his own material to fill out the three acts of *Marina.* But he did retain almost intact the well-known brothel scene (the one to which Davies objected), which is perhaps Shakespeare's best work in *Pericles.* But repairing the scenes "injurious" to Shakespeare's name was only a secondary consideration for Lillo, although an important one. His more immediate concern was to exploit the thematic possibilities of the Marina episodes.

In the course of Lillo's play we see Marina tossed back and forth on the waves of fortune. She is, in rapid succession, depicted as the fortunate and well-treated ward of Queen Philoten; the subject of Philoten's jealousy as she orders Marina's death; the object of the compassion of her would-be executioner, Leonine; the well-treated prize of pirates; the slave of a brothel owner; the recipient of the assistance of Lysimachus, governor of Ephesus, who had come to the brothel for pleasure but who fell in love with the virtuous Marina; a votary of Diana's temple; and, finally, the long-lost child reunited with parents, both of whom believed each other and the child to be dead. This wild and rapid alternation of the fortunes and misfortunes of Marina, and of her parents, and the depiction of solid and unbending virtue, is encapsulated by Pericles in the closing couplet of *Marina*: "Virtue preserv'd from fell destruction's blast, / Led on by heav'n, and crown'd with joy at last." Davies rightly comments on the play's impact and intentions: "A love of truth, in-

nocence, and virtue, a firm resignation to the will of Providence, and a detestation of vice and falsehood, are constantly insisted upon, and strongly inculcated in all the compositions of honest LILLO."

Shortly after Lillo's death the Drury Lane company mounted yet another of his original tragedies, *Elmerick, or Justice Triumphant.* This play opened on 23 February 1740 and ran for six nights, garnering two benefits for "the Author's poor Relations." The prologue, spoken by Quin, states that Lillo wrote "Deprest by want, afflicted by disease." The latter may well be true, but the former claim can and has been questioned on many grounds. According to Davies, Lillo was "far from being poor, he died in very easy circumstances and rather in affluence than want; . . . he bequeathed several legacies, and left the bulk of his estate to Mr. John Underwood his nephew, in which was included an estate of 60[0]*l. per annum.*" Thus while the author's relations may have been quite poor, Lillo was scarcely of "distressed fortune."

As we have seen with Lillo's oeuvre so far, he is interested in the ways in which people react under unusual duress. In *Elmerick,* unlike *Marina,* however, we do not witness oscillations of fortune: the play begins with Ismena, Elmerick's wife, describing their happiness but fearing a turn for the worse:

> When we are bless'd even to our utmost wish,
> Is it the nature of the restless mind
> To work its own disquiet, and extract
> Pain from delight?
> ....
> Yet [I] fear, I know not why, some fatal change
> May rob me of my happiness.

Ismena, we soon learn, has good reasons to fear for the future: relating to her father, Bathori, that she and Elmerick have recently "chang'd our solid peace for courts and senates," the inevitable line of the tragedy begins to unfold. The fortunes of the admirable but doomed couple rapidly proceed downhill in relentless fashion. Passion and intrigue have their turns as Matilda, the concupiscent queen of Hungary, attempts to seduce the chaste Elmerick.

The story is easy to summarize. Good King Andrew embarks upon a crusade to the Holy Land leaving Elmerick as regent with an ominous command:

Shou'd any dare,
Presuming on their birth or place for safety,
Disturb my subjects peace with bold injustice;
Let no consideration hold your hand,
As you shall answer it to me and heaven:
Think well how I wou'd act, or ought to act,
Were I in person here, and do it for me.

The subject who ultimately breaks the law is, of course, the queen, and Elmerick must order her execution. Here, then, is one sense of the meaning of the play's subtitle, "Justice Triumphant," that is, even a queen must live by laws. But the queen's plots involve others too. In order to gain Elmerick's attentions, she wrongly believes that if her brother, Prince Conrade, can win Ismena's charms, then Elmerick will readily succumb to the queen's wiles. Conrade, a lecherous brute, proceeds to rape Ismena, presuming that his princely station will protect him from any reprisals. Elmerick soon comprehends the plot, confronts and condemns Matilda, and anxiously awaits the recalling of Andrew. Meanwhile Ismena has died of shame, believing herself defiled and no longer suitable for Elmerick's embraces. At the king's return: the queen's plot is rapidly revealed and proven beyond doubt; Elmerick is redeemed; Conrade commits suicide (yet further sacrilegious proof of his evilness, that he was, as he says, "born to err"); and King Andrew announces that he will mourn with Elmerick for the loss of the virtuous Ismena.

Again Lillo saw in the forced circumstances, the head-on clash of virtue and temptation, the materials for an in-depth study of human motivations. Instead of misconceptions of duty, as portrayed in *The London Merchant* or *Fatal Curiosity* (and as we shall see in his version of *Arden of Feversham*), we have the painful but finally justified adherence to virtuous actions, as in *The Christian Hero* and *Marina*. The latter two plays, of course, are not tragedies, and the decidedly glum ending of *Elmerick* shows that Lillo wishes the audience to realize that the ending may be painful but *not unhappy*. In a sense this play is not a tragedy but merely another example of the mysterious workings of providence. Elmerick ties together these thoughts in his final speech:

Unerring power! whose deep and secret counsels
No finite mind can fathom and explore;
It must be just to leave your creatures free,
And wise to suffer what you most abhor:
Supreme and absolute of these your ways
You render no account—we ask for none.
For mercy, truth, and righteous retribution

Attend at length your high and awful throne.
Ismena is aveng'd—let me be wretched.

So while Elmerick's virtuous actions contributed to Ismena's death, he recognizes that he should not have acted otherwise and that heaven will reward all who abide by higher laws. In this sense justice is triumphant a second way: the misery and suffering of all just parties will be amply repaid in heaven. The human condition, then, consists of suffering and serving without question, for God's grand design "no finite mind can fathom."

Elmerick, like Scanderbeg, Pericles, Thaisa, and Marina, never swerves from the correct course of action, not even for a moment. We must see *Elmerick*, then, as perhaps Lillo's most interesting play because the hero is *not* rewarded on earth for his virtuous adherence to duty. Lillo's point is that if Elmerick can trust in providence in the face of his extreme misfortune, then lesser folk might learn to abide their lesser vagaries.

Lillo's final produced play, *Arden of Feversham*, reached the boards on 12 July 1759, again at Drury Lane. The entire stage history is brief: the play ran for one night only and was revived on only one occasion, 14 April 1790 at Covent Garden, as a benefit for actor Joseph Holman, who reduced the five acts of the original to three. Trudy Drucker states that at the first performance of Lillo's *Arden of Feversham* "the audience hooted it down," but Davies says that it was "much applauded."

This tragedy is based on the well-known, anonymous play of the same title, first known to have been performed in 1591. Since the first appearance of Lillo's version all have known that it was completed in 1759 by Dr. John Hoadly (brother of Benjamin Hoadly, author of the wildly popular *The Suspicious Husband*, 1747). But the circumstances of Lillo's original attempts at adaptation have given rise to a puzzle based on an anecdote first related to Davies by the actor John Roberts. Roberts told Davies that Lillo's *Arden of Feversham* "was written before the year 1736. How it came to lie dormant till 1762 [*sic*], when it was first acted in the summer season, I have not been able to learn." C. F. Burgess, taking this remark as his lead, hypothesizes that Lillo, a multidimensional playwright who did not always work in the "sentimental" mode, did not complete the play in 1736 because "it was destined to be a failure, as he himself recognized." But perhaps bearing more on Lillo's decision was the appearance of a rival contemporary version by Eliza Haywood on 21 January 1736.

Since Haywood's adaptation was not published, we cannot be sure of precise textual details, but Lillo would certainly have been aware of her play. Perhaps Lillo did not press for the staging of his own *Arden of Feversham* because the Haywood version, by chance, appeared just when he was creating his own adaptation; thus the play lay unfinished in manuscript form until 1759 when the talented Hoadly, who had assisted his brother with *The Suspicious Husband,* completed it. (The manuscript of the final version may be found in the Larpent collection of the Huntington Library.) Rather than a stunning stroke of artistic insight, Lillo's decision to leave the play unfinished was more likely based on his bad luck–that is, Haywood's play got to the stage first.

In Lillo's version of *Arden of Feversham,* the action concerns the conspiracy between Alicia, Arden's wife, and her lover, Mosby, to murder Arden. The complex motivations boil down to a dastardly plot founded on avarice, lust, and revenge; Arden is portrayed as a paragon of virtue, a man who both inspires and revolts the less virtuous people who surround him. The psychological struggles of Alicia and others to justify the impending foul deed serve as the focal points for the play's action. Time after time Arden barely escapes death because of the overwhelming sense of guilt or remorse felt by Alicia and Michael, Arden's protegé. For example, just as Barnwell drops the knife before attempting to murder his uncle, so Alicia lets fall her weapon; but, of course, Barnwell follows through due to the circumstances whereas Alicia does not. Arden, at last, becomes the victim of the combined machinations of several parties, including two hired assassins.

In Alicia we find one of Lillo's best female characters. Like Millwood, Alicia is attractive and cunning; and, also like Barnwell's nemesis, her past gives rise to an understandable if not forgivable rationale for her malicious acts. But Alicia also differs from Millwood in important ways. She does not stand to gain a great deal by her part in the conspiracy, but most important she comes to realize that Arden is a good husband and a much better man than her lover, Mosby. Wracked with torment at every step after learning that Mosby intends to murder Arden, Alicia either fails in her assigned tasks in the evil plot or refuses to assist. When in the conclusion the mayor announces that the whole crew will be executed, Alicia accepts her fate willingly: "I adore / Th' unerring hand of justice." The role demands a very experienced actress because of the wide range of emotions required. As Davies rightly suggests, the play may well have failed precisely because the part of Alicia was given to "a raw young actress, unacquainted with the stage, and utterly incapable of comprehending, much less of representing a character which required the strongest expression of violent and conflicting passions."

The theme of the play is justice, as we have seen in so many of Lillo's scripts. The Franklin states the message in the closing speech:

> You shall have justice all, and rig'rous justice.
> So shall the growth of enormous crimes,
> By their dread fate be check'd in future times.
> Of avarice, Mosby a dread instance prove,
> And poor Alicia of unlawful love.

Even Maria, who had no direct hand in the murder, is not exempt: despite Alicia's pleas, the mayor arrests Maria, observing, "She has undone herself–Behold how innocence / May suffer in bad fellowship." And so the play severely advocates a total dedication to the causes of virtue and justice; man must adhere to the highest standards in emulation of heavenly decrees.

In conclusion, while Lillo's attention to Calvinistic doctrine and elements of the "sentimental" ethos (which he shared with so many of his contemporaries) seems central to a complete understanding all six of his serious plays (*Silvia* and *Britannia and Batavia* are not serious plays), it is possible to take yet another approach to his drama, based on what appear to be experimental variations on the twin axes of general thematic tendencies and the status of the protagonist at each play's conclusion: whether the play depicts the central character as exhibiting morally "right" or "wrong" actions (by Christian standards, of course), and whether the play ends happily or unhappily for the central character (and whether he is dead or alive). Lillo seems to have systematically worked his way through three mathematical variations of the right/wrong and happy/unhappy axes in the following fashion:

The London Merchant	wrong	unhappy (dead)
The Christian Hero	right	happy
Arden of Feversham	right	unhappy (dead)
Fatal Curiosity	right	unhappy (dead)
Marina	right	happy
Elmerick	right	unhappy (alive)

After one recognizes that Lillo never depicts an immoral central character who is happy at play's end (a variation of interest to twentieth-century readers and writers but anathema to Lillo), several points emerge from this model. First, we see that Barnwell is a simple case: he acted incorrectly according to Christian mores, so he got his just punishment. Although one may be tempted to say that Barnwell is "happy" at the end, being pleased with the idea that God might forgive him after all, still, he has caused many people—most of all his dead uncle—great harm. In *The Christian Hero* Lillo worked with the next easiest variation: a good man (Scanderbeg) acts correctly and is appropriately rewarded by God. The play ends on a distinctly positive note. *Arden of Feversham*, chronologically next in date of composition, explores the next variation. Arden acts in a morally correct way, but he becomes the victim of others. He is a victim of evil, though he himself is virtuous (largely because of his passive nature). God's justice, as we have observed, however, is duly served at the end, but not before Arden has fallen. He is an odd hero; the play is more about Alicia and Mosby. Nonetheless, the play ends unhappily for the hero, forgiveness or no.

Fatal Curiosity appears to be another version of the variation which Lillo was exploring in *Arden of Feversham* but was forced to abandon when Haywood's play of the same title unluckily appeared. Young Wilmot acts in a "good" if excessive fashion; he harms no one and does no wrong, just like Arden, and yet he dies. A good man done in by the avarice of others is the theme of both *Arden of Feversham* and *Fatal Curiosity*. *Marina* explores old territory but through romance rather than tragedy. Here Lillo wished to show once again a good person (actually, several good people) rewarded for virtuous travails. Lillo seems to be interested at this point in coming to terms with the positive potential inherent in human suffering, especially when the individuals trust in providence. We see, then, that in his last play, *Elmerick*, Lillo tackles the most difficult variation, an active hero who acts correctly at *every* turn (Young Wilmot and Arden are passive victims) and yet lives on to suffer intense sorrow. Burgess argues that *Fatal Curiosity* is Lillo's greatest play, a conclusion well worth considering, but in light of the model proposed above, perhaps *Elmerick* is Lillo's most interesting play, if only because Elmerick suffers precisely because he embodies the closest thing to Christian perfection on earth one can imagine: he is a character of greatest importance to an audience seeking to understand the deity. Lillo's answer is, of course, that no amount of reasoning will allow one to understand or alleviate Elmerick's suffering: one must simply have faith in providence in the face of all adversity. Elmerick is the *living* exemplar at the play's conclusion; he must carry on, bearing his load of grief to his grave, trusting in a better life to come—hence, he is the greatest of Lillo's Christian heroes, surpassing even Scanderbeg.

Biographies:

David Erskine Baker, *The Companion to the Play-House*, 2 volumes (London: T. Becket & P. A. Dehondt, 1764); augmented and revised by Isaac Reed as *Biographia Dramatica*, 2 volumes (London: Printed for Rivingtons, 1782); augmented and revised again by Stephen Jones, 3 volumes (London: Longman, Hurst, Rees, Orme & Brown, 1812);

Thomas Davies, "Some Account of the Life of Mr. George Lillo," in *The Works of Mr. George Lillo* (London: Printed for T. Davies, 1775), pp. ix-xlviii;

Drew B. Palette, "Notes for a Biography of George Lillo," *Philological Quarterly*, 19 (July 1940): 261-267;

C. F. Burgess, "Further Notes for a Biography of George Lillo," *Philological Quarterly*, 46 (July 1967): 424-428;

Stephen L. Trainor, "Context for a Biography of George Lillo," *Philological Quarterly*, 64 (Winter 1985): 51-67.

References:

Bernard Beckerman, "Schemes of Show: A Search for Critical Norms," in *The Stage and the Page*, edited by George Winchester Stone, Jr. (Berkeley: University of California Press, 1981), pp. 209-228;

Ernest Bernbaum, *The Drama of Sensibility: A Sketch of the History of English Sentimental Comedy and Domestic Tragedy, 1696-1780* (Boston & London: Ginn, 1915);

Roberta F. S. Borkat, "The Evil of Goodness: Sentimental Morality in *The London Merchant*," *Studies in Philology*, 76 (Summer 1979): 288-312;

C. F. Burgess, "Lillo sans Barnwell, or the Playwright Revisited," *Modern Philology*, 66 (August 1968): 5-29;

Ralph Cohen, "Literary History and the Ballad of George Barnwell," in *Augustan Studies: Essays in Honor of Irvin Ehrenpreis,* edited by Douglas Lane Patey (Newark: University of Delaware Press, 1985), pp. 13-31;

F. E. De Boer, "George Lillo," Ph.D. dissertation, University of Wisconsin, 1965;

Trudy Drucker, Introduction to *The Plays of George Lillo,* 2 volumes (New York & London: Garland, 1979), I: vii-xxxii;

Edmond McAdoo Gagey, *Ballad Opera* (New York: Columbia University Press, 1937);

Raymond D. Havens, "The Sentimentalism of *The London Merchant,*" *ELH,* 12 (September 1945): 183-187;

W. H. McBurney, Introduction to *Fatal Curiosity* (Lincoln: University of Nebraska Press, 1966);

McBurney, Introduction to *The London Merchant* (Lincoln: University of Nebraska Press, 1965);

McBurney, "What George Lillo Read: A Speculation," *Huntington Library Quarterly,* 29 (May 1966): 275-286;

Allardyce Nicoll, *A History of Early Eighteenth Century Drama 1700-1750* (Cambridge: Cambridge University Press, 1925); revised as volume 2 of *A History of English Drama, 1660-1900,* 6 volumes (Cambridge: Cambridge University Press, 1952-1959);

Harry W. Pedicord, "George Lillo and Speculative Masonry," *Philological Quarterly,* 53 (Summer 1974): 401-412;

William Popple, Review of *The Christian Hero,* in *The Prompter,* no. 29 (18 February 1735); republished in *The Prompter: A Theatrical Paper,* modern edition, edited by William A. Appleton and Kalman A. Burnim (New York: Benjamin Blom, 1966), p. 29;

Jeremy Rifkin, *Time Wars* (New York: Holt, 1987);

G. B. Rodman, "Sentimentalism in Lillo's Merchant," *ELH,* 12 (1945): 45-61;

Stephen L. Trainor, Jr., "Suicide and Seneca in Two Eighteenth-Century Tragedies," *Comparative Drama,* 14 (1980): 216-229;

Trainor, "Tears Abounding: *The London Merchant* as Puritan Tragedy," *Studies in English Literature,* 18 (Summer 1978): 509-521;

Calhoun Winton, "The Tragic Music in Enlightened England," in *Greene Centennial Essays,* edited by Paul J. Korshin and Robert D. Allen (Charlottesville: University Press of Virginia, 1984), pp. 125-142.

Papers:

The manuscript for Lillo's version of *Arden of Feversham,* as completed by Dr. John Hoadly, is in the Larpent Collection at the Henry E. Huntington Library, in San Marino, California.

Nicholas Rowe

(June 1674-6 December 1718)

J. Douglas Canfield
University of Arizona
and
Alfred W. Hesse

PLAY PRODUCTIONS: *The Ambitious Stepmother,* London, Lincoln's Inn Fields, circa December 1700;

Tamerlane, London, Lincoln's Inn Fields, December 1701;

The Fair Penitent, London, Lincoln's Inn Fields, May 1703;

The Biter, London, Lincoln's Inn Fields, late November-early December 1704;

Ulysses, London, Queen's Theatre, 23 November 1705;

The Royal Convert, London, Queen's Theatre, 25 November 1707;

The Tragedy of Jane Shore, London, Theatre Royal in Drury Lane, 2 February 1714;

The Tragedy of the Lady Jane Gray, London, Theatre Royal in Drury Lane, 20 April 1715.

BOOKS: *The Ambitious Step-Mother. A Tragedy. As t'was Acted at the New Theatre in Little-Lincolns-Inn-Fields. By His Majesty's Servants. By N. Rowe, Esq.* (London: Printed for Peter Buck, 1701);

Tamerlane. A Tragedy. As it is Acted at the New Theater in Little Lincolns-Inn-Fields By His Majesty's Servants. Written by N. Rowe, Esq. (London: Printed for Jacob Tonson, 1702); modern edition, edited by Landon Crawford Burns, Jr., The Matthew Carey Library of English and American Literature (Philadelphia: University of Pennsylvania Press, 1966);

The Fair Penitent. A Tragedy. As it is Acted at the New Theatre in Little Lincolns-Inn-Fields. By Her Majesty's Servants. Written by N. Rowe, Esq. (London: Printed for Jacob Tonson, 1703); modern edition, edited by Malcolm Goldstein, Regents Restoration Drama Series (Lincoln: University of Nebraska Press, 1969);

*The Biter. A Comedy. As it is Acted at the Theatre in Lincolns-Inn-Fields, By Her Majesty's sworn Ser-*vants. *Written by N. Rowe, Esq.* (London: Printed for Jacob Tonson, 1705);

Ulysses: A Tragedy. As it is Acted at the Queen's Theatre in the Hay-Market. By Her Majesty's Sworn Servants. Written by N. Rowe, Esq. (London: Printed for Jacob Tonson, 1706);

A Poem upon the Late Glorious Successes of Her Majesty's Arms, &c. (London: Printed for Jacob Tonson, 1707);

The Royal Convert. A Tragedy. As it is Acted at the Queen's Theatre in the Hay-Market. By Her Majesty's Sworn Servants. Written by N. Rowe, Esq. (London: Printed for Jacob Tonson, 1708);

Epilogue Spoken by Mrs. Barry, April the 7th, 1709. At a Representation of Love for Love. For the Benefit of Mr. Betterton At His Leaving the Stage (London: Printed for E. Sanger & E. Curll, 1709);

Colin's Complaint for His Mistress's Unkindness. By Mr. Addison [single sheet] (N.p., circa 1712-1715?);

The Tragedy of Jane Shore. Written in Imitation of Shakespear's Style. By N. Rowe, Esq. (London: Printed for Bernard Lintott, 1714; facsimile, London: Scolar Press, 1973); modern edition [based on uncorrected state of first quarto], edited by Harry William Pedicord, Regents Restoration Drama Series (Lincoln: University of Nebraska Press, 1974);

Poems on Several Occasions. By N. Rowe, Esq. (London: Printed for E. Curll, 1714);

Maecenas. Verses occasion'd by the honours conferr'd on the Right Honourable the Earl of Halifax. By N. Rowe, Esq. (London: Printed for Bernard Lintott, 1714);

Ajax of Sophocles. Translated from the Greek, with Notes, possibly translated, with notes, by Rowe (London: Printed for Bernard Lintott, 1714);

The Tragedy of the Lady Jane Gray. As it is Acted at the Theatre-Royal in Drury Lane. By N. Rowe,

Nicholas Rowe (by permission of the National Portrait Gallery, London)

Esq. (London: Printed for Bernard Lintott, 1715);

The Poetical Works of Nicholas Rowe, Esq. (London: Printed for E. Curll, 1715) [*Poems on Several Occasions* bound with the 1712 edition of *Callipaedia*];

Ode for the New Year MDCCXVI. By N. Rowe (London: Printed for J. Tonson, 1716);

Lucan's Pharsalia, translated by Rowe (London: Printed for Jacob Tonson, 1718 [i.e., 1719]).

Collections: *The Dramatick Works of Nicholas Rowe, Esq.,* 2 volumes (London: Printed & sold by T. Jauncy, 1720; facsimile, Farnborough, U.K.: Gregg International Publishers, 1971);

The Works of Nicholas Rowe, 3 volumes (London: J. Darby, 1728);

The Miscellaneous Works of Nicholas Rowe, Esq., 3 volumes (London: Printed & sold by W. Feales, 1733);

The Works of Nicholas Rowe, Esq., 2 volumes, edited by Anne Deanes Devenish (London: Printed for H. Lintot, J. & R. Tonson & S. Draper, 1747);

The Works of Nicholas Rowe, Esq. . . . A New Edition. Ornamented with Copper-Plates. To which is Prefixed a Life of the Author [by Samuel Johnson], 2 volumes (London: Printed for W. Lowndes, J. Nichols, S. Bladon & W. Nicoll, 1792);

Three Plays: Tamerlane, The Fair Penitent, Jane Shore, edited by James R. Sutherland (London: Scholartis, 1929).

OTHER: *A New Miscellany of Original Poems, on Several Occasions,* includes poems by Rowe and others (London: Printed for Peter Buck, 1701);

Poems on Several Occasions: Together with some Odes in Imitation of Mr. Cowley's stile and Manner, includes poems by Rowe and others (London: L. Stokoe & G. Harris, 1703);

Poetical Miscellanies: The Fifth Part. Containing a Collection of Original Poems, With Several New Translations, By the most Eminent Hands, edited, with contributions, by Rowe (London: Printed for Jacob Tonson, 1704);

Prologue, in *The Gamester,* by Susanna Centlivre (London: Printed for William Turner & William Davis, 1705);

"The Golden Verses of Pythagoras," translated by Rowe, in *The Life of Pythagoras, with His Symbols and Golden Verses, Together with the Life of Hierocles, and his commentaries upon the verses. Collected out of the Choisest Manuscripts, and tr. into French, with annotations. By M. [André] Dacier. Now done into English* (London: Printed for Jacob Tonson, 1707);

"Some Account of Boileau's Writings, and of this Translation," in *Boileau's Lutrin: A Mock-Heroic Poem,* translated by John Ozell (London: Printed for R. Burrough & J. Baker, E. Sanger & E. Curll, 1708);

"Of the Manner of Living with Great Men," an "original chapter" added to *Characters: or The Manner of the Age, with the Moral Characters of Theophrastus. Translated from the Greek. To which is Prefix'd, an account of His Life and Writings. By Monsieur [Jean] de La Bruyère. Made English by Several Hands,* fifth edition (London: Printed for E. Curll, E. Sanger & J. Pemberton, 1709);

The Works of Mr. William Shakespear; in Six Volumes. Adorn'd with Cuts. Revis'd and Corrected, with an Account of the Life and Writings of the Author, edited by Rowe (London: Printed for Jacob Tonson, 1709);

Poetical Miscellanies: The Sixth Part. Containing a Collection of Original Poems, With Several New Translations. By the most Eminent Hands, edited, with contributions, by Rowe (London: Printed for Jacob Tonson, 1709);

Squire Bickerstaff Detected; or, The Astrological Impostor Convicted, by John Partridge, includes an undetermined contribution by Rowe (London: 1709-1710?);

Callipaedia. A Poem. In Four Books. With Some Other Pieces. Written in Latin by Claudius Quillet.

Made English by N. Rowe, Esq., book 1 translated by Rowe (London: Printed for E. Sanger & E. Curll, 1712);

"On the Last Judgment, and Happiness of the Saints in Heaven," in *Sacred Miscellanies, or Divine Poems upon Several Subjects* (London: Printed for E. Curll, 1713);

A Collection of Original Poems, Translations and Imitations, by Mr. Prior, Mr. Rowe, Dr. Swift, and Other Eminent Hands (London: Printed for E. Curll, 1714);

"Verses upon the Sickness and Recovery of the Right Honourable Robert Walpole, Esq," in *State Poems* (London: Printed for J. Roberts, 1716);

"The Episode of Glaucus and Scylla," translated by Rowe, in *Ovid's Metamorphoses in Fifteen Books. Translated by the most Eminent Hands. Adorn'd with Sculptures,* edited by Samuel Garth (London: Printed for Jacob Tonson, 1717);

Epilogue, in *The Cruel Gift,* by Centlivre (London: Printed for E. Curl & A. Bettesworth, 1717).

Nicholas Rowe is still famous today as the first editor and biographer of Shakespeare. Most of his act and scene divisions and several of his emendations are still retained in editions of Shakespeare's plays, and he preserved valuable anecdotes from the acting tradition through Thomas Betterton. Samuel Johnson implied that his best work, his translation of Lucan's *Pharsalia,* the great Latin epic on the civil war between Julius Caesar and Pompey, was "one of the greatest productions of English poetry." But Rowe was best known in his own time, as he should be in ours, for his plays. After some temporary early successes, he scored a major hit with *The Tragedy of Jane Shore* in 1714, and from that time on, several of his plays were regularly performed and reprinted for more than a century. Three of his tragedies (*Tamerlane, The Fair Penitent,* and *Jane Shore*) were among the most frequently performed, after Shakespeare's, in the eighteenth century, and *The Fair Penitent* and *Jane Shore* had a profound impact on the development of bourgeois tragedy, not only in England but on the Continent as well. Those two tragedies, although they have not held the boards since the early nineteenth century, remain standard fare in college courses on the drama of the period. They are classics of the genre of *she-tragedies,* so-called because their protagonists are women. Following in the tradition of Thomas Otway, John Banks, and Thomas Southerne, Rowe was a master at portraying women characters under stress. He thus provided great vehicles for the premier actresses of the eighteenth century–Elizabeth Barry, Anne Oldfield, Susannah Cibber, and Sarah Siddons. And his women, particularly Calista from *The Fair Penitent* and Jane Shore, now provide excellent subjects for feminist criticism. Their complaints against the tyranny of men ring poignant over the centuries.

Rowe was descended from several generations of squires settled in the village of Lamerton in southwest Devon, where he inherited property from his father, John Rowe, and his namesake-uncle, Nicholas Rowe, but Rowe himself probably spent little more than occasional brief holidays in Devon. He was born at the home of his mother's father, Jasper Edwards, lord of the manor of Little Barford, Bedfordshire, where he was baptized 30 June 1674 by the local curate, probably "John Bennett, Clerk," who had married Frances Edwards a month earlier. Elizabeth, his mother, continued to live in her father's house with periodic visits from her husband until 1679, when both she and a second son, John, died and were buried–followed in February 1686 by the only daughter, Elizabeth–at Little Barford.

Although Rowe probably received some early instruction from his clergymen-uncles, John Bennett and William Merriden, by 1686 he was a private pupil, presumably, of the master of the charity school at Highgate, London. Within a few more years he was elected a King's Scholar (1688-1691) of the prestigious Westminster School in the precincts of Westminster Abbey, under its greatest headmaster, Richard Busby. One of his first experiences at Westminster was Whig history in the making when at Sunday services on 20 and 27 May 1688 King James II required all churches to read from the pulpit the Declaration of Indulgence (or Toleration) that was then execrated by the clergy and the people. Rowe's schoolmate William Legge, later earl of Dartmouth, remembered the scene many years after–"I was then at Westminster school, and heard [the Declaration] read in the abbey. As soon as bishop Sprat, who was dean, gave order for reading it, there was so great a murmur and noise in the church, that nobody could hear him: but before he had finished, there was none left but a few prebends in their stalls, the queristers, and Westminster scholars. The bishop could hardly hold the proclamation in his hands for

trembling." It was at Westminster Rowe must have learned his liberal arts and languages, for he did not go on to a university, as most King's Scholars did, but rather, in 1691, he entered the Middle Temple to study in his father's law chambers there.

His father, John Rowe, while maintaining business contacts in Devon, had become a barrister of the Middle Temple and a distinguished lawyer, publishing a textbook of law cases in 1689. He was called by royal writ in April 1692 to the degree of serjeant-at-law, the highest order of counsel at the English bar, but before John Rowe could be installed in this new honor, he had died and was buried (7 May) in Temple Church. Young Nicholas, as sole heir, inherited a modest income of three hundred pounds a year from the Devon property as well as the Middle Temple chambers. He was less than eighteen years old with about half a year of law studies; it would not have been unusual or surprising if Rowe had given up law for other interests. But with persistence and determination–personal qualities which were to reappear throughout his life–Rowe went on to complete his studies in shorter time than any of the other eleven to finish, out of sixty-six who initially enrolled for study in 1691. Rowe was called to the bar on 22 May 1696.

Life at the Middle Temple, however, was not all work for Rowe in those years. On 6 July 1693, little more than a year after his father's death, Rowe married Antonia Parsons, the seventeen-year-old daughter of Anthony Parsons, an auditor of the land revenues and probably a business acquaintance of Rowe's father. The wedding did not take place at the bride's home church of St. Dunstan-in-the-West, on Fleet Street opposite the Temple, as one might expect. Rather the wedding party traveled quite across old London from its western to its eastern perimeter to the Church of the Holy Trinity, Minories, near the Tower of London–a "peculiar" church exempt from any bishop's requirement of banns or license for marriage. This was no runaway marriage, however, for it was preceded by a formal legal Indenture Tripartite arranging a property settlement and involving parents, relatives, and other important participants. On 15 November 1695 a son, John, was baptized at the Church of St. Dunstan-in-the-West in Fleet Street, the parish church of the Parsonses and now of Antonia and Nicholas Rowe; for Rowe and his bride apparently moved in with the Parsons family in their house on Fetter Lane off Fleet Street. The survival of baby

John for six months motivated the making of an Indenture of Lease and Release on 22 and 23 June 1696, by which Rowe entailed his Devon properties to his young son, thus limiting himself and his wife to life tenancies in the property–a common legal device to preserve an estate in a family. This first son, unfortunately, died before his first birthday (buried 31 October 1696). The next child of the marriage was a son, also named John, who in turn was to receive the entailed property. He was baptized in the neighboring parish of St. Andrew, Holborn, where Nicholas and Antonia were then residing in Blewitts Court, on 24 August 1699, and was the only child of this marriage to survive his parents.

Rowe's legal studies and new family were only part of his London life, however. He continued or renewed friendships from Westminster School days and gained new friends in various walks of life. At the Middle Temple he renewed friendships with William Shippen and with Bertram Stote, Old Westminsters both. Shippen particularly found in Rowe a helpful mentor, as he acknowledged in a Latin verse, "Epistola ad N. R.," published in 1698 but probably written three or four years earlier during his initial period at the Temple. In these years Rowe himself, in his imitation of Horace's ode "To Venus," printed in the 1701 *New Miscellany of Original Poems,* seems to hark back to his boyhood scenes by his reference to the town of Odell about fifteen miles from Little Barford, both along the river Ouse. In this youthful setting Rowe poetically envisions a friend creating a temple to Venus but ends with the sweet-sad pursuit of love. Odell was the seat of Sir Thomas Alston, a young man who succeeded to the baronetcy in 1697 and whom Shippen probably was addressing in "Epistola ad amicissimum T. A. Baronettum" in the 1701 *New Miscellany.* It may be, indeed, that Rowe too had Alston in mind in "To Venus." Rowe must also have known William Congreve, a somewhat older and less assiduous student at the Temple but a published author, and, perhaps through him Jacob Tonson, who became Rowe's publisher (1702-1709) at his shop across Fleet Street from the Temple. Richard Thornhill and Charles Finch, third earl of Winchilsea, Kentish neighbors and more tenuously associated with the Temple, were friends and regular tavern companions of Rowe. It may have been through them that Rowe exchanged verses with the earl's aunt, Anne Finch, then a crypto-poetess living on the Winchilsea estate in Kent, whom Rowe helped to introduce to the reading public by his "Epistle to Flavia," praising Anne's "The Spleen," both included with three of her other poems in the 1701 *New Miscellany.* Life for Rowe was obviously active and pleasant at the turn of the century.

Certainly Rowe was interested in writing; it would seem that no man of spirit and learning could resist the urge. His early verses are mostly imitations of Horace, although he also wrote some original pieces. It was almost inevitable, however, that an Old Westminster, with the example of Dryden still fresh in his mind, would try writing plays. Such was the case with Rowe, who gave a sign of his change of career by relinquishing his Temple chambers after May 1700. By December 1700 his first play, *The Ambitious Stepmother,* was in production, and on 29 January 1701 it was published by Peter Buck. Early in July 1701 Buck also published a volume of poetry, *A New Miscellany of Original Poems, on Several Occasions,* on the title page of which the names of eight selected contributors, including Rowe, are listed in red ink. There are indeed so many of Rowe's friends and associates represented in this collection that it could be thought a publisher's puff for his new playwright. The table of contents begins with a translation from Bion "by the Right Honourable the Earl of W[inchilsea]," and then three imitations of Horace and an original poem by Rowe. Within a few pages come a Latin and an English verse epistle and an imitation of Horace all signed "W. S." (very probably Shippen) followed, after an interval of one, by Shippen's signed "Epistle to N. Rowe Esq." translated into English. After another interval Rowe's "Epistle to Flavia, on the sight of two Pindaric Odes on the Spleen and Vanity, Written by a Lady her Friend [Anne Finch]" introduces "The Spleen" and three other pieces "By the same hand." Although Charles Gildon was the ostensible editor of *A New Miscellany,* Rowe's friends were firmly in control of at least the first quarter of its text.

The title character of Rowe's first play, *The Ambitious Stepmother,* is descended from the powerful villainess of the Restoration heroic play. Her very name, Artemisa, relates her to the patriarchal stereotype of the Amazon who appropriates male characteristics and who must be put back in her place. Indeed, in her first soliloquy she complains that the gods have imprisoned her great spirit in the body of a woman, that "inferior Part of the Creation." Shades of Bathsheba, she has arranged to have her husband murdered in order to marry the king and bear him a son,

AMBITIOUS STEPMOTHER.

Lud. Du Guernier inv. et Sculp.

Illustration from the 1792 edition of Rowe's works

Artaban, for whom she now plans to usurp the throne from the eldest son, Artaxerxes, upon the death of the aging king. Abetted by Mirza, the typical Machiavellian statesman, Artemisa has nothing but contempt for virtue and piety. Their gods are Epicurean at best, their ethic Hobbist: "Power gives a Sanction, and makes all things just." So they plan to capture Artaxerxes and his main supporter, the general Memnon, while they are unarmed during a holy festival in the sacred temple. Despite their protestations to the gods, Artaxerxes and Memnon are imprisoned and await their execution. Moreover, Memnon's daughter and Artaxerxes' new bride, Amestris, is at the mercy of the goatish Mirza.

Artemisa and Mirza generate their own defeat, however. Mirza's lust for Amestris causes him improvidently to ignore the people, who are enraged at the sacrilege, and ironically to put himself into her power, for she grabs his knife and stabs him to death. Furthermore, Mirza's own daughter, Cleone, loves Artaxerxes, frees him and Memnon, and kills herself to convince them of her trustworthiness, an action they interpret as an atonement for her father's evil. Meanwhile, the people tear Magas, the complicit high priest, to shreds, an action Artaban interprets as divine justice. And the queen's own son, whom she has been unable to convert to her nominalism, puts her in her place as he assumes the throne.

Artaban becomes king because Artaxerxes is dead by the end of the play. Although she has mortally wounded Mirza, Amestris is dragged to him and stabbed; the despondent Artaxerxes and Memnon both commit suicide. Critics from the eighteenth to the twentieth centuries have objected that Rowe has violated poetic justice. But, as he explains in the dedication, he rejects distributive justice as a dramatic principle. Instead, he portrays retributive justice as a sign of divine vengeance on evil but, following Otway, arranges an ending that will evoke the maximum pity. This is a tragedy of suffering innocence, filled with signs that there are gods who ultimately, if only eschatologically, vindicate virtue. If Artaxerxes and Memnon despair, they have missed the significance of Cleone's atoning self-sacrifice. Rowe's central metaphor throughout his tragedies is that life is a trial.

If such is the moral meaning of Rowe's first play, its political meaning is more ambiguous—and perhaps more interesting. While the action of the play punishes usurpers and while, like Dryden's Dorax, Rowe's Memnon rails against those who would tamper with the natural law of primogeniture, nevertheless, Artaban *is* king at the end not just by accident but by merit. Even while defending primogeniture against, in this instance, parliamentary action interrupting succession, Memnon has pointed out that the system protects those very "worst-deserving" lords who have made the decision and who have power only by the accident of birth: "What Titles had they had, if Merit only / Could have confer'd a Right?" And despite his mother's machinations, Artaban seeks the throne because he believes he is "Worthy" of it, and he is willing to fight Artaxerxes for it man-to-man: "let us stake at once / Our Rights of Merit and of Eldership, / And prove like Men our Title," for "Arms . . . give the noblest Right to Kings" and "Nature's Error only gave him Preference." Since Artaban becomes king and obviously merits succession because of his resistance to his mother and his pious reaction to her sacrilege, perhaps the play marks the transition from Memnon's residual traditional, aristocratic, even Jacobite, political theory of hereditary monarchy to Artaban's emergent bourgeois theory of meritocracy.

Finally, although Rowe may give voice to Artemisa's desire for equal rights and equal power sharing, his gender politics are clear: Artaban reasserts "The Majesty of Manly Government," insisting that women are "form'd to obey" and that "Desire of Government is monstrous" in them. Even if we view the relationship between Artemisa's and Artaban's positions as dialectical, Rowe's real heroines in the play are the faithful, submissive Amestris and the self-sacrificing Cleone. And if Rowe's play moves from aristocratic to bourgeois political theory, it nevertheless reinforces patriarchal control of genealogy. At one point Artaban complains to his beloved Cleone, who conceals her love for Artaxerxes behind a vow to die a "Virgin Votary" to Diana, that she cannot thus "give away / Mine and thy Father's Right." Rape is portrayed as the worst violation in the play, and both Artaxerxes and Memnon insist that Amestris is better off dead than adulterated. Artemisa the Amazon is as bad as a woman can be: she has murdered her husband in ambitious self-assertion; she has thus adulterated her marriage; and she would go so far as to dabble in politics. In the dedication Rowe justifies the "Poetical Justice" of her fate: "the Queen is depos'd from her Authority by her own Son; which, I suppose, will be allow'd as the severest Mortification that could happen to a Woman of her imperious Temper."

After Rowe's second son, John, was born and his first play produced, a succession of five more children born and of five more plays produced seemed to march almost in step to the year 1709. The five children unfortunately all died in infancy, while the plays, except *The Biter*, lived on in subsequent performances. All except the very first play were published by Jacob Tonson, with whom Rowe apparently succeeded to editorial responsibilities, after Dryden's death, for *Poetical Miscellanies*, parts 5 and 6, in 1703 (with 1704 on the title page) and 1709. Tonson also published Rowe's slender translation of "The Golden Verses of Pythagoras" in *The Life of Pythagoras,* on 31 October 1706 (with 1707 on the title page), and on 6 January 1707 Tonson published Rowe's long *Poem upon the Late Glorious Successes,* celebrating Marlborough's victories, in the *London Gazette.*

Rowe's friendship with Jonathan Swift also dates from this period of his life. *The Ambitious Stepmother* and Rowe's second play, *Tamerlane* (produced in December 1701 and published in January 1702), together in quarto format must have

Henry Mossop as Bajazet in Tamerlane, *a role he played for the first time in 1751*

formed the gift volume in Swift's library, recorded as "Rowe's Plays; with the Author's Compliment to Doctor Swift," probably presented to Swift between April and October 1702 during his visit to England.

Perhaps reflecting the political ambiguity of the play, *The Ambitious Stepmother* was dedicated to the new lord chamberlain, Edward Villiers, earl of Jersey, later suspected of Jacobitism. There is no such ambiguity in Rowe's second play. Dedicated to a safe Whig, William Cavendish, the heir of William Cavendish, first duke of Devonshire, who had been strong in the councils to call William of Orange to England in 1688, *Tamerlane*

was immediately interpreted politically, as Rowe acknowledges in the dedication: "Some People . . . have fancy'd, that in the Person of *Tamerlane* I have alluded to the greatest Character of the present Age," that is, King William. Rowe owns the parallel, though he insists that the "*Hero* has *transcended the Poet's Thought.*" The play is essentially a portrait of the ideal Christian bourgeois monarch, defined against his antithesis, the Hobbist, nominalist, atheistical tyrant. Rowe appropriates the traditional aristocratic motif of word-as-bond of political and sexual fidelity and alters it for eighteenth-century significance. Bajazet is the traditional villainous troth breaker, but he breaks

TAMERLANE.

Barralet ad viv del.

Walker sculp

M^r. PALMER as BAJAZET and
Miss HOPKINS as SELIMA.

Baj. Now, now thou Traitress.

Act 5.

Illustration from the 1792 edition of Rowe's works

leagues and treaties and alliances. He is the absolute autocrat, bound by no laws, human or divine. He has wreaked havoc in Asia Minor, and Tamerlane has come to conquer him as "Champion" of liberty from oppression. Tamerlane is an early version of the Christian stoic hero that Joseph Addison would portray as the ultimate bourgeois statesman in *Cato* (1713). Although sorely tempted to wrath by Bajazet, he maintains rational control. He attempts to turn Bajazet from captive to convert, from lawless, willful tyrant to benevolent leader. Bajazet mocks Tamerlane for the weakness of his Christian ethic. At first,

Bajazet appears to be right, for he turns Tamerlane's leniency against him, plotting the murder of Tamerlane and his own escape. But like Cleone, Bajazet's own daughter, Selima, whose name significantly means *peace* in Arabic, out of her love for the Christian Axalla, Tamerlane's lieutenant, betrays her father's designs and offers herself as a sacrifice to his wrath. In the end, Tamerlane and Axalla rescue Selima, capture Bajazet, and secure the bestial rebel to law in a cage once and for all. Axalla and Selima are united, and the Christian world is safe from the tyrannical oppression of the likes of Bajazet (read: Louis XIV).

While Bajazet is portrayed as absolute monarch exalted in "the Pride of Pow'r" on his throne, where "like an Idol" he is "vainly worshipp'd / By prostrate Wretches," Tamerlane is portrayed as divinely sanctioned champion of "an injur'd People's Wrongs." He boasts of nothing except "to have been Heaven's happy Instrument, / The means of Good to all my Fellow-Creatures." The emergent bourgeois political model is fraternal rather than paternal. Tamerlane *merits* to be first among equals. Bajazet mocks not only his piety but his dependence upon the advice and consent of "debating Senates," with whom he shares "a precarious Scepter." In the prologue Rowe underlines this bourgeois appropriation of the Roman model of government. When Tamerlane was roused to war against the tyrant, Rowe anachronistically narrates,

> The peaceful Fathers, who in Senates meet,
> Approve an Enterprize so Just, so Great;
> While with their Prince's Arms, their Voice thus join'd,
> Gains half the Praise of having sav'd Mankind.

Moreover, Rowe again suggests that meritocracy has supplanted aristocracy. Tamerlane's followers insist that "had not Nature made him Great by Birth, / Yet all the Brave had sought him for their Friend." When accused by Bajazet of "vile Obscurity," Axalla, who has come to court his daughter as well as peace, scorns to "borrow Merit from the Dead" by citing his Roman lineage but asserts instead "that inborn Merit, / That Worth" of his own "Virtue" that distinguishes him. Besides, the most salient feature of those "Heroes, and God-like Patriots" among his ancestors is that they "Scorn'd to be Kings."

Into this bourgeois heroic romance Rowe weaves the tragic story of Moneses and Arpasia, Greek lovers whose solemn betrothal has been ruptured by Bajazet's lust. As her name implies, Bajazet has raped Arpasia, seized her and forced her into marriage with him. Again, Rowe's gender politics are manifest. When Moneses appeals to Tamerlane, in effect, to annul the forced marriage and reinstate the prior vows, Tamerlane is as absolute as a legislature or tribunal of men refusing to allow an abortion after rape: "would'st thou have my partial Friendship break / That holy Knot, which ty'd once, all Mankind / Agree to hold Sacred, and Undissolvable?" "All Mankind" has established a system of genealogical control in which woman is nothing more than an incu-

bator. Tamerlane enjoins Moneses to "cure this amorous Sickness of thy Soul" and come engage with him in the manly martial arts: "Nor will I lose thee poorly for a Woman." Meanwhile, Arpasia is allowed divorce only in her sleep with its song-induced dream.

The tragedy of Moneses and Arpasia is one of suffering innocence. Trying to possess not only her body but her affections solely, Bajazet has Moneses cruelly strangled in Arpasia's sight. Rowe uses the subplot as a vehicle to stress his theme of stoic endurance. As he has appropriated the motif of word-as-bond, so he here appropriates the related theme of constancy and changes its emphasis from constancy or fidelity to a person to constancy of mind. Yet, like the martial arts, this too is manly activity: Arpasia must overcome the "Woman" in her "Soul" and endure this "Tryal" of her resolve. She does, then dies from the strain, confident that she and Moneses will be united in an afterlife. Bajazet has been defeated by those who stand fixed on the firm center of self-control and self-reliance, a self-reliance that is, of course, properly subordinate to a patriarchal god.

Rowe's third play, *The Fair Penitent*, produced and published in 1703, did not have great initial success and, revived after the smashing success of *Jane Shore*, remained subordinate to that play in popularity until the twentieth century. Today it is Rowe's most popular play in the academy, primarily because of its title character's tirades against the tyranny of male oppression. Calista has been seduced by the gay Lothario, who has wooed her partly out of spite because her father rejected him as an acceptable suitor to his daughter. She, in turn, has married Lothario's rival, Altamont, partly in sullen obedience to her father's wishes but mostly in order to spite Lothario for his diminished affection. Wishing to see him one more time to vent her spleen, Calista sends Lothario an invitation to an assignation, which he carelessly drops. Altamont's friend and mentor Horatio discovers it and, consequently, Calista's ruined honor. Not only has she adulterated herself as sacred vessel, she has brought her contaminated goods into marriage with a noble young man and, therefore, turned him into a retroactive cuckold.

Taking upon himself the role of admonitor, Horatio accosts Calista with the letter, which she tears to bits, railing at Horatio for being a spy. When Altamont enters and demands to know the problem, he is forced to take sides with his brand-

I. Aikin and Sarah Siddons, illustrations from the 1792 edition of Rowe's works

new bride and draws on his best friend, who is also his sister Lavinia's husband. They are saved from killing each other only by her intervention.

Calista stubbornly proceeds to meet Lothario, and, although she scorns his libertinism, Altamont catches them together, duels with Lothario, and kills him. Calista's shame is now public with a vengeance, and her father, Sciolto, attempts to kill her but is stayed by Altamont, who would not have the old man pollute his honors! Yet, eventually Sciolto brings Calista the dagger Western patriarchy dictates she must employ to remove her contamination. Meanwhile, Lothario's faction seeks revenge, and Sciolto is mortally wounded in a skirmish. Upon hearing the news, Calista fatally stabs herself. Before she dies, she obtains her dying father's forgiveness, wishes she had loved Altamont first, and begs heaven's "Mercy" with her last breath. Sciolto bequeaths his estate to the reconciled Altamont and Horatio, the latter reciting the moral of the play: "By such Examples are we taught to prove, / The Sorrows that attend unlawful Love."

The play thus typically embodies patriarchal concerns. Lothario is a Don Juan, whose libertinism threatens male control of genealogy. Sciolto is the patriarch who has the right to dispense with his daughter as an exchange item and to annihilate her if she brings pollution into the lineage. Horatio is fundamentally a misogynist who believes all women false, with the rare exception of his faithful, submissive wife. Lavinia is an emergent bourgeois version of that wife, whose nothingness takes meaning only from her husband's significance. And however much a modern audience responds to Calista's rebellious spirit, she is finally brought to kneel submissively to the father and the god who represent the superego that enforces male dominance. The innovation in Rowe's treatment of these typical figures lies partly in the power he gives to Calista's articulation of her plight but even more in his creation of a husband who eschews the Italian (patriarchal) stance of revenge and is willing to forgive his wife's pollution, forget the past, and live with her anyway, presumably producing a lineage that traditional patriarchy would consider contaminated. But of course the patriarchal configuration of the ending allows no such heresy. The uppity Calista is safely dead.

Rowe's only comedy, *The Biter,* produced in late 1704, is generally considered a failure. He had tried to hearken back to Ben Jonson, perhaps by way of Congreve. As in Jonson's *Epicoene* (1609 or 1610), Rowe has created a humorous uncle, Sir Timothy Tallapoy, a rich merchant obsessed with the Orient, who has become estranged from his nephew, Clerimont, over the latter's failure to retain investments in the East India Company, and who plans to marry the beautiful young Mariana and beget a race of mandarins. Moreover, with no respect for her wishes Sir Timothy has arranged a marriage for his daughter Angelica with the son of a rich country squire. Of course, the young people have other designs. Mariana is already married to Clerimont, and they abet her cousin Friendly's efforts to get both Angelica and her fortune. Part of their plot is to discredit the intended husband, Pinch, who is the title character. Sir Timothy thinks the fashionable biting, that is, tricking someone with a practical joke or lie then revealing it and laughing at the dupe's embarrassment, is an abomination. So the wits conceal Pinch's identity until he has thoroughly offended Sir Timothy, then bite Sir Timothy with news of their own trick: not only has Mariana wheedled Sir Timothy into signing over a significant portion of his estate to the disguised Friendly—who turns it into a portion for Angelica, whom he secretly marries in the last act—but Mariana reveals that she is already married into Sir Timothy's family. The twice-bitten Sir Timothy retires in a rage, but Clerimont is confident that they will be able to mollify him.

Rowe also seems to have Jonson in mind in setting the play during a country fair and parading across the stage a series of humorous characters who engage in a good deal of slapstick. Like Jonson's, Rowe's purpose is to establish class distinctions between the town wits and not only the country boobies but the cits, including the stuttering city solicitor, Scribblescrabble, and his boozy, indecorous wife. Scribblescrabble's inordinate concern with status instability is echoed by Lady Stale, a superannuated amorous widow (similar to both Jonson's Lady Wouldbe and Congreve's Lady Wishfort), who brags about her insignificant family and is assured by the real wit, Mrs. Clever, "Positively no Body can be out of Humour that has Mony enough."

Rowe's satire on merchants and cits cannot disguise the fundamental middle-class morality of his play, however. On the surface the relationship between Friendly and Lady Stale resembles that between Dorimant and Mrs. Loveit in Sir George Etherege's *Man of Mode* (1676). But like Congreve's bourgeois Mirabel, Friendly has never gone so far as to debauch Lady Stale. Despite all of her protestations of his deep "penetration" of her "Merit," she has simply and willfully misinterpreted his signs to her. Friendly appears to be as much a virgin on his wedding day as Angelica, protests he has been no Don Juan, has never been "false" in his life. And Clerimont and Mariana unfashionably bill and coo with each other even though they are already married. Thus Rowe's comedy, however unentertaining it be—even though he crafted it as a vehicle for Betterton as Sir Timothy, Barry as Lady Stale, and Francis Leigh, son of the great comic actor Tony Leigh, as Scribblescrabble—nevertheless is a good indicator of the shift from aristocratic to bourgeois values. The real threats in the play are not genealogical but economic.

A year later, in late November of 1705, Rowe's fourth "tragedy" was produced at the Queen's new theater in Haymarket. In *Ulysses* Rowe returns to the genre of heroic romance and to the figure of a champion. The theme of the return of Odysseus has always been treated as a theodicy, a vindication of Odysseus's rights through divine assistance, especially that of Pallas Athena. Rowe's play is no exception, and the beleaguered faithful few are vouchsafed a theophany in the middle of the play as Pallas appears to inspire hope and endows the undisguised hero with Jove's thunder. But Rowe's hero stands so fixed upon his own firm center, upon his own

Illustration for The Biter, *from the 1792 edition of Rowe's works*

identity as Ulysses, that despite all the acknowledgment of divine assistance he seems sufficient unto himself. He boasts to the Ithacan traitor Antinous,

> Were there no Gods in Heav'n, or were they
>   careless,
> And *Jove* had long forgot to wield his Thunder,
> And dart Destruction down on Crimes like thine;
> Yet, Traitor, hope not thou to 'scape from Justice,
> Nor let rebellious Numbers swell thy Pride;

> For know, *Ulysses* is alone sufficient
> To punish thee, and on thy perjur'd Head
> Revenge the Wrongs of Love and injur'd Majesty.

Of course, in Rowe's play the dynamic of the denouement is attributable not to Ulysses himself but to the gods, who inspire the injured Semanthe, another daughter of an evil plotter, to be moved to self-sacrifice, to commit the pious fraud of imputing her father's death not to Telemachus but to Antinous and turning her Sa-

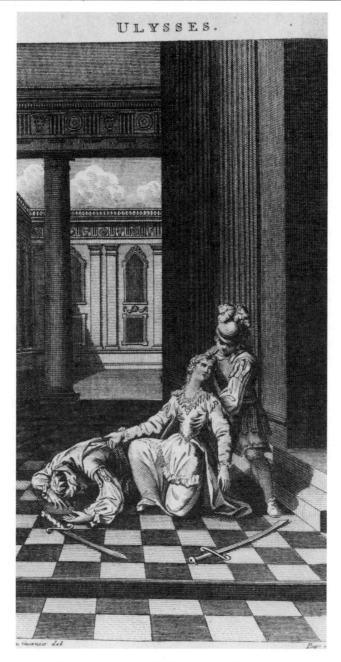

Illustration from the 1792 edition of Rowe's works

mian warriors upon his troops. But the lesson of self-reliance is taught also in this Cornelian subplot, where Ulysses employs his son not at the scene of his vengeance against the suitors of Penelope but in the corridors outside her chambers. Ulysses, disguised as the beggar Aethon, has tried his wife's fidelity by soliciting her for the suitor Eurymachus, to whom she has granted an evening's assignation. Telemachus has fallen in love with and secretly married Eurymachus's daughter Semanthe. Ulysses detects their rela-

tionship, so when he stations his son outside Penelope's door, he knows how severe will be Telemachus's trial. For like Corneille's young Cid, Telemachus will have to fight not only a seasoned warrior but his beloved's father. Telemachus is forced to stand firm on his own center, to affirm his identity as the son of Ulysses, and to defend his mother's name–alone against all odds.

Telemachus triumphs, but he must learn two other lessons associated with emergent bourgeois heroism. First, his disguised father, that master of craft and deceit, has enjoined Telemachus to "trust the Secret of thy Soul to none." Rowe's world–the emerging modern world–was becoming preoccupied with secrecy and spying, with trade secrets, military secrets, secret treaties, secret alliances. Loose lips sink ships, and–from Silhouette to Benedict Arnold to Mata Hari to Herb Philbrick to Oliver North–the modern landscape is populated by secret agents. One cannot tell even one's wife about one's special assignment, one's mission impossible. But Telemachus makes the tragic error of telling his best "friend," the opportunistic Antinous, and as a result, the latter gathers his forces, seizes Penelope, and very nearly wins the day. A chastened Telemachus is rescued by the pious fraud of Semanthe, an early example of the modern world's legitimate disinformation in defense of liberty. But he now must learn the second of his important lessons. When he complains to his father that, because Semanthe has determined never to see the slayer of her father again, he alone must mourn during the celebratory close of the romance, Ulysses calls upon him to endure as he has done, indeed to mourn alone in stoic self-reliance.

The essence of the trials of Penelope and Semanthe is also self-reliant endurance. In Ulysses' absence, Penelope has had to endure the insolence of her suitors and has had to rely on her own wits, her Odyssean craft. Thus she promises to marry after she has finished weaving a tapestry that she secretly unweaves every night. When this ruse is discovered, she must rely solely upon her commanding presence, her ability to stand up to the suitors' verbal assaults with her own indignant rhetoric. Finally, when she appears to yield to Eurymachus's threat against Telemachus, like Racine's Andromaque, she exacts a pledge of Telemachus's safety, then tries to kill herself rather than yield to Eurymachus's pollution. Upon such proof of not just fidelity but endurance, Ulysses, who up till now has slipped into those misogynistic generalizations that lie just beneath the surface of patriarchy, finally reveals himself and comforts his beleaguered wife.

Semanthe had pledged herself to Diana and thus was supposed to remain for the rest of her life essentially alone. Just as Telemachus must suffer the consequences of his tragic error, so also must Semanthe suffer the consequences of breaking her vow to Diana and secretly marrying Telemachus. The consequences are that her own father has been killed by her own husband, and she must now live alone after all, perhaps wiser but certainly sadder. Like Penelope, she is thrown back on her own resources and must use (manly) craft to indulge the woman in her soul and save the man she still loves. But she must subdue that woman and resist the impulse to remain with her parricide husband. She must endure her fate like a stoic. After all, like Corneille's Chimène, she cannot be less honorable, less pious to her parents, than Telemachus; in short, less of a man than Telemachus. Ulysses' admonition applies to her as well as to Telemachus: "Sigh not, nor of the common Lot complain, / Thou that art born a Man, art born to Pain."

In late November 1706 Rowe wrote another heroic romance, this one developing his theme of endurance through a pair of protagonists who rather than champions are passive sufferers, rewarded at last for their constancy of mind. Apparently to celebrate the Treaty of Union between England and Scotland, completed in 1707 and alluded to in the final lines of the play, Rowe turned to English pseudohistory for *The Royal Convert* (1707). Hengist, king of Kent and son of the first Saxon invader of Britain, is betrothed for alliance purposes to Rodogune, sister of the great Saxon chief, Offa. But while hunting one day he spies a beautiful young woman in a cottage in the forest and seizes her for his own. Stalling with his Saxon allies for time to secure his prize yet save the alliance, he turns to his younger brother, Aribert, the Royal Convert of the title, hoping Aribert can marry Rodogune instead. To his rage he discovers that Aribert is already married to the woman Ethelinda, sister to the Briton chief, Lucius. Hengist also discovers that, despite both the brothers' (enforced) vows before Woden's altar, Ethelinda has converted Aribert to Christianity. This fact provides Hengist with the excuse to remove the brother who has become his deadly rival. He plans to commit two of patriarchy's most heinous crimes, fratricide and incest.

Meanwhile, Aribert secures Ethelinda's escape to her brother, and Rodogune, who has fallen in love with Aribert rather than the intended Hengist, rescues him at the moment of his execution. Of course, she expects the reward of his affection; yet he retains his constancy of mind against this temptation too. When her troops bring in Ethelinda, whom they have captured in her attempt to escape, Rodogune, another of Rowe's termagants, waxes wroth at the sight of her rival and condemns both of the lov-

Anne Oldfield, who created the role of Ethelinda in The Royal Convert *and the title characters in* The Tragedy of Jane
Shore *and* The Tragedy of the Lady Jane Gray *(mezzotint by I. Simon, based on a portrait by Jonathan Richardson)*

ers to death. Teaching him to endure by relying upon the hope of an afterlife, Ethelinda, Rowe's faithful wife figure elevated to sainthood and martyrdom, repeats her favorite refrain, that she was born "to suffer." However, the desperate Hengist, bent on defying all social and natural bonds, returns to seize Ethelinda once more and carry her to his private castle, reminiscent of Lancelot's Joyous Gard, site of medieval literature's most radical rebellion. Aided by the Britons, his attack succeeds in driving off Rodogune's Saxons, but in an action reminiscent of the servant's resistance to Cornwall's similar violation of bonds in *King Lear,* a common soldier, as if to prove such violation offends the meanest member of the

human community, deals Hengist his death wound, and he dies unrepentant. Thus, their values affirmed by an underwriting Providence operating through secondary causes, the suffering innocents are vindicated and rewarded. Aribert becomes king, Ethelinda his queen, a combination that represents the union of Briton and Saxon and foreshadows the Act of Union.

Rowe concludes the play with another interesting combination. Rodogune is a termagant in the tradition of Rowe's Artemisa and Calista (all roles played by and probably consciously written for the aging but still apparently passionate and powerful Elizabeth Barry). She also relies solely on her "self." And when she is thwarted at the end, she leaves the stage recalcitrant, hurling her

ROYAL CONVERT.

Illustration from the 1792 edition of Rowe's works

unyielding defiance at men and demanding from nature not just equality but sovereignty:

> Be just for once, and equal the Command;
> Let Woman once be Mistress in her turn,
> Subdue Mankind beneath her haughty Scorn,
> And smile to see the proud Oppressor mourn.

This is patriarchy's paranoid image of what supporters of the Equal Rights Amendment really want. But Rowe domesticates Rodogune's energy by combining her figure with that of Ethelinda in her prophecy of a "Great" but "Pious" British queen, Anne Stuart, who will preside over her dominions with a "Mother's Love." Rowe's queen is no matriarch, however. Part of her function as

mother is to produce male heirs, a desideratum devoutly wished by Rowe's fellow Whigs as the death blow to the hopes of the Jacobites and their king-across-the-water.

Meanwhile, in January 1706 Rowe, apparently convinced that he was not and would not likely ever be a country squire, undertook the lengthy procedure of a private act of Parliament to break the entail of his property in Devon and Cornwall, set up at his marriage settlement. He pleaded the remoteness of the property from London and the low return received from its rental and was granted the privilege of selling the property to set up a trust fund of eighteen hundred pounds; the annual income from it would be his

Woodcuts from Rowe's Works of Mr. William Shakespear *(1709), the first illustrated edition: (top)* Hamlet *and* Measure for
Measure; *(bottom)* Macbeth *and* Henry VIII

and his wife's during their lives, but at their deaths the fund would pass to son John. Any residue from the sale of the property would be used for the payment of debts (Rowe mentions "paying several of his Father's Debts, which he was not obliged to have done"). The private bill was introduced to the Commons on 14 January 1706, was approved, and passed to the Lords, where it was also approved. On 19 March 1706 the Rowe Estate Act received the royal assent. (On the same day Rowe's friend Richard Thornhill received the royal permission for a similar bill concerning his property in Kent.) Clearly Rowe's action signaled that he was making the transition from country gentry to bourgeois intellectual, from absentee landlord to civil servant, in one act of law. His action, moreover, has political overtones, dissociating him from his background of Country Whigs and associating him more closely with the Court Whigs, who were and continued to be his patrons as an unpropertied civil servant and an author.

Finally in June 1709 came the crowning achievement of the Rowe-Tonson association with the publication of the first new edition of Shakespeare's works since the folio edition of 1623, for which Rowe received £36 10s. The idea was to publish a popular, familiar, moderately priced edition–modern in format (six volumes octavo rather than a scholarly folio) with an engraved frontispiece for each play and with all the usual aids for play readers (a list of dramatis personae, the scene location, and regular act and scene divisions for each play). All of these, together with a start toward contemporary spelling and some happy emendations, brought Rowe's Shakespeare into the hands and minds of a much larger public. Rowe added a new life of Shakespeare, brief (forty short pages) but incorporating the research of his friend the aged actor Betterton, the first to seek primary source material at Stratford–for which Rowe expresses "a particular Obligation to him." Altogether it was a major publishing and scholarly achievement. (In mid March Tonson advertised in the *London Gazette* and the *Daily Courant* for "Materials . . . that may be serviceable to this Design," but we do not know if he had any response.)

With good reason, Rowe's edition of Shakespeare was dedicated to the powerful Charles Seymour, duke of Somerset, for the duke had worked hard to secure for Rowe a good government position as an undersecretary of state to James Douglas, duke of Queensberry–the same

position that Addison held early in his public service. Queensberry became a new third secretary of state, ostensibly for Scotland following the Union in 1707, but at the duke's insistence, for a few foreign diplomatic posts as well. Although Narcissus Luttrell reports these appointments on 5 February 1709, notations in the State Papers record that Queensberry "enter'd upon" his duties of foreign representation on 15 June 1710. The files show that Rowe worked conscientiously but with seemingly little personal initiative as undersecretary, maintaining correspondence with British diplomatic posts in northern Europe. One of his more interesting letters, reporting the notorious stabbing of Robert Harley in Council meeting by the marquis de Guiscard, was sent to the English envoys in Denmark and Poland on the day following the event. Some letters have a scattering of five-digit code groups in the text. During this period Rowe clearly was very much a man-about-town, dining or meeting on at least four occasions with various groupings of Jonathan Swift, George Delaval, William Congreve, Richard Steele, Anthony Henley, and Sir Richard Temple, as well as joining with Swift and Matthew Prior on 22 November 1710 in a facetious letter to *The Tatler* (no. 258) ridiculing the current popularity of the words "Britain" and "British" following the Union. Early in July 1711, however, the duke of Queensberry died, and Rowe, as his last duty in this office, sent a circular letter to the foreign posts concerned announcing the death and the suspension of business in the duke's office.

This misfortune after so brief a tenure initiated a series of distressing events which must have been the nadir of Rowe's life. In February 1712 Antonia, his wife for almost nineteen years, died and was buried in St. Dunstan-in-the-West. She had borne him seven children, of whom only the second son, John, still lived. At her death Rowe was not only bereaved but soon to be homeless, since by 12 August 1712 tax records list their house in Fetter Lane "Empty." It was in this period, probably, that Rowe studied Spanish intensively, inferring from a brief conversation with Robert Harley, by then earl of Oxford, that he was being prepared for foreign service in Spain, only to be mortified when Oxford greeted his mastery of Spanish with the comment, "Then, Sir, I envy you the pleasure of reading Don Quixote in the original." This may, indeed, be all that resulted from Swift's claim, "Row I have recommended, and got a Promise of a Place." In September 1712 Elizabeth Spann, the widow of a Royal

Navy captain, approached Rowe seeking his help in promoting a petition to the government for her benefit. Rowe, fresh from the office of the secretary of state, where fees for services were a recognized perquisite of office, agreed to do what he could to advance her petition through his friends Erasmus Lewis and William Legge, earl of Dartmouth. But when sums totaling about ten pounds were mentioned as required and the accounts given by Rowe and Lewis about that money did not seem to agree, the widow Spann in January 1713 swore out a deposition accusing Rowe of peculation of that sum. The outcome of the case is not known, but needless to say the matter did not help Rowe's morale nor his reputation. Later in 1713 Rowe was living in the village of Stockwell, about a mile south of the Thames at Vauxhall–a kind of exile from the precincts of the City of London and of Westminster, where he had lived from boyhood, and a measure of the depth of his misfortune.

But at this point Alexander Pope enters, or perhaps reenters, Rowe's life. In early May 1713 Pope was witness to, and probably helpful in arranging, Rowe's contract with Pope's publisher, Bernard Lintot, for the publication of a new tragedy by Rowe, *Jane Shore*. Obviously with a little help from his friends, Rowe was started on the renewal of his career as a dramatist. When published in February 1714, amidst a great deal of hype, this play was dedicated to the teenaged Charles Douglas, duke of Queensberry, son of the duke under whom Rowe had served, who is urged in the opening paragraph to emulate his father. From this time on the letters of Pope suggest how warmly Pope fostered and encouraged Rowe's work in drama (reporting that this play "has been worth about five hundred pounds to Mr. Rowe") and in the translation of Lucan, despite the difference in their personalities and their politics.

The Tragedy of Jane Shore premiered on 2 February 1714 and had an initial run of thirteen nights, a run, among plays produced up till that time, second only to Addison's *Cato* in the previous year. It outdistanced all but Otway's *Orphan* and Rowe's own *Tamerlane* (revived every year to honor William III and, by extension, the revolution) in performances of serious plays, outside Shakespeare's, over the next two-thirds of a century and was still in the repertory more than a century later. It was translated into French, German, and Spanish and, along with other plays by Rowe

and Otway, influenced the development of domestic tragedy abroad.

Part of *Jane Shore*'s success is its providing of a wonderful vehicle for the successor to Elizabeth Barry as the greatest actress of her age, Anne Oldfield. Another part is its excellent blank verse, written in imitation of Shakespeare. As James R. Sutherland has correctly averred, no other Englishman of his time could write blank verse as well as Rowe. Part, too, may well have been its religiosity, which probably appealed to emergent middle-class morality of the day, with all its societies for reformation. But perhaps what else contributed to the play's immense popularity was a political ambiguity that allowed both Whig and Tory to consider it as espousing the Truth.

The historical Jane Shore was married to a gold merchant in London when she was espied, courted, and carried off by King Edward IV. Her story was recorded in many versions over the years. She remained at court as Edward's mistress till he died, the point at which Rowe's play takes up the action. Edward's brother Richard, the duke of Gloucester infamous in Tudor historiography and Shakespeare's *Richard III*, wants to usurp the succession from Edward's infant sons, the eldest of whom was Edward V. In order to do so he needs the support of sufficient powerful barons, among them Lord Hastings, a member of his Council. Richard's equally infamous advisers, Ratcliffe and Catesby (known popularly as the Rat and the Cat), counsel him to employ Hastings's new mistress, Jane Shore, to manage him, since she is totally dependent now on Richard's bounty.

Jane is Hastings's mistress only in his desire, however. Rowe portrays her as thoroughly penitent for her transgressive behavior, and when Hastings believes he has secured Jane's position at court and comes in the middle of the night to take his reward, she steadfastly resists him. When Hastings resorts to force, Jane's husband, disguised as one of the servants of her household, protects her and disarms him. Yet, although Jane has proved her firm purpose of amendment, her troubles have only begun. Her protector is ordered imprisoned by the powerful Hastings. Moreover, Hastings's cast mistress, Alicia, is furiously jealous and betrays Jane, supposedly her best friend, to Richard, accusing her of being the cause of Hastings's support of the young Edward. Richard orders Hastings summarily executed and Jane turned out on the streets, supposedly to do public penance but really to starve.

Sarah Siddons and Mary Ann Yates, illustrations from the 1792 edition of Rowe's works

Granted a last-minute audience with the condemned Hastings, Alicia confesses her treachery, and he interprets his fate as divine retribution for his libertinism. He admonishes Alicia to calm herself and offer succor to Jane, but by the time Jane arrives at her door Alicia has gone mad and refuses to help her. Rowe contrasts Alicia's unrepentant, vindictive behavior with Jane's repentant, charitable behavior throughout, a behavior that merits her succor and forgiveness even from her offended husband at the end. But it is too late. Hastings is executed; Richard's soldiers seize Shore; Jane dies; and Richard will go on to murder the royal princes in the Tower and become a usurping tyrant. Jane's faithful servant Bellmour

reads the middle-class moral of the play as the curtain closes: "Let those, who view this sad Example, know, / What Fate attends the broken Marriage Vow."

Rowe gives Jane one of his great speeches decrying the double standard of patriarchal morality, especially the fact that men may engage in sexual promiscuity with virtual impunity, whereas women become soiled goods in the system of sexual commodity exchange. But Rowe's morality remains patriarchal. Alicia and Hastings are punished for sexual transgressions, as is Jane, although she is granted the reconstitution of her middle-class domestic bliss before she dies, properly submissive to both her husband and her (male) god. And Rowe's major preoccupation in the play seems to be with stoic endurance in both causes of morality and political allegiance. Alicia and Hastings demonstrate fatal lack of self-control. Yet Hastings seems redeemable; for in the face of sure death, he stands up for legitimate succession, and Jane, who the night before had nearly been raped by him, when she hears of his patriotism praises him and prays for him. Ironically, it is Ratcliffe who enunciates the imperative of this bourgeois reappropriation of stoicism: "Summon your Courage, / And be your self."

The exaltation of self, largely negative in the seventeenth century, becomes positive in the heroic literature of the eighteenth: *Robinson Crusoe* (1719), *Moll Flanders* (1722), *Cato* (1713). And it is connected with a blossoming rhetoric of democracy. Jane properly maintains that "Highborn" beauties of the court are far worthier than she, but Alicia—and we—remain impressed that she was raised to a monarch's attention and remains attractive to Hastings. We are further impressed by the dignity and fortitude she exhibits in the face of calamity despite her class, for which Richard and his cohorts demean her. Even more, when Jane's husband stands up to Hastings, and with his sword at that—a very aristocratic martial art—he boasts, "no gaudy Titles grac'd my Birth, . . . / Yet Heav'n that made me Honest, made me more / Than ever King did, when he made a Lord." After he disarms Hastings, Shore credits his own "inborn Virtue" and triumphantly asks, "where is our difference now? . . . a Lord / Oppos'd against a Man is but a Man."

Contemporary Whigs would have been comforted by this kind of rhetoric. And they also would have read Richard's attempt at usurpation as the threat of the return of arbitrary government if ever a Stuart were to return. They would have welcomed the lines describing Edward IV's entailing of the royal succession "in Concurrence / With his Estates assembled." Hastings's characterization of the evils of faction and Jane's admonition to leave government to the professionals also seem supportive of at least republican if not democratic theory.

But Jane and Hastings's strident defense of the principle of hereditary succession, especially as expressed in the rhetoric of Catesby's description of Hastings—"he bears a most religious Reverence / To his dead Master *Edward*'s Royal Memory"—and Jane's refusal to "see [Edward's] Children robb'd of Right" must have given aid and comfort to Jacobites. Perhaps it is no wonder that Pope helped Rowe get his play published. Rowe may have intended that his play serve as a warning, as the death of Queen Anne approached, against the breaking of the Protestant succession established by Parliament and against the return of arbitrary, tyrannical (read: Catholic, Stuart) government. But Jane's and Hastings's defenses of hereditary succession must have seemed, at least to the Jacobites, as the political Truth, hurled in the teeth of those about to ignore the son of their legitimate monarch and seek for "hereditary" Protestant succession in the ranks of distant cousins in the distant provinces of Germany. Was Rowe conscious of the ambiguity? Was he himself ambivalent?

Whatever Rowe's real political allegiances, his economic fortunes improved tremendously with the success of *Jane Shore*, for that success contributed to his being named in the following year poet laureate to the first of the Hanoverians, George I. Meanwhile, Rowe's rehabilitation from despair was being aided in another way. It probably began in July 1711 with Rowe's playful letter to the dowager countess of Warwick enclosing his verse jeu d'esprit, "Occasioned by his First Visit to Lady Warwick at Holland House." It does not seem likely that this was anything more than an exercise in verse or "that Rowe was ever a serious rival of Addison" for the hand of the countess, as Arthur L. Cooke expressed it some thirty years ago. Indeed, Rowe was to become more enamored of Anne Devenish, who was "so dear to the Countess, that they were in a Manner inseparable," as William Ayre expressed it some two hundred forty years ago. Some of Rowe's own verses, published first in 1747 by his widow, record the courtship and witness that Anne spurred him to seek the laureateship, which he achieved in August 1715 on the death of Nahum Tate. In March 1716 Rowe took out a license from the bishop of London to marry Anne Devenish. Although no church record of the actual marriage has been found in the designated "parish church of Fulham," the newlyweds settled into the Devenish household in King Street, opening west from the northwest corner of Covent Garden, the house in which Rowe eventually died.

Rowe's ascension to the laureateship was aided most by his last play, *The Tragedy of the Lady Jane Gray*, produced in April 1715. In it Rowe's politics no longer seem the slightest bit ambiguous.

John Loftis has properly characterized the play as Whig propaganda. It dramatizes a radical Protestant attempt to keep Mary Tudor from the throne at the death of the boy-king, Edward VI. Justly fearing Roman retribution for Henry VIII's break with Catholicism, a powerful clique, led by the ambitious John Dudley, duke of Northumberland, attempted to alter the succession, bypassing Henry's daughters, Mary and Elizabeth, having his niece, Mary, duchess of Suffolk, who was next in line, abdicate, and having Henry's grandniece, Lady Jane Gray, named queen of England by Edward's will and decree of Council.

Rowe portrays Jane as a pious, educated young woman who has no ambition but agrees to try to save her country from *oppressive tyranny*, terms that were by this time buzzwords for Catholic monarchs and a rallying cry against Jacobites. Rowe's incessant descriptions of what would ensue if the Catholics return to power, and his portrayal of the sadism of Stephen Gardiner, bishop of Winchester, when they do, is meant for his contemporary audience in the year of the Jacobite revolution referred to as The Fifteen. At the same time, Rowe's play affirms the stoic morality of constancy of mind and self-reliance. Jane and her husband, Guilford Dudley, son of Northumberland, are portrayed not as ambitious opportunists but Protestant saints (straight out of John Foxe's *Book of Martyrs*) who gladly sacrifice their lives for the Whig buzzwords of Liberty, Country, and the Protestant Religion. In the subplot the earl of Pembroke, Guilford's rival for Lady Jane, must also learn to overcome his passions and endure his loss of Jane. Converted by the virtue of Guilford, he tries to win the royal couple a reprieve, but Gardiner's cruelty prevails and Queen Mary seems embarked on the career properly characterized as *bloody*.

At one point Jane raises the kind of questions the Royalists raised during the Exclusion Crisis:

> Can *Edward*'s Will,
> Or Twenty met in Council, make a Queen?
> . . . where are those . . . who make the Law?
> Where are the Ancient Honours of the Realm,
> The Nobles, with the Mitre'd Fathers join'd?
> The Wealthy Commons solemnly Assembled?
> Where is that Voice of a Consenting People,
> To pledge the Universal Faith with mine,
> And call me justly Queen?

But such reservations could not give the Jacobites of 1715 much comfort, for when Northumberland promises Jane that just such Parliamentary approval is forthcoming, she accepts the crown. The implication is that when such approval is present, succession can be altered—and should be in order to avoid oppressive tyranny. The play concludes with prophecies of future heroes (read: William III, George I, and his son, the Prince of Wales, to whose wife Rowe dedicated the play) who would finally complete the Protestant Reformation in England.

After *Jane Shore* and *Lady Jane Gray*, not only Rowe's domestic situation but his financial and social positions improved. Almost as soon as the Hanoverian royalty arrived, Rowe was appointed clerk of the Council of the Prince—Samuel Molyneaux was the secretary—and in September 1716 one of the land surveyors of the customs in London. This position paid a good salary (two hundred pounds), but John Dennis, Rowe's friend, writing to congratulate him, almost seems to commiserate with him, since it is an appointment by warrant, which required personal attendance rather than an appointment by patent, which could be filled by a hired replacement, such as Dennis held.

Meanwhile, Rowe was still working at his translation of Lucan, did a one-hundred-line conclusion (Glaucus and Scylla) to book 13 of the joint translation of Ovid's *Metamorphoses* edited by Samuel Garth in 1717, and prepared his required two odes (for the New Year and the King's Birthday) each year except 1717, when he produced only a New Year's ode. (His desperate pleas to Thomas Tickell and John Hughes for their help on this ode were apparently unrewarded.) In May 1718 he was appointed clerk of the presentations by the new lord chancellor, Thomas Parker. His wife's illness (probably during pregnancy) led Rowe to write a rare sad song, "Ah Willow." Fortunately Anne recovered from her illness and was delivered in late May of a daughter, who was baptized Charlotte at St. Paul's Church, Covent Garden, 1 June 1718.

"When he had just got to be easy in his Fortune," as Dr. James Wellwood was to write in 1719, Rowe became ill in early November 1718 and grew steadily worse. On 20 November he signed his will, witnessed by Pope and Thomas Hill, and on 6 December he died. He was buried six days later, at night in the south transept (now Poet's Corner) of Westminster Abbey, where Francis Atterbury, "the Bishop of Rochester [and concurrently Dean of Westminster] out of a particular Mark of Esteem for him, as being his

JANE GRAY.

Mr HARTLEY as JANE GRAY.

Wom. ———— her Knee
Has known that Posture only, and her Eye
Or fixed upon the Sacred Page before her,
Or lifted with her rising hopes to Heaven.

Illustration from the 1792 edition of Rowe's works

School-Fellow, honoured his Ashes by performing the last Offices himself," as Stephen Hales, the editor of a memorial volume of verses to Rowe, records. Rowe's body was carried to the abbey by the Company of Upholders, of which his father-in-law, Joseph Devenish, was a past master. The fine monument by Rysbrack, designed with a bust of Rowe and a medallion bust of his daughter Charlotte Fane (1718-1739), as well as a seated mourning figure (presumably his wife Anne), was not installed until after 29 October 1742, when the Chapter of Westminster Abbey gave consent to place it against the south wall "between Shakespears and Mr. Gays." In the 1930s the monuments to both Rowe and Gay were moved out of normal access to the triforium immediately above their original locations.

When Rowe died, his translation of Lucan was yet to be published, and before that a few friends of Rowe compiled a slim volume of verses, *Musarum Lachrymae; or, Poems to the Memory of Nicholas Rowe, Esq.,* dedicated to William Congreve and brought out by Curll on 31 January 1719. The contributors were Charles Beck-

Nicholas Rowe (engraving based on a portrait by Sir Godfrey Kneller)

ingham, Nicholas Amhurst, Susanna Centlivre, and Thomas Newcomb. Of these the best known by far must be Centlivre; she had received from Rowe a prologue for her *The Gamester* in 1704 and an epilogue for her *The Cruel Gift* in 1717, and it is clear from her own verse that she was a member of the circle of Mrs. Rowe, Dr. Wellwood, and young Edward Henry Rich, Lord Warwick. The rest of the contributors were quite young and not socially well acquainted (Beckingham addressed his dedication to Congreve, whom he confesses never to have met); Newcomb cannot even be found in *The New Cambridge Bibliography of English Literature*. More important, perhaps, in this little volume was an eleven-page memoir of Rowe, dated "Dec. the 26th,

1718" and signed "S. Hales," which qualifies as the earliest biography, although it probably includes as much error as fact.

The big event, however, was the posthumous publication of Rowe's *Lucan's Pharsalia* early in March 1719. The subscription list of 391 names for 431 copies, beginning with the Prince and Princess of Wales, was impressive but not overwhelming—Prior's *Poems on Several Occasions*, published by Tonson nearly simultaneously with Rowe's book, was among the largest with 1,446 names, while John Gay's volume in 1720 had 365 and the median was about 250. Apparently the death of Rowe prevented completion of his prefatory life of Lucan, and Dr. Wellwood explains that Rowe had prevailed upon him to fulfill this task. So he did, with the addition of a minimal life of Rowe, signing it on 26 February 1719. Tonson did a magnificent piece of work on this subscription edition, a large folio (pages about 18 1/2 inches tall) with many engravings, a handsome typeface, and ample margins. Anne Rowe, in accordance with her husband's wishes, dedicated the work to King George in one simple, dignified paragraph (a letter from James Brydges, earl of Carnarvon, later duke of Chandos, to Rowe on 3 April 1718 is a polite rejection of a proposed dedication, possibly of Lucan). During the early spring of 1719 (before 21 May) Pope had completed his early eight-line epitaph for Rowe, which, while honoring Rowe's memory, was also designed to remind wealthy patrons of the great Dryden's burial place nearby, still unmarked and unhonored almost twenty years after his death. On 19 June the widow Anne probated the simple will, which, except for twenty pounds for mourning and "those two pictures of mine" to his son John (explaining "that he is sufficiently provided for otherwise," that is, by the eighteen-hundred-pound trust fund set up by the Rowe Estate Act of 1706), and except for ten pounds for mourning to "my sister Sarah Peele" (that is, half-sister of Anne, his wife), everything went to the widow and daughter. Finally on 26 August 1719 Rowe's library of just over six hundred titles and thirty-one volumes of manuscripts (mostly "Law") was offered for sale and dispersed.

From the perspective of the end of Rowe's dramatic career, perhaps we can view clearly in retrospect the ideology to which his dramatic themes contributed. In an age when bourgeois ideologues were appropriating the rhetoric of the Roman Republic to gild their political goal of a plutocracy sanctioned by a ceremonial monarchy (witness Rowe's giveaway characterization of Commons as "Wealthy"), it is no accident that the Rowes and the Defoes and the Addisons and the Steeles were creating heroes who were stoic, self-reliant, patriarchal patriots. Even satirists no longer attacked primarily those who break their word but those who abuse the new ethos of the self in solipsism (for example, not only Swift and Pope but Rowe himself in the figure of Sir Timothy Tallapoy). Even Rowe's most interesting creations, at least to the late twentieth century, his female rebels, are absorbed into patriarchal paradigms: they remain uppity women providentially marginalized from the centers of power, or they become penitents, properly submissive to their human and divine fathers. Yet, perhaps these fig-

ures can be said to have evolved, through the domestic she-tragedies of playwrights like Lessing (who called Rowe "mein Dichter") and Goethe into the successful female rebels of Ibsen and the twentieth century. Rowe's plays might then be said to have contributed to the ideology not only of his own but to a more "enlightened" age.

Bibliography:

J. Douglas Canfield, "A Tentative Twentieth-Century Bibliography on Rowe's Tragedies," in his *Nicholas Rowe and Christian Tragedy* (Gainesville: University Presses of Florida, 1977), pp. 197-199.

Biographies:

James R. Sutherland, Introduction to *Three Plays: Tamerlane, The Fair Penitent, Jane Shore*, edited by Sutherland (London: Scholartis, 1929);

Norman Ault, "Pope and Rowe," in his *New Light on Pope* (London: Methuen, 1949), pp. 128-155;

Alfred W. Hesse, "Nicholas Rowe's Knowledge of Spanish: A Commentary on Spence and Birbeck Hill," *Papers of the Bibliographical Society of America*, 69 (1975): 546-552;

Hesse, "Some Neglected Life Records of Nicholas Rowe," *Notes and Queries*, 220 (1975): 348-353, 484-488;

Hesse, "Pope's Role in Tonson's 'Loss of Rowe,'" *Notes and Queries*, 222 (1977): 234-235.

References:

Janet E. Aikins, "To Know Jane Shore 'think on all time backward,'" *Papers on Language and Literature*, 18 (Summer 1982): 258-277;

J. M. Armistead, "Calista and the 'Equal Empire' of Her 'Sacred Sex,'" in *Studies in Eighteenth-Century Culture*, volume 15, edited by O. M. Brack, Jr. (Madison: University of Wisconsin Press, 1985), pp. 173-186;

Laura Brown, "The Defenseless Woman and the Development of English Tragedy," *Studies in English Literature*, 22 (Summer 1982): 429-443;

Brown, *English Dramatic Form, 1660-1760: An Essay in Generic History* (New Haven: Yale University Press, 1981), pp. 148-154;

Landon Crawford Burns, Jr., *Pity and Tears: The Tragedies of Nicholas Rowe*, Salzburg Studies in English Literature: Poetic Drama & Poetic Theory 8 (Salzburg: Institut für Englische Sprache und Literatur, University of Salzburg, 1974);

J. Douglas Canfield, "Female Rebels and Patriarchal Paradigms in Some Neoclassical Works," in *Studies in Eighteenth-Century Culture*, volume 18, edited by John Yolton (Madison: University of Wisconsin Press, 1988), pp. 204-227;

Canfield, *Nicholas Rowe and Christian Tragedy* (Gainesville: University Presses of Florida, 1977);

Canfield, Review of *Pity and Tears: The Tragedies of Nicholas Rowe*, by Landon Crawford Burns (1974), in *The Eighteenth Century: A Current Bibliography*, new series 1 (for 1975) (Philadelphia & Los Angeles: American Society for Eighteenth-Century Studies, 1978), pp. 366-367;

Canfield, Review of *The Tragedy of Jane Shore*, edited by Harry William Pedicord, Regents Restoration Drama Series (1974), in *The Eighteenth Century: A Current Bibliography*, new series 1, pp. 367-368;

Donald Bettice Clark, "An Eighteenth-Century Adaptation of Massinger," *Modern Language Quarterly*, 13 (September 1952): 239-252;

Clark, "Nicholas Rowe: A Study in the Development of the Pathetic Tragedy," Ph.D. dissertation, George Washington University, 1947;

Clark, "The Source and Characterization of Nicholas Rowe's *Tamerlane*," *Modern Language Notes*, 65 (March 1950): 145-152;

Derek Cohen, "Nicholas Rowe, Aphra Behn, and the Farcical Muse," *Papers on Language and Literature*, 15 (Fall 1979): 383-395;

Richard H. Dammers, "Female Characterization in English Platonic Drama: A Background for the Eighteenth Century Tragedies of Nicholas Rowe," *Restoration and 18th Century Theatre Research*, second series 1, no. 2 (1986): 34-41;

Dammers, "The Female Experience in the Tragedies of Nicholas Rowe," *Women and Literature*, 6 (Spring 1978): 28-35;

Dammers, "The Importance of Being Female in the Tragedies of Nicholas Rowe," *McNeese Review*, 26 (1979-1980): 13-20;

Malcolm Goldstein, "Pathos and Personality in the Tragedies of Nicholas Rowe," in *English Writers of the Eighteenth Century*, edited by John H. Middendorf (New York: Columbia University Press, 1971), pp. 172-185;

Jacques Gury, "Le Monstre et la pécheresse: Richard III et Jane Shore entre Shakespeare et Rowe vus par les Français de Louis XV à Louis-Philippe," *Moreana*, 20, nos. 79-80 (November 1983): 123-133;

Jean Hagstrum, *Sex and Sensibility: Ideal and Erotic Love from Milton to Mozart* (Chicago: University of Chicago Press, 1980), pp. 117-121, 173-175;

James L. Harner, Introduction to *The Tragedy of Jane Shore*, facsimile of 1714 edition (London: Scolar Press, 1973);

Alfred W. Hesse, "Who Was Bit by Rowe's Comedy *The Biter?*," *Philological Quarterly*, 62 (Fall 1983): 477-485;

Hesse and Richard J. Sherry, "Two Unrecorded Editions of Rowe's *Lady Jane Gray*: The Early Editions," *Papers of the Bibliographical Society of America*, 72 (1978): 220-226;

Alfred Jackson, "Rowe's Historical Tragedies," *Anglia*, 54 (1930): 307-330;

Annibel Jenkins, *Nicholas Rowe*, Twayne's English Authors Series 200 (Boston: G. K. Hall, 1977);

Frank J. Kearful, "The Nature of Tragedy in Rowe's *The Fair Penitent*," *Papers on Language and Literature*, 2 (Fall 1966): 351-360;

John Clyde Loftis, *The Politics of Drama in Augustan England* (Oxford: Clarendon, 1963);

Cynthia S. Matlack, " 'Spectatress of the Mischief Which She Made': Tragic Woman Perceived and Perceiver," in *Studies in Eighteenth-Century Culture*, volume 6, edited by Ronald C. Rosbottom (Madison: University of Wisconsin Press, 1977), pp. 317-330;

Judith Milhous, "The First Production of Rowe's *Jane Shore*," *Theatre Journal*, 38 (October 1986): 309-321;

Alfred Schwarz, "An Example of Eighteenth-Century Pathetic Tragedy: Rowe's *Jane Shore*," *Modern Language Quarterly*, 22 (September 1961): 236-247;

Richard J. Sherry, " 'Restoring and Preserving . . . Learning': Rowe's *Ulysses*, 1705," *Restoration and 18th Century Theatre Research*, second series 3, no. 1 (1988): 10-19;

Willard Thorp, "A Key to Rowe's *Tamerlane*," *Journal of English and Germanic Philology*, 39 (First Quarter 1940): 124-127;

George W. Whiting, "Rowe's Debt to *Paradise Lost*," *Modern Philology*, 32 (February 1935): 271-279;

Matthew H. Wikander, *The Play of Truth and State: Historical Drama from Shakespeare to Brecht* (Baltimore: Johns Hopkins University Press, 1986), pp. 119-125;

Lindley A. Wyman, "The Tradition of the Formal Meditation in Rowe's *The Fair Penitent,*" *Philological Quarterly*, 42 (July 1963): 412-416.

Papers:
Harvard University's Houghton Library houses the earliest Rowe manuscript, a schoolbook. The British Library has a manuscript of a translation of the first book of Lucan. Letters by Rowe are held by the British Library, the Historical Society of Pennsylvania's Dreer Collection, the London Public Record Office, Huntington Library, Hoare's Bank in London, Guildhall Library, the Folger Shakespeare Library, and the City of London Record Office. Ecclesiastical records pertaining to Rowe survive in the Guildhall Library, London.

Frances Sheridan
(1724-1766)

Ann Messenger
Simon Fraser University

See also the Sheridan entry in *DLB 39: British Novelists, 1660-1800.*

PLAY PRODUCTIONS: *The Discovery*, London, Theatre Royal in Drury Lane, 3 February 1763;
The Dupe, London, Theatre Royal in Drury Lane, 10 December 1763.

BOOKS: *Memoirs of Miss Sidney Bidulph, Extracted from Her Own Journal*, 3 volumes (London: Printed for R. & J. Dodsley, 1761); modern edition, introduction by Sue Townsend (London & New York: Pandora, 1987);
The Discovery: A Comedy. As It Is Performed at the Theatre-Royal in Drury-Lane. Written by the Editor of Miss Sidney Bidulph (London: Printed for T. Davies, 1763);
The Dupe: A Comedy. As It Is Now Acting at the Theatre-Royal in Drury-Lane, by His Majesty's Servants. By the Author of The Discovery (London: Printed for A. Millar, 1764);
Conclusion of the Memoirs of Miss Sidney Bidulph, as Prepared for the Press by the Late Editor of the Former Part, 2 volumes (London: Printed for J. Dodsley, 1767);
The History of Nourjahad, by the Editor of Sidney Bidulph (London: Printed for J. Dodsley, 1767); modern edition, edited by H. V. M. (H. V. Marrot) (London: Elkin Mathews & Marrot, 1927); modern edition, introduction by Maurice Johnson (Norwood, Pa.: Norwood Editions, 1977);

Eugenia and Adelaide: A Novel, 2 volumes (London: Printed for C. Dilly, 1791).
Collection: *The Plays of Frances Sheridan*, edited by Robert Hogan and Jerry C. Beasley (Newark: University of Delaware Press / London & Toronto: Associated University Presses, 1984).

Until Frances Chamberlaine Sheridan was in her late teens, she had never seen or even read a play, but the theater was to play a major role in the rest of her life. Her own role in the history of the theater is small but significant: her plays were an important influence on the comedies of her son Richard Brinsley Sheridan, and the reception of her two comedies which reached the stage reveals much about the public's taste at the time, especially its attitude toward feminist ideas.

She was born in Dublin, the youngest of five children of the Reverend Dr. Philip Chamberlaine and Anastasia Whyte; her mother did not live long after Frances's birth. She was never a pretty child, and her physical unattractiveness was increased by an accident, occurring when she was "an infant," that left her lame for life, as her biographer and granddaughter, Alicia LeFanu, reports. But her mind was good, so good and so hungry that she disobeyed her father (who had grudgingly allowed her minimal instruction in reading) and got her brothers to teach her writing, Latin, and botany. By the time she was in her midteens, she had written a two-volume novel on paper that had been doled out

Mrs Frances Sheridan

Author of Sidney Biddulp, Nourjahad, The Discovery &c.

Mother of the late Rt. Hon. Richard Brinsley Sheridan.

to her for the housekeeping accounts; she may also have written some sermons. When her father's mind gave way, she tended him faithfully, but apparently she took advantage of his slackened control to go to the theater with her brothers. When Philip Chamberlaine died in the early 1740s, she was free.

At the theater she would have seen young Thomas Sheridan on stage. Born in 1719, he made his debut, as Richard III, at Smock Alley theater in 1743, although with some hesitation because he was a gentleman. He became a star overnight. In two years he was the manager of Smock Alley, and before much longer he was "King Tom," theatrical dictator of all Dublin. His career flourished for ten years, despite the snags inevitably associated with theatrical temperaments. The first such snag appeared only a few months after his debut when he refused to perform as Cato because his costume had mysteriously disappeared; his costar, the visiting Theophilus Cibber, went on without him, speaking both their parts. The uproar that followed filled the public press with attacks, often grossly abusive, and defenses by friends and strangers alike. One of the strangers, who wrote a tribute to Thomas Sheridan in

Frances and Thomas Sheridan (collection of the Comtesse de Renéville)

verse, "The Owls," and another in prose, was Frances Chamberlaine. Versions of the dates and events involved differ, but the most reliable is that given by Esther Sheldon in *Thomas Sheridan of Smock-Alley* (1967), who reports that apparently Sheridan asked his sister (who knew Frances) to arrange a meeting; they met, courted for several years, and married, most probably in 1747.

The Sheridans spent the early years of their marriage in Dublin and at Quilca, a small country house Thomas had inherited. His work was absorbing: acting, managing, traveling to England to recruit actors, coping with the crisis of the Kelly riot (1747, when the theater was wrecked by "gentlemen" because Thomas Sheridan had declared himself their equal), trying to control a disorderly audience. During these early years, Frances bore five of her six children, four boys (including Richard Brinsley) and one girl. Two boys died in infancy, the second apparently as a consequence of another crisis in the theater, one which Thomas bungled badly and which put an end to his career as a manager. On 2 March 1754 a riot broke out at Smock Alley over the performance of James Miller and John Hoadly's *Mahomet the Imposter*, a play with implications for the Irish political scene. A fire was started, and a frightened

man rushed to the Sheridans' home to report, erroneously, that the whole theater was in flames. Thomas soon appeared unhurt, but Frances had been so disturbed that the child which was born shortly thereafter died in convulsions three months later. Although not burned down, the theater was seriously damaged by the rioters; Thomas's career and finances were also in ruins.

Although the Sheridan finances had never been really secure, from this point on money was a serious and a perpetual problem. Their first move was to London in 1754, where Thomas hoped to prosper in an educational career, writing books and giving lectures on rhetoric and elocution. Prosperity eluded him, however, and he was forced to return now and then to acting, in London and in Dublin, necessitating various family moves during the 1750s. In London, Frances bore her sixth child, Betsy, in 1758 and met the literary lights of the day, including Catherine Macaulay, Samuel Johnson, James Boswell, and Samuel Richardson.

Her letters to Richardson, written from Ireland in 1757, give some insight into the Sheridans' marriage, which Sheldon claims was "a lifelong romance." Frances does not exactly complain about her lot, but she longs to return

Betsy Sheridan, the youngest child of Frances and Thomas Sheridan (collection of William LeFanu)

to England. The solitude of Quilca is "profound," and her husband is not much of a companion: "he contrives to be busy from morn to night, and he is now as much immersed in turf-bogs, and a variety of other country occupations, as he was in Dublin in studies of another nature." Months later, the situation is unchanged: "Mr. Sheridan is up to the ears in ink; he is preparing another course of Lectures, compiling an English Grammar. . . . I have taken up my residence in the chimney corner, and should lose the use of my speech, if I did not find pretty constant employment for it with my little ones. . . ." With Thomas's imprudence in money matters added to this neglect and in the light of Frances's "Ode to Patience," the picture of the marriage is somewhat less rosy than that painted by both Sheldon and LeFanu. True, the Sheridans agreed on a conservative morality–Thomas did not introduce his wife to Peg Woffington, even when that lively actress was working for him in Dublin–but otherwise he appears to have been an inconsiderate husband.

Back in England again and living for a time at Windsor in winter 1759-1760, Frances Sheridan wrote her second novel, the first to be published, *Memoirs of Miss Sidney Bidulph* (1761). LeFanu claims that financial need, not "vanity," was her motive, which may well have been the case, even though the ladylike excuse is typical of the biography's tone and bias. Margaret Doody has analyzed Richardson's influence on this novel and describes its theme as the inescapability of the past. Despite her success with the novel, Sheridan turned to another genre for her next literary venture–comedy. In Windsor again (which she found dull) for the summer of 1762, she worked on *The Discovery*, which she showed to friends when she returned to London. She wrote to her cousin Sam Whyte that she was encouraged so much that she finished it and found that "Mr. Garrick was pressing to see it." When she read it to him, he immediately asked permission to produce it that season. It opened on 3 February 1763.

The play that Garrick was so pressing about is an interesting mixture of convention and innovation. Like most comedy, it deals in courtship and marital relations with, predictably, the triumph of youth and love over age and avarice. Also predictably, for its period, laughter and tears alternate, misbehaving characters reform, and nobody goes to bed outside of wedlock, comic conventions noted in the prologue. And although the prologue claims that "the story's new," the "discovery" of the title is yet another convention–a variation on the old revelation-of-parentage device: young Medway, in love with poor Miss Richly, is about to marry wealthy Mrs. Knightly to redeem the family fortunes which his father has lost, when Mrs. Knightly is discovered to be his illegitimate half sister. Overcome with family feeling, Mrs. Knightly gives half her money to her stepsister Miss Richly, thus enabling the true lovers to marry and Lord Medway, Mrs. Knightly's father, to pay his debts.

Yet in the epilogue Sheridan claims, and rightly so, that the play contains "innovations," which she lists as negatives: "not one pleasant sally!... /No sprightly rendezvous, no pretty fellows, / No wife intriguing, nor no husband jealous!" The list is reasonably accurate, but there are sprightliness and pleasantness of an unusual kind–and instead of an intriguing wife, an intriguing husband.

Much of the liveliness of the play emanates from Sir Harry and Lady Flutter, a pair of silly young newlyweds with fixed, wrong ideas about how they should behave in their new roles, ideas productive of constant friction which Lord Medway actively cultivates. He has an eye on Lady Flutter and believes his chances of an intrigue with her will improve as her marital misery increases. He instructs Sir Harry in the art of controlling his wife and then consoles and flatters the suffering bride. But Lady Medway accidentally overhears his plans for a private rendezvous, and, in an interesting if somewhat improbable scene, she warns Lady Flutter of her peril and explains that submissiveness to a husband's whims will make him and their marriage happy. Although Lady Medway's own submissiveness to her husband has not produced the promised result, Lady Flutter agrees to try the experiment, which in her case meets with immediate

and total success, Sir Harry instantly becoming both loving and manageable.

Sir Anthony Branville, not a "pretty fellow," is a comic character just because he is incapable of the "pleasant sallies" mentioned in the epilogue. He is the elderly suitor designed for young Louisa Medway by her impecunious father. Garrick chose that role for himself even though it was not the leading part, and his deadpan portrayal of the verbose, pompous, cautious old lover was a great success. Sir Anthony, Harry Flutter's "uncle Parenthesis," attempts to transfer his passion from Mrs. Knightly to Miss Medway because the former has "discarded" him. Louisa Medway hates him but is forced to accept his addresses, which she does willingly enough when she realizes they will probably never come to fruition. In a wonderfully funny scene, she artfully pleads with him to indulge her female delicacy with a slow-paced courtship, an arrangement that suits both of them perfectly despite Sir Anthony's professed passion. In the end, the well-named Mrs. Knightly solves this problem as well as young Medway's: she reasserts her power over Sir Anthony, leaving Miss Medway free to marry young Branville, Sir Anthony's nephew (who never appears in the play); Mrs. Knightly even persuades her devoted Sir Anthony to bestow enough money on his nephew to make the match possible.

Another innovation, or at least a rarity, one not listed in the epilogue, is the play's gentle feminism, consisting in part of Mrs. Knightly's sudden change from a jealous tormentor of her stepsister to the fairy godmother of both distressed maidens. Lady Medway is more consistent in her sense of sisterhood as she advises the unhappy Lady Flutter and tries to persuade Lord Medway to let Louisa marry for love. Far from militant or even rebellious, Lady Medway is nevertheless a strong woman: she is a model of patience and forbearance, virtues which eventually triumph as her husband declares himself "perfectly blessed in domestick joys" and "thoroughly reformed." That husband has been the villain of the piece, creating all the problems the women solve: he has made his wife unhappy; he lusts after Lady Flutter and undermines her marriage; and he has squandered the family fortunes, thus necessitating money marriages for his two children. At first, he resolves never "to urge [his] son against his inclination" while expecting complete obedience from Louisa in marrying the hated Sir Anthony–a direct and clearly disapproving exam-

Mary Ann Yates, who played Mrs. Knightly in The Discovery

ple of patriarchal values. But as his financial affairs deteriorate, he does beg his son to marry wealthy Mrs. Knightly instead of poor Miss Richly and young Medway agrees. Young Branville had also resolved to give up his love when he found that his uncle was addressing the same young lady. Interestingly, the two heroes of the play possess the peculiarly feminine virtue of self-sacrifice. (Lord Medway himself is not called upon to exercise that virtue, though perhaps the actor who played the role was. Thomas Sheridan shone in the part, but one wonders how he felt as, in his wife's play, a patient wife transformed him nightly from a spendthrift, neglectful husband into a model of "domestick joys.")

The Discovery had an initial run of seventeen nights, indicating considerable success, despite a few grumbles from Oliver Goldsmith and from Boswell (who was not feeling well and whose prologue for the play had been rejected). *The London Chronicle* approved its "excellent moral" and praised the acting. In Dublin, two theaters competed for the privilege of being the first to produce the play there. *The London Stage* lists six revivals in the eighteenth century, and the play was published several times in separate editions and in anthologies in the eighteenth and nineteenth centuries. Clearly, the gentle tone of its feminism was acceptable. Except for Aldous Huxley's patchwork adaptation of 1924–which includes no "discovery" and makes the title meaningless–*The Discovery* had largely vanished in the twentieth century until it was republished in the scholarly edition of Sheridan's plays by Robert Hogan and Jerry Beasley in 1984. Given both its recent invisibility and the conventional nature of much comedy, it is difficult to demonstrate specific influences *The Discovery* may have had, although Hogan and Beasley claim that Richard Brinsley Sheridan's *The Rivals* (1775) and *The School for Scandal* (1777) "owe more than a little" to his mother's play, especially the fluency of the comic language, which they admire.

Having done well with her first play, Sheridan promptly set about writing a second. *The Dupe* was produced ten months after *The Discovery*, opening on 10 December 1763. But it only ran for three nights. Both Alicia LeFanu and Sam Whyte blame one of the actresses in the production, suspecting that it was Kitty Clive's fault that the play failed, but the reviewers found it was well acted. The play itself was probably the culprit.

The double plot is fairly complex, yet clear: elderly Sir John Woodall, the dupe of the title, is tricked into revealing his secret marriage to his mistress, Mrs. Etherdown, and settling an income on her, whereupon she drops her pose of loving submissiveness and turns into such a termagant that he is more than willing to grant her the separation she desires. Mrs. Etherdown has temporarily managed to pass off a boy baby as hers and Sir John's, thus disinheriting his niece Emily, whom she keeps virtually a prisoner in the house. She plots with her pretended brother, Sharply, to abduct Emily and ruin her; but Sharply, having carried Emily off, offers her marriage instead. Emily rejects him with scorn; he interprets her reaction as ill-concealed desire for his person and offers instead the superior delights of a clandestine affair. But when she names Wellford as the man she loves, Sharply, who is afraid of Wellford (as well as owing him his life), does a quick about-face and promises to restore her to her lover. Gratefully, she gives him her hand just as Wellford charges into the room to rescue her. Wellford concludes at once that she is "light" and "debase[d]" and stomps off. This misunderstanding, which Emily deeply resents, and her apparent poverty stand in the way of the match. Eventually she forgives Wellford for his degrading assumption about her moral character, but only later, when the baby is proved to be an imposter and Emily once again be-

comes Sir John's heir, does she agree to marry him.

Three other characters are involved in these plots: Rose and the Friendlys. Rose is Mrs. Etherdown's maid and Sharply's mistress; she assists Mrs. Etherdown in her trickery but reveals the baby's origins to Sharply, who has promised her marriage. Mr. Friendly unravels the intrigues and lectures Sir John on morality, while Mrs. Friendly, the funniest character in the play, talks endlessly and pointlessly no matter how urgent her message may be. Sheridan's ability to create character in language, which made stuffy Sir Anthony Branville so good in *The Discovery*, brings this clacking female vividly to life.

Sheridan's modern editors, Hogan and Beasley, have mixed opinions about *The Dupe*. They suggest that its relative failure might have been due to its "flabby verbosity" combined with "the author's generally unconventional treatment of love and marriage and her avoidance of conventional morality." They have some praise for the characterization and language, however. Richard Bevis, who found *The Discovery* trite and sentimental, sees nothing to commend in *The Dupe*.

True, it is a rather talky play, and perhaps, as Bevis suggests, Mrs. Friendly's chatter bored some of the audience as much as it bores and frustrates the other characters. None of the love affairs or marriages appear in an attractive light, not even that of Emily and Wellford, which is marred by his nasty suspicions. And the morality, which has feminist overtones, is at times unconventional: Sharply refuses to make an honest woman of Rose, and Friendly advises her against the marriage anyway because she would be subject "for life to a man who must despise her." Mrs. Etherdown, who has had a series of lovers when Sir John was absent, is reasonably successful in profiting from her trickery. Perhaps this is why Horace Walpole called it "vulgar" and *The St. James's Chronicle* said it was "gross and indelicate." The question of conventional morality is addressed directly when Wellford doubts that "it is a christian office to part a man and his wife," which the Friendlys are attempting to do for Sir John, but he is assured by Mrs. Friendly, "From *such* a wife . . . it is "; it would have been more conventional if Sheridan had reformed the erring wife and repaired the marriage. Even the obviously conventional morality mouthed by Friendly–about self-knowledge, Christian forgiveness, and suffering for the sins of one's youth–is not quite central to the sentimental ethic and could have

Hannah Pritchard, who played Lady Medway in The Discovery *and Mrs. Etherdown in* The Dupe

been perceived as out of place.

Yet *The Dupe* was a success in print. Whyte and LeFanu report that the bookseller found it so profitable that he voluntarily sent Sheridan one hundred pounds in addition to the original purchase price of the manuscript, along with a letter deploring the play's "undeserved treatment on the stage." Hogan and Beasley read this as partly compassionate, but clearly the play was selling. Perhaps such a difference in the play's reception supports the story that the performance was sabotaged. More interesting is the light thus cast on audience psychology and on the eighteenth-century readership.

The Dupe is not a pleasant play. An audience expecting to laugh together at amusing fools and to nod companionably at the expected morality, to share an experience of likable characters, and to rejoice together at the reformation of rakes would have been disappointed. A reader, however, in relative solitude, could dwell on the real evils in human character and behavior that the play presents and the resulting problems for court-

ship and marriage that are not happily resolved. He or she could consider at leisure the ambiguities of Sir John's quasi reform and of Friendly's ethical standards in the grim moral atmosphere of the real world that the play depicts. The female reader–and the eighteenth-century readership included many women–would find particular pleasures in the play, pleasures which she might not want to applaud in the public theater. *The Dupe* shows a woman, Mrs. Etherdown, pretending to the kind of loving submissiveness that is genuine in Lady Medway of *The Discovery*, and tricking the unattractive, coarse-mannered Sir John Woodall out of a small but steady income and a heap of good jewelry. Her crime, and her sexual politics, did pay, as she exercised her power and gained her freedom. Mrs. Friendly, though insulted and once physically stifled by male characters, nevertheless runs her life and her tongue as she chooses, while her listeners can only expostulate ineffectually or leave the room. Even the powerless and victimized Emily, in many ways a typical sentimental heroine, has re-

William Havard, who played Mr. Friendly in The Dupe *(engraving by Fisher, based on an engraving by Worlidge)*

markable strength. Like some of her sisters in the novel, including Sheridan's own Sidney Bidulph, she is scrupulous about money and refuses to marry Wellford when she believes she is a beggar. Yet it is partly her own interests, not merely conventional self-sacrifice to his, that motivate her refusal: she tells him that she has "pride— perhaps too much; and cannot bear to lay myself under obligations where I once hoped to have the power of conferring them." Furthermore, she resents his mistrust and suspicion about Sharply and tells him so in no uncertain terms: "you ought to know me better. The woman whom you have debased by your mean suspicions, will not, on such terms, condescend to be your wife." This is a far cry from the sentimental heroine as doormat, her more conventional role.

It is conceivable, then, that the unconventional, feminist point of view in the play contributed to its failure in the public arena while promoting its popularity in the privacy of the ladies' closets.

Not surprisingly, considering its relative failure in the theater, *The Dupe* had little or no influence on the comedy that followed, with the possible exception of one detail in Richard Brinsley Sheridan's *The Rivals*, in which Faulkland, the sentimental hero, insults Julia by doubting her constancy, as Wellford had insulted Emily. The two ladies react very differently, however. Unlike Emily, who announced her resentment, Julia thinks only of her lover's well-being: on one occasion, she leaves the room in tears, hoping selflessly thus to spare Faulkland regret for having hurt her feelings; on another, she decides not to

Thomas Sheridan (engraved by Scott, based on a portrait by Stewart)

marry him—not, like Emily, because he has mistrusted her, but because she would be unable to help him reform the fault in his character. This alteration brings Richard Brinsley's heroine more into line with comic convention than his mother's and, because Julia is supposedly the less foolish character of the pair, creates some questions about the degree to which the play is satirizing sentimentalism.

With *The Dupe* a failure, the Sheridan finances looked bleak indeed. The next spring (1764), they went to Bristol and to Bath, where Thomas gave a series of lectures on oratory. Then it was back to London and on to an acting job in Edinburgh, with the creditors snapping at their heels. By autumn the danger was intense. A visit to London failed to adjust matters, so in September the family fled to France, taking three of

the children and leaving Richard Brinsley at school. They settled at Blois, where the children learned French faster than their mother and where Thomas, when his health permitted, got on with his books on grammar and elocution.

Frances too, despite declining health, picked up her pen yet again and wrote two more volumes of *Sidney Bidulph* and an oriental tale, *The History of Nourjahad* (1767), both of which were published after her death, as was her juvenile novel, *Eugenia and Adelaide* (1791). She also wrote another comedy, *A Journey to Bath*, which she sent to Garrick at Drury Lane. Garrick rejected it on several grounds, and Sheridan responded to them point by point in an effort to get him to change his mind. Hogan and Beasley quote her letter, which is her most detailed commentary on her own writing. Despite Garrick's criticisms, she believed the play contained "a good moral and some character" and that it was, as comedy should be, amusing rather than pathetic. But Garrick stood firm.

After her death, Richard Brinsley Sheridan inherited–and used–the manuscript of *A Journey to Bath*, but today only part of that manuscript survives, containing the first three acts. It is not possible to be sure of the outcome of the plots and thus to judge the play's "moral." But one can judge the characters. In what remains, an assortment of people have come to take the waters and shop in the marriage market of Bath. They all live in the lodging house of Mrs. Surface, whose name Richard Brinsley borrowed for his equally hypocritical Joseph in *The School for Scandal* and whose character supplied some hints for his Mrs. Candour. Scandal is a minor theme in *A Journey to Bath*; snobbery and money are its focus, as wealthy citizens strive to arrange marriages with titles. The usual pair of young lovers are of the citizen class, but the boy's uncle wants a better match for him and likes Lady Filmot, a lonely older woman who wants both the boy's money and his handsome person. Some of the best scenes show her educating the boy in social graces and the duties of a "cissisbey." The girl, even more naive and awkward than her lover, is in the care of her mother, the socially ambitious Mrs. Tryfort, who has her eye on a willing, impoverished lord. He takes on the hopeless task of polishing the rough-diamond girl. The mother, as gauche and awkward as her daughter, considers herself already polished because she imitates the vocabulary of her betters, but she always gets it wrong. Sheridan's sensitivity to rhetoric serves her well here as it has before. Mrs. Tryfort is the most direct source of Richard Brinsley's famous Mrs. Malaprop, even to some specific examples of wrong usage, though the two playwrights use the old device to define otherwise different character types: Mrs. Malaprop is proud of her learning, Mrs. Tryfort of her upper-class style. Both are wonderfully comic. Bath, with its "rooms" and Parade and Spring Garden, provides a colorful setting for the intrigues. The fragment of the play that survives has the kind of rough edges, such as abrupt exit lines, that show it was never revised in rehearsal, but its humor and point are such that one thinks Garrick must have been wrong to reject it.

The fatigue of writing both fiction and drama and the disappointment over *A Journey to Bath* could not have improved Sheridan's health,

although her husband wrote to friends in England that it was completely restored in the salubrious air of Blois. When, in September 1766, she contracted an apparently insignificant fever, accompanied by fainting fits (which she had often had before), he was concerned enough to postpone a trip to Dublin; yet he found her death two weeks later unexpected. His letter to Sam Whyte reporting it shows both profound grief and surprise. Obviously puzzled, he ordered a post-mortem, which revealed "four internal maladies," any one of which could have killed her. She was buried in a private Protestant cemetery near Blois.

Frances Sheridan left no record of the years of pain those four maladies must have caused her beyond the occasional mention of ill health in her letters. She did leave an enduring record, however, in her writing, which includes two and a half valuable comedies.

Biography:

Alicia LeFanu, *Memoirs of the Life and Writings of Mrs. Frances Sheridan, Mother of the Late Right Hon. Richard Brinsley Sheridan, and Author of "Sidney Bidulph," "Nourjahad," and "The Discovery"* (London: Whittaker, 1824).

References:

Richard Bevis, *The Laughing Tradition: Stage Comedy in Garrick's Day* (Athens: University of Georgia Press, 1980);

Margaret Anne Doody, "Frances Sheridan: Morality and Annihilated Time," in *Fetter'd or Free?*, edited by Mary Anne Schofield and Cecilia Macheski (Athens: Ohio University Press, 1985), pp. 324-358;

Aldous Huxley, *The Discovery; A Comedy in Five Acts . . . Adapted for the Modern Stage by Aldous Huxley* (London: Chatto & Windus, 1924);

David W. Meredith, Entry on Frances Sheridan, in *A Dictionary of British and American Women Writers 1660-1800*, edited by Janet Todd (Totowa, N.J.: Roman & Allanheld, 1985), pp. 282-284;

Samuel Richardson, *The Correspondence of Samuel Richardson . . .* , edited by Anna Laetitia Barbauld, volume 4 (London: Richard Philips, 1804);

Esther K. Sheldon, *Thomas Sheridan of Smock-Alley* (Princeton: Princeton University Press, 1967);

Horace Walpole, *Correspondence*, edited by W. S. Lewis and others, volume 38 (New Haven: Yale University Press / London: Oxford University Press, 1974);

Samuel Whyte, *Miscellanea Nova* (Dublin: Printed by R. Marchbank for the editor, E. A.

White, 1800; facsimile, New York & London: Garland, 1974).

Papers:
A manuscript for the first three acts of *A Journey to Bath* is in the British Library.

Richard Steele

(March 1672-1 September 1729)

Calhoun Winton
University of Maryland at College Park

PLAY PRODUCTIONS: *The Funeral*, London, Theatre Royal in Drury Lane, between 9 October and 11 December 1701;

The Lying Lover, Theatre Royal in Drury Lane, 2 December 1703;

The Tender Husband, Theatre Royal in Drury Lane, 23 April 1705;

The Conscious Lovers, Theatre Royal in Drury Lane, 7 November 1722.

BOOKS: *The Procession. A Poem on Her Majesties Funeral. By a Gentleman of the Army* (London: Printed for Thomas Bennet, 1695);

The Christian Hero: An Argument Proving that no Principles but Those of Religion Are Sufficient to make a Great Man (London: Printed for J. Tonson, 1701);

The Funeral: or, Grief a-la-Mode. A Comedy. As it is Acted at The Theatre Royal in Drury-Lane, By His Majesty's Servants (London: Printed for Jacob Tonson, 1702);

The Lying Lover, or, The Ladies Friendship. A Comedy. As it is acted at the Theatre Royal *By Her Majesty's Servants* (London: Printed for Bernard Lintott, 1704);

The Tender Husband, or, The Accomplish'd Fools. A Comedy. As it is Acted at the Theatre-Royal in Drury-Lane. By Her Majesty's Servants (London: Printed for Jacob Tonson, 1705);

Prologue to the University of Oxford. Written by Mr. Steel, and spoken by Mr. Wilks [broadside] (London: Printed for B. Lintott, 1706);

The Tatler. By Isaac Bickerstaff, Esq., nos. 1-271 (London: Printed by John Nutt for John Morphew, 12 April 1709-2 January 1711); modern edition, 2 volumes, edited by

Donald F. Bond (London: Oxford University Press, 1987);

The Spectator, nos. 1-555, by Steele and Joseph Addison (London: Printed for Samuel Buckley & J. Tonson, 1 March 1711-6 December 1712); modern edition, 5 volumes, edited by Bond (London: Oxford University Press, 1965);

The Englishman's Thanks to the Duke of Marlborough (London: Printed for A. Baldwin, 1712);

The Guardian, by Steele, Addison, and others, nos. 1-175 (London: Printed for J. Tonson, 12 March-1 October 1713); modern edition, edited by John Calhoun Stephens (Lexington: University Press of Kentucky, 1982);

The Englishman: Being the Sequel of the Guardian, first series, nos. 1-56 (London: Printed for Sam. Buckley, 6 October 1713-11 February 1714); *The Englishman: Being the Close of the Paper so called,* no. 57 (London: Printed for Ferd: Burleigh, 15 February 1714); *The Englishman,* second series nos. 1-38 (London: Printed & sold by R. Burleigh, 11 July 1715-21 November 1715); modern edition, edited by Rae Blanchard (Oxford: Clarendon Press, 1955);

The Importance of Dunkirk Consider'd: In Defence of the Guardian of August the 7th. In a Letter to the Bailiff of Stockbridge (London: Printed for A. Baldwin, 1713);

The Crisis: Or, A Discourse Representing, from the most Authentick Records, the just Causes of the late Happy Revolution: and the several Settlements of the Crowns of England and Scotland on Her Majesty; and on the Demise of Her Majesty without Issue, upon the Most Illustrious Princess Sophia, Electress and Dutchess Dowager of Hano-

Sir Richard Steele (portrait by Sir Godfrey Kneller; by permission of the National Portrait Gallery, London)

ver, and The Heirs of Her Body Being Protestants . . . With Some Seasonable Remarks on the Danger of a Popish Successor (London: Printed by S. Buckley & sold by F. Burleigh, 1714);

A Letter to a Member of Parliament Concerning the Bill for Preventing the Growth of Schism (London: Printed & sold by Ferd. Burleigh, 1714);

The French Faith Represented in the Present State of Dunkirk. A Letter to the Examiner, In Defense of Mr. S——le (London: Printed & sold by Ferd. Burleigh, 1714);

The Lover. Written in Imitation of the Tatler. By Marmaduke Myrtle, Gent., nos. 1-40 (London: Printed & sold by Ferd. Burleigh, 25 February-27 March 1714); *The Reader*, nos. 1-9 (London: Printed by Sam. Buckley, 22 April-10 May 1714); *Town-Talk. In a Letter to a lady in the country*, nos. 1-9 (London:

Printed by R. Burleigh & sold by Burleigh, Anne Dodd, James Roberts & J. Graves, 17 December 1715-15 February 1716); *Chit-Chat. In a letter to a lady in the country. By Humphrey Philroye*, nos. 1-3 (London: Printed & sold by R. Burleigh, March 1716); modern edition: *Richard Steele's Political Journalism, 1714-16*, edited by Blanchard (Oxford: Clarendon Press, 1959);

Mr. Steele's Apology for Himself and His Writings; Occasioned by his Expulsion from the House of Commons (London: Printed & sold by R. Burleigh, 1714);

A Letter from the Earl of Mar to the King, Before His Majesty's Arrival in England. With some Remarks on my Lord's subsequent Conduct (London: Printed for Jacob Tonson, 1715);

A Letter to a Member, &c. concerning the Condemn'd Lords, in Vindication of Gentlemen Calumniated in the St. James's Post *of Friday* March *the 2d*

(London: Printed & sold by J. Roberts, J. Graves & A. Dodd, 1716);

An Account of the Fish-Pool, by Steele and Joseph Gillmore (London: Printed & sold by H. Meere, J. Pemberton & J. Roberts, 1718);

The Plebeian. . . . By a Member of the House of Commons, nos. 1-4 (London, 14 March-6 April 1719);

The Antidote, in a Letter to the Free-Thinker (London: Printed for J. Roberts, 1719);

The Antidote. Number II. In a Letter to the Free-Thinker (London: Printed for J. Roberts, 1719);

A Letter to the Earl of O——d, Concerning the Bill of Peerage (London: Printed for J. Roberts, 1719);

The Spinster: In Defence of the Woolen Manufactures (London: Printed for J. Roberts, 1719);

The Crisis of Property (London: Printed for W. Chetwood, J. Roberts, J. Brotherton & Charles Lillie, 1720);

A Nation a Family: Being the Sequel of the Crisis of Property (London: Printed for W. Chetwood, J. Roberts, J. Brotherton & Charles Lillie, 1720);

The State of the Case Between the Lord-Chamberlain of His Majesty's Household, and the Governor of the Royal Company of Comedians. With The Opinions of Pemberton, Northey, and Parker, concerning the Theatre (London: Printed for W. Chetwood, J. Roberts, J. Graves & Charles Lillie, 1720);

The Theatre. By Sir John Edgar (London: Printed for W. Chetwood, J. Roberts & C. Lillie, 2 January-5 April 1720); modern edition, edited by John Loftis (Oxford: Clarendon Press, 1962);

A Prologue to the Town, as it was spoken at the theatre in Little Lincoln's Inn Fields. Written by Mr. Welstead. With an Epilogue on the same occasion, by Sir Richard Steele (London: Printed & sold by J. Brotherton & W. Meadows, J. Roberts, A. Dodd, W. Lewis & J. Graves, 1721);

The Conscious Lovers. A Comedy. As it is Acted at the Theatre Royal in Drury-Lane, By His Majesty's Servants (London: Printed for Jacob Tonson, 1723 [i.e., 1722]);

Pasquin, nos. 46 and 51 (London: Sold by J. Peele, 9 and 26 July 1723).

Collections: *Richard Steele,* edited, with an introduction and notes, by G. A. Aitken, Mermaid Series (London: Unwin/New York: Scribners, 1894)—includes notes and fragments of "The School of Action" from the Blenheim manuscripts, apparently since lost;

Tracts and Pamphlets by Richard Steele, edited by Rae Blanchard (Baltimore: Johns Hopkins Press, 1944);

The Plays of Richard Steele, edited by Shirley Strum Kenny (Oxford: Clarendon Press, 1971).

OTHER: "To Mr. Congreve, Occasion'd by the Way of the World," in *A New Collection of Poems On Several Occasions,* edited by Charles Gildon (London: Printed for Peter Buck & George Strahan, 1701);

Prologue to *The Mistake,* by Sir John Vanbrugh (London: Printed for Jacob Tonson, 1706);

Prologue to *The Distrest Mother,* by Ambrose Philips (London: Printed for S. Buckley & J. Tonson, 1712);

Verses addressed to Joseph Addison, in *Cato,* by Addison, seventh edition (London: Printed for Jacob Tonson, 1713);

Prologue to *Lucius,* by Delarivière Manley (London: J. Barber, 1717).

Although Richard Steele was principally recognized in his own era as an editor, essayist, and pamphleteer, it was as a young practicing dramatist that he first caught the attention of literary London, with three plays produced in five years' time. Steele's tenuous hold on critical attention in this century, however, so far as the theater and drama are concerned, has to do with his last published play, *The Conscious Lovers,* produced in 1721 but almost certainly written much earlier: is it or is it not "sentimental," and, if it is, does it then signify a major change in the direction of stage comedy, is it the first or an early example of a new genre, sentimental comedy? The critical focus on this single play has diverted attention from some of Steele's substantial achievements in the world of theater and drama. Three of his plays (*The Funeral, The Tender Husband,* and *The Conscious Lovers*) were among the ten or fifteen most popular of the eighteenth century, remaining in English dramatic repertory for decades.

Perhaps more important, in the long run, were the insights Steele derived from his experience as an editor. He was the inventor, for example, of regular theatrical reviewing: in the first issue of *The Tatler* (12 April 1709) he included an item about what was going on at the theater in Drury Lane; more followed in later issues, and from 1709, for the first time in stage history, dra-

Richard Steele, 1712 (portrait by Jonathan Richardson; by permission of the National Portrait Gallery, London)

matic authors and actors could expect to see in public print immediate reactions to the plays they had written or appeared in. Audiences, he discovered, could be attracted to plays or driven away by what they read in the press; acting and managing careers could hang in the balance. It was a momentous discovery, and, although Steele was personally too benevolent to take much advantage of the newfound power, others would–and have.

The son of Richard Steele and Elinor Sheyles Symes Steele, Richard Steele was born in Dublin, probably in early March 1672, for he was christened in St. Bride's parish church on 12 March of that year. St. Bride's was a Church of Ireland, or Protestant, parish in the midst of a sea of Roman Catholics, and Steele was thus born into the Protestant Ascendancy. Whatever its faults, and it had plenty, the Ascendancy produced a remarkable number of excellent writers, particularly comic writers: Steele's contemporaries included Jonathan Swift and William Congreve, and later in the eighteenth century Oliver

Goldsmith and Richard Brinsley Sheridan came to London, as in the following century did Oscar Wilde and Bernard Shaw. Perhaps being always in a minority–a West Briton in Dublin, an Irishman in London–developed in these men a differing, comic angle of vision.

Whether Steele acquired any knowledge of the drama in Ireland we do not know. When his father, a lawyer, died young–in 1676 or 1677–Steele was adopted, formally or informally, by his paternal aunt Katherine and her second husband, Henry Gascoigne. Gascoigne served as private secretary to James Butler, the great first duke of Ormonde, lord-lieutenant of Ireland. Some time in the early 1680s, probably correctly sensing troubles ahead in Ireland, Gascoigne decided to move his family to London, where Steele was enrolled, through Ormonde's influence, as a student in the Charterhouse, in November 1684. The wholesale doses of required Latin and Greek probably kept Steele's nose in his books most of the time, but the Charterhouse was close enough to the theaters for an enterprising teenager to spot the famous actors and actresses, the stage-door Johnnies, the foreign musicians and singers, the expensive whores, the harried playwrights; to experience, that is, the life of the theater. No doubt Richard Steele did so; from the beginning this Irishman writes as a London insider. This is supposition; what is fact is that Joseph Addison, just Steele's age, enrolled at the Charterhouse in 1686. This was the beginning of a famous friendship which, though centered in the three great periodicals they edited jointly, extended to each man's efforts in the drama.

The Charterhouse was one of those sorting houses which English society, the English class system, has maintained for centuries: schools where particularly able young men without much in the way of personal means could be identified and set on the path to education, leadership, and success. If one had inherited wealth and position, of course, one did not have to go through the tiresome process of learning to translate Catullus and Horace, but for boys of intelligence and little money, boys such as Addison and Steele—or John Dryden, or Matthew Prior, or Samuel Johnson—schools like the Charterhouse were steps up the social ladder. Brains and ability were essential, but influence helped too. When Steele was ready for university in 1689, his foster father was ready to help him: Gascoigne now had a place in the King's household, and he saw to it that young Richard was admitted to Christ Church, Oxford, the duke of Ormonde's old college. Aunt Katherine, who knew something about the value of appearances if not much about spelling, wrote Gasciogne, "Pray give him a pare of gloves and Send him a Sord and Show him how to put it one, That he may be like The young Lads nex doer...."

Oxford, unlike London, did not provide much food for Steele's aesthetic imagination. Years later he looked back to his university days with an alumnus' fondness, but he never settled into the academic track, unlike his friend Addison, who had preceded him by two years and was already recognized as being on the way to a brilliant career. Lack of money probably made Steele restless, especially in a fashionable college such as Christ Church. In 1691 he migrated to Merton College as a portionista or postmaster, the name Merton has used over the centuries for its endowed scholarships. Legend has it that Steele wrote a comedy while he was at Merton but destroyed it on the advice of one of his fellow post-

masters; given his later career the legend is credible.

In the spring of 1692 King William was recruiting a larger army to pursue his campaign on the Continent against the French; in May of that year Steele went down from Merton, not to return as a student. At some time, presumably that spring, he enlisted as a trooper in the Second Troop of Life Guards, the royal bodyguard, then commanded by young James Butler, the second duke of Ormonde, who had succeeded his grandfather, Gascoigne's patron, in 1688. Like their successors at Buckingham Palace today, the Life Guards were both a ceremonial and a fighting outfit. The Second Troop was on active service in Flanders for the campaigns of 1692 and 1693, and, although the muster rolls do not exist to prove it, there seems no reason to doubt Steele's statement that he was there with them, as he reminisced years later, with "a broad sword, jack-boots, and shoulder-belt, under the command of the unfortunate Duke of Ormonde...."

When he was back in London, on guard duty in Whitehall and at St. James's Palace, Steele had plenty of time to pursue the advancement of his career and his interest in the stage and drama. Troopers of the Life Guards were officially referred to as "private gentlemen" and addressed as "Mister." With the Gascoignes living in London, providing a convenient address, Steele could see and be seen. In 1695 he left the Life Guards and joined the Coldstreamers, the Second Foot Guards, commanded by John Baron Cutts, to whom Steele had, not coincidentally, dedicated *The Procession,* a poem published in April. In April 1697 he was commissioned ensign in Lord Cutts's own company, with the brevet rank of captain. Hence, hereafter, Captain Steele.

By 1700, though, his life and career seemed stalled: the Treaty of Ryswick (1697) had brought peace to Europe and unemployment to soldiers, though not to Steele; much of what little money he had had literally gone up in smoke in alchemical experiments; he had fathered an illegitimate daughter and was financing her support; he had fought and won a duel in Hyde Park; he had no doubt seen every play offered in London. Everything was in the past tense; at twenty-eight he had no prospects.

Like his fellow officers, John Vanbrugh and George Farquhar, Steele turned to writing, producing in April 1701 a religious self-help book entitled *The Christian Hero* and in December of that year his first play (not counting the legendary at-

Draft in Steele's hand of a prologue for an unknown occasion (Maggs Bros., sale number 527, December 1929)

Mary Scurlock Steele (portrait by Sir Godfrey Kneller; George A. Aitken, The Life of Richard Steele, *1889)*

tempt at Merton), *The Funeral*. Both were successes.

The Christian Hero, a serious work of piety, has relevance to Steele's drama in two ways: first and most obviously, its literary success (it ran to ten editions in his lifetime) provided an impetus for the production and publication of his plays, on the familiar grounds that if an author can do something well, he can do anything well. Second, it shows Steele's seriousness of purpose, which would be reflected in the ethical concerns of his plays and his periodicals. His own observation had told him that the drama and stage were in trouble, most notoriously from the attacks of the reforming clergyman Jeremy Collier, whose *A Short View of the Immorality, and Profaneness of the English Stage* (1698) was, we now recognize, only part of a widespread hostility toward the stage. Signs of this were clearly evident several years before the appearance of the *Short View*. It was at least theoretically possible to imagine a kind of

comedy that met some of the reformers' objections by taking ethical questions seriously, even as the audience laughed. Fielding later did this in his novels and so, much later, did Shaw in his plays. There is nothing inherently "sentimental" about such an approach, unless one stretches the term to the point of meaninglessness.

After the publication of *The Christian Hero*, Steele took some time off from his army duties and retired to lodgings in Wandsworth, on the Surrey side of the Thames, to work on *The Funeral*. From there he wrote a fellow company commander in the Coldstreams, "I shall I [hope] pay my debts with my play, and then . . . be very easy, for . . . nothing can really make my heart ache but a dun. . . ." Always optimistic, Steele in this case saw his hopes come true. In October Christopher Rich, manager of the Theatre Royal in Drury Lane, read the play and accepted it for production. Rich had a group of young actors and actresses just coming into their own; for the next thirty years they would dominate the London legitimate theater: Robert Wilks, Colley Cibber, Anne Oldfield, the great knockabout comedians Richard Norris and William "Pinky" Penkethman. Steele was fortunate in his cast.

He was evidently making some of his own good luck. William Cavendish, duke of Devonshire, Lord Steward of the Royal Household, attended a rehearsal and announced that he liked the play. Irish connections. The duke was married to the daughter of the first duke of Ormonde and had been the employer of Steele's foster father, Henry Gascoigne. Army connections. In the preface to the first edition Steele wrote, "I know not in what words to thank my Fellow-Soldiers for their Warmth and Zeal in my behalf, nor to what to attribute their Undeserv'd favour, except it be that 'tis Habitual to 'em to run to the Succour of those they see in Danger."

As it turned out, Steele did not need connections, Irish or army. First produced in early December 1701, *The Funeral* was an instant success. It was an early example of what Shirley Strum Kenny has termed "humane comedy," new theatrical practice for the new century, with simplified plot lines, greater emphasis on sight comedy and dialect, and generally broader acting styles than had been the norm in the wit comedies of the high Restoration. *The Funeral*'s plot line is simple enough: Lord Brumpton, who has disinherited his son, the young army officer Lord Hardy, in favor of his second wife, recovers from an illness of which he has been declared dead and secretly observes his widow in the preparations for his funeral, learning of her previous infidelities and present indifference to his death. Brumpton has as wards two orphan sisters, Lady Sharlot and Lady Harriot, who are pursued by Lord Hardy and his friend Tom Campley. Sable, the undertaker, and his mourners and gravediggers add comic effects in their preparations for a fashionable funeral, as do a large cast of saucy servants. After minor complications the lovers are of course in the end united, and the play ends with singing and dancing. Steele had introduced songs in every act, several of them written by Daniel Purcell, thereby taking advantage of Drury Lane's accomplished musicians and singers.

Those of Steele's friends who saw the play would have noticed that the author had drawn heavily on personal experience. Lord Hardy, the protagonist, is a young army officer and a Christ Church man. Some of the action involves recruiting, an activity with which Steele was thoroughly

familiar. The heroines are orphans and almost everyone is in debt. Though remembered by those who have not read it as a satire on undertaking, *The Funeral* is hardly a satire on anything. There are satirical touches on marital duplicity, on gossips, on hypocritical mourning, but the play is a thoroughly good-humored comedy. Toward the end Steele introduced some blank-verse dialogue for the reunion of the lovers, and there is more blank verse in the high style for Lord Brumpton's patriotic resolve to follow his son onto the field of battle. In spite of the blank verse—though it may be that the audience liked it—the play was successful because it deserved to be; it is a competent piece of dramaturgy, with some excellent sight-comedy scenes and generally good theatrical construction. It entered the professional repertory in London, the provinces, and abroad, and was played right through the eighteenth century.

It is still uncertain what financial rewards Steele derived from *The Funeral* beyond, presumably, the third night's net proceeds; but as Kenny has noted, "he clearly gained fame." In an autobiographical essay written more than a decade later Steele recalled that "Nothing can make the town so fond of a man as a successful play," and went on to assert that King William himself had noted Steele as someone to be provided for. William died soon after the opening but his favor may have materialized in March 1702 in the form of an assignment for Steele as a captain in the Thirty-Fourth Foot. His assignment, unfortunately, took him out of town just when it was becoming fond of him, to Landguard Fort in Suffolk, overlooking one of the approaches to Harwich. The war was on again, but nothing much was happening at Landguard in the way of action.

With time on his hands, Steele began to write a new comedy, to be called "The Election of Gotham." Rich, in an unusual burst of confidence, advanced Steele seventy-two pounds with the understanding, he later asserted, that the play would be provided for production in February 1703. The play was never finished, Steele presumably applied the advance against his other debts, and the transaction boiled over into a very complicated lawsuit in 1707 which was eventually dismissed without a finding one way or the other. Before feeling sympathy for Rich, however, one might reflect that managing one of the two monopoly theaters was a lucrative business and that Steele later supplied Rich with two other plays, compensation for which Rich was able to minimize by citing the earlier advance. The dramatic author was still in no very favorable position vis-à-vis bookseller and theater manager. No more is known about the ill-fated "Election of Gotham." Perhaps it was based on Steele's observations of electoral processes in rural England.

He continued to write. According to local tradition (agrees with what is known about the composition of *The Funeral*), Steele would from time to time withdraw to a farmhouse nearby or to an inn in Harwich, there to work on his plays. On 2 December 1703 his comedy *The Lying Lover* opened at Drury Lane and played for six nights, a successful run from Steele's point of view, providing two benefit performances. The success was only apparent, however; few in the audience desired to see the play a second time. It was not revived in his lifetime.

Steele had taken Collier's pronouncement and the general feeling of the time seriously, probably anticipating the queen's order of January 1704, which prohibited the playhouses from acting anything contrary to religion and good manners. In the preface to the first edition of *The Lying Lover*, which appeared in that month, Steele declared that he thought it "an honest Ambition to attempt a Comedy, which might be no improper Entertainment in a Christian Commonwealth." A severe critic might judge that Steele was joining the side of the angels in order to cover the defects of a bad play. As its stage history attests, *The Lying Lover* is the poorest of Steele's known plays, not because of its moral instruction–although there is enough of that–but because of imprecise characterization and a curious mixture of styles. Some of the plot is derived from Pierre Corneille's *Le Menteur* (1643) and the parts are not well articulated. As in *The Funeral* there are two pairs of lovers finding their way to final happiness through various blocking actions. There are no parts for older women, which probably represents Steele's writing for the youthful Drury Lane company.

We may imagine Steele, pressed as he almost always was for time and money, hurriedly translating extended passages from Corneille, revising them quickly, and copying onto manuscript. Young Bookwit, the hero, for example, in the first act observes the approach of his friends Lovemore and Frederick, noting "they seem amaz'd at something by their Action." This is a literal translation of Corneille (Ils semblent étonnés, à voir leur action), but limping English.

Once again Steele has introduced good comic roles for the servants, especially that of Latine, young Bookwit's Oxford companion who has lost a drawing of lots with Bookwit to determine who should play the servant. This is, of course, a device Farquhar was to use three years later in *The Beaux Stratagem* with his Aimwell and Archer. Cibber played Latine, Wilks Young Bookwit, Anne Oldfield and Jane Rogers took the female leads, all the now-experienced young regulars of Drury Lane, but they were not enough. The public's anticipations were disappointed, and after six performances the play disappeared from the repertory (barring a single revival in 1734), constituting Steele's only stage failure.

Swamped with debts, author of a failed play, unsuccessful in his quest for further promotion in the army, Steele found that his fortunes had bumped to another low point in 1704. The following year was very different: in April or May he married Margaret Ford Stretch, a rich widow formerly of Barbados, sold his commission in the Thirty-Fourth Foot, and wrote another hit play. In August 1706 he was appointed gentleman-waiter to Queen Anne's husband, Prince George of Denmark, a position worth one hundred pounds a year. From Landguard Fort to St. James's Palace in a year's time.

In late March or early April 1705, Steele presented still another play to Rich, this one entitled *The Tender Husband, or, The Accomplish'd Fools*. Steele, Rich declared in the 1707 lawsuit, knew that April was an unfavorable month for openings but nevertheless pressed for the play's production. Opening on 23 April, it had an initial run of five nights, with indifferent success. Steele thus missed his second benefit (sixth night) performance, postponed by agreement until November, when Rich had skimmed the cream of the potential audience by staging performances in May, June, and October. In December both *The Funeral* and *The Tender Husband* were presented at Drury Lane, without remuneration for the author.

In the main plot Clerimont Senior, the "tender husband" of the ironic title, tests the virtue of his somewhat addle-brained wife by having his mistress, Fainall, court her, disguised as a young man. In the subplot Captain Clerimont, Clerimont's younger brother, an impoverished army officer, is campaigning to win the hand of the romance-reading Bridget (Biddy) Tipkin, who is the daughter of the Lombard Street

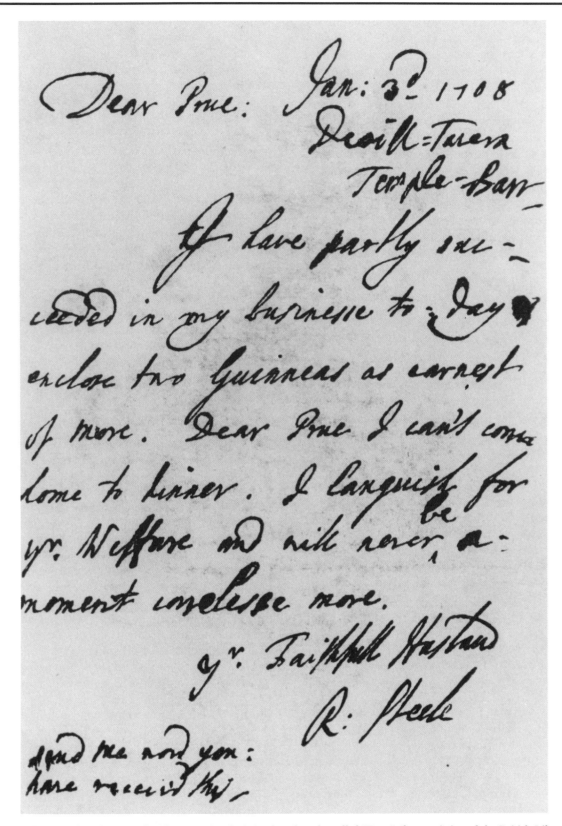

Letter from Steele to his second wife, Mary Scurlock Steele, whom he called "Prue" (by permission of the British Library)

banker Hezekiah Tipkin. Biddy is being forced into marriage with loutish Humphry Gubbin, son of Tipkin's brother-in-law, Sir Harry Gubbin, a country squire. At the end Clerimont Senior and his wife are reconciled, and Captain Clerimont, with the aid of his ally, Lawyer Pounce, averts Humphry's marriage and wins Biddy Tipkin and her inheritance.

The search for the play's sources has continued from Steele's time to ours, revealing mainly that his knowledge of European drama was considerable. There are motifs and characters from Roman comedy (for example, the tyrannical father, Sir Harry Gubbin), from Molière, from Spanish literature, from the English theatrical tradition, but all of these are integrated into a pleasing theatrical whole. The exact nature of Addison's contributions has never been determined. Kenny traces the sources carefully and concludes that Addison's hand is principally to be seen in the Clerimont Senior main plot.

Steele treats a wide spectrum of society in the *The Tender Husband:* the country gentry, the mercantile community of the City, the fashionable world of Westminster. It is a good play, the best balanced of all of Steele's dramatic works, tightly constructed and, all in all, one of the better comedies of the century. Years later Goldsmith and perhaps Fielding found the play a source of ideas: Humphry Gubbin, the loutish heir from the country who discovers he is of age and conspires with his cousin against their marriage, is certainly the lineal ancestor of Tony Lumpkin. The play has, in fact, much of the spirit of *She Stoops to Conquer* (1773) and is little inferior to it. Although, as noted earlier, the play was not an immediate success, by the following year *The Tender Husband* was securely in the repertory. It was revived in London every season except three for the next forty years, and was acted in the provinces and the American colonies for decades.

The original production should have satisfied author and audience. Robert Wilks and Anne Oldfield, both at the peak of their careers, created the roles of Captain Clerimont and Biddy Tipkin, and the comedian Penkethman, the role of Humphry Gubbin. Daniel Purcell, brother of Henry, set the songs "Why, lovely charmer, tell me why" and "While gentle Parthenissa walks," both of which were to become popular. Steele had sprinkled songs through the play and had closed the final act

with a dance, making use of Drury Lane's experienced–and expensive–dancers.

The Tender Husband is not a sentimental comedy, but it does reflect some of the changes which were taking place in stage comedy. The language is inoffensive; double entendres are reduced in number and thrust. The clergy are kept offstage (Collier, himself a clergyman, had been most vehement in his criticism of the drama's treatment of the cloth). Steele has accepted the traditional protagonist of Restoration wit comedy and split him in two, giving the ruthless aspects of the libertine to the older brother, Clerimont Senior, and retaining the more attractive characteristics, including that of superior wisdom, for the younger, Captain Clerimont. And perhaps most important, the satire is gentler: apart from Clerimont Senior there are in fact no genuinely reprehensible characters.

After *The Tender Husband* became successful, one would have expected Richard Steele to go on with his writing for the stage. He did not benefit from that success, other than in whatever modest remuneration he had worked out for the printed editions with the publisher Jacob Tonson, who held the copyright. The lawsuit against Christopher Rich apparently came to nothing as far as Steele was concerned, except for more legal fees. The next play, he must have resolved, "I'll manage differently." That next production, of *The Conscious Lovers*, was to be seventeen years in the future, and Steele would indeed manage it differently, but why the long delay?

As John Loftis has shown most convincingly in *Steele at Drury Lane* (1952), Steele was working on *The Conscious Lovers* years before it opened. This was during the period when he was inaugurating, writing for, and editing the series of periodicals which made his fortune (the first three edited with Joseph Addison): *The Tatler, The Spectator, The Guardian,* and *The Englishman.* The immediate cause for the delay was, of course, the fact that he was getting these started; in effect, inventing the genre of the essay periodical. The expenditure of time and energy involved in beginning and continuing these papers must have been enormous. This endeavor would have absorbed his time even if he had not taken a second wife on 9 September 1707–his first having died in 1706 not long after their marriage. Mary Scurlock Steele, "Dear Prue" of literary fame, was a reasonably understanding spouse but as the couple produced four children, two sons and two daughters in four years' time, she and the chil-

ISAAC BICKERSTAFF Esq.

Frontispiece to The Lucubrations of Isaac Bickerstaff Esq. *(1710-1711), the first collected edition of*
The Tatler *(1709-1711), the periodical for which Steele invented theatrical reviewing*

dren required parts of Steele's day, too–time that bachelor writers such as Joseph Addison, Alexander Pope, and Jonathan Swift could devote to literary matters. Periodicals and paternity: these almost certainly were what delayed *The Conscious Lovers'* completion for so long.

Not that Steele forgot the stage when he stopped writing for it. His periodicals were full of material about the stage and drama. The very first *Tatler* (12 April 1709), given away free to potential customers, that is, to everyone, reported on a recent benefit night for the great actor and theater manager Thomas Betterton. The play presented had been Congreve's *Love for Love*. Steele, writing as Isaac Bickerstaff, the persona of *The*

Tatler, presents a brief critique of the acting and a pious hope for the theater's future: "All the Parts were acted to Perfection; the Actors were careful of their Carriage, and no one was guilty of the Affectation to insert Witticisms of his own, but a due Respect was had to the Audience, for encouraging this accomplished Player. It is not now doubted but Plays will revive, and take their usual Place in the Opinions of Persons of Wit and Merit. . . ." Theater reviewing was born.

Steele, as Bickerstaff, shows the author's hand in his remark about actors not inserting witticisms of their own. Much as he admired Penkethman, the great farce comedian who had acted in every one of his plays, Steele could not forbear grinding his teeth when Pinky let the spirit of improvisation flow over him and ad-libbed not only stage business–surely a legitimate area for improvisation–but also lines of dialogue. Bickerstaff reports in *Tatler* no. 89 that he was pleased to hear a gentleman become indignant at "a practice which I myself have been very much offended at. There is nothing (said he) more ridiculous, than for an actor to insert words of his own in the part he is to act, so that it is impossible to see the poet for the player: you'll have Pinkethman and Bullock helping out Beaumont and Fletcher." Here is author, and critic, contending with actor for the favorable opinion of the audience. In the short run, of course, a competent actor is almost certain to win: Penkethman never changed his ways. But the point is that a powerful new medium, print, has been introduced into the equation. Much more is known about Penkethman's acting than about Shakespeare's companion Will Kemp because regular theatrical reviewing had been invented.

Another aspect of the relationship between the drama and print culture in which Steele interested himself was that of play publication. Before plays opened, if he liked the play or the author, Steele often made it his practice to include brief previews or "puffs" of the upcoming production. He did this, for example, for the first two of John Gay's plays, and for Addison's *Cato* (1713), among many others, including his own *The Conscious Lovers.* Then, after opening, he would sometimes reveal where the printed play could be purchased, or if he did not the publisher would often insert an advertisement to that effect. Inexpensive collections of plays were also beginning to be published, following the lead of Nicholas Rowe's collection of Shakespeare (1709). Steele saw these printed plays not through the eyes of a literary scholar, not as ends in themselves but as adjuncts to the theatrical process–a process which he assumes, importantly, has an ethical end. As he writes in the preface to *The Conscious Lovers,* "the greatest Effect of a Play in reading [that is, in reading a play] is to excite the Reader to go see it; and when he does so, it is then a Play has the Effect of Example and Precept."

Here Steele touches on one of his bedrock beliefs, the potential moral utility of the drama. If, as the reformers maintained, the drama was capable of affecting human conduct adversely, then the reverse was logically also true: it could be morally beneficial to humankind. This belief was widespread in the Age of the Enlightenment; such diverse thinkers as Thomas Jefferson, Adam Ferguson, and Denis Diderot endorsed it. It was behind most of Steele's theatrical criticism in his periodicals. The question Steele and these others were asking, implicitly, is controversial but not contemptible: is there a relationship between the theater and moral life, and if so, what is it? It is a question that has preoccupied many playwrights and television critics of our own time.

The proper vehicle of a playwright's ideas is, of course, not literary criticism but a play, and Steele had one in mind, was in fact working on it, on and off, as early as 1710 or perhaps earlier. Various matters in addition to his own procrastination got in the way of his finishing it. The labor involved in writing and editing his periodicals has already been mentioned. Then in 1714, with the death of Queen Anne and the accession of George I, Steele found himself the recipient of Royal favor: he was offered and accepted the governorship of the Theatre Royal in Drury Lane.

This appointment was partly a reward for his service as Whig propagandist and Member of Parliament (to which he had been elected in 1713); the Tories were turned out of office on the death of the queen and the Whigs began a long period of political dominance. There was, however, much more than politics involved. He was well known, from his plays and periodicals, for his views on theater reform, and the reformers had been demanding action for years. Most important, he seemed to be uniquely qualified for the position. He had known the London theatrical scene since his days as a schoolboy at the Charterhouse, first as a member of the audience, then as a practicing playwright, finally as a working journalist: he knew personally the theatrical professionals. From Drury Lane's perspective, the fact that he was a Whig was, in 1714, only a fringe benefit, and a minor one at that. In point of fact, Robert Harley's Tory ministry had offered him the same or a similar post in 1713. Whatever his political opinions, he was widely judged to be the man for the job.

Under terms of the license, day to day conduct of the theater's affairs was and remained in the hands of three actor-managers, Robert Wilks, Colley Cibber, and Barton Booth. They had invited Steele to seek the appointment in the first place, conscious, as Cibber later put it, "that many Days had our House been particularly fill'd, by the Influence, and Credit of his Pen." Steele did not have in mind merely serving as a fig-

Sir Richard Steele, circa 1713 (perhaps a copy of the portrait by Sir James Thornhill;
Willard Connely, Sir Richard Steele, *1934)*

urehead, however. A manager, he knew, who could supply an occasional play would be able to benefit not only as a shareholder in the enterprise but as the author. Steele had found during the first run of *The Tender Husband* that the day of the week and the month of the season could drastically affect the author's benefit from the third and sixth nights' performances; a theater manager could see to it that his play was produced at the right time and in the proper manner.

On 9 April 1715 knighthood was bestowed on Steele by King George at St. James's Palace. This was a purely political reward and Sir Richard, reelected to Parliament, found that parliamentary business in all its forms, including writing propaganda for the ministry, took up time he had assumed he could devote to the theater. Nevertheless, he performed effectively the duties of the governor, largely in the area of what we

would term public relations but no less important for that, as the actor-managers later affirmed, recalling "that they have frequently acknowledged the great services done them by [Steele]."

In one of its aspects a public-relations venture, in another striking testimony to Steele's zeal for enlightenment, his Censorium was a quasi-theatrical undertaking. He had rented a large room in York Buildings and as early as 1713 was seeing to its refurbishing, installing lighting, upholstered seats, decorative panels, and the like, with an eye to performances, the first of which took place in 1715 on the King's Birthday. Steele had in mind mingling entertainment and edification; in the prologue which he wrote for that occasion (spoken by Elizabeth Younger, an actress at Drury Lane) he at once complimented the specially invited aristocratic audience and gave them a seasonable reminder of their cultural responsibility: "The Land shall grow Polite from You, who

The Steele children–Elizabeth, Eugene, and Mary–in 1722 or 1723 (miniatures on ivory, attributed to Christian Richter; by permission of the National Portrait Gallery, London)

sit / In chosen Ranks, *the Cabinet of Wit.*" Songs and instrumental numbers were performed, a collation of sweetmeats and champagne was followed by country (that is, contra, square) dances for all the guests. Steele intended these performances, which continued for a number of years, as an alternative to Italian opera, he and Addison having denounced it repeatedly as a mindless fad. Italian opera survived.

About 1718 Steele's luck changed decisively for the worse. That year his wife died; in the next, so did his old friend and collaborator Joseph Addison. Steele had his new play almost ready for the stage in 1719 but found himself on the losing side of a dispute with the lord chamberlain, Thomas Pelham-Holles, duke of Newcastle. Steele had angered the ministry by opposing in Parliament a bill it was sponsoring. Newcastle's retaliation was swift and severe: using the powers he possessed as lord chamberlain, he revoked the license of the Drury Lane managers and issued a new license in the king's name to Cibber, Wilks, and Booth. Steele thus had no voice in the company and received no financial benefits. He began a new periodical, *The Theatre,* in which he argued his side of the case and gave a puff for his new play, "which had not some Accidents prevented, would have been performed before this time...." Those "Accidents" were speedily set right in 1721 when Sir Robert Walpole came to power and, acting on Steele's request, ordered Newcastle to settle with him for his share of the

Drury Lane profits. The actor-managers could overlook whatever differences of opinion they had with Steele, at the prospect of staging a new play by him who enjoyed Walpole's and therefore the king's favor.

Casting the play gathered professionals who had worked together for decades. The managers themselves took leading roles: Barton Booth as Bevil, Jr., Robert Wilks as Myrtle, and Colley Cibber in another substantial comic part as Tom the servant. Anne Oldfield, who had played Biddy Tipkin to Wilks's Captain Clerimont in *The Tender Husband* seventeen years earlier, created the long-lost and long-suffering Indiana. New settings and new costumes had been ordered, and the managers had thoughtfully raised admission prices to take care of the crowds they anticipated. An extensive advertising campaign was laid on.

At opening night, 7 November 1722, the house was packed; a "greater Concourse of People was never known to be assembled," according to the *Daily Journal.* What they saw was a play with a pathetic, or tragicomic, main plot and a comic subplot. The main plot, largely derived from Terence's *Andria,* depicts the difficult relationship between Sir John Bevil and his son Bevil, Jr., who is in love with the apparent orphan Indiana but is forced by his father to marry Lucinda, daughter of the wealthy merchant Sealand. In the subplot Bevil, Jr.'s friend Myrtle pursues Lucinda, and after various plot complications it is revealed that Indiana is the long-lost

Sir Richard Steele, 1722 or 1723 (miniature on ivory, attributed to Christian Richter;
by permission of the National Portrait Gallery, London)

daughter of Sealand by his first wife. There are rich comic parts for the servants. Bevil, Jr.'s moralizing and the pathetic reunion of Indiana and her father do not go down well with modern readers, but Steele knew his own audience, and the play was enormously successful. Jean Hagstrum has explained, "The play was successful on stage because it portrayed the sensibility that was gaining the day and because it addressed itself to a subject that concerned almost everyone, the possible conflict between duty to one's heart and to one's parents."

Steele's health began to give way badly about this time. In order to pay his debts and leave something to his two living daughters he retired to Carmarthen in Wales, where he had inherited a house from his wife. There he worked on a comedy, *The School of Action*, surviving fragments of which were printed in Aitken's Mermaid edition. The play has an interesting premise: the relationships between the law and the stage, Steele using "action" in its dual sense of a

legal move and of stage action, that is, acting. He intended to use play-within-a-play, reflexive techniques that Fielding would exploit in the next decade. But Steele knew his days were numbered; the play was never finished, and in one of his notes to himself he wrote, "For the Prologue take notice of this play as a *Posthumous Work.*" As indeed it was: Steele died in Carmarthen on the night of 1 September 1729 and was buried in St. Peter's Church there.

In the eighteenth century Steele's literary reputation was very high. In this century he has come to be seen as the junior partner of the Addison and Steele partnership, but his devaluation should not apply to his work in the theater. Here he was clearly the innovator, and his three principal comedies were a major influence in the trend toward reformed or "humane" comedy. Whether they were also sentimental comedies is still debated, and debatable. They were effective stage vehicles, designed for the Drury Lane company which first performed them, and they remained in the repertory of the English-language theater for decades. More important than his plays, probably, were the theater news and dramatic criticism which he presented in his periodicals, thus instituting journalistic treatment of the stage and drama. From Steele's time, theater companies and dramatic authors would see their efforts subjected to the critical judgments not only of audiences but of readers, perhaps millions of them. This was a momentous innovation.

Letters:

The Correspondence of Richard Steele, edited by Rae Blanchard (London: Oxford University Press, 1941).

Biographies:

George A. Aitken, *The Life of Richard Steele,* 2 volumes (London: Wm. Isbister, 1889);

Calhoun Winton, *Captain Steele* (Baltimore: Johns Hopkins Press, 1964);

Winton, *Sir Richard Steele, M.P.* (Baltimore & London: Johns Hopkins Press, 1970).

References:

Rae Blanchard, Introduction to *Steele's The Englishman,* edited by Blanchard (Oxford: Clarendon Press, 1955);

Blanchard, Introduction to *Steele's Periodical Journalism 1714-16,* edited by Blanchard (Oxford: Clarendon Press, 1959);

Donald F. Bond, Introduction to *The Spectator,* 5 volumes, edited by Bond (London: Oxford University Press, 1965);

Bond, Introduction to *The Tatler,* 2 volumes, edited by Bond (London: Oxford University Press, 1987);

Richmond P. Bond, *The Tatler: The Making of a Literary Journal* (Cambridge, Mass.: Harvard University Press, 1971);

Jean Hagstrum, *Sex and Sensibility* (Chicago: University of Chicago Press, 1980);

Robert D. Hume, ed., *The London Theatre World, 1660-1800* (Carbondale: Southern Illinois University Press, 1980);

Shirley Strum Kenny, "Humane Comedy," *Modern Philology,* 75 (August 1977): 29-43;

Kenny, "Perennial Favorites: Congreve, Vanbrugh, Cibber, Farquhar, and Steele," *Modern Philology,* 73 (May 1976): S4-S11;

Michael G. Ketcham, *Transparent Designs* (Athens: University of Georgia Press, 1985);

John Loftis, *Comedy and Society from Congreve to Fielding* (Stanford: Stanford University Press, 1959);

Loftis, *Steele at Drury Lane* (Berkeley & Los Angeles: University of California Press, 1952);

Paul E. Parnell, "The Sentimental Mask," *PMLA,* 78 (December 1963): 529-535;

Peter Smithers, *The Life of Joseph Addison* (Oxford: Clarendon Press, 1954);

John Calhoun Stephens, Introduction to *The Guardian,* edited by Stephens (Lexington: University Press of Kentucky, 1982);

Calhoun Winton, "Sentimentalism and Theater Reform in the Early Eighteenth Century," in *Quick Springs of Sense,* edited by Larry S. Champion (Athens: University of Georgia Press, 1974), pp. 98-112.

Papers:

The British Library holds the most important collection of Steele's papers, mostly correspondence. The collection at Blenheim, seat of the dukes of Marlborough, which was consulted by Aitken and others earlier in this century, has apparently been dispersed in recent years, presumably by private sale. Yale has a number of Steele's letters.

Catharine Trotter

(16 August 1679-11 May 1749)

Sophia B. Blaydes
West Virginia University

PLAY PRODUCTIONS: *Agnes de Castro*, London, Theatre Royal in Drury Lane, December 1695 or 27-31 January 1696;

Fatal Friendship, London, Lincoln's Inn Fields, circa late May or early June 1698;

Love at a Loss, or, Most Votes Carry It (later rewritten as *The Honourable Deceiver; or, All Right at the Last*), London, Theatre Royal in Drury Lane, 23 November 1700;

The Unhappy Penitent, London, Theatre Royal in Drury Lane, 4 February 1701;

The Revolution of Sweden, London, Queen's Theatre, 11 February 1706.

BOOKS: *Agnes de Castro, A Tragedy. As it is Acted at the Theatre Royal, By His Majesty's Servants. Written By a Young Lady* (London: Printed for H. Rhodes, R. Parker & S. Briscoe, 1696);

Fatal Friendship. A Tragedy. As it is Acted at the New-Theatre in Little-Lincolns-Inn-Fields (London: Printed for Francis Saunders, 1698); modern edition, in *The Female Wits: Women Playwrights on the London Stage 1660-1720*, edited by Fidelis Morgan (London: Virago, 1981);

Love at a Loss, or, Most Votes Carry It. A Comedy. As it is now Acted at the Theatre Royal in Drury-Lane, by His Majesty's Servants (London: Printed for William Turner, 1701);

The Unhappy Penitent, A Tragedy. As it is Acted, At the Theatre Royal in Drury Lane, by his Majesty's Servants (London: Printed for William Turner & John Nutt, 1701);

A Defence of Mr. Lock's Essay of Human Understanding, Wherein its Principles with reference to Morality, Reveal'd Religion, and the Immortality of the Soul, are Consider'd and Justify'd: In Answer to Some Remarks on that Essay (London: Printed for Will. Turner & John Nutt, 1702);

The Revolution of Sweden. A Tragedy. As it is Acted at the Queens Theatre in the Hay-Market (London: Printed for James Knapton & George Strahan, 1706);

A Discourse concerning a Guide in Controversies, in Two Letters. Written to One of the Church of Rome, By a Person lately Converted from that Communion (London: Printed for A. & J. Churchill, 1707);

A Letter to Dr. Holdsworth, Occasioned by His Sermon Preached before the University of Oxford: On Easter-Monday, Concerning the Resurrection of the Same Body In which the Passages That Concern Mr. Lock are chiefly considered, By the Author of "A Defence of Mr. Lock's Essay" . . . in Answer to Some Remarks on that Essay [by Thomas Burnet] (London: Printed for Benjamin Motte, 1726);

Remarks upon the Principles and Reasonings of Dr. Rutherforth's Essay on the Nature and Obligations of Virtue: in Vindication of the contrary Principles and Reasonings inforced in the Writings of the late Dr. Samuel Clarke, Published by Mr. Warburton, with a Preface (London: Printed for J. & P. Knapton, 1747);

The Works of Mrs. Catharine Cockburn, Theological, Moral, Dramatic, and Poetical, Several of them now first printed, Revised and published, With an Account of the Life of the Author, By Thomas Birch, M.A.F.R.S. Rector of the United Parishes of St. Margaret Pattens, and St. Gabriel Fenchurch, 2 volumes (London: Printed for J. & P. Knapton, 1751)—includes first printings of the following: "A Vindication of an Essay Concerning Human Understanding," I: 51-112; "A Vindication of Mr. Locke's Christian Principles, from the injurious Imputations of Dr. Holdsworth, Part I," I: 155-251; "A Vindication of Mr. Locke, in the Controversy concerning the Resurrection of the Same Body, Part II," I: 253-378; "Answer to a Question in the *Gentleman's Magazine*, over the Jurisdiction of the Magistrate over the Life of the Subject," II: 139-143; "These Remarks are, with the utmost Deference, inscribed to Alexander Pope, Esq. by an admirer of his Moral Character," I: 450-455; "Notes on Christianity as

Catharine Trotter Cockburn (frontispiece to volume 1 of The Works of Mrs. Catharine Cockburn, *1751; courtesy of the Folger Shakespeare Library)*

old as the Creation," II: 129-131; "On his Grace the Duke of *Marlborough*, after his victory at *Ramellies*, in *1706*," II: 566-567; "On his Grace the Duke of *Marlborough's* return from his expedition into *Germany*, after the Battle of *Blenheim, 1704*," II: 561-564; "On the Credibility of the historical Parts of Scripture," II: 128-129; "On the Infallibility of the Church of Rome," II: 134-138; "On the Usefulness of Schools and Universities for the Improvement of the Mind in the right Notions of God," II: 125-127; "Remarks on Mr. Seed's Sermon on Moral Virtue," II: 143-144; "Remarks upon an Inquiry into the Origin of Human Appetites and Affec-

tions," II: 144-149; "Songs: The Vain Advice, The Relapse, The needless Deceit, The Fair Insensible," II: 568-571; "Sunday's Journal," II: 121-125; "The rapture of an affectionate soul to *JESUS* on the Cross, composed in Latin by St. *Francis Xaverius*; paraphrased," II: 575-576; "To Mr. *Congreve*, on his Tragedy, the *Mourning Bride*," II: 564-565; "Verses sent to Mr. Bevil Higgons, On his sickness and recovery from the Smallpox, in the Year 1693," II: 557-559.

Collection: *The Plays of Mary Pix and Catharine Trotter*, edited by Edna L. Steeves, volume 2 (New York: Garland, 1982).

OTHER: *Olinda's Adventures; or, The Amours of a Young Lady*, in volume 1 of *Letters of Love and Gallantry and Several Other Subjects. All Written by Ladies* (London: Printed for Samuel Briscoe, 1693); republished in *The Second Volume of Familiar Letters of Love, Gallantry and several Occasions, By the Wits of the Last and Present Age . . .* (London: Printed for Sam. Briscoe, 1718), pp. 133-198; facsimile, Augustan Reprint Society Publication Number 138 (Los Angeles: William Andrews Clark Memorial Library, 1969);

Epilogue, in *Queen Catharine or, The Ruines of Love*, by Mary Pix (London: Printed for William Turner & Richard Basset, 1698);

"Calliope: The Heroick Muse: On the Death of John Dryden, Esq; By Mrs. C. T.," in *The Nine Muses. Or, Poems Written by Nine severall Ladies Upon the Death of the late Famous John Dryden, Esq.*, possibly compiled by Delarivière Manley (London: Printed for Richard Basset, 1700);

"Poetical Essays; May 1737: Verses, occasion'd by the Busts in the Queen's Hermitage, and Mr. Duck being appointed Keeper of the Library in Merlin's Cave, By the Authoress of a Treatise (not yet publish'd) in Vindication of the Resurrection of the same Body," *Gentleman's Magazine*, 7 (1737): 308.

Literary history has not been kind to Catharine Trotter. Once a celebrated dramatist, Trotter is now a curiosity, and not just because she was a female writer. Her misfortune was that she was only fourteen when her novel was published, sixteen when her first play was produced, and twenty-six when she retired. Yet she is more than a curiosity, despite her odd career. Shifts in taste may justify Trotter's literary oblivion, but it just may be that Thomas Birch unwittingly hastened it. A minister and historian, Birch published a two-volume edition of Trotter's work (1751) that emphasized her life after 1706. To Birch, Trotter brought honor to her sex by "a genius equal to most . . . in the study of a real philosophy, and a theology worthy of human nature, and its all-perfect author." As evidence, he printed 916 pages of Trotter's philosophical and religious works, leaving 115 pages for a play and some poems. Soon, Trotter appeared only in anthologies of "Learned Women" or "Female Writers." Furthermore, Trotter did not fare any better as a philosopher or religious writer. Even in

relation to John Locke, her major philosophical interest, she is a footnote in others' studies.

An aristocrat by birth, Trotter was poor for most of her life. She was born in London to Scottish parents, navy captain David Trotter and his wife, Sarah Ballenden (or Bellenden) Trotter. Her father served splendidly during the Dutch War and was dubbed "Honest Dave" by Charles II and the duke of York. Unfortunately, Captain Trotter died in 1684, leaving his widow and two children penniless. After King Charles II's death in 1685, Sarah's pension stopped, and, until 1702, when it was granted again by Queen Anne, Sarah was forced to depend upon her relatives and friends.

Only four when her father died, Catharine soon impressed her family with her precocity and her will. She extemporized in verse and wrote in English and French, having taught herself. With a little help from her friends, she mastered logic and Latin grammar. Although raised a Protestant, young Catharine soon converted. According to Birch, "several [Catholic] families of distinction . . . exposed her, while very young, to impressions in favour of that church until 1707," when she returned to the Church of England.

To Birch, Trotter was an attractive, "private" person. She was "extremely amiable," modest, and innocent, "small, [with] remarkable liveliness in her eye, and delicacy of complexion." However, Birch's description falls short of George Farquhar's impression of "the beautiful" Trotter. Birch's appreciation and Farquhar's testimonial underscore their biases: one admired Trotter's spiritual excellence; the other, her youthful public image.

That public image began in 1693 with the anonymous publication in *Letters of Love and Gallantry* of Trotter's poem to her sick friend Bevil Higgons. A conventional lament, the poem is most noteworthy for the age and sex of the poet. Birch republished it, but he ignored Trotter's novel, *Olinda's Adventures*, also published anonymously in 1693, in *Letters of Love and Gallantry and Several Other Subjects*. A rare example of early modern juvenile writings, the novel sheds light on courtship and marriage practices of the period. Moreover, it reveals Trotter's skill as a creator of character, scenes, and action, all of which she soon employed in her plays. Although Trotter was not identified in the book, Robert Adams Day suggests that readers knew she wrote it. The character Olinda is so much like her creator that Delarivière Manley may be forgiven for insisting

Illustration for Olinda's Adventures *in* The Second Volume of Familiar Letters
of Love, Gallantry and several Occasions *(1718)*

in her epistolary novel *The Adventures of Rivella* (1714) that incidents in *Olinda's Adventures* are from Trotter's life. Birch dismisses the idea, warning us to consider the source, but one may easily confuse beautiful Olinda with Trotter. Trotter was just thirteen when she wrote the novel, and Olinda at fifteen writes of events that occurred after she was thirteen because "about that time I began to fancy my self a Woman." Like Trotter, Olinda is intelligent and lives with her widowed mother, who wants her daughter to marry advantageously.

The novel comprises eight letters, seven of them to a confidant. Olinda writes: "tho' . . . I have not always been so nicely cautious as a Woman in strictness ought, I have never gone beyond the bounds of solid Virtue." She confronts di-

lemmas of love and honor, appearance and reality, and marriage and money. Tightly structured, the novel links episodes without repeating devices or conflicts. Trotter's humor and insight enliven Olinda, who reveals her triumphs and her errors, no matter how embarrassing. For example, Olinda writes of Berontus the goldsmith: "I was well enough pleas'd with the Love, tho' not with the Lover; for 'tis natural at that unthinking Age to covet a croud of Admirers, tho' we despise them." Encouraged, Berontus sends a note to Olinda that her mother intercepts. Olinda writes: "she ask'd what Answer I wou'd return. I told her I was wholly to be Govern'd by her; but if I was to follow my own inclination I wou'd not answer it at all." Olinda's mother takes charge—"she did not think it an ill Match, considering my

Circumstances"–and writes to Berontus for Olinda, until he complains "of the strange contradictions in what I [Olinda] did, and what I Writ." At one point the readers are treated to a session where her mother and Berontus "talk of . . . Joynture, and Settlements, etc." Yet, Olinda dismisses him, declaring she is "too young to think of Love, or Marriage."

By the end Olinda and her mother have fled from an old married suitor; another has died of smallpox; and Olinda has learned that men are "more capable to instruct and form our Minds, than the wisest of our own," while women are "more apt to curb that Licentiousness, which Men encourage one another in." She cynically concludes, "what happiness will it be for us, to see our selves the Instruments of all the Men's becoming Good, and all the Women Wise? (A more extraordinary Reformation than *Luther's*.)"

Trotter's achievement is not well known, in part because even her strongest advocate, Birch, did not mention the short novel. More recently, Day praised the book as a step in the development of the novel, citing the middle-class milieu, where Olinda is courted by goldsmiths rather than princes, where she is shown living in London without much money, and where she is deferential to her anxious mother. To Day, Trotter "ably anticipates the English domestic and realistic novel" and is more experienced and mature than her years would suggest. Day notes, "we must look to the juvenilia of Jane Austen for the first comparable phenomenon." Further, the novel shows a budding dramatist with an eye for detail and character and an ethic that will define her life.

Only fourteen when *Olinda's Adventures* was published, Trotter was just sixteen when *Agnes de Castro* was presented anonymously at the Theatre Royal in Drury Lane. By the next season she would be familiar enough to be the subject of a satire, *The Female Wit* (1696), with Manley and Mary Pix. She was "Calista, a lady who pretends to the learned languages and assumes to herself the name of critic." Like her authorship of *Olinda's Adventures*, Trotter's authorship of *Agnes de Castro* was an open secret. In her unsigned dedication to the lord chamberlain, she alludes to the "little Off-spring of my early Muse." Then, in the poem that follows the dedication, Manley declares, "the Author of Agnes de Castro" fills "the Vacant Throne" left by "Orinda" (Katherine Phillips) and "Astrea" (Aphra Behn). Further, the prologue by William Wycherley identifies "Our Fe-

male Wit" and asks that readers "be not, as Poor Women often find, / Less kind to her." In the epilogue Trotter begs the audience to "judge aright" this "New Author" who "is Virtuous, Young, and Fair." Who in London would not have known that the playwright was a young and pretty woman?

A blank-verse tragedy, *Agnes de Castro* was Christopher Rich's challenge to Thomas Betterton's production of Congreve's *Love for Love* at Lincoln's Inn Fields. Rich may have chosen it because of London's curiosity about Trotter or because its title had already been popularized by Behn's 1689 novel. The cast included Thomas Simpson as the King, John Verbruggen as Alvaro, Jane Rogers as Agnes, Mrs. Temple as the Princess, and Frances Maria Knight as Elvira. All would appear not only in other plays by Trotter but also in the play that satirized her, *The Female Wits*; Mrs. Temple played Calista.

Trotter's play should have pleased the audience–it kept the unities and its characters confronted the popular heroic dilemma of love and honor. However, Trotter's characters were depicted in ways unexpected and, for some, unacceptable from a sixteen-year-old girl. Indeed, Trotter's play might have fared better if it had been written by a man, for Agnes compares favorably with Belvidera in Thomas Otway's *Venice Preserv'd* (1682) and Marcia in Joseph Addison's *Cato* (1713). Like these other heroines, Agnes is torn between love and honor, and she is the innocent target of unwarranted jealousy and unsolicited love. Unlike Belvidera or Marcia, however, Agnes is a forceful, active agent who adheres to her principles despite her passions.

Set in Portugal, the play centers on conflicts with the Spaniards. The Prince of Portugal secretly loves Agnes, a Spanish aristocrat who has the exclusive affection of the prince's second wife, Constantia, a Spanish princess. The princess confesses to Agnes that her husband does not love her. Agnes loves her friend and is bound to serve her, but she secretly loves the prince. The unhappy triangle is tested by Elvira, Alvaro, and Bianca. Bianca, the prince's first wife, and Elvira, the prince's former mistress, conspire against Agnes because the princess's bond with Agnes insults them, as if Portuguese women are not equal to Spanish women. Elvira vows, "Revenge is Justice, Born in Noble Souls." She is seconded by Bianca, who introduces the theme of women's powers and duties: " 'T would make all

TO THE
AUTHOR
OF
Agnes de Castro.

O Rinda, *and the Fair Aftrea gone,*
    Not one was found to fill the Vacant Throne:
Afpiring Man had quite regain'd the Sway,
Again had Taught us humbly to Obey ;
Till you (Natures third ftart, in favour of our Kind)
With ftronger Arms, their Empire have disjoyn'd,
And fnatcht a Lawrel which they thought their Prize,
Thus Conqu'ror, with your Wit, as with your Eyes.
Fired by the bold Example, I would try
To turn our Sexes weaker Deftiny.
O ! How I long in the Poetick Race,
To loofe the Reins, and give their Glory Chafe ;
For thus Encourag'd, and thus led by you,
Methinks we might more Crowns than theirs Subdue.

                                        Dela Manley.

A PROLOGUE; *Written by Mr.*
Wycherly *at the Authors requeft: De-*
fign'd to be Spoke.

L Adies and Gallants, you we hope to find,
    To her, who brings you now together, kind ;
    That you, will to your pleafing her confent,
    Not out of your own Nicety prevent,
But to fpight her, your own divertifement ;
And will not your Difpleafure to her fhow,
Who your fcorn Ventures, but to pleafure you,
Nay, her own pleafure, does for yours, forego ;
And like the Pregnant of her Sex, to gain,
Bet for your pleafure, more Difgrace, and Pain,
Who, but becaufe fhe'd do you, a good Turn,
unask'd, unfu'd to, may become your fcorn ;
But you ; the Men of Honour, or of Wit,
To fet yours to a Woman can't think fit,
And Ladies ; as neceffitous of Fame,
Ne'er raife your Credit, by another's fhame,
Cenfuring others, to 'fcape others blame ;
And Gallants ; as y'are Men of Honour, you,
Will ne'er fpeak ill, of her you do not know ;
The more fhe ftrives, to give you Pleafure too,
Which is moft often, (as we Women find,)
The fole caufe, you prove to us, but lefs kind ;
As well-bred *Beaux's* with Noife too, ne'er thinks fit,
To filence on the Stage, as in the Pit,
Another's Senfe, to hide your want of Wit ;
But Beaux's and Wits, I pray be filent now,
And hear without Noife, nay with Patience too,
Our Female Wit, if you'd have her, hear you ;
Efpecially, fince your own talking does,
Your Pleafure interupt, your Senfe Expofe,
Whilft Silence, good Senfe, and good Breeding fhows ;
And each Man's manners, Honour, Wit appear,
More, as he's lefs a Woman's Cenfurer,
Then Cenfures, which wou'd fpoil your fport forbear :
Think not the Ladies Wit, or Honour lefs,
Becaufe fhe feeks thofe who have lefs to pleafe ;
Let not her aim, to pleafe the Publick now,
Defign'd her Credit, but your Scandal grow,
Make not her proffer'd favour, her Difgrace,
Nay, though it fhou'd not pleafe th'intention praife,
'Tis merit only, to defire to pleafe ;
Then be not, as Poor Women often find,
Lefs kind to her, but as fhe's more inclin'd,
At venture of her Fame, to pleafe Mankind.

                                        PRO-

Commendatory verse by Delarivière Manley and prologue by William Wycherley from the 1696 edition of Agnes de Castro

Men be Faithless as the Prince, / If Women bore their Wrongs without return." Their passions are matched by Alvaro, Elvira's brother, who has "boundless Rage and Jealousie" that "must be fatal to the Prince, or *Agnes.*"

Like *Olinda's Adventures,* Trotter's drama depends upon the desires and decisions of women. At one point Alvaro observes: "No Monarch's Pow'rs so vast, as Woman's Empire." He can neither subdue nor win Agnes. Confounding love with lust, he uses passion to justify revenge: "T'enjoy her were for Love a happy Fate, / But 'tis the Rape, wou'd satisfy my Hate." He tells Agnes, "What but Pow'r Makes Actions Right, or Wrong?" The confusion in the play of power with right, lust with love, and revenge with honor most often pits women against men. All confront conditions defined by their adversaries; some are defeated by their excesses. For example, having mistaken the princess for Agnes, upon whom she hopes to avenge her honor, Elvira stabs the princess and accuses Agnes of

the murder. In act 4 a mad Elvira is haunted by the princess's ghost and, by act 5, stabs her confidant, Bianca. Elvira's brother, Alvaro, vows vengeance on Agnes: "When I have reap'd what to my passion's due, / She dies[,] *Elvira,* she shall bleed for you." Jealousy continues to bring tragedy: Alvaro stabs Agnes instead of his intended victim, the prince, who wounds Alvaro.

Trotter's adaptation of Behn's novel strengthens the dramatic action. For example, where Behn's princess dies of natural causes, Trotter's is stabbed by mistake. Where Behn has Agnes secretly marry the prince, Trotter keeps Agnes true to her ideals. Other changes compress the action of the play enabling Trotter to observe the unities and focus on the characters' heroic dimensions.

According to Charles Gildon, the play "met with good success," an opinion seconded a century later by David Erskine Baker. However, subsequent critics have ignored their judgment. Edmund Gosse, for one, equivocates: " 'Agnes de

Castro' is an immature production, and shows a juvenile insensibility to plagiarism. . . . But, as the dramatic work of a girl of sixteen, the play is rather extraordinary for nimble movement and adroit theatrical arrangements." He applauds Trotter's "meritorious character-drawing," especially "her conception of a benevolent and tenderly forgiving Princess [who is] well contrasted with the fierce purity of Agnes and the infatuation of the Prince." After noting "a capital scene of exquisite confusion between this generous and distracted trio," he concludes, "It is a bad play, but not at all an unpromising one." More recently, Nancy Cotton faults its poetry of "one or two extra syllables," its "peculiar" dialogue, and its "duologues and soliloquies." She concludes, "The total effect is of a Senecan tragedy a hundred years out of date." Less harsh, Robert D. Hume (1975) finds *Agnes de Castro* exemplifies the female writers' preference for the heroic mode because it is "a standard mixture of court intrigue, heated heroic sentiment in blank verse, and fairly limited pathos." However, Constance Clark sees the play as an early eighteenth-century "She-tragedy" with "two heroines of unassailable virtue who meet tragic ends through no fault of their own." To Clark, Agnes and the princess are "larger-than-life" because of their virtue and extraordinary friendship.

Three years later Trotter's second play, *Fatal Friendship*, premiered at Lincoln's Inn Fields. Although her name does not appear on the title page, Trotter signed the dedication to Princess Anne of Denmark, later Queen of England. It is Trotter's best-known play, in part because Birch included it in *The Works of Mrs. Catharine Cockburn* (1751), stating that it "met with great applause, and is still thought the most perfect of all her dramatic performances." Ironically, theater history attends mostly to a stage direction in act 2, scene 2, that is "a striking example" of two flats being drawn apart to suggest a door or a gate. Similarly, recent interest in Trotter stems from gender, not dramatic achievement, a problem that Trotter notes in her dedication: "when a Woman appears in the World under any distinguishing Character, she must expect to be the mark of ill Nature," especially if she ventures into "what the other Sex think their peculiar Prerogative." Her play is "an undertaking few of my Sex, have ventur'd at" and so "may draw some Malice on me," she writes. Yet, the play has "most noble" purposes, "to discourage Vice, and recommend a firm unshaken Virtue."

Like *Olinda's Adventures*, *Fatal Friendship* has characters, situations, and themes that seem autobiographical. For example, the central characters, like Trotter and her mother, are impoverished aristocrats who see marriage in economic terms. As she did in *Olinda's Adventures* Trotter includes the problems of the second-born son of an aristocrat, and, like the novel, the play has a misguided parent, this time a father. The play is set in France, after a war with Spain. Ostensibly about the heroic dilemma of love and honor, it is really about money. Gramont, Count Roquelaure's younger son, has returned from the war and is secretly married to Felicia, who has borne him a son. Felicia's brother, Bellgard, another poor aristocrat, wants Felicia to marry Gramont's rich father, Count Roquelaure, who arranges a marriage for his son with Lamira, a wealthy young widow. Further complicating the plot is Gramont's best friend, Castalio, a Neapolitan French officer, who loves Lamira. Lamira, however, refuses to marry Castalio because he is poor.

When Count Roquelaure finds that Felicia will not marry him, he wants her even more. His frustration increases after his son refuses to marry Lamira. When the count argues that Lamira deserves Gramont's love, Gramont responds:

> It is not merit only gives us love,
> Else every heart wou'd take the same impression,
> But each we see receives a different Image,
> As it were fitted for that stamp alone.

In a startling echo of John Locke's ideas, Trotter betrays her early interest in philosophy. However, Gramont's view of love does not persuade the count, who imprisons Castalio and blackmails his son: Gramont is to marry Lamira, or Castalio will remain a prisoner. At the same time the count continues to pursue Felicia. However, Gramont's fatal friendship with Castalio ruins them all. Gramont agrees to marry Lamira to free his friend from prison but wonders, "shall I give up my honour, / To save my self, and all I love from ruine?" Gramont submits when he learns his son is held for ransom, and the count's blackmail works. Gramont may have married Lamira, but he refuses to bed her. Insulted, Lamira seeks revenge. Meanwhile Gramont's confusion deepens after he learns that Castalio loves Lamira. Similarly, Bellgard tells Felicia of Gramont's betrayal only to learn that Felicia is married to Gramont. When he calls her "Traitress . . . pollution of my blood," she agrees: "O I deserve all this, that cou'd deceive / And disobey the best of Brothers." The tragedy reaches a bloody close: Gramont stabs himself after interceding in a fight between Bellgard and Castalio and accidently killing his friend. Before dying, Gramont learns that the count has cleared the false charges against Castalio and has assumed the care of Felicia and her son.

A summary does not do justice to the structure, the characterization, and the dilemmas that Trotter's audience applauded in the only successful new play of the season. Yet, it still earned mixed responses, first from Gildon: "I think it deserved the applause it met with, which every play that has the advantage of being clap't, cannot get from the severer and abler judges," and then from Sullen and Ramble, who claim that they "hate these Petticoat-Authors" in *A Comparison Between the Two Stages* (1702), yet toast Trotter and her play:

> R. To the Fair Author of the *Fatal Friendship*.
> C. Ay, come . . . any thing that the Glass may go round.

It was during the heady season that Farquhar found the "representation of *Fatal Friendship*" almost as affecting as the "sight of the beautiful author."

Not many since her day agree. Like Gildon, John Genest equivocates: "The story is domestic and the play on the whole not a very bad one, but the distress arises from improbable circumstances." James Beattie is disturbed that Trotter "at eighteen [was more] adept in love matters than unmarried women of her age ought to be." Jane Williams finds the play "undecorous," without "a single line of poetry," and the plot "commonplace, but well complicated," leading her to wonder why Birch wanted to include more of Trotter's plays if this was the best. Earlier this century, Herbert Carter did not find *Fatal Friendship* a good tragedy. More recently, it has earned qualified praise. Fidelis Morgan includes it in her edition of *The Female Wits* (1981) because its "plot is extraordinary, for a tragedy, in its ingenious obsession with money, its advantages, and the problems resulting from the lack of it." Morgan cites Trotter's debt to Otway, and in her comparison of the two writers finds Trotter stronger: "where Otway's heroines were pitiable victims, there only to wail, the women in *The Fatal Friendship* are as active as anyone in bringing about calamity. Mor-

gan also praises the suspense that depends upon the characters' own uncertainties and applauds the relationship of Felicia and Lamira where "it is never clear which is torturer, which victim."

Yet, for Edna Steeves, Trotter's tragedy centers "on the private lives of the hero and heroine." She finds that "The emotional strength of the play lies in the psychological effects upon the domestic lives of the main characters who are faced with intolerable situations." She suggests that Barry and Bracegirdle, who were frequently cast in confrontational parts, brought success to the play: "They represented the Restoration audience's view of the opposite extremes of feminine psychology, and it is of interest to see a woman dramatist exploring the minds and emotions of her leading female characters." However, Clark sees weaknesses in the play, especially the nature of the tragedy. The hero's crimes, she finds, are "impetuosity and parental disobedience." The murder is not the result of tragic dilemmas, but an accident, and the father's remorse and capitulation at the end are "dei ex machina." All of the weaknesses lead Clark to conclude that Trotter was beginning to question "whether romantic love was . . . important enough . . . for a tragedy."

Trotter addressed that question more directly in her only comedy, *Love at a Loss, or, Most Votes Carry It*. It premiered at the Theatre Royal in Drury Lane on 23 November 1700 with Colley Cibber as Cleon, "a vain affected Fellow," Frances Knight as Lesbia, and Anne Oldfield as Lucilia. Trotter insists she wrote the comedy "when the Town had been little pleas'd with Tragedy intire." Further confounding her understanding of the London audience, the comedy was *not* well received. Yet, she published it on 3 May 1701, shortly after *The Unhappy Penitent* opened, because its censure "endear'd it to me, made me earnest to have it clear it self of the injurious Report it suffer'd under, by appearing in Print." Even Trotter's dedication to Lady Sarah Piers is defensive, for it criticizes any who view "Wives . . . as the impediments of a Man's Pleasure, or at best a Convenience in the setling his Affairs, without aiming at a Satisfaction her self." Her polemic continues in the prologue, where she insists "Mother Wit defend an *English* Maid," only to despair in the epilogue: "What certain Hazard's do Poor Women run!"

Set in France, the play, in prose, completes its action on a day when Lesbia, Miranda, and Lucilia confront romantic dilemmas. On the rebound from Grandfoy, who still loves her, Lesbia is engaged to Beaumine, "a Gay Roving Spark," with whom she has prematurely consummated their marriage. Quickly losing interest in Lesbia, Beaumine has been seeking liaisons with others, among them Miranda. "A Gay Coquet," Miranda is engaged to Constant, who, as his name suggests, is her opposite. Completing the lovers' combinations are Lucilia and Phillabell, who are to wed the following day. Their problem? Lucilia has bogus love letters that she sent to Cleon, the fop who still hopes to win her. She resorts to intrigue to hide them from Phillabell.

Love is always at a loss in the play, especially when called upon by the women. In act 1, for example, Lysetta, Lucilia's governess, belatedly instructs her charge: "more Women have sacrific'd their Vertue to Reputation, than ever Love has ruin'd; and if [men] can but make us kind, why need they care why we are so?" Outraged, Lucilia responds, "Shou'd you not have warn'd me of the Deceit and Treachery of Men?" Lysetta agrees, lamenting, "Is there any Man that would not rather have another Man's Wife than make her his own?" As for Lesbia, her problem is Beaumine. She explains to Lucilia, "agreeable as [Beaumine] is, I never lov'd him much, and yet I don't know how he found the yielding Minute."

Trotter implies that good matches are impossible. Phillabell wants to marry Lucilia because she "is reserv'd and prudent, her Fortune equals mine . . . I have all the Security for a lasting Love and Happiness, that Reason can desire or give." To Beaumine, "over-fondness" cloys; he looks for a "fresh Appetite." For Grandfoy, only honor stands between him and his beloved Lesbia. Knowing of her lapse with Beaumine, Grandfoy tells her, "would you consent to be mine, I should receive you as the greatest earthly Blessing, but that you have refus'd me, unless *Beaumine* . . . by a declared infidelity, entirely release you." Lesbia is trapped: her love *is* at a loss because neither Beaumine's love nor his honor matches her own. Beaumine tells her, "You have now a great deal of my Love, 'tis certain Marriage won't add one Jot to it, and very possibly it may extreamly lessen it."

A secondary theme in the play is Trotter's ubiquitous problem parent, this time Beaumine's mother. Never onstage, she is important because she is Beaumine's excuse to postpone his marriage and because she is verbally abused. For example, Beaumine claims that he cannot marry, for "the old Woman" is near death. Lesbia responds,

"But will the old Woman ever die, Beaumine?" Parents in Trotter's hands do not fare well, especially when they affect marriage plans.

Some of the conflict, however, has more acceptable wit. At the end of act 1, Beaumine exalts the hypocrisy of lovers: "We all are false alike in love, 'tis clear, / He that dissembles best, is most sincere." That same idea occurs in act 3, when he says, "What should hinder people from being false, when they are certain not to be suspected?" Viewing love and faithfulness cynically, Beaumine sings in act 3: "Wou'd you, wou'd you love the Nymph for ever, / Never, never, never, never, never let her be your wife." With his wit and independence, Beaumine is a better match for Miranda, the coquette who wants to satisfy her desires without sacrificing her "honor," her freedom, or her pleasure. She claims to love Constant and Beaumine, but "I like the Squeaking of a Fiddle, better than the Squalling of Brats, and an obsequious humble Servant, better than a surly Lord and Master." Later, Miranda permits her rival Lesbia to hide and observe Beaumine's infidelity. In the same scene, Lesbia returns the favor by keeping Miranda from losing Constant. Through both the action and the theme of the play, Miranda and Lesbia complement one another.

Comic though the play may be, Trotter uses it to show society how ineffectual its ideals are in the face of human nature. In an indictment of love and marriage, Trotter displaces romantic ideals with majority rule. Unable to choose between her obligation to Beaumine and her love of Grandfoy, Lesbia begins the final action with her comment, "they had best throw Dice for me." To Cleon, "This is extreamly new; but I don't know why it shou'd not be brought into a Custom to Marry, as well as to Divorce by Vote." They vote and Beaumine wins, five to one, but the reasons for each vote are as illuminating as the results. Cleon votes for Beaumine, who will "soonest be weary of her." Constant alone votes for Grandfoy, using an argument not supported by the text, that Grandfoy "loves her best." Bonsot, "a good-natured officious Fool," votes for Beaumine, who "won't quarrel with her." Lucilia agrees–Beaumine "can plead most right in her." Phillabell and Miranda both vote for Beaumine because Lesbia "loves him best," despite contrary evidence. When the voting ends, Lesbia's only comment is, "The odds are on *Beaumine*'s side." Forestalling criticism of her unromantic views, Trotter offers a reformed Beaumine at the end.

Yet, Grandfoy's lot shows us that truth and goodness are not enough. His future is decided by people motivated more by their passions and purses than by love and honor. They have revealed their hypocrisy and faithlessness. How else could their votes go but to one most like themselves, to Beaumine?

The comedy disappointed Trotter's audiences, and Trotter herself was disappointed by its publication. She was not in London during its printing, and upon her return she was so distressed by the errors that, according to Birch, if she could have, she would have suppressed it. Later, after she had retired from the stage, she revised the play under a new title, *The Honourable Deceiver; or, All Right at the Last,* but it was neither performed nor published. Over the years, many critics, including Herbert Carter and Leslie Stephen (in the *Dictionary of National Biography*), assumed the original version of *Love at a Loss* had not been produced. After Allardyce Nicoll discovered a copy, he identified it as a comedy of manners of the rakish Beaumine and "sentimental" Lesbia with "many of Jonson's devices." More recently, Clark suggests that the main plot line runs parallel to that of *Fatal Friendship.* She finds the Miranda/Constant plot juxtaposes humours characters and the Lucinda plot hints at an autobiographical indiscretion. Clark speculates that the lost version reinforced the "dominance of Lesbia's story with its improbable theme of a seduced woman who gets her man in the end" and assumes that Lesbia wanted Beaumine, not Grandfoy. To Cotton, the play fails because it "is more moral than merry." Steeves, however, sees good comedy and satire in the play. She writes, "the generally high quality of wit . . . comes as a surprise. The dialogue often sparkles." Like Trotter's other work, the play offers solutions to problems of money, marriage, and mothers, all of which may have faced the young and pretty playwright. Her contributions are its wit and a message that spoke to women of her day.

Trotter's concern for women continued in her blank-verse tragedy *The Unhappy Penitent,* which opened 4 February 1701 at Drury Lane. The cast included Anne Oldfield as Ann of Brittanie, Jane Rogers as Margarite of Flanders, William Mills as Charles VIII of France, and Charles Williams as the duke of Brittanie. When the play was published on 2 August 1701, Trotter's name was on a title page for the first time.

For the first time, too, Trotter ventured into criticism. In her dedication to Charles Montague,

lord Halifax, she discusses honored playwrights, including Dryden, who "little moves our concern for those he represents" because "his Genius seems not turn'd to work upon the softer Passions," and Otway, who moved "Compassion . . . and excell'd in the Pathetick." However, Nathaniel Lee, who aimed "at the sublime," she writes, should have "intirely apply'd himself to describe . . . Love . . . if that be allow'd a proper subject for *Tragedy.*" She finds Shakespeare alone is "secure . . . from attack." Then she criticizes her own play, admitting "the Distress is not great enough, the Subject of it only the misfortune of Lovers." She doubts "whether Love a proper Subject for . . . *Tragedy*" because it "becomes a Vice, when cherish'd as an exalted Vertue." It fixes the mind "on one object, and sets all our happiness at Stake on so great hazard as the caprice or fidelity of another." She regrets that she presents love as the "shining Vertue of our Heroes." However, the "doting lovers" deserve our pity because they recognize they hurried their passion and are punished for it.

Set in fifteenth-century France, the "Bloodless *Tragedy*" concerns Charles VIII (1470-1498), whose father died in 1483 when Charles was too young to rule. From infancy, Charles was betrothed to Margarite of Flanders, but in 1491 he married Ann, duchess of Brittany. Using historical facts, Trotter transforms the politics of marriage into the dilemmas of love and honor. Ann, the "Pattern of Perfection," warns Margarite, who is "with Passion Blinded" and loves Lorrain, "Be Mistriss of your self, and firm to Virtue." Margarite follows Ann's advice and asks the king to nullify their engagement, but he is too proud to let Lorrain have her. Margarite frantically turns on Ann, her friend: "Alas, I rave, When calm Deliberation's necessary." The king reconsiders, but Lorrain blames Margarite and her "Sexes art To charge th'effects of your inconstancy, On Conscience." Yet, they reconcile and marry. When the duke of Brittanie learns that the king released Margarite from her vows, he claims Margarite is the king's discarded mistress. Lorrain believes it, rants of his wife's faithlessness, instructs her to "Look into [her] Soul," and claims that woman is "The worst, and weakest part of the Creation."

Meanwhile, Brittanie finds Margarite and convinces her that Lorrain is imprisoned. He tells her that she may free him by compromising her honor. For Lorrain's sake Margarite lies to her brother, the archduke of Austria, confessing

THE

Unhappy Penitent

A

TRAGEDY.

As it is ACTED,

At the Theatre Royal *in* Drury
Lane, *by his Majesty's Servants.*

Written by Mrs. TROTTER.

LONDON,

Printed for *William Turner,* at the *Angel* at *Lincolns-Inn Back-Gate,* and *John Nutt* near
Stationers-Hall. 1701.

Dramatis Personæ.

CHarles the 8th King of *France*.   Mr. *Mills*.
  Duke of *Lorrain*.   Mr. *Wilks*.
Arch-Duke of *Austria*.   Mr. *Williams*.
Duke of *Brittanie*.   Capt. *Griffin*.
Graville, ⎱ of the Privy Council.   ⎰ Mr. *Thomas*.
Du Law.   ⎰   ⎱ Mr. *Simpson*.
Brisson, a Gentleman of the Bed-Chamber. Mr. *Smith*.
Du Croy, a Gentleman belonging to the D. of *Brit.* Mr. *Toms*.
Two *Neapolitan* Lords.   Mr. *Kent* and Mr. *Fairbank*.

Margarite of *Flanders*.   Mrs. *Rogers*
Ann of *Brittanie*.   Mrs. *Oldfield*.
Madame de Bourbon, the King's Sister. Mrs. *Powell*.

Men and Women, Attendants.

PROLOGUE

Spoken by Mrs. Oldfeild.

OF *late we've heard of nothing but of War,
    The Cry is young* Gustavus, *and the Czar:
How to Finall the Gallick Squadrons fly;
What Schemes are form'd 'gainst our old Ally,
But now the peaceful Tattle of the Town,
Is how to join both Houses into one,
And whilst the blustering hot-brain'd Heroes fight,
Our softer Sex pleads gently to unite.
No Wounds but* Cupid's *discompose our Mind,
And if we're cruel, 'tis when we are kind.
Our calm Complection Love's soft Mansion seeks,
We swoon at Blood, unless 'tis in our Cheeks,
Hence you've to Night a Bloodless Tragedy,
Our Authoress cannot let her Heroe dye.
'Tis not an Age to drown, tho' burn for Love,
Will nought but Death your barbarous pitty move!
Here's what is worse to one that's well enclin'd,
The desperate Nymph renounces all Mankind.*

To

Title page, cast list, and prologue from the first of Trotter's plays to bear her name on its title page

dishonor. He blames himself for putting "so great a Trust, Into the hands of such frail things!" He then urges her to "Dye . . . to expiate thy foul Sin." Margarite accepts his judgment, echoing Felicia in the *Fair Favorite,* and confesses, "*Lorrain*'s my crime." When her brother blames her "deceitful, ruinous Passions," she pledges her life to "Heav'n" and prepares to enter the convent. Lorrain's instability leads him to madness. Margarite is exonerated by the king after Brittanie confesses his lies. However, she has pledged to enter the convent "if Heav'n wou'd clear My Fame." As Margarite vacillates, Ann despairs, "She's lost! What resolution can be trusted!" Finally, Margarite keeps her word and leaves.

The play is readable and, when considered in the light of a young woman's literary and personal development, it is fascinating. Trotter has enough confidence both to evaluate and print her views of male dramatists and to warn us that love is not tragic, contrary to dramatic tradition. Critical opinion over the centuries, however, has

not been swayed. Genest finds the play "indifferent" and "Margarite's conduct . . . not very natural." Cotton agrees: "The king and Ann are left not only to marry but also, considering that the king's delay caused much of Margarite's trouble, to draw rather priggish morals in the same haste-makes-waste spirit as those at the end of *Fatal Friendship*." She finds the play legalistic: "Margarite violates her contract with the king, but redeems her mistake by keeping a contract with heaven." However, Hume sees the play as pathetic tragedy, not heroic drama, despite "a technically heroic setting" and "love-and-honour misunderstandings. The pathetic parting of the Duke of Lorrain and Margarite of Flanders . . . is . . . sentimental mush of the most contrived sort." According to Clark, the play resembles *Agnes de Castro* with its pair of "high-minded women" who are involved with one man. To Clark, the play has "basically decent people caught up in conflicts of interest . . . without any dastardly deeds."

In her next play, *The Revolution of Sweden,* Trotter continued to question love as motive in he-

Preface from the 1706 edition of The Revolution of Sweden

roic tragedy and to express growing concern with the conditions of women. Predictably, the play had problems. Even after its early draft was revised in light of Congreve's suggestions that Trotter had solicited, the play suffered at least one four-day delay before its premiere on Monday, 11 February 1706. It opened with Betterton's company, the same company that had performed *Fatal Friendship* in 1698. Thomas Betterton played Count Arwide; Elizabeth Barry, Constantia; and Mary Hook (Harcourt), Christina. The play was performed in the Haymarket at the Queen's Theatre, London's newest and largest theater, designed by Sir John Vanbrugh.

Three years before, in 1703, Congreve responded in a lengthy letter to Trotter's plea for help, praising the play's "great and noble" design. However, he warned her away from any "businesse" that could "run into length or obscurity." He then systematically examined Trotter's characters, plot, and action. He questioned the women's "heroic virtue," wondering "whether those of yr: own sex will approve." He cautioned against "noise" in act 2 lest it "do too much dis-

turb an audience." He warned her against offending "probability, in supposing a man not to discover his own wife." He cautioned that "intricacy in the fourth act must by all means be avoided." He found act 5 had "many harangues . . . which is dangerous in a Catastrophe if long."

Although it probably benefited from Congreve's advice, Betterton's acting, and Vanbrugh's theater, the play was not warmly received. Trotter was so stung by the criticisms that she retaliated in her published dedication to Lady Harriett Godolphin. First, Trotter blames society and suggests that the English, like the French, should invite learned women to be "Members of their Societies," and she offers her play as evidence of merit because its "particular Virtue [is that] it tends to incite a disinterested and resolute Care of the Publick Good." In her preface to the play Trotter more directly attacks her critics. Contradicting John Downes's comment that it "expir'd the Sixth Day" because it lacked "the just Decorum of Plays," Trotter blames "the present tast of the Town" because the play was censured by people who either did not see it or who did not understand what they saw. She admonishes, "one who comes to a Play, shou'd be attentive at it; those who find in the Audience a better Entertainment, . . . shou'd not judge at all, of what they have no leisure to mind." She then ridicules the critics: "Some finding that *Arwide* has [signed] . . . a Paper, in which there are Articles that he knows nothing of, conclude that he sign'd a Treaty with his Enemy, without ever reading it, and . . . laugh at a *Womans Plot*, when the least attention . . . must have satisfy'd them that the deceit was a little more artfully laid." She accuses her critics of irresponsibility, especially those who said she deviated from the history of the revolution. Referring to Aristotle, she writes: "Tragedy is confin'd to represent only such incidents as immediately conduce to the effecting the one great Action it proposes, all which must be suppos'd to happen in a small space of Time." She did confine the plot to the election of Gustavus to the throne, and, she explains, "those who know the History, will find . . . I have us'd the Poetick License in bringing several Incidents and Places, much nearer together . . . as far as probability wou'd allow." Then Trotter strengthens her position by addressing the queen and a noblewoman as her patrons and her champions. She writes in the prologue that those who expect a "soft Effeminate Feast" will find "a Noble Heroine" who saves her nation because of "publick Virtues." No one, not even "the vainest haughtiest Man," can disdain the play by a woman, especially "in Great *ANNA*'s Reign."

The play follows two Swedish couples—Count Arwide and his wife, Constantia, and Beron and his wife, Christina. Arwide, Constantia, and Christina are loyal to Gustavus, while Beron is loyal to the viceroy of Sweden. Instead of Gustavus Vasa, the young leader of Sweden's revolution of June 1523, the women are the center of the play, heroically facing danger for the "Publick Good." Christina first appears disguised as her cousin, Fredage, to escape her husband, Beron, who has betrayed Gustavus. Meanwhile, a captive of the Danish forces, Constantia is courageous and steadfast despite the overtures of her captor, the viceroy, who claims that her husband has sacrificed her to the enemy. Released, Constantia returns to the Swedish camp, informs Gustavus of her husband's treachery, and Arwide is arrested. He denies the charges, assuring his wife of the truth. Christina, however, has learned the true villainy of Beron. Just as Congreve suggested to Trotter, Christina reveals both her iden-

tity and her husband's treachery at the same time; she clears Arwide and then dies.

The women are models of virtue and courage. Arwide says of his wife, "O wou'd Men emulate thy great Example." They follow a higher ethic and sacrifice their husbands for honor, knowing that their "Sufferings . . . are [their] greatest Glory." Trotter subtly extols women by having them reprimanded for assuming more than their sex justifies. At one point the archbishop berates Constantia, who has lectured him. At her challenge he says: "Is it for you / To judge of your Superiors, t'instruct your Guide? / When Women preach, 'twill be with *Luther*'s Aid; / A blessed Reformation." Such exchanges abound, but none is as philosophical nor as criticized as this.

Despite Trotter's heavy thesis, Downes admits the playwright is faithful to the history of the revolution. Genest writes that "it is not a bad play" but warns that Trotter used Vertot's *Histoire des revolutions de Suede* (1695) and omitted "the early part of Gustavus's exploits." To Genest, while "Arwide and Christina are real characters, all that they say and do . . . is fiction." Nicoll, like other recent commentators, is not as concerned with the play's authenticity. He sees it as "a poor piece of work with a strained and chaotic plot, and passions atrophied and chill," and dismisses it as a "classic treatment of otherwise heroic subject-matter." Disagreeing, Montague Summers finds that, despite its lack of "fire and spirit," it "is not an uninteresting drama." He sees the "historical characters . . . transformed into purely romantic figures," suggesting Trotter should have kept to "the heroic manner."

Recently, women have been more positive. Cotton finds the play is "an early feminist statement." Likening Trotter's play to the closet dramas of Margaret Cavendish, duchess of Newcastle, Cotton suggests that "Christina is the military-patriotic lady," and that "Constantia fulfills the duchess' ideal of the oratorical heroine, capable of arguing theology with learned prelates." Morgan applauds "Trotter's usual care for language." She notes that the play "is well constructed, but because of the subject matter . . . leaves a distinct impression of dullness." Steeves offers more on the history of the Swedish revolution, finding that J. Mitchell in his 1696 translation of Vertot's book "compared the history of Gustavus Vasa to political events taking place in England during the reign of William III." She suggests it is to Trotter's credit "that in this, her one attempt to write a drama based on a political theme, she has succeeded in fusing history and contemporary political feeling in an emotionally affecting tragedy." Finally, Clark faults Trotter for "haranguing" her audience through Constantia and "bringing the action to a standstill." Nonetheless, she praises the intelligent and brave women who are "exquisitely moral" and Trotter's use of theater as "a platform for her feminist theories and a sort of sermon 'vivant.' "

In her last play Trotter's heroes are women who place honor and courage above romantic or married love. That thesis began to appear in much of Trotter's nondramatic work although it was not so evident in her poem to Higgons in 1693, her congratulatory poem in 1697 to Congreve when *The Mourning Bride* premiered, and her epilogue for Mary Pix's *Queen Catharine or, The Ruines of Love* in June 1698. By 1700, however, Trotter's feminism and philosophy were clearer when, in the guise of Calliope, the heroic muse, she wrote an elegy in Dryden's memory. A few years later, in December 1704 and May 1706, her celebrations of Marlborough's victories at Blenheim and Ramellies reflected her treatment of women in *The Revolution of Sweden*. The focus on women continued in her poem ". . . the Queen's Hermitage," but by 1737, when it was published in *Gentleman's Magazine*, Trotter was not identified as a dramatist but as "the Authoress of a Treatise (not yet publish'd) in Vindication of Mr LOCK. . . ." That shift in her identity reflects Birch's view of Trotter's primary achievement. In May 1702, while still writing for the stage, Trotter had published her first philosophical tract, *A Defence of Mr. Lock's Essay of Human Understanding*, in response to Dr. Thomas Burnet's attack on Locke as a materialist. She published her essay anonymously, for according to Birch, "being more apprehensive of appearing before the great writer, whom she defended, than of the public censure, and conscious, that the name of a woman would be a prejudice against a work of that nature, she resolved to conceal herself with the utmost care."

Changes in Trotter's attitudes extended beyond her play writing and philosophizing. Not long after she left the theater in 1707, Trotter also left Catholicism. She explained her decision in *A Discourse concerning a Guide in Controversies* (1707). Her conversions, she wrote, arose from "free and impartial Enquiries." Published with a preface by Bishop Gilbert Burnet, the essay had a second edition in her lifetime.

Soon after her conversion, Trotter decided to marry. According to Birch, "finding a general libertinism amongst the men, she thought the best security of her happiness in the conjugal state would be the choice of a clergyman." He reports that piety was for Trotter the "true ground of mutual affection." Through Bishop Burnet, Trotter first met George Burnet, who was assigned to Europe for religious missions. After reading the correspondence between Trotter and Burnet, Clark suggests that Burnet wished to court Trotter, "but it was clearly not reciprocated or encouraged. [Trotter] especially balked at his suggestion that on his return from his travels, in 1707, he visit and stay in the house where she was summering in Ockam Mills, Surrey." However, Steeves reads money into the relationship and cites Burnet's engagement to "a young lady of birth and wealth" shortly before Trotter's marriage to Cockburn. Steeves reasons, "If Catharine had received from her aristocratic patrons the recognition her literary output merited, Burnet might have returned to England and proposed to her." Supporting Steeves is Birch's suggestion that, by 1708, after her mother's pension was restored, Trotter "was free to make her love-match."

Although she was courted by a Mr. Fenn, another young clergyman, Trotter set out to win Patrick Cockburn. A record of their courtship survives in letters, and, in some, Trotter casts Cockburn as "Arwide" from *The Revolution of Sweden*; she is "Constantia," Fenn is "Gustavus," and her rival for Cockburn's affection is "Christina." Early in 1708 she married Cockburn, even though, as she wrote Burnet, "I have always been very fearful of putting my happiness entirely in the power of any one." Unhappily, that fear was prophetic. At first, the couple prospered. In June of 1708 Cockburn became curate of Nayland, Suffolk, and later of St. Dunstan's in Fleet Street, London, until the death of Queen Anne and the accession of George I in 1714. For twelve years, from 1714 to 1726, the family suffered because Cockburn refused to take the Oath of Abjuration. By 29 November 1726 Cockburn overcame his scruples, took the oath, and was appointed to St. Paul's Episcopal Church in Aberdeen. He was preferred to the vicarage of Long Horsley, Northumberland, but did not reside there until 1737. He died on 4 January 1749.

After her marriage, Trotter gave up writing until 1726, when she began another defense of Locke in response to Dr. Winch Holdsworth of Oxford. His attack, however, was six years old. She explained, "My young family was grown up . . . and beginning to have some taste of polite literature, my inclination revived with my leisure." She had been so much out of the public eye that when she completed her essay on moral obligation she could not find a publisher for it. It finally appeared in August 1743 in *History of the Works of the Learned* with a dedication to Alexander Pope. Then in 1747 Trotter published an essay in response to Rutherforth's *Essay on the Nature and Obligations of Virtue*, which advocated a system of egoistic utilitarianism. The preface to Trotter's work was by William Warburton, Pope's friend.

While in Aberdeen, she decided to "correct" her tragedies just as she had corrected her comedy. She thought the plays suffered "from too great simplicity of style . . . unequal to the dignity of that poetry." Her friends encouraged her to prepare an edition of her work, and she gave some materials to Birch. Before she was able to complete her task, she died on 11 May 1749, just a few months after her husband's death. She is buried near him in Long Horsely. They left two daughters and one son.

One wonders how Trotter adjusted to being a clergyman's wife, especially after leading a celebrity's life since she was thirteen. In a letter to Pope that she never sent, Trotter offers some answers. Regretting that Pope "did not come sooner into the world, or I later," she writes that she knows they would have met because of their mutual friends, who "are all gone before me, though I was in a manner dead long before them. You had just begun to dawn upon the world when I retired from it. Being married in 1708, I bid adieu to the muses . . . gave myself up to the cares of a family, and the education of my children, that scarce knew, whether there was any such thing as books, plays, or poems . . . in Great Britain."

Even a brief survey of Trotter's life and work will raise questions, especially in light of Mary Pilkington's 1804 evaluation of Trotter. Pilkington suggests that it would have been a far, far better thing to be a wife than to be a playwright, and she is thus able to applaud Trotter "for relinquishing the flattering distinctions of an author, to fulfill those duties which are attached to the character of a wife. . . ." To Pilkington, Trotter "excites a greater degree of interest, superintending the education of her children, than when she was metaphysically defending the opinions of

Mr. Lock." Others agree, finding Trotter respectable in her reticence. Gosse eloquently concurs: to him, Trotter buried "her youth, her beauty, her accomplishments and her ambitions in a small country parsonage in the wildest wilds of Northumberland. Perhaps it would be wrong to believe that she was not, after all, happier so, helping a good man in the exercise of his duties, and bringing up her children . . . than if she had remained admired and envied in the stormy life of authorship in London, or the peaceful and philosophic cloisters of Salisbury."

Gosse forces the question: Would there have been much loss if Trotter had not existed? If she had married a real-life goldsmith when she was fourteen and never written, what would we have missed? Judging from her limited exposure over the centuries, one must answer, "Little," and that was the view of Charles Didbin as well in 1800. Myra Reynolds agrees, for Trotter "has no wit, no fancy, no imagination, no sprightliness of thought, no humor." Carter, too, could not accept her eminence even in her own day. He suggests, "The secret [of her theatrical success] probably lay in her vigorous and charming little personality."

In 1699, during the height of Trotter's triumphs, Gildon was among those who praised the wit and beauty of two plays: "we like the first, but are transported with the last. There is the Chastity of her Person and the Tenderness of her Mind in both; the Passions are natural and moving, the Style just and familiar, and adapted to the Subject; if there be not the Sublime, 'tis because there was no room for it, not because she had not Fire and Genius enough to write it." In 1754 John Duncombe included Trotter in his poem *The Feminead* and exalted her as the "matron" who "now walks musing forth." He shouted, "Hail Cockburn Hail!" However, those who praised Trotter were gradually disappearing. For example, about a century later, Williams praised Trotter, but not her plays. To Williams, Trotter had knowledge, love of truth, and a clear sense of right and wrong. "Her eloquence has the force of manly argument, with the charm of feminine persuasion." A few years later, John Doran was still able to find Trotter's plays "all of a sentimental but refined class—illustrating love, friendship, repentance and conjugal faith."

Perhaps now, late in the twentieth century, the balance is being redressed. Articles and books by critics such as Clark and Cotton are discussing Trotter and her work. Her plays and her novel are available in editions with useful and informative commentary by scholars such as Day and Steeves. In addition the restoration of women writers to our literary canon has brought her before a new public, and, today, Trotter is a refreshing discovery. She offers surprising insight into the impact of money on marriage, probably because she was so affected by it. Without a father for most of her life and driven by her mother, if we are to believe Trotter's fictional parents, she gives us a new perspective. She offers a view of virtue through heroines who will not barter their love for their safety or their economic security. Trotter consistently gives us characters who are driven to the right action, Olinda for her own reputation, Christina for the "Publick Good." In her plays Trotter gives us more-or-less successful women subjected to traps laid by their friends, enemies, and relatives. In each case Trotter's women dominate the action, for good or ill, and resolve the conflicts, usually for good.

Perhaps it is ironic that Trotter has been as much a victim of her reputation as she was of her sex. Two years after her death, through Birch, she became an icon for women, and that icon was offered with the broad, leaden edges and vivid hues of stained glass. Her reality lost, she remained for more than two centuries the model of the submissive, selfless woman who finally saw how right it was to serve her husband and nurture her children. With the current interest in the creative artist regardless of sex or religion, with a freedom-of-opportunity school of criticism, if you will, Trotter returns for a reappraisal that may find her drama of special interest for its reflection of its day. It may also find that plays by a woman during the time of Otway, Lee, and Addison have much to offer students of the drama.

Letters:

"Letter of Advice to her Son," "Letters between Mrs. Cockburn and several of her Friends," and "Letters between the Rev. Dr. Sharp, Archdeacon of Northumberland, and Prebendary of Durham, and Mrs. Cockburn, concerning the Foundation of Moral Virtue," in *The Works of Mrs. Catharine Cockburn, Theological, Moral, Dramatic, and Poetical, Several of them now first printed, Revised and published, With an Account of the Life of the Author* (London: Printed for J. and P. Knapton, 1751), II: 11-20, 153-352, 353-460.

Bibliography:

Thomas Birch, Table of Contents, in *The Works of Mrs. Catharine Cockburn, Theological, Moral, Dramatic, and Poetical, Several of them now first printed, Revised and published, With an Account of the Life of the Author* (London: Printed for J. & P. Knapton, 1751).

Biographies:

Gerard Langbaine, *The Lives and Characters of the English Dramatic Poets. Also an Exact Account of all the Plays that Were Ever Yet Printed in the English Tongue,* revised by Charles Gildon (London: Turner, 1699);

Giles Jacob, *The Poetical Register; or, The Lives and Characters of all the English Poets, with an Account of Their Writings,* 2 volumes (London: Bettesworth, 1723);

Thomas Birch, "The Life of Mrs. Cockburn," in *The Works of Mrs. Catharine Cockburn, Theological, Moral, Dramatic, and Poetical, Several of them now first printed, Revised and published, With an Account of the Life of the Author* (London: Printed for J. & P. Knapton, 1751), I: i-xlviii;

David Erskine Baker, *The Companion to the Play-House* (London: T. Becket & P. A. Dehondt, 1764); augmented and revised by Isaac Reed as *Biographia Dramatica,* 2 volumes (London: Printed for Rivingtons, 1782); augmented and revised again by Stephen Jones, 3 volumes (London: Hurst, Rees, Orme & Brown, 1812);

Charles Didbin, *A Complete History of the English Stage,* 5 volumes (London: Charles Didbin, 1800);

Mary Pilkington, *Memoirs of Celebrated Female Characters* (London: Albion, 1804);

Mary Hays, *Female Biography; or Memoirs of Illustrious and Celebrating Women* (Philadelphia: Byrch & Small, 1807);

John Genest, *Some Account of the English Stage,* 10 volumes (Bath: H. E. Carrington, 1832);

Frederic Rowton, *The Female Poets of Great Britain, Chronologically Arranged: With Copious Selections and Critical Remarks* (Philadelphia: Henry C. Baird, 1853); a facsimile of the 1853 edition, with a critical introduction and bibliographical appendices, by Marilyn L. Williamson (Detroit: Wayne State University Press, 1981), pp. 112-114, 544;

Sarah Josepha Hale, *Woman's Record, or, Sketches of All Distinguished Women, from Creation to A.D. 1854* (New York: Harper, 1855);

Doris Mary Stenton, *The English Woman in History* (London: Allen & Unwin, 1957; New York: Schocken, 1977).

References:

Alison Adburgham, *Women in Print: Writing Women and Women's Magazines from the Restoration to the Accession of Victoria* (London: Allen & Unwin, 1972);

Herbert Carter, "Three Women Dramatists of the Restoration," *Bookman's Journal,* 13 (1925): 91-97;

Constance Clark, "Catherine Trotter," in her *Three Augustan Women Playwrights,* American University Studies Series 4, English Language and Literature, volume 40 (New York: Lang, 1986), pp. 35-95;

Nancy Cotton, "The Female Wits: Catherine Trotter, Delariviere Manley, Mary Pix," in her *Women Playwrights in England: c. 1363-1750* (Lewisburg, Pa.: Bucknell University Press, 1980), pp. 81-121;

Robert Adams Day, Introduction to *Olinda's Adventures; or, The Amours of a Young Lady,* Augustan Reprint Society Publication Number 138 (Los Angeles: William Andrews Clark Memorial Library, University of California, 1969), pp. i-viii;

John Doran, *Their Majesties' Servants: Annals of the English Stage from Thomas Betterton to Edmund Kean,* 2 volumes (New York: W. J. Widdleton, 1865);

John Duncombe, *The Feminead; or, Female Genius. A Poem* (London: M. Cooper, 1754);

The Female Wits: or, The Triumvirate of Poets at Rehearsal. A Comedy. As it was acted several days successively with great applause at the Theatre-Royal in Drury-Lane. By Her Majesty's Servants. Written by Mr. W. M. (London: W. Turner, 1704); facsimile, edited by Lucyle

Hook, Augustan Reprint Society Publication Number 124 (Los Angeles: William Andrews Clark Memorial Library, University of California, 1967); modern edition, in *The Female Wits: Women Playwrights on the London Stage 1660-1720,* edited by Fidelis Morgan (London: Virago, 1981), pp. 390-433;

Laurie A. Finke, "The Satire of Women Writers in *The Female Wits,*" *Restoration: Studies in English Literary Culture,* 8 (Fall 1984): 64-71;

Alison Fleming, "Catherine Trotter–the Scots Sappho," *Scots Magazine,* 33 (1940): 305-314;

Sir Edmund W. Gosse, "Catharine Trotter, the Precursor of the Bluestockings," *Transactions of the Royal Society of Literature,* 34 (1916): 87-118;

Margaret Maison, "Pope and Two Learned Nymphs," *Review of English Studies,* 29 (November 1978): 405-414;

Fidelis Morgan, "Catharine Trotter," in *The Female Wits: Women Playwrights on the London Stage 1660-1720,* edited by Morgan (London: Virago, 1981), pp. 24-31;

Myra Reynolds, *The Learned Lady in England, 1650-1760* (Boston: Houghton Mifflin, 1920);

Gunnar Sorelius, "Catharine Trotter's *The Revolution of Sweden (1706); A Libertarian Drama about Gustavus Vasa,*" Kungl. Humanistiska Vetenskaps-Samfundet i Uppsala, *Annales Societatis Litterarum Humaniorum Regiae Upsaliensis* (Aarsbok, 1977-1978);

Edna L. Steeves, Introduction to volume 2 of *The Plays of Mary Pix and Catharine Trotter* (New York & London: Garland, 1982), pp. ix-xlii;

Thomas Whincop, *A Compleat List of all English Dramatic Poets* (London: T. W., 1747);

Jane Williams, *Literary Women of England* (London: Saunders, Otley, 1861).

Papers:

The British Library's collection of Trotter's works and correspondence is in the Birch Mss. 4264-4267.

William Whitehead

(February 1715-14 April 1785)

Martin J. Wood
University of Wisconsin–Eau Claire

PLAY PRODUCTIONS: *The Roman Father*, translation and adaptation of Pierre Corneille's *Horace*, London, Theatre Royal in Drury Lane, 24 February 1750;

Creusa, Queen of Athens, translation and adaptation of Euripides' *Ion*, London, Theatre Royal in Drury Lane, 20 April 1754;

The School for Lovers, translation and adaptation of Bernard le Bovier Fontenelle's *Le Testament*, London, Theatre Royal in Drury Lane, 10 February 1762;

A Trip to Scotland, London, Theatre Royal in Drury Lane, 6 January 1770.

BOOKS: *The Danger of Writing Verse. An Epistle* (London: Printed for R. Dodsley & sold by T. Cooper, 1741);

Ann Boleyn to Henry the Eighth. An Epistle (London: Printed for R. Dodsley, sold by M. Cooper, 1743);

An Essay on Ridicule (London: Printed for R. Dodsley, 1743);

Atys and Adrastus. A Tale in the Manner of Dryden's Fables (London: Printed for R. Manby & sold by M. Cooper, 1744);

On Nobility: An Epistle to the Right Honble. the Earl of ****** (London: Printed for R. Dodsley & sold by M. Cooper, 1744);

The Roman Father. A Tragedy, As it is Acted at the Theatre Royal in Drury-Lane, By His Majesty's Servants (London: Printed for R. Dodsley, sold by M. Cooper, 1750);

A Hymn to the Nymph of Bristol Spring (London: Printed for R. Dodsley, sold by M. Cooper, 1751);

Poems on Several Occasions. With The Roman Father, a Tragedy (London: Printed for R. & J. Dodsley, 1754)–includes *Fatal Constancy, or Love in Tears*, pp. 153-165;

Creusa, Queen of Athens. A Tragedy, As it is Acted at the Theatre Royal in Drury-Lane, By His Majesty's Servants (London: Printed for R. & J. Dodsley, 1754);

William Whitehead (engraving based on a portrait by R. Wilson)

Elegies. With an Ode to the Tiber. Written Abroad (London: Printed for R. & J. Dodsley, 1757);

Verses to the People of England (London: Printed for R. & J. Dodsley, sold by M. Cooper, 1758);

The School for Lovers. A Comedy, As it is Acted at the Theatre Royal in Drury-Lane (London: Printed for R. & J. Dodsley & sold by J. Hinxman, 1762);

A Charge to the Poets (London: Printed for R. & J. Dodsley & sold by J. Hinxman, 1762);

A Trip to Scotland. As it is Acted at the Theatre Royal in Drury-Lane, anonymous (London: Printed for J. Dodsley, 1770);

Variety. A Tale for Married People, anonymous (London: Printed for J. Dodsley, 1776);

The Goat's Beard. A Fable, as "Goat" (London: Printed for J. Dodsley, 1777).

Collection: *Plays and Poems. By Mr. William White-head, Esq., Poet Laureat,* 2 volumes (London: Printed for J. Dodsley, 1774); volume 3: *Poems,* edited, with a memoir, by William Mason (York: Printed by A. Ward, sold by J. Robson & W. Clarke, London, and J. Todd, York, 1788).

OTHER: "Observations on the Shield of Aeneas," in volume 3 of *The Works of Virgil, in Latin and English,* edited by Joseph Warton, 4 volumes (London: Printed for R. Dodsley, 1753).

Among the minor dramatists of the later eighteenth century whose work has virtually disappeared, few deserve their fates less than William Whitehead. He rose from poverty to comfort and ease, from utter obscurity to national renown, and from schoolboy versifier to poet laureate, all on the strength of his own ability. He employed his considerable poetic talent extremely well if not often, always gently instructing his readers in morality and virtue, occasionally making enough money to defray family debts. His weaknesses included a hesitance to try new poetic or dramatic forms, too much reliance on the suggestions of David Garrick, and too little ambition. In an age that revised even Shakespeare's plays, he adhered too closely to contemporary standards of correct dramatic practice. Yet his plays were among the most popular of his day, and he considered his lack of ambition not a weakness but a sign that he was content with his life. He injured no one, so was criticized for being too mild; he wrote subtle satire, and was misunderstood; he rejected empty fame, and so has been forgotten.

William Whitehead was born in Cambridge in February 1715, the second son of a prosperous baker who served Cambridge University's Pembroke Hall. The income from Richard Whitehead's bakery provided a liberal education for his older son, John, who finished his schooling and became a clergyman while William was still in grammar school. When William turned fourteen, he enrolled at Winchester College, Cambridge, no doubt expecting to duplicate his brother's success. Unfortunately, his father squandered his wealth and, two years into William's schooling, died deeply in debt. Despite the hard times that followed for the family, William continued his studies, thanks mostly to his mother's sacrifice and his own economy.

One of Whitehead's outstanding personal assets, an extremely congenial nature, readily impressed his professors and teachers. They remembered him warmly many years later and spoke highly of his intelligence, grace, and excellent conversation. He quickly formed intimate friendships with them that were to last for life. His poetical talents also impressed them, and when he won one of several modest prizes in a poetry competition sponsored by Charles Mordaunt, lord Peterborough, his entry earned the praise of the contest's judge, Alexander Pope. Indeed, Pope later employed the youth to translate the first Epistle of his *Essay on Man* (1733-1734) into Latin. Whitehead displayed dramatic talents as well, at sixteen composing an entire comedy at Winchester and playing women's parts in school plays.

A delicate youth, Whitehead, even in his school years, clearly preferred poetry to any kind of sport. He associated with those who were wealthy or noble, not because he could gain by them, but because they shared his sensibilities. Certainly he enjoyed good company; or, more to the point, good company enjoyed him. His conversation and amiable wit must have made him attractive indeed, for despite his poverty he was a frequent visitor in the homes of these well-born friends.

In 1735, two years after the Peterborough competition, Whitehead became eligible for election to New College, Oxford, where he hoped to continue his studies as a fellow. Unfortunately, despite his considerable merit, his academic success, and his own connections—he had been a tutor to a nobleman's son—his prospects were thwarted by connections superior to his. Too old now to stay at Winchester College, Whitehead retired from school disappointed. Soon after he left Winchester, however, his mother discovered a way to continue his education, obtaining a scholarship specifically set aside at Clare College for the orphaned sons of bakers. A very meager stipend accompanied the scholarship, but once again his mother and his economy served him well.

During this time he began publishing poetry, motivated not by ambition but by a professed desire to cover some of his own expenses. His mother, still encumbered by Richard's foolish debts, continued to sacrifice for her son, and Whitehead sincerely wished to lessen the additional burden his education imposed. Had he ambitiously sought fame, he might have been more daring in his subjects or more experimental in his selected forms. As it was, his first works revealed a pattern that was to become characteristic of him: he closely imitated his predecessors in style, in form, and in subject. Pope served as his early model, and Whitehead enjoyed a few small successes by following this lead. With *The Danger of Writing Verse* (1741), a mildly satirical work in heroic couplets that Pope himself praised highly, Whitehead demonstrated that he could do an old thing very well. But the practical reasons that motivated his publications also restricted them to a marketable style.

Circumstances soon obliged Whitehead to consider his future. His mother passed away in 1742 just months after his earning the bachelor's degree, bequeathing him the burden of his father's debt. A fellowship at Clare Hall followed, and in 1743 his master's, but with these achievements he could do little to defray the debt. He lived frugally for another two years. By then, however, his diligence, amiability, and unfailing discretion had brought him to the attention of William Villiers, the third earl of Jersey, who hired him as tutor to his son, the Viscount Villiers (George Bussy Villiers). This appointment freed Whitehead from his duties at Clare College, and he moved to the earl's house in London. He proved an excellent tutor as well as an excellent companion, retaining the position virtually for life.

As tutor, Whitehead had two pupils, Villiers and a companion named Stephens. Life at the earl's residence was comfortable, and Whitehead found leisure to pursue other interests. Chief among these, especially now that he was in London, was the theater, which he began to attend regularly. He wrote a farce almost immediately upon his arrival, entitled the "Edinburgh Ball." Although this piece is occasionally listed among Whitehead's dramatic works, it was never printed or performed. A couple of years later he wrote and published a verse epistle to the actor David Garrick, who had just obtained control of the Drury Lane theater. This gesture appealed to Garrick, whose vanity was well known. Whitehead was soon at work on a classic tragedy, and in February 1750 Drury Lane enacted his first surviving play, *The Roman Father*, with Garrick himself in the title role. The play, an adaptation of Pierre Corneille's *Horace* (1635), was a great success, running twelve more times that year alone, and being revived in London either at Drury Lane or Covent Garden on many occasions in succeeding years and decades. According to G. H. Nettleton,

its success was "only second to that of *The Distrest Mother* among the English versions of French classical tragedy."

The Roman Father strictly observes the neoclassical principles of its era, portraying the action of a single day and a single place in ancient Rome. As if these were not restrictions enough, Whitehead strove also to limit his language, incorporating only such speech as would be natural for each character. As he notes in his prologue to *The Roman Father*, every line "Where not the character, but poet spoke" was discarded. The result of all this neoclassicism is a spare play indeed. The story concerns a father, Horatius, his three sons, the Horatii, and his daughter, Horatia. Father and daughter argue over an upcoming battle between Rome and Alba, two peoples united by their Trojan ancestry. To the delight of nearly everyone except Horatius and Horatia, the armies have agreed to forgo a general battle in favor of combat among three champions from each side. Horatius had hoped for the glory of battle for his sons; Horatia had wished to avoid anything that might endanger her betrothed, Curiatius, an Alban hero. Now, however, the proper Roman father Horatius fervently hopes his three sons will be Rome's representatives, while Horatia secretly hopes Curiatius will not be Alba's. Her worst fear comes true: the Horatii must battle the Curiatii to the death. The situation allows Garrick as Horatius, angered by her "woman's weakness," to thunder several orations on Roman honor and glory, roaring, "Had I a thousand Sons, in such a Cause / I could behold them bleeding at my Feet, / And thank the Gods with Tears!" But Horatia's love nourishes a different kind of honor, causing her to rage against an abstract virtue that forces her to choose among her own most deeply held passions; she later declares such virtue to be merely "over-weening Pride." Indeed, she strikes the modern reader as eminently sensible, even though her era (or at least her play) casts her in the role of one for whom the emotional conflict "Transcends a Woman's Weakness." Late in act 4 she rebels, cursing "my Country's Love, the Trick ye teach us / To make us slaves beneath the Mask of Virtue." In the end, however, the Curiatii die at the hands of the Horatii, and a maddened Horatia intentionally provokes her victorious brother to anger so that he will murder her. When he does so and an enraged mob shows up to demand justice, Horatius defends the murder of his daughter by his son and convinces the unruly citizens

Sarah Ward as Valeria, Hannah Pritchard as Horatia, Spranger Barry as Plobius, and David Garrick as Horatius in the first production of The Roman Father *(by permission of the Folger Shakespeare Library)*

that they should be grateful to their city's savior. The play ends on this patriotic if not paternal note.

The Roman Father has little to offer modern audiences. Though it satisfied Garrick's appetite for grand declamations, it has little action, and minuscule character development. Horatius's archaic values would move audiences far less than Horatia's terribly divided loyalties. In its own day, however, all eyes were on Garrick, the father. Whitehead's fellow playwright Arthur Murphy reports that the play was "a great favorite" during its run and praises Whitehead for restoring the classical unities Corneille had violated, as well as for discarding "all redundancies and superfluous characters."

With this great success, Whitehead might have begun to establish himself as one of his era's leading dramatists. It is doubtful, however, that he ever seriously attempted that kind of fame. He wrote because he still owed his father's debt. It is also true, as he himself confessed, that he loved an easy life. In 1751, six years after he

had begun tutoring Villiers, he wrote a verse epistle to a friend, a Reverend Wright, who had criticized Whitehead for remaining dependent upon the earl of Jersey instead of entering upon a profession. In this poem Whitehead reveals much about his own love of comfort and lack of ambition:

> Many men of less worth, you partially cry,
>   To splendour and opulence soar;
> Suppose I allow it; yet, pray sir, am I
>   Less happy because they are more?

At any rate, he continues, "He who rules his own bosom is lord of himself, / And lord of all nature beside." And so he remained tutor to Villiers, occasionally published a piece of poetry, but did not pursue fame with any passion. The success of *The Roman Father* led to no fervent work on new productions. Although he wrote a sketch for a play entitled *Fatal Constancy, or Love in Tears,* the work never became a fully realized drama; it appeared in Whitehead's 1754 collection, *Poems on*

Several Occasions, simply as a dramatic monologue.

Whitehead's next complete work was *Creusa, Queen of Athens,* based on the *Ion* of Euripides, the central action of which is a sudden, mutual recognition between mother and son just before they kill each other. The story featured so many fabulous events, like oracles and visitations from gods, that scholars of Whitehead's time could not imagine its success as drama. Once again, however, Whitehead strips the story to its bones. Observing strict adherence to the vaunted unities, he concocts a plot wherein the attendants at the Delphic temple are outright frauds, their oracles calculated instruments of policy. Creusa, supposedly childless, and Xuthus, her husband of fifteen years, visit Delphi to ask the gods who should succeed to the Athenian throne when she dies. The audience soon learns that a secret child of hers had been spirited out of Athens seventeen years before along with her secret husband, a man of low birth named Nicander. Nicander had been banished from Athens, and within days his garments had been found bloodied on the road. But the apparent murder was a sham, fooling even Creusa; Nicander took their newborn son, Ion, with him to Delphi, placed him on the doorstep of the temple, and for seventeen years sought a way to return the youth to Athens and his rightful throne. Ion, raised by the temple's unsuspecting attendants, was called Ilyssus; Nicander became Aletes, a local sage, teaching the boy moral virtue. Naturally, Garrick played Aletes. Thus all the elements have fallen into place for high drama when the king and queen come to call at Delphi. And because Creusa is also furnished with a scheming counselor, Phorbas, who hates Xuthus and oracles, tragedy is guaranteed. At Aletes' behest, a fraudulent oracle recommends Ilyssus as heir to the throne. To extend the plot, Aletes passes up numerous occasions to reveal true identities. In the end, after Phorbas has convinced her to help kill Ilyssus, and then Aletes has told her the secret, Creusa drinks the poison she had meant for Ilyssus.

Once again, our time would find little reason to admire Whitehead's play. Its bare plot reveals just enough complications to delay the recognition scene as long as possible. Modern audiences would probably find its action oddly contrived, especially for a play intended to be realistic. John Butt, who deems Whitehead and Murphy two of "the few good structural crafts-

men" among the day's dramatists, points out that even these two considered a play's structure subservient "not to story, theme, or character . . . but to the depiction of emotion, or better still, emotional conflict. . . ." Emotion was Garrick's strength, and the fate of those who wrote during his career was to write more or less for him. Fairness demands we evaluate these plays not as works of art but as vehicles for Garrick's delivery and elocution.

Whitehead himself considered *Creusa* a far better tragedy than *The Roman Father.* Garrick's biographer Thomas Davies did not agree, because the language was not vigorous nor the sentiments moving. But Davies thought Garrick had saved the play by his portrayal of Aletes, skillfully "delivering didactics" and proving himself "a perfect master of elocution." On the other hand, Murphy concurred with Whitehead, praising the improvements of *Creusa* over the original, especially its new sense of historical probability, and added his hope that it would be revived "whenever the public taste shall undergo a thorough reform."

Although *Creusa* was repeated nine times immediately after its debut in Garrick's theater in 1754, this tragedy never achieved the popular appeal of *The Roman Father.* It was revived briefly in 1757 and again in 1759, then disappeared from the stage. This mattered little to its pragmatic author; the financial success of his first two plays enabled Whitehead to discharge his father's entire debt, and he did not write another play for eight years. Whitehead elected instead, at the request of Lord Jersey, to accompany young Villiers on a European tour. In addition, the Lord Harcourt wanted his own son Viscount Nuneham (George Simon Harcourt) to complete his education in the same way, so Whitehead became governor to both young men.

For a little over two years, Whitehead and his charges traveled the Continent. They visited France, Germany, Austria, Italy, Switzerland, and Holland; as poets must, Whitehead reacted to such scenes, especially Rome, by writing odes and elegies, among them his "Ode to the Tiber" (1757). But Whitehead was not especially inspired since he wrote only some half-dozen poems during the entire journey. These did not sell well, but this fact no longer concerned him; while in Italy he learned he had received appointment to two patent places, the secretary and registrar of the Order of the Bath. Such honorary offices, conferring income without obligations, can only have gone to Whitehead through the efforts of his friends in high places. Whatever spur fame might have represented to him was rapidly losing its effect. When the tour ended, Whitehead returned to England a comfortable man. Furthermore, despite the fact that the tour signaled the end of the young lords' traditional education, Whitehead remained at the Jersey estate even without his pupils. His presence there, and his renowned congeniality, wit, and lively conversation, had proved to be indispensable to the happiness of the elderly Lord and Lady Jersey; he found himself always welcome at Lord Harcourt's home as well.

Two years later, in 1758, poet laureate Colley Cibber died, leaving that office vacant for the first time since 1730. During Cibber's reign the laureateship had been worse than vacant. Twice annually, for the new year and the king's birthday, Cibber had produced his obligatory odes, poetically weak and bloated with flattery; twice annually he earned the ridicule of all the wits in England. The office of poet laureate held little respect throughout the century, but by the end of Cibber's reign its degradation was complete. Upon his death none knew whether any decent poet would accept the post. It was first offered to Thomas Gray, whose *Elegy Written in a Country Churchyard* (1750) earned universal praise. But Gray declined the honor, despite the fact that in his case no odes would have been required. According to E. K. Broadus, Gray wrote in a letter to the poet William Mason, "I would rather be sergeant-trumpeter or pin-maker to the palace." The post thus vacant, Whitehead's friendships once again served him well; the earl of Harcourt, who was governor to the Prince of Wales, secured the offer, and Whitehead accepted readily, even with the requirement for obligatory odes restored.

As it turned out, Whitehead became the best poet laureate of the eighteenth century. He rejected Mason's idea of hiring hungry poets to compose the annual odes and took seriously the notion that a laureate might actually serve his nation. Indeed, Whitehead's official odes honored his nation rather than his king, exhorting all Britons instead of flattering their ruler. In 1758 he published *Verses to the People of England*, urging divided citizens to unite against their common enemy, the French. Such a patriotic use of the laureateship was unique in his century. Also unusual was his satiric address, *A Charge to the Poets* (1762), humorously advising poets to get along bet-

ter with one another and to ignore their critics. He wrote whimsically, as though a laureate could speak to poets the way a bishop instructs his clergymen. Thinking of his own experience, he cautioned poets against hoping to survive only by writing, because "Few fortunes have been raised by lofty rhyme," advising them instead, "Some soberer province for your business choose, / Be that your helmet, and your plume the Muse." Unfortunately this advice was not taken in the jocund spirit in which Whitehead offered it. Some poets thought he was lecturing from an office he had not earned, or that such advice came too easily from a chronic dependent. No reaction was more violent than that of Charles Churchill, an indefatigable satirist whose poem "Ghost" nearly became a force to immortalize Whitehead the way Pope's *Dunciad* had Cibber. Churchill was not as good, nor Whitehead as bad, as Pope and Cibber, and the heavy-handed attack has left no lasting impression. For Whitehead, however, it proved devastating.

Part of Churchill's rage arose from Whitehead's venture into comedy. In early 1762 Garrick's theater had produced Whitehead's newest play, *The School for Lovers*. This comedy, based on an unacted play by Fontenelle, saw thirteen performances in 1762 and was popular enough to be revived in London on numerous occasions even into the next century. For Whitehead, this play is almost daring. Though as usual he borrowed the story and again observed the unities, he departed radically from the century's invariable practice of ridiculing vice. Instead, he chose to mix mirth and sorrow, producing a comedy that was kindly called "mixed" or, less kindly, "sentimental." Indeed, he forthrightly declared in his prologue that his comedy "Would play politely with your hopes and fears, / And sometimes smiles provoke, and sometimes tears." But this passage is not part of the prologue that Garrick spoke; he wanted it revised. Garrick also changed the prologue's discussion of Whitehead's adherence to the unity of location, assuring the audience instead, "Change you shall have; so set your hearts at ease: / Write as *he* will, we'll act it as *you* please." As usual, Whitehead revised as Garrick suggested, a practice he followed too readily.

But pleasing Garrick and his audiences was not the same as pleasing the critics. As Alexander Chalmers notes, the comedy was "written on a plan so very different from all that is called comedy, that the critics were at a loss where to place it . . . ." Furthermore, whatever its plan, *The*

School for Lovers lacked anything like vigor. The lovers in the play include a guardian, Dorilant, and his young ward, Caelia, an attractive girl of seventeen. Caelia is also the target of another lover, Modely, a modern young man-about-town, with whom Caelia's mother conspires in an effort to secure Dorilant for herself. Modely has all along been betrothed to Dorilant's sister, but as a fashionable man Modely can consider this deceit an appropriate stratagem. Most of the play's action concerns the inability of Dorilant and Caelia to express their true fondness for one another and the confusion that results when, for a time, Dorilant thinks Caelia truly loves Modely. Dorilant withdraws, his honor forbidding him to interfere with her happiness, and Caelia's perception of his sudden coldness convinces her that he does not love her. Little else happens throughout the play; the scheming is not very complicated nor the loving very warm. In the end virtue is certainly rewarded, for Dorilant and Caelia find one another's arms, but vice is not sufficiently punished for comic purists of the age. His inconstancy notwithstanding, Modely displays enough sincerity at the end that Dorilant's injured sister will marry him after all, and Caelia's mother escapes punishment for her treachery.

Whitehead pokes fun at sentimentality and rises above ridicule by allowing Modely to redeem himself. But these are subtle innovations; his audience saw only an inoffensive piece of light comedy. Churchill despised its tameness and ridiculed Whitehead's banal writing and gentle personality. This unfortunate characterization endured; James Boswell later referred to Whitehead as "a man so still and so tame, as to be contented to pass many years as the domestick companion of a superannuated lord and lady." From this Boswell judged Whitehead unable to make interesting conversation, which is patently false. But Churchill's influence prevailed, perhaps even causing Garrick to refuse Whitehead's next play. According to August Bitter, this play was a new kind, a bourgeois tragedy; never published or performed, it is now lost. Because its plan was so different from the classical tragedies Whitehead had produced before, we can only speculate about its quality or its potential contribution to the drama.

The years between this episode and his next production were comfortable ones. Whitehead had remained a resident of the Jersey household ever since his return from the Continent in 1756; his former pupils, who never ceased to be very fond of him, had ceded their share of his company to the Lord and Lady Jersey, and except for two official odes each year, Whitehead's sole responsibility was to amuse his patron. This was the kind of ease he had sought all his life, and since he could have it honorably, he never asked for anything else. A poet of immense ambition would eagerly have capitalized upon such an opportunity; Whitehead remained content.

When Whitehead next had a play produced, his 1770 farce, *A Trip to Scotland,* he asked Garrick to stage it without identifying him as its author, and he published it anonymously the same year. Perhaps this had nothing to do with Churchill, who had died in 1764; perhaps the poet laureate did not want a mere farce to bear his name. Much more lively, humorous, and fantastic than *The School for Lovers, A Trip to Scotland* played on more than twenty occasions in 1770, and continued to enjoy popularity and success at Drury Lane for a number of years.

The farce, Whitehead's only fully original dramatic work, portrays young people evading both English law and their parents' wishes by fleeing to Scotland, where liberal marriage laws allow them to follow their own impulses. Whitehead's road to Scotland is jammed with coaches and bordered with inns, all conspiring to assist the elopers. Whitehead characteristically apologizes for neglecting to observe the unities; Cupid, dressed as a postilion, speaks a prologue explaining how he can transport scenes here and there by magic. The story shows Griskin, a wealthy citizen, falling victim to his housekeeper's schemes. The housekeeper, Fillagree, helps Griskin's daughter conspire with a smooth city apprentice to elope to Scotland, after which the father's opposition will surely vanish, and the couple will be restored to a full inheritance. Once they have left, Griskin, motivated mostly by fears of a sensible neighbor's censure, sets off in pursuit, accompanied by Fillagree, only to arrive too late at the inn where the youngsters have shared a marriage bed. Fillagree's schemes mature when Griskin cannot resist her charms, and he agrees to marry her. Griskin exults when the sensible neighbor's daughter, too, appears at the inn, along with an actor who has just broken off their intended marriage, having learned that her father's money was no longer available. The actor thinks he has done the right thing in breaking off, saying, "Whatever the effect the late run of sentimental comedies may have had upon their audiences, they have at least made the players men of honor."

The satire on sentimentality was again too subtle, and while audiences loved the farce they detected no moralizing in it. After *A Trip to Scotland* Whitehead produced no more drama. In 1774 he published his collected works, *Plays and Poems,* in two volumes. Aside from his official odes, two anonymous moral pieces completed his poetical work. Perhaps his most popular poem, *Variety. A Tale for Married People,* appeared in 1776, selling out five editions. *The Goat's Beard,* another moral work, was published in 1777 but had far less popular appeal. Whitehead spent his last years at ease among his friends, whom he never failed to entertain, and, when a mild illness confined him to his home in the spring of 1785, he received them there as well. Even Lord Harcourt paid him visits, one day finding him at work revising the next birthday ode. Whitehead died suddenly the very next day, 14 April 1785.

For our time Whitehead's legacy is meager indeed. None of his plays has been reprinted in this century, nor have even his best poems graced many anthologies. But William Whitehead could have been a major dramatist and poet. As his poetry clearly demonstrates, he wrote with considerable talent. But he was too cautious and revised the plays too readily; the finest touches in them are often too subtle. Had he written a great deal more, remained more independent of Garrick, and experimented with other forms and styles, his work would now be better known. But he would have needed a consuming drive and abundant energy. To a large extent his stature in the history of literature is a thing of his own creation, the logical result of a life conducted exactly as he desired. We should consider this before judging him too harshly.

Bibliography:

Carl J. Stratman and others, eds., *Restoration and Eighteenth Century Theatre Research: A Bibliographical Guide, 1900-1968* (Carbondale: Southern Illinois University Press, 1971).

Biographies:

William Mason, "Memoirs," in *Poems by William Whitehead, Esq., Late Poet Laureate, and Register and Secretary to the Most Honorable Order of the Bath. Volume III. To Which Are prefixed, Memoirs of His Life and Writings* (York: Printed by A. Ward, sold by J. Robson & W. Clarke, London, and J. Todd, York, 1788);

Alexander Chalmers, "The Life of Whitehead," in *The Works of the English Poets from Chaucer to Cowper,* 21 volumes, edited by Samuel Johnson, with additions by Chalmers (London: J. Johnson, 1810), XVII: 189-197.

References:

August Bitter, *William Whitehead—poeta laureatus; eine Studie zu den Literarischen Strömugen um die mitte des 18 Jahrhunderts* (Halle [Saale]: M. Niemeyer, 1933);

Edmund Kemper Broadus, "William Whitehead," in his *The Laureateship: A Study of the Office of the Poet Laureate in England* (London: Oxford at the Clarendon Press, 1921), pp. 135-146;

John Butt, *The Mid-Eighteenth Century* (Oxford: Oxford University Press, 1979);

Alexander Chalmers, "Poems of William Whitehead," in *The Works of the English Poets from Chaucer to Cowper,* 21 volumes, edited by Samuel Johnson, with additions by Chalmers (London: J. Johnson, 1810), XVII: 199-278;

Thomas Davies, *Memoirs of the Life of David Garrick, Esq.* (London: Longman, Hurst, Rees & Orme, 1808);

Austin Dobson, "Laureate Whitehead," in his *Old Kensington Palace and Other Papers* (London: Oxford University Press, 1910), pp. 140-172;

Arthur Murphy, *The Life of David Garrick, Esq.* (London: J. Wright, 1801);

George Henry Nettleton, *English Drama of the Restoration and Eighteenth Century (1642-1780)* (New York: Macmillan, 1921).

Appendix I:

THE LICENSING ACT OF 1737

The single most important document for the history of the theater in the first half of the eighteenth century is the Licensing Act. It effectively ended the careers of playwrights like John Gay and Henry Fielding, restricted the subject matter of a generation of playwrights, and ended the vigorous competition among theaters when it went into effect at the end of the 1737 season.

An Act to explain and amend so much of an Act made in the Twelfth Year of the Reign of Queen Anne Intituled An Act for reducing the Laws relating to Rogues Vagabonds Sturdy Beggars and Vagrants into one Act of Parliament and for the more effectual punishing such Rogues Vagabonds Sturdy Beggars and Vagrants and Sending them whither they ought to be sent as relates to Common Players of Interludes. Anno 10.° Georg ÿ 2.ᵈⁱ

Le Roy le Veult.

Soit baillé aux Seigneurs
Aceste Bille les Seigneurs sont Assentus.

Whereas by an act of Parliament made in the Twelfth Year of the Reign of her Late Majesty Queen Anne Intituled an act for reducing the Laws relating to Rogues Vagabonds Sturdy Beggars and Vagrants into one act of Parliament and for the more effectual punishing such Rogues Vagabonds Sturdy Beggars and Vagrants and Sending them whither they ought to be sent It was Enacted that all persons pretending themselves to be Patent Gatherers or Collectors for Prisons Gaols or hospitals and wandring abroad for that purpose all ffencers Bear Wards Common Players of Interludes and other persons therein named and Expressed shall be deemed Rogues and Vagabonds

And Whereas some Doubts have arisen concerning so much of the said act as relates to Common Players of Interludes

Now for Explaining and Amending the same

Be it Declared and *Enacted* by the Kings Most Excellent Majesty by and with the Advice and Consent of the Lords Spiritual and Temporal and Commons in this present Parliament assembled and by the authority of the same that from and after the twenty fourth day of June One Thousand seven hundred and thirty seven every person who shall for hire Gain or Reward act represent or perform or cause to be acted represented or performed any Interlude Tragedy Comedy opera Play ffarce or other Entertainment of the Stage or any part or parts therein in case such person shall not have any Legal Settlement in the place where the same shall be acted represented or performed without authority by vertue of Letters Patent from His Majesty His Heirs Successors or Predecessors or without Licence from the Lord Chamberlain of His Majestys Household for the time being shall be deemed to be a Rogue and a Vagabond within the intent and meaning of the said recited act and shall be Liable and Subject to all such penalties and punishments and by such methods of Conviction as are inflicted on or appointed by the said act for the punishment of Rogues and Vagabonds who shall be found wandring Begging and Misordering themselves within the intent and meaning of the said recited act

And Be it further *Enacted* by the authority aforesaid that if any person having or not having a Legal Settlement as aforesaid shall without such authority or License as aforesaid act represent or perform or cause to be acted represented or performed for hire Gain or reward any Interlude Tragedy Comedy opera Play ffarce or other Entertainment of the Stage or any part or parts therein every such person shall for every such offence forfeit the sum of fifty pounds and in case the said sum of fifty pounds shall be paid Levied or recovered such offender shall not for the same offence suffer any of the Pains or penalties inflicted by the said recited act

And Be it further *Enacted* by the authority aforesaid that from and after the said twenty fourth day of June one thousand seven hundred and thirty seven no person shall for hire Gain or reward act perform represent or cause to be acted performed or represented any new Interlude Tragedy Comedy Opera Play ffarce or other Entertainment of the Stage or any part or parts therein or any new act scene or other part added to any old Interlude Tragedy Comedy Opera Play ffarce or other Entertainment of the / Stage or any new Prologue or Epilogue unless a true Copy thereof be sent to the Lord Chamberlain of the Kings Household for the time being fourteen days at least before the acting representing or performing thereof together with an account of the Playhouse or other place where the same shall be and the time when the same is intended to be first acted represented or performed signed by the Master or Manager or one of the Masters or Managers of such Playhouse or Place or Company of actors therein

And Be it *Enacted* by the authority aforesaid that from and after the said twenty fourth day of June one thousand seven hundred and thirty seven it shall and may be Lawful to and for the said Lord Chamberlain for the time being from time to time and when and as often as he shall think fit to prohibit the acting performing or representing any Interlude Tragedy Comedy opera Play ffarce or Other Entertainment of the Stage or any act scene or part thereof or any Prologue or Epilogue and in case any person or persons shall for hire Gain or reward act perform or represent or cause to be acted performed or represented any new Interlude Tragedy Comedy Opera Play ffarce or other Entertainment of the Stage or any act scene or part thereof or any new Prologue or Epilogue before a Copy thereof shall be sent as aforesaid with such account as aforesaid or shall for hire Gain or reward act perform or represent or cause to be acted performed or represented any Interlude Tragedy Comedy opera Play ffarce or other Entertainment of the Stage or any act scene or part thereof or any Prologue or Epilogue contrary to such Prohibition as aforesaid every person so offending shall for every such Offence forfeit the sum of fifty pounds and every Grant License and authority in case there be any such by or under which the said Master or Masters or Manager or Managers set up formed or continued such Playhouse or such Company of actors shall cease determine and become absolutely void to all intents and purposes whatsoever

Provided always that no person or persons shall be authorized by virtue of any Letters Patent from His Majesty His Heirs successors or Predecessors orby the Licence of the Lord Chamberlain of His Majestys Household for the time being to act represent or perform for hire gain or reward any Interlude Tragedy Comedy Opera Play ffarce or other Entertainment of the Stage or any part or parts therein in any part of Great Britain Except in the City of Westminster and within the Liberties thereof and in such places where His Majesty His Heirs or successors shall in their Royal Persons reside and during such residence only any thing in this act contained to the contrary in any wise notwithstanding

And Be it further *Enacted* by the authority aforesaid that all the pecuniary penalties inflicted by this act for offences committed within that part of Great Britain called England Wales and the Town of Berwick upon Tweed shall be recovered by Bill Plaint or Information in any of His Majestys Courts of Record at Westminster in which no Essoign Protection or Wager of Law shall be allowed and for offences committed in that part of Great Britain called Scotland by action or summary Complaint before the Court of Session or Justiciary there or for offences committed in any part of Great Britain in a summary way before two Justices of the Peace for any County Stewartry Riding Division or Liberty where any such offence shall be committed by the Oath or Oaths of one or more credible Witness or Witnesses or by the confession of the offender the same to be levied by distress and sale of the offenders Goods and Chattels rendring the Overplus to such offender if any there be above the penalty and charge of Distress and for want of Sufficient Distress the offender shall be committed to any House of Correction in any such County Stewartry Riding or Liberty for any time not exceeding Six months there to be Kept to hard Labour or to the common Gaol of any such County Stewartry Riding or Liberty for any time not exceeding Six months there to remain without Bail or Mainprize and if any person or persons shall think him her or themselves aggrieved by the Order or Orders of such Justices of the Peace it shall and may be lawful for such person or persons tc appeal therefrom to the next General Quarter Sessions to be held for the said County Stewartry Riding or Liberty whose Order therein shall be final and conclusive and the said penalties for any offence against this act shall belong one moiety thereof to the Informer or person suing or prosecuting for the same the other moiety to the Poor of the Parish where such offence shall be committed

And Be it further *Enacted* by the authority aforesaid that if any Interlude Tragedy Comedy opera Play ffarce or other Entertainment of the Stage or any act scene or part thereof shall be acted represented or performed in any House or place where Wine ale Beer or other Liquors shall be sold or Retailed the same shall be deemed to be acted represented and performed for Gain Hire and Reward

And Be it further *Enacted* by the authority aforesaid that no person shall be Liable to be prosecuted for any offence against this act unless such Prosecution shall be commenced within the space of Six Calendar Months after the offence committed and if any action or suit shall be commenced or brought against any Justice of the Peace or any other person for doing or causing to be done any thing in pursuance of this act such action or suit shall be commenced within Six Calendar months next after the fact done and the Defendant or Defendants in such action or suit shall and may plead the General Issue and give the special matter in Evidence and if upon such action or suit a Verdict shall be given for the Defendant or Defendants or the plaintiff or plaintiffs or Prosecutor shall become Nonsuit or shall not prosecute his or their said action or suit then the Defendant or Defendants shall have Treble Costs and shall have the like remedy for the same as any Defendant or Defendants have in other cases by Law.

Appendix II:
PLAYS, PLAYWRIGHTS, AND PLAYGOERS

Throughout the Restoration and eighteenth century dramatists used prologues and epilogues to make direct contact with their audiences. They tried to charm, cajole, or coerce playgoers into applauding their plays, and, in their unending search for novel ways to entertain, they composed prologues and epilogues to be spoken by children, women in breeches, favorite characters like Shakespeare's Malvolio, and even comic actors seated on donkeys. Often, however, these short theater pieces were also important critical statements, and they have left us with permanent records of playwrights' opinions and purposes.

I. PROLOGUE CONVENTIONS

In this prologue, William Penkethman, one of the foremost comic actors of the century, appealed directly to the most admiring segment of his audience in behalf of Susanna Centlivre's The Basset-Table *(1706). Such appeals were conventional in prologues—but not ones so exclusively to the footmen and others in the topmost seats. "Clap your grimy Hands," their beloved "Pinky" commanded.*
[*From* The Basset-Table. A Comedy. As it is Acted at the Theatre-Royal in Drury-Lane, by Her Majesty's Servants *(London: Printed for William Turner & sold by J. Nutt, 1706)]*

PROLOGUE
Spoke by Mr. Penkethman.

In all the Faces that to Plays Resort,
Whether of Country, City, Mob or Court;
I've always found that none such hopes Inspire,
As you–dear Brethren of the Upper Tire.
Poets in Prologues, may both Preach and Rail,
Yet all their Wisdom, nothing will avail,
Who writes not up to you, 'tis ten to one will fail.
Your thundring plaudit 'tis that deals out Fame,
You make Plays run, tho' of themselves but Lame:
How often have we known your Noise Commanding,
Impose on your Inferior Masters Understanding;
Therefore, Dear Brethren, (since I am one of you)
Whether adorn'd in Grey, Green, Brown or Blue,
This day stand all by me, as I will fall by you,
And now to let—
The poor Pit see how Pinky's Voice Commands,
Silence–Now rattle all your Sticks, and clap your grimy Hands.
I greet your Love–and let the vainest Author show,
Half this Command on clearer Hands below,
Nay, more to prove your Interest, let this Play live by you.
So may you share good Claret with your Masters,
Still free in your Amours from their Disasters;
Free from poor House-keeping, where Peck is under Locks.
Free from Cold Kitchings, and no Christmas Box:
So may no long Debates i' th' House of Commons,
Make you in the Lobby Starve, when hungar Summons;
But may your plentious Vails come flowing in,
Give you a lucky hit, and make you Gentlemen;
And thus preferr'd, ne'er fear the World's Reproaches,
But shake your Elbows with my Lord, and keep your Coaches.

For Henry Fielding's The Old Debauchees *(1732) a leading actor plays the part of one complaining of the tedium he feels when he must recite yet another prologue. His complaint summarizes many of the stock statements to be found in prologues.*
[From The Old Debauchees. A Comedy. As it is acted at the Theatre-Royal in Drury-Lane *(London: Printed for J. W. & sold by J. Roberts, 1732)]*

PROLOGUE
Spoken by Mr. *William Mills.*
I Wish, with all my Heart, the Stage and Town
Would both agree to cry all Prologues down,
That we, no more oblig'd to say or sing,
Might drop this useless necessary Thing:
No more with awkward Strut, before the Curtain,
Chaunt out some Rhimes—there's neither good nor hurt in;

What is this Stuff the Poets make us deal in,
But some old worn-out Jokes of their Retailing:
From Sages of our own, or former Times,
Transvers'd from Prose, perhaps transpros'd from Rhimes.

How long the Tragick Muse her Station kept,
How Guilt was humbl'd, and how Tyrants wept,
Forgetting still how often Hearers slept.

Perhaps, for Change, you, now and then, by Fits,
Are told that Criticks are the Bane of Wits;
How they turn Vampyres, being dead and damn'd,
And with the Blood of living Bards are cramm'd:
That Poets thus tormented die, and then
The Devil gets in them, and they suck agen.

Thus modern Bards, like Bays, their Prologues frame
For this, and that, and every Play the same,
Which you, most justly, neither praise nor blame.

As something must be spoke, no matter what,
No Friends are now by Prologues lost or got,
By such Harangues we raise nor Spleen, nor Pity—
Thus ends this idle, but important Ditty.

By the time David Garrick wrote a prologue for Fielding's The Fathers *(1778) the tradition of having popular characters speak was well established. In this effective prologue, most of Fielding's best-known novel characters speak in favor of the play.*
[From The Complete Works of Henry Fielding, Esq., *volume 12 (New York: Croscup & Sterling, 1903)]*

PROLOGUE
WRITTEN BY MR. GARRICK, SPOKEN BY MR. KING

WHEN from the world departs a son of fame,
His deeds or works embalm his precious name;
Yet not content, the Public call for art
To rescue from the tomb his mortal part;
Demand the painter's and the sculptor's hand,
To spread his mimic form throughout the land:
A form, perhaps, which living, was neglected,
And when it could not feel respect, respected.
This night no bust or picture claims your praise,
Our claim's superior, we his spirit raise:
From time's dark storehouse, bring a long-lost play,
And drag it from oblivion into day.

But who the Author? Need I name the wit,
Whom nature prompted as his genius writ?
Truth smiled on Fancy for each well-wrought story,
Where characters live, act, and stand before ye:
Suppose these characters, various as they are,
The knave, the fool, the worthy, wise, and fair,
For and against the Author pleading at your bar.
First pleads Tom Jones—grateful his heart and warm—
Brave, generous Britons, shield this play from harm;
My best friend wrote it; should it not succeed,
Though with my Sophy blest—my heart will bleed—
Then from his face he wipes the manly tear;
Courage, my master, Partridge cries, don't fear:
Should Envy's serpent hiss, or malice frown,
Though I'm a coward, zounds! I'll knock 'em down:
Next, sweet Sophia comes—she cannot speak—
Her wishes for the play o'erspread her cheek;
In every look her sentiments you read:
And more than eloquence her blushes plead.
Now Blifil bows—with smiles his false heart gilding,
He was my foe—I beg you'll damn this FIELDING;
Right! Thwackum roars—no mercy, sirs, I pray—
Scourge the dead Author, through his orphan play.
What words! cries Parson Adams, fie, fie, disown 'em,
Good Lord!—*de mortuis nil nisi bonum*:
If such are Christian teachers, who'll revere 'em—
And thus they preach, the Devil alone shall hear 'em.
Now Slipslop enters—though this scrivening vagrant,
Salted my virtue, which was ever flagrant,
Yet, like black 'Thello, I'd bear scorns and whips,
Slip into poverty to the very hips,

T' exalt this play—may it increase in favour;
And be its fame immortalized for ever!
'Squire Western, reeling, with October mellow,
Tall, yo!—Boys!—Yoax—Critics! hunt the fellow!
Damn 'em, those wits are varmint not worth breeding,
What good e'er came of writing and of reading?
Next comes, brimful of spite and politics,
His sister Western—and thus deeply speaks:
Wits are armed powers, like France attack the foe;
Negotiate till they sleep—then strike the blow!
Allworthy last, pleads to your noblest passions—
Ye generous leaders of the taste and fashions;
Departed genius left his orphan play
To your kind care—what the dead wills, obey:
O then, respect the FATHER'S fond bequest,
And make his widow smile, his spirit rest.

II. CRITICAL STATEMENTS

The great actor Thomas Betterton's performance of this prologue prepared the audience for Nicholas Rowe's Ambitious Stepmother *(1700) by championing compassion, an emotion the play was written to evoke. Implicit as well in the prologue are somewhat uncomplimentary comparisons between Rowe's play and the popular fare usually provided the audience.*
[From The Dramatick Works of Nicholas Rowe, Esq., *volume 1 (London: Printed & sold by T. Jauncy, 1720)]*

PROLOGUE
Spoken by Mr. Betterton.
If dying Lovers yet deserve a Tear,
If a sad Story of a Maid's Despair,
Yet move Compassion in the pitying Fair;
This Day the Poet does his Art employ,
The soft Accesses of your Souls to try.
Nor let the Stoick boast his Mind unmov'd;
The Brute Philosopher, who ne'er has prov'd
The Joy of Loving or of being Lov'd;
Who scorns his Human Nature to confess,
And striving to be more than Man, is less.
Nor let the Men the weeping Fair accuse,
Those kind Protectors of the Tragick Muse,
Whose Tears did moving *Otway's* Labours crown,
And made the poor *Monimia's* Grief their own:
Those Tears, their Art, not Weakness has confest,
Their Grief approv'd the Niceness of their Taste,
And they wept most, because they judg'd the best.
O could this Age's Writers hope to find
An Audience to Compassion thus inclin'd,
The Stage would need no Farce, nor Song, nor Dance,
Nor Capering Monsieur brought from active *France*.
Clinch and his Organ-Pipe, his Dogs and Bear,
To native *Barnet* might again repair,
Or breathe with Captain *Otter Bankside* Air:
Majestick Tragedy should once agen
In Purple Pomp adorn the swelling Scene.
Her Search should ransack all the Antients Store,
The Fortunes of their Loves and Arms explore,
Such as might grieve you, but shou'd please you more.
What *Shakespear* durst not, this bold Age shou'd do,
And famous *Greek* and *Latin* Beauties shew.
Shakespear, whose Genius to it self a Law,
Could Men in every Height of Nature draw,
And copy'd all but Women that he saw.
Those antient Heroines your Concern shou'd move,
Their Grief and Anger much, but most their Love;
For in the Account of every Age we find
The best and fairest of that Sex were kind,
To Pity always and to Love inclin'd.

Assert, ye Fair-ones, who in Judgment sit,
Your antient Empire over Love and Wit;
Reform our Sense, and teach the Men t' obey;
They'll leave their Tumbling if you lead the way.
Be but what those before to *Otway* were;
O were you but as kind, we know you are as fair.

This epilogue to Susanna Centlivre's Love's Contrivance (1703) *makes a common complaint: that audiences prefer familiar stage effects and predictable plots.*
[From Love's Contrivance, or, Le Medecin malgré Lui. A Comedy. As it is Acted at the Theatre Royal in Drury-Lane *(London: Printed for Bernard Lintott, 1703)]*

EPILOGUE

What, if to end this Fortune-telling Play,
I tell you all your Fortunes here to Day;
And, faith, to judge by here and there a Face,
Fortune has Fav'rites scatter'd in this place:
The Beaus, whose Garb of late such Lustre darts,
To draw fair Ladies Eyes, and break poor Tradesmens Hearts,
Their Fortune is what still attends the Great,
Still borrowing, still dunn'd, and still in Debt.
Pit-masks this Season are grown mighty bare,
They scarce got Pattings to ply round May-Fair.
But when the Term, and Winter comes agen,
Bawds, Brims, and Lawyers flourish bravely then.
Vintners and Taylors thro' such Knavish Lives,
With honest Citts, and virtuous City Wives;
I fear (tho' wishing it might be uncivil)
Like Pawn-Brokers, they'll all go to the Devil:
The City Prentices, those upstart Beaus,
In short spruce Puffs, and *Vigo* Colour Clothes,
Who with a Brace of Trulls stole here to Day,
And muster'd up a Crown to see this Play;
Lewdness and Gaming will run them aground,
And Masters Cash fall short a hundred Pound.
Our upper Friends, whose Height Respect denotes,
Since Liv'ries too are not unlike lac'd Coats,
By coming will such Criticks grow at last,
Nothing but Standard-Wit will please their Taste,
Till learning here how well the Town's harangu'd,
They'll make ingenious Speeches when they're hang'd.
Our Fidlers will, be scraping as before,
Spend ev'ry Groat they get upon a Whore,
Lead merry Lives, damn'd shabby, and damn'd poor:
But where at last they'll go, is hard to tell,
For really they're too impudent for Hell.
The Ladies, by their melting Looks, I see,
Will die for Love, perhaps for Love of me;
My Pity flows apace to save their Life,
I cou'd be kind, but must not wrong my Wife.
But lastly, for the Fortune of this Play,
Humour's a Hazard, yet thus much I'll say,
The Author purely for your Mirth design'd it,
And whether good or bad, 'tis—*As you find it.*

This prologue to Colley Cibber's The Careless Husband *(1704) argues the virtue of satiric plays.*
[From Plays Written by Mr. Cibber. In Two Volumes, *volume 1 (London: Printed for Jacob Tonson, Bernard Lintot, William Mears & William Chetwood, 1721)]*

THE PROLOGUE

Of all the various Vices of the Age,
And Shoals of Fools expos'd upon the Stage,
How few are lasht that call for Satyr's Rage!
What can you think, to see our Plays so full
Of Madmen, Coxcombs, and the driveling Fool;
Of Citts, of Sharpers, Rakes and roaring Bullies,
Of Cheats, of Cuckolds, Aldermen and Cullies?
Wou'd not one swear, 'twere taken for a Rule,
That Satyr's Rod in the Dramatick School
Was only meant for the Incorrigible Fool?
As if too Vice and Folly were confin'd
To the vile Scum alone of Human Kind;
Creatures a Muse should Scorn, such abject Trash
Deserve not Satyr's, but the Hangman's Lash.
Wretches so far shut out from Sense of Shame
Newgate or *Bedlam* only shou'd reclaim;
For Satyr ne'er was meant to make wild Monsters tame.
No, Sirs—
    We rather think the Persons fit for Plays,
Are they whose Birth and Education Says
They've ev'ry Help that shou'd improve Mankind,
Yet still live Slaves to a vile tainted Mind;
Such as in Wit are often seen t' abound
And yet have some weak Part, where Folly's found:
For Follies sprout like Weeds, highest in Fruitful Ground.
And 'tis observ'd, the Garden of the Mind
To no infestive Weed's so much inclin'd,
As the rank Pride that some from Affectation find.
A Folly too well known to make its Court
With most Success among the better Sort.
Such are the Persons we to day provide,
And Nature's Fools for once are laid aside.
This is the Ground on which our Play we build;
But in the Structure must to Judgment yield:
And where the Poet fails in Art, or Care,
We beg your wonted Mercy to the Player.

The characteristically beautiful rhythm of Alexander Pope's poetry provides an appropriate introduction to Joseph Addison's Roman play, Cato *(1713). Pope's statement of the pleasures and purposes of tragedy summarizes the century's opinion well.*
[From Cato. A Tragedy. As it is Acted at the Theatre-Royal in Drury-Lane, By Her Majesty's Servants *(London: Sold by M. Gunne & R. Gunne, 1713)]*

PROLOGUE
By Mr. *POPE.*
Spoken by Mr. *Wilks*

To wake the Soul by tender Strokes of Art,
To raise the Genius, and to mend the Heart,
To make Mankind in conscious Virtue bold,
Live ov'r each Scene, and Be what they behold:
For this the Tragic-Muse first trod the Stage,
Commanding Tears to stream thro' every Age;
Tyrants no more their Savage Nature kept,
And Foes to Virtue wonder'd how they wept.
Our Author shuns by vulgar Springs to move
The Hero's Glory, or the Virgin's Love;
In pitying Love we but our Weakness show,
And wild Ambition well deserves its Woe.
Here Tears shall flow from a more gen'rous Cause,
Such Tears as Patriots shed for dying Laws:
He bids your Breasts with Ancient Ardor rise,
And calls forth *Roman* Drops from *British* Eyes.
Virtue confess'd in human Shape he draws,
What *Plato* Thought, and God-like *Cato* Was:
No common Object to your Sight displays,
But what with Pleasure Heav'n it self surveys;
A brave Man struggling in the Storms of Fate,
And greatly falling with a falling State!
While *Cato* gives his little Senate Laws,
What Bosom heats not in his Country's Cause?
Who sees him act, but envies ev'ry Deed?
Who hears him groan, and does not wish to bleed?
Ev'n when proud *Ceasar* 'midst triumphal Cares,
The Spoils of Nations, and the Pomp of Wars.
Ignobly Vain, and impotently Great,
Show'd *Rome* her *Cato*'s Figure drawn in State;
As her dead Father's rev'rend Image past,
The Pomp was darken'd, and the Day o'ercast,
The Triumph ceas'd—Tears gush'd from ev'ry Eye;
The World's great Victor past unheeded by;
Her last good Man dejected *Rome* ador'd,
And honour'd *Ceasar*'s less than *Cato*'s Sword.

Britans attend: Be worth like this approv'd,
And show you have the Virtue to be mov'd.
With honest Scorn the first fam'd *Cato* view'd
Rome learning Arts from *Greece,* whom she Subdu'd;
Our Scene precariously subsists too long

On *French* translation, and *Italian* Song.
Dare to have Sense your selves; Assert the Stage;
Be justly warm'd with your own Native Rage.
Such Plays alone shou'd please a *British* Ear,
As *Cato*'s self had not disdain'd to hear.

In this 1714 epilogue to Jane Shore, *Nicholas Rowe inadvertently provided the name for an entire group of eighteenth-century plays about women: the "she-tragedy."*
[From The Tragedy of Jane Shore. Written in Imitation of Shakespear's Style. *By N. Rowe, Esq. (London: Printed for Bernard Lintott, 1714)]*

EPILOGUE; spoken by Mrs. *Oldfield.*

Ye modest Matrons all, ye virtuous Wives,
Who lead with horrid Husbands, decent Lives,
You who for all you are in such a taking,
To see your Spouses Drinking, Gaming, Raking,
Yet make a Conscience still of Cuckold-making,
What can we say your Pardon to obtain?
This Matter here was prov'd against poor *Jane*:
She never once deny'd it, but in short,
Whimper'd,—and Cry'd,—*sweet Sir,—I'm sorry for't.*
'Twas well she met a kind, good natur'd Soul,
We are not all so easy to controul:
I fancy one might find in this good Town
Some wou'd ha' told the Gentleman his own;
Have answer'd smart,—*To what do you pretend,*
Blockhead!—As if I must n't see a Friend:
Tell me of Hackney-Coaches—Jaunts to th' City—
Where shou'd I buy my China—Faith, I'll fit ye—
Our Wife was of a milder, meeker Spirit:
You!—Lords and Masters!—was not that some Merit?
Don't you allow it to be virtuous Bearing,
When we submit thus to your Domineering.
Well, peace be with her, she did Wrong most surely;
But so do many more who look demurely:
Nor shou'd our mourning Madam weep alone,
There are more Ways of Wickedness than one.
If the reforming Stage shou'd fall to shaming
Ill-nature, Pride, Hypocrisy, and Gaming;
The Poets frequently might move Compassion,
And with *She* Tragedies o'er-run the Nation.
Then judge the fair Offender, with good Nature;
And let your Fellow-feeling curb your Satyr.
What if our Neighbours have some little Failing,
Must we needs fall to damning and to railing;
For Her Excuse too, be it understood,
That if the Woman was not quite so good,
Her Lover was a King, she Flesh and Blood.
And since she has dearly paid the sinful Score,
Be kind at last, and pity poor *Jane Shore.*

In his prologue to The Coffee-House Politician *(1730), Henry Fielding explained the serious purposes of comedy and set his own satiric comedy in the classical tradition.* [*From* The Complete Works of Henry Fielding, Esq., *volume 9 (New York: Crosscup & Sterling, 1903)*]

PROLOGUE
SPOKEN BY MR. MILWARD

IN ancient Greece, the infant Muse's school,
Where vice first felt the pen of ridicule,
With honest freedom and impartial blows
The Muse attacked each vice as it arose:
No grandeur could the mighty villain screen
From the just satire of the comic scene:
No titles could the daring poet cool,
Nor save the great right honourable fool.
They spared not even the aggressor's name,
And public villainy felt public shame.

   Long hath this generous method been disused,
For vice hath grown too great to be abused;
By power defended from the piercing dart,
It reigns, and triumphs in the lordly heart;
While beaus, and cits, and squires, our scenes afford,
Justice preserves the rogues who wield her sword;
All satire against her tribunal's quash'd,
Nor lash the bards, for fear of being lash'd.

   But the heroic Muse, who sings to-night,
Through these neglected tracts attempts her flight.
Vice, clothed with power, she combats with her pen,
And, fearless, dares the lion in his den.

   Then only reverence to power is due,
When public welfare is its only view:
But when the champions, whom the public arm
For their own good with power, attempt their harm,
He sure must meet the general applause,
Who 'gainst those traitors fights the public cause.

   And while these scenes the conscious knave displease,
Who feels within the criminal he sees,
The uncorrupt and good must smile, to find
No mark for satire in his generous mind.

This prologue to Fielding's The Modern Husband *(1732) briefly reviews the author's successful dramatic career (sure to incline them favorably toward the author and the play) and announces Fielding's return to serious comedy. The age's opinion of the highest purposes of theater are summarized in the concluding lines.*

[From The Modern Husband. A Comedy. As it is Acted at the Theatre-Royal in Drury-Lane. By His Majesty's Servants *(London: Printed for J. Watts, 1732)]*

PROLOGUE.
Spoken by Mr. *WILKS*.

IN early Youth, our *Author* first begun,
To Combat with the *Follies* of the *Town*;
Her want of Art, his unskill'd *Muse* bewail'd,
And where his *Fancy* pleas'd his *Judgment* fail'd.
Hence, your nice Tastes he strove to entertain,
With unshap'd Monsters of a wanton Brain!
  He taught *Tom Thumb* strange Victories to boast,
Slew Heaps of Giants, and then–kill'd a Ghost!
  To Rules, or Reason, scorn'd the dull Pretence,
And fought your *Champion*, 'gainst the Cause of Sense!
  At length, repenting Frolick Flights of Youth,
Once more he flies to Nature, and to Truth:
In Virtue's just Defence, aspires to Fame,
And courts Applause without the Applauder's Shame!
  Impartial let your *Praise*, or *Censure* flow,
For, as he brings *no Friend*, he hopes to find *no Foe*.
His *Muse* in Schools too unpolite was bred,
To apprehend each Critick–that can Read:
For, sure, no Man's Capacity's less ample
Because he's been at *Oxford* or the *Temple*!
He shews but little Judgment, or discerning,
Who thinks Taste banish'd from the Seats of Learning.
  Nor is less false, or scandalous th' Aspersion,
That such will ever damn their own Diversion.
But, *Poets damn'd*, like *Thieves* convicted, act,
Rail at their *Jury*, and deny the Fact!
To Night (yet Strangers to the Scene) you'll view,
A Pair of Monsters most entirely new!
Two Characters scarce ever found in Life,
A *willing Cuckold*–sells his *willing Wife*!
But, from whatever Clime the Creatures come,
Condemn 'em not–because not found at home:
If then, true Nature in his Scenes you trace,
Not Scenes, that *Comedy* to *Farce* debase;
If Modern Vice detestable be shewn,
And vicious, as it is, he draws the Town;
Tho' no loud Laugh applaud the serious Page,
Restore the sinking Honour of the Stage!
The Stage which was not for low Farce design'd,
But to *divert, instruct,* and *mend* Mankind.

The prologue to John Gay's Achilles *(1733) may have been written by the playwright's friend the great poet Alexander Pope. In any event, it is above-average verse. Amusing, vivid comparisons of the poet to rope dancers, combined with serious critical observations, capture the literary force of the "Scriblerians," the literary club to which Pope and Gay belonged.*

[From John Gay: Dramatic Works, *edited by John Fuller, volume 2 (Oxford: Clarendon Press, 1983)]*

PROLOGUE.
Written by Mr. *GAY.*
Spoken by Mr. *QUIN.*

I WONDER not our Author doubts Success,
One in his Circumstance can do no less.
The Dancer on the Rope that tries at all,
In each unpractis'd Caper risques a Fall:
I own I dread his ticklish Situation,
Critics detest Poetic Innovation.
Had *Ic'rus* been content with solid Ground,
The giddy vent'rous Youth had ne'er been drown'd.
The *Pegasus* of old had Fire and Force,
But your true Modern is a Carrier's Horse,
Drawn by the foremost Bell, afraid to stray,
Bard following Bard jogs on the beaten Way.
Why is this Man so obstinate an Elf ?
Will he, alone, not imitate himself ?
   His Scene now shews the Heroes of old *Greece*;
But how? 'tis monstrous! In a Comic Piece.
To Buskins, Plumes and Helmets what Pretence,
If mighty Chiefs must speak but common Sense?
Shall no bold Diction, no Poetic Rage,
Fome at our Mouths and thunder on the Stage?
No—'tis *Achilles*, as he came from *Chiron*,
Just taught to sing as well as wield cold Iron;
And whatsoever Criticks may suppose,
Our Author holds, that what He spoke was Prose.

III. THE AUDIENCE

Susanna Centlivre often shaped her prologues and epilogues around extended meta-phors. In this epilogue to her Basset-Table *(1706) she compared the performance and the audience to ships that might meet in a fatal engagement for her play. In describing the audience, she moved through the familiar kinds of playgoers. Her own play, "well mann'd, and not ill Woman'd neither," she described as awaiting their signal—friendship or attack.*
[From The Basset-Table. A Comedy. As it is Acted at the Theatre-Royal in Drury-Lane, by Her Majesty's Servants *(London: Printed for William Turner & sold by J. Nutt, 1706)]*

EPILOGUE.
Spoke by Mr. Esthcourt.

THis goodly Fabrick to a gazing Tarr,
Seems Fore and Aft, a Three Deckt-man of War.
Abaft, the Hold's the Pit, from thence look up,
Aloft! that Swabber's Nest, that's the Main-Top.
Side-boxes mann'd with Beau, and modish Rake,
Are like the Fore-castle, and Quarter-Deck.
Those dark disguised, advent'rous, black-nos'd few,
May pass for Gunners, or a Fire-Ship's Crew.
Some come like Privateers a Prize to seize,
And catch the *French* within the Narrow Seas.
The Orange-Ladies, Virgins of Renown,
Are Powder-Monkies running up and down.
We've here our Calms, our Storms, and prosp'rous Gales,
And shift our Scenes as Seamen shift their Sails.
The Ship's well mann'd, and not ill Woman'd neither,
So Ballast'd and Stow'd, my Lads, she'll bear the Weather.
But greater Dangers ventring Players alarm,
This Night's Engagement's worse than any Storm.
The Poet's Captain, but half dead with fright,
She leaves her Officers to maintain the Fight;
Yon'd middle Teer with Eighteen Pounders mauls us,
That Upper-Deck with Great and Small-Shot gauls us.
But from this Lower-Teer most Harm befals,
There's no opposing their prevailing Balls.
As either Foe or Friend their Chain-shot flies,
We sink or swim, we Conquer, Fall or Rise.
To fit and rig our Ships much Pains we take;
Grant we may now a Saving-Voyage make.
Here we're Embark'd, and as you Smile or Frown,
You are our Stars, by You we Live or Drown.

The Spectator *sometimes reviewed plays and often commented on the state of British drama. In this essay for no. 361 (24 April 1712) Joseph Addison explains a distinctively eighteenth-century feature of the theater: the cat-call. These tiny "musical" instruments were available in a variety of pitches, and the audience came armed with them to express their disapproval.*
[*From* The Spectator, *edited by Donald F. Bond, volume 3 (Oxford: Clarendon Press, 1965)]*

*Tartaream intendit vocem, quâ protinus omne
Contremuit domus . . .*

Virg.

I HAVE lately received the following Letter from a Country Gentleman.

Mr. SPECTATOR,
'THE Night before I left *London* I went to see a Play called *The Humorous Lieutenant.* Upon the rising of the Curtain I was very much surprised with the great Consort of Cat-calls which was exhibited that Evening, and began to think with my self that I had made a Mistake, and gone to a Musick Meeting instead of the Play-house. It appeared indeed a little odd to me to see so many Persons of Quality of both Sexes assembled together at a kind of Catter-wawling, for I cannot look upon that Performance to have been any thing better, whatever the Musicians themselves might think of it. As I had no Acquaintance in the House to ask Questions of, and was forced to go out of Town early the next Morning, I could not learn the Secret of this Matter. What I wou'd therefore desire of you is, to give some Account of this strange Instrument which I found the Company called a Cat-call; and particularly to let me know whether it be a Piece of Musick lately come from *Italy.* For my own part, to be free with you, I wou'd rather hear an *English* Fiddle; tho' I durst not shew my Dislike whilst I was in the Play-house, it being my Chance to sit the very next Man to one of the Performers.
I am, SIR,
*Your most Affectionate Friend,
and Servant,*
John Shallow, *Esq;'*

In compliance with Squire *Shallow*'s Request, I design this Paper as a Dissertation upon the Cat-call. In order to make my self a Master of the Subject, I purchased one the beginning of last Week, tho' not without great difficulty, being inform'd at two or three Toyshops that the Players had lately bought them all up. I have since consulted many learned Antiquaries in relation to its Original, and find them very much divided among themselves upon that particular. A Fellow of the Royal Society, who is my good Friend, and a great Proficient in the Mathematical part of Musick, concludes from the Simplicity of its Make, and the Uniformity of its Sound, that the Cat-call is older than any of the Inventions of *Jubal.* He observes very well, that Musical Instruments took their first rise from the Notes of Birds, and other melodious Animals; and what, says he, was more natural than for the first Ages of Mankind to imitate the Voice of a Cat that lived under the same Roof with them? He added, that the Cat had contributed more to Harmony than any other Animal, as we are not only beholden to her for this Wind Instrument, but for our String Musick in general.

Another Virtuoso of my Acquaintance will not allow the Cat-call to be older than *Thespis,* and is apt to think it appear'd in the World soon after the Ancient Comedy; for which reason it has still a place in our Dramatick Entertainments: Nor must I here omit what a very curious Gentleman, who is lately return'd from his Travels, has more than once assured me, namely, that there was lately dug up at *Rome* the Statue of a *Momus,* who holds an Instrument in his Right Hand, very much resembling our Modern Cat-call.

There are others who ascribe this Invention to *Orpheus,* and look upon the Cat-call to be one of those Instruments which that famous Musician made use of to draw the Beasts about him. It is certain, that the roasting of a Cat does not call together a greater Audience of that Species, than this Instrument, if dexterously play'd upon in proper Time and Place.

But notwithstanding these various and learned Conjectures, I cannot forbear thinking that the Cat-call is originally a Piece of *English* Musick. Its Resemblance to the Voice of some of our *British* Songsters, as well as the use of it, which is peculiar to our Nation, confirms me in this Opinion. It has at least received great Improvements among us, whether we consider the Instrument it self, or those several Quavers and Graces which are thrown into the playing of it. Every one might be sensible of this, who heard that remarkable overgrown Cat-call which was placed in the Center of the Pit, and presided over all the rest at that celebrated Performance lately exhibited in *Drury-Lane.*

Having said thus much concerning the Original of the Cat-call, we are in the next place to consider the Use of it. The Cat-call exerts it self to most advantage in the *British* Theatre: It very much improves the sound of Nonsense, and often goes along with the Voice of the Actor who pronounces it, as the Violin or Harpsicord accompanies the *Italian* Recitativo.

It has often supplied the place of the ancient *Chorus,* in the Works of Mr. *** In short, a bad Poet has as great an Antipathy to a Cat-call as many People have to a real Cat.

Mr. *Collier,* in his Ingenious Essay upon Musick, has the following Passage:

I believe 'tis possible to invent an Instrument *that shall have a quite contrary Effect to those Martial ones now in use. An* Instrument *that shall sink the Spirits, and shake the Nerves, and curdle the Blood, and inspire Despair, and Cowardise, and Consternation, at a surprizing rate. 'Tis probable the Roaring of Lions, the Warbling of Cats and Scritch-Owls, together with a mixture of the Howling of Dogs, judiciously imitated and compounded, might go a great way in this Invention. Whether such Anti-musick as this might not be of Ser-*

vice in a Camp, I shall leave to the Military Men to consider.

What this learned Gentleman supposes in Speculation, I have known actually verified in Practice. The Cat-call has struck a Damp into Generals, and frighted Heroes off the Stage. At the first sound of it I have seen a Crowned Head tremble, and a Princess fall into Fits. The *Humorous Lieutenant* himself could not stand it, nay, I am told that even *Almanzor* looked like a Mouse, and trembled at the Voice of this terrifying Instrument.

As it is of a Dramatick Nature, and peculiarly appropriated to the Stage, I can by no means approve the Thought of that angry Lover; who after an unsuccessful Pursuit of some Years took leave of his Mistress in a Serenade of Cat-calls.

I must conclude this Paper with the Account I have lately received of an ingenious Artist who has long studied this Instrument, and is very well versed in all the Rules of the Drama. He teaches to play on it by Book, and to express by it the whole Art of Criticism. He has his Base and his Treble Cat-call; the former for Tragedy, the latter for Comedy; only in Tragy-Comedies they may both play together in Consort. He has a particular Squeak to denote the Violation of each of the Unities, and has different Sounds to shew whether he aims at the Poet or the Player. In short, he teaches the Smut-note, the Fustian-note, the Stupid-note, and has composed a kind of Air that may serve as an Act-tune to an incorrigible Play, and which takes in the whole Compass of the Cat-call.

In a somewhat earlier piece, the prologue to Thomas Jevon's Devil of a Wife *(1686) gave the dramatist's opinion of the cat-call.*
[From The Devil of a Wife, or A Comical Transformation. As it is Acted by Their Majesties Servants at the Queens Theatre in Dorset Garden *(London: Printed by J. Heptinstall for J. Eaglesfield, 1686)]*

PROLOGUE,
Spoke by Mr. *Jevon.*

How long is't since you saw I pray,
That strange old fashion'd thing call'd a New Play.
Or how long indeed d'ye think 'twill be,
Before you tast that long'd for Novelty?
T'ou may set your hearts at rest for this Age,
Union and Catcalls have quite spoyl'd the Stage.
Time was the Poets cou'd cock, look bigg, and cry,
Damn these fancy Players, let's all agree,
And starve the Rogues, the Times friends turned be,
And I am turn'd Poet, there's Farce d'ye see.
But now to my *Geatheration* friends,   ⎤ Points to some particular People in the Pit
What quick return, or what concise amends   ⎦
Have you my ever honour'd ever dear,
Renowned, whistling Patrons made appear
To him that is your servant everywhere?
My Name's Mr. *Jevon,* I'm known far and near.
But no more words in so much Company,
Satisfaction I must have and quickly;
Or Gad, Il'e leave off writing directly.
Let me have a pledge of it now y'are here,
Or in your Balls you may forget I fear.
Be favourable to this same piece at hand,
And d'ye hear friends don't; shall I, shall I stand.
If I in Pocket find you dive for Catcall,
Il'e let down Curtain, Il'e tell ye that all.
Catcalls well tun'd might do well in Opera's,
They'd serve for Hoboys to fill up a *Chorus.*
Or in a *French* Love Song, observe you now,
A *Cadmeus Pur Qua, Pur Qua, meme Vou.*   [sings.]
Begar Monsieur it be *De* pretty *Whyne,*
Ki La D'ance De Mineway, on it be very fine.
Dances you have and various here to Night,
But they are *English* all, all *English* quite.
Throughout, *English* Songs, Farce *English* too,
That's *French* Sence,
All Non-sense without any more adoe.
Knickshaws like this serve for a *Lenten* Dish,
If not for Flesh, pray let it serve for Fish.
And since Pennance at this Time's in fashion.
Come three Days for Mortification.

I Made a Visit the other Morning to a Friend, at his Chambers in the *Temple*, and found him engaged with an ingenious Mechanick, who is the Maker of a certain little Musical Instrument, which, of late, is carried in the Pockets of all your Men of Wit and Pleasure about the Town. He gave me to understand, at the same Time, that this Expence was owing to an Accident which happened to him the Night before: For it being his Chance to pass thro' *Temple-Bar* at a Time when the Multitude were giving the Discipline of the Kennel to one of those Beasts of Prey commonly stil'd Informers, an Artist, known among the Vulgar by the Name of a Pick-pocket, found Means of diving his nimble Fingers to the Bottom of one of his Pockets, and convey'd from thence the following Moveables, the Goods of *Frank Townly*, of the *Middle Temple*, Esq; *viz.*

A Letter-Case, finely wrought and gilt, in which were no Bank Notes.

It contain'd, four Subscription Receipts for Books not yet printed, and which, perhaps, never will be printed:

A Blank Ticket in the Bridge Lottery, worth now about as much as before it was drawn:

Two Milliners, and three Taylors Bills, unpay'd:

A Billet-doux from a celebrated Toast of *Covent-Garden*, commonly call'd, the *Kitten*.

Besides the Letter-Case, he lost a silk Garter with a Buckle, snatch'd from one of the Legs of the said *Kitten*:–By the same Token, she garters above Knee:

A Box of Pills, with Directions for taking two over Night, and three in the Morning–to drink Something warm after they begin to operate, and to be careful not to catch Cold:

Two Catcals–the one a Base, the other a Treble.

It was the last of these Losses which my Friend was about to supply.–There were a great many of them lying upon the Table, some in *Pinchbeck*, some in Silver. The Artist had employ'd the utmost of his Skill in adorning them:–On one Side, you might see the comick Mask and tragick Buskin curiously engraved; on the other, a felonious Critick snatching a Laurel from a poor Poet's Brow:–The Workmanship exceeded the Materials.

While I was viewing all the Wonders of this little Tube, now become the Terror of the Poet and the Player, a thousand Reflections rose in my Mind. I thought on the cruel Palpitations it would cause in the Hearts of many unfortunate Adventurers for Fame, as yet unborn.

Being in the Midst of my Meditations, my Friend, the Templar, taking one of them in his Hand, and looking round it, repeated the following Verses:

> *Pretty Tube of mighty Power,*
> *Charmer of an idle Hour, &c.*

When he had finished his Soliloquy, I applied it to my Lips, and giving it Breath, it sent forth the most harsh unmusical Sound had ever wounded my Ears. My Friend smiled to see me frighten'd at my own Noises, and, taking it from me, was so good as to give me a Solo upon it himself, which he perform'd with a Skill and Mastery not to be acquired without great Practice. This Flourish of his was answer'd with the like Harmony by a Couple of Cats, who, at the Call of *Venus*, were met upon the Top of a House facing the Window of the Room wherein we sat.

After the most curious Examination I could make of it, I do not think that I ever saw any Thing like it, either in the *Museum* at *Oxford*, or in the Collection of Sir *H—— S——*, who, to his own immortal Honour, as well as to the great Emolument of his Country, has spared neither Pains or Expence in accumulating Rarities of equal Use and Importance to Mankind.

It differs very much from the *Tibia* of the Antients, as may be seen by several antique *Basso Relievos* in *Italy*, where that Instrument appears perfect, to this Day: Nor has it any Resemblance to the *Calamus*, or Shepherds Pipe of *Arcadia*, one of which I myself saw, upon my Travels, in the Cabinet of that learned Antiquary *Signor Cosone Bagatello* of *Padua*. Besides, had it been in Use among the Antients, it could not have escaped the Observation of the *German Literati*, and we should has seen two or three Folios written upon it by *Thrumbobergius*, or some other, the Sages of a Nation who have supplied the Commonwealth of Learning with such Loads of Lumber.–From all which I conclude, it must be of modern Invention.

What confirms me more in this Opinion is, that my Friend, the *Templar*, who is a Man of Reading, assures me, that *Pancirollus* has not mention'd it in his Treatise *de rebus inventis & deperditis*, I take it, therefore, that the Invention of it is later than the Use of the Compass, and more modern than either Gunpowder or Printing. Be that as it will, *Frank Townly* is of Opinion, that it is an Invention which may be of infinite Utility to our Country; and he told me, that this little Tube, placed in judicious Hands, would contribute more towards reforming the Stage, and introducing a good Taste in Dramatick Poetry, than all the Criticisms of *Rapin* and *Rymer:*–That a good Critick ought no more to be without his Cat-cal, than a Soldier without his Sword;–and desired me to write something upon it in one of my Papers.

The Artist who made it was very attentive all this While to our Discourse. He began to put on a Look of Importance, and told us, that perhaps it might come at first from Out-landish Countries; but it was quite a different Thing, from what it was when he first knew it, for that we can improve tho' we cannot invent; and that, since the late Act to license Plays and the Players of Interludes, *&c.* he himself had sat up Night and Day to try Experiments upon it; and that, by long Study, he had so enlarged the Compass of it, that it now took in three Notes more of the Gamot than ever it had done before.–As Operas were going down, he did not doubt but *Myn Heer Handel* himself would compose for it; that he hoped to get a Patent to be the sole Maker and Vender of it, for he had a Sister who was a Servant to the kept Mistress of a Man in Power, by whose Interest he hoped to procure it; and he was pretty sure he should soon get an Estate by it, provided the Laureat would leave off writing Odes, and would write again for the Stage.

There being a New Play in the Bills for that Night, *Townly* proposed to me to accompany him, and some others of our Acquaintance, to it.–They are a Set of Gentlemen who never fail to assist the first Night at every Thing new which is exhibited upon the Stage. The Artist, hearing us talk of going to the Play, desired me to carry one of his Instruments with me, and if, upon Trial, I did not like it, I should pay nothing for it.–Tho' I refused his generous Offer, I resolved to see

the Play. We went at the proper Hour, and placed ourselves in the Center of the Pit, amidst a Sort of People who come to that Place, not to shew their Cloaths, but to improve their Understandings; it is they who set a Value upon Works of this Nature, and from their Opinions the Publick pronounces a Thing to be either good or bad.

I believe the Author might design it for a Comedy, but it was of that Kind which the *French* call *Assoupissant*.–However, all due Attention was paid to it for the Space of two Acts.–*Townly*, at length, finding nothing in it to keep up his Attention, began to tune his Flagellet, which, like the Sound of the last Trumpet, roused the whole Audience from that quiet Slumber into which they had been laid by the Scenes upon the Stage.–He lead this Orchaestra all that Night, and I will do him the Justice to say, he never founded in the wrong Place. He was accompanied by such a Number of others, in various Keys, that it became a *Concerto grosso:* I will not say it was quite so sweet as the Musick of the Spheres, and yet I suspected that a Party from the *Italian* Opera in the *Haymarket* had thrust themselves into this Consort, in Hopes to revive their sinking Opera again by damning all Plays; for methought I could plainly distinguish some of *Farinelli*'s Notes, as well as certain Graces of *Gaferelli*, not to mention a Squeek in Imitation of *Strada*.

But commend me to a certain Critick in the Gallery, who damn'd the Play with a Yawn.–This Person kept his Fire to the last; whether he had been really asleep, and waked from some Dream, or only pretended it, he fetch'd a Yawn, or rather a Groan, making Night hideous, and so scared the whole Audience, that it put an End to the Consort below.

But I should have taken Notice before, that some Sparks behind the Scenes, Enemies to *English* Liberty (I wish I knew them) were for compelling us to like the Play by Force of Arms, and threaten'd to bring the Guards upon the Stage to bully us out of Applause. Upon which, I did not think it inconsistent either with my Age or Gravity to hiss for the Good of my Country, and I became almost reconciled to the squawling of the Cat-cal, when I heard its Musick exerted in the Cause of Liberty: Nor was I less pleased with the Spirit of an Audience who would not give up their Opinions to Criticks who were to dispute the Rules of the Dramma with Bayonets fix'd to the End of their Muskets; for had I been in the Place of that Logician who disputed with a

Roman Emperor, I should not, like him, have given up my Opinion, when I was in the Right, because his Imperial Majesty commanded fifty Legions.

Tho' I shall oppose every Thing which looks like Tyranny, either in Criticism or in Politicks, yet I will own I could with that some Method, less tumultuous, could be found out of giving our Judgments upon the Works of the ingenious: I would not have the Seat of Wit, and the Empire of the Muses, disturb'd with Noise and Confusion.–That a Spirit of Opposition should rise up against the licensing of Dramatick Poetry, is no Wonder:–A true *Briton* would no more have our Wit excised, than our Wine;–it will render both spiritless and adulterate. But my Objection to the present Practice is, that where the Resentment is only intended against the Licenser, the Poet may suffer;–like the Frogs in the Fable when pelted by Boys, he may say to the Audience, that, tho' it be Sport to them, it is Death to him.

As I have consider'd this Affair with all the Attention which a Matter of such Importance deserves, I will, *ex officio*, and, by Vertue of that Authority which I vested in myself when I assumed the Character of a Publick Writer, offer some Regulations for a more orderly Judgment to be stamp'd upon the Works of our Dramatick Writers.

I therefore humbly propose, that a certain Number of Criticks, from our several Inns of Courts, shall meet in one of the *Temple* Halls, to consider and draw up proper Rules and Directions for the Use of the Cat-cal the first Night of every New Play.

That they shall have Power to send for Persons, Papers, and Records.

That they shall appoint some Person, duly qualified, to compose for the said Instrument.

That the Composition shall consist of three select Pieces of Musick, different in their Kind.

That the first shall be play'd at the End of the Prologue, and at no other Time, and shall be understood to be for the Entertainment of the Licensers.

That the second shall never be play'd but when an Actor commits some flagrant Fault.

That neither of these shall be taken to reflect in the least upon the Poet.

That the third shall be play'd at the End, and only when the Play merits to be damn'd.

That no Person shall be allow'd to assist in this Consort who has not read *Horace, Rapin,* and *Rymer.*

That no Gentleman of the University be allow'd to found a Cat-cal till he has been two Years in Town.

That *Frank Townly,* or some other Critick of equal Lungs, be appointed to lead the Orchaestra, and likewise to beat Time.

That Ladies be allow'd to use Cat-cals if they please.

That a *Tibicina,* or small Flagellet, of a more curious Workmanship, and of a sweeter Tone, be made on Purpose for their use.

That it shall be tied, with a Silver or Gold Ribbon, to the Sticks of their Fans.

That the Ladies which constitute the *Shakespeare's* Club be the principal Persons to appoint such of their own Sex as may use these Flagellets.

That no Lady be judg'd qualified to play in this Consort that has not read the *Spectators.*

That the Criticks in the Pit, out of Respect, shall be silent, when the Ladies begin to sound.

That all Expressions which are offensive to Modesty or good Manners, be left to the Censure of the Ladies.

That no Lady, under the Degree of a Toast, be appointed to lead their Orchaestra.

That the Critick in the Gallery have full Liberty to yawn when the Play is over, provided he does not like it: Any Thing contain'd in these Orders to the contrary notwithstanding.

N. B. *We beg Pardon of our Correspondent,* RECTA RATIO, *for having so long deferr'd the Publication of his Letter,–the Truth of it is, it was, by Chance, mislaid; but being now recover'd, shall be inserted in our next.*

Richard Steele satirically proposed a panel to select plays sure to please the fickle London audience in the third number (9 January 1720) of his periodical The Theatre. *The composition of this panel and his descriptions provide a comic but accurate look at the audience.*
[*From* Richard Steele's The Theatre, 1720, *edited by John Loftis (Oxford: Clarendon Press, 1962)]*

—His dantem Jura Catonem.

UPON my producing my second Paper at *Sophronia's* Tea-Table, the Ladies had the Goodness to express a Delight, in that they now began to be convinc'd of my being determin'd to go on with the Work. And in order to it, I had leave to lay before them a new Scheme for the Government of the publick Diversions. I told them, that it had long been a great Cause of Distress to the Actors, to know who were properly the Town, and who not; they having been often under the nicest Perplexities, from the very different Opinions of People of Quality and Condition.

There is, they tell me, scarce any Play put up in their Bills, or that they propose to revive, but has as much the Dislike of some, as the Approbation of others, even before it comes on, and that the same happens in most of their private Affairs. Whenever they fall into publick Company, it is very difficult to preserve that Deference due to the Opinion of their Superiors, and at the same time to pursue their own Measures, and what their Experience convinces them will most probably contribute to the publick Entertainment. Therefore, that the Players may be better justified in what they shall do hereafter, I have propos'd:

1. That a select Number of Persons shall be chosen, as real Representatives of a *British* Audience.

2. These Persons so elected, shall be stil'd *Auditors of the* Drama.

3. No Persons to have free Voices in these Elections, but such as shall produce Certificates from the respective Door-keepers of the Theatre, that they never refus'd to pay for their Places.

4. The Players shall chuse two of their own Society, *viz.* one Male, and one Female, to take care of their Interest, and for the better Information of these *Auditors,* in Matters immediately relating to their Customs and private Oeconomy.

5. One Dramatick Poet, to serve for the Liberties of *Parnassus*; to be chosen only by Tragick or Comick Writers.

6. Three of the Fair Sex shall represent the Front-Boxes.

7. Two Gentlemen of Wit and Pleasure for the Side-Boxes.

8. Three Substantial Citizens for the Pit.

9. One Lawyer's Clerk, and one *Valet de Chambre* for the first Gallery. One Journeyman-Baker for the Upper-Gallery.

10. And one Footman that can write and read shall be *Mercury* to the Board.

11. This Body so chosen, shall have full Power, in the Right of the Audiences of *Great Britain,* to approve, condemn, or rectify whatever shall be exhibited on the *English* Theatre.

And the Players guiding themselves by their Laws, shall not be accountable to, or controuled by any other Opinions or Suggestions whatever, nor ever appeal from the Judgments of these duly elected *Auditors.* Provided notwithstanding, that any daily Spectators shall have reserv'd to them, and their Successors for ever, their full Right of Applauding, or Disliking the Performance of any particular Actor, whenever his Care, or Negligence, shall appear to deserve either the one, or the other: But in Matters merely relating to the Conduct of the Theatre, the said elected *Auditors,* from time to time, shall be deemed able, and to have Right, to give Laws for ever.

This Scheme was approv'd by the whole Assembly at the Lady *Sophronia's,* and they desir'd me accordingly to appoint the Day of the Election of *Auditors.* I am therefore to acquaint the Town, that due Notice shall be given of some Play to be acted, after which the Audience will proceed to chuse Representatives for the *British* Theatre, by way of Ballot; which every Door-keeper is hereby impower'd to receive, at the same time he takes their Money.

This Matter has already taken Air, and there are Candidates who already appear, and have desir'd my Interest and Recommendation. The first who address'd me with a modest Discovery of that Ambition, is *Lucinda,* who hopes to be chosen for the Boxes.

Lucinda is the Daughter of Mr. *Sealand,* an eminent Merchant; she is a young Woman of a most unaffected, easy, and engaging Behaviour, which has brought her much into Fashion among all the great Families she visits: She is conversant in Books, and no Stranger to Houshold Affairs, of a discerning and quick Spirit in Conversation, and has a mortal Aversion to all Coxcombs; she has the Modesty, in the Account of herself, to pretend only to a Judgment in the Dresses and Habits of the Theatre. But as I love to be fair in all Representations, I must give the Electors Notice (who may act accordingly) that she is a great Favourer of the Woollen Manufactures; and she intends on the Election-day to appear in a White Stuff Suit, lin'd with Cherry-colour'd Silk, in the second Row of the Front-Boxes: For, besides the Consideration of her Country's Good, she has skill enough to know that no Woman is the better dress'd for being in rich Clothes, and that 'tis the Fancy and Elegance of an Habit, and not the Cost, that makes it always becoming to the Wearer. She is in Hopes too, as I am privately inform'd, to introduce, even on the Stage, Dresses of our own Growth and Labour, which shall be as good, as cheap, and becoming, as any imported from Abroad. This Method, she imagines, will give the World a very advantagious Opportunity of judging of the Commodiousness, Beauty, and Ease of those Habits, by the Appearance they make upon the Players, in Parts proper to them. She concludes that the Theatre should be made serviceable to all Parts of Life, and all Trades and Professions, that it may the better deserve the Support of the Publick.

Mr. *Charles Myrtle* stands for the Side-Box. He is a Gentleman of a very plentiful Fortune; a Student, or rather an Inhabitant of the *Temple*; he has a fine Taste of Letters, and from thence bears some Reputation of a Scholar, which makes him much more valuable in that of a Gentleman. He has many agreeable Qualities, besides the Distinction of a good Understanding, and more good Nature. But he has little Imperfections, that frequently indispose his Temper; and when Jealousy takes hold of him, he becomes untractable, and unhappily positive in his Opinions and Resolutions; but I must not say too much on the less advantagious Side of his Character, because my Son *Harry Edgar* offers himself at the same time to the Town, and hopes for their Votes and Interest for the Side-Box.

We have a Candidate for the Pit, an eminent *East-India* Merchant, Mr. *Sealand,* Father of *Lucinda.* This Gentleman was formerly what is call'd a Man of Pleasure about the Town; and having, when young, lavish'd a small Estate, retir'd to *India,* where by Marriage, and falling into the Knowlege of Trade, he laid the Foundation of the great Fortune, of which he is now Master. I am in great Hopes he will carry his Election, for his Thoughts and Sentiments against the unworthy Representations of Citizens on the Stage, may highly contribute to the Abolition of such ridiculous Images for the future: His Knowledge and Experience, by living in mix'd Company, as well as in the busy World here, ballanc'd him against approving what is either too frivolous, or too abstracted for publick Entertainments. He is a true Pattern of that kind of third Gentry, which has arose in the World this last Century: I mean the great, and rich Families of Merchants, and eminent Traders, who in their Furniture, their Equipage, their Manner of Living, and especially their Oeconomy, are so far from being below the Gentry, that many of them are now the best Representatives of the ancient ones, and deserve the Imitation of the modern Nobility. If this Gentleman should carry his Election, (as from his having the whole City-Interest of *Jews,* as well as Gentiles, in the Pit, it is very likely he will) we shall have great Assistance from him, with relation both to the real and imaginary World. He is a Man that does Business with the Candour of a Gentleman, and performs his Engagements with the Exactness of a Citizen.

The Players are in much Hurry about the Election of their proper Representatives, there being but two female Candidates, who are both remarkable for their great Merit and Industry in their Profession. My Son tells me, he finds by their Discourse about the Playhouse, that every one, consulted apart, speaks of them in different Modes. I'll vote, says one, for a Lady that values her self only as she is eminent in the Theatre, that never when she is in her Part has her Hero in the Side-Box, instead of on the Stage, but is acting as well when another is speaking, as when she speaks herself; who expresses in her Countenance as much what she hears, as what she utters. This Description could relate to but two of all the House; but it is thought the Actors will chuse the less Handsome, out of their Complaisance to those Ladies who are Candidates for the Audience, because it is remarkable that People of Quality bear to see their Inferiors in Fortune, their Equals in Wit and Knowledge, with Patience enough, provided they do not also come up to them in their Manners and Beauty.

The first Gallery has offer'd to it a Representative who is an Underling of the Law, one who knows a great deal, as the Querks of it may perplex, but not a Word as the Reason of it may protect and serve Mankind. I hope he will not carry it, because such a Creature can be in no Place, where he does not consider rather how he can, as he is situated, disturb his Neighbour, than enjoy his own. And this kind of Creature will show himself as much during his Term in a Seat at a Play, as in the Possession of an Estate for ever and ever.

My Man *Humphrey,* who has liv'd with me for many Years, proposes himself for the first Gallery. He is a diligent, careful, sensible Man, and has had a Right in all that comes off my Person these forty Years; for so long has he been my *Valet de Chambre,* or Gentleman, as they call it. I cannot accuse him but of one ungentlemanly Thing, during our whole Time together; and that was, He brought a Taylor to see me, as I walk'd in *Lincoln's-Inn* Garden, and sold him the Coat I had then on my Back, while I was musing concerning the Course of humane Affairs in the upper Walk. This I cannot call an Injustice, for I had given him the Suit, and he put me in it, because it was warm, the Day after I gave it him being cold. However, I may call it an Unpoliteness, and an *Indecorum,* because his Master had it on while he was making the Bargain. After I have said all

this, I think I may put up a Man for the Gallery, whose greatest Offence he ever committed was only against Decency.

I had, when I propos'd this Scheme, a Journeyman-Baker in my Eye, as well that in case of Danger of Famine, from any outward Cause, the House might bake for themselves, as also that he is a robust Critick, and can by Way of Cudgel keep Silence about him in the Upper-Gallery, where the Wit and Humour of the Play will not always command Attention.

I have not yet heard of any other Candidates; but when I do, shall give timely Notice: In the mean time shall rest with great Content, in the Hopes I conceive from the Assistance of a well chosen Board. The Election of a Poet for the landed Interest of *Parnassus,* as well as the Choice of the Actors who are to accompany the *Auditors* of the *Drama,* are Matters that deserve to be treated of distinctly; but the Qualification of so much *per Annum,* in order to be deem'd a Man of Capacity for this Service, I cannot allow to be necessary, tho' I have very good Friends of another Mind, who will also take upon them to say, that for the Dignity and Safety of *Arcadia,* a Comick, or Tragick Poet, should have three hundred Pounds a-year; and an Epick Poet cannot be truly such, except he have six hundred a-year: From which worthy Gentlemen I must beg leave to differ; and I take the Liberty to say, that there is no such Accomplishment mention'd by *Aristotle, Horace,* or any other Critick, ancient or modern.

Richard Steele wrote this prologue for John Vanbrugh's The Mistake *(1706), and it is a delightful series of insults aimed at the audience's frivolous tastes: "With Audiences compos'd of Belles and Beaux, / The first Dramatick Rule is, have good Clothes."*
[From The Mistake. A Comedy. As it is Acted at the Theatre-Royal in the Hay-Market *(London: Printed for J. & R. Tonson, 1736)]*

PROLOGUE,
Written by Mr. STEELE.
Spoken by Mr. BOOTH.

OUR Author's Wit and Rallery to-night
Perhaps might please, but that your Stage delight
No more is in your Minds, but Ears and Sight.
With Audiences compos'd of Belles and Beaux,
The first Dramatick Rule is, have good Clothes.
To charm the gay Spectator's gentle Breast,
In Lace and Feather Tragedy's express'd,
And Heroes die unpity'd, if ill-dress'd.

The other Stile you full as well advance;
If 'tis a Comedy, you ask—Who dance?
For oh! what dire Convulsions have of late
Torn and distracted each Dramatick State,
On this great Question, which House first should sell
The New *French* Steps, imported by *Ruel*?
Desbarques can't rise so high, we must agree,
They've half a Foot in Height more Wit than we.
But tho' the Genius of our Learned Age
Thinks fit to Dance and Sing quite off the Stage.
True Action, Comick Mirth, and Tragick Rage;
Yet as your Taste now stands, our Author draws
Some hopes of your Indulgence and Applause.
For that great End this Edifice he made,
Where humble Swain at Lady's Feet is laid;
Where the pleas'd Nymph her conquer'd Lover spies,
Then to Glass Pillars turns her conscious Eyes,
And points a-new each Charm, for which he dies.

The Muse, before nor Terrible nor Great,
Enjoys by him this awful gilded Seat:
By him Theatrick Angels mount more high,
And Mimick Thunders shake a broader Sky.

Thus all must own, our Author has done more
For your Delight, than ever Bard before.
His Thoughts are still to raise your Pleasures fill'd;
To Write, Translate, to Blazon, or to Build.
Then take him in the Lump, nor nicely pry
Into small Faults, that 'scape a busy Eye;
But kindly, Sirs, consider, he to-day
Finds you the House, the Actors, and the Play
So, tho' we Stage-Mechanick Rules omit,
You must allow it in a Whole-Sale Wit.

IV. THE AUTHOR AND THE AUDIENCE

John Dryden's prologue for John Vanbrugh's revision of John Fletcher's The Pilgrim
*(1700) laments from personal experience how uncertain the reception of a play is and
how anxious playwrights are at its performance.*
[From The Prologues and Epilogues of John Dryden, *edited by William Bradford
Gardner (New York: Published for the University of Texas by Columbia University
Press, 1951)]*

PROLOGUE

How wretched is the Fate of those who write!
Brought muzled to the Stage, for fear they bite.
Where, like *Tom Dove,* they stand the Common Foe;
Lugg'd by the *Critique,* Baited by the *Beau.*
Yet worse, their Brother *Poets* Damn the Play,
And Roar the loudest, tho' they never Pay.
The Fops are proud of Scandal, for they cry,
At every lewd, low Character,–That's I.
He who writes Letters to himself, wou'd Swear
The World forgot him, if he was not there.
What shou'd a Poet do? 'Tis hard for One
To pleasure all the Fools that wou'd be shown:
And yet not Two in Ten will pass the Town,
Most Coxcombs are not of the Laughing kind;
More goes to make a Fop, than Fops can find.
    Quack *Maurus,* tho' he never took Degrees
In either of our Universities;
Yet to be shown by some kind Wit he looks,
Because he plaid the fool and writ Three Books.
But if he wou'd be worth a Poet's Pen,
He must be more a Fool, and write again:
For all the former Fustian stuff he wrote,
Was Dead-born Doggrel, or is quite forgot;
His Man of *Uz,* stript of his *Hebrew* Robe,
Is just the Proverb, and *As poor as* Job.
One wou'd have thought he cou'd no longer Jog;
But *Arthur* was a Level, *Job*'s a Bog.
There, tho' he crept, yet still he kept in sight;
But here, he founders in, and sinks down right.
Had he prepar'd us, and been dull by Rule,
Tobit had first been turn'd to Ridicule:
But our bold *Britton,* without Fear or Awe,
O're-leaps at once, the whole *Apocrypha*;
Invades the *Psalms* with Rhymes, and leaves no room
For any Vandal *Hopkins* yet to come.
    But what if, after all, this Godly Geer,
Is not so Senceless as it wou'd appear?
Our Mountebank has laid a deeper Train,
His Cant, like *Merry Andrew*'s Noble Vein,
Cat-Call's the Sects, to draw 'em in again.
At leisure Hours, in Epique Song he deals,

Writes to the rumbling of his Coaches Wheels,
Prescribes in hast, and seldom kills by Rule,
But rides Triumphant between Stool and Stool.
    Well, let him go; 'tis yet too early day,
To get himself a Place in Farce or Play.
We know not by what Name we should Arraign him,
For no one Category can contain him;
A Pedant, Canting Preacher, and a Quack,
Are Load enough to break one Asses Back:
At last, grown wanton, he presum'd to write,
Traduc'd Two Kings, their kindness to requite;
One made the Doctor, and one dubb'd the Knight.

The prologue to Joseph Trapp's play, Abra-mule: or, Love and Empire *(1708), is a typical plea to the audience whom he addresses as "Men of Sense." He prepares them for the fact that his play will not provide some of the most popular elements: music, a ghost, thunder and lightning, and farcical interludes. This dignified prologue was written to be spoken by one of the greatest actors of the time, Thomas Betterton. His prologues, and others like it, help us understand what the audiences expected and enjoyed.*
[From Abra-mule: or, Love and Empire. A Tragedy. As it is acted at the New Theatre in Little Lincolns-Inn Fields, by Her Majesty's Servants. The second edition, corrected *(London: Printed for John Stephens, 1708)]*

PROLOGUE
Spoken by Mr. Betterton.

WHAT various Thoughts a Poet's Breast divide,
When brought before an Audience, to be try'd!
Guilty of Scribling, with beseeching Hands,
Before your Bar the Malefactor stands.
Now hopes 'twill please, now doubts 'twill prove but dull;
Mourns a thin Pit, yet dreads it when 'tis full.
These are at best the anxious Writers Cares:
But he, who now your fatal Censure fears,
Has no great Man to Countenance his Muse,
And shield him from the Arts which Rival Factions use.
No necessary Friends to start Applause,
T o'erpower Ill-nature, and support his Cause.
Then 'tis all Tragedy which he prepares,
With no relieving Interval of Farce.
Nay, but one Song; his Numbers rarely chime,
Nor bless the Gall'ries with the Sweets of Rhime.
Few Actors are to fall, no Ghosts to rise;
No Fustian roars, nor mimick Lightning flies;
No Thunder from his Heroes, or the Skies.

With all these Disadvantages oppress'd,
He still has Hopes, and makes his bold Request
To Men of Sense; and here are none, I know,
But either are, or think at least they're so.
To you, with modest Awe, he dares to speak;
Will not assume too much, yet Scorns to Sneak:
He boasts not of his Genius, or his Rules;
Nor insolently calls his Judges, Fools.
Yet to Desert disclaims not all Pretence;
To be so Modest would be Impudence.
For surely his Presumptions must be great,
Who dares invite his Betters to no Treat.
He not expects you should gross Dulness flatter,
Yet leaves you room enough to shew good Nature.
Begs you would come, of all ill Passion eas'd;
Patient to hear, and willing to be pleas'd.
Cowards and Fools are barbarous, and think
All Wit and Valour is to damn and sink;
But Weakness in Distress still finds Defence
From Men of Courage, and from Men of Sense.

The Tatler *was the first English periodical to review plays consistently. These essays from* The Tatler's *first months are typical. [From* The Tatler, *edited by Donald F. Bond (London: Oxford University Press, 1987).]*

[From no. 1 for 12 April 1709]

Will's Coffee-house, April 8.

On *Thursday* last was acted, for the Benefit of Mr. *Betterton,* the Celebrated Comedy, call'd *Love for Love.* Those Excellent Players, Mrs. *Barry,* Mrs. *Bracegirdle,* and Mr. *Dogget,* tho' not at present concern'd in the House, acted on that Occasion. There has not been known so great a Concourse of Persons of Distinction as at that Time; the Stage it self was cover'd with Gentlemen and Ladies, and when the Curtain was drawn, it discovered even there a very splendid Audience. This unusual Encouragement which was given to a Play for the Advantage of so Great an Actor, gives an undeniable Instance, That the True Relish for Manly Entertainment and Rational Pleasures is not wholly lost. All the Parts were acted to Perfection; the Actors were careful of their Carriage, and no one was guilty of the Affectation to insert Witticisms of his own, but a due Respect was had to the Audience, for encouraging this accomplish'd Player. It is not now doubted but Plays will revive, and take their usual Place in the Opinion of Persons of Wit and Merit, notwithstanding their late Apostacy in Favour of Dress and Sound. This Place is very much alter'd since Mr. *Dryden* frequented it; where you us'd to see *Songs, Epigrams,* and *Satyrs,* in the Hands of every Man you met, you have now only a Pack of Cards; and instead of the Cavils about the Turn of the Expression, the Elegance of the Style, and the like, the Learned now dispute only about the Truth of the Game. But, however the Company is alter'd, all have shewn a great Respect for Mr. *Betterton*; and the very Gaming Part of this House have been so much touch'd with a Sence of the Uncertainty of Humane Affairs, (which alter with themselves every Moment) that in this Gentleman, they pitied *Mark Anthony* of *Rome, Hamlett* of *Denmark, Mithridates* of *Pontus, Theodosius* of *Greece,* and *Henry* the Eighth of *England.* It is well known, he has been in the Condition of each of those illustrious Personages for several Hours together, and behav'd himself in those high Stations, in all the Changes of the Scene, with suitable Dignity. For these Reasons, we intend to repeat this Favour[n] to him on a proper Occasion, lest he who can instruct us so well in personating Feigned Sorrows, should be lost to us by suffering under Real Ones. . . .

[From no. 9 for 30 April 1709]

Will's Coffee-house, April 28.

This Evening we were entertain'd with *The Old Batchelor,* a Comedy of deserved Reputation. In the Character which gives Name to the Play, there is excellently represented the Reluctance of a Batter'd Debauchee to come into the Trammels of Order and Decency: He neither languishes nor burns, but frets for Love. The Gentlemen of more Regular Behaviour are drawn with much Spirit and Wit, and the *Drama* introduc'd by the Dialogue of the first Scene with uncommon, yet natural Conversation. The Part of *Fondlewife* is a lively Image of the unseasonable Fondness of Age and Impotence. But instead of such agreeable Works as these, the Town has this half Age been tormented with Insects call'd *Easie Writers,* whose Abilities Mr. *Wycherly* one Day describ'd excellently well in one Word. *That,* said he, *among these Fellows is call'd* Easy Writing, *which any one may easily Write.*

[From no. 19 for 24 May 1709]

Will's Coffee-house, May 23.

On *Saturday* last was presented, *The Busie Body,* a Comedy, written (as I have heretofore remark'd) by a Woman. The Plot and Incidents of the Play are laid with that Subtilty of Spirit which is peculiar to Females of Wit, and is very seldom well perform'd by those of the other Sex, in whom Craft in Love is an Act of Invention, and not, as with Women, the Effect of Nature and Instinct.

To Morrow will be acted a Play call'd, *The Trip to the Jubilee.* This Performance is the greatest Instance that we can have of the irresistible Force of proper Action. The Dialogue in it self has something too low to bear a Criticism upon it: But Mr. *Wilks* enters into the Part with so much Skill, that the Gallantry, the Youth, and Gaiety of a young Man of a plentiful Fortune, is look'd upon with as much Indulgence on the Stage, as in real Life, without any of those Intermixtures of Wit and Humour, which usually prepossess us in Favour of such Characters in other Plays.

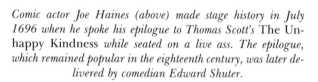

Comic actor Joe Haines (above) made stage history in July 1696 when he spoke his epilogue to Thomas Scott's The Unhappy Kindness *while seated on a live ass. The epilogue, which remained popular in the eighteenth century, was later delivered by comedian Edward Shuter.*

In 1732 Henry Fielding provided an epilogue for Charles Boden's The Modish Couple. *He describes the fearful playwright, perspiring in anxiety until he sweats away to
half his size. As a practicing playwright, Fielding surely could sympathize with the statement, "I think he has shewn his Spirit bolder,/in listing* Poet, *than in listing* Soldier."
[From The Female Husband and Other Writings, *edited by Claude E. Jones (Liverpool: Liverpool University Press, 1960)]*

EPILOGUE
Written by *HENRY FIELDING,* Esq;
Spoken by Mrs. *CIBBER*

I Hear some honest Citizens are humming,
Jogging their Wives–ay–now, my Dear! 'tis coming:
The Fans, I see, are marshall'd, Rank and File,
Some to hide Blushes, more to hide a Smile,
While spindle Beaux their meagre Sides are straining
To raise a Laugh, tho' they scarce know one's Meaning.
Faith! you're all bit. Let Tragedy still deal
Such whetting Acids at its palling Meal;
Where Virtue in such sad Extremes is drest,
That first they make her dreadful, then a Jest;
In painting Vice, so well they know to charm ye,
Our Poets make more Cuckolds, than our Army:
They raise such Spirits in a Female Brain,
That the poor Husband toils to lay in vain.
She, who before was well enough contented,
Now told what Flames the *Greeks* and *Romans* vented;
Her Fancy fir'd with *Hector* or with *Caesar,*
What can a *Haberdasher* do to please her?
But Ways, like these, our Comic *Captain* scorns;
He swears no Spouse to him shall owe his Horns.
Our *Captain....* Gad! I almost had forgot him,
To such sad Plight this sweating Night has brought him,
Nine Nights together shou'd he lessen so,
Our plump, round Bard will dwindle to a Beau;
His *Pegasus,* when next he mounts, will know it,
And wonder what's become of *half* the Poet.
I'faith! I think he has shewn his Spirit bolder,
In listing *Poet,* than in listing *Soldier*:
To mount the Stage, who'd not be more afraid,
Than to *mount* Guard at *Court* or *Masquerade*!
Which is more dangerous? (What say you Sparks?)
To march around *Parnassus,* or the *Parks*?
How happy were the Bard, how void of Fear,
Were he as sure to find no En'my here,
As he is sure to march in Safety there.
But here no Prowess serve's the brave Commander,
One *Critic Clerk* wou'd rout an *Alexander.*
Soldiers, give *Quarter* to a valiant Brother,
Courtiers are too well bred to Dam each other.
As the first Fault, ye *Criticks,* spare what's past,
And spare him, *Wits,* in hopes 'twill be his last.

This sustained attack on pantomime comes from a periodical, The Prompter, *written by William Popple and the successful dramatist Aaron Hill. This essay from no. 128 for 30 January 1736 does not overestimate the preference contemporary audiences had for the form.*

[From The Prompter: A theatrical paper (1734-1736), *edited by William W. Appleton and Kalman A. Burnim (New York: Blom, 1966)]*

The saying attributed to the late Mr. Booth—viz. That empty boxes were the greatest disgrace the stage could suffer—has, by being made the managers' regular apology, done more disservice to the stage than any one thing I know. The constant rotation of old plays having by experience been found to bring on that disgrace, our managers, instead of providing in time a fresh and constant supply of new ones, have called in the aid of pantomime, and to prevent one evil have incurred a greater one—*viz.* a corruption of the public taste—which must end in the downfall of the stage.

It is alleged in favour of pantomime that the Town requires it, as experience has shown this season, in the case of the gentleman at the head of the new theatre in Covent Garden, who, excepting the days Mrs. Porter performed, and the first of Mr. Delane's appearance there, has acted to thin houses or else been obliged to dismiss, till Friday last, when he was agreeably pleased to find his expectations confirmed by an overflowing house, occasioned by pantomime only.

I will allow the whole of the argument, provided in return it be allowed me that the introduction of pantomime was the occasion of plays becoming less entertaining than they were before, and not filling the houses as usual, and that an audience, now, will not go home satisfied unless the good impressions made and generous sentiments imbibed during the play are quite worn out and erased by the succeeding pantomime. . . . Without entering into the particular detail of all the expenses attending the theatre, it is certain that the extraordinary number of pantomime-persons, together with their salaries, dresses, scenes, and machinery (all absolutely needless without pantomime) increase the expense of each night 25 or 30 £. at a medium. Now where the difference as to profit, whether a manager acts to a 90 £. house at 30 £. expense, or to an 120 £. house at 60 £. lies, I own I can't see. I believe a 120 £. house to an entertainment, thro' the whole of its run is a fair computation, and a 90 £. house for mere plays as just.

But the people will not come to see plays only. Not while they are encouraged to expect pantomime. But I would ask those who maintain this argument, what would become of that number of people that constantly spend the hours between six and ten at a playhouse if pantomime were abolished? Would they stay at home? No. Believe me, besides the pleasure of the representation, there will always be reasons enough to make the fashionable and gay frequent playhouses. What will they do then? Why they'll come to plays as usual, and after a little time, the manager's profit will rise to an excessive height by this very great saving.

The two principal reasons, then, for the continuation of pantomime are that the people now require it and that it puts money in the pockets of the managers, which, it is said, plays will not as plentifully do. I have already answered both, and shall now proceed to show the evil consequences resulting from pantomime which I defy them to answer.

First (but that has already been observed)—it wipes away all the impressions made by the play and leaves the mind of the auditor unbenefited. It is (to use no very pleasing image) like taking an emetic immediately upon a dose of physic to prevent the good of its operation by making you throw it up before it can work.

Secondly, the stage has, in all ages, been looked upon as a school where riper persons may receive lessons for their conduct. . . . The immediate effect of pantomime is sapping the foundations of the stage and dispersing corruption through the minds of a whole people by rendering the best means of reformation (pleasure mixed with monition) less productive of its effect, and turning the inclinations of the spectators to covet the sight of feats of activity from whence no instruction can be derived. . . .

Thirdly, it debases the stage and sinks it to the lowest species of entertainment. It makes that which should be an honour to a nation, an infamy. Our neighbour nation, France (as contemptible as we are pleased to think it), has too just and noble a notion of what the stage is to admit any representation on theirs but Tragedy, Comedy, or Farce. For which reason, after the Greek and Roman stage, the French claims the right of excellence which we might, if we were proof against the force of corruption, contest with them. M. Voltaire, during the short stay he made among us, is a strong example that he thought some English pieces not unworthy being transplanted on the stage of France. They have indeed a theatre on which Harlequin exerts his talents, but their Harlequin, at times, might make some of our comedies blush, in being more moral, more chaste, and more rationally pleasing, and what is now called The New Italian Comedy treads on the heels of true comedy. Instead of sinking their principal stage, they are every day raising the lower. I forbear the parallel of our conduct with theirs.

The next evil flowing from the spreading of pantomime, and [it] is no slight one, affects the very heart of the stage–the actors. The actors are a body as little blind to their interests as their head. Without a great reach of thought they can easily foresee that when once their art falls into contempt, their talent will fall short of its reward. If plays lose the power of pleasing, by the superior charms of pantomime, the consequence is plain. But this is not all. Instead of exerting their power, they will, by reflecting how little regard is had to the pains they take, learn to take none at all and become tame vocal puppets, obliged to utter words put in their mouths, but not under the necessity of personating characters, which no longer please. And who can blame them? I need not mention that this way of thinking tends directly to the destruction of the art itself and by deduction, not forced, to the utter ruin of the stage.

Another evil arising from the distaste pantomime occasions for plays touches authors and merits a particular disquisition which I may give in a future paper. I shall content myself for the present with observing that a new play, brought on by itself, cannot make head against pantomime, and that as each house strives to distress the other, the first new play that shall appear will have a battery of pantomime levelled against it and must receive (perhaps its death) wounds thro' its naked sides; that if poets do not receive the aid of pantomime to support their new pieces, it is a monstrous injustice to tax them with the charge of it, for thus it will stand with them: they contribute to the extra charge of pantomime, which pantomime is employed to take away the taste of the public to new plays: that is, they pay for a knife to cut their own throats. . . .

Checklist of Further Readings

Bateson, Frederick. *English Comic Drama (1700-1750)*. Oxford: Clarendon Press, 1929.

Bevis, Richard W. *The Laughing Tradition: Stage Comedy in Garrick's Day*. Athens: University of Georgia Press, 1980.

Braunmiller, A. R., and J. C. Bulman, eds. *Comedy from Shakespeare to Sheridan: Change and Continuity in the English and European Dramatic Tradition*. Newark: University of Delaware Press, 1986.

Brown, Laura. *English Dramatic Form, 1660-1760*. New Haven: Yale University Press, 1981.

Danchin, Pierre. *The Prologues and Epilogues of the Restoration*, 4 volumes. Nancy: Presses Universitaires de Nancy, 1981.

Donaldson, Ian. *The World Upside-Down: Comedy from Jonson to Fielding*. Oxford: Clarendon Press, 1970.

Fiske, Roger. *English Theatre Music in the Eighteenth Century*. London, New York & Toronto: Oxford University Press, 1973.

Fujimura, Thomas H. *The Restoration Comedy of Wit*. Princeton: Princeton University Press, 1952.

Gagey, Edmond McAdoo. *Ballad Opera*. New York: Columbia University Press, 1937.

Griswold, Wendy. *Renaissance Revivals: City Comedy and Revenge Tragedy*. Chicago: University of Chicago Press, 1986.

Holland, Norman N. *The First Modern Comedies: The Significance of Etherege, Wycherley, and Congreve*. Cambridge, Mass.: Harvard University Press, 1959.

Holland, Peter. *The Ornament of Action: Text and Performance in Restoration Comedy*. Cambridge: Cambridge University Press, 1979.

Hotson, Leslie. *The Commonwealth and Restoration Stage*. Cambridge, Mass.: Harvard University Press, 1928.

Hughes, Leo. *The Drama's Patrons: A Study of the Eighteenth-Century London Audience*. Austin: University of Texas Press, 1971.

Hume, Robert D. *The Development of English Drama in the Late Seventeenth Century*. Oxford: Clarendon Press, 1976.

Hume. *Henry Fielding and the London Theatre, 1728-1737*. Oxford: Oxford University Press, 1988.

Hume. *The Rakish Stage: Studies in English Drama, 1660-1800*. Carbondale: Southern Illinois University Press, 1983.

Hume, ed. *The London Theatre World, 1660-1800*. Carbondale: Southern Illinois University Press, 1980.

Kenny, Shirley S. " 'Elopement, Divorces, and the Devil Knows What': Love and Marriage in English Comedy, 1690-1720," *South Atlantic Quarterly,* 78 (Winter 1979): 84-106.

Kenny, ed. *British Theatre and the Other Arts, 1660-1800.* Washington, D.C.: Folger Books, 1984.

Kern, Jean B. *Dramatic Satire in the Age of Walpole 1720-1750.* Ames: Iowa State University Press, 1976.

Leach, Robert. *The Punch and Judy Show: History, Tradition and Meaning.* Athens: University of Georgia Press, 1985.

Leacroft, Richard. *The Development of the English Playhouse.* Ithaca: Cornell University Press, 1973.

Lewis, Peter. *Fielding's Burlesque Drama: Its Place in the Tradition.* Edinburgh: Edinburgh University Press for the University of Durham, 1987.

Liesenfeld, Vincent J. *The Licensing Act of 1737.* Madison: University of Wisconsin Press, 1984.

Lindley, David, ed. *The Court Masque.* Manchester & Dover, N.H.: Manchester University Press, 1984.

Loftis, John. *Comedy and Society from Congreve to Fielding.* Stanford: Stanford University Press, 1959.

Loftis. *Politics of Drama in Augustan England.* Oxford: Clarendon Press, 1963.

Loftis, ed. *Restoration Drama: Modern Essays in Criticism.* New York: Oxford University Press, 1966.

Manifold, John S. *The Music in English Drama from Shakespeare to Purcell.* London: Rockliff, 1956.

Milhous, Judith, and Robert D. Hume. *Producible Interpretation: Eight English Plays 1675-1707.* Carbondale & Edwardsville: Southern Illinois University Press, 1985.

Mills, John A. *Hamlet on Stage: The Great Tradition.* Westport, Conn.: Greenwood Press, 1985.

Nicoll, Allardyce. *A History of English Drama, 1660-1900,* 6 volumes, fourth edition revised. Cambridge: Cambridge University Press, 1952-1959.

Powell, Jocelyn. *Restoration Theatre Production.* London & Boston: Routledge & Kegan Paul, 1984.

Price, Curtis A. *Henry Purcell and the London Stage.* London, New York & Cambridge: Cambridge University Press, 1984.

Price. *Music in the Restoration Theatre.* Ann Arbor, Mich.: UMI Research Press, 1979.

Prior, Moody. *The Language of Tragedy.* New York: Columbia University Press, 1947.

Rosenfeld, Sybil M. *A Short History of Scene Design in Great Britain.* Oxford: Blackwell, 1973.

Rothstein, Eric. *Restoration Tragedy: Form and the Process of Change.* Madison: University of Wisconsin Press, 1967.

Sawyer, Paul. *Christopher Rich of Drury Lane.* Lanham, Md.: University Press of America, 1986.

Southern, Richard. *Changeable Scenery: Its Origin and Development in the British Theatre.* London: Faber & Faber, 1952.

Staves, Susan. *Players' Sceptres*. Lincoln & London: University of Nebraska Press, 1979.

Stone, George Winchester, ed. *The Stage and the Page: London's "Whole Show" in the Eighteenth-Century Theatre*. Berkeley: University of California Press, 1981.

Styan, J. L. *Restoration Comedy in Performance*. New York: Cambridge University Press, 1986.

Taney, Retta. *Restoration Revivals on the British Stage, 1944-1979*. Lanham, Md.: University Press of America, 1985.

Van Lennep, William, and others. *The London Stage 1660-1800: A Calendar of Plays, Entertainments, and Afterpieces,* 5 parts. Carbondale: Southern Illinois University Press, 1960-1968.

Waith, Eugene. *Ideas of Greatness: Heroic Drama in England*. New York: Barnes & Noble, 1971.

Weber, Harold. *The Restoration Rake Hero: Transformations in Sexual Understanding in Seventeenth-Century England*. Madison: University of Wisconsin Press, 1986.

Winton, Calhoun. "The Tragic Muse in Enlightened England," in *Greene Centennial Studies,* edited by Paul J. Korshin and Robert R. Allen. Charlottesville: University Press of Virginia, 1984.

Worthen, William B. *The Idea of the Actor: Drama and the Ethics of Performance*. Princeton: Princeton University Press, 1984.

Zimbardo, Rose A. *A Mirror to Nature: Transformations in Drama and Aesthetics, 1600-1732*. Lexington: University Press of Kentucky, 1986.

Contributors

Paula R. Backscheider ....*University of Rochester*
Barbara M. Benedict ....*Trinity College, Connecticut*
Sophia B. Blaydes ....*West Virginia University*
William J. Burling ....*Auburn University*
J. Douglas Canfield ....*University of Arizona*
Charles Michael Carroll...*St. Petersburg Junior College*
Jean Gagen ....*University of Kansas*
Alfred W. Hesse...*Silver Spring, Maryland*
Peter Holland... *Cambridge University*
Shirley Strum Kenny ....*Queens College, City University of New York*
Linda E. Merians...*La Salle University*
Ann Messenger ....*Simon Fraser University*
Douglas H. White...*Loyola University of Chicago*
Calhoun Winton..*University of Maryland at College Park*
Martin J. Wood...*University of Wisconsin–Eau Claire*

Cumulative Index

Dictionary of Literary Biography, Volumes 1-84
Dictionary of Literary Biography Yearbook, 1980-1988
Dictionary of Literary Biography Documentary Series, Volumes 1-6

Cumulative Index

DLB before number: *Dictionary of Literary Biography,* Volumes 1-84
Y before number: *Dictionary of Literary Biography Yearbook,* 1980-1988
DS before number: *Dictionary of Literary Biography Documentary Series,* Volumes 1-6

A

Abbey Press...DLB-49

The Abbey Theatre and Irish
Drama, 1900-1945.................................DLB-10

Abbot, Willis J. 1863-1934 ....DLB-29

Abbott, Jacob 1803-1879..................................DLB-1

Abbott, Lyman 1835-1922 ....DLB-79

Abbott, Robert S. 1868-1940 ....DLB-29

Abelard-Schuman DLB-46

Abell, Arunah S. 1806-1888 ....DLB-43

Abercrombie, Lascelles 1881-1938 ....DLB-19

Abrams, M. H. 1912- DLB-67

Abse, Dannie 1923- DLB-27

Academy Chicago Publishers DLB-46

Ace Books DLB-46

Acorn, Milton 1923-1986 ....DLB-53

Acosta, Oscar Zeta 1935?- DLB-82

Actors Theatre of Louisville DLB-7

Adair, James 1709?-1783?................................DLB-30

Adame, Leonard 1947- DLB-82

Adamic, Louis 1898-1951.................................DLB-9

Adams, Alice 1926- Y-86

Adams, Brooks 1848-1927 ....DLB-47

Adams, Charles Francis, Jr. 1835-1915.............DLB-47

Adams, Douglas 1952- Y-83

Adams, Franklin P. 1881-1960 ....DLB-29

Adams, Henry 1838-1918.........................DLB-12, 47

Adams, Herbert Baxter 1850-1901 ....DLB-47

Adams, J. S. and C. [publishing house]............DLB-49

Adams, James Truslow 1878-1949.....................DLB-17

Adams, John 1735-1826...................................DLB-31

Adams, John Quincy 1767-1848........................DLB-37

Adams, Léonie 1899-1988 ....DLB-48

Adams, Samuel 1722-1803............................DLB-31, 43

Adams, William Taylor 1822-1897 ....DLB-42

Adcock, Fleur 1934- DLB-40

Ade, George 1866-1944 ....DLB-11, 25

Adeler, Max (see Clark, Charles Heber)

Advance Publishing Company DLB-49

AE 1867-1935 ....DLB-19

Aesthetic Poetry (1873), by Walter Pater...........DLB-35

Afro-American Literary Critics:
An Introduction DLB-33

Agassiz, Jean Louis Rodolphe 1807-1873 ....DLB-1

Agee, James 1909-1955...............................DLB-2, 26

Aiken, Conrad 1889-1973.............................DLB-9, 45

Ainsworth, William Harrison 1805-1882 ....DLB-21

Aitken, Robert [publishing house].....................DLB-49

Akins, Zoë 1886-1958......................................DLB-26

Alain-Fournier 1886-1914 ....DLB-65

Alba, Nanina 1915-1968...................................DLB-41

Albee, Edward 1928- DLB-7

Alcott, Amos Bronson 1799-1888 ....DLB-1

Alcott, Louisa May 1832-1888 ....DLB-1, 42, 79

Alcott, William Andrus 1798-1859......................DLB-1

Alden, Henry Mills 1836-1919 ....DLB-79

Alden, Isabella 1841-1930................................DLB-42

Alden, John B. [publishing house] DLB-49

Alden, Beardsley and Company DLB-49

Aldington, Richard 1892-1962 ....DLB-20, 36

Aldis, Dorothy 1896-1966 ....DLB-22

Aldiss, Brian W. 1925- DLB-14

Aldrich, Thomas Bailey 1836-1907
....DLB-42, 71, 74, 79

Alexander, Charles Wesley
[publishing house] DLB-49

Alexander, James 1691-1756 ....DLB-24

Alexander, Lloyd 1924- DLB-52

Alger, Horatio, Jr. 1832-1899.....................DLB-42

Algonquin Books of Chapel Hill.......................DLB-46

Algren, Nelson 1909-1981....................DLB-9; Y-81, 82

Allan, Ted 1916- DLB-68

Alldritt, Keith 1935- DLB-14

Allen, Ethan 1738-1789 ....DLB-31

Allen, George 1808-1876 ....DLB-59

Allen, Grant 1848-1899.............................DLB-70

Allen, Henry W. 1912- Y-85

Allen, Hervey 1889-1949 ....DLB-9, 45

Allen, James 1739-1808............................DLB-31

Allen, James Lane 1849-1925 ....DLB-71

Allen, Jay Presson 1922- DLB-26

Allen, John, and Company DLB-49

Allen, Samuel W. 1917- DLB-41

Allen, Woody 1935- DLB-44

Allingham, Margery 1904-1966.....................DLB-77

Allingham, William 1824-1889 ....DLB-35

Allison, W. L. [publishing house] DLB-49

Allott, Kenneth 1912-1973.........................DLB-20

Allston, Washington 1779-1843 ....DLB-1

Alsop, George 1636-post 1673......................DLB-24

Alsop, Richard 1761-1815..........................DLB-37

Altemus, Henry, and Company...................DLB-49

Altenberg, Peter 1885-1919 ....DLB-81

Alurista 1947- DLB-82

Alvarez, A. 1929- DLB-14, 40

Ambler, Eric 1909- DLB-77

*America: or, a Poem on the Settlement of the
    British Colonies* (1780?), by Timothy
    Dwight.......................................DLB-37

American Conservatory Theatre DLB-7

American Fiction and the 1930s......................DLB-9

American Humor: A Historical Survey
    East and Northeast
    South and Southwest
    Midwest
    West.......................................DLB-11

American News Company................................DLB-49

The American Poets' Corner: The First
    Three Years (1983-1986)........................Y-86

American Publishing Company DLB-49

American Stationers' Company........................DLB-49

American Sunday-School Union DLB-49

American Temperance Union...........................DLB-49

American Tract Society DLB-49

The American Writers Congress
    (9-12 October 1981) Y-81

The American Writers Congress: A Report
    on Continuing Business........................Y-81

Ames, Fisher 1758-1808.............................DLB-37

Ames, Mary Clemmer 1831-1884.......................DLB-23

Amini, Johari M. 1935- DLB-41

Amis, Kingsley 1922- DLB-15, 27

Amis, Martin 1949- DLB-14

Ammons, A. R. 1926- DLB-5

Amory, Thomas 1691?-1788...........................DLB-39

Anaya, Rudolfo A. 1937- DLB-82

Andersch, Alfred 1914-1980.........................DLB-69

Anderson, Margaret 1886-1973.......................DLB-4

Anderson, Maxwell 1888-1959 ....DLB-7

Anderson, Patrick 1915-1979........................DLB-68

Anderson, Paul Y. 1893-1938........................DLB-29

Anderson, Poul 1926- DLB-8

Anderson, Robert 1917- DLB-7

Anderson, Sherwood 1876-1941...........DLB-4, 9; DS-1

Andreas-Salomé, Lou 1861-1937......................DLB-66

Andres, Stefan 1906-1970...........................DLB-69

Andrews, Charles M. 1863-1943......................DLB-17

Andrieux, Louis (see Aragon, Louis)

Andrian, Leopold von 1875-1951 ....DLB-81

Andrus, Silas, and Son DLB-49

Angell, James Burrill 1829-1916 ....DLB-64

Angelou, Maya 1928- DLB-38

The "Angry Young Men"................................DLB-15

Anhalt, Edward 1914- DLB-26

Anners, Henry F. [publishing house]................DLB-49

Anthony, Piers 1934- DLB-8

Anthony Burgess's *99 Novels:* An Opinion Poll Y-84

Antin, Mary 1881-1949 ....Y-84

Antschel, Paul (see Celan, Paul)

Apodaca, Rudy S. 1939- DLB-82

Appleton, D., and Company DLB-49

Appleton-Century-Crofts DLB-46

Apple-wood Books DLB-46

Aquin, Hubert 1929-1977 ....DLB-53

Aragon, Louis 1897-1982 ....DLB-72

Arbor House Publishing Company DLB-46

Arcadia House DLB-46

Arce, Julio G. (see Ulica, Jorge)

Archer, William 1856-1924 ....DLB-10

Arden, John 1930- DLB-13

Arden of Faversham DLB-62

The Arena Publishing Company DLB-49

Arena Stage...DLB-7

Arensberg, Ann 1937- Y-82

Arias, Ron 1941- DLB-82

Arland, Marcel 1899-1986 ....DLB-72

Arlen, Michael 1895-1956.............................DLB-36, 77

Armed Services Editions DLB-46

Arno Press...DLB-46

Arnold, Edwin 1832-1904 ....DLB-35

Arnold, Matthew 1822-1888 ....DLB-32, 57

Arnold, Thomas 1795-1842 ....DLB-55

Arnow, Harriette Simpson 1908-1986..................DLB-6

Arp, Bill (see Smith, Charles Henry)

Arthur, Timothy Shay 1809-1885 ....DLB-3, 42, 79

As I See It, by Carolyn Cassady.........................DLB-16

Asch, Nathan 1902-1964.................................DLB-4, 28

Ash, John 1948- DLB-40

Ashbery, John 1927- DLB-5; Y-81

Asher, Sandy 1942- Y-83

Ashton, Winifred (see Dane, Clemence)

Asimov, Isaac 1920- DLB-8

Atheneum Publishers DLB-46

Atherton, Gertrude 1857-1948.......................DLB-9, 78

Atkins, Josiah circa 1755-1781 ....DLB-31

Atkins, Russell 1926- DLB-41

The Atlantic Monthly Press DLB-46

Attaway, William 1911-1986 ....DLB-76

Atwood, Margaret 1939- DLB-53

Aubert, Alvin 1930- DLB-41

Aubin, Penelope 1685-circa 1731 ....DLB-39

Aubrey-Fletcher, Henry Lancelot (see Wade, Henry)

Auchincloss, Louis 1917- DLB-2; Y-80

Auden, W. H. 1907-1973.............................DLB-10, 20

Audio Art in America: A Personal
      Memoir...Y-85

Auernheimer, Raoul 1876-1948 ....DLB-81

Austin, Alfred 1835-1913...................................DLB-35

Austin, Mary 1868-1934................................DLB-9, 78

Austin, William 1778-1841................................DLB-74

The Author's Apology for His Book
      (1684), by John Bunyan DLB-39

An Author's Response, by Ronald Sukenick..........Y-82

Authors and Newspapers Association DLB-46

Authors' Publishing Company DLB-49

Avalon Books..DLB-46

Avendaño, Fausto 1941- DLB-82

Avison, Margaret 1918- DLB-53

Avon Books...DLB-46

Ayckbourn, Alan 1939- DLB-13

Aymé, Marcel 1902-1967 ....DLB-72

Aytoun, William Edmondstoune 1813-1865 ......DLB-32

B

Babbitt, Irving 1865-1933 ....DLB-63

Babbitt, Natalie 1932- DLB-52

Babcock, John [publishing house] DLB-49

Bache, Benjamin Franklin 1769-1798 ....DLB-43

Bacon, Delia 1811-1859......................................DLB-1

Bacon, Thomas circa 1700-1768.......................DLB-31

Badger, Richard G., and Company DLB-49

Bage, Robert 1728-1801....................................DLB-39

Bagehot, Walter 1826-1877...............................DLB-55

Bagnold, Enid 1889-1981 ....DLB-13

Bahr, Hermann 1863-1934 ....DLB-81

Bailey, Alfred Goldsworthy 1905- DLB-68

Bailey, Francis [publishing house] DLB-49

Bailey, H. C. 1878-1961 ....DLB-77

Bailey, Paul 1937- DLB-14

Bailey, Philip James 1816-1902..........................DLB-32

Baillie, Hugh 1890-1966 ....DLB-29

Bailyn, Bernard 1922- DLB-17

Bainbridge, Beryl 1933- DLB-14

Baird, Irene 1901-1981.....................................DLB-68

The Baker and Taylor Company DLB-49

Baker, Houston A., Jr. 1943- DLB-67

Baker, Walter H., Company
    ("Baker's Plays").....................................DLB-49

Bald, Wambly 1902- DLB-4

Balderston, John 1889-1954 ....DLB-26

Baldwin, James 1924-1987 ....DLB-2, 7, 33; Y-87

Baldwin, Joseph Glover 1815-1864 ....DLB-3, 11

Ballantine Books...DLB-46

Ballard, J. G. 1930- DLB-14

Ballou, Maturin Murray 1820-1895....................DLB-79

Ballou, Robert O. [publishing house]................DLB-46

Bambara, Toni Cade 1939- DLB-38

Bancroft, A. L., and Company DLB-49

Bancroft, George 1800-1891 ....DLB-1, 30, 59

Bancroft, Hubert Howe 1832-1918...................DLB-47

Bangs, John Kendrick 1862-1922..............DLB-11, 79

Banks, John circa 1653-1706 ....DLB-80

Bantam Books..DLB-46

Banville, John 1945- DLB-14

Baraka, Amiri 1934- DLB-5, 7, 16, 38

Barber, John Warner 1798-1885 ....DLB-30

Barbour, Ralph Henry 1870-1944.....................DLB-22

Barbusse, Henri 1873-1935...............................DLB-65

Barclay, E. E., and Company DLB-49

Bardeen, C. W. [publishing house]....................DLB-49

Baring, Maurice 1874-1945...............................DLB-34

Barker, A. L. 1918- DLB-14

Barker, George 1913- DLB-20

Barker, Harley Granville 1877-1946 ....DLB-10

Barker, Howard 1946- DLB-13

Barker, James Nelson 1784-1858.....................DLB-37

Barker, Jane 1652-1727?.................................DLB-39

Barks, Coleman 1937- DLB-5

Barlach, Ernst 1870-1938................................DLB-56

Barlow, Joel 1754-1812 ....DLB-37

Barnard, John 1681-1770 ....DLB-24

Barnes, A. S., and Company............................DLB-49

Barnes, Djuna 1892-1982 ....DLB-4, 9, 45

Barnes, Margaret Ayer 1886-1967 ....DLB-9

Barnes, Peter 1931- DLB-13

Barnes, William 1801-1886................................DLB-32

Barnes and Noble Books...................................DLB-46

Barney, Natalie 1876-1972................................DLB-4

Baron, Richard W., Publishing Company DLB-46

Barr, Robert 1850-1912 ....DLB-70

Barrax, Gerald William 1933- DLB-41

Barrie, James M. 1860-1937 ....DLB-10

Barrio, Raymond 1921- DLB-82

Barry, Philip 1896-1949 ....DLB-7

Barse and Hopkins...DLB-46

Barstow, Stan 1928- DLB-14

Barth, John 1930- DLB-2

Barthelme, Donald 1931- DLB-2; Y-80

Barthelme, Frederick 1943- Y-85

Bartlett, John 1820-1905...................................DLB-1

Bartol, Cyrus Augustus 1813-1900.....................DLB-1

Bartram, John 1699-1777 ....DLB-31

Bartram, William 1739-1823............................DLB-37

Basic Books DLB-46

Bass, T. J. 1932- Y-81

Bassett, John Spencer 1867-1928 ....DLB-17

Bassler, Thomas Joseph (see Bass, T. J.)

Bate, Walter Jackson 1918- DLB-67

Bates, Katharine Lee 1859-1929........................DLB-71

Baum, L. Frank 1856-1919 ....DLB-22

Baumbach, Jonathan 1933- Y-80

Bawden, Nina 1925- DLB-14

Bax, Clifford 1886-1962 ....DLB-10

Bayer, Eleanor (see Perry, Eleanor)

Bazin, Hervé 1911- DLB-83

Beach, Sylvia 1887-1962....................................DLB-4

Beacon Press DLB-49

Beadle and Adams..DLB-49

Beagle, Peter S. 1939- Y-80

Beal, M. F. 1937- Y-81

Beale, Howard K. 1899-1959.............................DLB-17

Beard, Charles A. 1874-1948.............................DLB-17

A Beat Chronology: The First Twenty-five

Years, 1944-1969 ....DLB-16

Beattie, Ann 1947- Y-82

Beauchemin, Yves 1941- DLB-60

Beaulieu, Victor-Lévy 1945- DLB-53

Beaumont, Francis circa 1584-1616
    and Fletcher, John 1579-1625 ....DLB-58

Beauvoir, Simone de 1908-1986...............Y-86, DLB-72

Becher, Ulrich 1910- DLB-69

Becker, Carl 1873-1945.......................DLB-17

Becker, Jurek 1937- DLB-75

Becker, Jürgen 1932- DLB-75

Beckett, Samuel 1906- DLB-13, 15

Beckford, William 1760-1844 ....DLB-39

Beckham, Barry 1944- DLB-33

Beecher, Catharine Esther 1800-1878.................DLB-1

Beecher, Henry Ward 1813-1887.................DLB-3, 43

Beer, George L. 1872-1920......................DLB-47

Beer, Patricia 1919- DLB-40

Beerbohm, Max 1872-1956......................DLB-34

Beer-Hofmann, Richard 1866-1945 ....DLB-81

Beers, Henry A. 1847-1926 ....DLB-71

Behan, Brendan 1923-1964 ....DLB-13

Behn, Aphra 1640?-1689.................DLB-39, 80

Behn, Harry 1898-1973 ....DLB-61

Behrman, S. N. 1893-1973 ....DLB-7, 44

Belasco, David 1853-1931 ....DLB-7

Belford, Clarke and Company.................DLB-49

Belitt, Ben 1911- DLB-5

Belknap, Jeremy 1744-1798.................DLB-30, 37

Bell, James Madison 1826-1902.................DLB-50

Bell, Marvin 1937- DLB-5

Bell, Robert [publishing house] DLB-49

Bellamy, Edward 1850-1898 ....DLB-12

Bellamy, Joseph 1719-1790 ....DLB-31

Belloc, Hilaire 1870-1953 ....DLB-19

Bellow, Saul 1915- DLB-2, 28; Y-82; DS-3

Belmont Productions.................DLB-46

Bemelmans, Ludwig 1898-1962.................DLB-22

Bemis, Samuel Flagg 1891-1973.................DLB-17

Benchley, Robert 1889-1945.................DLB-11

Benedictus, David 1938- DLB-14

Benedikt, Michael 1935- DLB-5

Benét, Stephen Vincent 1898-1943.................DLB-4, 48

Benét, William Rose 1886-1950.................DLB-45

Benford, Gregory 1941- Y-82

Benjamin, Park 1809-1864 ....DLB-3, 59, 73

Benn, Gottfried 1886-1956 ....DLB-56

Bennett, Arnold 1867-1931 ....DLB-10, 34

Bennett, Charles 1899- DLB-44

Bennett, Gwendolyn 1902- DLB-51

Bennett, Hal 1930- DLB-33

Bennett, James Gordon 1795-1872 ....DLB-43

Bennett, James Gordon, Jr. 1841-1918 ....DLB-23

Bennett, John 1865-1956 ....DLB-42

Benoit, Jacques 1941- DLB-60

Benson, Stella 1892-1933 ....DLB-36

Bentley, E. C. 1875-1956.................DLB-70

Benton, Robert 1932-   and Newman,
    David 1937- DLB-44

Benziger Brothers.................DLB-49

Beresford, Anne 1929- DLB-40

Berford, R. G., Company.................DLB-49

Berg, Stephen 1934- DLB-5

Bergengruen, Werner 1892-1964 ....DLB-56

Berger, John 1926- DLB-14

Berger, Meyer 1898-1959 ....DLB-29

Berger, Thomas 1924- DLB-2; Y-80

Berkeley, Anthony 1893-1971 ....DLB-77

Berkeley, George 1685-1753.................DLB-31

The Berkley Publishing Corporation DLB-46

Bernal, Vicente J. 1888-1915.................DLB-82

Bernanos, Georges 1888-1948 ....DLB-72

Bernard, John 1756-1828 ....DLB-37

Berrigan, Daniel 1921- DLB-5

Berrigan, Ted 1934-1983 ....DLB-5

Berry, Wendell 1934- DLB-5, 6

Berryman, John 1914-1972.................DLB-48

Bersianik, Louky 1930- DLB-60

Berton, Pierre 1920- DLB-68

Bessette, Gerard 1920- DLB-53

Bessie, Alvah 1904-1985.................DLB-26

Bester, Alfred 1913- DLB-8

The Bestseller Lists: An Assessment Y-84

Betjeman, John 1906-1984 ....DLB-20; Y-84

Betts, Doris 1932- Y-82

Beveridge, Albert J. 1862-1927 ....DLB-17

Beverley, Robert circa 1673-1722.................DLB-24, 30

Bichsel, Peter 1935- DLB-75

Biddle, Drexel [publishing house] DLB-49

Bidwell, Walter Hilliard 1798-1881 ....DLB-79

Bienek, Horst 1930- DLB-75

Bierbaum, Otto Julius 1865-1910 ....DLB-66

Bierce, Ambrose 1842-1914?......DLB-11, 12, 23, 71, 74

Biggle, Lloyd, Jr. 1923- DLB-8

Biglow, Hosea (see Lowell, James Russell)

Billings, Josh (see Shaw, Henry Wheeler)

Binding, Rudolf G. 1867-1938............................DLB-66

Bingham, Caleb 1757-1817 ....DLB-42

Binyon, Laurence 1869-1943 ....DLB-19

Biographical Documents I.....................................Y-84

Biographical Documents II Y-85

Bioren, John [publishing house] DLB-49

Bird, William 1888-1963 ....DLB-4

Bishop, Elizabeth 1911-1979................................DLB-5

Bishop, John Peale 1892-1944 ....DLB-4, 9, 45

Bissett, Bill 1939- DLB-53

Black, David (D. M.) 1941- DLB-40

Black, Walter J. [publishing house] DLB-46

Black, Winifred 1863-1936 ....DLB-25

The Black Arts Movement, by Larry Neal.........DLB-38

Black Theaters and Theater Organizations in
    America, 1961-1982: A Research List.........DLB-38

Black Theatre: A Forum [excerpts]....................DLB-38

Blackamore, Arthur 1679-? DLB-24, 39

Blackburn, Alexander L. 1929- Y-85

Blackburn, Paul 1926-1971......................DLB-16; Y-81

Blackburn, Thomas 1916-1977........................DLB-27

Blackmore, R. D. 1825-1900 ....DLB-18

Blackmur, R. P. 1904-1965 ....DLB-63

Blackwood, Caroline 1931- DLB-14

Blair, Eric Arthur (see Orwell, George)

Blair, Francis Preston 1791-1876.......................DLB-43

Blair, James circa 1655-1743.............................DLB-24

Blair, John Durburrow 1759-1823 ....DLB-37

Blais, Marie-Claire 1939- DLB-53

Blaise, Clark 1940- DLB-53

Blake, Nicholas 1904-1972...............................DLB-77
    (see also Day Lewis, C.)

The Blakiston Company DLB-49

Blanchot, Maurice 1907- DLB-72

Bledsoe, Albert Taylor 1809-1877 ....DLB-3, 79

Blelock and Company DLB-49

Blish, James 1921-1975 ....DLB-8

Bliss, E., and E. White [publishing house] DLB-49

Bloch, Robert 1917- DLB-44

Block, Rudolph (see Lessing, Bruno)

Bloom, Harold 1930- DLB-67

Bloomer, Amelia 1818-1894 ....DLB-79

Blume, Judy 1938- DLB-52

Blunck, Hans Friedrich 1888-1961....................DLB-66

Blunden, Edmund 1896-1974............................DLB-20

Blunt, Wilfrid Scawen 1840-1922 ....DLB-19

Bly, Nellie (see Cochrane, Elizabeth)

Bly, Robert 1926- DLB-5

The Bobbs-Merrill Company DLB-46

Bobrowski, Johannes 1917-1965.......................DLB-75

Bodenheim, Maxwell 1892-1954 ....DLB-9, 45

Bodkin, M. McDonnell 1850-1933 ....DLB-70

Bodsworth, Fred 1918- DLB-68

Boehm, Sydney 1908- DLB-44

Boer, Charles 1939- DLB-5

Bogan, Louise 1897-1970...............................DLB-45

Bogarde, Dirk 1921- DLB-14

Boland, Eavan 1944- DLB-40

Böll, Heinrich 1917-1985.......................Y-85, DLB-69

Bolling, Robert 1738-1775 ....DLB-31

Bolt, Carol 1941- DLB-60

Bolt, Robert 1924- DLB-13

Bolton, Herbert E. 1870-1953 ....DLB-17

Bond, Edward 1934- DLB-13

Boni, Albert and Charles [publishing house].....DLB-46

Boni and Liveright DLB-46

Robert Bonner's Sons......................................DLB-49

Bontemps, Arna 1902-1973 ....DLB-48, 51

The Book League of America DLB-46

Book Reviewing in America: I Y-87

Book Reviewing in America: II Y-88

Book Supply Company DLB-49

The Booker Prize
    Address by Anthony Thwaite, Chairman
        of the Booker Prize Judges
        Comments from Former Booker Prize
        Winners Y-86

Boorstin, Daniel J. 1914- DLB-17

Booth, Mary L. 1831-1889 ....DLB-79

Booth, Philip 1925- Y-82

Booth, Wayne C. 1921- DLB-67

Borchardt, Rudolf 1877-1945 ....DLB-66

Borchert, Wolfgang 1921-1947 ....DLB-69

Borges, Jorge Luis 1899-1986 ....Y-86

Borrow, George 1803-1881 ....DLB-21, 55

Bosco, Henri 1888-1976 ....DLB-72

Bosco, Monique 1927- DLB-53

Botta, Anne C. Lynch 1815-1891 ....DLB-3

Bottomley, Gordon 1874-1948 ....DLB-10

Bottoms, David 1949- Y-83

Bottrall, Ronald 1906- DLB-20

Boucher, Anthony 1911-1968 ....DLB-8

Boucher, Jonathan 1738-1804 ....DLB-31

Bourjaily, Vance Nye 1922- DLB-2

Bourne, Edward Gaylord 1860-1908 ....DLB-47

Bourne, Randolph 1886-1918 ....DLB-63

Bousquet, Joë 1897-1950 ....DLB-72

Bova, Ben 1932- Y-81

Bove, Emmanuel 1898-1945 ....DLB-72

Bovard, Oliver K. 1872-1945 ....DLB-25

Bowen, Elizabeth 1899-1973 ....DLB-15

Bowen, Francis 1811-1890 ....DLB-1, 59

Bowen, John 1924- DLB-13

Bowen-Merrill Company DLB-49

Bowering, George 1935- DLB-53

Bowers, Claude G. 1878-1958 ....DLB-17

Bowers, Edgar 1924- DLB-5

Bowles, Paul 1910- DLB-5, 6

Bowles, Samuel III 1826-1878 ....DLB-43

Bowman, Louise Morey 1882-1944 ....DLB-68

Boyd, James 1888-1944 ....DLB-9

Boyd, John 1919- DLB-8

Boyd, Thomas 1898-1935 ....DLB-9

Boyesen, Hjalmar Hjorth 1848-1895 ....DLB-12, 71

Boyle, Kay 1902- DLB-4, 9, 48

Boyle, Roger, Earl of Orrery
    1621-1679 ....DLB-80

Boyle, T. Coraghessan 1948- Y-86

Brackenbury, Alison 1953- DLB-40

Brackenridge, Hugh Henry 1748-1816 ....DLB-11, 37

Brackett, Charles 1892-1969 ....DLB-26

Brackett, Leigh 1915-1978 ....DLB-8, 26

Bradburn, John [publishing house] DLB-49

Bradbury, Malcolm 1932- DLB-14

Bradbury, Ray 1920- DLB-2, 8

Braddon, Mary Elizabeth 1835-1915 ....DLB-18, 70

Bradford, Andrew 1686-1742 ....DLB-43, 73

Bradford, Gamaliel 1863-1932 ....DLB-17

Bradford, John 1749-1830 ....DLB-43

Bradford, William 1590-1657 ....DLB-24, 30

Bradford, William III 1719-1791 ....DLB-43, 73

Bradlaugh, Charles 1833-1891 ....DLB-57

Bradley, David 1950- DLB-33

Bradley, Ira, and Company DLB-49

Bradley, J. W., and Company DLB-49

Bradley, Marion Zimmer 1930- DLB-8

Bradley, William Aspenwall 1878-1939 ....DLB-4

Bradstreet, Anne 1612 or 1613-1672 ....DLB-24

Brady, Frederic A. [publishing house] DLB-49

Bragg, Melvyn 1939- DLB-14

Brainard, Charles H. [publishing house] DLB-49

Braine, John 1922-1986 ....DLB-15; Y-86

Braithwaite, William Stanley
    1878-1962 ....DLB-50, 54

Bramah, Ernest 1868-1942 ....DLB-70

Branagan, Thomas 1774-1843 ....DLB-37

Branch, William Blackwell 1927- DLB-76

Branden Press DLB-46

Brault, Jacques 1933- DLB-53

Braun, Volker 1939- DLB-75

Brautigan, Richard 1935-1984 ....DLB-2, 5; Y-80, 84

Braxton, Joanne M. 1950- DLB-41

Bray, Thomas 1656-1730 ....DLB-24

Braziller, George [publishing house] DLB-46

The Bread Loaf Writers' Conference 1983............Y-84

The Break-Up of the Novel (1922),
    by John Middleton Murry..........................DLB-36

Breasted, James Henry 1865-1935......................DLB-47

Brecht, Bertolt 1898-1956 ....DLB-56

Bredel, Willi 1901-1964...............................DLB-56

Bremser, Bonnie 1939- DLB-16

Bremser, Ray 1934- DLB-16

Brentano, Bernard von 1901-1964 ....DLB-56

Brentano's DLB-49

Brenton, Howard 1942- DLB-13

Breton, André 1896-1966 ....DLB-65

Brewer, Warren and Putnam DLB-46

Brewster, Elizabeth 1922- DLB-60

Bridgers, Sue Ellen 1942- DLB-52

Bridges, Robert 1844-1930.............................DLB-19

Bridie, James 1888-1951...............................DLB-10

Briggs, Charles Frederick 1804-1877 ....DLB-3

Brighouse, Harold 1882-1958...........................DLB-10

Brimmer, B. J., Company DLB-46

Brinnin, John Malcolm 1916- DLB-48

Brisbane, Albert 1809-1890............................DLB-3

Brisbane, Arthur 1864-1936 ....DLB-25

Broadway Publishing Company DLB-46

Brochu, André 1942- DLB-53

Brock, Edwin 1927- DLB-40

Brod, Max 1884-1968...................................DLB-81

Brodhead, John R. 1814-1873 ....DLB-30

Brome, Richard circa 1590-1652 ....DLB-58

Bromfield, Louis 1896-1956 ....DLB-4, 9

Broner, E. M. 1930-...................................DLB-28

Brontë, Anne 1820-1849 ....DLB-21

Brontë, Charlotte 1816-1855...........................DLB-21

Brontë, Emily 1818-1848 ....DLB-21, 32

Brooke, Frances 1724-1789.............................DLB-39

Brooke, Henry 1703?-1783 ....DLB-39

Brooke, Rupert 1887-1915..............................DLB-19

Brooke-Rose, Christine 1926- DLB-14

Brookner, Anita 1928- Y-87

Brooks, Charles Timothy 1813-1883 ....DLB-1

Brooks, Cleanth 1906- DLB-63

Brooks, Gwendolyn 1917- DLB-5, 76

Brooks, Jeremy 1926- DLB-14

Brooks, Mel 1926- DLB-26

Brooks, Noah 1830-1903................................DLB-42

Brooks, Richard 1912- DLB-44

Brooks, Van Wyck 1886-1963 ....DLB-45, 63

Brophy, Brigid 1929- DLB-14

Brossard, Chandler 1922- DLB-16

Brossard, Nicole 1943- DLB-53

Brother Antoninus (see Everson, William)

Brougham, John 1810-1880..............................DLB-11

Broughton, James 1913- DLB-5

Broughton, Rhoda 1840-1920............................DLB-18

Broun, Heywood 1888-1939..............................DLB-29

Brown, Alice 1856-1948 ....DLB-78

Brown, Bob 1886-1959..............................DLB-4, 45

Brown, Cecil 1943- DLB-33

Brown, Charles Brockden 1771-1810.....DLB-37, 59, 73

Brown, Christy 1932-1981..............................DLB-14

Brown, Dee 1908- Y-80

Browne, Francis Fisher 1843-1913 ....DLB-79

Brown, Frank London 1927-1962 ....DLB-76

Brown, Fredric 1906-1972 ....DLB-8

Brown, George Mackay 1921- DLB-14, 27

Brown, Harry 1917-1986 ....DLB-26

Brown, Marcia 1918- DLB-61

Brown, Margaret Wise 1910-1952 ....DLB-22

Brown, Oliver Madox 1855-1874.........................DLB-21

Brown, Sterling 1901-1989 ....DLB-48, 51, 63

Brown, T. E. 1830-1897 ....DLB-35

Brown, William Hill 1765-1793 ....DLB-37

Brown, William Wells 1814-1884....................DLB-3, 50

Browne, Charles Farrar 1834-1867......................DLB-11

Browne, Michael Dennis 1940- DLB-40

Browne, Wynyard 1911-1964.............................DLB-13

Brownell, W. C. 1851-1928 ....DLB-71

Browning, Elizabeth Barrett 1806-1861 ....DLB-32

Browning, Robert 1812-1889............................DLB-32

Brownjohn, Allan 1931- DLB-40

Brownson, Orestes Augustus
    1803-1876.........................DLB-1, 59, 73

Bruce, Charles 1906-1971 ....DLB-68

Bruce, Leo 1903-1979 ....DLB-77

Bruce, Philip Alexander 1856-1933.......DLB-47

Bruce Humphries [publishing house] DLB-46

Bruce-Novoa, Juan 1944- DLB-82

Bruckman, Clyde 1894-1955 ....DLB-26

Brundage, John Herbert (see Herbert, John)

Bryant, William Cullen 1794-1878.........DLB-3, 43, 59

Buchan, John 1875-1940..................DLB-34, 70

Buchanan, Robert 1841-1901 ....DLB-18, 35

Buchman, Sidney 1902-1975 ....DLB-26

Buck, Pearl S. 1892-1973 ....DLB-9

Buckingham, Joseph Tinker 1779-1861 and
    Buckingham, Edwin 1810-1833.........DLB-73

Buckler, Ernest 1908-1984...............DLB-68

Buckley, William F., Jr. 1925- Y-80

Buckminster, Joseph Stevens 1784-1812...DLB-37

Buckner, Robert 1906- DLB-26

Budd, Thomas ?-1698.....................DLB-24

Budrys, A. J. 1931- DLB-8

Buechner, Frederick 1926- Y-80

Buell, John 1927- DLB-53

Buffum, Job [publishing house]..........DLB-49

Bukowski, Charles 1920- DLB-5

Bullins, Ed 1935- DLB-7, 38

Bulwer-Lytton, Edward (also Edward Bulwer)
    1803-1873 ....DLB-21

Bumpus, Jerry 1937- Y-81

Bunce and Brother.......................DLB-49

Bunner, H. C. 1855-1896 ....DLB-78, 79

Bunting, Basil 1900-1985 ....DLB-20

Bunyan, John 1628-1688..................DLB-39

Burch, Robert 1925- DLB-52

Burciaga, José Antonio 1940- DLB-82

Burgess, Anthony 1917- DLB-14

Burgess, Gelett 1866-1951 ....DLB-11

Burgess, John W. 1844-1931..............DLB-47

Burgess, Thornton W. 1874-1965 ....DLB-22

Burgess, Stringer and Company...........DLB-49

Burk, John Daly circa 1772-1808.........DLB-37

Burke, Kenneth 1897- DLB-45, 63

Burlingame, Edward Livermore 1848-1922...DLB-79

Burnett, Frances Hodgson 1849-1924......DLB-42

Burnett, W. R. 1899-1982 ....DLB-9

Burney, Fanny 1752-1840 ....DLB-39

Burns, Alan 1929- DLB-14

Burns, John Horne 1916-1953.............Y-85

Burnshaw, Stanley 1906- DLB-48

Burr, C. Chauncey 1815?-1883............DLB-79

Burroughs, Edgar Rice 1875-1950 ....DLB-8

Burroughs, John 1837-1921...............DLB-64

Burroughs, Margaret T. G. 1917- DLB-41

Burroughs, William S., Jr. 1947-1981....DLB-16

Burroughs, William Seward 1914-
    ....DLB-2, 8, 16; Y-81

Burroway, Janet 1936- DLB-6

Burt, A. L., and Company DLB-49

Burton, Miles (see Rhode, John)

Burton, Richard F. 1821-1890............DLB-55

Burton, Virginia Lee 1909-1968..........DLB-22

Burton, William Evans 1804-1860.........DLB-73

Busch, Frederick 1941- DLB-6

Busch, Niven 1903- DLB-44

Butler, E. H., and Company DLB-49

Butler, Juan 1942-1981 ....DLB-53

Butler, Octavia E. 1947- DLB-33

Butler, Samuel 1835-1902................DLB-18, 57

Butor, Michel 1926- DLB-83

Butterworth, Hezekiah 1839-1905.........DLB-42

B. V. (see Thomson, James)

Byars, Betsy 1928- DLB-52

Byatt, A. S. 1936- DLB-14

Byles, Mather 1707-1788.................DLB-24

Bynner, Witter 1881-1968................DLB-54

Byrd, William II 1674-1744..............DLB-24

Byrne, John Keyes (see Leonard, Hugh)

C

Cabell, James Branch 1879-1958..........DLB-9, 78

Cable, George Washington 1844-1925 ....DLB-12, 74

Cahan, Abraham 1860-1951.....................DLB-9, 25, 28

Cain, George 1943- DLB-33

Caldwell, Ben 1937- DLB-38

Caldwell, Erskine 1903-1987..................DLB-9

Caldwell, H. M., Company......................DLB-49

Calhoun, John C. 1782-1850 ....DLB-3

Calisher, Hortense 1911- DLB-2

Callaghan, Morley 1903- DLB-68

Callaloo..Y-87

Calmer, Edgar 1907- DLB-4

Calverley, C. S. 1831-1884 ....DLB-35

Calvert, George Henry 1803-1889 ....DLB-1, 64

Cambridge Press....................................DLB-49

Cameron, Eleanor 1912- DLB-52

Camm, John 1718-1778 ....DLB-31

Campbell, Gabrielle Margaret Vere
   (see Shearing, Joseph)

Campbell, James Edwin 1867-1896 ....DLB-50

Campbell, John 1653-1728 ....DLB-43

Campbell, John W., Jr. 1910-1971 ....DLB-8

Campbell, Roy 1901-1957 ....DLB-20

Campion, Thomas 1567-1620....................DLB-58

Camus, Albert 1913-1960 ....DLB-72

Candelaria, Cordelia 1943- DLB-82

Candelaria, Nash 1928- DLB-82

Candour in English Fiction (1890),
   by Thomas Hardy DLB-18

Cannan, Gilbert 1884-1955....................DLB-10

Cannell, Kathleen 1891-1974...................DLB-4

Cannell, Skipwith 1887-1957 ....DLB-45

Cantwell, Robert 1908-1978....................DLB-9

Cape, Jonathan, and Harrison Smith
   [publishing house] DLB-46

Capen, Joseph 1658-1725 ....DLB-24

Capote, Truman 1924-1984..................DLB-2; Y-80, 84

Cardinal, Marie 1929- DLB-83

Carey, Henry circa 1687-1689-1743 ....DLB-84

Carey, M., and Company DLB-49

Carey, Mathew 1760-1839 ....DLB-37, 73

Carey and Hart......................................DLB-49

Carlell, Lodowick 1602-1675 ....DLB-58

Carleton, G. W. [publishing house] DLB-49

Carossa, Hans 1878-1956........................DLB-66

Carr, Emily 1871-1945 ....DLB-68

Carrier, Roch 1937- DLB-53

Carlyle, Jane Welsh 1801-1866 ....DLB-55

Carlyle, Thomas 1795-1881 ....DLB-55

Carpenter, Stephen Cullen ?-1820?..................DLB-73

Carroll, Gladys Hasty 1904- DLB-9

Carroll, John 1735-1815...........................DLB-37

Carroll, Lewis 1832-1898 ....DLB-18

Carroll, Paul 1927- DLB-16

Carroll, Paul Vincent 1900-1968 ....DLB-10

Carroll and Graf Publishers DLB-46

Carruth, Hayden 1921- DLB-5

Carryl, Charles E. 1841-1920...........................DLB-42

Carswell, Catherine 1879-1946 ....DLB-36

Carter, Angela 1940- DLB-14

Carter, Henry (see Leslie, Frank)

Carter, Landon 1710-1778...........................DLB-31

Carter, Lin 1930- Y-81

Carter, Robert, and Brothers...........................DLB-49

Carter and Hendee................................DLB-49

Caruthers, William Alexander 1802-1846............DLB-3

Carver, Jonathan 1710-1780 ....DLB-31

Carver, Raymond 1938-1988 ....Y-84, 88

Cary, Joyce 1888-1957...........................DLB-15

Casey, Juanita 1925- DLB-14

Casey, Michael 1947- DLB-5

Cassady, Carolyn 1923- DLB-16

Cassady, Neal 1926-1968...........................DLB-16

Cassell Publishing Company DLB-49

Cassill, R. V. 1919- DLB-6

Castlemon, Harry (see Fosdick, Charles Austin)

Caswall, Edward 1814-1878 ....DLB-32

Cather, Willa 1873-1947.................DLB-9, 54, 78; DS-1

Catherwood, Mary Hartwell 1847-1902 ....DLB-78

Catton, Bruce 1899-1978...........................DLB-17

Causley, Charles 1917- DLB-27

Caute, David 1936- DLB-14

Cawein, Madison 1865-1914 ....DLB-54

The Caxton Printers, Limited.........................DLB-46

Cayrol, Jean 1911- DLB-83

Celan, Paul 1920-1970.........................DLB-69

Céline, Louis-Ferdinand 1894-1961 ....DLB-72

Center for the Book Research Y-84

Centlivre, Susanna 1669?-1723 ....DLB-84

The Century Company DLB-49

Cervantes, Lorna Dee 1954- DLB-82

Chacón, Eusebio 1869-1948 ....DLB-82

Chacón, Felipe Maximiliano
      1873-?..DLB-82

Challans, Eileen Mary (see Renault, Mary)

Chalmers, George 1742-1825............................DLB-30

Chamberlain, Samuel S. 1851-1916....................DLB-25

Chamberland, Paul 1939- DLB-60

Chamberlin, William Henry 1897-1969 ....DLB-29

Chambers, Charles Haddon 1860-1921 ....DLB-10

Chandler, Harry 1864-1944 ....DLB-29

Chandler, Raymond 1888-1959 ....DS-6

Channing, Edward 1856-1931 ....DLB-17

Channing, Edward Tyrrell 1790-1856 ....DLB-1, 59

Channing, William Ellery 1780-1842 ....DLB-1, 59

Channing, William Ellery II 1817-1901 ....DLB-1

Channing, William Henry 1810-1884 ....DLB-1, 59

Chaplin, Charlie 1889-1977 ....DLB-44

Chapman, George 1559 or 1560-1634 ....DLB-62

Chappell, Fred 1936- DLB-6

Charbonneau, Robert 1911-1967 ....DLB-68

Charles, Gerda 1914- DLB-14

Charles, William [publishing house]..................DLB-49

The Charles Wood Affair:
      A Playwright Revived Y-83

Charlotte Forten: Pages from her Diary............DLB-50

Charteris, Leslie 1907- DLB-77

Charyn, Jerome 1937- Y-83

Chase, Borden 1900-1971 ....DLB-26

Chase-Riboud, Barbara 1936- DLB-33

Chauncy, Charles 1705-1787 ....DLB-24

Chávez, Fray Angélico 1910- DLB-82

Chayefsky, Paddy 1923-1981 ....DLB-7, 44; Y-81

Cheever, Ezekiel 1615-1708 ....DLB-24

Cheever, George Barrell 1807-1890.................DLB-59

Cheever, John 1912-1982 ....DLB-2; Y-80, 82

Cheever, Susan 1943- Y-82

Chelsea House DLB-46

Cheney, Ednah Dow (Littlehale) 1824-1904 ....DLB-1

Cherry, Kelly 1940 ....Y-83

Cherryh, C. J. 1942- Y-80

Chesnutt, Charles Waddell 1858-1932...DLB-12, 50, 78

Chester, George Randolph 1869-1924 ....DLB-78

Chesterton, G. K. 1874-1936............DLB-10, 19, 34, 70

Cheyney, Edward P. 1861-1947.........................DLB-47

Chicano History...DLB-82

Chicano Language.......................................DLB-82

Child, Francis James 1825-1896 ....DLB-1, 64

Child, Lydia Maria 1802-1880........................DLB-1, 74

Child, Philip 1898-1978 ....DLB-68

Childers, Erskine 1870-1922............................DLB-70

Children's Book Awards and Prizes DLB-61

Childress, Alice 1920- DLB-7, 38

Childs, George W. 1829-1894............................DLB-23

Chilton Book Company...................................DLB-46

Chittenden, Hiram Martin 1858-1917...............DLB-47

Chivers, Thomas Holley 1809-1858 ....DLB-3

Chopin, Kate 1850-1904 ....DLB-12, 78

Choquette, Adrienne 1915-1973.....................DLB-68

Choquette, Robert 1905- DLB-68

The Christian Publishing Company DLB-49

Christie, Agatha 1890-1976 ....DLB-13, 77

Church, Benjamin 1734-1778...........................DLB-31

Church, Francis Pharcellus 1839-1906.............DLB-79

Church, William Conant 1836-1917.................DLB-79

Churchill, Caryl 1938- DLB-13

Ciardi, John 1916-1986...........................DLB-5; Y-86

Cibber, Colley 1671-1757................................DLB-84

City Lights Books DLB-46

Cixous, Hélène 1937- DLB-83

Clapper, Raymond 1892-1944 ....DLB-29

Clare, John 1793-1864 ....DLB-55

Clark, Alfred Alexander Gordon (see Hare, Cyril)

Clark, Ann Nolan 1896- DLB-52

Clark, C. M., Publishing Company DLB-46

Clark, Catherine Anthony 1892-1977 ....DLB-68

Clark, Charles Heber 1841-1915 ....DLB-11

Clark, Davis Wasgatt 1812-1871 ....DLB-79

Clark, Eleanor 1913- DLB-6

Clark, Lewis Gaylord 1808-1873 ....DLB-3, 64, 73

Clark, Walter Van Tilburg 1909-1971 ....DLB-9

Clarke, Austin 1896-1974 ....DLB-10, 20

Clarke, Austin C. 1934- DLB-53

Clarke, Gillian 1937- DLB-40

Clarke, James Freeman 1810-1888 ....DLB-1, 59

Clarke, Rebecca Sophia 1833-1906 ....DLB-42

Clarke, Robert, and Company DLB-49

Clausen, Andy 1943- DLB-16

Claxton, Remsen and Haffelfinger...................DLB-49

Clay, Cassius Marcellus 1810-1903 ....DLB-43

Cleary, Beverly 1916- DLB-52

Cleaver, Vera 1919-   and
          Cleaver, Bill 1920-1981.........................DLB-52

Cleland, John 1710-1789...................................DLB-39

Clemens, Samuel Langhorne
          1835-1910.............................DLB-11, 12, 23, 64, 74

Clement, Hal 1922- DLB-8

Clemo, Jack 1916- DLB-27

Clifton, Lucille 1936- DLB-5, 41

Clode, Edward J. [publishing house].................DLB-46

Clough, Arthur Hugh 1819-1861......................DLB-32

Cloutier, Cécile 1930- DLB-60

Coates, Robert M. 1897-1973 ....DLB-4, 9

Coatsworth, Elizabeth 1893- DLB-22

Cobb, Jr., Charles E. 1943- DLB-41

Cobb, Frank I. 1869-1923 ....DLB-25

Cobb, Irvin S. 1876-1944...........................DLB-11, 25

Cobbett, William 1762-1835 ....DLB-43

Cochran, Thomas C. 1902- DLB-17

Cochrane, Elizabeth 1867-1922 ....DLB-25

Cockerill, John A. 1845-1896............................DLB-23

Cocteau, Jean 1889-1963..................................DLB-65

Coffee, Lenore J. 1900?-1984 ....DLB-44

Coffin, Robert P. Tristram 1892-1955 ....DLB-45

Cogswell, Fred 1917- DLB-60

Cogswell, Mason Fitch 1761-1830 ....DLB-37

Cohen, Arthur A. 1928-1986............................DLB-28

Cohen, Leonard 1934- DLB-53

Cohen, Matt 1942- DLB-53

Colden, Cadwallader 1688-1776..................DLB-24, 30

Cole, Barry 1936- DLB-14

Colegate, Isabel 1931- DLB-14

Coleman, Emily Holmes 1899-1974 ....DLB-4

Coleridge, Mary 1861-1907...............................DLB-19

Colette 1873-1954..DLB-65

Colette, Sidonie Gabrielle (see Colette)

Collier, John 1901-1980 ....DLB-77

Collier, P. F. [publishing house] DLB-49

Collin and Small...DLB-49

Collins, Isaac [publishing house] DLB-49

Collins, Mortimer 1827-1876.......................DLB-21, 35

Collins, Wilkie 1824-1889.............................DLB-18, 70

Collyer, Mary 1716?-1763? DLB-39

Colman, Benjamin 1673-1747...........................DLB-24

Colman, S. [publishing house] DLB-49

Colombo, John Robert 1936- DLB-53

Colter, Cyrus 1910- DLB-33

Colum, Padraic 1881-1972 ....DLB-19

Colwin, Laurie 1944- Y-80

Comden, Betty 1919-   and Green,
          Adolph 1918- DLB-44

The Comic Tradition Continued
          [in the British Novel]...................................DLB-15

Commager, Henry Steele 1902- DLB-17

The Commercialization of the Image of
          Revolt, by Kenneth Rexroth DLB-16

Community and Commentators: Black
          Theatre and Its Critics................................DLB-38

Compton-Burnett, Ivy 1884?-1969....................DLB-36

Conference on Modern Biography........................Y-85

Congreve, William 1670-1729 ....DLB-39, 84

Conkey, W. B., Company....................................DLB-49

Connell, Evan S., Jr. 1924- DLB-2; Y-81

Connelly, Marc 1890-1980..........................DLB-7; Y-80

Connolly, James B. 1868-1957............................DLB-78

Connor, Tony 1930- DLB-40

Conquest, Robert 1917- DLB-27

Conrad, John, and Company...........................DLB-49

Conrad, Joseph 1857-1924 ....DLB-10, 34

Conroy, Jack 1899- Y-81

Conroy, Pat 1945- DLB-6

The Consolidation of Opinion: Critical
    Responses to the Modernists DLB-36

Constantine, David 1944- DLB-40

Contempo Caravan: Kites in a Windstorm Y-85

A Contemporary Flourescence of Chicano
    Literature Y-84

The Continental Publishing Company DLB-49

A Conversation with Chaim Potok...........................Y-84

Conversations with Publishers I: An Interview
    with Patrick O'Connor.....................................Y-84

Conway, Moncure Daniel 1832-1907....................DLB-1

Cook, David C., Publishing Company DLB-49

Cook, Ebenezer circa 1667-circa 1732...............DLB-24

Cook, Michael 1933- DLB-53

Cooke, George Willis 1848-1923 ....DLB-71

Cooke, Increase, and Company DLB-49

Cooke, John Esten 1830-1886.............................DLB-3

Cooke, Philip Pendleton 1816-1850 ....DLB-3, 59

Cooke, Rose Terry 1827-1892 ....DLB-12, 74

Coolbrith, Ina 1841-1928...................................DLB-54

Coolidge, George [publishing house] DLB-49

Coolidge, Susan (see Woolsey, Sarah Chauncy)

Cooper, Giles 1918-1966....................................DLB-13

Cooper, James Fenimore 1789-1851.....................DLB-3

Cooper, Kent 1880-1965....................................DLB-29

Coover, Robert 1932- DLB-2; Y-81

Copeland and Day...DLB-49

Coppel, Alfred 1921- Y-83

Coppola, Francis Ford 1939- DLB-44

Corcoran, Barbara 1911- DLB-52

Corelli, Marie 1855-1924 ....DLB-34

Corle, Edwin 1906-1956......................................Y-85

Corman, Cid 1924- DLB-5

Cormier, Robert 1925- DLB-52

Corn, Alfred 1943- Y-80

Cornish, Sam 1935- DLB-41

Corpi, Lucha 1945- DLB-82

Corrington, John William 1932- DLB-6

Corrothers, James D. 1869-1917 ....DLB-50

Corso, Gregory 1930- DLB-5, 16

Cortez, Jayne 1936- DLB-41

Corvo, Baron (see Rolfe, Frederick William)

Cory, William Johnson 1823-1892......................DLB-35

Cosmopolitan Book Corporation......................DLB-46

Costain, Thomas B. 1885-1965...........................DLB-9

Cotter, Joseph Seamon, Sr.
    1861-1949 ....DLB-50

Cotter, Joseph Seamon, Jr.
    1895-1919 ....DLB-50

Cotton, John 1584-1652 ....DLB-24

Coulter, John 1888-1980....................................DLB-68

Cournos, John 1881-1966 ....DLB-54

Coventry, Francis 1725-1754 ....DLB-39

Coverly, N. [publishing house] DLB-49

Covici-Friede...DLB-46

Coward, Noel 1899-1973 ....DLB-10

Coward, McCann and Geoghegan.....................DLB-46

Cowles, Gardner 1861-1946................................DLB-29

Cowley, Malcolm 1898-1989.................DLB-4, 48; Y-81

Cox, A. B. (see Berkeley, Anthony)

Cox, Palmer 1840-1924 ....DLB-42

Coxe, Louis 1918- DLB-5

Coxe, Tench 1755-1824.....................................DLB-37

Cozzens, James Gould 1903-1978 ....DLB-9; Y-84; DS-2

Craddock, Charles Egbert (see Murfree, Mary N.)

Cradock, Thomas 1718-1770.............................DLB-31

Craig, Daniel H. 1811-1895 ....DLB-43

Craik, Dinah Maria 1826-1887 ....DLB-35

Cranch, Christopher Pearse 1813-1892..........DLB-1, 42

Crane, Hart 1899-1932 ....DLB-4, 48

Crane, R. S. 1886-1967 ....DLB-63

Crane, Stephen 1871-1900 ....DLB-12, 54, 78

Crapsey, Adelaide 1878-1914 ....DLB-54

Craven, Avery 1885-1980....................................DLB-17

Crawford, Charles 1752-circa 1815 ....DLB-31

Crawford, F. Marion 1854-1909.........................DLB-71

Crawley, Alan 1887-1975 ....DLB-68

Crayon, Geoffrey (see Irving, Washington)

Creasey, John 1908-1973 ....DLB-77

Creative Age Press...DLB-46

Creel, George 1876-1953 ....DLB-25

Creeley, Robert 1926- DLB-5, 16

Creelman, James 1859-1915 ....DLB-23

Cregan, David 1931- DLB-13

Crèvecoeur, Michel Guillaume Jean de
    1735-1813 ....DLB-37

Crews, Harry 1935- DLB-6

Crichton, Michael 1942- Y-81

A Crisis of Culture: The Changing Role
    of Religion in the New Republic DLB-37

Cristofer, Michael 1946- DLB-7

"The Critic as Artist" (1891), by Oscar Wilde....DLB-57

Criticism In Relation To Novels (1863),
    by G. H. Lewes DLB-21

Crockett, David (Davy) 1786-1836.................DLB-3, 11

Croft-Cooke, Rupert (see Bruce, Leo)

Crofts, Freeman Wills 1879-1957 ....DLB-77

Croly, Jane Cunningham 1829-1901 ....DLB-23

Crosby, Caresse 1892-1970 ....DLB-48

Crosby, Caresse 1892-1970 and Crosby,
    Harry 1898-1929 ....DLB-4

Crosby, Harry 1898-1929.....................................DLB-48

Crossley-Holland, Kevin 1941- DLB-40

Crothers, Rachel 1878-1958..................................DLB-7

Crowell, Thomas Y., Company...........................DLB-49

Crowley, John 1942- Y-82

Crowley, Mart 1935- DLB-7

Crown Publishers...DLB-46

Crowne, John 1641-1712 ....DLB-80

Croy, Homer 1883-1965 ....DLB-4

Crumley, James 1939- Y-84

Cruz, Victor Hernández 1949- DLB-41

Csokor, Franz Theodor 1885-1969 ....DLB-81

Cullen, Countee 1903-1946.....................DLB-4, 48, 51

Culler, Jonathan D. 1944- DLB-67

The Cult of Biography
    Excerpts from the Second Folio Debate:
      "Biographies are generally a disease of
      English Literature"–Germaine Greer,
      Victoria Glendinning, Auberon Waugh,
      and Richard Holmes........................Y-86

Cummings, E. E. 1894-1962 ....DLB-4, 48

Cummings, Ray 1887-1957 ....DLB-8

Cummings and Hilliard DLB-49

Cummins, Maria Susanna 1827-1866.................DLB-42

Cuney, Waring 1906-1976...................................DLB-51

Cuney-Hare, Maude 1874-1936..........................DLB-52

Cunningham, J. V. 1911- DLB-5

Cunningham, Peter F. [publishing house]..........DLB-49

Cuomo, George 1929- Y-80

Cupples and Leon DLB-46

Cupples, Upham and Company..........................DLB-49

Cuppy, Will 1884-1949 ....DLB-11

Currie, Mary Montgomerie Lamb Singleton,
    Lady Currie (see Fane, Violet)

Curti, Merle E. 1897- DLB-17

Curtis, George William 1824-1892 ....DLB-1, 43

D

D. M. Thomas: The Plagiarism Controversy Y-82

Dabit, Eugène 1898-1936....................................DLB-65

Daborne, Robert circa 1580-1628.......................DLB-58

Daggett, Rollin M. 1831-1901............................DLB-79

Dahlberg, Edward 1900-1977 ....DLB-48

Dale, Peter 1938- DLB-40

Dall, Caroline Wells (Healey) 1822-1912..............DLB-1

Dallas, E. S. 1828-1879..DLB-55

The Dallas Theater Center DLB-7

D'Alton, Louis 1900-1951 ....DLB-10

Daly, T. A. 1871-1948..DLB-11

Damon, S. Foster 1893-1971 ....DLB-45

Damrell, William S. [publishing house]..............DLB-49

Dana, Charles A. 1819-1897 ....DLB-3, 23

Dana, Richard Henry, Jr. 1815-1882 ....DLB-1

Dandridge, Ray Garfield DLB-51

Dane, Clemence 1887-1965.................................DLB-10

Danforth, John 1660-1730 ....DLB-24

Danforth, Samuel I 1626-1674 ....DLB-24

Danforth, Samuel II 1666-1727..........................DLB-24

Dangerous Years: London Theater,

1939-1945 ....DLB-10

Daniel, John M. 1825-1865 ....DLB-43

Daniel, Samuel 1562 or 1563-1619....................DLB-62

Daniells, Roy 1902-1979........................DLB-68

Daniels, Josephus 1862-1948 ....DLB-29

Danner, Margaret Esse 1915- DLB-41

Darwin, Charles 1809-1882........................DLB-57

Daryush, Elizabeth 1887-1977 ....DLB-20

Dashwood, Edmée Elizabeth Monica
    de la Pasture (see Delafield, E. M.)

d'Aulaire, Edgar Parin 1898- and
    d'Aulaire, Ingri 1904- DLB-22

Davenant, Sir William 1606-1668.................DLB-58

Davenport, Robert ?-? DLB-58

Daves, Delmer 1904-1977 ....DLB-26

Davey, Frank 1940- DLB-53

Davidson, Avram 1923- DLB-8

Davidson, Donald 1893-1968....................DLB-45

Davidson, John 1857-1909 ....DLB-19

Davidson, Lionel 1922- DLB-14

Davie, Donald 1922- DLB-27

Davies, Robertson 1913- DLB-68

Davies, Samuel 1723-1761.....................DLB-31

Davies, W. H. 1871-1940.......................DLB-19

Daviot, Gordon 1896?-1952 ....DLB-10
    (see also Tey, Josephine)

Davis, Charles A. 1795-1867 ....DLB-11

Davis, Clyde Brion 1894-1962....................DLB-9

Davis, Dick 1945- DLB-40

Davis, Frank Marshall 1905-? DLB-51

Davis, H. L. 1894-1960........................DLB-9

Davis, John 1774-1854 ....DLB-37

Davis, Margaret Thomson 1926- DLB-14

Davis, Ossie 1917- DLB-7, 38

Davis, Rebecca Harding 1831-1910.................DLB-74

Davis, Richard Harding 1864-1916 ....DLB-12,
    23, 78, 79

Davis, Samuel Cole 1764-1809........................DLB-37

Davison, Peter 1928- DLB-5

Davys, Mary 1674-1732........................DLB-39

DAW Books DLB-46

Dawson, William 1704-1752....................DLB-31

Day, Benjamin Henry 1810-1889 ....DLB-43

Day, Clarence 1874-1935 ....DLB-11

Day, Dorothy 1897-1980 ....DLB-29

Day, John circa 1574-circa 1640 ....DLB-62

Day, The John, Company DLB-46

Day Lewis, C. 1904-1972....................DLB-15, 20
    (see also Blake, Nicholas)

Day, Mahlon [publishing house] DLB-49

Day, Thomas 1748-1789 ....DLB-39

Deacon, William Arthur 1890-1977 ....DLB-68

Deal, Borden 1922-1985 ....DLB-6

de Angeli, Marguerite 1889-1987....................DLB-22

De Bow, James Dunwoody Brownson
    1820-1867 ....DLB-3, 79

de Bruyn, Günter 1926- DLB-75

de Camp, L. Sprague 1907- DLB-8

The Decay of Lying (1889),
    by Oscar Wilde [excerpt]...............DLB-18

Dedication, *Ferdinand Count Fathom* (1753),
    by Tobias Smollett DLB-39

Dedication, *Lasselia* (1723), by Eliza
    Haywood [excerpt] DLB-39

Dedication, *The History of Pompey the
    Little* (1751), by Francis Coventry DLB-39

Dedication, *The Wanderer* (1814),
    by Fanny Burney DLB-39

Defense of *Amelia* (1752), by Henry Fielding.....DLB-39

Defoe, Daniel 1660-1731.......................DLB-39

de Fontaine, Felix Gregory 1834-1896 ....DLB-43

De Forest, John William 1826-1906....................DLB-12

de Graff, Robert 1895-1981.......................Y-81

DeJong, Meindert 1906- DLB-52

Dekker, Thomas circa 1572-1632 ....DLB-62

Delafield, E. M. 1890-1943 ....DLB-34

de la Mare, Walter 1873-1956.....................DLB-19

Deland, Margaret 1857-1945 ....DLB-78

Delaney, Shelagh 1939- DLB-13

Delany, Martin Robinson 1812-1885................DLB-50

Delany, Samuel R. 1942- DLB-8, 33

de la Roche, Mazo 1879-1961 ....DLB-68

Delbanco, Nicholas 1942- DLB-6

De León, Nephtalí 1945- DLB-82

Delgado, Abelardo Barrientos 1931- DLB-82

DeLillo, Don 1936- DLB-6

Dell, Floyd 1887-1969 ....DLB-9

Dell Publishing Company......................DLB-46

delle Grazie, Marie Eugene 1864-1931 ....DLB-81

del Rey, Lester 1915- DLB-8

de Man, Paul 1919-1983 ....DLB-67

Demby, William 1922- DLB-33

Deming, Philander 1829-1915 ....DLB-74

Demorest, William Jennings 1822-1895 ....DLB-79

Denham, Sir John 1615-1669 ....DLB-58

Denison, T. S., and Company......................DLB-49

Dennie, Joseph 1768-1812................DLB-37, 43, 59, 73

Dennis, Nigel 1912- DLB-13, 15

Dent, Tom 1932- DLB-38

Denton, Daniel circa 1626-1703......................DLB-24

DePaola, Tomie 1934- DLB-61

Derby, George Horatio 1823-1861 ....DLB-11

Derby, J. C., and Company......................DLB-49

Derby and Miller DLB-49

Derleth, August 1909-1971 ....DLB-9

The Derrydale Press......................DLB-46

Desbiens, Jean-Paul 1927- DLB-53

des Forêts, Louis-René 1918- DLB-83

DesRochers, Alfred 1901-1978 ....DLB-68

Desrosiers, Léo-Paul 1896-1967......................DLB-68

Destouches, Louis-Ferdinand (see Céline,
    Louis-Ferdinand)

De Tabley, Lord 1835-1895 ....DLB-35

Deutsch, Babette 1895-1982 ....DLB-45

Deveaux, Alexis 1948- DLB-38

The Development of Lighting in the Staging
    of Drama, 1900-1945 [in Great Britain]......DLB-10

de Vere, Aubrey 1814-1902 ....DLB-35

The Devin-Adair Company......................DLB-46

De Voto, Bernard 1897-1955 ....DLB-9

De Vries, Peter 1910- DLB-6; Y-82

Dewdney, Christopher 1951- DLB-60

Dewdney, Selwyn 1909-1979 ....DLB-68

DeWitt, Robert M., Publisher DLB-49

DeWolfe, Fiske and Company......................DLB-49

de Young, M. H. 1849-1925......................DLB-25

The Dial Press......................DLB-46

Diamond, I. A. L. 1920-1988 ....DLB-26

Di Cicco, Pier Giorgio 1949- DLB-60

Dick, Philip K. 1928- DLB-8

Dick and Fitzgerald DLB-49

Dickens, Charles 1812-1870................DLB-21, 55, 70

Dickey, James 1923- DLB-5; Y-82

Dickey, William 1928- DLB-5

Dickinson, Emily 1830-1886 ....DLB-1

Dickinson, John 1732-1808......................DLB-31

Dickinson, Jonathan 1688-1747......................DLB-24

Dickinson, Patric 1914- DLB-27

Dickson, Gordon R. 1923- DLB-8

Didion, Joan 1934- DLB-2; Y-81, 86

Di Donato, Pietro 1911- DLB-9

Dillard, Annie 1945- Y-80

Dillard, R. H. W. 1937- DLB-5

Dillingham, Charles T., Company......................DLB-49

The G. W. Dillingham Company......................DLB-49

Dintenfass, Mark 1941- Y-84

Diogenes, Jr. (see Brougham, John)

DiPrima, Diane 1934- DLB-5, 16

Disch, Thomas M. 1940- DLB-8

Disney, Walt 1901-1966......................DLB-22

Disraeli, Benjamin 1804-1881......................DLB-21, 55

Ditzen, Rudolf (see Fallada, Hans)

Dix, Dorothea Lynde 1802-1887 ....DLB-1

Dix, Dorothy (see Gilmer, Elizabeth Meriwether)

Dix, Edwards and Company DLB-49

Dixon, Paige (see Corcoran, Barbara)

Dixon, Richard Watson 1833-1900......................DLB-19

Dobell, Sydney 1824-1874......................DLB-32

Döblin, Alfred 1878-1957 ....DLB-66

Dobson, Austin 1840-1921 ....DLB-35

Doctorow, E. L. 1931- DLB-2, 28; Y-80

Dodd, William E. 1869-1940 ....DLB-17

Dodd, Mead and Company......................DLB-49

Dodge, B. W., and Company......................DLB-46

Dodge, Mary Mapes 1831?-1905 ....DLB-42, 79

Dodge Publishing Company DLB-49

Dodgson, Charles Lutwidge (see Carroll, Lewis)

Dodson, Owen 1914-1983 ....DLB-76

Doesticks, Q. K. Philander, P. B. (see Thomson, Mortimer)

Donahoe, Patrick [publishing house]................DLB-49

Donald, David H. 1920- DLB-17

Donleavy, J. P. 1926- DLB-6

Donnadieu, Marguerite (see Duras, Marguerite)

Donnelley, R. R., and Sons Company DLB-49

Donnelly, Ignatius 1831-1901 ....DLB-12

Donohue and Henneberry.................................DLB-49

Doolady, M. [publishing house]........................DLB-49

Dooley, Ebon (see Ebon)

Doolittle, Hilda 1886-1961............................DLB-4, 45

Doran, George H., Company............................DLB-46

Dorgelès, Roland 1886-1973 ....DLB-65

Dorn, Edward 1929- DLB-5

Dorr, Rheta Childe 1866-1948 ....DLB-25

Dorst, Tankred 1925- DLB-75

Dos Passos, John 1896-1970 ....DLB-4, 9; DS-1

Doubleday and Company...................................DLB-49

Doughty, Charles M. 1843-1926................DLB-19, 57

Douglas, Keith 1920-1944 ....DLB-27

Douglas, Norman 1868-1952 ....DLB-34

Douglass, Frederick 1817?-1895.........DLB-1, 43, 50, 79

Douglass, William circa 1691-1752 ....DLB-24

Dover Publications..DLB-46

Dowden, Edward 1843-1913............................DLB-35

Downing, J., Major (see Davis, Charles A.)

Downing, Major Jack (see Smith, Seba)

Dowson, Ernest 1867-1900.............................DLB-19

Doxey, William [publishing house]....................DLB-49

Doyle, Sir Arthur Conan 1859-1930 ....DLB-18, 70

Doyle, Kirby 1932- DLB-16

Drabble, Margaret 1939- DLB-14

The Dramatic Publishing Company DLB-49

Dramatists Play Service.....................................DLB-46

Draper, John W. 1811-1882.............................DLB-30

Draper, Lyman C. 1815-1891 ....DLB-30

Dreiser, Theodore 1871-1945 ....DLB-9, 12; DS-1

Drewitz, Ingeborg 1923-1986 ....DLB-75

Drieu La Rochelle, Pierre 1893-1945 ....DLB-72

Drinkwater, John 1882-1937 ....DLB-10, 19

The Drue Heinz Literature Prize
    Excerpt from "Excerpts from a Report
      of the Commission," in David
      Bosworth's *The Death of Descartes*
    An Interview with David Bosworth Y-82

Dryden, John 1631-1700.................................DLB-80

Duane, William 1760-1835................................DLB-43

Dubé, Marcel 1930- DLB-53

Dubé, Rodolphe (see Hertel, François)

Du Bois, W. E. B. 1868-1963.......................DLB-47, 50

Du Bois, William Pène 1916- DLB-61

Ducharme, Réjean 1941- DLB-60

Duell, Sloan and Pearce DLB-46

Duffield and Green DLB-46

Duffy, Maureen 1933- DLB-14

Dugan, Alan 1923- DLB-5

Duhamel, Georges 1884-1966...........................DLB-65

Dukes, Ashley 1885-1959 ....DLB-10

Dumas, Henry 1934-1968 ....DLB-41

Dunbar, Paul Laurence 1872-1906 ....DLB-50, 54, 78

Duncan, Robert 1919-1988 ....DLB-5, 16

Duncan, Ronald 1914-1982..............................DLB-13

Dunigan, Edward, and Brother DLB-49

Dunlap, John 1747-1812 ....DLB-43

Dunlap, William 1766-1839..................DLB-30, 37, 59

Dunn, Douglas 1942- DLB-40

Dunne, Finley Peter 1867-1936 ....DLB-11, 23

Dunne, John Gregory 1932- Y-80

Dunne, Philip 1908- DLB-26

Dunning, Ralph Cheever 1878-1930....................DLB-4

Dunning, William A. 1857-1922.......................DLB-17

Plunkett, Edward John Moreton Drax,
    Lord Dunsany 1878-1957 ....DLB-10, 77

Durand, Lucile (see Bersianik, Louky)

Duranty, Walter 1884-1957................................DLB-29

Duras, Marguerite 1914- DLB-83

Durfey, Thomas 1653-1723 ....DLB-80

Durrell, Lawrence 1912- DLB-15, 27

Durrell, William [publishing house]..................DLB-49

Dürrenmatt, Friedrich 1921- DLB-69

Cumulative Index

Dutton, E. P., and Company..........................DLB-49

Duvoisin, Roger 1904-1980.........................DLB-61

Duyckinck, Evert Augustus 1816-1878..........DLB-3, 64

Duyckinck, George L. 1823-1863 ....DLB-3

Duyckinck and Company DLB-49

Dwight, John Sullivan 1813-1893 ....DLB-1

Dwight, Timothy 1752-1817 ....DLB-37

Dyer, Charles 1928- DLB-13

Dylan, Bob 1941- DLB-16

E

Eager, Edward 1911-1964..............................DLB-22

Earle, James H., and Company DLB-49

Early American Book Illustration,
    by Sinclair Hamilton DLB-49

Eastlake, William 1917- DLB-6

Eastman, Carol ?- DLB-44

Eberhart, Richard 1904- DLB-48

Ebner-Eschenbach, Marie von
    1830-1916 ....DLB-81

Ebon 1942- DLB-41

Ecco Press...DLB-46

Edes, Benjamin 1732-1803...........................DLB-43

Edgar, David 1948- DLB-13

The Editor Publishing Company DLB-49

Edmonds, Randolph 1900- DLB-51

Edmonds, Walter D. 1903- DLB-9

Edschmid, Kasimir 1890-1966 ....DLB-56

Edwards, Jonathan 1703-1758 ....DLB-24

Edwards, Jonathan, Jr. 1745-1801 ....DLB-37

Edwards, Junius 1929- DLB-33

Edwards, Richard 1524-1566 ....DLB-62

Effinger, George Alec 1947- DLB-8

Eggleston, Edward 1837-1902 ....DLB-12

Ehrenstein, Albert 1886-1950 ....DLB-81

Eich, Günter 1907-1972 ....DLB-69

1873 Publishers' Catalogues...........................DLB-49

Eighteenth-Century Aesthetic Theories...........DLB-31

Eighteenth-Century Philosophical
    Background DLB-31

Eigner, Larry 1927- DLB-5

Eisner, Kurt 1867-1919.................................DLB-66

Eklund, Gordon 1945- Y-83

Elder, Lonne III 1931- DLB-7, 38, 44

Elder, Paul, and Company DLB-49

Elements of Rhetoric (1828; revised, 1846),
    by Richard Whately [excerpt] DLB-57

Eliot, George 1819-1880 ....DLB-21, 35, 55

Eliot, John 1604-1690..................................DLB-24

Eliot, T. S. 1888-1965 ....DLB-7, 10, 45, 63

Elizondo, Sergio 1930- DLB-82

Elkin, Stanley 1930- DLB-2, 28; Y-80

Elles, Dora Amy (see Wentworth, Patricia)

Ellet, Elizabeth F. 1818?-1877......................DLB-30

Elliott, George 1923- DLB-68

Elliott, Janice 1931- DLB-14

Elliott, William 1788-1863 ....DLB-3

Elliott, Thomes and Talbot DLB-49

Ellis, Edward S. 1840-1916 ....DLB-42

The George H. Ellis Company DLB-49

Ellison, Harlan 1934- DLB-8

Ellison, Ralph 1914- DLB-2, 76

Ellmann, Richard 1918-1987 ....Y-87

The Elmer Holmes Bobst Awards
    in Arts and Letters Y-87

Emanuel, James Andrew 1921- DLB-41

Emerson, Ralph Waldo 1803-1882..........DLB-1, 59, 73

Emerson, William 1769-1811 ....DLB-37

Empson, William 1906-1984 ....DLB-20

The End of English Stage Censorship,
    1945-1968 ....DLB-13

Ende, Michael 1929- DLB-75

Engel, Marian 1933-1985 ....DLB-53

Engle, Paul 1908- DLB-48

English Composition and Rhetoric (1866),
    by Alexander Bain [excerpt]......................DLB-57

The English Renaissance of Art (1908),
    by Oscar Wilde DLB-35

Enright, D. J. 1920- DLB-27

Enright, Elizabeth 1909-1968 ....DLB-22

L'Envoi (1882), by Oscar Wilde DLB-35

Epps, Bernard 1936- DLB-53

Epstein, Julius 1909- and
  Epstein, Philip 1909-1952 ....DLB-26

Equiano, Olaudah circa 1745-1797 ....DLB-37, 50

Ernst, Paul 1866-1933 ....DLB-66

Erskine, John 1879-1951 ....DLB-9

Ervine, St. John Greer 1883-1971 ....DLB-10

Eshleman, Clayton 1935- DLB-5

Ess Ess Publishing Company DLB-49

Essay on Chatterton (1842),
  by Robert Browning DLB-32

Estes, Eleanor 1906-1988 ....DLB-22

Estes and Lauriat...DLB-49

Etherege, George 1636-circa 1692.....................DLB-80

Ets, Marie Hall 1893- DLB-22

Eudora Welty: Eye of the Storyteller.....................Y-87

Eugene O'Neill Memorial Theater Center...........DLB-7

Eugene O'Neill's Letters: A Review........................Y-88

Evans, Donald 1884-1921...................................DLB-54

Evans, George Henry 1805-1856........................DLB-43

Evans, M., and Company DLB-46

Evans, Mari 1923- DLB-41

Evans, Mary Ann (see Eliot, George)

Evans, Nathaniel 1742-1767...............................DLB-31

Evans, Sebastian 1830-1909 ....DLB-35

Everett, Alexander Hill 1790-1847.....................DLB-59

Everett, Edward 1794-1865 ....DLB-1, 59

Everson, William 1912- DLB-5, 16

Every Man His Own Poet; or, The
  Inspired Singer's Recipe Book (1877),
  by W. H. Mallock DLB-35

Ewart, Gavin 1916- DLB-40

Ewing, Juliana Horatia 1841-1885.....................DLB-21

Exley, Frederick 1929- Y-81

Experiment in the Novel (1929),
  by John D. Beresford DLB-36

F

"F. Scott Fitzgerald: St. Paul's Native Son
  and Distinguished American Writer":
  University of Minnesota Conference,
  29-31 October 1982...Y-82

Faber, Frederick William 1814-1863 ....DLB-32

Fair, Ronald L. 1932- DLB-33

Fairfax, Beatrice (see Manning, Marie)

Fairlie, Gerard 1899-1983 ....DLB-77

Fallada, Hans 1893-1947....................................DLB-56

Fancher, Betsy 1928- Y-83

Fane, Violet 1843-1905.......................................DLB-35

Fantasy Press Publishers DLB-46

Fante, John 1909-1983..Y-83

Farber, Norma 1909-1984...................................DLB-61

Farigoule, Louis (see Romains, Jules)

Farley, Walter 1920- DLB-22

Farmer, Philip José 1918- DLB-8

Farquhar, George circa 1677-1707 ....DLB-84

Farquharson, Martha (see Finley, Martha)

Farrar and Rinehart..DLB-46

Farrar, Straus and Giroux...................................DLB-46

Farrell, James T. 1904-1979 ....DLB-4, 9; DS-2

Farrell, J. G. 1935-1979......................................DLB-14

Fast, Howard 1914- DLB-9

Faulkner, William 1897-1962
  ....DLB-9, 11, 44; DS-2; Y-86

Fauset, Jessie Redmon 1882-1961 ....DLB-51

Faust, Irvin 1924- DLB-2, 28; Y-80

Fawcett Books DLB-46

Fearing, Kenneth 1902-1961..............................DLB-9

Federal Writers' Project.....................................DLB-46

Federman, Raymond 1928- Y-80

Feiffer, Jules 1929- DLB-7, 44

Feinberg, Charles E. 1899-1988 ....Y-88

Feinstein, Elaine 1930- DLB-14, 40

Fell, Frederick, Publishers.................................DLB-46

Fels, Ludwig 1946- DLB-75

Felton, Cornelius Conway 1807-1862 ....DLB-1

Fennario, David 1947- DLB-60

Fenno, John 1751-1798 ....DLB-43

Fenno, R. F., and Company DLB-49

Fenton, James 1949- DLB-40

Ferber, Edna 1885-1968.................................DLB-9, 28

Ferdinand, Vallery III (see Salaam, Kalamu ya)

Ferguson, Sir Samuel 1810-1886 ....DLB-32

Ferguson, William Scott 1875-1954 ....DLB-47

Ferlinghetti, Lawrence 1919- DLB-5, 16

Fern, Fanny (see Parton, Sara
Payson Willis)

Ferret, E., and Company.....................................DLB-49

Ferrini, Vincent 1913- DLB-48

Ferron, Jacques 1921-1985.............................DLB-60

Ferron, Madeleine 1922- DLB-53

Fetridge and Company......................................DLB-49

Feuchtwanger, Lion 1884-1958.........................DLB-66

Ficke, Arthur Davison 1883-1945......................DLB-54

Fiction Best-Sellers, 1910-1945.........................DLB-9

Fiction into Film, 1928-1975: A List of Movies
Based on the Works of Authors in
British Novelists, 1930-1959 ....DLB-15

Fiedler, Leslie A. 1917- DLB-28, 67

Field, Eugene 1850-1895 ....DLB-23, 42

Field, Nathan 1587-1619 or 1620.......................DLB-58

Field, Rachel 1894-1942....................................DLB-9, 22

A Field Guide to Recent Schools of
American Poetry.....................................Y-86

Fielding, Henry 1707-1754...........................DLB-39, 84

Fielding, Sarah 1710-1768 ....DLB-39

Fields, James Thomas 1817-1881 ....DLB-1

Fields, Julia 1938- DLB-41

Fields, W. C. 1880-1946 ....DLB-44

Fields, Osgood and Company.............................DLB-49

Fifty Penguin Years...Y-85

Figes, Eva 1932- DLB-14

Filson, John circa 1753-1788.............................DLB-37

Findley, Timothy 1930- DLB-53

Finlay, Ian Hamilton 1925- DLB-40

Finley, Martha 1828-1909 ....DLB-42

Finney, Jack 1911- DLB-8

Finney, Walter Braden (see Finney, Jack)

Firbank, Ronald 1886-1926...............................DLB-36

Firmin, Giles 1615-1697....................................DLB-24

First Strauss "Livings" Awarded to Cynthia
Ozick and Raymond Carver
An Interview with Cynthia Ozick
An Interview with Raymond Carver Y-83

Fish, Stanley 1938- DLB-67

Fisher, Clay (see Allen, Henry W.)

Fisher, Dorothy Canfield 1879-1958 ....DLB-9

Fisher, Leonard Everett 1924- DLB-61

Fisher, Roy 1930- DLB-40

Fisher, Rudolph 1897-1934...............................DLB-51

Fisher, Sydney George 1856-1927 ....DLB-47

Fisher, Vardis 1895-1968...................................DLB-9

Fiske, John 1608-1677......................................DLB-24

Fiske, John 1842-1901..................................DLB-47, 64

Fitch, Thomas circa 1700-1774.........................DLB-31

Fitch, William Clyde 1865-1909.........................DLB-7

FitzGerald, Edward 1809-1883 ....DLB-32

Fitzgerald, F. Scott 1896-1940......DLB-4, 9; Y-81; DS-1

Fitzgerald, Penelope 1916- DLB-14

Fitzgerald, Robert 1910-1985...........................Y-80

Fitzgerald, Thomas 1819-1891 ....DLB-23

Fitzgerald, Zelda Sayre 1900-1948..........................Y-84

Fitzhugh, Louise 1928-1974...............................DLB-52

Fitzhugh, William circa 1651-1701......................DLB-24

Flanagan, Thomas 1923- Y-80

Flanner, Hildegarde 1899-1987.........................DLB-48

Flanner, Janet 1892-1978...................................DLB-4

Flavin, Martin 1883-1967...................................DLB-9

Flecker, James Elroy 1884-1915 ....DLB-10, 19

Fleeson, Doris 1901-1970..................................DLB-29

Flei;dser, Marieluise 1901-1974.........................DLB-56

The Fleshly School of Poetry and Other
Phenomena of the Day (1872), by Robert
Buchanan...DLB-35

The Fleshly School of Poetry: Mr. D. G.
Rossetti (1871), by Thomas Maitland
(Robert Buchanan) DLB-35

Fletcher, J. S. 1863-1935...................................DLB-70

Fletcher, John (see Beaumont, Francis)

Fletcher, John Gould 1886-1950 ....DLB-4, 45

Flieg, Helmut (see Heym, Stefan)

Flint, F. S. 1885-1960 ....DLB-19

Flint, Timothy 1780-1840 ....DLB-73

Follen, Eliza Lee (Cabot) 1787-1860.....................DLB-1

Follett, Ken 1949- Y-81

Follett Publishing Company DLB-46

Folsom, John West [publishing house]...............DLB-49

Foote, Horton 1916- DLB-26

Foote, Shelby 1916- DLB-2, 17

Forbes, Calvin 1945- DLB-41

Forbes, Ester 1891-1967 ....DLB-22

Forbes and Company.......................DLB-49

Force, Peter 1790-1868 ....DLB-30

Forché, Carolyn 1950- DLB-5

Ford, Charles Henri 1913- DLB-4, 48

Ford, Corey 1902-1969....................DLB-11

Ford, Ford Madox 1873-1939 ....DLB-34

Ford, J. B., and Company DLB-49

Ford, Jesse Hill 1928- DLB-6

Ford, John 1586-? DLB-58

Ford, Worthington C. 1858-1941 ....DLB-47

Fords, Howard, and Hulbert DLB-49

Foreman, Carl 1914-1984.................DLB-26

Forester, Frank (see Herbert, Henry William)

Fornés, María Irene 1930- DLB-7

Forrest, Leon 1937- DLB-33

Forster, E. M. 1879-1970..................DLB-34

Forten, Charlotte L. 1837-1914.........DLB-50

Fortune, T. Thomas 1856-1928 ....DLB-23

Fosdick, Charles Austin 1842-1915.....DLB-42

Foster, Genevieve 1893-1979............DLB-61

Foster, Hannah Webster 1758-1840....DLB-37

Foster, John 1648-1681 ....DLB-24

Foster, Michael 1904-1956................DLB-9

Four Essays on the Beat Generation,
    by John Clellon Holmes..............DLB-16

Four Seas Company.........................DLB-46

Four Winds Press............................DLB-46

Fournier, Henri Alban (see Alain-Fournier)

Fowler and Wells Company...............DLB-49

Fowles, John 1926- DLB-14

Fox, John, Jr. 1862 or 1863-1919 ......DLB-9

Fox, Paula 1923- DLB-52

Fox, Richard K. [publishing house] DLB-49

Fox, Richard Kyle 1846-1922............DLB-79

Fox, William Price 1926- DLB-2; Y-81

Fraenkel, Michael 1896-1957 ....DLB-4

France, Richard 1938- DLB-7

Francis, C. S. [publishing house] DLB-49

Francis, Convers 1795-1863..............DLB-1

Francke, Kuno 1855-1930.................DLB-71

Frank, Leonhard 1882-1961 ....DLB-56

Frank, Melvin (see Panama, Norman)

Frank, Waldo 1889-1967..................DLB-9, 63

Franken, Rose 1895?-1988 ....Y-84

Franklin, Benjamin 1706-1790..........DLB-24, 43, 73

Franklin, James 1697-1735 ....DLB-43

Franklin Library DLB-46

Frantz, Ralph Jules 1902-1979..........DLB-4

Fraser, G. S. 1915-1980...................DLB-27

Frayn, Michael 1933- DLB-13, 14

Frederic, Harold 1856-1898 ....DLB-12, 23

Freeman, Douglas Southall 1886-1953..........DLB-17

Freeman, Legh Richmond 1842-1915 ....DLB-23

Freeman, Mary E. Wilkins 1852-1930..........DLB-12, 78

Freeman, R. Austin 1862-1943 ....DLB-70

French, Alice 1850-1934 ....DLB-74

French, David 1939- DLB-53

French, James [publishing house].......DLB-49

French, Samuel [publishing house] DLB-49

Freneau, Philip 1752-1832................DLB-37, 43

Friedman, Bruce Jay 1930- DLB-2, 28

Friel, Brian 1929- DLB-13

Friend, Krebs 1895?-1967? DLB-4

Fries, Fritz Rudolf 1935- DLB-75

Fringe and Alternative Theater
    in Great Britain.........................DLB-13

Frisch, Max 1911- DLB-69

Fritz, Jean 1915- DLB-52

Frost, Robert 1874-1963 ....DLB-54

Frothingham, Octavius Brooks 1822-1895..........DLB-1

Froude, James Anthony 1818-1894..........DLB-18, 57

Fry, Christopher 1907- DLB-13

Frye, Northrop 1912- DLB-67, 68

Fuchs, Daniel 1909- DLB-9, 26, 28

The Fugitives and the Agrarians:
    The First Exhibition Y-85

Fuller, Charles H., Jr. 1939- DLB-38

Fuller, Henry Blake 1857-1929 ....DLB-12

Fuller, John 1937- DLB-40

Fuller, Roy 1912- DLB-15, 20

Fuller, Samuel 1912- DLB-26

Fuller, Sarah Margaret, Marchesa
  D'Ossoli 1810-1850 ....DLB-1, 59, 73

Fulton, Len 1934- Y-86

Fulton, Robin 1937- DLB-40

Furman, Laura 1945- Y-86

Furness, Horace Howard 1833-1912.................DLB-64

Furness, William Henry 1802-1896....................DLB-1

Furthman, Jules 1888-1966............................DLB-26

The Future of the Novel (1899),
  by Henry James...DLB-18

G

Gaddis, William 1922- DLB-2

Gág, Wanda 1893-1946 ....DLB-22

Gagnon, Madeleine 1938- DLB-60

Gaine, Hugh 1726-1807 ....DLB-43

Gaine, Hugh [publishing house].......................DLB-49

Gaines, Ernest J. 1933- DLB-2, 33; Y-80

Gaiser, Gerd 1908-1976 ....DLB-69

Galaxy Science Fiction Novels..........................DLB-46

Gale, Zona 1874-1938 ....DLB-9, 78

Gallagher, William Davis 1808-1894 ....DLB-73

Gallant, Mavis 1922- DLB-53

Gallico, Paul 1897-1976..................................DLB-9

Galsworthy, John 1867-1933.....................DLB-10, 34

Galvin, Brendan 1938- DLB-5

Gambit..DLB-46

Gammer Gurton's Needle...................................DLB-62

Gannett, Frank E. 1876-1957............................DLB-29

García, Lionel G. 1935- DLB-82

Gardam, Jane 1928- DLB-14

Garden, Alexander circa 1685-1756.................DLB-31

Gardner, John 1933-1982 ....DLB-2; Y-82

Garis, Howard R. 1873-1962 ....DLB-22

Garland, Hamlin 1860-1940.................DLB-12, 71, 78

Garneau, Michel 1939- DLB-53

Garner, Hugh 1913-1979.................................DLB-68

Garnett, David 1892-1981 ....DLB-34

Garraty, John A. 1920- DLB-17

Garrett, George 1929- DLB-2, 5; Y-83

Garrick, David 1717-1779 ....DLB-84

Garrison, William Lloyd 1805-1879 ....DLB-1, 43

Gary, Romain 1914-1980 ....DLB-83

Gascoyne, David 1916- DLB-20

Gaskell, Elizabeth Cleghorn 1810-1865.............DLB-21

Gass, William Howard 1924- DLB-2

Gates, Doris 1901- DLB-22

Gates, Henry Louis, Jr. 1950- DLB-67

Gates, Lewis E. 1860-1924 ....DLB-71

Gay, Ebenezer 1696-1787................................DLB-24

Gay, John 1685-1732 ....DLB-84

The Gay Science (1866),
  by E. S. Dallas [excerpt] DLB-21

Gayarré, Charles E. A. 1805-1895 ....DLB-30

Gaylord, Charles [publishing house]...................DLB-49

Geddes, Gary 1940- DLB-60

Geddes, Virgil 1897- DLB-4

Geis, Bernard, Associates DLB-46

Geisel, Theodor Seuss 1904- DLB-61

Gelber, Jack 1932- DLB-7

Gellhorn, Martha 1908- Y-82

Gems, Pam 1925- DLB-13

A General Idea of the College of Mirania (1753),
  by William Smith [excerpts].........................DLB-31

Genet, Jean 1910-1986 ....Y-86, DLB-72

Genevoix, Maurice 1890-1980 ....DLB-65

Genovese, Eugene D. 1930- DLB-17

Gent, Peter 1942- Y-82

George, Henry 1839-1897................................DLB-23

George, Jean Craighead 1919- DLB-52

Gerhardie, William 1895-1977...........................DLB-36

Gernsback, Hugo 1884-1967............................DLB-8

Gerould, Katharine Fullerton 1879-1944..........DLB-78

Gerrish, Samuel [publishing house]..................DLB-49

Gerrold, David 1944- DLB-8

Geston, Mark S. 1946- DLB-8

Gibbon, Lewis Grassic (see Mitchell, James Leslie)

Gibbons, Floyd 1887-1939 ....DLB-25

Gibbons, William ?-?......................................DLB-73

Gibson, Graeme 1934- DLB-53

Gibson, Wilfrid 1878-1962 ....DLB-19

Gibson, William 1914- DLB-7

Gide, André 1869-1951 ....DLB-65

Giguère, Diane 1937- DLB-53

Giguère, Roland 1929- DLB-60

Gilbert, Anthony 1899-1973 ....DLB-77

Gilder, Jeannette L. 1849-1916 ....DLB-79

Gilder, Richard Watson 1844-1909 ....DLB-64, 79

Gildersleeve, Basil 1831-1924 ....DLB-71

Giles, Henry 1809-1882 ....DLB-64

Gill, William F., Company DLB-49

Gillespie, A. Lincoln, Jr. 1895-1950 ....DLB-4

Gilliam, Florence ?-? DLB-4

Gilliatt, Penelope 1932- DLB-14

Gillott, Jacky 1939-1980 ....DLB-14

Gilman, Caroline H. 1794-1888 ....DLB-3, 73

Gilman, W. and J. [publishing house] DLB-49

Gilmer, Elizabeth Meriwether 1861-1951 ....DLB-29

Gilmer, Francis Walker 1790-1826 ....DLB-37

Gilroy, Frank D. 1925- DLB-7

Ginsberg, Allen 1926- DLB-5, 16

Ginzkey, Franz Karl 1871-1963 ....DLB-81

Giono, Jean 1895-1970 ....DLB-72

Giovanni, Nikki 1943- DLB-5, 41

Gipson, Lawrence Henry 1880-1971 ....DLB-17

Giraudoux, Jean 1882-1944 ....DLB-65

Gissing, George 1857-1903 ....DLB-18

Gladstone, William Ewart 1809-1898 ....DLB-57

Glaeser, Ernst 1902-1963 ....DLB-69

Glanville, Brian 1931- DLB-15

Glapthorne, Henry 1610-1643? DLB-58

Glasgow, Ellen 1873-1945 ....DLB-9, 12

Glaspell, Susan 1876-1948 ....DLB-7, 9, 78

Glass, Montague 1877-1934 ....DLB-11

Glassco, John 1909-1981 ....DLB-68

Glauser, Friedrich 1896-1938 ....DLB-56

F. Gleason's Publishing Hall DLB-49

Glück, Louise 1943- DLB-5

Godbout, Jacques 1933- DLB-53

Goddard, Morrill 1865-1937 ....DLB-25

Goddard, William 1740-1817 ....DLB-43

Godey, Louis A. 1804-1878 ....DLB-73

Godey and McMichael DLB-49

Godfrey, Dave 1938- DLB-60

Godfrey, Thomas 1736-1763 ....DLB-31

Godine, David R., Publisher DLB-46

Godkin, E. L. 1831-1902 ....DLB-79

Godwin, Gail 1937- DLB-6

Godwin, Parke 1816-1904 ....DLB-3, 64

Godwin, William 1756-1836 ....DLB-39

Goes, Albrecht 1908- DLB-69

Goffe, Thomas circa 1592-1629 ....DLB-58

Goffstein, M. B. 1940- DLB-61

Gogarty, Oliver St. John 1878-1957 ....DLB-15, 19

Goines, Donald 1937-1974 ....DLB-33

Gold, Herbert 1924- DLB-2; Y-81

Gold, Michael 1893-1967 ....DLB-9, 28

Goldberg, Dick 1947- DLB-7

Golding, William 1911- DLB-15

Goldman, William 1931- DLB-44

Goldsmith, Oliver 1730 or 1731-1774 ....DLB-39

Goldsmith Publishing Company DLB-46

Gomme, Laurence James
[publishing house] DLB-46

González-T., César A. 1931- DLB-82

The Goodman Theatre DLB-7

Goodrich, Frances 1891-1984 and
Hackett, Albert 1900- DLB-26

Goodrich, S. G. [publishing house] DLB-49

Goodrich, Samuel Griswold 1793-1860 ...DLB-1, 42, 73

Goodspeed, C. E., and Company DLB-49

Goodwin, Stephen 1943- Y-82

Gookin, Daniel 1612-1687 ....DLB-24

Gordon, Caroline 1895-1981 ....DLB-4, 9; Y-81

Gordon, Giles 1940- DLB-14

Gordon, Mary 1949- DLB-6; Y-81

Gordone, Charles 1925- DLB-7

Gorey, Edward 1925- DLB-61

Gosse, Edmund 1849-1928 ....DLB-57

Gould, Wallace 1882-1940 ....DLB-54

Goyen, William 1915-1983 ....DLB-2; Y-83

Gracq, Julien 1910- DLB-83

Grady, Henry W. 1850-1889..............................DLB-23

Graf, Oskar Maria 1894-1967.........................DLB-56

Graham, George Rex 1813-1894.......................DLB-73

Graham, Lorenz 1902- DLB-76

Graham, Shirley 1896-1977 ....DLB-76

Graham, W. S. 1918- DLB-20

Graham, William H. [publishing house] DLB-49

Graham, Winston 1910- DLB-77

Grahame, Kenneth 1859-1932......................DLB-34

Gramatky, Hardie 1907-1979 ....DLB-22

Granich, Irwin (see Gold, Michael)

Grant, Harry J. 1881-1963..............................DLB-29

Grant, James Edward 1905-1966.....................DLB-26

Grass, Günter 1927- DLB-75

Grasty, Charles H. 1863-1924.........................DLB-25

Grau, Shirley Ann 1929- DLB-2

Graves, John 1920- Y-83

Graves, Richard 1715-1804............................DLB-39

Graves, Robert 1895-1985 ....DLB-20; Y-85

Gray, Asa 1810-1888 ....DLB-1

Gray, David 1838-1861..................................DLB-32

Gray, Simon 1936- DLB-13

Grayson, William J. 1788-1863.....................DLB-3, 64

The Great War and the Theater, 1914-1918
    [Great Britain]................................DLB-10

Greeley, Horace 1811-1872 ....DLB-3, 43

Green, Adolph (see Comden, Betty)

Green, Duff 1791-1875 ....DLB-43

Green, Gerald 1922- DLB-28

Green, Henry 1905-1973 ....DLB-15

Green, Jonas 1712-1767 ....DLB-31

Green, Joseph 1706-1780...............................DLB-31

Green, Julien 1900- DLB-4, 72

Green, Paul 1894-1981 ....DLB-7, 9; Y-81

Green, T. and S. [publishing house] DLB-49

Green, Timothy [publishing house]...................DLB-49

Greenberg: Publisher DLB-46

Green Tiger Press....................................DLB-46

Greene, Asa 1789-1838 ....DLB-11

Greene, Benjamin H. [publishing house]..........DLB-49

Greene, Graham 1904- DLB-13, 15, 77; Y-85

Greene, Robert 1558-1592................................DLB-62

Greenhow, Robert 1800-1854............................DLB-30

Greenough, Horatio 1805-1852..........................DLB-1

Greenwell, Dora 1821-1882 ....DLB-35

Greenwillow Books....................................DLB-46

Greenwood, Grace (see Lippincott, Sara Jane Clarke)

Greenwood, Walter 1903-1974 ....DLB-10

Greer, Ben 1948- DLB-6

Greg, W. R. 1809-1881..................................DLB-55

Gregg Press...DLB-46

Persse, Isabella Augusta,
    Lady Gregory 1852-1932 ....DLB-10

Gregory, Horace 1898-1982............................DLB-48

Greville, Fulke, First Lord Brooke
    1554-1628 ....DLB-62

Grey, Zane 1872-1939 ....DLB-9

Grieve, C. M. (see MacDiarmid, Hugh)

Griffith, Elizabeth 1727?-1793.........................DLB-39

Griffiths, Trevor 1935- DLB-13

Griggs, S. C., and Company.............................DLB-49

Griggs, Sutton Elbert 1872-1930 ....DLB-50

Grignon, Claude-Henri 1894-1976.....................DLB-68

Grigson, Geoffrey 1905- DLB-27

Grimké, Angelina Weld 1880-1958...............DLB-50, 54

Grimm, Hans 1875-1959................................DLB-66

Griswold, Rufus Wilmot 1815-1857 ....DLB-3, 59

Gross, Milt 1895-1953 ....DLB-11

Grosset and Dunlap....................................DLB-49

Grossman Publishers DLB-46

Groulx, Lionel 1878-1967 ....DLB-68

Grove Press...DLB-46

Grubb, Davis 1919-1980................................DLB-6

Gruelle, Johnny 1880-1938.............................DLB-22

Guare, John 1938- DLB-7

Guest, Barbara 1920- DLB-5

Guèvremont, Germaine 1893-1968 ....DLB-68

Guilloux, Louis 1899-1980.............................DLB-72

Guiney, Louise Imogen 1861-1920....................DLB-54

Guiterman, Arthur 1871-1943.........................DLB-11

Gunn, Bill 1934- DLB-38

Gunn, James E. 1923- DLB-8

Gunn, Neil M. 1891-1973 ....DLB-15

Gunn, Thom 1929- DLB-27

Gunnars, Kristjana 1948- DLB-60

Gurik, Robert 1932- DLB-60

Gütersloh, Albert Paris 1887-1973 ....DLB-81

Guthrie, A. B., Jr. 1901- DLB-6

Guthrie, Ramon 1896-1973..........................DLB-4

The Guthrie Theater.....................................DLB-7

Guy, Ray 1939- DLB-60

Guy, Rosa 1925- DLB-33

Gwynne, Erskine 1898-1948 ....DLB-4

Gysin, Brion 1916- DLB-16

H

H. D. (see Doolittle, Hilda)

Hackett, Albert (see Goodrich, Frances)

Hagelstange, Rudolf 1912-1984......................DLB-69

Haggard, H. Rider 1856-1925.......................DLB-70

Hailey, Arthur 1920- Y-82

Haines, John 1924- DLB-5

Hake, Thomas Gordon 1809-1895.................DLB-32

Haldeman, Joe 1943- DLB-8

Haldeman-Julius Company..............................DLB-46

Hale, E. J., and Son.....................................DLB-49

Hale, Edward Everett 1822-1909 ....DLB-1, 42, 74

Hale, Leo Thomas (see Ebon)

Hale, Lucretia Peabody 1820-1900...................DLB-42

Hale, Nancy 1908-1988 ....Y-80, 88

Hale, Sarah Josepha (Buell) 1788-1879 ...DLB-1, 42, 73

Haley, Alex 1921- DLB-38

Haliburton, Thomas Chandler 1796-1865.........DLB-11

Hall, Donald 1928- DLB-5

Hall, James 1793-1868 ....DLB-73, 74

Hall, Samuel [publishing house].....................DLB-49

Hallam, Arthur Henry 1811-1833...................DLB-32

Halleck, Fitz-Greene 1790-1867 ....DLB-3

Hallmark Editions DLB-46

Halper, Albert 1904-1984.............................DLB-9

Halstead, Murat 1829-1908..........................DLB-23

Hamburger, Michael 1924- DLB-27

Hamilton, Alexander 1712-1756 ....DLB-31

Hamilton, Alexander 1755?-1804...................DLB-37

Hamilton, Cicely 1872-1952..........................DLB-10

Hamilton, Edmond 1904-1977 ....DLB-8

Hamilton, Gail (see Corcoran, Barbara)

Hamilton, Ian 1938- DLB-40

Hamilton, Patrick 1904-1962.........................DLB-10

Hamilton, Virginia 1936- DLB-33, 52

Hammett, Dashiell 1894-1961 ....DS-6

Hammon, Jupiter 1711-died between
   1790 and 1806.....................................DLB-31, 50

Hammond, John ?-1663.................................DLB-24

Hamner, Earl 1923- DLB-6

Hampton, Christopher 1946- DLB-13

Handel-Mazzetti, Enrica von
   1871-1955 ....DLB-81

Handlin, Oscar 1915- DLB-17

Hankin, St. John 1869-1909 ....DLB-10

Hanley, Clifford 1922- DLB-14

Hannah, Barry 1942- DLB-6

Hannay, James 1827-1873.............................DLB-21

Hansberry, Lorraine 1930-1965 ....DLB-7, 38

Harcourt Brace Jovanovich DLB-46

Hardwick, Elizabeth 1916- DLB-6

Hardy, Thomas 1840-1928...........................DLB-18, 19

Hare, Cyril 1900-1958..................................DLB-77

Hare, David 1947- DLB-13

Hargrove, Marion 1919- DLB-11

Harlow, Robert 1923- DLB-60

Harness, Charles L. 1915- DLB-8

Harper, Fletcher 1806-1877 ....DLB-79

Harper, Frances Ellen Watkins
   1825-1911 ....DLB-50

Harper, Michael S. 1938- DLB-41

Harper and Brothers.....................................DLB-49

Harris, Benjamin ?-circa 1720 ....DLB-42, 43

Harris, George Washington 1814-1869.........DLB-3, 11

Harris, Joel Chandler 1848-1908 .....DLB-11, 23, 42, 78

Harris, Mark 1922- DLB-2; Y-80

Harrison, Charles Yale 1898-1954 ....DLB-68

Harrison, Frederic 1831-1923.........................DLB-57

Harrison, Harry 1925- DLB-8

Harrison, James P., Company......................DLB-49

Harrison, Jim 1937- Y-82

Harrison, Paul Carter 1936- DLB-38

Harrison, Tony 1937- DLB-40

Harrisse, Henry 1829-1910..........................DLB-47

Harsent, David 1942- DLB-40

Hart, Albert Bushnell 1854-1943 ....DLB-17

Hart, Moss 1904-1961 ....DLB-7

Hart, Oliver 1723-1795 ....DLB-31

Harte, Bret 1836-1902 ....DLB-12, 64, 74, 79

Hartlaub, Felix 1913-1945...........................DLB-56

Hartley, L. P. 1895-1972.............................DLB-15

Hartley, Marsden 1877-1943 ....DLB-54

Härtling, Peter 1933- DLB-75

Hartman, Geoffrey H. 1929- DLB-67

Hartmann, Sadakichi 1867-1944 ....DLB-54

Harwood, Lee 1939- DLB-40

Harwood, Ronald 1934- DLB-13

Haskins, Charles Homer 1870-1937..............DLB-47

The Hatch-Billops Collection DLB-76

A Haughty and Proud Generation (1922),
    by Ford Madox Hueffer............................DLB-36

Hauptmann, Carl 1858-1921 ....DLB-66

Hauptmann, Gerhart 1862-1946 ....DLB-66

Hauser, Marianne 1910- Y-83

Hawker, Robert Stephen 1803-1875 ....DLB-32

Hawkes, John 1925- DLB-2, 7; Y-80

Hawkins, Walter Everette 1883-?..................DLB-50

Hawthorne, Nathaniel 1804-1864 ....DLB-1, 74

Hay, John 1838-1905 ....DLB-12, 47

Hayden, Robert 1913-1980..........................DLB-5, 76

Hayes, John Michael 1919- DLB-26

Hayne, Paul Hamilton 1830-1886...........DLB-3, 64, 79

Haywood, Eliza 1693?-1756 ....DLB-39

Hazard, Willis P. [publishing house] DLB-49

Hazzard, Shirley 1931- Y-82

Headley, Joel T. 1813-1897 ....DLB-30

Heaney, Seamus 1939- DLB-40

Heard, Nathan C. 1936- DLB-33

Hearn, Lafcadio 1850-1904 ....DLB-12, 78

Hearst, William Randolph 1863-1951 ....DLB-25

Heath, Catherine 1924- DLB-14

Heath-Stubbs, John 1918- DLB-27

Hébert, Anne 1916- DLB-68

Hébert, Jacques 1923- DLB-53

Hecht, Anthony 1923- DLB-5

Hecht, Ben 1894-1964...................DLB-7, 9, 25, 26, 28

Hecker, Isaac Thomas 1819-1888 ....DLB-1

Hedge, Frederic Henry 1805-1890 ....DLB-1, 59

Heidish, Marcy 1947- Y-82

Heinlein, Robert A. 1907- DLB-8

Heinrich, Willi 1920- DLB-75

Hei;dsenbüttel 1921- DLB-75

Heller, Joseph 1923- DLB-2, 28; Y-80

Hellman, Lillian 1906-1984 ....DLB-7; Y-84

Helprin, Mark 1947- Y-85

Helwig, David 1938- DLB-60

Hemingway, Ernest
    1899-1961 ....DLB-4, 9; Y-81, 87; DS-1

Hemingway: Twenty-Five Years Later Y-85

Hemphill, Paul 1936- Y-87

Henchman, Daniel 1689-1761 ....DLB-24

Henderson, Alice Corbin 1881-1949..............DLB-54

Henderson, David 1942- DLB-41

Henderson, George Wylie 1904- DLB-51

Henderson, Zenna 1917- DLB-8

Henley, Beth 1952- Y-86

Henley, William Ernest 1849-1903................DLB-19

Henry, Buck 1930- DLB-26

Henry, Marguerite 1902- DLB-22

Henry, Robert Selph 1889-1970....................DLB-17

Henry, Will (see Allen, Henry W.)

Henschke, Alfred (see Klabund)

Henty, G. A. 1832-1902 ....DLB-18

Hentz, Caroline Lee 1800-1856.....................DLB-3

Herbert, Alan Patrick 1890-1971 ....DLB-10

Herbert, Frank 1920-1986 ....DLB-8

Herbert, Henry William 1807-1858 ....DLB-3, 73

Herbert, John 1926- DLB-53

Herbst, Josephine 1892-1969........................DLB-9

Herburger, Günter 1932- DLB-75

Hercules, Frank E. M. 1917- DLB-33

Herder, B., Book Company................................DLB-49

Hergesheimer, Joseph 1880-1954........................DLB-9

Heritage Press..DLB-46

Hermlin, Stephan 1915- DLB-69

Hernton, Calvin C. 1932- DLB-38

"The Hero as Man of Letters: Johnson,
    Rousseau, Burns" (1841), by Thomas
    Carlyle [excerpt] DLB-57

The Hero as Poet. Dante; Shakspeare (1841),
    by Thomas Carlyle DLB-32

Herrick, E. R., and Company DLB-49

Herrick, Robert 1868-1938....................DLB-9, 12, 78

Herrick, William 1915- Y-83

Herrmann, John 1900-1959..............................DLB-4

Hersey, John 1914- DLB-6

Hertel, François 1905-1985...............................DLB-68

Hervé-Bazin, Jean Pierre Marie (see Bazin, Hervé)

Herzog, Emile Salomon Wilhelm (see Maurois, André)

Hesse, Hermann 1877-1962..............................DLB-66

Hewat, Alexander circa 1743-circa 1824............DLB-30

Hewitt, John 1907- DLB-27

Hewlett, Maurice 1861-1923............................DLB-34

Heyen, William 1940- DLB-5

Heyer, Georgette 1902-1974.............................DLB-77

Heym, Stefan 1913- DLB-69

Heyward, Dorothy 1890-1961 and
    Heyward, DuBose 1885-1940 ....DLB-7

Heyward, DuBose 1885-1940...................DLB-7, 9, 45

Heywood, Thomas 1573 or 1574-1641 ....DLB-62

Hiebert, Paul 1892-1987 ....DLB-68

Higgins, Aidan 1927- DLB-14

Higgins, Colin 1941-1988 ....DLB-26

Higgins, George V. 1939- DLB-2; Y-81

Higginson, Thomas Wentworth 1823-1911 ...DLB-1, 64

Highwater, Jamake 1942?- DLB-52; Y-85

Hildesheimer, Wolfgang 1916- DLB-69

Hildreth, Richard 1807-1865 ....DLB-1, 30, 59

Hill, Aaron 1685-1750 ....DLB-84

Hill, Geoffrey 1932- DLB-40

Hill, George M., Company...............................DLB-49

Hill, "Sir" John 1714?-1775 ....DLB-39

Hill, Lawrence, and Company, Publishers.........DLB-46

Hill, Leslie 1880-1960 ....DLB-51

Hill, Susan 1942- DLB-14

Hill, Walter 1942- DLB-44

Hill and Wang DLB-46

Hilliard, Gray and Company DLB-49

Hillyer, Robert 1895-1961 ....DLB-54

Hilton, James 1900-1954.............................DLB-34, 77

Hilton and Company.......................................DLB-49

Himes, Chester 1909-1984............................DLB-2, 76

Hine, Daryl 1936- DLB-60

Hinojosa-Smith, Rolando 1929- DLB-82

The History of the Adventures of Joseph Andrews
    (1742), by Henry Fielding [excerpt].............DLB-39

Hirsch, E. D., Jr. 1928- DLB-67

Hoagland, Edward 1932- DLB-6

Hoagland, Everett H. III 1942- DLB-41

Hoban, Russell 1925- DLB-52

Hobsbaum, Philip 1932- DLB-40

Hobson, Laura Z. 1900- DLB-28

Hochman, Sandra 1936- DLB-5

Hodgins, Jack 1938- DLB-60

Hodgman, Helen 1945- DLB-14

Hodgson, Ralph 1871-1962 ....DLB-19

Hodgson, William Hope 1877-1918...................DLB-70

Hoffenstein, Samuel 1890-1947........................DLB-11

Hoffman, Charles Fenno 1806-1884 ....DLB-3

Hoffman, Daniel 1923- DLB-5

Hofmann, Michael 1957- DLB-40

Hofmannsthal, Hugo von 1874-1929.................DLB-81

Hofstadter, Richard 1916-1970 ....DLB-17

Hogan, Desmond 1950- DLB-14

Hogan and Thompson DLB-49

Hohl, Ludwig 1904-1980 ....DLB-56

Holbrook, David 1923- DLB-14, 40

Holcroft, Thomas 1745-1809............................DLB-39

Holden, Molly 1927-1981 ....DLB-40

Holiday House..DLB-46

Holland, Norman N. 1927- DLB-67

Hollander, John 1929- DLB-5

Holley, Marietta 1836-1926 ....DLB-11

Hollingsworth, Margaret 1940- DLB-60

Hollo, Anselm 1934- DLB-40

Holloway, John 1920- DLB-27

Holloway House Publishing Company DLB-46

Holme, Constance 1880-1955 ....DLB-34

Holmes, Oliver Wendell 1809-1894 ....DLB-1

Holmes, John Clellon 1926-1988 ....DLB-16

Holst, Hermann E. von 1841-1904 ....DLB-47

Holt, Henry, and Company DLB-49

Holt, John 1721-1784 ....DLB-43

Holt, Rinehart and Winston DLB-46

Holthusen, Hans Egon 1913- DLB-69

Home, Henry, Lord Kames 1696-1782 ....DLB-31

Home, John 1722-1808 ....DLB-84

Home Publishing Company DLB-49

Home, William Douglas 1912- DLB-13

Homes, Geoffrey (see Mainwaring, Daniel)

Honig, Edwin 1919- DLB-5

Hood, Hugh 1928- DLB-53

Hooker, Jeremy 1941- DLB-40

Hooker, Thomas 1586-1647 ....DLB-24

Hooper, Johnson Jones 1815-1862 ....DLB-3, 11

Hopkins, Gerard Manley 1844-1889 ....DLB-35, 57

Hopkins, John H., and Son DLB-46

Hopkins, Lemuel 1750-1801 ....DLB-37

Hopkins, Pauline Elizabeth 1859-1930 ....DLB-50

Hopkins, Samuel 1721-1803 ....DLB-31

Hopkinson, Francis 1737-1791 ....DLB-31

Horgan, Paul 1903- Y-85

Horizon Press DLB-46

Horne, Frank 1899-1974 ....DLB-51

Horne, Richard Henry (Hengist) 1802
   or 1803-1884 ....DLB-32

Hornung, E. W. 1866-1921 ....DLB-70

Horovitz, Israel 1939- DLB-7

Horton, George Moses 1797?-1883? DLB-50

Horwood, Harold 1923- DLB-60

Hosford, E. and E. [publishing house] DLB-49

Hotchkiss and Company DLB-49

Hough, Emerson 1857-1923 ....DLB-9

Houghton Mifflin Company DLB-49

Houghton, Stanley 1881-1913 ....DLB-10

Housman, A. E. 1859-1936 ....DLB-19

Housman, Laurence 1865-1959 ....DLB-10

Hovey, Richard 1864-1900 ....DLB-54

Howard, Maureen 1930- Y-83

Howard, Richard 1929- DLB-5

Howard, Roy W. 1883-1964 ....DLB-29

Howard, Sidney 1891-1939 ....DLB-7, 26

Howe, E. W. 1853-1937 ....DLB-12, 25

Howe, Henry 1816-1893 ....DLB-30

Howe, Irving 1920- DLB-67

Howe, Julia Ward 1819-1910 ....DLB-1

Howell, Clark, Sr. 1863-1936 ....DLB-25

Howell, Evan P. 1839-1905 ....DLB-23

Howell, Soskin and Company DLB-46

Howells, William Dean 1837-1920...DLB-12, 64, 74, 79

Hoyem, Andrew 1935- DLB-5

de Hoyos, Angela 1940- DLB-82

Hoyt, Henry [publishing house] DLB-49

Hubbard, Kin 1868-1930 ....DLB-11

Hubbard, William circa 1621-1704 ....DLB-24

Huch, Friedrich 1873-1913 ....DLB-66

Huch, Ricarda 1864-1947 ....DLB-66

Huck at 100: How Old Is
   Huckleberry Finn? Y-85

Hudson, Henry Norman 1814-1886 ....DLB-64

Hudson and Goodwin DLB-49

Huebsch, B. W. [publishing house] DLB-46

Hughes, David 1930- DLB-14

Hughes, John 1677-1720 ....DLB-84

Hughes, Langston 1902-1967 ....DLB-4, 7, 48, 51

Hughes, Richard 1900-1976 ....DLB-15

Hughes, Ted 1930- DLB-40

Hughes, Thomas 1822-1896 ....DLB-18

Hugo, Richard 1923-1982 ....DLB-5

Hugo Awards and Nebula Awards DLB-8

Hull, Richard 1896-1973 ....DLB-77

Hulme, T. E. 1883-1917 ....DLB-19

Hume, Fergus 1859-1932 ....DLB-70

Humorous Book Illustration DLB-11

Humphrey, William 1924- DLB-6

Humphreys, David 1752-1818 ....DLB-37

Humphreys, Emyr 1919- DLB-15

Huncke, Herbert 1915- DLB-16

Huneker, James Gibbons 1857-1921 ....DLB-71

Hunt, Irene 1907- DLB-52

Hunt, William Gibbes 1791-1833 ....DLB-73

Hunter, Evan 1926- Y-82

Hunter, Jim 1939- DLB-14

Hunter, Kristin 1931- DLB-33

Hunter, N. C. 1908-1971 ....DLB-10

Hurd and Houghton DLB-49

Hurst and Company DLB-49

Hurston, Zora Neale 1891-1960 ....DLB-51

Huston, John 1906- DLB-26

Hutcheson, Francis 1694-1746 ....DLB-31

Hutchinson, Thomas 1711-1780 ....DLB-30, 31

Hutton, Richard Holt 1826-1897 ....DLB-57

Huxley, Aldous 1894-1963 ....DLB-36

Huxley, Elspeth Josceline
    1907- DLB-77

Huxley, T. H. 1825-1895 ....DLB-57

Hyman, Trina Schart 1939- DLB-61

I

The Iconography of Science-Fiction Art DLB-8

Ignatow, David 1914- DLB-5

Iles, Francis (see Berkeley, Anthony)

Imbs, Bravig 1904-1946 ....DLB-4

Inchbald, Elizabeth 1753-1821 ....DLB-39

Inge, William 1913-1973 ....DLB-7

Ingelow, Jean 1820-1897 ....DLB-35

The Ingersoll Prizes Y-84

Ingraham, Joseph Holt 1809-1860 ....DLB-3

Inman, John 1805-1850 ....DLB-73

International Publishers Company DLB-46

An Interview with Peter S. Prescott Y-86

An Interview with Tom Jenks Y-86

Introduction to Paul Laurence Dunbar,
    Lyrics of Lowly Life (1896),
    by William Dean Howells DLB-50

Introductory Essay: *Letters of Percy Bysshe
    Shelley* (1852), by Robert Browning DLB-32

Introductory Letters from the Second Edition
    of *Pamela* (1741), by Samuel Richardson.....DLB-39

Irving, John 1942- DLB-6; Y-82

Irving, Washington
    1783-1859 ....DLB-3, 11, 30, 59, 73, 74

Irwin, Grace 1907- DLB-68

Irwin, Will 1873-1948 ....DLB-25

Isherwood, Christopher 1904-1986 ....DLB-15; Y-86

The Island Trees Case: A Symposium on School
        Library Censorship
    An Interview with Judith Krug
    An Interview with Phyllis Schlafly
    An Interview with Edward B. Jenkinson
    An Interview with Lamarr Mooneyham
    An Interview with Harriet Bernstein Y-82

Ivers, M. J., and Company DLB-49

J

Jackmon, Marvin E. (see Marvin X)

Jackson, Angela 1951- DLB-41

Jackson, Helen Hunt 1830-1885 ....DLB-42, 47

Jackson, Laura Riding 1901- DLB-48

Jackson, Shirley 1919-1965 ....DLB-6

Jacob, Piers Anthony Dillingham (see Anthony,
    Piers)

Jacobs, George W., and Company DLB-49

Jacobson, Dan 1929- DLB-14

Jahnn, Hans Henny 1894-1959 ....DLB-56

Jakes, John 1932- Y-83

James, Henry 1843-1916 ....DLB-12, 71, 74

James, John circa 1633-1729 ....DLB-24

James Joyce Centenary: Dublin, 1982 ....Y-82

James Joyce Conference Y-85

James, U. P. [publishing house] DLB-49

Jameson, Fredric 1934- DLB-67

Jameson, J. Franklin 1859-1937 ....DLB-17

Jameson, Storm 1891-1986 ....DLB-36

Jarrell, Randall 1914-1965 ....DLB-48, 52

Jasmin, Claude 1930- DLB-60

Jay, John 1745-1829 ....DLB-31

Jeffers, Lance 1919-1985 ....DLB-41

Jeffers, Robinson 1887-1962............................DLB-45

Jefferson, Thomas 1743-1826.........................DLB-31

Jellicoe, Ann 1927- DLB-13

Jenkins, Robin 1912- DLB-14

Jenkins, William Fitzgerald (see Leinster, Murray)

Jennings, Elizabeth 1926- DLB-27

Jens, Walter 1923- DLB-69

Jensen, Merrill 1905-1980.................................DLB-17

Jerome, Jerome K. 1859-1927 ....DLB-10, 34

Jesse, F. Tennyson 1888-1958............................DLB-77

Jewett, John P., and Company...........................DLB-49

Jewett, Sarah Orne 1849-1909.....................DLB-12, 74

The Jewish Publication Society DLB-49

Jewsbury, Geraldine 1812-1880........................DLB-21

Joans, Ted 1928- DLB-16, 41

John Edward Bruce: Three Documents............DLB-50

John O'Hara's Pottsville Journalism........................Y-88

John Steinbeck Research Center............................Y-85

John Webster: The Melbourne Manuscript............Y-86

Johnson, B. S. 1933-1973......................DLB-14, 40

Johnson, Benjamin [publishing house]..............DLB-49

Johnson, Benjamin, Jacob, and
 Robert [publishing house]...........................DLB-49

Johnson, Charles 1679-1748 ....DLB-84

Johnson, Charles R. 1948- DLB-33

Johnson, Charles S. 1893-1956 ....DLB-51

Johnson, Diane 1934- Y-80

Johnson, Edward 1598-1672.........................DLB-24

Johnson, Fenton 1888-1958 ....DLB-45, 50

Johnson, Georgia Douglas 1886-1966 ....DLB-51

Johnson, Gerald W. 1890-1980.........................DLB-29

Johnson, Helene 1907- DLB-51

Johnson, Jacob, and Company...........................DLB-49

Johnson, James Weldon 1871-1938 ....DLB-51

Johnson, Lionel 1867-1902 ....DLB-19

Johnson, Nunnally 1897-1977 ....DLB-26

Johnson, Owen 1878-1952 ....Y-87

Johnson, Pamela Hansford 1912- DLB-15

Johnson, Samuel 1696-1772.........................DLB-24

Johnson, Samuel 1709-1784.........................DLB-39

Johnson, Samuel 1822-1882........................DLB-1

Johnson, Uwe 1934-1984 ....DLB-75

Johnston, Annie Fellows 1863-1931....................DLB-42

Johnston, Basil H. 1929- DLB-60

Johnston, Denis 1901-1984 ....DLB-10

Johnston, Jennifer 1930- DLB-14

Johnston, Mary 1870-1936.........................DLB-9

Johnston, Richard Malcolm 1822-1898 ....DLB-74

Johnstone, Charles 1719?-1800? DLB-39

Jolas, Eugene 1894-1952................................DLB-4, 45

Jones, Charles C., Jr. 1831-1893.......................DLB-30

Jones, D. G. 1929- DLB-53

Jones, David 1895-1974.........................DLB-20

Jones, Ebenezer 1820-1860.........................DLB-32

Jones, Ernest 1819-1868.........................DLB-32

Jones, Gayl 1949- DLB-33

Jones, Glyn 1905- DLB-15

Jones, Gwyn 1907- DLB-15

Jones, Henry Arthur 1851-1929.........................DLB-10

Jones, Hugh circa 1692-1760.........................DLB-24

Jones, James 1921-1977.........................DLB-2

Jones, LeRoi (see Baraka, Amiri)

Jones, Lewis 1897-1939 ....DLB-15

Jones, Major Joseph (see Thompson, William
 Tappan)

Jones, Preston 1936-1979.........................DLB-7

Jones, William Alfred 1817-1900 ....DLB-59

Jones's Publishing House DLB-49

Jong, Erica 1942- DLB-2, 5, 28

Jonson, Ben 1572?-1637................................DLB-62

Jordan, June 1936- DLB-38

Joseph, Jenny 1932- DLB-40

Josephson, Matthew 1899-1978 ....DLB-4

Josiah Allen's Wife (see Holley, Marietta)

Josipovici, Gabriel 1940- DLB-14

Josselyn, John ?-1675.........................DLB-24

Joyaux, Philippe (see Sollers, Philippe)

Joyce, Adrien (see Eastman, Carol)

Joyce, James 1882-1941 ....DLB-10, 19, 36

Judd, Orange, Publishing Company.................DLB-49

Judd, Sylvester 1813-1853.................................DLB-1

June, Jennie (see Croly, Jane Cunningham)

Jünger, Ernst 1895- DLB-56

Justice, Donald 1925- Y-83

K

Kacew, Romain (see Gary, Romain)

Kafka, Franz 1883-1924 ....DLB-81

Kalechofsky, Roberta 1931- DLB-28

Kaler, James Otis 1848-1912 ....DLB-12

Kandel, Lenore 1932- DLB-16

Kanin, Garson 1912- DLB-7

Kant, Hermann 1926- DLB-75

Kantor, Mackinlay 1904-1977 ....DLB-9

Kaplan, Johanna 1942- DLB-28

Kasack, Hermann 1896-1966 ....DLB-69

Kaschnitz, Marie Luise 1901-1974 ....DLB-69

Kästner, Erich 1899-1974 ....DLB-56

Kattan, Naim 1928- DLB-53

Katz, Steve 1935- Y-83

Kauffman, Janet 1945- Y-86

Kaufman, Bob 1925- DLB-16, 41

Kaufman, George S. 1889-1961 ....DLB-7

Kavanagh, Patrick 1904-1967 ....DLB-15, 20

Kavanagh, P. J. 1931- DLB-40

Kaye-Smith, Sheila 1887-1956 ....DLB-36

Kazin, Alfred 1915- DLB-67

Keane, John B. 1928- DLB-13

Keats, Ezra Jack 1916-1983 ....DLB-61

Keble, John 1792-1866 ....DLB-32, 55

Keeble, John 1944- Y-83

Keeffe, Barrie 1945- DLB-13

Keeley, James 1867-1934 ....DLB-25

W. B. Keen, Cooke and Company DLB-49

Keillor, Garrison 1942- Y-87

Keller, Gary D. 1943- DLB-82

Kelley, Edith Summers 1884-1956 ....DLB-9

Kelley, William Melvin 1937- DLB-33

Kellogg, Ansel Nash 1832-1886 ....DLB-23

Kellogg, Steven 1941- DLB-61

Kelly, George 1887-1974 ....DLB-7

Kelly, Piet and Company DLB-49

Kelly, Robert 1935- DLB-5

Kemble, Fanny 1809-1893 ....DLB-32

Kemelman, Harry 1908- DLB-28

Kempowski, Walter 1929- DLB-75

Kendall, Claude [publishing company] DLB-46

Kendell, George 1809-1867 ....DLB-43

Kenedy, P. J., and Sons DLB-49

Kennedy, Adrienne 1931- DLB-38

Kennedy, John Pendleton 1795-1870 ....DLB-3

Kennedy, Margaret 1896-1967 ....DLB-36

Kennedy, William 1928- Y-85

Kennedy, X. J. 1929- DLB-5

Kennelly, Brendan 1936- DLB-40

Kenner, Hugh 1923- DLB-67

Kennerley, Mitchell [publishing house] DLB-46

Kent, Frank R. 1877-1958 ....DLB-29

Keppler and Schwartzmann DLB-49

Kerouac, Jack 1922-1969 ....DLB-2, 16; DS-3

Kerouac, Jan 1952- DLB-16

Kerr, Charles H., and Company DLB-49

Kerr, Orpheus C. (see Newell, Robert Henry)

Kesey, Ken 1935- DLB-2, 16

Kessel, Joseph 1898-1979 ....DLB-72

Kessel, Martin 1901- DLB-56

Kesten, Hermann 1900- DLB-56

Keun, Irmgard 1905-1982 ....DLB-69

Key and Biddle DLB-49

Keyserling, Eduard von 1855-1918 ....DLB-66

Kiely, Benedict 1919- DLB-15

Kiggins and Kellogg DLB-49

Kiley, Jed 1889-1962 ....DLB-4

Killens, John Oliver 1916- DLB-33

Killigrew, Thomas 1612-1683 ....DLB-58

Kilmer, Joyce 1886-1918 ....DLB-45

King, Clarence 1842-1901 ....DLB-12

King, Florence 1936 ....Y-85

King, Francis 1923- DLB-15

King, Grace 1852-1932 ....DLB-12, 78

King, Solomon [publishing house] DLB-49

King, Stephen 1947- Y-80

King, Woodie, Jr. 1937- DLB-38

Kinglake, Alexander William 1809-1891............DLB-55

Kingsley, Charles 1819-1875.........................DLB-21, 32

Kingsley, Henry 1830-1876.............................DLB-21

Kingsley, Sidney 1906- DLB-7

Kingston, Maxine Hong 1940- Y-80

Kinnell, Galway 1927- DLB-5; Y-87

Kinsella, Thomas 1928- DLB-27

Kipling, Rudyard 1865-1936 ....DLB-19, 34

Kirk, John Foster 1824-1904.............................DLB-79

Kirkconnell, Watson 1895-1977..........................DLB-68

Kirkland, Caroline M. 1801-1864 ....DLB-3, 73, 74

Kirkland, Joseph 1830-1893 ....DLB-12

Kirkup, James 1918- DLB-27

Kirsch, Sarah 1935- DLB-75

Kirst, Hans Hellmut 1914-.............................DLB-69

Kitchin, C. H. B. 1895-1967 ....DLB-77

Kizer, Carolyn 1925- DLB-5

Klabund 1890-1928 ....DLB-66

Klappert, Peter 1942- DLB-5

Klass, Philip (see Tenn, William)

Klein, A. M. 1909-1972.................................DLB-68

Kluge, Alexander 1932- DLB-75

Knapp, Samuel Lorenzo 1783-1838 ....DLB-59

Knickerbocker, Diedrich (see Irving, Washington)

Knight, Damon 1922- DLB-8

Knight, Etheridge 1931- DLB-41

Knight, John S. 1894-1981.............................DLB-29

Knight, Sarah Kemble 1666-1727.........................DLB-24

Knister, Raymond 1899-1932 ....DLB-68

Knoblock, Edward 1874-1945.............................DLB-10

Knopf, Alfred A. 1892-1984.............................Y-84

Knopf, Alfred A. [publishing house].................DLB-46

Knowles, John 1926- DLB-6

Knox, Frank 1874-1944 ....DLB-29

Knox, John Armoy 1850-1906.............................DLB-23

Knox, Ronald Arbuthnott 1888-1957.................DLB-77

Kober, Arthur 1900-1975 ....DLB-11

Koch, Howard 1902- DLB-26

Koch, Kenneth 1925- DLB-5

Koenigsberg, Moses 1879-1945 ....DLB-25

Koeppen, Wolfgang 1906- DLB-69

Koestler, Arthur 1905-1983 ....Y-83

Kolb, Annette 1870-1967 ....DLB-66

Kolbenheyer, Erwin Guido 1878-1962.............DLB-66

Kolodny, Annette 1941- DLB-67

Komroff, Manuel 1890-1974 ....DLB-4

Konigsburg, E. L. 1930- DLB-52

Kopit, Arthur 1937- DLB-7

Kops, Bernard 1926?- DLB-13

Kornbluth, C. M. 1923-1958.............................DLB-8

Kosinski, Jerzy 1933- DLB-2; Y-82

Kraf, Elaine 1946- Y-81

Krasna, Norman 1909-1984.............................DLB-26

Krauss, Ruth 1911- DLB-52

Kreuder, Ernst 1903-1972 ....DLB-69

Kreymborg, Alfred 1883-1966 ....DLB-4, 54

Krieger, Murray 1923- DLB-67

Krim, Seymour 1922- DLB-16

Krock, Arthur 1886-1974 ....DLB-29

Kroetsch, Robert 1927- DLB-53

Krutch, Joseph Wood 1893-1970.........................DLB-63

Kubin, Alfred 1877-1959 ....DLB-81

Kubrick, Stanley 1928- DLB-26

Kumin, Maxine 1925- DLB-5

Kunnert, Günter 1929- DLB-75

Kunitz, Stanley 1905- DLB-48

Kunjufu, Johari M. (see Amini, Johari M.)

Kunze, Reiner 1933- DLB-75

Kupferberg, Tuli 1923- DLB-16

Kurz, Isolde 1853-1944.................................DLB-66

Kusenberg, Kurt 1904-1983 ....DLB-69

Kuttner, Henry 1915-1958.............................DLB-8

Kyd, Thomas 1558-1594 ....DLB-62

Kyger, Joanne 1934- DLB-16

Kyne, Peter B. 1880-1957 ....DLB-78

L

Laberge, Albert 1871-1960 ....DLB-68

Laberge, Marie 1950- DLB-60

Lacretelle, Jacques de 1888-1985........................DLB-65

Ladd, Joseph Brown 1764-1786........................DLB-37

La Farge, Oliver 1901-1963................................DLB-9

Lafferty, R. A. 1914- DLB-8

Laird, Carobeth 1895- Y-82

Laird and Lee DLB-49

Lalonde, Michèle 1937-....................................DLB-60

Lamantia, Philip 1927- DLB-16

Lambert, Betty 1933-1983 ....DLB-60

L'Amour, Louis 1908?- Y-80

Lamson, Wolffe and Company DLB-49

Lancer Books DLB-46

Landesman, Jay 1919- and
    Landesman, Fran 1927- DLB-16

Lane, Charles 1800-1870..................................DLB-1

The John Lane Company DLB-49

Lane, M. Travis 1934- DLB-60

Lane, Patrick 1939- DLB-53

Lane, Pinkie Gordon 1923- DLB-41

Laney, Al 1896- DLB-4

Langevin, André 1927- DLB-60

Langgässer, Elisabeth 1899-1950......................DLB-69

Lanham, Edwin 1904-1979 ....DLB-4

Lanier, Sidney 1842-1881 ....DLB-64

Lardner, Ring 1885-1933...................DLB-11, 25

Lardner, Ring, Jr. 1915- DLB-26

Lardner 100: Ring Lardner
    Centennial Symposium...............................Y-85

Larkin, Philip 1922-1985 ....DLB-27

La Rocque, Gilbert 1943-1984 ....DLB-60

Laroque de Roquebrune, Robert
    (see Roquebrune, Robert de)

Larrick, Nancy 1910- DLB-61

Larsen, Nella 1893-1964 ....DLB-51

Lasker-Schüler, Else 1869-1945 ....DLB-66

Lathrop, Dorothy P. 1891-1980........................DLB-22

Lathrop, George Parsons 1851-1898..................DLB-71

Lathrop, John, Jr. 1772-1820 ....DLB-37

Latimore, Jewel Christine McLawler (see Amini,
    Johari M.)

Laughlin, James 1914- DLB-48

Laumer, Keith 1925- DLB-8

Laurence, Margaret 1926-1987.........................DLB-53

Laurents, Arthur 1918- DLB-26

Laurie, Annie (see Black, Winifred)

Lavin, Mary 1912- DLB-15

Lawless, Anthony (see MacDonald, Philip)

Lawrence, David 1888-1973..............................DLB-29

Lawrence, D. H. 1885-1930....................DLB-10, 19, 36

Lawson, John ?-1711 ....DLB-24

Lawson, Robert 1892-1957 ....DLB-22

Lawson, Victor F. 1850-1925 ....DLB-25

Lea, Henry Charles 1825-1909........................DLB-47

Lea, Tom 1907- DLB-6

Leacock, John 1729-1802 ....DLB-31

Lear, Edward 1812-1888..................................DLB-32

Leary, Timothy 1920- DLB-16

Leary, W. A., and Company DLB-49

Léautaud, Paul 1872-1956 ....DLB-65

Leavitt and Allen..DLB-49

Lécavelé, Roland (see Dorgelès, Roland)

Lechlitner, Ruth 1901- DLB-48

Leclerc, Félix 1914- DLB-60

Le Clézio, J. M. G. 1940- DLB-83

Lectures on Rhetoric and Belles Lettres (1783),
    by Hugh Blair [excerpts].............................DLB-31

Leder, Rudolf (see Hermlin, Stephan)

Lederer, Charles 1910-1976..............................DLB-26

Ledwidge, Francis 1887-1917 ....DLB-20

Lee, Dennis 1939- DLB-53

Lee, Don L. (see Madhubuti, Haki R.)

Lee, George W. 1894-1976 ....DLB-51

Lee, Harper 1926- DLB-6

Lee, Harriet (1757-1851) and
    Lee, Sophia (1750-1824) DLB-39

Lee, Laurie 1914- DLB-27

Lee, Nathaniel circa 1645 - 1692.....................DLB-80

Lee, Vernon 1856-1935....................................DLB-57

Lee and Shepard DLB-49

Le Fanu, Joseph Sheridan 1814-1873 ....DLB-21, 70

Leffland, Ella 1931- Y-84

le Fort, Gertrud von 1876-1971..........................DLB-66

Le Gallienne, Richard 1866-1947........................DLB-4

Legaré, Hugh Swinton 1797-1843 ....DLB-3, 59, 73

Legaré, James M. 1823-1859 ....DLB-3

Le Guin, Ursula K. 1929- DLB-8, 52

Lehman, Ernest 1920- DLB-44

Lehmann, John 1907- DLB-27

Lehmann, Rosamond 1901- DLB-15

Lehmann, Wilhelm 1882-1968 ....DLB-56

Leiber, Fritz 1910- DLB-8

Leinster, Murray 1896-1975 ....DLB-8

Leitch, Maurice 1933- DLB-14

Leland, Charles G. 1824-1903 ....DLB-11

L'Engle, Madeleine 1918- DLB-52

Lennart, Isobel 1915-1971 ....DLB-44

Lennox, Charlotte 1729 or 1730-1804 ....DLB-39

Lenski, Lois 1893-1974 ....DLB-22

Lenz, Hermann 1913- DLB-69

Lenz, Siegfried 1926- DLB-75

Leonard, Hugh 1926- DLB-13

Leonard, William Ellery 1876-1944 ....DLB-54

Le Queux, William 1864-1927...........................DLB-70

Lerner, Max 1902- DLB-29

LeSieg, Theo. (see Geisel, Theodor Seuss)

Leslie, Frank 1821-1880...............................DLB-43, 79

The Frank Leslie Publishing House DLB-49

Lessing, Bruno 1870-1940...............................DLB-28

Lessing, Doris 1919- DLB-15; Y-85

Lettau, Reinhard 1929- DLB-75

Letter to [Samuel] Richardson on *Clarissa*
(1748), by Henry Fielding...........................DLB-39

Lever, Charles 1806-1872 ....DLB-21

Levertov, Denise 1923- DLB-5

Levi, Peter 1931- DLB-40

Levien, Sonya 1888-1960 ....DLB-44

Levin, Meyer 1905-1981 ....DLB-9, 28; Y-81

Levine, Philip 1928- DLB-5

Levy, Benn Wolfe 1900-1973....................DLB-13; Y-81

Lewes, George Henry 1817-1878 ....DLB-55

Lewis, Alfred H. 1857-1914.............................DLB-25

Lewis, Alun 1915-1944....................................DLB-20

Lewis, C. Day (see Day Lewis, C.)

Lewis, Charles B. 1842-1924...........................DLB-11

Lewis, C. S. 1898-1963 ....DLB-15

Lewis, Henry Clay 1825-1850 ....DLB-3

Lewis, Janet 1899- Y-87

Lewis, Matthew Gregory 1775-1818 ....DLB-39

Lewis, Richard circa 1700-1734.......................DLB-24

Lewis, Sinclair 1885-1951 ....DLB-9; DS-1

Lewis, Wyndham 1882-1957 ....DLB-15

Lewisohn, Ludwig 1882-1955....................DLB-4, 9, 28

The Library of America.................................DLB-46

The Licensing Act of 1737...............................DLB-84

Liebling, A. J. 1904-1963 ....DLB-4

Lieutenant Murray (see Ballou, Maturin Murray)

Lilar, Françoise (see Mallet-Joris, Françoise)

Lillo, George 1691-1739..................................DLB-84

Lilly, Wait and Company DLB-49

Limited Editions Club DLB-46

Lincoln and Edmands DLB-49

Lindsay, Jack 1900- Y-84

Lindsay, Vachel 1879-1931...............................DLB-54

Linebarger, Paul Myron Anthony (see
Smith, Cordwainer)

Link, Arthur S. 1920- DLB-17

Linn, John Blair 1777-1804 ....DLB-37

Linton, Eliza Lynn 1822-1898..........................DLB-18

Linton, William James 1812-1897 ....DLB-32

Lion Books...DLB-46

Lionni, Leo 1910- DLB-61

Lippincott, J. B., Company DLB-49

Lippincott, Sara Jane Clarke 1823-1904............DLB-43

Lippmann, Walter 1889-1974 ....DLB-29

Lipton, Lawrence 1898-1975 ....DLB-16

Literary Documents: William Faulkner
and the People-to-People Program Y-86

Literary Documents II: *Library Journal–*
Statements and Questionnaires from
First Novelists.......................................Y-87

Literary Effects of World War II
[British novel] DLB-15

Literary Prizes [British] DLB-15

Literary Research Archives: The Humanities
Research Center, University of Texas..............Y-82

Literary Research Archives II: Berg

Collection of English and American Literature
of the New York Public Library........................Y-83

Literary Research Archives III:
The Lilly Library..Y-84

Literary Research Archives IV:
The John Carter Brown Library....................Y-85

Literary Research Archives V:
Kent State Special Collections.......................Y-86

Literary Research Archives VI: The Modern
Literary Manuscripts Collection in the
Special Collections of the Washington
University Libraries....................................Y-87

"Literary Style" (1857), by William
Forsyth [excerpt]......................................DLB-57

Literatura Chicanesca:
The View From Without............................DLB-82

Literature at Nurse, or Circulating Morals (1885),
by George Moore......................................DLB-18

Littell, Eliakim 1797-1870.............................DLB-79

Littell, Robert S. 1831-1896...........................DLB-79

Little, Brown and Company...........................DLB-49

Littlewood, Joan 1914-................................DLB-13

Lively, Penelope 1933-.................................DLB-14

Livesay, Dorothy 1909-................................DLB-68

Livings, Henry 1929-...................................DLB-13

Livingston, Anne Howe 1763-1841................DLB-37

Livingston, Myra Cohn 1926-.......................DLB-61

Livingston, William 1723-1790......................DLB-31

Lizárraga, Sylvia S. 1925-.............................DLB-82

Llewellyn, Richard 1906-1983......................DLB-15

Lobel, Arnold 1933-....................................DLB-61

Lochridge, Betsy Hopkins (see Fancher, Betsy)

Locke, David Ross 1833-1888......................DLB-11, 23

Locke, John 1632-1704................................DLB-31

Locke, Richard Adams 1800-1871.................DLB-43

Locker-Lampson, Frederick 1821-1895..........DLB-35

Lockridge, Ross, Jr. 1914-1948......................Y-80

Locrine and *Selimus*....................................DLB-62

Lodge, David 1935-.....................................DLB-14

Lodge, George Cabot 1873-1909...................DLB-54

Lodge, Henry Cabot 1850-1924....................DLB-47

Loeb, Harold 1891-1974...............................DLB-4

Logan, James 1674-1751..............................DLB-24

Logan, John 1923-.......................................DLB-5

Logue, Christopher 1926-.............................DLB-27

London, Jack 1876-1916........................DLB-8, 12, 78

Long, H., and Brother..................................DLB-49

Long, Haniel 1888-1956................................DLB-45

Longfellow, Henry Wadsworth 1807-1882....DLB-1, 59

Longfellow, Samuel 1819-1892......................DLB-1

Longley, Michael 1939-................................DLB-40

Longmans, Green and Company....................DLB-49

Longstreet, Augustus Baldwin
1790-1870.......................................DLB-3, 11, 74

Longworth, D. [publishing house]..................DLB-49

Lonsdale, Frederick 1881-1954......................DLB-10

A Look at the Contemporary Black Theatre
Movement..DLB-38

Loos, Anita 1893-1981.......................DLB-11, 26; Y-81

Lopate, Phillip 1943-....................................Y-80

López, Diana (see Isabella, Ríos)

The Lord Chamberlain's Office and Stage
Censorship in England...............................DLB-10

Lorde, Audre 1934-.....................................DLB-41

Loring, A. K. [publishing house]....................DLB-49

Loring and Mussey......................................DLB-46

Lossing, Benson J. 1813-1891........................DLB-30

Lothar, Ernst 1890-1974...............................DLB-81

Lothrop, D., and Company............................DLB-49

Lothrop, Harriet M. 1844-1924......................DLB-42

The Lounger, no. 20 (1785), by Henry
Mackenzie...DLB-39

Lounsbury, Thomas R. 1838-1915.................DLB-71

Lovell, John W., Company.............................DLB-49

Lovell, Coryell and Company.........................DLB-49

Lovingood, Sut (see Harris, George Washington)

Low, Samuel 1765-?....................................DLB-37

Lowell, Amy 1874-1925................................DLB-54

Lowell, James Russell 1819-1891.......DLB-1, 11, 64, 79

Lowell, Robert 1917-1977.............................DLB-5

Lowenfels, Walter 1897-1976........................DLB-4

Lowndes, Marie Belloc 1868-1947.................DLB-70

Lowry, Lois 1937-.......................................DLB-52

Lowry, Malcolm 1909-1957...........................DLB-15

Lowther, Pat 1935-1975................................DLB-53

Loy, Mina 1882-1966 ....DLB-4, 54

Lucas, Fielding, Jr. [publishing house]..............DLB-49

Luce, John W., and Company DLB-46

Lucie-Smith, Edward 1933- DLB-40

Ludlum, Robert 1927- Y-82

Ludwig, Jack 1922- DLB-60

Luke, Peter 1919- DLB-13

The F. M. Lupton Publishing Company DLB-49

Lurie, Alison 1926- DLB-2

Lyly, John circa 1554-1606 ....DLB-62

Lyon, Matthew 1749-1822..............................DLB-43

Lytle, Andrew 1902- DLB-6

Lytton, Edward (see Bulwer-Lytton, Edward)

Lytton, Edward Robert Bulwer 1831-1891 ....DLB-32

M

Maass, Joachim 1901-1972 ....DLB-69

Mabie, Hamilton Wright 1845-1916...................DLB-71

Mac A'Ghobhainn, Iain (see Smith, Iain Crichton)

MacArthur, Charles 1895-1956...............DLB-7, 25, 44

Macaulay, David 1945- DLB-61

Macaulay, Rose 1881-1958 ....DLB-36

Macaulay, Thomas Babington 1800-1859 ....DLB-32, 55

Macaulay Company DLB-46

MacBeth, George 1932- DLB-40

MacCaig, Norman 1910- DLB-27

MacDiarmid, Hugh 1892-1978 ....DLB-20

MacDonald, George 1824-1905 ....DLB-18

MacDonald, John D. 1916-1986 ....DLB-8; Y-86

MacDonald, Philip 1899?-1980 ....DLB-77

Macdonald, Ross (see Millar, Kenneth)

MacEwen, Gwendolyn 1941- DLB-53

Macfadden, Bernarr 1868-1955..........................DLB-25

Machen, Arthur Llewelyn Jones 1863-1947.......DLB-36

MacInnes, Colin 1914-1976 ....DLB-14

MacKaye, Percy 1875-1956 ....DLB-54

Macken, Walter 1915-1967...............................DLB-13

Mackenzie, Compton 1883-1972.........................DLB-34

Mackenzie, Henry 1745-1831 ....DLB-39

Mackey, William Wellington 1937- DLB-38

Mackintosh, Elizabeth (see Tey, Josephine)

MacLean, Katherine Anne 1925- DLB-8

MacLeish, Archibald 1892-1982.......DLB-4, 7, 45; Y-82

MacLennan, Hugh 1907- DLB-68

MacLeod, Alistair 1936- DLB-60

Macleod, Norman 1906- DLB-4

The Macmillan Company...................................DLB-49

MacNamara, Brinsley 1890-1963 ....DLB-10

MacNeice, Louis 1907-1963 ....DLB-10, 20

Macpherson, Jay 1931- DLB-53

Macpherson, Jeanie 1884-1946..........................DLB-44

Macrae Smith Company DLB-46

Macy-Masius...DLB-46

Madden, David 1933- DLB-6

Maddow, Ben 1909- DLB-44

Madgett, Naomi Long 1923- DLB-76

Madhubuti, Haki R. 1942- DLB-5, 41

Madison, James 1751-1836 ....DLB-37

Mahan, Alfred Thayer 1840-1914.....................DLB-47

Maheux-Forcier, Louise 1929- DLB-60

Mahin, John Lee 1902-1984 ....DLB-44

Mahon, Derek 1941- DLB-40

Mailer, Norman 1923-
................................DLB-2, 16, 28; Y-80, 83; DS-3

Maillet, Adrienne 1885-1963 ....DLB-68

Maillet, Antonine 1929- DLB-60

Main Selections of the Book-of-the-Month Club,
    1926-1945 ....DLB-9

Main Trends in Twentieth-Century
    Book Clubs DLB-46

Mainwaring, Daniel 1902-1977..........................DLB-44

Major, André 1942- DLB-60

Major, Clarence 1936- DLB-33

Major, Kevin 1949- DLB-60

Major Books...DLB-46

Makemie, Francis circa 1658-1708.....................DLB-24

Malamud, Bernard 1914-1986.......DLB-2, 28; Y-80, 86

Malleson, Lucy Beatrice (see Gilbert, Anthony)

Mallet-Joris, Françoise 1930- DLB-83

Mallock, W. H. 1849-1923.........................DLB-18, 57

Malone, Dumas 1892-1986................................DLB-17

Malraux, André 1901-1976...............................DLB-72

Malzberg, Barry N. 1939- DLB-8

Mamet, David 1947- DLB-7

Mandel, Eli 1922- DLB-53

Mandiargues, André Pieyre de 1909- DLB-83

Manfred, Frederick 1912- DLB-6

Mangan, Sherry 1904-1961..............................DLB-4

Mankiewicz, Herman 1897-1953 ....DLB-26

Mankiewicz, Joseph L. 1909- DLB-44

Mankowitz, Wolf 1924- DLB-15

Manley, Delarivière 1672?-1724 ....DLB-39, 80

Mann, Abby 1927- DLB-44

Mann, Heinrich 1871-1950..............................DLB-66

Mann, Horace 1796-1859.................................DLB-1

Mann, Klaus 1906-1949 ....DLB-56

Mann, Thomas 1875-1955 ....DLB-66

Manning, Marie 1873?-1945 ....DLB-29

Manning and Loring DLB-49

Mano, D. Keith 1942- DLB-6

Manor Books DLB-46

March, William 1893-1954...............................DLB-9

Marchessault, Jovette 1938- DLB-60

Marcus, Frank 1928- DLB-13

Marek, Richard, Books....................................DLB-46

Marion, Frances 1886-1973.............................DLB-44

Marius, Richard C. 1933- Y-85

The Mark Taper Forum...................................DLB-7

Markfield, Wallace 1926- DLB-2, 28

Markham, Edwin 1852-1940............................DLB-54

Markle, Fletcher 1921- DLB-68

Marlatt, Daphne 1942- DLB-60

Marlowe, Christopher 1564-1593 ....DLB-62

Marmion, Shakerley 1603-1639 ....DLB-58

Marquand, John P. 1893-1960.........................DLB-9

Marquis, Don 1878-1937.............................DLB-11, 25

Marriott, Anne 1913- DLB-68

Marryat, Frederick 1792-1848 ....DLB-21

Marsh, George Perkins 1801-1882 ....DLB-1, 64

Marsh, James 1794-1842...............................DLB-1, 59

Marsh, Capen, Lyon and Webb DLB-49

Marsh, Ngaio 1899-1982.................................DLB-77

Marshall, Edward 1932- DLB-16

Marshall, James 1942- DLB-61

Marshall, Paule 1929-......................................DLB-33

Marshall, Tom 1938- DLB-60

Marston, John 1576-1634.................................DLB-58

Marston, Philip Bourke 1850-1887.................DLB-35

Martens, Kurt 1870-1945.................................DLB-66

Martien, William S. [publishing house]............DLB-49

Martin, Abe (see Hubbard, Kin)

Martin, Claire 1914- DLB-60

Martin du Gard, Roger 1881-1958...................DLB-65

Martineau, Harriet 1802-1876.....................DLB-21, 55

Martínez, Max 1943- DLB-82

Martyn, Edward 1859-1923 ....DLB-10

Marvin X 1944- DLB-38

Marzials, Theo 1850-1920................................DLB-35

Masefield, John 1878-1967 ....DLB-10, 19

Mason, A. E. W. 1865-1948 ....DLB-70

Mason, Bobbie Ann 1940- Y-87

Mason Brothers...DLB-49

Massey, Gerald 1828-1907 ....DLB-32

Massinger, Philip 1583-1640...........................DLB-58

Masters, Edgar Lee 1868-1950 ....DLB-54

Mather, Cotton 1663-1728...........................DLB-24, 30

Mather, Increase 1639-1723 ....DLB-24

Mather, Richard 1596-1669 ....DLB-24

Matheson, Richard 1926- DLB-8, 44

Matheus, John F. 1887- DLB-51

Mathews, Cornelius 1817?-1889 ....DLB-3, 64

Mathias, Roland 1915- DLB-27

Mathis, June 1892-1927 ....DLB-44

Mathis, Sharon Bell 1937- DLB-33

Matthews, Brander 1852-1929....................DLB-71, 78

Matthews, Jack 1925-......................................DLB-6

Matthews, William 1942- DLB-5

Matthiessen, F. O. 1902-1950 ....DLB-63

Matthiessen, Peter 1927- DLB-6

Maugham, W. Somerset 1874-1965 ....DLB-10, 36, 77

Mauriac, Claude 1914- DLB-83

Mauriac, François 1885-1970..........................DLB-65

Maurice, Frederick Denison 1805-1872 ....DLB-55

Maurois, André 1885-1967 ....DLB-65

Maury, James 1718-1769.........................DLB-31

Mavor, Elizabeth 1927- DLB-14

Mavor, Osborne Henry (see Bridie, James)

Maxwell, H. [publishing house] DLB-49

Maxwell, William 1908- Y-80

May, Elaine 1932- DLB-44

May, Thomas 1595 or 1596-1650 ....DLB-58

Mayer, Mercer 1943- DLB-61

Mayer, O. B. 1818-1891 ....DLB-3

Mayes, Wendell 1919- DLB-26

Mayfield, Julian 1928-1984.....................DLB-33; Y-84

Mayhew, Henry 1812-1887.........................DLB-18, 55

Mayhew, Jonathan 1720-1766.........................DLB-31

Mayne, Seymour 1944- DLB-60

Mayor, Flora Macdonald 1872-1932...................DLB-36

Mazursky, Paul 1930- DLB-44

McAlmon, Robert 1896-1956 ....DLB-4, 45

McBride, Robert M., and Company DLB-46

McCaffrey, Anne 1926- DLB-8

McCarthy, Cormac 1933- DLB-6

McCarthy, Mary 1912- DLB-2; Y-81

McCay, Winsor 1871-1934 ....DLB-22

McClatchy, C. K. 1858-1936 ....DLB-25

McClellan, George Marion 1860-1934 ....DLB-50

McCloskey, Robert 1914- DLB-22

McClure, Joanna 1930- DLB-16

McClure, Michael 1932- DLB-16

McClure, Phillips and Company.......................DLB-46

McClurg, A. C., and Company DLB-49

McCluskey, John A., Jr. 1944- DLB-33

McCollum, Michael A. 1946.....................Y-87

McCord, David 1897- DLB-61

McCorkle, Jill 1958- Y-87

McCorkle, Samuel Eusebius 1746-1811 ....DLB-37

McCormick, Anne O'Hare 1880-1954...............DLB-29

McCormick, Robert R. 1880-1955...............DLB-29

McCoy, Horace 1897-1955.........................DLB-9

McCullagh, Joseph B. 1842-1896 ....DLB-23

McCullers, Carson 1917-1967.........................DLB-2, 7

McDonald, Forrest 1927- DLB-17

McDougall, Colin 1917-1984 ....DLB-68

McDowell, Obolensky DLB-46

McEwan, Ian 1948- DLB-14

McFadden, David 1940- DLB-60

McGahern, John 1934- DLB-14

McGeehan, W. O. 1879-1933.........................DLB-25

McGill, Ralph 1898-1969 ....DLB-29

McGinley, Phyllis 1905-1978.........................DLB-11, 48

McGirt, James E. 1874-1930 ....DLB-50

McGough, Roger 1937- DLB-40

McGraw-Hill DLB-46

McGuane, Thomas 1939- DLB-2; Y-80

McGuckian, Medbh 1950- DLB-40

McGuffey, William Holmes 1800-1873 ....DLB-42

McIlvanney, William 1936- DLB-14

McIntyre, O. O. 1884-1938.........................DLB-25

McKay, Claude 1889-1948.........................DLB-4, 45, 51

The David McKay Company.........................DLB-49

McKean, William V. 1820-1903.........................DLB-23

McKinley, Robin 1952- DLB-52

McLaren, Floris Clark 1904-1978 ....DLB-68

McLaverty, Michael 1907- DLB-15

McLean, John R. 1848-1916 ....DLB-23

McLean, William L. 1852-1931.........................DLB-25

McLoughlin Brothers DLB-49

McMaster, John Bach 1852-1932.....................DLB-47

McMurtry, Larry 1936- DLB-2; Y-80, 87

McNally, Terrence 1939- DLB-7

McNeil, Florence 1937- DLB-60

McNeile, Herman Cyril 1888-1937 ....DLB-77

McPherson, James Alan 1943- DLB-38

McPherson, Sandra 1943- Y-86

McWhirter, George 1939- DLB-60

Mead, Matthew 1924- DLB-40

Mead, Taylor ?- DLB-16

Medill, Joseph 1823-1899 ....DLB-43

Medoff, Mark 1940- DLB-7

Meek, Alexander Beaufort 1814-1865 ....DLB-3

Meinke, Peter 1932- DLB-5

Melançon, Robert 1947- DLB-60

Mell, Max 1882-1971.........................DLB-81

Meltzer, David 1937- DLB-16

Meltzer, Milton 1915- DLB-61

Melville, Herman 1819-1891 ....DLB-3, 74

Memoirs of Life and Literature (1920),
    by W. H. Mallock [excerpt].........................DLB-57

Mencken, H. L. 1880-1956 ....DLB-11, 29, 63

Méndez M., Miguel 1930- DLB-82

Mercer, Cecil William (see Yates, Dornford)

Mercer, David 1928-1980................................DLB-13

Mercer, John 1704-1768 ....DLB-31

Meredith, George 1828-1909.................DLB-18, 35, 57

Meredith, Owen (see Lytton, Edward Robert Bulwer)

Meredith, William 1919- DLB-5

Meriwether, Louise 1923- DLB-33

Merriam, Eve 1916- DLB-61

The Merriam Company DLB-49

Merrill, James 1926- DLB-5; Y-85

Merrill and Baker...DLB-49

The Mershon Company DLB-49

Merton, Thomas 1915-1968 ....DLB-48; Y-81

Merwin, W. S. 1927- DLB-5

Messner, Julian [publishing house]....................DLB-46

Metcalf, J. [publishing house] DLB-49

Metcalf, John 1938- DLB-60

The Methodist Book Concern DLB-49

Mew, Charlotte 1869-1928 ....DLB-19

Mewshaw, Michael 1943- Y-80

Meyer, E. Y. 1946- DLB-75

Meyer, Eugene 1875-1959 ....DLB-29

Meynell, Alice 1847-1922 ....DLB-19

Meyrink, Gustav 1868-1932 ....DLB-81

Micheaux, Oscar 1884-1951.............................DLB-50

Micheline, Jack 1929- DLB-16

Michener, James A. 1907?- DLB-6

Micklejohn, George circa 1717-1818 ....DLB-31

Middleton, Christopher 1926- DLB-40

Middleton, Stanley 1919- DLB-14

Middleton, Thomas 1580-1627.........................DLB-58

Miegel, Agnes 1879-1964................................DLB-56

Miles, Josephine 1911-1985.............................DLB-48

Milius, John 1944- DLB-44

Mill, John Stuart 1806-1873 ....DLB-55

Millar, Kenneth 1915-1983 ....DLB-2; Y-83; DS-6

Millay, Edna St. Vincent 1892-1950 ....DLB-45

Miller, Arthur 1915- DLB-7

Miller, Caroline 1903- DLB-9

Miller, Eugene Ethelbert 1950- DLB-41

Miller, Henry 1891-1980 ....DLB-4, 9; Y-80

Miller, J. Hillis 1928- DLB-67

Miller, James [publishing house] DLB-49

Miller, Jason 1939- DLB-7

Miller, May 1899- DLB-41

Miller, Perry 1905-1963 ....DLB-17, 63

Miller, Walter M., Jr. 1923- DLB-8

Miller, Webb 1892-1940 ....DLB-29

Millhauser, Steven 1943- DLB-2

Millican, Arthenia J. Bates 1920- DLB-38

Milne, A. A. 1882-1956................................DLB-10, 77

Milner, Ron 1938- DLB-38

Milnes, Richard Monckton (Lord Houghton)
    1809-1885 ....DLB-32

Minton, Balch and Company...........................DLB-46

Miron, Gaston 1928- DLB-60

Mitchel, Jonathan 1624-1668 ....DLB-24

Mitchell, Adrian 1932- DLB-40

Mitchell, Donald Grant 1822-1908....................DLB-1

Mitchell, Gladys 1901-1983.............................DLB-77

Mitchell, James Leslie 1901-1935......................DLB-15

Mitchell, John (see Slater, Patrick)

Mitchell, John Ames 1845-1918......................DLB-79

Mitchell, Julian 1935- DLB-14

Mitchell, Ken 1940- DLB-60

Mitchell, Langdon 1862-1935 ....DLB-7

Mitchell, Loften 1919- DLB-38

Mitchell, Margaret 1900-1949...........................DLB-9

Modern Age Books DLB-46

"Modern English Prose" (1876),
    by George Saintsbury DLB-57

The Modern Language Association of America
    Celebrates Its Centennial Y-84

The Modern Library DLB-46

Modern Novelists–Great and Small (1855), by
    Margaret Oliphant.....................................DLB-21

"Modern Style" (1857), by Cockburn
Thomson [excerpt] DLB-57

The Modernists (1932), by Joseph Warren
Beach..DLB-36

Modiano, Patrick 1945- DLB-83

Moffat, Yard and Company DLB-46

Monkhouse, Allan 1858-1936 ....DLB-10

Monro, Harold 1879-1932 ....DLB-19

Monroe, Harriet 1860-1936................DLB-54

Monsarrat, Nicholas 1910-1979 ....DLB-15

Montague, John 1929- DLB-40

Montgomery, John 1919- DLB-16

Montgomery, Marion 1925- DLB-6

Montherlant, Henry de 1896-1972 ......DLB-72

Moody, Joshua circa 1633-1697 ....DLB-24

Moody, William Vaughn 1869-1910..............DLB-7, 54

Moorcock, Michael 1939- DLB-14

Moore, Catherine L. 1911- DLB-8

Moore, Clement Clarke 1779-1863 ....DLB-42

Moore, George 1852-1933.......................DLB-10, 18, 57

Moore, Marianne 1887-1972 ....DLB-45

Moore, T. Sturge 1870-1944 ....DLB-19

Moore, Ward 1903-1978 ....DLB-8

Moore, Wilstach, Keys and Company DLB-49

The Moorland-Spingarn
Research Center DLB-76

Moraga, Cherríe 1952- DLB-82

Morales, Alejandro 1944- DLB-82

Morency, Pierre 1942- DLB-60

Morgan, Berry 1919- DLB-6

Morgan, Charles 1894-1958................DLB-34

Morgan, Edmund S. 1916- DLB-17

Morgan, Edwin 1920- DLB-27

Morgner, Irmtraud 1933- DLB-75

Morison, Samuel Eliot 1887-1976........DLB-17

Morley, Christopher 1890-1957............DLB-9

Morley, John 1838-1923......................DLB-57

Morris, George Pope 1802-1864.........DLB-73

Morris, Lewis 1833-1907....................DLB-35

Morris, Richard B. 1904- DLB-17

Morris, William 1834-1896...................DLB-18, 35, 57

Morris, Willie 1934- Y-80

Morris, Wright 1910- DLB-2; Y-81

Morrison, Arthur 1863-1945 ....DLB-70

Morrison, Toni 1931- DLB-6, 33; Y-81

Morrow, William, and Company DLB-46

Morse, James Herbert 1841-1923.......DLB-71

Morse, Jedidiah 1761-1826 ....DLB-37

Morse, John T., Jr. 1840-1937............DLB-47

Mortimer, John 1923- DLB-13

Morton, John P., and Company DLB-49

Morton, Nathaniel 1613-1685.............DLB-24

Morton, Sarah Wentworth 1759-1846 ....DLB-37

Morton, Thomas circa 1579-circa 1647.............DLB-24

Mosley, Nicholas 1923- DLB-14

Moss, Arthur 1889-1969 ....DLB-4

Moss, Howard 1922- DLB-5

The Most Powerful Book Review in America
[*New York Times Book Review*] Y-82

Motion, Andrew 1952- DLB-40

Motley, John Lothrop 1814-1877............DLB-1, 30, 59

Motley, Willard 1909-1965..................DLB-76

Motteux, Peter Anthony 1663-1718 ....DLB-80

Mottram, R. H. 1883-1971..................DLB-36

Mouré, Erin 1955- DLB-60

Movies from Books, 1920-1974 ....DLB-9

Mowat, Farley 1921- DLB-68

Mowrer, Edgar Ansel 1892-1977........DLB-29

Mowrer, Paul Scott 1887-1971............DLB-29

Mucedorus..DLB-62

Muhajir, El (see Marvin X)

Muhajir, Nazzam Al Fitnah (see Marvin X)

Muir, Edwin 1887-1959.......................DLB-20

Muir, Helen 1937- DLB-14

Mukherjee, Bharati 1940- DLB-60

Muldoon, Paul 1951- DLB-40

Mumford, Lewis 1895- DLB-63

Munby, Arthur Joseph 1828-1910........DLB-35

Munday, Anthony 1560-1633 ....DLB-62

Munford, Robert circa 1737-1783 ....DLB-31

Munro, Alice 1931- DLB-53

Munro, George [publishing house].........DLB-49

Munro, H. H. 1870-1916 ....DLB-34

Munro, Norman L. [publishing house] DLB-49

Munroe, James, and Company DLB-49

Munroe, Kirk 1850-1930 ....DLB-42

Munroe and Francis DLB-49

Munsell, Joel [publishing house].......................DLB-49

Munsey, Frank A. 1854-1925.............................DLB-25

Munsey, Frank A., and Company.......................DLB-49

Murdoch, Iris 1919- DLB-14

Murfree, Mary N. 1850-1922 ....DLB-12, 74

Muro, Amado 1915-1971 ....DLB-82

Murphy, Beatrice M. 1908- DLB-76

Murphy, John, and Company DLB-49

Murphy, Richard 1927- DLB-40

Murray, Albert L. 1916- DLB-38

Murray, Gilbert 1866-1957 ....DLB-10

Murray, Judith Sargent 1751-1820....................DLB-37

Murray, Pauli 1910-1985 ....DLB-41

Muschg, Adolf 1934- DLB-75

Musil, Robert 1880-1942 ....DLB-81

Mussey, Benjamin B., and Company.................DLB-49

Myers, Gustavus 1872-1942 ....DLB-47

Myers, L. H. 1881-1944 ....DLB-15

Myers, Walter Dean 1937- DLB-33

N

Nabbes, Thomas circa 1605-1641 ....DLB-58

Nabl, Franz 1883-1974.......................................DLB-81

Nabokov, Vladimir 1899-1977 ....DLB-2; Y-80; DS-3

Nabokov Festival at Cornell...............................Y-83

Nafis and Cornish...DLB-49

Naipaul, Shiva 1945-1985...................................Y-85

Naipaul, V. S. 1932- Y-85

Nancrede, Joseph [publishing house]................DLB-49

Nasby, Petroleum Vesuvius (see Locke, David Ross)

Nash, Ogden 1902-1971.....................................DLB-11

Nathan, Robert 1894-1985.................................DLB-9

The National Jewish Book Awards........................Y-85

The National Theatre and the Royal Shakespeare
    Company: The National Companies...........DLB-13

Naughton, Bill 1910- DLB-13

Neagoe, Peter 1881-1960 ....DLB-4

Neal, John 1793-1876 ....DLB-1, 59

Neal, Joseph C. 1807-1847................................DLB-11

Neal, Larry 1937-1981.......................................DLB-38

The Neale Publishing Company DLB-49

Neely, F. Tennyson [publishing house] DLB-49

"The Negro as a Writer," by
    G. M. McClellan DLB-50

"Negro Poets and Their Poetry," by
    Wallace Thurman......................................DLB-50

Neihardt, John G. 1881-1973 ....DLB-9, 54

Nelson, Alice Moore Dunbar
    1875-1935 ....DLB-50

Nelson, Thomas, and Sons.................................DLB-49

Nelson, William Rockhill 1841-1915 ....DLB-23

Nemerov, Howard 1920- DLB-5, 6; Y-83

Ness, Evaline 1911-1986.....................................DLB-61

Neugeboren, Jay 1938- DLB-28

Neumann, Alfred 1895-1952 ....DLB-56

Nevins, Allan 1890-1971 ....DLB-17

The New American Library.................................DLB-46

New Directions Publishing Corporation.............DLB-46

A New Edition of *Huck Finn* Y-85

New Forces at Work in the American Theatre:
    1915-1925 ....DLB-7

New Literary Periodicals: A Report
    for 1987...Y-87

New Literary Periodicals: A Report
    for 1988...Y-88

The New *Ulysses* Y-84

The New Variorum Shakespeare Y-85

A New Voice: The Center for the Book's First
    Five Years Y-83

The New Wave [Science Fiction] DLB-8

Newbolt, Henry 1862-1938................................DLB-19

Newbound, Bernard Slade (see Slade, Bernard)

Newby, P. H. 1918- DLB-15

Newcomb, Charles King 1820-1894 ....DLB-1

Newell, Peter 1862-1924 ....DLB-42

Newell, Robert Henry 1836-1901 ....DLB-11

Newman, David (see Benton, Robert)

Newman, Frances 1883-1928 ....Y-80

Newman, John Henry 1801-1890 ....DLB-18, 32, 55

Newman, Mark [publishing house]....................DLB-49

Newsome, Effie Lee 1885-1979 ....DLB-76

Newspaper Syndication of American Humor....DLB-11

Nichol, B. P. 1944- DLB-53

Nichols, Dudley 1895-1960 ....DLB-26

Nichols, John 1940- Y-82

Nichols, Mary Sargeant (Neal) Gove
    1810-1884 ....DLB-1

Nichols, Peter 1927- DLB-13

Nichols, Roy F. 1896-1973 ....DLB-17

Nichols, Ruth 1948- DLB-60

Nicholson, Norman 1914- DLB-27

Ní Chuilleanáin, Eiléan 1942- DLB-40

Nicol, Eric 1919- DLB-68

Nicolay, John G. 1832-1901 and
    Hay, John 1838-1905 ....DLB-47

Niebuhr, Reinhold 1892-1971 ....DLB-17

Niedecker, Lorine 1903-1970 ....DLB-48

Nieman, Lucius W. 1857-1935............................DLB-25

Niggli, Josefina 1910- Y-80

Niles, Hezekiah 1777-1839 ....DLB-43

Nims, John Frederick 1913- DLB-5

Nin, Anaïs 1903-1977..................................DLB-2, 4

1985: The Year of the Mystery:
    A Symposium...Y-85

Nissenson, Hugh 1933- DLB-28

Niven, Larry 1938- DLB-8

Nizan, Paul 1905-1940 ....DLB-72

Nobel Peace Prize
    The 1986 Nobel Peace Prize
        Nobel Lecture 1986: Hope, Despair
            and Memory
        Tributes from Abraham Bernstein,
            Norman Lamm, and John R. Silber Y-86

The Nobel Prize and Literary
    Politics...Y-88

Nobel Prize in Literature
    The 1982 Nobel Prize in Literature
        Announcement by the Swedish Academy
            of the Nobel Prize
        Nobel Lecture 1982: The Solitude of Latin
            America

        Excerpt from *One Hundred Years
            of Solitude*
        The Magical World of Macondo
        A Tribute to Gabriel García Márquez Y-82
    The 1983 Nobel Prize in Literature
        Announcement by the Swedish
            Academy
        Nobel Lecture 1983
        The Stature of William Golding................Y-83
    The 1984 Nobel Prize in Literature
        Announcement by the Swedish
            Academy
        Jaroslav Seifert Through the Eyes of the
            English-Speaking Reader
        Three Poems by Jaroslav Seifert............Y-84
    The 1985 Nobel Prize in Literature
        Announcement by the Swedish
            Academy
        Nobel Lecture 1985.................................Y-85
    The 1986 Nobel Prize in Literature
        Nobel Lecture 1986: This Past Must
            Address Its Present..............................Y-86
    The 1987 Nobel Prize in Literature
        Nobel Lecture 1987.................................Y-87
    The 1988 Nobel Prize in Literature
        Nobel Lecture 1988.................................Y-88

Noel, Roden 1834-1894 ....DLB-35

Nolan, William F. 1928- DLB-8

Noland, C. F. M. 1810?-1858............................DLB-11

Noonday Press DLB-46

Noone, John 1936- DLB-14

Nordhoff, Charles 1887-1947 ....DLB-9

Norman, Marsha 1947- Y-84

Norris, Charles G. 1881-1945 ....DLB-9

Norris, Frank 1870-1902....................................DLB-12

Norris, Leslie 1921- DLB-27

Norse, Harold 1916- DLB-16

North Point Press...DLB-46

Norton, Alice Mary (see Norton, Andre)

Norton, Andre 1912- DLB-8, 52

Norton, Andrews 1786-1853..............................DLB-1

Norton, Caroline 1808-1877 ....DLB-21

Norton, Charles Eliot 1827-1908...................DLB-1, 64

Norton, John 1606-1663 ....DLB-24

Norton, Thomas (see Sackville, Thomas)

Norton, W. W., and Company............................DLB-46

Nossack, Hans Erich 1901-1977 ....DLB-69

A Note on Technique (1926), by Elizabeth
    A. Drew [excerpts].........................DLB-36

Nourse, Alan E. 1928- DLB-8

The Novel in [Robert Browning's] "The Ring
    and the Book" (1912), by Henry James DLB-32

Novel-Reading: *The Works of Charles Dickens,*
    The Works of W. Makepeace Thackeray (1879),
    by Anthony Trollope.................................DLB-21

The Novels of Dorothy Richardson (1918), by
    May Sinclair DLB-36

Novels with a Purpose (1864),
    by Justin M'Carthy DLB-21

Nowlan, Alden 1933-1983................................DLB-53

Noyes, Alfred 1880-1958.................................DLB-20

Noyes, Crosby S. 1825-1908.............................DLB-23

Noyes, Nicholas 1647-1717..............................DLB-24

Noyes, Theodore W. 1858-1946.......................DLB-29

Nugent, Frank 1908-1965...............................DLB-44

Nye, Edgar Wilson (Bill) 1850-1896 ....DLB-11, 23

Nye, Robert 1939- DLB-14

O

Oakes, Urian circa 1631-1681 ....DLB-24

Oates, Joyce Carol 1938- DLB-2, 5; Y-81

Oberholtzer, Ellis Paxson 1868-1936 ....DLB-47

O'Brien, Edna 1932- DLB-14

O'Brien, Fitz-James 1828-1862..........................DLB-74

O'Brien, Kate 1897-1974.................................DLB-15

O'Brien, Tim 1946- Y-80

O'Casey, Sean 1880-1964................................DLB-10

Ochs, Adolph S. 1858-1935 ....DLB-25

O'Connor, Flannery 1925-1964.................DLB-2; Y-80

O'Dell, Scott 1903- DLB-52

Odell, Jonathan 1737-1818 ....DLB-31

Odets, Clifford 1906-1963 ....DLB-7, 26

O'Faolain, Julia 1932- DLB-14

O'Faolain, Sean 1900- DLB-15

O'Flaherty, Liam 1896-1984 ....DLB-36; Y-84

Off Broadway and Off-Off-Broadway DLB-7

Off-Loop Theatres DLB-7

Offord, Carl Ruthven 1910- DLB-76

Ogilvie, J. S., and Company...............................DLB-49

O'Grady, Desmond 1935- DLB-40

O'Hagan, Howard 1902-1982 ....DLB-68

O'Hara, Frank 1926-1966..............................DLB-5, 16

O'Hara, John 1905-1970............................DLB-9; DS-2

O. Henry (see Porter, William Sydney)

Old Franklin Publishing House DLB-49

Older, Fremont 1856-1935 ....DLB-25

Oliphant, Laurence 1829?-1888.........................DLB-18

Oliphant, Margaret 1828-1897 ....DLB-18

Oliver, Chad 1928- DLB-8

Oliver, Mary 1935- DLB-5

Ollier, Claude 1922- DLB-83

Olsen, Tillie 1913?- DLB-28; Y-80

Olson, Charles 1910-1970............................DLB-5, 16

Olson, Elder 1909- DLB-48, 63

On Art in Fiction (1838), by
    Edward Bulwer...DLB-21

On Learning to Write.......................................Y-88

On Some of the Characteristics of Modern
    Poetry and On the Lyrical Poems of Alfred
    Tennyson (1831), by Arthur Henry
    Hallam DLB-32

"On Style in English Prose" (1898), by Frederic
    Harrison..DLB-57

"On Style in Literature: Its Technical Elements"
    (1885), by Robert Louis Stevenson..............DLB-57

"On the Writing of Essays" (1862),
    by Alexander Smith....................................DLB-57

Ondaatje, Michael 1943- DLB-60

O'Neill, Eugene 1888-1953 ....DLB-7

Oppen, George 1908-1984...............................DLB-5

Oppenheim, E. Phillips 1866-1946....................DLB-70

Oppenheim, James 1882-1932...........................DLB-28

Oppenheimer, Joel 1930- DLB-5

Optic, Oliver (see Adams, William Taylor)

Orczy, Emma, Baroness 1865-1947 ....DLB-70

Orlovitz, Gil 1918-1973................................DLB-2, 5

Orlovsky, Peter 1933- DLB-16

Ormond, John 1923- DLB-27

Ornitz, Samuel 1890-1957 ....DLB-28, 44

Orton, Joe 1933-1967.....................................DLB-13

Orwell, George 1903-1950 ....DLB-15

The Orwell Year Y-84

Osbon, B. S. 1827-1912..............................DLB-43

Osborne, John 1929- DLB-13

Osgood, Herbert L. 1855-1918...........................DLB-47

Osgood, James R., and Company.....................DLB-49

O'Shaughnessy, Arthur 1844-1881....................DLB-35

O'Shea, Patrick [publishing house]...................DLB-49

Oswald, Eleazer 1755-1795 ....DLB-43

Otero, Miguel Antonio 1859-1944 ....DLB-82

Otis, James (see Kaler, James Otis)

Otis, James, Jr. 1725-1783 ....DLB-31

Otis, Broaders and Company...........................DLB-49

Ottendorfer, Oswald 1826-1900 ....DLB-23

Otway, Thomas 1652-1685 ....DLB-80

Ouellette, Fernand 1930- DLB-60

Ouida 1839-1908 ....DLB-18

Outing Publishing Company........................DLB-46

Outlaw Days, by Joyce Johnson.......................DLB-16

The Overlook Press......................................DLB-46

Overview of U.S. Book Publishing, 1910-1945....DLB-9

Owen, Guy 1925- DLB-5

Owen, John [publishing house].........................DLB-49

Owen, Wilfred 1893-1918 ....DLB-20

Owsley, Frank L. 1890-1956 ....DLB-17

Ozick, Cynthia 1928- DLB-28; Y-82

P

Pack, Robert 1929- DLB-5

Packaging Papa: *The Garden of Eden* Y-86

Padell Publishing Company DLB-46

Padgett, Ron 1942- DLB-5

Page, L. C., and Company DLB-49

Page, P. K. 1916- DLB-68

Page, Thomas Nelson 1853-1922 ....DLB-12, 78

Page, Walter Hines 1855-1918.......................DLB-71

Paget, Violet (see Lee, Vernon)

Pain, Philip ?-circa 1666..............................DLB-24

Paine, Robert Treat, Jr. 1773-1811 ....DLB-37

Paine, Thomas 1737-1809 ....DLB-31, 43, 73

Paley, Grace 1922- DLB-28

Palfrey, John Gorham 1796-1881..................DLB-1, 30

Palgrave, Francis Turner 1824-1897 ....DLB-35

Paltock, Robert 1697-1767..............................DLB-39

Panama, Norman 1914-   and
    Frank, Melvin 1913-1988   ....DLB-26

Pangborn, Edgar 1909-1976 ....DLB-8

"Panic Among the Philistines": A Postscript,
    An Interview with Bryan Griffin Y-81

Panneton, Philippe (see Ringuet)

Panshin, Alexei 1940- DLB-8

Pansy (see Alden, Isabella)

Pantheon Books...DLB-46

Paperback Library DLB-46

Paperback Science Fiction DLB-8

Paquet, Alfons 1881-1944 ....DLB-66

Paradis, Suzanne 1936- DLB-53

Parents' Magazine Press DLB-46

Parisian Theater, Fall 1984: Toward
    A New Baroque Y-85

Parizeau, Alice 1930- DLB-60

Parke, John 1754-1789.......................................DLB-31

Parker, Dorothy 1893-1967..........................DLB-11, 45

Parker, James 1714-1770.................................DLB-43

Parker, Theodore 1810-1860..............................DLB-1

Parkman, Francis, Jr. 1823-1893 ....DLB-1, 30

Parks, Gordon 1912- DLB-33

Parks, William 1698-1750 ....DLB-43

Parks, William [publishing house] DLB-49

Parley, Peter (see Goodrich, Samuel Griswold)

Parrington, Vernon L. 1871-1929 ....DLB-17, 63

Parton, James 1822-1891 ....DLB-30

Parton, Sara Payson Willis 1811-1872.........DLB-43, 74

Pastan, Linda 1932- DLB-5

Pastorius, Francis Daniel 1651-circa 1720 ....DLB-24

Patchen, Kenneth 1911-1972.......................DLB-16, 48

Pater, Walter 1839-1894..................................DLB-57

Paterson, Katherine 1932- DLB-52

Patmore, Coventry 1823-1896 ....DLB-35

Paton, Joseph Noel 1821-1901.........................DLB-35

Patrick, John 1906- DLB-7

Pattee, Fred Lewis 1863-1950 ....DLB-71

Patterson, Eleanor Medill 1881-1948 ....DLB-29

Patterson, Joseph Medill 1879-1946 ....DLB-29

Pattillo, Henry 1726-1801 ....DLB-37

Paul, Elliot 1891-1958 ....DLB-4

Paul, Peter, Book Company DLB-49

Paulding, James Kirke 1778-1860 ....DLB-3, 59, 74

Paulin, Tom 1949- DLB-40

Pauper, Peter, Press DLB-46

Paxton, John 1911-1985 ....DLB-44

Payn, James 1830-1898 ....DLB-18

Payne, John 1842-1916 ....DLB-35

Payne, John Howard 1791-1852 ....DLB-37

Payson and Clarke DLB-46

Peabody, Elizabeth Palmer 1804-1894 ....DLB-1

Peabody, Elizabeth Palmer [publishing
    house] DLB-49

Peabody, Oliver William Bourn 1799-1848 ....DLB-59

Peachtree Publishers, Limited DLB-46

Pead, Deuel ?-1727 ....DLB-24

Peake, Mervyn 1911-1968 ....DLB-15

Pearson, H. B. [publishing house] DLB-49

Peck, George W. 1840-1916 ....DLB-23, 42

Peck, H. C., and Theo. Bliss [publishing
    house] DLB-49

Peck, Harry Thurston 1856-1914 ....DLB-71

Peele, George 1556-1596 ....DLB-62

Pellegrini and Cudahy DLB-46

Pemberton, Sir Max 1863-1950 ....DLB-70

Penguin Books DLB-46

Penn Publishing Company DLB-49

Penn, William 1644-1718 ....DLB-24

Penner, Jonathan 1940- Y-83

Pennington, Lee 1939- Y-82

Percy, Walker 1916- DLB-2; Y-80

Perec, Georges 1936-1982 ....DLB-83

Perelman, S. J. 1904-1979 ....DLB-11, 44

Periodicals of the Beat Generation DLB-16

Perkins, Eugene 1932- DLB-41

Perkoff, Stuart Z. 1930-1974 ....DLB-16

Permabooks DLB-46

Perry, Bliss 1860-1954 ....DLB-71

Perry, Eleanor 1915-1981 ....DLB-44

"Personal Style" (1890), by John Addington
    Symonds DLB-57

Perutz, Leo 1882-1957 ....DLB-81

Peter, Laurence J. 1919- DLB-53

Peterkin, Julia 1880-1961 ....DLB-9

Petersham, Maud 1889-1971 and
    Petersham, Miska 1888-1960 ....DLB-22

Peterson, Charles Jacobs 1819-1887 ....DLB-79

Peterson, Louis 1922- DLB-76

Peterson, T. B., and Brothers DLB-49

Petry, Ann 1908- DLB-76

Pharr, Robert Deane 1916- DLB-33

Phelps, Elizabeth Stuart 1844-1911 ....DLB-74

Philippe, Charles-Louis 1874-1909 ....DLB-65

Phillips, David Graham 1867-1911 ....DLB-9, 12

Phillips, Jayne Anne 1952- Y-80

Phillips, Stephen 1864-1915 ....DLB-10

Phillips, Ulrich B. 1877-1934 ....DLB-17

Phillips, Willard 1784-1873 ....DLB-59

Phillips, Sampson and Company DLB-49

Phillpotts, Eden 1862-1960 ....DLB-10, 70

Philosophical Library DLB-46

"The Philosophy of Style" (1852), by
    Herbert Spencer DLB-57

Phinney, Elihu [publishing house] DLB-49

Phoenix, John (see Derby, George Horatio)

PHYLON (Fourth Quarter, 1950),
    The Negro in Literature:
    The Current Scene DLB-76

Pickard, Tom 1946- DLB-40

Pictorial Printing Company DLB-49

Pike, Albert 1809-1891 ....DLB-74

Pilon, Jean-Guy 1930- DLB-60

Pinckney, Josephine 1895-1957 ....DLB-6

Pinero, Arthur Wing 1855-1934 ....DLB-10

Pinget, Robert 1919- DLB-83

Pinnacle Books DLB-46

Pinsky, Robert 1940- Y-82

Pinter, Harold 1930- DLB-13

Piontek, Heinz 1925- DLB-75

Piper, H. Beam 1904-1964 ....DLB-8

Piper, Watty DLB-22

Pisar, Samuel 1929- Y-83

Pitkin, Timothy 1766-1847 ....DLB-30

The Pitt Poetry Series: Poetry
  Publishing Today Y-85

Pitter, Ruth 1897- DLB-20

Pix, Mary 1666-1709 ....DLB-80

The Place of Realism in Fiction (1895), by
  George Gissing DLB-18

Plante, David 1940- Y-83

Plath, Sylvia 1932-1963 ....DLB-5, 6

Platt and Munk Company DLB-46

Playboy Press DLB-46

Plays, Playwrights, and Playgoers DLB-84

Playwrights and Professors, by Tom
  Stoppard DLB-13

Playwrights on the Theater DLB-80

Plenzdorf, Ulrich 1934- DLB-75

Plessen, Elizabeth 1944- DLB-75

Plievier, Theodor 1892-1955 ....DLB-69

Plomer, William 1903-1973.....................DLB-20

Plumly, Stanley 1939- DLB-5

Plumpp, Sterling D. 1940- DLB-41

Plunkett, James 1920- DLB-14

Plymell, Charles 1935- DLB-16

Pocket Books DLB-46

Poe, Edgar Allan 1809-1849..............DLB-3, 59, 73, 74

Poe, James 1921-1980.............................DLB-44

The Poet Laureate of the United States
  Statements from Former Consultants
  in Poetry..Y-86

Pohl, Frederik 1919- DLB-8

Poirier, Louis (see Gracq, Julien)

Poliakoff, Stephen 1952- DLB-13

Polite, Carlene Hatcher 1932- DLB-33

Pollard, Edward A. 1832-1872.................DLB-30

Pollard, Percival 1869-1911....................DLB-71

Pollard and Moss DLB-49

Pollock, Sharon 1936- DLB-60

Polonsky, Abraham 1910- DLB-26

Poole, Ernest 1880-1950..........................DLB-9

Poore, Benjamin Perley 1820-1887.....................DLB-23

Popular Library......................................DLB-46

Porlock, Martin (see MacDonald, Philip)

Porter, Eleanor H. 1868-1920..............................DLB-9

Porter, Henry ?-? DLB-62

Porter, Katherine Anne 1890-1980........DLB-4, 9; Y-80

Porter, Peter 1929- DLB-40

Porter, William Sydney 1862-1910.........DLB-12, 78, 79

Porter, William T. 1809-1858........................DLB-3, 43

Porter and Coates DLB-49

Portis, Charles 1933- DLB-6

Poston, Ted 1906-1974 ....DLB-51

Postscript to [the Third Edition of] *Clarissa*
  (1751), by Samuel Richardson DLB-39

Potok, Chaim 1929- DLB-28; Y-84

Potter, David M. 1910-1971 ....DLB-17

Potter, John E., and Company DLB-49

Pottle, Frederick A. 1897-1987 ....Y-87

Poulin, Jacques 1937- DLB-60

Pound, Ezra 1885-1972............................DLB-4, 45, 63

Powell, Anthony 1905- DLB-15

Pownall, David 1938- DLB-14

Powys, John Cowper 1872-1963 ....DLB-15

Powys, T. F. 1875-1953 ....DLB-36

The Practice of Biography: An Interview with
  Stanley Weintraub...............................Y-82

The Practice of Biography II: An Interview with
  B. L. Reid...Y-83

The Practice of Biography III: An Interview with
  Humphrey Carpenter Y-84

The Practice of Biography IV: An Interview with
  William Manchester.............................Y-85

The Practice of Biography V: An Interview with
  Justin Kaplan Y-86

The Practice of Biography VI: An Interview with
  David Herbert Donald Y-87

Praeger Publishers.................................DLB-46

Pratt, Samuel Jackson 1749-1814 ....DLB-39

Preface to *Alwyn* (1780), by Thomas
  Holcroft..DLB-39

Preface to *Colonel Jack* (1722), by Daniel
  Defoe..DLB-39

Preface to *Evelina* (1778), by Fanny Burney.......DLB-39

Preface to *Ferdinand Count Fathom* (1753), by
   Tobias Smollett DLB-39

Preface to *Incognita* (1692), by William
   Congreve..DLB-39

Preface to *Joseph Andrews* (1742), by
   Henry Fielding DLB-39

Preface to *Moll Flanders* (1722), by Daniel
   Defoe...DLB-39

Preface to *Poems* (1853), by Matthew
   Arnold..DLB-32

Preface to *Robinson Crusoe* (1719), by Daniel
   Defoe...DLB-39

Preface to *Roderick Random* (1748), by Tobias
   Smollett DLB-39

Preface to *Roxana* (1724), by Daniel Defoe DLB-39

Preface to *St. Leon* (1799),
   by William Godwin......................................DLB-39

Preface to Sarah Fielding's *Familiar Letters*
   (1747), by Henry Fielding [excerpt] DLB-39

Preface to Sarah Fielding's *The Adventures of
   David Simple* (1744), by Henry Fielding.......DLB-39

Preface to *The Cry* (1754), by Sarah Fielding DLB-39

Preface to *The Delicate Distress* (1769), by
   Elizabeth Griffin DLB-39

Preface to *The Disguis'd Prince* (1733), by Eliza
   Haywood [excerpt] DLB-39

Preface to *The Farther Adventures of Robinson
   Crusoe* (1719), by Daniel Defoe DLB-39

Preface to the First Edition of *Pamela* (1740), by
   Samuel Richardson..DLB-39

Preface to the First Edition of *The Castle of
   Otranto* (1764), by Horace Walpole..............DLB-39

Preface to *The History of Romances* (1715), by
   Pierre Daniel Huet [excerpts].......................DLB-39

Preface to *The Life of Charlotta du Pont* (1723),
   by Penelope Aubin DLB-39

Preface to *The Old English Baron* (1778), by
   Clara Reeve...DLB-39

Preface to the Second Edition of *The Castle of
   Otranto* (1765), by Horace Walpole..............DLB-39

Preface to *The Secret History, of Queen Zarah, and
   the Zarazians* (1705), by Delarivière
   Manley..DLB-39

Preface to the Third Edition of *Clarissa* (1751),
   by Samuel Richardson [excerpt].................DLB-39

Preface to *The Works of Mrs. Davys* (1725), by

Mary Davys DLB-39

Preface to Volume 1 of *Clarissa* (1747), by
   Samuel Richardson......................................DLB-39

Preface to Volume 3 of *Clarissa* (1748), by
   Samuel Richardson......................................DLB-39

Préfontaine, Yves 1937- DLB-53

Prelutsky, Jack 1940- DLB-61

Prentice, George D. 1802-1870..........................DLB-43

Prentice-Hall DLB-46

Prescott, William Hickling 1796-1859......DLB-1, 30, 59

The Present State of the English Novel (1892),
   by George Saintsbury DLB-18

Preston, Thomas 1537-1598 ....DLB-62

Price, Reynolds 1933- DLB-2

Price, Richard 1949- Y-81

Priest, Christopher 1943- DLB-14

Priestley, J. B. 1894-1984 ....DLB-10, 34, 77; Y-84

Prime, Benjamin Young 1733-1791....................DLB-31

Prince, F. T. 1912- DLB-20

Prince, Thomas 1687-1758 ....DLB-24

The Principles of Success in Literature (1865), by
   George Henry Lewes [excerpt]....................DLB-57

Pritchett, V. S. 1900- DLB-15

Procter, Adelaide Anne 1825-1864 ....DLB-32

The Progress of Romance (1785), by Clara Reeve
   [excerpt]..DLB-39

Prokosch, Frederic 1906- DLB-48

The Proletarian Novel..DLB-9

Propper, Dan 1937- DLB-16

The Prospect of Peace (1778), by Joel Barlow DLB-37

Proud, Robert 1728-1813..................................DLB-30

Proust, Marcel 1871-1922 ....DLB-65

Prynne, J. H. 1936- DLB-40

Przybyszewski, Stanislaw 1868-1927 ....DLB-66

The Public Lending Right in America
   Statement by Sen. Charles McC. Mathias, Jr.
   PLR and the Meaning of Literary Property
   Statements on PLR by American Writers.........Y-83

The Public Lending Right in the United Kingdom
   Public Lending Right: The First Year in the
   United Kingdom Y-83

The Publication of English Renaissance
   Plays DLB-62

Publications and Social Movements
[Transcendentalism] DLB-1

Publishers and Agents: The Columbia
Connection Y-87

Publishing Fiction at LSU Press Y-87

Pugin, A. Welby 1812-1852 ....DLB-55

Pulitzer, Joseph 1847-1911 ....DLB-23

Pulitzer, Joseph, Jr. 1885-1955 ....DLB-29

Pulitzer Prizes for the Novel, 1917-1945 ....DLB-9

Purdy, James 1923- DLB-2

Pusey, Edward Bouverie 1800-1882 ....DLB-55

Putnam, George Palmer 1814-1872 ....DLB-3, 79

Putnam, Samuel 1892-1950 ....DLB-4

G. P. Putnam's Sons DLB-49

Puzo, Mario 1920- DLB-6

Pyle, Ernie 1900-1945 ....DLB-29

Pyle, Howard 1853-1911 ....DLB-42

Pym, Barbara 1913-1980 ....DLB-14; Y-87

Pynchon, Thomas 1937- DLB-2

Pyramid Books...............................DLB-46

Pyrnelle, Louise-Clarke 1850-1907 ....DLB-42

Q

Quad, M. (see Lewis, Charles B.)

The Queen City Publishing House....................DLB-49

Queneau, Raymond 1903-1976 ....DLB-72

The Question of American Copyright
in the Nineteenth Century
Headnote
Preface, by George Haven Putnam
The Evolution of Copyright, by Brander
Matthews
Summary of Copyright Legislation in the
United States, by R. R. Bowker
Analysis of the Provisions of the Copyright
Law of 1891, by George Haven Putnam
The Contest for International Copyright,
by George Haven Putnam
Cheap Books and Good Books,
by Brander Matthews...................DLB-49

Quin, Ann 1936-1973........................DLB-14

Quincy, Samuel of Georgia ?-? DLB-31

Quincy, Samuel of Massachusetts 1734-1789.....DLB-31

Quintana, Leroy V. 1944- DLB-82

Quist, Harlin, Books.........................DLB-46

Quoirez, Françoise (see Sagan, Françoise)

R

Rabe, David 1940- DLB-7

Radcliffe, Ann 1764-1823 ....DLB-39

Raddall, Thomas 1903- DLB-68

Radiguet, Raymond 1903-1923...........DLB-65

Radványi, Netty Reiling (see Seghers, Anna)

Raine, Craig 1944- DLB-40

Raine, Kathleen 1908- DLB-20

Ralph, Julian 1853-1903....................DLB-23

Ralph Waldo Emerson in 1982 ....Y-82

Rambler, no. 4 (1750), by Samuel Johnson
[excerpt].......................................DLB-39

Ramée, Marie Louise de la (see Ouida)

Ramsay, David 1749-1815 ....DLB-30

Rand, Avery and Company.................DLB-49

Rand McNally and Company..............DLB-49

Randall, Dudley 1914- DLB-41

Randall, Henry S. 1811-1876..............DLB-30

Randall, James G. 1881-1953.............DLB-17

The Randall Jarrell Symposium: A Small
Collection of Randall Jarrells
Excerpts From Papers Delivered at
the Randall Jarrell Symposium Y-86

Randolph, Anson D. F. [publishing house]........DLB-49

Randolph, Thomas 1605-1635............DLB-58

Random House................................DLB-46

Ranlet, Henry [publishing house].....................DLB-49

Ransom, John Crowe 1888-1974 ....DLB-45, 63

Raphael, Frederic 1931- DLB-14

Raphaelson, Samson 1896-1983.........DLB-44

Raskin, Ellen 1928-1984...................DLB-52

Rattigan, Terence 1911-1977 ....DLB-13

Rawlings, Marjorie Kinnan 1896-1953...........DLB-9, 22

Raworth, Tom 1938- DLB-40

Ray, David 1932- DLB-5

Ray, Henrietta Cordelia 1849-1916 ....DLB-50

Raymond, Henry J. 1820-1869................DLB-43, 79

Raymond Chandler Centenary Tributes

from Michael Avallone, James Elroy, Joe Gores,
and William F. Nolan Y-88

Reach, Angus 1821-1856....................................DLB-70

Read, Herbert 1893-1968 ....DLB-20

Read, Opie 1852-1939..DLB-23

Read, Piers Paul 1941- DLB-14

Reade, Charles 1814-1884....................................DLB-21

Reader's Digest Condensed Books DLB-46

Reading, Peter 1946- DLB-40

Reaney, James 1926- DLB-68

Rechy, John 1934- Y-82

Redding, J. Saunders 1906-1988 ....DLB-63, 76

Redfield, J. S. [publishing house] DLB-49

Redgrove, Peter 1932- DLB-40

Redmon, Anne 1943- Y-86

Redmond, Eugene B. 1937- DLB-41

Redpath, James [publishing house] DLB-49

Reed, Henry 1808-1854.......................................DLB-59

Reed, Henry 1914- DLB-27

Reed, Ishmael 1938- DLB-2, 5, 33

Reed, Sampson 1800-1880...................................DLB-1

Reese, Lizette Woodworth 1856-1935 ....DLB-54

Reese, Thomas 1742-1796 ....DLB-37

Reeve, Clara 1729-1807.......................................DLB-39

Regnery, Henry, Company DLB-46

Reid, Alastair 1926- DLB-27

Reid, Christopher 1949- DLB-40

Reid, Helen Rogers 1882-1970............................DLB-29

Reid, James ?-?..DLB-31

Reid, Mayne 1818-1883..DLB-21

Reid, Thomas 1710-1796......................................DLB-31

Reid, Whitelaw 1837-1912 ....DLB-23

Reilly and Lee Publishing Company DLB-46

Reimann, Brigitte 1933-1973 ....DLB-75

Reisch, Walter 1903-1983....................................DLB-44

Remarque, Erich Maria 1898-1970....................DLB-56

"Re-meeting of Old Friends": The Jack Kerouac
Conference..Y-82

Remington, Frederic 1861-1909 ....DLB-12

Renaud, Jacques 1943- DLB-60

Renault, Mary 1905-1983 ....Y-83

Representative Men and Women: A Historical
Perspective on the British Novel,
1930-1960 ....DLB-15

(Re-)Publishing Orwell Y-86

Reuter, Gabriele 1859-1941 ....DLB-66

Revell, Fleming H., Company..............................DLB-49

Reventlow, Franziska Gräfin zu
1871-1918 ....DLB-66

Review of [Samuel Richardson's] *Clarissa* (1748),
by Henry Fielding DLB-39

The Revolt (1937), by Mary
Colum [excerpts] DLB-36

Rexroth, Kenneth 1905-1982 ....DLB-16, 48; Y-82

Rey, H. A. 1898-1977...DLB-22

Reynal and Hitchcock DLB-46

Reynolds, G. W. M. 1814-1879 ....DLB-21

Reynolds, Mack 1917- DLB-8

Reznikoff, Charles 1894-1976.......................DLB-28, 45

"Rhetoric" (1828; revised, 1859), by
Thomas de Quincey [excerpt] DLB-57

Rhett, Robert Barnwell 1800-1876....................DLB-43

Rhode, John 1884-1964 ....DLB-77

Rhodes, James Ford 1848-1927 ....DLB-47

Rhys, Jean 1890-1979 ....DLB-36

Ricardou, Jean 1932- DLB-83

Rice, Elmer 1892-1967.......................................DLB-4, 7

Rice, Grantland 1880-1954 ....DLB-29

Rich, Adrienne 1929- DLB-5, 67

Richards, David Adams 1950- DLB-53

Richards, George circa 1760-1814 ....DLB-37

Richards, I. A. 1893-1979 ....DLB-27

Richards, Laura E. 1850-1943 ....DLB-42

Richards, William Carey 1818-1892 ....DLB-73

Richardson, Charles F. 1851-1913......................DLB-71

Richardson, Dorothy M. 1873-1957 ....DLB-36

Richardson, Jack 1935- DLB-7

Richardson, Samuel 1689-1761..........................DLB-39

Richardson, Willis 1889-1977 ....DLB-51

Richler, Mordecai 1931- DLB-53

Richter, Conrad 1890-1968...................................DLB-9

Richter, Hans Werner 1908- DLB-69

Rickword, Edgell 1898-1982 ....DLB-20

Riddell, John (see Ford, Corey)

Ridge, Lola 1873-1941 ....DLB-54

Ridler, Anne 1912- DLB-27

Riffaterre, Michael 1924- DLB-67

Riis, Jacob 1849-1914 ....DLB-23

Riker, John C. [publishing house] DLB-49

Riley, John 1938-1978....................................DLB-40

Rilke, Rainer Maria 1875-1926..........................DLB-81

Rinehart and Company....................................DLB-46

Ringuet 1895-1960 ....DLB-68

Rinser, Luise 1911- DLB-69

Ríos, Isabella 1948- DLB-82

Ripley, Arthur 1895-1961 ....DLB-44

Ripley, George 1802-1880 ....DLB-1, 64, 73

The Rising Glory of America: Three Poems DLB-37

The Rising Glory of America: Written in 1771
    (1786), by Hugh Henry Brackenridge and
    Philip Freneau DLB-37

Riskin, Robert 1897-1955.................................DLB-26

Risse, Heinz 1898- DLB-69

Ritchie, Anna Mowatt 1819-1870 ....DLB-3

Ritchie, Anne Thackeray 1837-1919 ....DLB-18

Ritchie, Thomas 1778-1854 ....DLB-43

Rites of Passage [on William Saroyan]...................Y-83

The Ritz Paris Hemingway Award.........................Y-85

Rivera, Tomás 1935-1984.................................DLB-82

Rivers, Conrad Kent 1933-1968 ....DLB-41

Riverside Press..DLB-49

Rivington, James circa 1724-1802......................DLB-43

Rivkin, Allen 1903- DLB-26

Robbe-Grillet, Alain 1922- DLB-83

Robbins, Tom 1936- Y-80

Roberts, Elizabeth Madox 1881-1941.............DLB-9, 54

Roberts, Kenneth 1885-1957 ....DLB-9

Roberts Brothers..DLB-49

Robertson, A. M., and Company.......................DLB-49

Robinson, Casey 1903-1979 ....DLB-44

Robinson, Edwin Arlington 1869-1935 ....DLB-54

Robinson, James Harvey 1863-1936...................DLB-47

Robinson, Lennox 1886-1958 ....DLB-10

Robinson, Mabel Louise 1874-1962...................DLB-22

Robinson, Therese 1797-1870 ....DLB-59

Roblès, Emmanuel 1914- DLB-83

Rodgers, Carolyn M. 1945- DLB-41

Rodgers, W. R. 1909-1969 ....DLB-20

Rodriguez, Richard 1944- DLB-82

Roethke, Theodore 1908-1963 ....DLB-5

Rogers, Will 1879-1935....................................DLB-11

Rohmer, Sax 1883-1959...................................DLB-70

Roiphe, Anne 1935- Y-80

Rojas, Arnold R. 1896-1988.............................DLB-82

Rolfe, Frederick William 1860-1913...................DLB-34

Rolland, Romain 1866-1944 ....DLB-65

Rolvaag, O. E. 1876-1931.................................DLB-9

Romains, Jules 1885-1972................................DLB-65

Roman, A., and Company.................................DLB-49

Romero, Orlando 1945- DLB-82

Roosevelt, Theodore 1858-1919.........................DLB-47

Root, Waverley 1903-1982 ....DLB-4

Roquebrune, Robert de 1889-1978 ....DLB-68

Rose, Reginald 1920- DLB-26

Rosen, Norma 1925- DLB-28

Rosenberg, Isaac 1890-1918 ....DLB-20

Rosenfeld, Isaac 1918-1956...............................DLB-28

Rosenthal, M. L. 1917- DLB-5

Ross, Leonard Q. (see Rosten, Leo)

Rossen, Robert 1908-1966 ....DLB-26

Rossetti, Christina 1830-1894............................DLB-35

Rossetti, Dante Gabriel 1828-1882.....................DLB-35

Rossner, Judith 1935- DLB-6

Rosten, Leo 1908- DLB-11

Roth, Henry 1906?- DLB-28

Roth, Philip 1933- DLB-2, 28; Y-82

Rothenberg, Jerome 1931- DLB-5

Rowe, Elizabeth 1674-1737 ....DLB-39

Rowe, Nicholas 1674-1718 ....DLB-84

Rowlandson, Mary circa 1635-circa 1678...........DLB-24

Rowley, William circa 1585-1626.......................DLB-58

Rowson, Susanna Haswell circa 1762-1824.......DLB-37

Roy, Gabrielle 1909-1983.................................DLB-68

Roy, Jules 1907- DLB-83

The Royal Court Theatre and the English

Stage Company...DLB-13

The Royal Court Theatre and the New
  Drama DLB-10

The Royal Shakespeare Company
  at the Swan...Y-88

Royall, Anne 1769-1854....................................DLB-43

The Roycroft Printing Shop DLB-49

Rubens, Bernice 1928- DLB-14

Rudd and Carleton...DLB-49

Rudkin, David 1936- DLB-13

Ruffin, Josephine St. Pierre 1842-1924.............DLB-79

Ruggles, Henry Joseph 1813-1906 ....DLB-64

Rukeyser, Muriel 1913-1980 ....DLB-48

Rule, Jane 1931- DLB-60

Rumaker, Michael 1932- DLB-16

Rumens, Carol 1944- DLB-40

Runyon, Damon 1880-1946 ....DLB-11

Rush, Benjamin 1746-1813 ....DLB-37

Ruskin, John 1819-1900....................................DLB-55

Russ, Joanna 1937- DLB-8

Russell, B. B., and Company DLB-49

Russell, Benjamin 1761-1845............................DLB-43

Russell, Charles Edward 1860-1941 ....DLB-25

Russell, George William (see AE)

Russell, R. H., and Son DLB-49

Rutherford, Mark 1831-1913............................DLB-18

Ryan, Michael 1946- Y-82

Ryan, Oscar 1904- DLB-68

Ryga, George 1932- DLB-60

Ryskind, Morrie 1895-1985 ....DLB-26

S

The Saalfield Publishing Company DLB-46

Saberhagen, Fred 1930- DLB-8

Sackler, Howard 1929-1982..............................DLB-7

Sackville, Thomas 1536-1608
  and Norton, Thomas 1532-1584 ....DLB-62

Sackville-West, V. 1892-1962 ....DLB-34

Sadlier, D. and J., and Company.......................DLB-49

Saffin, John circa 1626-1710............................DLB-24

Sagan, Françoise 1935- DLB-83

Sage, Robert 1899-1962 ....DLB-4

Sagel, Jim 1947- DLB-82

Sahkomaapii, Piitai (see Highwater, Jamake)

Sahl, Hans 1902- DLB-69

Said, Edward W. 1935- DLB-67

St. Johns, Adela Rogers 1894-1988 ....DLB-29

St. Martin's Press DLB-46

Saint-Exupéry, Antoine de 1900-1944 ....DLB-72

Saint Pierre, Michel de 1916-1987.....................DLB-83

Saintsbury, George 1845-1933 ....DLB-57

Saki (see Munro, H. H.)

Salaam, Kalamu ya 1947- DLB-38

Salas, Floyd 1931- DLB-82

Salemson, Harold J. 1910-1988 ....DLB-4

Salinas, Luis Omar 1937- DLB-82

Salinger, J. D. 1919- DLB-2

Salt, Waldo 1914- DLB-44

Sampson, Richard Henry (see Hull, Richard)

Sanborn, Franklin Benjamin 1831-1917 ....DLB-1

Sánchez, Ricardo 1941- DLB-82

Sanchez, Sonia 1934- DLB-41

Sandburg, Carl 1878-1967...........................DLB-17, 54

Sanders, Ed 1939- DLB-16

Sandoz, Mari 1896-1966....................................DLB-9

Sandys, George 1578-1644...............................DLB-24

Santayana, George 1863-1952 ....DLB-54, 71

Santmyer, Helen Hooven 1895-1986.....................Y-84

Sapper (see McNeile, Herman Cyril)

Sargent, Pamela 1948- DLB-8

Saroyan, William 1908-1981...................DLB-7, 9; Y-81

Sarraute, Nathalie 1900- DLB-83

Sarrazin, Albertine 1937-1967 ....DLB-83

Sarton, May 1912- DLB-48; Y-81

Sartre, Jean-Paul 1905-1980 ....DLB-72

Sassoon, Siegfried 1886-1967 ....DLB-20

Saturday Review Press......................................DLB-46

Saunders, James 1925- DLB-13

Saunders, John Monk 1897-1940 ....DLB-26

Savage, James 1784-1873 ....DLB-30

Savage, Marmion W. 1803?-1872 ....DLB-21

Savard, Félix-Antoine 1896-1982 ....DLB-68

Sawyer, Ruth 1880-1970 ....DLB-22

Sayers, Dorothy L. 1893-1957 ....DLB-10, 36, 77

Sayles, John Thomas 1950- DLB-44

Scannell, Vernon 1922- DLB-27

Scarry, Richard 1919- DLB-61

Schaeffer, Albrecht 1885-1950 ....DLB-66

Schaeffer, Susan Fromberg 1941- DLB-28

Schaper, Edzard 1908-1984 ....DLB-69

Scharf, J. Thomas 1843-1898 ....DLB-47

Schickele, René 1883-1940 ....DLB-66

Schlesinger, Arthur M., Jr. 1917- DLB-17

Schlumberger, Jean 1877-1968 ....DLB-65

Schmid, Eduard Hermann Wilhelm
    (see Edschmid, Kasimir)

Schmidt, Arno 1914-1979 ....DLB-69

Schmidt, Michael 1947- DLB-40

Schmitz, James H. 1911- DLB-8

Schnitzler, Arthur 1862-1931 ....DLB-81

Schnurre, Wolfdietrich 1920- DLB-69

Schocken Books DLB-46

The Schomburg Center for Research
    in Black Culture DLB-76

Schouler, James 1839-1920 ....DLB-47

Schrader, Paul 1946- DLB-44

Schreiner, Olive 1855-1920 ....DLB-18

Schroeder, Andreas 1946- DLB-53

Schulberg, Budd 1914- DLB-6, 26, 28; Y-81

Schulte, F. J., and Company DLB-49

Schurz, Carl 1829-1906 ....DLB-23

Schuyler, George S. 1895-1977 ....DLB-29, 51

Schuyler, James 1923- DLB-5

Schwartz, Delmore 1913-1966 ....DLB-28, 48

Schwartz, Jonathan 1938- Y-82

Science Fantasy DLB-8

Science-Fiction Fandom and Conventions DLB-8

Science-Fiction Fanzines: The Time Binders DLB-8

Science-Fiction Films DLB-8

Science Fiction Writers of America and the
    Nebula Awards DLB-8

Scott, Evelyn 1893-1963 ....DLB-9, 48

Scott, Harvey W. 1838-1910 ....DLB-23

Scott, Paul 1920-1978 ....DLB-14

Scott, Sarah 1723-1795 ....DLB-39

Scott, Tom 1918- DLB-27

Scott, William Bell 1811-1890 ....DLB-32

Scott, William R. [publishing house] DLB-46

Scott-Heron, Gil 1949- DLB-41

Charles Scribner's Sons DLB-49

Scripps, E. W. 1854-1926 ....DLB-25

Scudder, Horace Elisha 1838-1902 ....DLB-42, 71

Scudder, Vida Dutton 1861-1954 ....DLB-71

Scupham, Peter 1933- DLB-40

Seabrook, William 1886-1945 ....DLB-4

Seabury, Samuel 1729-1796 ....DLB-31

Sears, Edward I. 1819?-1876 ....DLB-79

Sears Publishing Company DLB-46

Seaton, George 1911-1979 ....DLB-44

Seaton, William Winston 1785-1866 ....DLB-43

Sedgwick, Arthur George 1844-1915 ....DLB-64

Sedgwick, Catharine Maria 1789-1867 ....DLB-1, 74

Seeger, Alan 1888-1916 ....DLB-45

Segal, Erich 1937- Y-86

Seghers, Anna 1900-1983 ....DLB-69

Seid, Ruth (see Sinclair, Jo)

Seidel, Frederick Lewis 1936- Y-84

Seidel, Ina 1885-1974 ....DLB-56

Séjour, Victor 1817-1874 ....DLB-50

Séjour Marcou et Ferrand,
    Juan Victor (see Séjour, Victor)

Selby, Hubert, Jr. 1928- DLB-2

Selden, George 1929- DLB-52

Selected English-Language Little Magazines and
    Newspapers [France, 1920-1939] DLB-4

Selected Humorous Magazines (1820-1950) DLB-11

Selected Science-Fiction Magazines and
    Anthologies DLB-8

Seligman, Edwin R. A. 1861-1939 ....DLB-47

Seltzer, Chester E. (see Muro, Amado)

Seltzer, Thomas [publishing house] DLB-46

Sendak, Maurice 1928- DLB-61

Sensation Novels (1863), by H. L. Manse..........DLB-21

Seredy, Kate 1899-1975 ....DLB-22

Serling, Rod 1924-1975.............................DLB-26

Settle, Mary Lee 1918- DLB-6

Seuss, Dr. (see Geisel, Theodor Seuss)

Sewall, Joseph 1688-1769.........................DLB-24

Sewell, Samuel 1652-1730 ....DLB-24

Sex, Class, Politics, and Religion [in the British
    Novel, 1930-1959] DLB-15

Sexton, Anne 1928-1974 ....DLB-5

Shaara, Michael 1929-1988 ....Y-83

Shadwell, Thomas 1641?-1692 ....DLB-80

Shaffer, Anthony 1926- DLB-13

Shaffer, Peter 1926- DLB-13

Shairp, Mordaunt 1887-1939.....................DLB-10

Shakespeare, William 1564-1616 ....DLB-62

Shange, Ntozake 1948- DLB-38

Shapiro, Karl 1913- DLB-48

Sharon Publications DLB-46

Sharpe, Tom 1928- DLB-14

Shaw, Bernard 1856-1950...................DLB-10, 57

Shaw, Henry Wheeler 1818-1885 ....DLB-11

Shaw, Irwin 1913-1984 ....DLB-6; Y-84

Shaw, Robert 1927-1978 ....DLB-13, 14

Shay, Frank [publishing house]...................DLB-46

Shea, John Gilmary 1824-1892 ....DLB-30

Shearing, Joseph 1886-1952 ....DLB-70

Shebbeare, John 1709-1788 ....DLB-39

Sheckley, Robert 1928- DLB-8

Shedd, William G. T. 1820-1894 ....DLB-64

Sheed, Wilfred 1930- DLB-6

Sheed and Ward DLB-46

Sheldon, Alice B. (see Tiptree, James, Jr.)

Sheldon, Edward 1886-1946 ....DLB-7

Sheldon and Company...............................DLB-49

Shepard, Sam 1943- DLB-7

Shepard, Thomas I 1604 or 1605-1649 ....DLB-24

Shepard, Thomas II 1635-1677.....................DLB-24

Shepard, Clark and Brown DLB-49

Sheridan, Frances 1724-1766....................DLB-39, 84

Sherriff, R. C. 1896-1975 ....DLB-10

Sherwood, Robert 1896-1955 ....DLB-7, 26

Shiels, George 1886-1949..........................DLB-10

Shillaber, B.[enjamin] P.[enhallow]
    1814-1890 ....DLB-1, 11

Shine, Ted 1931- DLB-38

Shirer, William L. 1904- DLB-4

Shirley, James 1596-1666 ....DLB-58

Shockley, Ann Allen 1927- DLB-33

Shorthouse, Joseph Henry 1834-1903...............DLB-18

Showalter, Elaine 1941- DLB-67

Shulevitz, Uri 1935- DLB-61

Shulman, Max 1919-1988 ....DLB-11

Shute, Henry A. 1856-1943 ....DLB-9

Shuttle, Penelope 1947- DLB-14, 40

Sidney, Margaret (see Lothrop, Harriet M.)

Sidney's Press DLB-49

Siegfried Loraine Sassoon: A Centenary Essay
    Tributes from Vivien F. Clarke and
        Michael Thorpe Y-86

Sierra Club Books.................................DLB-49

Sigourney, Lydia Howard (Huntley)
    1791-1865 ....DLB-1, 42, 73

Silkin, Jon 1930- DLB-27

Silliphant, Stirling 1918- DLB-26

Sillitoe, Alan 1928- DLB-14

Silman, Roberta 1934- DLB-28

Silverberg, Robert 1935- DLB-8

Simak, Clifford D. 1904-1988 ....DLB-8

Simcox, George Augustus 1841-1905.................DLB-35

Simenon, Georges 1903- DLB-72

Simmel, Johannes Mario 1924- DLB-69

Simmons, Herbert Alfred 1930- DLB-33

Simmons, James 1933- DLB-40

Simms, William Gilmore 1806-
    1870..........................DLB-3, 30, 59, 73

Simon, Claude 1913- DLB-83

Simon, Neil 1927- DLB-7

Simon and Schuster.................................DLB-46

Simons, Katherine Drayton Mayrant 1890-1969.....Y-83

Simpson, Helen 1897-1940 ....DLB-77

Simpson, Louis 1923- DLB-5

Simpson, N. F. 1919- DLB-13

Sims, George R. 1847-1922.....................DLB-35, 70

Sinclair, Andrew 1935- DLB-14

Sinclair, Jo 1913- DLB-28

Sinclair Lewis Centennial Conference Y-85

Sinclair, May 1863-1946 ....DLB-36

Sinclair, Upton 1878-1968.....................DLB-9

Sinclair, Upton [publishing house] DLB-46

Singer, Isaac Bashevis 1904- DLB-6, 28, 52

Singmaster, Elsie 1879-1958 ....DLB-9

Siodmak, Curt 1902- DLB-44

Sissman, L. E. 1928-1976 ....DLB-5

Sisson, C. H. 1914- DLB-27

Sitwell, Edith 1887-1964 ....DLB-20

Skelton, Robin 1925- DLB-27, 53

Skinner, John Stuart 1788-1851 ....DLB-73

Skipsey, Joseph 1832-1903.....................DLB-35

Slade, Bernard 1930- DLB-53

Slater, Patrick 1880-1951 ....DLB-68

Slavitt, David 1935- DLB-5, 6

A Slender Thread of Hope: The Kennedy
    Center Black Theatre Project.....................DLB-38

Slick, Sam (see Haliburton, Thomas Chandler)

Sloane, William, Associates DLB-46

Small, Maynard and Company DLB-49

Small Presses in Great Britain and Ireland,
    1960-1985 ....DLB-40

Small Presses I: Jargon Society Y-84

Small Presses II: The Spirit That
    Moves Us Press Y-85

Small Presses III: Pushcart Press.....................Y-87

Smiles, Samuel 1812-1904....................DLB-55

Smith, Alexander 1829-1867 ....DLB-32, 55

Smith, Betty 1896-1972 ....Y-82

Smith, Carol Sturm 1938- Y-81

Smith, Charles Henry 1826-1903 ....DLB-11

Smith, Charlotte 1749-1806 ....DLB-39

Smith, Cordwainer 1913-1966 ....DLB-8

Smith, Dave 1942- DLB-5

Smith, Dodie 1896- DLB-10

Smith, Doris Buchanan 1934- DLB-52

Smith, E. E. 1890-1965.........................DLB-8

Smith, Elihu Hubbard 1771-1798.....................DLB-37

Smith, Elizabeth Oakes (Prince) 1806-1893 ....DLB-1

Smith, George O. 1911-1981 ....DLB-8

Smith, H. Allen 1907-1976 ....DLB-11, 29

Smith, Harrison, and Robert Haas
    [publishing house] DLB-46

Smith, Iain Crichten 1928- DLB-40

Smith, J. Allen 1860-1924....................DLB-47

Smith, J. Stilman, and Company DLB-49

Smith, John 1580-1631 ....DLB-24, 30

Smith, Josiah 1704-1781.....................DLB-24

Smith, Ken 1938- DLB-40

Smith, Lee 1944- Y-83

Smith, Mark 1935- Y-82

Smith, Michael 1698-circa 1771 ....DLB-31

Smith, Red 1905-1982.......................DLB-29

Smith, Roswell 1829-1892 ....DLB-79

Smith, Samuel Harrison 1772-1845....................DLB-43

Smith, Samuel Stanhope 1751-1819.....................DLB-37

Smith, Seba 1792-1868.......................DLB-1, 11

Smith, Stevie 1902-1971......................DLB-20

Smith, Sydney Goodsir 1915-1975 ....DLB-27

Smith, W. B., and Company DLB-49

Smith, William 1727-1803....................DLB-31

Smith, William 1728-1793....................DLB-30

Smith, William Gardner 1927-1974....................DLB-76

Smith, William Jay 1918- DLB-5

Smollett, Tobias 1721-1771 ....DLB-39

Snellings, Rolland (see Touré, Askia Muhammad)

Snodgrass, W. D. 1926- DLB-5

Snow, C. P. 1905-1980 ....DLB-15, 77

Snyder, Gary 1930- DLB-5, 16

Sobiloff, Hy 1912-1970 ....DLB-48

The Society for Textual Scholarship
    and *TEXT*.....................................Y-87

Solano, Solita 1888-1975 ....DLB-4

Sollers, Philippe 1936- DLB-83

Solomon, Carl 1928- DLB-16

Solway, David 1941- DLB-53

Solzhenitsyn and America Y-85

Sontag, Susan 1933- DLB-2, 67

Sorrentino, Gilbert 1929- DLB-5; Y-80

Soto, Gary 1952- DLB-82

Sources for the Study of Tudor
    and Stuart Drama.....................................DLB-62

Southerland, Ellease 1943- DLB-33

Southern, Terry 1924- DLB-2

Southern Writers Between the Wars...................DLB-9

Southerne, Thomas 1659-1746.......................DLB-80

Spark, Muriel 1918- DLB-15

Sparks, Jared 1789-1866..............................DLB-1, 30

Sparshott, Francis 1926-..........................DLB-60

Späth, Gerold 1939- DLB-75

Spellman, A. B. 1935-.............................DLB-41

Spencer, Anne 1882-1975.........................DLB-51, 54

Spencer, Elizabeth 1921-..........................DLB-6

Spencer, Herbert 1820-1903........................DLB-57

Spencer, Scott 1945-..............................Y-86

Spender, Stephen 1909-............................DLB-20

Spicer, Jack 1925-1965............................DLB-5, 16

Spielberg, Peter 1929-............................Y-81

Spier, Peter 1927- DLB-61

Spinrad, Norman 1940-.............................DLB-8

Spofford, Harriet Prescott 1835-1921..............DLB-74

Squibob (see Derby, George Horatio)

Stafford, Jean 1915-1979 ....DLB-2

Stafford, William 1914-...........................DLB-5

Stage Censorship: "The Rejected Statement"
    (1911), by Bernard Shaw [excerpts]............DLB-10

Stallings, Laurence 1894-1968.....................DLB-7, 44

Stallworthy, Jon 1935- DLB-40

Stampp, Kenneth M. 1912- DLB-17

Stanford, Ann 1916-...............................DLB-5

Stanton, Elizabeth Cady 1815-1902.................DLB-79

Stanton, Frank L. 1857-1927.......................DLB-25

Stapledon, Olaf 1886-1950.........................DLB-15

Star Spangled Banner Office.......................DLB-49

Starkweather, David 1935-.........................DLB-7

Statements on the Art of Poetry...................DLB-54

Steadman, Mark 1930-..............................DLB-6

The Stealthy School of Criticism (1871), by
    Dante Gabriel Rossetti...........................DLB-35

Stearns, Harold E. 1891-1943......................DLB-4

Stedman, Edmund Clarence 1833-1908.............DLB-64

Steele, Max 1922- Y-80

Steele, Richard 1672-1729.........................DLB-84

Steere, Richard circa 1643-1721 ....DLB-24

Stegner, Wallace 1909- DLB-9

Stehr, Hermann 1864-1940 ....DLB-66

Steig, William 1907- DLB-61

Stein, Gertrude 1874-1946.........................DLB-4, 54

Stein, Leo 1872-1947..............................DLB-4

Stein and Day Publishers..........................DLB-46

Steinbeck, John 1902-1968................DLB-7, 9; DS-2

Steiner, George 1929- DLB-67

Stephen, Leslie 1832-1904 ....DLB-57

Stephens, Alexander H. 1812-1883..................DLB-47

Stephens, Ann 1810-1886...........................DLB-3, 73

Stephens, Charles Asbury 1844?-1931 ....DLB-42

Stephens, James 1882?-1950........................DLB-19

Sterling, George 1869-1926 ....DLB-54

Sterling, James 1701-1763.........................DLB-24

Stern, Richard 1928- Y-87

Stern, Stewart 1922- DLB-26

Sterne, Laurence 1713-1768........................DLB-39

Sternheim, Carl 1878-1942.........................DLB-56

Stevens, Wallace 1879-1955 ....DLB-54

Stevenson, Anne 1933- DLB-40

Stevenson, Robert Louis 1850-1894.............DLB-18, 57

Stewart, Donald Ogden 1894-1980.........DLB-4, 11, 26

Stewart, Dugald 1753-1828.........................DLB-31

Stewart, George R. 1895-1980......................DLB-8

Stewart and Kidd Company..........................DLB-46

Stickney, Trumbull 1874-1904......................DLB-54

Stiles, Ezra 1727-1795 ....DLB-31

Still, James 1906- DLB-9

Stith, William 1707-1755..........................DLB-31

Stockton, Frank R. 1834-1902...............DLB-42, 74

Stoddard, Ashbel [publishing house] DLB-49

Stoddard, Richard Henry 1825-1903.............DLB-3, 64

Stoddard, Solomon 1643-1729 ....DLB-24

Stoker, Bram 1847-1912............................DLB-36, 70

Stokes, Frederick A., Company DLB-49

Stokes, Thomas L. 1898-1958.......................DLB-29

Stone, Herbert S., and Company DLB-49

Stone, Lucy 1818-1893.................................DLB-79

Stone, Melville 1848-1929 ....DLB-25

Stone, Samuel 1602-1663 ....DLB-24

Stone and Kimball......................................DLB-49

Stoppard, Tom 1937- DLB-13; Y-85

Storey, Anthony 1928- DLB-14

Storey, David 1933- DLB-13, 14

Story, Thomas circa 1670-1742 ....DLB-31

Story, William Wetmore 1819-1895.....................DLB-1

Storytelling: A Contemporary Renaissance.............Y-84

Stoughton, William 1631-1701 ....DLB-24

Stowe, Harriet Beecher 1811-1896 ....DLB-1, 12, 42, 74

Stowe, Leland 1899- DLB-29

Strand, Mark 1934- DLB-5

Stratemeyer, Edward 1862-1930......................DLB-42

Stratton and Barnard DLB-49

Straub, Peter 1943- Y-84

Street, Cecil John Charles (see Rhode, John)

Street and Smith....................................DLB-49

Streeter, Edward 1891-1976 ....DLB-11

Stribling, T. S. 1881-1965 ....DLB-9

Stringer and Townsend DLB-49

Strittmatter, Erwin 1912- DLB-69

Strother, David Hunter 1816-1888......................DLB-3

Stuart, Jesse 1906-1984....................DLB-9, 48; Y-84

Stuart, Lyle [publishing house]........................DLB-46

Stubbs, Harry Clement (see Clement, Hal)

The Study of Poetry (1880), by Matthew
    Arnold...DLB-35

Sturgeon, Theodore 1918-1985 ....DLB-8; Y-85

Sturges, Preston 1898-1959.............................DLB-26

"Style" (1840; revised, 1859), by Thomas
    de Quincey [excerpt]...............................DLB-57

"Style" (1888), by Walter Pater DLB-57

Style (1897), by Walter Raleigh [excerpt]............DLB-57

"Style" (1877), by T. H. Wright [excerpt] DLB-57

"Le Style c'est l'homme" (1892),
    by W. H. Mallock DLB-57

Styron, William 1925- DLB-2; Y-80

Suárez, Mario 1925- DLB-82

Such, Peter 1939- DLB-60

Suckling, Sir John 1609-1642 ....DLB-58

Suckow, Ruth 1892-1960.................................DLB-9

Suggs, Simon (see Hooper, Johnson Jones)

Sukenick, Ronald 1932- Y-81

Suknaski, Andrew 1942- DLB-53

Sullivan, C. Gardner 1886-1965 ....DLB-26

Sullivan, Frank 1892-1976 ....DLB-11

Summers, Hollis 1916- DLB-6

Sumner, Henry A. [publishing house] DLB-49

Surtees, Robert Smith 1803-1864 ....DLB-21

A Survey of Poetry
    Anthologies, 1879-1960 ....DLB-54

Surveys of the Year's Biography
    A Transit of Poets and Others: American
        Biography in 1982 ....Y-82
    The Year in Literary Biography Y-83
    The Year in Literary Biography Y-84
    The Year in Literary Biography Y-85
    The Year in Literary Biography Y-86
    The Year in Literary Biography Y-87
    The Year in Literary Biography Y-88

Surveys of the Year's Book Publishing
    The Year in Book Publishing...............Y-86

Surveys of the Year's Drama
    The Year in Drama...................................Y-82
    The Year in Drama...................................Y-83
    The Year in Drama...................................Y-84
    The Year in Drama...................................Y-85
    The Year in Drama...................................Y-87
    The Year in Drama...................................Y-88

Surveys of the Year's Fiction
    The Year's Work in Fiction: A Survey.............Y-82
    The Year in Fiction: A Biased View................Y-83
    The Year in Fiction...................................Y-84
    The Year in Fiction...................................Y-85
    The Year in Fiction...................................Y-86
    The Year in the Novel................................Y-87
    The Year in Short Stories............................Y-87
    The Year in the Novel................................Y-88
    The Year in Short Stories............................Y-88

Surveys of the Year's Poetry
    The Year's Work in American Poetry.............Y-82
    The Year in Poetry Y-83
    The Year in Poetry Y-84
    The Year in Poetry Y-85
    The Year in Poetry Y-86
    The Year in Poetry Y-87
    The Year in Poetry Y-88

Sutherland, John 1919-1956 ....DLB-68

Sutro, Alfred 1863-1933 ....DLB-10

Swados, Harvey 1920-1972 ....DLB-2

Swain, Charles 1801-1874 ....DLB-32

Swallow Press...DLB-46

Swenson, May 1919- DLB-5

Swerling, Jo 1897- DLB-44

Swift, Jonathan 1667-1745 ....DLB-39

Swinburne, A. C. 1837-1909.........................DLB-35, 57

Swinnerton, Frank 1884-1982...........................DLB-34

Swisshelm, Jane Grey 1815-1884 ....DLB-43

Swope, Herbert Bayard 1882-1958 ....DLB-25

Swords, T. and J., and Company DLB-49

Swords, Thomas 1763-1843 and
    Swords, James ?-1844 ....DLB-73

Symonds, John Addington 1840-1893...............DLB-57

Symons, Arthur 1865-1945..........................DLB-19, 57

Symons, Scott 1933- DLB-53

Synge, John Millington 1871-1909 ....DLB-10, 19

T

Tafolla, Carmen 1951- DLB-82

Taggard, Genevieve 1894-1948.........................DLB-45

Tait, J. Selwin, and Sons..................................DLB-49

Talvj or Talvi (see Robinson, Therese)

Taradash, Daniel 1913- DLB-44

Tarbell, Ida M. 1857-1944 ....DLB-47

Tarkington, Booth 1869-1946............................DLB-9

Tashlin, Frank 1913-1972 ....DLB-44

Tate, Allen 1899-1979................................DLB-4, 45, 63

Tate, James 1943- DLB-5

Tate, Nahum circa 1652-1715...........................DLB-80

Taylor, Bayard 1825-1878 ....DLB-3

Taylor, Bert Leston 1866-1921 ....DLB-25

Taylor, Charles H. 1846-1921 ....DLB-25

Taylor, Edward circa 1642-1729 ....DLB-24

Taylor, Henry 1942- DLB-5

Taylor, Sir Henry 1800-1886 ....DLB-32

Taylor, Mildred D. ?- DLB-52

Taylor, Peter 1917- Y-81

Taylor, William, and Company..........................DLB-49

Taylor-Made Shakespeare? Or Is
    "Shall I Die?" the Long-Lost Text
    of Bottom's Dream?...Y-85

Teasdale, Sara 1884-1933..................................DLB-45

The Tea-Table (1725), by Eliza Haywood
    [excerpt] DLB-39

Tenn, William 1919- DLB-8

Tennant, Emma 1937- DLB-14

Tenney, Tabitha Gilman 1762-1837 ....DLB-37

Tennyson, Alfred 1809-1892 ....DLB-32

Tennyson, Frederick 1807-1898 ....DLB-32

Terhune, Albert Payson 1872-1942....................DLB-9

Terry, Megan 1932- DLB-7

Terson, Peter 1932- DLB-13

Tesich, Steve 1943- Y-83

Tey, Josephine 1896?-1952 ....DLB-77

Thacher, James 1754-1844 ....DLB-37

Thackeray, William Makepeace
    1811-1863 ....DLB-21, 55

Thanet, Octave (see French, Alice)

The Theater in Shakespeare's Time DLB-62

The Theatre Guild DLB-7

Thério, Adrien 1925- DLB-53

Theroux, Paul 1941- DLB-2

Thoma, Ludwig 1867-1921................................DLB-66

Thoma, Richard 1902- DLB-4

Thomas, Audrey 1935- DLB-60

Thomas, D. M. 1935- DLB-40

Thomas, Dylan 1914-1953.........................DLB-13, 20

Thomas, Edward 1878-1917..............................DLB-19

Thomas, Gwyn 1913-1981 ....DLB-15

Thomas, Isaiah 1750-1831........................DLB-43, 73

Thomas, Isaiah [publishing house]....................DLB-49

Thomas, John 1900-1932...................................DLB-4

Thomas, Joyce Carol 1938- DLB-33

Thomas, Lorenzo 1944- DLB-41

Thomas, R. S. 1915- DLB-27

Thompson, Dorothy 1893-1961.........................DLB-29

Thompson, Francis 1859-1907 ....DLB-19

Thompson, George Selden (see Selden, George)

Thompson, John 1938-1976...............................DLB-60

Thompson, John R. 1823-1873 ....DLB-3, 73

Thompson, Maurice 1844-1901...................DLB-71, 74

Thompson, Ruth Plumly 1891-1976 ....DLB-22

Thompson, William Tappan 1812-1882 ....DLB-3, 11

Thomson, James 1834-1882................................DLB-35

Thomson, Mortimer 1831-1875.........................DLB-11

Thoreau, Henry David 1817-1862 ....DLB-1

Thorpe, Thomas Bangs 1815-1878................DLB-3, 11

Thoughts on Poetry and Its Varieties (1833),
    by John Stuart Mill.....................................DLB-32

Thurber, James 1894-1961......................DLB-4, 11, 22

Thurman, Wallace 1902-1934...........................DLB-51

Thwaite, Anthony 1930- DLB-40

Thwaites, Reuben Gold 1853-1913 ....DLB-47

Ticknor, George 1791-1871...........................DLB-1, 59

Ticknor and Fields DLB-49

Ticknor and Fields (revived)...........................DLB-46

Tietjens, Eunice 1884-1944..............................DLB-54

Tilton, J. E., and Company................................DLB-49

Time and Western Man (1927), by Wyndham
    Lewis [excerpts] DLB-36

Time-Life Books..DLB-46

Times Books..DLB-46

Timothy, Peter circa 1725-1782.......................DLB-43

Timrod, Henry 1828-1867.................................DLB-3

Tiptree, James, Jr. 1915- DLB-8

Titus, Edward William 1870-1952......................DLB-4

Toklas, Alice B. 1877-1967 ....DLB-4

Tolkien, J. R. R. 1892-1973 ....DLB-15

Tolson, Melvin B. 1898-1966.......................DLB-48, 76

Tom Jones (1749), by Henry
    Fielding [excerpt] DLB-39

Tomlinson, Charles 1927- DLB-40

Tomlinson, Henry Major 1873-1958 ....DLB-36

Tompkins, Abel [publishing house]..................DLB-49

Tompson, Benjamin 1642-1714.........................DLB-24

Tonks, Rosemary 1932- DLB-14

Toole, John Kennedy 1937-1969 ....Y-81

Toomer, Jean 1894-1967.............................DLB-45, 51

Tor Books DLB-46

Torrence, Ridgely 1874-1950...........................DLB-54

Toth, Susan Allen 1940- Y-86

Tough-Guy Literature DLB-9

Touré, Askia Muhammad 1938- DLB-41

Tourgée, Albion W. 1838-1905.........................DLB-79

Tourneur, Cyril circa 1580-1626 ....DLB-58

Tournier, Michel 1924- DLB-83

Tousey, Frank [publishing house].....................DLB-49

Tower Publications..DLB-46

Towne, Benjamin circa 1740-1793.....................DLB-43

Towne, Robert 1936- DLB-44

Tracy, Honor 1913- DLB-15

The Transatlantic Publishing Company DLB-49

Transcendentalists, American DS-5

Traven, B. 1882? or 1890?-1969? DLB-9, 56

Travers, Ben 1886-1980 ....DLB-10

Tremain, Rose 1943- DLB-14

Tremblay, Michel 1942- DLB-60

Trends in Twentieth-Century
    Mass Market Publishing DLB-46

Trent, William P. 1862-1939.............................DLB-47

Trescot, William Henry 1822-1898....................DLB-30

Trevor, William 1928- DLB-14

Trilling, Lionel 1905-1975 ....DLB-28, 63

Triolet, Elsa 1896-1970....................................DLB-72

Tripp, John 1927- DLB-40

Trocchi, Alexander 1925- DLB-15

Trollope, Anthony 1815-1882 ....DLB-21, 57

Trollope, Frances 1779-1863 ....DLB-21

Troop, Elizabeth 1931- DLB-14

Trotter, Catharine 1679-1749 ....DLB-84

Trotti, Lamar 1898-1952...................................DLB-44

Trottier, Pierre 1925- DLB-60

Troupe, Quincy Thomas, Jr. 1943- DLB-41

Trow, John F., and Company DLB-49

Trumbo, Dalton 1905-1976..............................DLB-26

Trumbull, Benjamin 1735-1820........................DLB-30

Trumbull, John 1750-1831................................DLB-31

T. S. Eliot Centennial Y-88

Tucholsky, Kurt 1890-1935...............................DLB-56

Tucker, George 1775-1861 ....DLB-3, 30

Tucker, Nathaniel Beverley 1784-1851 ....DLB-3

Tucker, St. George 1752-1827 ....DLB-37

Tuckerman, Henry Theodore 1813-1871 ....DLB-64

Tunis, John R. 1889-1975 ....DLB-22

Tuohy, Frank 1925- DLB-14

Tupper, Martin F. 1810-1889 ....DLB-32

Turbyfill, Mark 1896- DLB-45

Turco, Lewis 1934- Y-84

Turnbull, Gael 1928- DLB-40

Turner, Charles (Tennyson) 1808-1879 ....DLB-32

Turner, Frederick 1943- DLB-40

Turner, Frederick Jackson 1861-1932 ....DLB-17

Turner, Joseph Addison 1826-1868 ....DLB-79

Turpin, Waters Edward 1910-1968 ....DLB-51

Twain, Mark (see Clemens, Samuel Langhorne)

Tyler, Anne 1941- DLB-6; Y-82

Tyler, Moses Coit 1835-1900 ....DLB-47, 64

Tyler, Royall 1757-1826 ....DLB-37

Tylor, Edward Burnett 1832-1917 ....DLB-57

U

Udall, Nicholas 1504-1556 ....DLB-62

Uhse, Bodo 1904-1963 ....DLB-69

Ulibarrí, Sabine R. 1919- DLB-82

Ulica, Jorge 1870-1926 ....DLB-82

Under the Microscope (1872), by A. C.
    Swinburne DLB-35

United States Book Company DLB-49

Universal Publishing and Distributing
    Corporation DLB-46

The University of Iowa Writers'
    Workshop Golden Jubilee Y-86

"The Unknown Public" (1858), by
    Wilkie Collins [excerpt] DLB-57

Unruh, Fritz von 1885-1970 ....DLB-56

Upchurch, Boyd B. (see Boyd, John)

Updike, John 1932- DLB-2, 5; Y-80, 82; DS-3

Upton, Charles 1948- DLB-16

Upward, Allen 1863-1926 ....DLB-36

Urista, Alberto Baltazar (see Alurista)

Ustinov, Peter 1921- DLB-13

V

Vail, Laurence 1891-1968 ....DLB-4

Vailland, Roger 1907-1965..................................DLB-83

Vajda, Ernest 1887-1954 ....DLB-44

Valgardson, W. D. 1939- DLB-60

Van Allsburg, Chris 1949- DLB-61

Van Anda, Carr 1864-1945.................................DLB-25

Vanbrugh, Sir John 1664-1726 ....DLB-80

Vance, Jack 1916?- DLB-8

Van Doren, Mark 1894-1972 ....DLB-45

van Druten, John 1901-1957 ....DLB-10

Van Duyn, Mona 1921- DLB-5

Van Dyke, Henry 1852-1933...............................DLB-71

Van Dyke, Henry 1928- DLB-33

Vane, Sutton 1888-1963 ....DLB-10

Vanguard Press...DLB-46

van Itallie, Jean-Claude 1936- DLB-7

Vann, Robert L. 1879-1940................................DLB-29

Van Rensselaer, Mariana Griswold
    1851-1934 ....DLB-47

Van Rensselaer, Mrs. Schuyler (see Van
    Rensselaer, Mariana Griswold)

Van Vechten, Carl 1880-1964 ....DLB-4, 9

van Vogt, A. E. 1912- DLB-8

Varley, John 1947- Y-81

Vassa, Gustavus (see Equiano, Olaudah)

Vega, Janine Pommy 1942- DLB-16

Veiller, Anthony 1903-1965................................DLB-44

Venegas, Daniel ?-? DLB-82

Verplanck, Gulian C. 1786-1870.........................DLB-59

Very, Jones 1813-1880 ....DLB-1

Vian, Boris 1920-1959...DLB-72

Vickers, Roy 1888?-1965 ....DLB-77

Victoria 1819-1901 ....DLB-55

Vidal, Gore 1925- DLB-6

Viebig, Clara 1860-1952 ....DLB-66

Viereck, George Sylvester 1884-1962.................DLB-54

Viereck, Peter 1916- DLB-5

Viewpoint: Politics and Performance, by David
    Edgar..DLB-13

Vigneault, Gilles 1928- DLB-60

The Viking Press DLB-46

Villanueva, Tino 1941- DLB-82

Villard, Henry 1835-1900 ....DLB-23

Villard, Oswald Garrison 1872-1949 ....DLB-25

Villarreal, José Antonio 1924- DLB-82

Villemaire, Yolande 1949- DLB-60

Villiers, George, Second Duke
    of Buckingham 1628-1687 ....DLB-80

Viorst, Judith ?- DLB-52

Volkoff, Vladimir 1932- DLB-83

Volland, P. F., Company DLB-46

von der Grün, Max 1926- DLB-75

Vonnegut, Kurt 1922- DLB-2, 8; Y-80; DS-3

Vroman, Mary Elizabeth circa 1924-1967 ....DLB-33

W

Waddington, Miriam 1917- DLB-68

Wade, Henry 1887-1969 ....DLB-77

Wagoner, David 1926- DLB-5

Wah, Fred 1939- DLB-60

Wain, John 1925- DLB-15, 27

Wainwright, Jeffrey 1944- DLB-40

Waite, Peirce and Company DLB-49

Wakoski, Diane 1937- DLB-5

Walck, Henry Z. DLB-46

Walcott, Derek 1930- Y-81

Waldman, Anne 1945- DLB-16

Walker, Alice 1944- DLB-6, 33

Walker, George F. 1947- DLB-60

Walker, Joseph A. 1935- DLB-38

Walker, Margaret 1915- DLB-76

Walker, Ted 1934- DLB-40

Walker and Company DLB-49

Walker, Evans and Cogswell Company DLB-49

Walker, John Brisben 1847-1931 ....DLB-79

Wallace, Edgar 1875-1932 ....DLB-70

Wallant, Edward Lewis 1926-1962 ....DLB-2, 28

Walpole, Horace 1717-1797 ....DLB-39

Walpole, Hugh 1884-1941 ....DLB-34

Walrond, Eric 1898-1966 ....DLB-51

Walser, Martin 1927- DLB-75

Walser, Robert 1878-1956 ....DLB-66

Walsh, Ernest 1895-1926 ....DLB-4, 45

Walsh, Robert 1784-1859 ....DLB-59

Wambaugh, Joseph 1937- DLB-6; Y-83

Ward, Artemus (see Browne, Charles Farrar)

Ward, Arthur Henry Sarsfield
    (see Rohmer, Sax)

Ward, Douglas Turner 1930- DLB-7, 38

Ward, Lynd 1905-1985........................DLB-22

Ward, Mrs. Humphry 1851-1920 ....DLB-18

Ward, Nathaniel circa 1578-1652 ....DLB-24

Ward, Theodore 1902-1983................DLB-76

Ware, William 1797-1852......................DLB-1

Warne, Frederick, and Company.......DLB-49

Warner, Charles Dudley 1829-1900 ....DLB-64

Warner, Rex 1905- DLB-15

Warner, Susan Bogert 1819-1885..............DLB-3, 42

Warner, Sylvia Townsend 1893-1978 ....DLB-34

Warner Books DLB-46

Warren, John Byrne Leicester (see De Tabley, Lord)

Warren, Lella 1899-1982.........................Y-83

Warren, Mercy Otis 1728-1814.............DLB-31

Warren, Robert Penn 1905- DLB-2, 48; Y-80

Washington, George 1732-1799.............DLB-31

Wassermann, Jakob 1873-1934 ....DLB-66

Wasson, David Atwood 1823-1887 ......DLB-1

Waterhouse, Keith 1929- DLB-13, 15

Waterman, Andrew 1940- DLB-40

Waters, Frank 1902- Y-86

Watkins, Tobias 1780-1855 ....DLB-73

Watkins, Vernon 1906-1967.................DLB-20

Watmough, David 1926- DLB-53

Watson, Sheila 1909- DLB-60

Watson, Wilfred 1911- DLB-60

Watt, W. J., and Company DLB-46

Watterson, Henry 1840-1921 ....DLB-25

Watts, Alan 1915-1973 ....DLB-16

Watts, Franklin [publishing house].....DLB-46

Waugh, Auberon 1939- DLB-14

Waugh, Evelyn 1903-1966....................DLB-15

Way and Williams DLB-49

Wayman, Tom 1945- DLB-53

Weatherly, Tom 1942- DLB-41

Webb, Frank J. ?-? DLB-50

Webb, James Watson 1802-1884 ....DLB-43

Webb, Mary 1881-1927...........................DLB-34

Webb, Phyllis 1927- DLB-53

Webb, Walter Prescott 1888-1963 ....DLB-17

Webster, Augusta 1837-1894 ....DLB-35

Webster, Charles L., and Company DLB-49

Webster, John 1579 or 1580-1634? DLB-58

Webster, Noah 1758-1843 ....DLB-1, 37, 42, 43, 73

Weems, Mason Locke 1759-1825...........DLB-30, 37, 42

Weidman, Jerome 1913- DLB-28

Weinbaum, Stanley Grauman 1902-1935 ....DLB-8

Weisenborn, Günther 1902-1969 ....DLB-69

Weiß, Ernst 1882-1940 ....DLB-81

Weiss, John 1818-1879 ....DLB-1

Weiss, Peter 1916-1982 ....DLB-69

Weiss, Theodore 1916- DLB-5

Welch, Lew 1926-1971? DLB-16

Weldon, Fay 1931- DLB-14

Wellek, René 1903- DLB-63

Wells, Carolyn 1862-1942...............................DLB-11

Wells, Charles Jeremiah circa 1800-1879 ....DLB-32

Wells, H. G. 1866-1946 ....DLB-34, 70

Wells, Robert 1947- DLB-40

Wells-Barnett, Ida B. 1862-1931...........................DLB-23

Welty, Eudora 1909- DLB-2; Y-87

Wendell, Barrett 1855-1921 ....DLB-71

Wentworth, Patricia 1878-1961 ....DLB-77

Werfel, Franz 1890-1945 ....DLB-81

The Werner Company...............................DLB-49

Wersba, Barbara 1932- DLB-52

Wescott, Glenway 1901- DLB-4, 9

Wesker, Arnold 1932- DLB-13

Wesley, Richard 1945- DLB-38

Wessels, A., and Company DLB-46

West, Anthony 1914-1988 ....DLB-15

West, Dorothy 1907- DLB-76

West, Jessamyn 1902-1984 ....DLB-6; Y-84

West, Mae 1892-1980...........................DLB-44

West, Nathanael 1903-1940 ....DLB-4, 9, 28

West, Paul 1930- DLB-14

West, Rebecca 1892-1983 ....DLB-36; Y-83

West and Johnson DLB-49

Western Publishing Company DLB-46

Wetherell, Elizabeth (see Warner, Susan Bogert)

Whalen, Philip 1923- DLB-16

Wharton, Edith 1862-1937 ....DLB-4, 9, 12, 78

Wharton, William 1920s?- Y-80

What's Really Wrong With Bestseller Lists Y-84

Wheatley, Dennis Yates 1897-1977 ....DLB-77

Wheatley, Phillis circa 1754-1784 ....DLB-31, 50

Wheeler, Charles Stearns 1816-1843....................DLB-1

Wheeler, Monroe 1900-1988 ....DLB-4

Wheelock, John Hall 1886-1978 ....DLB-45

Wheelwright, John circa 1592-1679 ....DLB-24

Wheelwright, J. B. 1897-1940...........................DLB-45

Whetstone, Colonel Pete (see Noland, C. F. M.)

Whipple, Edwin Percy 1819-1886 ....DLB-1, 64

Whitaker, Alexander 1585-1617.........................DLB-24

Whitaker, Daniel K. 1801-1881 ....DLB-73

Whitcher, Frances Miriam 1814-1852 ....DLB-11

White, Andrew 1579-1656 ....DLB-24

White, Andrew Dickson 1832-1918....................DLB-47

White, E. B. 1899-1985 ....DLB-11, 22

White, Edgar B. 1947- DLB-38

White, Ethel Lina 1887-1944 ....DLB-77

White, Horace 1834-1916 ....DLB-23

White, Richard Grant 1821-1885........................DLB-64

White, Walter 1893-1955...............................DLB-51

White, William, and Company...........................DLB-49

White, William Allen 1868-1944 ....DLB-9, 25

White, William Anthony Parker (see Boucher, Anthony)

White, William Hale (see Rutherford, Mark)

Whitechurch, Victor L. 1868-1933 ....DLB-70

Whitehead, James 1936- Y-81

Whitehead, William 1715-1785...........................DLB-84

Whitfield, James Monroe 1822-1871.................DLB-50

Whiting, John 1917-1963 ....DLB-13

Whiting, Samuel 1597-1679 ....DLB-24

Whitlock, Brand 1869-1934 ....DLB-12

Whitman, Albert, and Company DLB-46

Whitman, Albery Allson 1851-1901 ....DLB-50

Whitman, Sarah Helen (Power) 1803-1878.........DLB-1

Whitman, Walt 1819-1892 ....DLB-3, 64

Whitman Publishing Company DLB-46

Whittemore, Reed 1919- DLB-5

Whittier, John Greenleaf 1807-1892 ....DLB-1

Whittlesey House...DLB-46

Wideman, John Edgar 1941- DLB-33

Wiebe, Rudy 1934- DLB-60

Wiechert, Ernst 1887-1950..............................DLB-56

Wieners, John 1934- DLB-16

Wier, Ester 1910- DLB-52

Wiesel, Elie 1928- DLB-83; Y-87

Wiggin, Kate Douglas 1856-1923 ....DLB-42

Wigglesworth, Michael 1631-1705 ....DLB-24

Wilbur, Richard 1921- DLB-5

Wild, Peter 1940- DLB-5

Wilde, Oscar 1854-1900 ....DLB-10, 19, 34, 57

Wilde, Richard Henry 1789-1847 ....DLB-3, 59

Wilde, W. A., Company DLB-49

Wilder, Billy 1906- DLB-26

Wilder, Laura Ingalls 1867-1957......................DLB-22

Wilder, Thornton 1897-1975 ....DLB-4, 7, 9

Wiley, Bell Irvin 1906-1980..............................DLB-17

Wiley, John, and Sons DLB-49

Wilhelm, Kate 1928- DLB-8

Wilkes, George 1817-1885 ....DLB-79

Wilkinson, Sylvia 1940- Y-86

Wilkinson, William Cleaver 1833-1920 ....DLB-71

Willard, L. [publishing house] DLB-49

Willard, Nancy 1936- DLB-5, 52

Willard, Samuel 1640-1707............................DLB-24

Williams, A., and Company DLB-49

Williams, C. K. 1936- DLB-5

Williams, Chancellor 1905- DLB-76

Williams, Emlyn 1905- DLB-10, 77

Williams, Garth 1912- DLB-22

Williams, George Washington 1849-1891 ....DLB-47

Williams, Heathcote 1941- DLB-13

Williams, Hugo 1942- DLB-40

Williams, Isaac 1802-1865...............................DLB-32

Williams, Joan 1928- DLB-6

Williams, John A. 1925- DLB-2, 33

Williams, John E. 1922- DLB-6

Williams, Jonathan 1929- DLB-5

Williams, Raymond 1921- DLB-14

Williams, Roger circa 1603-1683 ....DLB-24

Williams, Samm-Art 1946- DLB-38

Williams, Sherley Anne 1944- DLB-41

Williams, T. Harry 1909-1979.........................DLB-17

Williams, Tennessee 1911-1983........DLB-7; Y-83; DS-4

Williams, Valentine 1883-1946........................DLB-77

Williams, William Appleman 1921- DLB-17

Williams, William Carlos 1883-1963 ....DLB-4, 16, 54

Williams, Wirt 1921- DLB-6

Williams Brothers DLB-49

Williamson, Jack 1908- DLB-8

Willingham, Calder Baynard, Jr. 1922- DLB-2, 44

Willis, Nathaniel Parker 1806-1867 ...DLB-3, 59, 73, 74

Wilmer, Clive 1945- DLB-40

Wilson, A. N. 1950- DLB-14

Wilson, Angus 1913- DLB-15

Wilson, Arthur 1595-1652 ....DLB-58

Wilson, Augusta Jane Evans 1835-1909 ....DLB-42

Wilson, Colin 1931- DLB-14

Wilson, Edmund 1895-1972 ....DLB-63

Wilson, Ethel 1888-1980 ....DLB-68

Wilson, Harriet E. Adams 1828?-1863? DLB-50

Wilson, Harry Leon 1867-1939 ....DLB-9

Wilson, John 1588-1667................................DLB-24

Wilson, Lanford 1937- DLB-7

Wilson, Margaret 1882-1973............................DLB-9

Wilson, Michael 1914-1978 ....DLB-44

Wilson, Woodrow 1856-1924 ....DLB-47

Wimsatt, William K., Jr. 1907-1975...................DLB-63

Winchell, Walter 1897-1972............................DLB-29

Winchester, J. [publishing house]....................DLB-49

Windham, Donald 1920- DLB-6

Winsor, Justin 1831-1897................................DLB-47

John C. Winston Company DLB-49

Winters, Yvor 1900-1968 ....DLB-48

Winthrop, John 1588-1649 ....DLB-24, 30

Winthrop, John, Jr. 1606-1676.......................DLB-24

Wirt, William 1772-1834................................DLB-37

Wise, John 1652-1725 ....DLB-24

Wisner, George 1812-1849..............................DLB-43

Wister, Owen 1860-1938...............................DLB-9, 78

Witherspoon, John 1723-1794 ....DLB-31

Wittig, Monique 1935- DLB-83

Wodehouse, P. G. 1881-1975 ....DLB-34

Wohmann, Gabriele 1932- DLB-75

Woiwode, Larry 1941- DLB-6

Wolcott, Roger 1679-1767 ....DLB-24

Wolf, Christa 1929- DLB-75

Wolfe, Gene 1931- DLB-8

Wolfe, Thomas 1900-1938................DLB-9; DS-2; Y-85

Wollstonecraft, Mary 1759-1797 ....DLB-39

Wondratschek, Wolf 1943- DLB-75

Wood, Benjamin 1820-1900............................DLB-23

Wood, Charles 1932- DLB-13

Wood, Mrs. Henry 1814-1887 ....DLB-18

Wood, Samuel [publishing house] DLB-49

Wood, William ?-?...DLB-24

Woodberry, George Edward 1855-1930.............DLB-71

Woodbridge, Benjamin 1622-1684 ....DLB-24

Woodhull, Victoria C. 1838-1927 ....DLB-79

Woodmason, Charles circa 1720-? DLB-31

Woodson, Carter G. 1875-1950 ....DLB-17

Woodward, C. Vann 1908- DLB-17

Woolf, David (see Maddow, Ben)

Woolf, Virginia 1882-1941 ....DLB-36

Woollcott, Alexander 1887-1943.......................DLB-29

Woolman, John 1720-1772...............................DLB-31

Woolner, Thomas 1825-1892 ....DLB-35

Woolsey, Sarah Chauncy 1835-1905..................DLB-42

Woolson, Constance Fenimore 1840-1894....DLB-12, 74

Worcester, Joseph Emerson 1784-1865 ....DLB-1

The Works of the Rev. John Witherspoon
    (1800-1801) [excerpts]............................DLB-31

A World Chronology of Important Science
    Fiction Works (1818-1979) DLB-8

World Publishing Company DLB-46

Worthington, R., and Company........................DLB-49

Wouk, Herman 1915- Y-82

Wright, Charles 1935- Y-82

Wright, Charles Stevenson 1932- DLB-33

Wright, Frances 1795-1852..............................DLB-73

Wright, Harold Bell 1872-1944 ....DLB-9

Wright, James 1927-1980.................................DLB-5

Wright, Jay 1935- DLB-41

Wright, Louis B. 1899-1984..............................DLB-17

Wright, Richard 1908-1960 ....DS-2, DLB-76

Wright, Richard B. 1937- DLB-53

Wright, Sarah Elizabeth 1928- DLB-33

Writers' Forum Y-85

Writing for the Theatre, by Harold Pinter DLB-13

Wycherley, William 1641-1715 ....DLB-80

Wylie, Elinor 1885-1928................................DLB-9, 45

Wylie, Philip 1902-1971 ....DLB-9

Y

Yates, Dornford 1885-1960...............................DLB-77

Yates, J. Michael 1938- DLB-60

Yates, Richard 1926- DLB-2; Y-81

Yeats, William Butler 1865-1939 ....DLB-10, 19

Yep, Laurence 1948- DLB-52

Yerby, Frank 1916- DLB-76

Yezierska, Anzia 1885-1970..............................DLB-28

Yolen, Jane 1939- DLB-52

Yonge, Charlotte Mary 1823-1901 ....DLB-18

A Yorkshire Tragedy DLB-58

Yoseloff, Thomas [publishing house] DLB-46

Young, Al 1939- DLB-33

Young, Stark 1881-1963 ....DLB-9

Young, Waldeman 1880-1938 ....DLB-26

Young, William [publishing house].....................DLB-49

Yourcenar, Marguerite 1903-1987............DLB-72; Y-88

"You've Never Had It So Good," Gusted by
    "Winds of Change": British Fiction in the
    1950s, 1960s, and After DLB-14

Z

Zamora, Bernice 1938- DLB-82

Zangwill, Israel 1864-1926 ....DLB-10

Zebra Books DLB-46

Zebrowski, George 1945- DLB-8

Zech, Paul 1881-1946 ....DLB-56

Zelazny, Roger 1937- DLB-8

Zenger, John Peter 1697-1746 ....DLB-24, 43

Zieber, G. B., and Company DLB-49

Zieroth, Dale 1946- DLB-60

Zimmer, Paul 1934- DLB-5

Zindel, Paul 1936- DLB-7, 52

Zolotow, Charlotte 1915- DLB-52

Zubly, John Joachim 1724-1781 ....DLB-31

Zu-Bolton II, Ahmos 1936- DLB-41

Zuckmayer, Carl 1896-1977 ....DLB-56

Zukofsky, Louis 1904-1978 ....DLB-5

zur Mühlen, Hermynia 1883-1951 ....DLB-56

Zweig, Arnold 1887-1968 ....DLB-66

Zweig, Stefan 1881-1942 ....DLB-81

(Continued from front endsheets)

71: *American Literary Critics and Scholars, 1880-1900,* edited by John W. Rathbun and Monica M. Grecu (1988)

72: *French Novelists, 1930-1960,* edited by Catharine Savage Brosman (1988)

73: *American Magazine Journalists, 1741-1850,* edited by Sam G. Riley (1988)

74: *American Short-Story Writers Before 1880,* edited by Bobby Ellen Kimbel, with the assistance of William E. Grant (1988)

75: *Contemporary German Fiction Writers,* Second Series, edited by Wolfgang D. Elfe and James Hardin (1988)

76: *Afro-American Writers, 1940-1955,* edited by Trudier Harris (1988)

77: *British Mystery Writers, 1920-1939,* edited by Bernard Benstock and Thomas F. Staley (1988)

78: *American Short-Story Writers, 1880-1910,* edited by Bobby Ellen Kimbel, with the assistance of William E. Grant (1988)

79: *American Magazine Journalists, 1850-1900,* edited by Sam G. Riley (1988)

80: *Restoration and Eighteenth-Century Dramatists,* First Series, edited by Paula R. Backscheider (1989)

81: *Austrian Fiction Writers, 1875-1913,* edited by James Hardin and Donald G. Daviau (1989)

82: *Chicano Writers,* First Series, edited by Francisco A. Lomelí and Carl R. Shirley (1989)

83: *French Novelists Since 1960,* edited by Catharine Savage Brosman (1989)

84: *Restoration and Eighteenth-Century Dramatists,* Second Series, edited by Paula R. Backscheider (1989)

Documentary Series

1: *Sherwood Anderson, Willa Cather, John Dos Passos, Theodore Dreiser, F. Scott Fitzgerald, Ernest Hemingway, Sinclair Lewis,* edited by Margaret A. Van Antwerp (1982)

2: *James Gould Cozzens, James T. Farrell, William Faulkner, John O'Hara, John Steinbeck, Thomas Wolfe, Richard Wright,* edited by Margaret A. Van Antwerp (1982)

3: *Saul Bellow, Jack Kerouac, Norman Mailer, Vladimir Nabokov, John Updike, Kurt Vonnegut,* edited by Mary Bruccoli (1983)

4: *Tennessee Williams,* edited by Margaret A. Van Antwerp and Sally Johns (1984)

5: *American Transcendentalists,* edited by Joel Myerson (1988)

6: *Hardboiled Mystery Writers,* edited by Matthew J. Bruccoli and Richard Layman (1988)

Yearbooks

1980, edited by Karen L. Rood, Jean W. Ross, and Richard Ziegfeld (1981)

1981, edited by Karen L. Rood, Jean W. Ross, and Richard Ziegfeld (1982)

1982, edited by Richard Ziegfeld; associate editors: Jean W. Ross and Lynne C. Zeigler (1983)

1983, edited by Mary Bruccoli and Jean W. Ross; associate editor: Richard Ziegfeld (1984)

1984, edited by Jean W. Ross (1985)

1985, edited by Jean W. Ross (1986)

1986, edited by J. M. Brook (1987)

1987, edited by J. M. Brook (1988)

1988, edited by J. M. Brook (1989)